BIODIVERSITY CONSERVATION, LAW + LIVELIHOODS

The IUCN Academy of Environmental Law Research Studies' third colloquium brought together more than 130 experts from 27 nations on nearly every continent. This book brings together a number of the papers presented there and offers a global perspective on biodiversity conservation and the maintenance of sustainable cultures. It addresses issues from international, regional, and country-specific perspectives. The book is organized thematically to present a broad spectrum of issues, including the history and major governance structures in this area; the needs, problems, and prerequisites for biodiversity; area-based, species-based, and ecosystem-based conservation measures; the use of components of biodiversity and the processes affecting it; biosecurity; and access to and sharing of benefits from components of biodiversity and their economic value.

Michael I. Jeffery, QC, is Professor of Law at Macquarie University and Director of its Centre for Environmental Law. He served as Dean of Law in 1999. He received his LLB degree from the University of Toronto and his LLM degree from Osgoode Hall Law School, York University. A former Chair of the Province of Ontario's Environmental Assessment Board, he was appointed a Queen's Counsel in 1978 and headed the environmental law practice of one of Canada's largest law firms in the 1990s. He has served as Deputy Chair of the IUCN's Commission on Environmental Law and has been the Editor-in-Chief of the *Macquarie Journal of International and Comparative Environmental Law* since its inception.

Jeremy Firestone is an Associate Professor of Marine Policy and Legal Studies at the University of Delaware. He holds a JD from the University of Michigan and a PhD in Public Policy from the University of North Carolina. Previously, he served as an environmental protection lawyer for the U.S. Environmental Protection Agency and the state of Michigan. Professor Firestone's research and teaching interests include ocean governance, wildlife conservation, energy policy, and indigenous rights.

Karen Bubna-Litic is a senior lecturer in the Faculty of Law at the University of Technology, Sydney, and Assistant Director of the UTS Centre for Corporate Governance. She received her LLB degree from the University of Western Australia and her LLM degree from the University of Sydney. She has been a visiting professor at the Boalt School of Law, University of California, Berkeley; the School of Environmental Negotiation, University of Virginia; and the Program for Research and Documentation for a Sustainable Society at the University of Oslo. She is a Solicitor and Barrister of the Supreme Court of Western Australia and was Director of Research in the Faculty of Law from 2003–2005.

IUCN ACADEMY OF ENVIRONMENTAL LAW RESEARCH STUDIES

Biodiversity Conservation, Law + Livelihoods

Bridging the North–South Divide

Edited by

MICHAEL I. JEFFERY, QC
Macquarie University

JEREMY FIRESTONE
University of Delaware

KAREN BUBNA-LITIC
University of Technology, Sydney

CAMBRIDGE
UNIVERSITY PRESS

CAMBRIDGE UNIVERSITY PRESS
Cambridge, New York, Melbourne, Madrid, Cape Town, Singapore, São Paulo, Delhi

Cambridge University Press
32 Avenue of the Americas, New York, NY 10013-2473, USA

www.cambridge.org
Information on this title: www.cambridge.org/9780521885034

First published 2008

Printed in the United States of America

A catalog record for this publication is available from the British Library.

Library of Congress Cataloging in Publication Data

Biodiversity conservation, law + livelihoods : bridging the north-south
divide / edited by Michael I. Jeffery, Jeremy Firestone, Karen Bubna-Litic.
p. cm. – (IUCN Academy of environmental law research studies)
ISBN 978-0-521-88503-4 (hardback)
1. Biodiversity conservation – Law and legislation. 2. North and south.
I. Jeffery, Michael I. (Michael Irwin). II. Firestone, Jeremy M.
III. Bubna-Litic, Karen. IV. IUCN Academy of Environmental Law.
Colloquium (3rd: 2005: Sydney, Australia) V. Title. VI. Series.
K3488.B566 2008
346.04′–dc22 2007024349

ISBN 978-0-521-88503-4 hardback

Contents

Acknowledgments

We wish to warmly acknowledge the contributions of the many individuals and institutions that enabled us to bring together in this volume the majority of the research papers presented at the third Colloquium of the IUCN Academy of Environmental Law hosted by Macquarie University's Centre for Environmental Law in Sydney, Australia, in July 2005.

After five years of diligent work on the part of members of the International Union for the Conservation of Nature and Natural Resources (IUCN) and in particular the members and former Chairs of the IUCN Commission on Environmental Law (CEL) and the IUCN Environmental Law Centre, the Academy was formally launched in Shanghai, China, in November 2003. Shanghai was also the location of the Academy's first Colloquium hosted by Shanghai Jiao Tong University. The second annual Colloquium was held in Nairobi, Kenya, with Sydney being chosen as the site of the third Colloquium in what has developed in a short space of time into one of the most important annual events on the international environmental law calendar.

Macquarie University's former Vice-Chancellor, Professor Di Yerbury, enthusiastically supported the activities of the Academy and ensured the success of the third Colloquium through a generous grant from the University's Millennium Fund. Special thanks must be accorded to both Professor Tony Adams, Pro Vice-Chancellor (International), who filled in at the opening ceremony for Professor Yerbury, who was overseas and unable to officiate, and Professor Elizabeth More, Vice-Chancellor (Administration), who represented the University at the closing banquet held at Sydney's Taronga Zoo overlooking Sydney Harbour.

The leadership of Professor Michael Jeffery, QC, Director of the University's Centre for Environmental Law and Coordinator of the Colloquium Committee, was essential to the success of the week-long event. His job was made easier with the enthusiastic support and around-the-clock work of his Centre colleagues Donna Craig, David Leary, and Susan Shearing.

Much of the success of the Colloquium was due to the tireless yet cheerful administrative support provided by a dedicated cadre of student volunteers, and special thanks must be given to Kate McLoughlan, Michael Collins, and Marcia Valsinger-Clarke for their roles. The Biodiversity Conservation Day Tour to Kuring-gai Chase National Park led by Professor Ben Boer (University of Sydney) and Chief Judge Brian Preston of the NSW Land and Environment Court was a memorable highlight of the Colloquium, and we owe them both a debt of gratitude for their superb efforts. Likewise, we wish to thank Professor Liz Deane, the Dean of Macquarie University's Division of Environmental and Life Sciences, and her staff for arranging for delegates to enjoy "lunch with the wallabies" and tour the University's wallaby research facility.

We thank United Nations Secretary-General Kofi A. Annan for his support of the Academy and for providing the introduction to this publication. Essential financial support was provided by the United Nations Development Programme, and we wish to warmly acknowledge the assistance provided by UNEP's Bakari Kante and Lal Kurukulasuriya. Financial support was also provided by the NSW government, represented at the Colloquium by the Hon. Bob Debus, Attorney-General and Minister for the Environment, and the Commonwealth government, represented by Mr. Howard Bamsey, Acting Secretary, Department of Environment and Heritage.

Australian Commonwealth Senator and IUCN Vice-President Christine Milne lent her strong support as outlined in her opening remarks.

We also wish to warmly acknowledge the contributions of Professor Joseph Sax, who gave the Academy's Distinguished Lectures and contributed throughout the Colloquium, and Dr. Francoise Burhenne-Guilmin, who delivered the Keynote Address.

We are most appreciative of the support and hospitality of the Hon. Justice Keith Mason AC, President of the NSW Court of Appeal, who graciously hosted a reception at the Court and conducted a tour of the Banco Court for invitees.

The Colloquium could not have been a success without the participation and contributions of the more than 130 leading environmental lawyers, judges, and academics representing 27 countries around the world, and the research papers comprising this volume attest to the exceptional expertise and experience of those involved. A special thanks must be given to Professor Robert Percival and Associate Professor Lye Lin Heng for their assistance in crafting a statement, to be known as the "Macquarie Statement," which was adopted by consensus on the last day of the Colloquium.

Thanks also to those who assisted the Editorial Committee in working on this publication, including Macquarie students Jane Scanlon, Emiliano Schivazappa, and Nik Hughes. We are grateful to Cambridge University Press and its representative, John Berger, for the publication of these research papers and the compendium material. And of course this volume would not have been possible without the devotion and enthusiasm of the project manager, Mary Paden, of Aptara Inc., on behalf of Cambridge University Press.

We would be remiss in failing to accord Professor Nicholas A. Robinson, Chair of the Academy, a special note of thanks; without his inspiration and dedication neither the Academy nor the impressive body of research knowledge contained in this and earlier colloquia publications would have seen the light of day. His guidance, leadership, and scholarship are evident throughout all Academy activities.

The Editors

UNITED NATIONS NATIONS UNIES

THE SECRETARY-GENERAL

MESSAGE TO THE THIRD COLLOQUIUM OF THE IUCN ACADEMY OF ENVIRONMENTAL LAW

Sydney, 11 July 2005

The Millennium Ecosystem Assessment released earlier this year was the first comprehensive global evaluation of the world's major ecosystems. The product of an unprecedented, four-year study involving natural scientists, scholars and environmental leaders from all over the world, it offers a sobering look at how human activities are causing environmental damage on a massive scale. It challenges all countries, all people and the IUCN Academy of Environmental Law to do more to protect the environment on which our lives depend.

The report tells us how biodiversity is declining at an alarming rate. Twenty-five percent of commercially exploited marine fish stocks are over-harvested. The conversion of wetlands, forests, and mangroves is reducing the capacity of ecosystems to mitigate the effects of extreme weather events such as the recent tsunami in the Indian Ocean. If the world is to meet the agreed target of reducing the loss of biological diversity by 2010, and achieve the Millennium Development Goals by 2015, we will need dramatic steps to change course.

Laws, regulations, enforcement measures, policy reforms, market mechanisms, and investments in the management of critical ecosystems must all be part of the picture. Your colloquium on the law of biodiversity can provide essential guidance. We need legal tools that will turn recommendations into practice. And we need your suggestions as to how environmental law can bring about the policy, institutional, and behavioural changes needed to deal with the root causes of environmental degradation.

The Millennium Ecosystem Report did not only sound an alarm; it also proposes solutions and strategies for restoring and maintaining ecosystems. It is encouraging to know that the World Conservation Union is involved in the search for solutions on an issue of great urgency to all humankind. Please accept my best wishes for the success of your deliberations.

Kofi A. Annan

Macquarie Statement

14 July 2005
Sydney, Australia

Delegates at the IUCN Academy of Environmental Law's Third Annual Colloquium hosted by Macquarie University through its Centre for Environmental Law reached a consensus on the need to protect biological diversity as a fundamental part of efforts to ensure a healthy environment for present and future generations of humans and other living species.

The statement, to be known as the "Macquarie Statement" was debated in the final plenary session of the five-day gathering in Sydney of more than 130 environmental experts from 27 nations to consider the theme of "Biodiversity Conservation, Law + Livelihoods: Bridging the North–South Divide." The complete text of the statement follows:

MACQUARIE STATEMENT
Statement of the Third Colloquium of the IUCN Academy of Environmental Law

At the Third Colloquium of the IUCN Academy of Environmental Law, more than 130 environmental experts from 27 nations representing universities from each continent gathered to consider the theme of "Biodiversity Conservation, Law + Livelihoods: Bridging the North–South Divide." Papers presented by the participants and discussions in both plenary and panel sessions reflected a broad recognition that efforts to protect biological diversity are a fundamental part of efforts to ensure a healthy environment for present and future generations of humans and other living species.

The colloquium took into account the findings of the Millennium Ecosystems Assessment that, despite past warnings, threats to biodiversity and general environmental degradation have continued unabated, making it difficult to meet the original target of reducing the loss of biodiversity by the year 2010 and to meet Millennium Development Goals by 2015. To improve our capacity to meet these goals, the colloquium emphasized the following themes.

Human activity, including anthropogenic causes of climate change, is contributing to an alarming rate of species extinction that is reducing the diversity of the biosphere to the detriment of present and future generations.

Environmental law must focus on redressing the factors that contribute to the reduction in biological diversity at their sources by creating appropriate incentives for changing behaviour. Further, environmental law must develop and put into effect the legal tools that will turn established and evolving scientific and policy recommendations into enforceable norms, institutions and procedures. At a global level, this must build on the established principle of common but differentiated responsibilities.

The establishment and maintenance of protected areas on a national, regional or global basis can play an important role in protecting endangered species and preserving biodiversity by conserving ecosystems and natural habitats on which species depend.

Recognizing the complex interdependencies of living organisms in ecosystems, efforts to preserve biodiversity must emphasize a broad ecosystem approach, rather than focusing primarily on preventing extinction on a species-by-species basis or park-by-park basis.

As globalization spreads concepts of private property, it is important that concepts of property law be reconceptualized to ensure the protection of public values and to prevent the destruction of the economy of nature and the environmental services that ecosystems provide.

Measures that promote the conservation and sustainable use of biodiversity ultimately will contribute to a more peaceful and prosperous world for the benefit of both current and future generations. All countries should follow sustainable development paths, learning from, and avoiding, the mistakes of the past.

As knowledge of the causes and consequences of environmental problems continues to improve, it is imperative that legal concepts be adapted to take into account new information and to improve the capacity of law to respond to environmental imperatives. The considerable expertise possessed by members of the Academy of Environmental Law can be leveraged to make significant contributions to improved public policy through collaborative and comparative law research projects. These projects can help improve our understanding of what policies work and why and enhance our ability to employ law to achieve our shared goals.

Special and deliberate efforts should be made to develop a critical mass of expertise and institutional arrangements in developing countries, paying particular attention to the interests of minority, indigenous and marginalized peoples to ensure equitable national and regional sustainable development.

Every country and regional entity must put into place legal and policy mechanisms as well as institutional procedures that protect the rights of minorities, indigenous and marginalized people in relation to their settlements, knowledge, customary law and access to justice, ensuring that they have priority in benefits derived from sustainable use of biodiversity.

Contributors

Abdul Haseeb Ansari Professor, AIKOL, International Islamic University, Malaysia.

Patryck de Araújo Ayala PhD Candidate in Law, Universidade Federal de Santa Catarina, Brazil.

Karen Bubna-Litic Senior Lecturer in the Faculty of Law, University of Technology, Sydney.

Dr. Françoise Burhenne-Guilmin Senior Counsel, IUCN Environmental Law Centre, Germany.

Arlindo Daibert Attorney-General's Office, City of Rio de Janeiro, Brazil.

The Hon. R. J. Debus Attorney-General and Minister for the Environment, State of New South Wales, Australia.

Dr. Qun Du Professor, Environmental Law and Natural Resource Management, Tongji – UNEP Institute of Environmental Sustainable Development, Tongji University, Wuhan, Hubei, People's Republic of China.

Loretta Feris Associate Professor of Law, Faculty of Law, University of Pretoria.

Heline Sivini Ferreira PhD Candidate in Law, Universidade Federal de Santa Catarina, Brazil.

Jeremy Firestone Associate Professor of Marine Policy and Legal Studies, University of Delaware, USA.

D. E. Fisher Professor of Law, Queensland University of Technology, Australia; consultant, Phillips Fox Lawyers.

Ian Hannam Associate Professor, Australian Centre for Agriculture and Law, University of New England, Australia.

Dr. Alan D. Hemmings Senior Fellow Gateway Antarctica Centre for Antarctic Studies and Research, University of Canterbury, Christchurch, New Zealand.

David R. Hodas Professor, Widener University School of Law, Wilmington, Delaware, USA.

Zhang Hui Lawyer, Legal advisor to Jilin Forest Bureau, People's Republic of China.

Michael I. Jeffery QC, Professor of Law and Director of the Centre for Environmental Law, Macquarie University, Sydney.

Yasuhiko Kagami Ocean Policy Research Foundation, Japan.

Isoa Korovulavula Institute of Applied Science, University of the South Pacific, Suva, Fiji Island.

Na Li Professor of Law, Jilin University, People's Republic of China.

Jonathan Lilley PhD Candidate, College of Marine and Earth Studies, University of Delaware, USA.

Rosemary Lyster Associate Professor in the Faculty of Law at Sydney University; Director of the Australian Centre for Environmental Law, Sydney.

Brendan Mackey Fenner School of Resources, Environment and Society/Faculty of Science, The Australian National University, Canberra.

Pio E. Manoa School of Marine Studies, University of the South Pacific, Suva, Fiji Islands.

Paul Martin Australian Centre for Agriculture and Law, University of New England Armidale, New South Wales, Australia.

Bo (Kevin) Miao PhD Candidate, Center for Environmental Law, Macquarie University, Sydney.

Ilona Miller Principal Solicitor, Environmental Defender's Office, New South Wales, Australia.

José Rubens Morato-Leite Professor of Environmental Law, Universidade Federal de Santa Catarina, Brazil.

Burton Ong Associate Professor, Faculty of Law, National University of Singapore.

Nicholas A. Robinson Gilbert and Sarah Kerlin Distinguished Professor of Environmental Law, Pace University School of Law, USA.

Dr. Michelle Rogan-Finnemore Centre Manager of Gateway Antarctica Centre for Antarctic Studies and Research, University of Canterbury, Christchurch, New Zealand.

Justin Rose PhD Candidate, Centre for Environmental Law, Macquarie University, Sydney.

Nicholas de Sadeleer Professor of Law, University of Oslo, Norway.

George A. Sarpong Senior Lecturer, Faculty of Law, University of Ghana, Legon.

Joseph L. Sax James H. House and Hiram H. Hurd Professor of Environmental Regulation, Emeritus, University of California, Berkeley, USA.

Jessica Wood Environmental Defender's Office, Sydney.

Desalegn Wana Lecturer, Department of Geography and Environmental Studies, Addis Ababa University, Ethiopia.

Liu Yanchun Head of Jilin Provincial Forest Administrative Bureau, People's Republic of China.

Yuhong Zhao Assistant Professor, School of Law, City University of Hong Kong.

Introduction

Michael I. Jeffery, Jeremy Firestone, and Karen Bubna-Litic

The threats to biological diversity are well known, and include overharvesting of flora and fauna, species introductions, habitat loss and fragmentation, pollution, tourism, globalization, and climate change. These factors threaten the sustainability of culture as well. This volume, addressing as it does the conservation of biodiversity and the divide between developed and developing states, appropriately focuses international and comparative environmental law scholars, practitioners, and policy makers on ways to engage cooperatively to meet the broader imperatives of a sustainable biosphere and sustainable cultures. It also usefully ties these concepts together in one volume given the interrelationship between the two. The tension between nature conservation, on the one hand, and sustainable cultures, on the other, is perhaps best reflected in international law by section 8(j) of the 1992 Convention on Biological Diversity (CBD). There states are called on to conserve biological diversity and to "respect, preserve, and maintain" indigenous cultures while at the same time promoting the wider sustainable use of the components of biological diversity. Appropriately, the Convention recognizes that the conservation of biological diversity is a "common concern of humankind." We would suggest that sustainable cultures should likewise be recognized. It is to these twin goals – rather, obligations – that we now turn.

This book places the issues threatening biological diversity – the variability of life on Earth and their interaction at the level of genes, species, and ecosystems – in a contemporary context. We have moved beyond the debates of the early 1990s at the time of the Rio Conference, which focused primarily on economic development in an environmentally sustainable manner, to where we find ourselves today with an increased awareness that the way forward must necessarily address poverty eradication on a sustainable basis. Any realistic hope of achieving the Millennium Development Goals lies with reducing poverty through the conservation and sustainable use of biodiversity on a truly global scale. This reduction in poverty will be evidenced in five main areas: security of food production; sustainable livelihoods; improvements to health; reduced vulnerability to natural disasters and conflict over shared resources, such as food and water; and, finally, in the area of ecosystem services. This volume, although only an introduction to some of these areas, represents the aspirations of the participants to the colloquium and the Academy to be built on in future fora.

To this end, the World Conservation Union (IUCN) Academy of Environmental Law assembled many of the world's most distinguished experts in all areas of biodiversity law at its third annual colloquium in July 2005 hosted by Macquarie University's Centre for Environmental Law in Sydney, Australia. This followed the Academy's inaugural colloquium on the Law of Energy for Sustainable Development hosted by Shanghai's Jiao Tong University in 2003 and the second colloquium on Land Use Law for Sustainable Development in 2004 hosted by the University of Nairobi.

The Academy's third colloquium, entitled Biodiversity Conservation, Law + Livelihoods: Bridging the North-South Divide, brought together more than 130 environmental experts from 27 nations representing universities from each continent to consider issues related to the colloquium's theme. The exceptional level of expertise represented by the author/presenters of the papers contained in this book with respect to the myriad of biodiversity issues addressed throughout the five-day colloquium was reflected by the preeminence of two participants in particular: Dr. Françoise Burhenne-Guilmin, the presenter of the colloquium's Keynote Address and a coauthor of the "Guides" to both the CBD and the Cartagena (Biosafety) Protocol, and Professor Joseph L. Sax, who presented the Distinguished Lectures and is recognized as one of the true pioneers responsible for the development of environmental law as a separate and important legal academic discipline. The participation of Australian traditional owners throughout the colloquium was greatly appreciated by all.

The message by then United Nations Secretary-General Kofi Annan, which is presented at the beginning of this book, attests to the gravity of the ecological dangers facing humankind and, indeed, all living organisms, and acknowledges "the role that environmental law can play in bringing about the policy, institutional, and behavioural changes needed to deal with the root causes of environmental degredation."

The level of synergy and positive interaction among the participants was evident throughout the colloquium both in the plenary sessions and the more thematic breakout sessions. Nowhere was this more evident than in the final plenary session, when, after extensive debate, a consensus was reached on a final statement of principles, referred to as the "Macquarie Statement" and reproduced on page xiii.

We decided on a thematic structure to organize the material contained in the various sections as it was felt that the broad spectrum of issues covered by the concept of biodiversity could best be presented in this manner. This in no way is meant to distract from the fact that the presenters represented every major region of the world and that the chapters address many of the same issues from a country-specific or regional perspective. Notwithstanding this thematic structure, it will be readily apparent that the book in its entirety also presents a global perspective on a matter of global concern.

The sections in the book represent seven themes. Part I sets the context in terms of history and the major governance structures in this area. Joseph L. Sax, in, "Environmental Law Forty Years Later: Looking Back and Looking Ahead," sets a challenge to environmental lawyers worldwide. He confronted us with the notion that there has been widespread failure to address the incentive systems that generate environmental degradation and that our legal systems need to reconstitute themselves to tackle the new values and understandings of contemporary environmental issues such as biodiversity. He shows how property law has developed to encourage exploitation of the land for human purposes and points out that even though we now have environmental laws to conserve land and water, the underlying property law has not changed. Environmental values have not been integrated into the basic structure of the law and so the old incentives remain. The theme of challenging the conference was continued with Dr Françoise Burhenne-Guilmin's chapter, "Biodiversity and International Law: Historical Perspectives and Present Challenges – Where Do We Come From, Where Are We Going?"

Dr Burhenne-Guilmin poses the challenge to lawyers of operationalising the ecosystem approach and promoting sustainable use within the CBD. Brendan Mackey considers the contribution that the Earth Charter plays in building a global moral community and its role in the foundation of new legal instruments, institutions and processes on global governance. Finally, Paul Martin examines how the role of law must change to meet the challenge of ecological sustainability.

Part II encompasses the conservation of biodiversity and is divided into three sections with the first identifying the needs, problems, and prerequisites in relation to biodiversity. Michael Jeffery questions the effectiveness of developing countries' implementation of the CBD's environmental protection and sustainable human development mandates, and, more specifically, he analyzes the CBD's role in poverty eradication and the "poverty-environment paradigm." He advocates improving environmental governance, developing strategies that meet the economic and social needs of people who depend on biodiversity products and the surrounding ecosystem, and resolving intellectual property issues that are inequitable to poorer countries. In his chapter, "Legal and Paralegal Rules for Biodiversity Conservation: A Sequence of Conceptual, Linguistic, and Legal Challenges," Douglas Fisher identifies the legal challenge resulting from the use of language in the field of biodiversity conservation. He questions our perceptions, understandings, and construction of the concept and value of nature and biodiversity and suggests how it should be expressed and treated in the legal system. Abdul Haseeb Ansari examines biodiversity issues from an Islamic, ethical, legal, and policy viewpoint. Implementation of the CBD is considered in "Experience, Mistakes and Challenges: The Implementation of the Convention on Biological Diversity in Brazil," by Jose Rubens Morato-Leite, Heline Sivini Ferreira, and Patryck de Araújo Ayala. The authors conclude that, although implementation of the CBD is crucial in a megadiverse country like Brazil, impediments, such as politics, institutional weakness, little or no access to information, economic issues, limited exchange and collaboration, social factors, and lack of appropriate policies and laws need to be overcome through a multidisciplinary and qualified group working together. Nicholas de Sadeleer looks at the unique position that European community law plays in the protection of biodiversity and concludes that although it may have an advantage over international law in terms of efficacy, there is a danger that the principle of subsidiarity may lead to a race to the bottom in terms of environmental protection. Justin Rose's chapter investigates the legal and institutional aspects of the region-wide promotion of community-based conservation and natural resources management as an environmental governance mechanism in the Pacific Island region.

The theme of Part III is conservation measures, which are divided into area-based and species-based. The Minister for the Environment in New South Wales, the Hon. Robert Debus, sets out his government's new initiatives on land management. These are community conservation areas, which are essentially multi-use reserves that are managed consistent with sustainability principles, where community involvement and input is encouraged. The other two chapters on area-based conservation are case studies from Ethiopia and Japan. Desalegn Wana's chapter, "Local People's Perceptions and Attitudes towards Nech-Sar National Park, Ethiopia," emphasizes the importance of a participatory approach for the conservation of biodiversity in ensuring the local people's involvement in park management. Yasuhiko Kagami examines the processes involved in the nomination of Shiretoko for world heritage status. The species-based approach is critically examined in Karen Bubna-Litic's chapter, "Ten Years of Threatened Species Legislation in NSW – What Are the Lessons?" She concludes that the approach that has been used in New South Wales has resulted in costly disputes and that an ecosystem approach needs to be taken to ensure a long-term view of biodiversity protection. Ecosystem-based approaches are considered by Ilona Miller and Jessica Simpson in their chapter, "Sanctuaries, Protected Species and Politics: How Effective Is Australia at Protecting Its Marine Biodiversity under the Environment Protection and Biodiversity Conservation Act 1999?" and by Nicholas Robinson's chapter, "Legal Stewardship of Mountain Regions: The Emerging Ecoregime."

Part IV concerns the use of components of biodiversity. Ian Hannam advocates the need for a specific international soil instrument, as soil is an ecological element that needs to be protected against degradation from world population and increased food production. George Sarpong examines the legal regime for forestry in Ghana with emphasis on the role of the political will of, necessary incentives by, and goodwill on behalf of the government. The chapter by Jeremy Firestone and Jonathan Lilley, "Bridging the Dominant-Indigenous People's Cultural Divide: Reflections on Makah Whaling," examines the debate surrounding the resumption of subsistence whaling by the Makah tribe to illustrate how nation-states and indigenous peoples can bridge the divide and work together to achieve a sustainable biosphere and a sustainable culture.

One group of chapters within the "processes affecting biodiversity" theme in Part V begins by considering the issue of global warming. For example, David Hodas, in his chapter, "Do Biodiversity and Climate Change Laws Mix?" asserts that the laws on biodiversity and endangered species, on the one hand, and the laws on climate change, on the other, do not appropriately address and incorporate the other vital issue. He offers the solution that policy approaches be developed to integrate biodiversity and climate change into routine decision making. Bo Miao considers China's potential adoption of an emissions-trading scheme to combat global warming. Another group in this theme considers the role of sustainable land use in protecting ecosystem functions. Arlindo Daibert compares the private land disposal policies in Brazil and the United States, whereas Du Qun discusses how a new instrument in China, ecological function zoning, can achieve its aim of enhancing the ecological functions of the national key river basins and watersheds. Na Li, Liu Yanchun, and Zhang Hui discuss the positive environmental and economic outcomes of the Ecograss Project on land that has been seriously degraded through agricultural overuse and climate change.

The book then moves in Part VI to consider biosecurity issues of both invasive alien species and genetically modified organisms (GMOs). Yuhong Zhao's chapter, "Prevention and Control of Alien Invasive Species – China's Implementation of the CBD," argues that China's legal regime for dealing with alien invasive species is piecemeal and fragmented and offers suggestions for a more effective outcome. Loretta Feris examines liability and redress schemes in the context of the CBD and the Cartegena Protocol on Biosafety in, "The Reality and Effect of 'Advanced Informed Agreement' under the Cartegena Protocol." Rosemary Lyster questions the reality of informed consent in many developing countries and the effect of the protocol in light of trade law.

The final two sections of Part VII look at access and benefit-sharing in two different contexts. Alan D. Hemmings and Michelle Rogan-Finnemore in their chapter, "Access, Obligations and Benefits: Regulating Bioprospecting in the Antarctic," contend that bioprospecting activities in Antarctica exist in somewhat of a legal and regulatory vacuum as a result of unresolved territorial sovereignty claims. They offer potential solutions to this complex issue. The last two chapters tackle the issue of indigenous intellectual and cultural property rights. Burton Ong examines the response of the World Intellectual Property Organisation (WIPO) to the exploitation of genetic resources and traditional knowledge and the development of protection of these resources. Finally, Pio Manoa and Isoa Korovulavula, in their chapter, "Sharing All the Benefit: The Challenge of Legal Recognition of Indigenous Intellectual and Cultural Property Rights in the Fiji Islands," use frameworks from Costa Rica, Brazil, and Peru to show how Fijian national law could recognize indigenous intellectual and cultural property rights.

PART ONE

THE CONTEXT

1 Environmental Law Forty Years Later: Looking Back and Looking Ahead

Joseph L. Sax

Nearly forty years ago, when environmental law was first emerging as a subject, the background was effectively one of legal anarchy. Industrial emissions into the air and water were uncontrolled and unlimited. Waste materials, however toxic, were buried at any convenient site, and records were not even routinely maintained of their location or magnitude, nor was there monitoring of their movement into water courses or aquifers. DDT and other chlorinated hydrocarbon pesticides were liberally applied and the only regulation (in the United States, for example) was whether the labels under which they were sold accurately described their contents. As an example of how different things were then, in one of our earliest environmental cases, in 1967, where an effort was being made to protect a wildlife sanctuary against the expropriation of a right-of-way for a gas transmission line, the judge said in open court, "Before this case started I looked up the meaning of [the word] ecology in the dictionary because I noted it [in the case documents before me]. I was not aware of that word before."[1]

The situation was extreme, and attention was focused, as it should have been, on the sometimes disastrous consequences of then-current and commonplace practices, notably on such tragic matters as the methyl mercury poisoning in Japan that came to be known as Minamata disease; and leading to such catalyzing events as the Tokyo International Conference on Environment organized in March 1970, under the leadership of Professor Shigeto Tsuru.

Although many countries have in the ensuing years have done a great deal to bring such activities under management and control, the nature and magnitude of environmental problems still confronting us – global warming and biodiversity impoverishment, to name only the most familiar – is daunting. Moreover, the positive energy that once impelled us forward to tackle challenges in this realm has at least in some places lost momentum or even become retrograde. The United States, which once offered forward-looking leadership in both the legal and administrative spheres, does not under its current governance, alas, play that role.

My concerns reach beyond the failures of a particular political regime. I see a set of deeper problems that I would like to put forward as the theme of this chapter. My thesis is that there is a widespread failure to address some of the incentive systems that generate our environmental degradation, and as a result there has been a failure of our domestic legal systems to reconstitute themselves to respond to the new values and understandings

[1] Harold W. Helfrich Jr., ed., *The Environmental Crisis* (New Haven, CT: Yale University Press, 1970), 108–109.

that constitute contemporary appreciation of issues such as biodiversity. Insofar as that is the case, environmental protection tends to float at the surface of our legal system, despite a plethora of environmental laws and regulations, and thus, at the profoundest level, the legal system is handicapped in doing the job it needs to do. Because of the limits of my own work and experience, I shall use as examples my own country, the United States, and its domestic law to illustrate my thesis. But I sense that what is true of our domestic law is, at least in the large, true of the domestic law situation in many countries.[2] And, unless basic domestic law adapts itself to the fundamental needs of environmental protection, all our efforts, including those at the international level, will continue to be severely handicapped. Thus, I want to consider why our efforts seem always to be such an uphill battle, struggling against such intense counterforces.

Let's begin by considering the legal system in general, and with an observation of the greatest generality, so much so as to be platitudinous: Legal systems are functional. That is, a legal system is structured to promote goals that the society desires to advance. That is why we observe the basic rules of law changing as a society moves from a feudal to a preindustrial and then industrial world. Such changes are summed up in phrases like "from status to contract."

Insofar as the physical world is concerned, modern societies generally have been concerned with promoting agriculture, manufacturing, housing, transportation, and the like, and with the transformations of the physical world that facilitate these activities. That is to say, prairies become farms, forests are harvested for lumber, and mountains and streambeds are mined for minerals. In these processes, wildlife is replaced with stock such as cattle and sheep, wetlands are filled and planted with food and forage crops, or with houses, and rivers are stopped up to produce hydropower and used as conduits to carry away wastes.[3]

This is what we do; it is the essential functioning of the modern economy. One may call it developmental or industrial, or postindustrial, but essentially it is an economy that has devoted itself to modifying or terminating the services the natural world was previously providing, such as species diversity, and substituting in its place things such as monocultural, large-scale agriculture.

Our law has been functional in that it is designed to permit and to reward activities that advance these conversions and to discourage activities that undermine them. Of all our basic legal categories, none is more important in this respect than the law of property, and, in particular, land law. That law, for example, encourages one to fence one's land, which is good for raising cattle and sheep, but does not permit one to tear down fences, which is good for wildlife. Of course, we can point to many enactments that are designed to promote environmental values, among them the establishment of parks and refuges, and the broad panoply of environmental regulatory laws that are now in force. But I want to emphasize strongly a distinction between the basic structural laws of the legal system (such as the property regime) and these regulatory enactments. For it is those foundational laws that essentially drive behavior by creating a deep structure of incentives and disincentives, and that fundamentally describe the directions the society

[2] There are, of course, notable exceptions, such as the provision in the German Constitution recognizing the social responsibility of the property owner, and the many nations that restrict or deny private ownership in heritage resources such as antiquities.

[3] See Joseph L. Sax, "Property Rights and the Economy of Nature: Understanding *Lucas v. South Carolina Coastal Council.*" 45 *Stanford L. Rev* (1993), 1442.

is going. I suggest that we learn more about how people are actually going to behave by looking at the incentive structure of these laws than by looking at expressions of environmental goals or at most environmental regulatory regimes.

This basic point is illustrated in every field of law. During the period when society desired rapid industrialization, tort law reflected that goal and made it functional. We saw rules like assumption of risk and the fellow servant rule, and union organizing characterized as a criminal conspiracy. Similarly, the old property rule of natural flow in water disappeared when it became desirable to allow mills to stop rivers in order to furnish hydropower for burgeoning industries. On the social side, one saw an analogous evolution of basic property rules. Women were desired to be subservient to their husbands, and the property law embodied that desire by putting a married woman's property into the hands of her husband. The true beginning of womens' rights came with the Married Womens' Property Acts dispossessing husbands of legal power over their wives' property.

In 1850, our Congress enacted a law called the Swamp Lands Grant Act, which authorized the grant of publicly owned wetlands to the states so that they could be transferred to settlers who were encouraged to fill them and to convert them to farmlands.[4] Similarly, throughout the arid regions of the western United States, where water was scarce, it was the law that the only way one could obtain a legally protected property right in water was to physically remove it from a river or stop it and apply it to irrigation, domestic supply, or the production of hydropower.[5] No right could be obtained to simply leave water in a river for what today are called instream flows (to maintain fish populations). Leaving water to flow in its natural course was legally considered waste.

The mechanism for promoting the goals of the developmental society was largely the law of private property. And it has been an enormously successful mechanism. You can go just about anywhere in the world today, look around you, and you will see the product of this potent legal tool, the property system. What you see – houses, commercial areas, cultivated farmland, factories, and so forth – is its visible product. The extirpation of the natural services of land and water (what is no longer there) is its invisible product.

Today, some forty years into the era of modern environmental law, we are all intensely aware – as our parents and grandparents were not – of the benefits provided by natural service, of wetlands and free-flowing rivers, and of habitat that maintains diverse ecosystems and populations of plants and animals that are the product of millions of years of evolutionary activity. Today, we have many environmental laws and environmental law courses at our law faculties. But how much has our property law changed so as to create incentives to preserve and restore those natural services that we have learned to value? How much have the basic rules of property that we teach today in the law faculties changed from what we taught forty years ago? The answer is, "not very much at all." The same engines are still generating the same developmental incentives that we had before the age of what is called modern environmental law.

To be sure, we have a good deal more regulatory law intended to protect environmental values than we did a few decades ago, and that is certainly a positive and important development. But the point I wish to call to your attention, and to emphasize, is how little environmental values have been integrated into the basic structure of the law.

[4] For example, ch. 84, Act of 28 September 1850, 9 Stat. 519.

[5] For example, *Empire Water & Power Co. v. Cascade Town Co.*, 205 F. 123 (8th Cir. 1913).

Thus, we still have nothing in the structure of property law that provides inducement to owners and managers to maintain and restore the natural services that land and water provide; on the contrary, we have a system that continues to incentivize the uses I described earlier that terminate those services and convert them to the purposes of the modern developmental economy. Specifically, I am referring to activities such as the diminution of wetlands and the transformation of habitat.

The point is an important and insufficiently noted one, I suggest, precisely because of the observation that is so familiar in economic discourse that the market (that is, the existing property system) functions of its own momentum to generate the goods and services that the society wants. That is exactly the sense in which the law is functional. The existing property system incentivizes the manipulation of land and water to produce precisely those things that promote the displacement of natural services in favor of various kinds of manufactured services, such as housing, corn, and pork. Although regulatory laws operate to moderate the way in which such activities are carried on, and at best to diminish the displacement of natural services, one hardly needs to be a keen observer to note that such regulatory efforts are always a struggle against the unrelenting, autonomic momentum of the property system and the rewards it promotes and encourages. It is an unequal battle.

Of course we need houses, corn, and pork, and no one would or should seriously suggest that the property system be reconceived in a way that would cease to provide adequate means to generate those goods, or that would return us to some version of a pristine natural world full of bears and wolves and no people, or only people who submitted to all the habitat demands of those creatures. The question I wish to raise is what a legal (and in particular, a property) regime for an age of environmental knowledge and sophistication would look like, as contrasted with the regime we have notwithstanding the so-called environmental law revolution.

I start by noting that at least in the Anglo-American legal system we have a highly individualistic conception of property. And although I recognize that a more limited and nuanced view of ownership exists in some other systems, I would suggest that economic globalization is bringing with it a quite strong sense of that individualistic version of ownership to many other places; and that just as ships in world trade carry with them exotic species that found they are able to thrive in foreign environments, the same may be said of the ownership concepts to which I am referring.

Let me begin with a brief description of that system. It consists of the view that almost anything can be owned,[6] and that ownership embraces the full range of uses that can be made, so long as one does not invade the like rights of others – what might be called the trespassory or nuisance limit on ownership. In this system, there is almost no notion of use entitlements that are withheld because of some interest of the public; nor is there any affirmative obligation to use one's property in a way that is beneficial to the public. The system rests on a fundamental market-driven assumption that ultimately what is good for the owner is good for the public, as public demand will generate private supply of that demand and not of what is not wanted or needed.[7]

[6] There are a few familiar exceptions: human slavery, trade in children, human organs, and so on (although even these restrictions are not universally observed).

[7] A recent and usefully documented debate over the importance of modifying property concepts as a means to reshaping environmental protection is found in chapters 6 and 7 of C. A. Arnold, ed., *Wet*

The most extreme example of this absolutist view is the right of destruction, formally called the "jus abutendi" or right of abuse, essentially the notion that one can do as he wishes with his own property, even wasting or destroying it, however much of a loss that might be to the society at large.[8] Indeed, as I pointed out in a recent book,[9] under our law the owner of a very great painting – a cultural treasure of incalculable value – is perfectly free to throw it into his furnace and turn it to ashes, for any reason or out of pure caprice. The same is dramatically true as to natural resources, as we saw some decades ago in the struggle to preserve the ancient redwoods, some of which predated the life of Jesus, but that are ordinary property entirely amenable in law – as they were in fact – to the "jus abutendi."

The harmful implications of this highly individualized conception of property for the environment have, in my view, not been sufficiently emphasized. Thus, to take a more contemporary example, absent some specific law prohibiting such action, the owner of a tract of land that contains the sole habitat of some species – whatever its scientific or cultural value – is entirely free to extirpate it. It is a notable inadequacy that the basic concept of ownership rights in our law takes no note of contemporary appreciation of the fundamental importance of biodiversity.

A striking example of this conception of property arose about a dozen years ago when the fossil remains of a Tyrannosaurus rex (T-rex), said to be the most complete and best articulated skeleton of a T-rex ever found, was unearthed on a ranch in South Dakota by a lady named Sue Hendrickson, an employee of a commercial company that collects and restores fossils. The question was who owned the remains, and that question came before a federal appellate court. Its explanation of its decision is profoundly revealing about the way we conceive the property system. Here is what the court said:

> We hold that the fossil was "land," ... Sue Hendrickson found the fossil embedded in the land. Under South Dakota law, the fossil was an "ingredient" comprising part of the "solid material of the earth." It was a component part of [the] land, just like the soil, the rocks, and whatever other naturally-occurring materials make up the earth of the ranch.... That the fossil once was a dinosaur which walked on the surface of the earth ... [is] irrelevant.[10]

Equally irrelevant to the legal system was the scientific importance of the fossil. The pervasiveness of this view of property in juridical thought is also revealed by a decision of the United States Supreme Court in a recent case that has been much cited as a leading precedent, a case entitled *Lucas v. South Carolina Coastal Commission.*[11] As part of a modern coastal protection program, regulations had been adopted that effectively prevented development of shoreline land that consisted of coastal dunes, the basic

Growth: Should Water Law Control Land Use (Washington, DC: Env. Law. Inst., 2005), in articles by Robert W. Adler and Holly Doremus.

[8] There is one area in which the law does routinely intercede, invalidating testamentary orders to destroy property (usually to keep it from disliked relatives), the ground effectively being that the testator must not have been of sound mind if – for example – he orders a valuable home demolished, or wants his automobile buried with him. See, generally, Strahilevitz, "The Right to Destroy." 114 *Yale L. J* (2005), 781.

[9] Joseph L. Sax, *Playing Darts with a Rembrandt*: *Public and Private Rights in Cultural Treasures* (Ann Arbor: University of Michigan Press, 1999), 181.

[10] *Black Hills Inst. v. South Dakota School of Mines and Technology*, 12 F.3d 737, 742 (8th Cir. 1993), *cert. denied*, 513 U.S. 810 (1994)

[11] *Lucas v. South Carolina Coastal Council*, 505 U.S. 1003 (1992).

idea being that dunes provided an important natural protective barrier to the region. When the law was applied to one owner's small undeveloped tract, he asserted that the regulation amounted to an uncompensated expropriation of his property, as it left him with an economically worthless piece of land.[12] In granting the owner compensation, the Court's decision emphasized that, under the regulation, the owner couldn't even build a single house on his land, and quoted the from Coke's Institutes, "for what is land but the profits thereof?"[13]

The possibility that some property may not be suitable for developmental use because of the natural services it provides to the public never seems to have been contemplated as a possibility by the Justice who wrote the Court's opinion. The regulation as applied in this particular area may not have been – probably was not – very well conceived from an environmental perspective, which was neither the basis for the decision nor of significance to the Court. The important lesson of that decision is that, from the perspective of our law, the economy of nature is as irrelevant as the dinosaur's scientific significance was in the case noted earlier. Natural values can be protected, but they do not shape the property system. As the courts see it, they can be protected only to the extent that they are compatible with property rights, or insofar as the public acquires the property right in a sale. The right of destruction is the base and starting point, the sun to which everything else is satellite. Is it surprising that environmental protection always seems to be struggling, inch by inch, to climb a vast mountain, sometimes rising a bit only to slip backward?

Unfortunately, the environmentally handicapped perspective of the Lucas case is representative of our legal system today, and it has played a central role in stimulating a so-called property rights movement in the United States that has mounted a sustained challenge to environmental protection laws as constitutionally uncompensated expropriations of private property. The operative message of this movement is that the public must buy back the right to maintain the remaining elements of its biodiversity from owners who have a property right to destroy it. Although this may seem an extreme position, it has been given legitimacy and powerful impetus by decisions from the U.S. Supreme Court such as that in the *Lucas* case, and we can only hope that the Court is now ready to moderate the extreme implications of that approach, as some of its more recent decisions suggest.[14]

Sad to say, the unintended consequences of the property right definitions crafted in the mid-nineteenth century when the western United States was settled have been taken up as an entitlement by today's property rights movement. Today, as diversions by irrigators are restricted in order to provide downstream flows and to protect the extirpation of various species of endangered fish, lawsuits are brought asserting a property right to remove all the water from our rivers for developmental purposes, in effect a claimed private ownership right to exterminate fisheries. And some courts, in the spirit of the *Lucas* decision described earlier, have held that the public must pay to stop the

[12] The case was unusual in a number of respects. It was stipulated (surely erroneously) that the tract was made totally worthless. This was the last undeveloped coastal site in the region, raising questions about the usefulness of the regulation as applied there. And, ultimately, the State withdrew the regulation, emphasizing its questionable importance as applied to that place. Nonetheless, the case is notable for the language and perspective on property rights that it elicited from the Supreme Court.

[13] *Lucas*, 505 U.S., at 1017.

[14] *Lingle v. Chevron, Inc.*, 125 S. Ct. 2074 (2005); *Tahoe-Sierra Preservation Council v. Tahoe Regional Planning Agency*, 535 U.S. 302 (2002).

destruction of fisheries, and recently, the U.S. federal government paid many millions of dollars in just such a case.

In that case, agricultural irrigators who had been receiving water from a state water project had their contractual allotments cut back in order to allow downstream flows to maintain a fish species listed under the federal Endangered Species Act (ESA).[15] The farmers claimed that they had a property right to the water and that their entitlements to receive water were not limited by a public right to protect native species from being extirpated by diversions out of the river. When a federal trial court ruled in favor of the farmers against the federal government (which was responsible for the endangered species law and listing), the Bush administration declined to appeal to a higher court, instead, settling with the farmers for a payment of approximately $16 million. In light of this outcome, a number of other lawsuits claiming property rights violations on behalf of irrigators who have similarly been limited in their diversions have been initiated. Fortunately, the judge in another similar case has rejected such claims, and rejected the reasoning of the previous decision.[16] So far, no appellate courts have considered this issue.

Fortunately, the environmentally insensitive perspective of the *Lucas* decision and its followers does not reflect the view that has been taken by all American jurists. A very different position had been put forward in the early years of the modern environmental era, but it has been pushed into the background, and in many quarters virtually forgotten. It deserves a quite different fate because it illustrates what a property regime would look like in a society whose basic law is environmentally functional.

In 1972, a case rather similar in its facts to *Lucas* came before the Supreme Court of the State of Wisconsin. A shoreline zoning ordinance effectively prohibited development of a landowner's lakeshore property, and was challenged as confiscatory.[17] The Wisconsin Court described the case before it as "a conflict between the public interest in stopping the despoliation of natural resources, which our citizens until recently have taken as inevitable and for granted, and an owner's asserted right to use his property as he wishes."[18] The Court said the following:

> Is the ownership of a parcel of land so absolute that man can change its nature to suit any of his purposes? The great forests of our state were stripped on the theory that man's ownership was unlimited.... An owner of land has no absolute and unlimited right to change the essential natural character of his land so as to use it for a purpose for which it was unsuited in its natural state and which injures the rights of others.... Too much stress is laid on the right of an owner to change commercially valueless land when that change does damage to the rights of the public.[19]

The Court went on to distinguish the fundamental rule of eminent domain law – that is, that when the public wants to improve the public condition the public as a whole ought to pay for it rather than letting the burden of such improvements fall upon any individual.[20] "This observation," the Court said, "refers to the improvement of the

[15] *Tulare Lake Basin Water District v. United States*, 49 Fed. Cl. 313 (2001), 59 Fed. Cl. 246 (2003), 61 Fed. Cl. 624 (2004).
[16] *Klamath Irrigation District v. United States*, 64 Fed. Cl. 328 (2005), *modified by*, 67 Fed. Cl. 504 (2005).
[17] *Just v. Marinette County*, 201 N.W.2d 761 (1972). The cases differed in one important factual respect: *Just* did not claim his land had been totally devalued.
[18] Ibid. at 767.
[19] Ibid. at 768, 770.
[20] Citing *Pennsylvania Coal Co. v. Mahon*, 260 U.S. 393, 416 (1922).

public condition, the securing of a benefit not presently enjoyed and to which the public is not entitled. The shoreland zoning ordinance preserves nature, the environment, and natural resources as they were created, and to which the people have a present right. The ordinance does not create or improve the public condition but only preserves nature from the despoilage and harm resulting from the unrestricted activities of humans."[21]

The decision in the *Just* case is the only modern opinion I know in our legal system that spells out an inherent limit on the scope and definition of the rights that can be acquired in land, defined by the ecological services performed by that land in its natural condition (in that case, the protection of water quality in a lake performed by adjacent wetlands); and that identifies those natural services as benefits to which the public is entitled. It is a chastening fact that the phrase "rights of the public" found in the *Just* case is as rare as an endangered species in American environmental jurisprudence, as rare as the phrase "rights of the private property owner" is commonplace. Although there was at one time a fairly strong interest in embodying an environmental right in state constitutions that had some success, those efforts have not had anything like the power or significance that some had hoped for. Although they are occasionally of more than rhetorical importance (as in Hawaii, as I describe later), there has yet to be a willingness to confront the blunt fact that to mean something by speaking of the "rights of the public" means to engage in a zero sum game with the established regime of property law.

I will return to the concept of legally enforceable rights held by the public – a fundamental point in the *Just* decision. For the moment, I only want to call attention to the interlocking elements that underlie the remarkable decision of the Wisconsin Supreme Court in *Just*: ecological services performed by land in its natural condition; limitations on the permissible scope of private ownership implied by those preexisting services; and legally cognizable rights in those services held by the public (not the state!).

The basic point of the case, that no one has a property right to destroy the benefits of a natural system (such as a lake), may seem obvious, yet its opposite has been the (unarticulated) watchword of the developmental economy's property system. As I noted earlier, water rights in our appropriation system could only be acquired by physical diversions out of a stream, the notion being that only such applications were "beneficial," and that leaving water in the river was effectively wasting it. The practical result was that irrigators and cities were permitted to dry up rivers by their diversions, thereby destroying the rivers as habitat for fish. And dry riverbeds, devoid of the fish that once flourished there, can be found today throughout the irrigated West. To be sure, those who crafted the legal rules for property rights in water did not set out to promote the destruction of fisheries as a positive element of a property right; and no doubt the implicit assumption was that fisheries would continue to prevail elsewhere, and despite significant diversions. That is, however, what they accomplished.

Although the *Just* case stands apart from the dominant judicial view today, it is in tune with a more environmentally sympathetic view that can be found in cases from an earlier era, at least as applied to wildlife. In 1900, in response to the virtual extermination of its beaver population, the State of New York enacted a law prohibiting the hunting, molestation, or disturbance of beavers, which it had restocked in a number of streams in the Adirondack Mountains. One of the restocking streams abutted land owned by a

[21] *Just*, at 771.

man named Barrett, whose land was valuable for its many trees. Not surprisingly, the new beaver population – legally protected from molestation – promptly set to work felling hundreds of Barrett's trees, significantly reducing the value of his land. Barrett then sued the State, claiming the beavers were in effect agents of the State of New York, and had trespassed on his land. Barrett cannot prevail, the Court said, against a law designed to protect wild animals, despite the harm they do. "Wherever protection is accorded, harm may be done to the individual. Deer or moose may browse on his crops, mink or skunks kill his chickens, robins eat his cherries . . . and no one can complain of [these] incidental injuries."[22]

"This is as it should be," the Court continued, "because the public authority is not to be limited to guarding merely the physical or material interests of the citizen. . . . The eagle is preserved not for its use, but for its beauty. . . . The same thing may be said of the beaver. . . . Observation of the animals at work or play is a source of never-failing interest and instruction. . . . [Their] preservation does not unduly oppress individuals. . . . [It] is no different . . . from that . . . when [the law] prohibits the destruction of the nests and eggs of wild birds even when the latter are found upon private property."

In short, in law as in morals, as the great American naturalist Aldo Leopold put it, "The landowner has an obligation to manage land in the interest of the community, as well as his own interest."[23]

I have so far noted some important tasks that still lie before us in developing an adequate body of environmental law. First among them is to reconsider our general legal principles (in particular, the law of private property) to reflect the values of what I have called the economy of nature, so that they encourage resource uses consistent with protecting and restoring the natural services of land and water, rather than giving incentives to disturb and destroy those services.

In the pages that follow, I shall have something to say about the law's understanding (or more precisely its misunderstanding) of the true nature of environmental problems, and how that failure impacts environmental protection; and I then shall comment briefly on one area of U.S. domestic law to which we can look for the sort of principled conception of public rights and state responsibilities that will at some point have to flourish more broadly if we are to produce a body of environmental law adequate to the challenges we face.

In the United States, action by private individuals and nonprofit organizations has always been an important element of environmental law. Although day-to-day law enforcement is carried out by government officials, both through enforcement and by negotiation (sometimes called reg-neg), the prospect of citizen enforcement continues to be an important prod both to public officials and to industry. To be sure, as regulatory statutes have proliferated, and environmental enforcement has become a more accepted governmental activity, the role of the judiciary is not as central as it was thirty or forty years ago.[24] But judicial action remains a vital element of environmental law, and that element has provided a revealing aspect of what I see as a misunderstanding of environmental harm.

[22] *Barrett v. State*, 116 N.E. 99 (Ct. Appeals, New York, 1917).

[23] Quoted in C. Meine, *Aldo Leopold: His Life and Work* (Madison: University of Wisconsin Press, 1988), 481.

[24] See, for example, Joseph L. Sax., *Defending the Environment: A Strategy for Citizen Action* (New York: Borzoi Books, 1970).

American courts have always been very concerned about the limits of the judicial role. In general, courts do not give advisory opinions about the law, nor do they decide generalized questions, such as whether a law is being adequately enforced. They much prefer to decide particularized controversies, such as a contract dispute between A and B, or a claim by an individual that his or her right has been violated by some specific conduct. The federal constitutional formula for this limitation of judicial authority is the "case or controversy" clause in Article III, section 2, of the U.S. Constitution.

Our Supreme Court in particular (and particularly in recent years) has been especially interested in defining the limits of the judicial role, and has written a number of opinions about the doctrine that we call standing-to-sue, or *locus standi*. Environmental cases have been of particular interest to the Court in this respect. That is not surprising because environmental cases often are quite unlike the conventional cases that come to court. For example, no one has the usual legal interest in environmental benefits, such as a deed, a lease, or a contract. Nor is there commonly the sort of immediate personal injury in environmental cases that one finds in an auto accident or a train derailment.

When the question of environmental standing-to-sue first reached the courts, back in the early 1970s in a case known as *Mineral King*, it got a quite sympathetic response, although in a very conventional way. A private company proposed to build a resort in a national forest under a permit, and the question was whether a U.S. federal government agency had done an adequate environmental assessment.[25] When the project was challenged by some environmentally concerned citizens, their standing-to-sue was questioned on the ground that they had no legally recognized interest in the forest, as would someone who had a lease to harvest timber, or owned a nearby vacation home. The Court found, however, that because they regularly used the area for recreation, their use interest (although not a traditional one) was sufficient to permit them to sue to assure that the environmental values of the forest were given the protection the law required.

At the time, the decision in the case was seen as a significant victory for environmental law, insofar as it rejected the view that only one with a conventional legal, ownership-type, interest could have standing, and it acknowledged the interest of hikers and birdwatchers in protecting the aesthetic values of a forest. Several decades later, we were to see how much less significant a victory that was than it seemed to be at the time, and how far we still had to go in communicating to our judges what environmental controversies were really about.

In 1992, a case entitled *Lujan v. Defenders of Wildlife* found its way to the U.S. Supreme Court.[26] The substantive question in the case was whether the Endangered Species Act (ESA) was intended to have extraterritorial application, so that a U.S.-funded project in another country that jeopardized the continued existence of a listed species triggered the consultation requirements of the ESA. The real plaintiff in the case was an environmental organization, Defenders of Wildlife, but because we do not have conventional organizational standing in the United States, the standard practice is for such organizations to join individual members who have a sufficient interest to meet the judiciary's standing-to-sue requirement. Following the precedent set by *Mineral King* and later cases, the individual plaintiffs were people who had previously gone as

[25] *Sierra Club v. Morton*, 405 U.S. 727 (1972).

[26] 504 U.S. 555 (1992).

tourists to the project's location to see the listed, threatened animals, and who alleged that they had a definite intent to return for one or more additional visits. For example, one plaintiff alleged that she had traveled to Sri Lanka and observed the habitat of the endangered Asian elephant, and intended to return and hoped to be able to see the endangered elephants again.

Of course, this was not the real motivation behind the *Defenders of Wildlife* challenge, which was interested in safeguarding the elephant's habitat without regard to its capacity to entertain foreign tourists. But it was, it seemed, exactly in line with the sort of allegation the courts required under the *Mineral King* approach. Nonetheless, taking an extraordinarily narrow view, the Supreme Court decided that it was not sufficient that the plaintiffs had visited in the past, for that could not support a claim that the project was currently harming them, or would definitely harm them subsequently. Moreover, it said, a mere statement of a future intent to visit was not sufficient, as the plaintiffs had no definite plan of visitation. Thus, the individuals could not demonstrate sufficient injury to their recreational or study interests to be allowed standing-to-sue.

You will not be surprised to learn that the decision was the subject of considerable criticism, even by some of the other Justices, who suggested that the plaintiffs' failed solely because they had neglected to buy round-trip air tickets, which would have shown a sufficient interest in revisitation of the elephants to support a claim of definite prospective injury. The decision is, indeed, worthy of derision on that ground, and – as many have noted – indicative of a distinct lack of sympathy with environmental litigation on the part of a number of the present Justices. But I find the case disturbing for a much more fundamental reason; and my concern extends even to the views of the Justices who dissented in one or another way from the decision that I have just described. What is genuinely significant about the *Defenders* case, and deeply distressing, is what it shows about how the Justices perceive the significance of the ESA, what it means to be "injured" by violations of the Act, and who is thereby injured. The Court put it this way: "Of course, the desire to use or observe an animal species, even for purely esthetic purposes, is undeniably a cognizable interest for purpose of standing,"[27] citing the *Mineral King* case for its "generous" view of what can constitute a legally cognizable interest. But, as indicated earlier, the Court found that this interest of the plaintiffs had not been injured, as there was no proof of their future "use or observation." And the Court apparently could not conceive of any other legally recognizable interest in biodiversity protection that could be injured.

The Court rejected other somewhat more expansive claims, in particular the assertion that anyone who has an interest in studying or seeing the endangered animals anywhere on earth has standing, or that anyone with a professional interest in such animals would have standing. "Under these theories," the opinion says, "anyone who goes to see Asian elephants in the Bronx Zoo [in New York] has standing" to challenge the habitat-threatening project under challenge in Sri Lanka in this case. "This," it says, "is beyond all reason."[28] Furthermore, according to the decision, it is "pure speculation and fantasy, to say that anyone who observes or works with an endangered species anywhere in the world is appreciably harmed by a single project affecting some portion of that species with which he has no more specific connection."[29]

[27] Ibid. at 562–563.
[28] Ibid. at 566.
[29] Ibid. at 567.

Other Justices, although not taking quite so narrow a view, were equally wide of the mark. One of them, also equating injury with "studying or enjoying a species," did not think it disqualifying that the plaintiffs had no return trip planned. Another felt that a zookeeper would have standing, despite physical distance from the project, because of a "professional nexus" to the species. Even the two Justices who thought that Congress could create a broad legal interest in species protection nonetheless said that "the party bringing suit must show that the action injures him in a concrete and personal way."[30] One must wonder how that could be done with many of the most endangered species that, unlike elephants, have no visitors and are not the subject of vacations or aesthetic enjoyment. For such creatures or plants, it seems only a scientist engaged in a current research project on the species would qualify.

It is instructive to compare the Justices' various conceptions of what the interests are that the ESA allows to be judicially protected with a statement about the meaning of biodiversity, articulated by the knowledgeable and distinguished scientist E. O. Wilson of Harvard University. The following brief excerpt is from his 2002 book, *The Future of Life*:[31]

> Agriculture is one of the vital industries most likely to be upgraded by attention to the remaining wild species. The world's food supply hangs by a slender thread of biodiversity. Ninety percent is provided by slightly more than a hundred plant species out of a quarter-million known to exist. Twenty species carry most of the load, of which only three – wheat, maize and rice – stand between humanity and starvation. For the most part the premier twenty are those that happened to be present in the regions where agriculture was independently invented some ten thousand years ago. . . . Yet some thirty thousand species of wild plants, most occurring outside these regions, have edible parts consumed at one time or another by hunter-gatherers. Of these, at least ten thousand can be adapted as domestic crops. A few, including the three species of New World amaranths . . . are immediately available for commercial development.

This, for one important example, is what biodiversity protection is really about, and it is in this context that we have to ask who is injured "concretely and personally" by species loss.

Oddly enough, in the *Defenders* decision, the Court at least implicitly acknowledged that the legislators who enacted the ESA understood very well what people such as Edward Wilson were talking about. The Court was quite aware that the purpose of the ESA had little to do with protecting recreational activity, or with protecting against what the Court in its decision understood to be "concrete and personal" injuries. Indeed, it quotes the purposive provision of the ESA which says the law was intended "to provide a means whereby the ecosystems upon which endangered species and threatened species depend may be conserved."[32] However, the Justices seem to doubt that the constitutional limits on the judicial role would permit the Congress to create or to recognize a judicially enforceable right in persons who have been injured in the way the Professor Wilson explains we are all injured by the decline of biodiversity. For such injury, as the Justices of our Supreme Court see it, cannot

[30] Ibid. at 581 (Kennedy, J. concurring).
[31] Edward O. Wilson, *The Diversity of Life* (Cambridge, MA: Belknap Press, 1992), 114.
[32] *Lucas*, at 566.

legally amount to a person being "injured in fact"[33] regardless of the purpose or intent of legislation dealing with biodiversity.

This last observation is the very essence of the decision. The Court cannot conceive of anyone having a legal entitlement in the safeguarding of biodiversity. Yet it hardly seems an exaggeration to say that the protection of biodiversity is at the very core of the environmental enterprise. Indeed, the essential things that the Court rejects as being legally cognizable are the very essence of environmental perils: the fact that the most significant hazards are pervasive; that they threaten essentially everyone across the globe; that they are generally impending rather than actualized, and thus not injurious in the conventional legal sense; and that they most often present hazards – such as loss of sustainability and impoverishment of future generations – that are not within the conventional legal category of "concrete injury." The risk – in the setting of matters such as species loss – is to what is usually called existence value.

For this reason, I consider the decision in the *Defenders of the Wildlife* case, once stripped of its technical theorizing about standing-to-sue, to reveal a vast chasm between what environmental protection is all about and what our jurists think legal rights are all about. In the profoundest sense, they are denying the very possibility of environmental law in the sense that they cannot conceive of the most fundamental concerns of environmental protection as having the status of basic legal rights. Of course, not every legitimate interest must be capable of judicial vindication. And no doubt my country is more focused on litigation than many others. But ask yourself this question: Can you imagine a legal system in which other basic legal rights such as property and contract and personal security are not subject to the protective shield of the courts?

The perceptual failure of our courts to give appropriate status to environmental rights reveals itself in many ways, and under various doctrines. Another recent example of the importance of having environmental interests recognized as rights is revealed by a 2004 case entitled *Norton v. Southern Utah Wilderness Alliance*, also a decision of the U.S. Supreme Court.[34] That case involved one of a number of pristine natural areas designated as wilderness study areas, where the law imposes a nonimpairment standard for management pending final legislative decision as to whether they will be designated as formal wilderness and given protection from all disturbing use and construction. A federal land management agency was mandated to administer those lands, keeping them unimpaired. In violation of this mandate the agency admittedly permitted impairment to occur by allowing recreational use of off-road machines known as all-terrain vehicles (ATVs). An alliance of wilderness defenders brought suit to compel the agency to take steps to control these admittedly illegal destructive uses, which it had not done.

The Court denied the plaintiffs any relief. Technically, the case was decided on a very narrow interpretation of the Administrative Procedure Act, the Court holding that the Act did not specify exactly what the land management agency should do, and thus its mandate was not "discrete" and specific enough to give rise to an enforceable violation. But essentially the case reveals a judicial view that the protection of wilderness is not the sort of interest that can give rise to an ordinary enforceable legal right on the part of the public, even those members of the public who would otherwise have standing-to-sue based on their presence on the land and present use of it. Wilderness preservation, it

[33] Ibid.

[34] 542 U.S. 55 (2004).

seems, is too indistinct and untraditional a concept to command the intervention of the courts – the sort of judicial intervention that would indisputably be afforded to one who claimed a right under a lease or a contract to cut down a wilderness forest, or mine in a wilderness desert.

I want to make my point clear. I am not suggesting that we lack any significant means of environmental law enforcement. Of course, I recognize that law can be used, and is today commonly invoked, to protect against many environmental wrongs, particularly those wrongs that resemble conventional nuisances, such as air and water pollution that directly threaten the health or economic interest of identifiable individuals.[35] I also appreciate that under the oddity of the *Mineral King* approach to standing, it may be possible to address species degradation, or the ravaging of an ancient forest at the behest of an individual who can qualify as a current tourist or recreationist. So, too, I understand that government can – and sometimes does – act to deal with fundamental issues such as loss of biodiversity, and empower public officials to protect against such loss. And I understand that some governments sometimes act effectively to address issues of the greatest environmental importance, such as global warming, epidemic disease, and burgeoning population growth.

But there is a very significant difference between receiving the benefit of legal support as a matter of contemporary policy or politics, and having a right recognized as one of the fundamental pillars of the legal system. Although we may talk about fundamental rights to environmental quality, and even embody those precepts in major declarations or constitutions, we need to understand at the same time how far we are from embracing any real conception of public rights as legal entitlements in matters like biodiversity protection. The examples that I have provided exemplify the sort of results that one can expect when such rights remain unrecognized, that is, when the environment remains at best only a second-order legal interest.

Let me now turn to a more positive aspect of this exploration of the essentials of environmental law. What does a domestic field of law look like when it is attuned to environmental values?

The best example, at least in the American system, is that subcategory of property jurisprudence that we call water law. Despite the way in which the law was implemented during the era of unrestrained development (as I noted earlier), the fundamental principle of our water law is a rejection of the individualist theory of ownership, and a focus on the needs of the public that, the law recognizes, can change over time.[36] Public ownership of the water and private rights as only usufructuary are the central juridical concepts of this distinctive subsystem of property law. The public trust doctrine is one of its elaborations.[37]

The waters within every jurisdiction belong to the people in perpetuity, and the only private rights that can be acquired are use rights. For example, the law and the State Constitution in California provides that "All water within the State is the property of the

[35] For example, commercial salmon fishermen were allowed to intervene in irrigators' inverse condemnation suit against government for reducing water deliveries to protect flows for migrating salmon listed under the *Endangered Species Act. Klamath Irrigation District v. United States,* supra note 16).

[36] "What is a beneficial use at one time may, because of changed conditions, become a waste of water at a later time." *Tulare District v. Lindsay-Strathmore District,* 3 Cal.2d 489, 567 45 P.2d 972, 1007 (1935).

[37] Joseph L. Sax, "The Public Trust Doctrine in Natural Resource Law: Effective Judicial Intervention." 68 *Michigan Law Review* (1970), 471.

people of the State . . ." and "the people of the State have a paramount interest in the use of all the water of the State" and "the protection of the public interest in the development of the water resources of the State is of vital concern to the people . . . and . . . the State shall determine in what way the water . . . should be developed for the greatest public benefit."[38] One may acquire a right of use, but that right may be exercised only in ways that are consistent with the public interest. Thus, for example, there is no right to waste water, and no right to contaminate it so as to make it unusable by others. The California Constitution not only prohibits waste and unreasonable use but also requires that water be employed "with a view to the reasonable and beneficial use thereof in the interest of the people and for the public welfare."[39]

State laws require anyone wishing to acquire a right to use water to obtain a permit, and to demonstrate that the proposed use is in the public interest.[40] In considering that question, the permitting authority is directed to consider the "effect of loss of alternative uses that might be made if not precluded by this application [and] the effect of the proposed use upon access to navigable or public waters."[41] This is the law throughout the arid regions of the United States. Public interest determinations may involve whether further abstraction from a source will have an impact on water quality, or waste – as in a case in which pumping from a geothermal aquifer for irrigation was rejected as not in the public interest where the water could have been used for heating.[42] The public interest standard also has been employed to help a rural and traditional community maintain its distinctive way of life, by denying water to a proposed resort that would have driven up the cost of water and made the agricultural way of life in a traditional, but viable, community unsustainable.[43]

Moreover, there are a variety of public rights in water with which no one may interfere to advance private interests, such as the right of navigation (which in many places extends beyond commercial navigation to recreational boating and fishing), and the protection of natural values.[44] These are not merely public interests that government *may* protect under its regulatory police power; they are entitlements held by each of us as members of the public, and they not only limit the nature of one's private property interest but also impose mandatory duties on the State. An interesting example arose in the 1920s when oil drilling was first proposed off the coast of California. The question arose whether such activity had to be prevented altogether because of the risk oil rigs in the ocean might present to public navigation and to contamination of coastal areas. The California Supreme Court ruled that offshore drilling was permissible, but that it was a usufructuary right in the ocean and was thus subject to continual supervision by the State, so that if at any time it was found to intrude on public entitlements, it would have to be restricted or even stopped altogether.[45] No greater private right than that conditional one could be acquired in the use of the waters of the state.

[38] California Water Code §§102, 104, 105.

[39] California Constitution, Art X, section 2.

[40] California Water Code §§1253, 1255.

[41] Alaska Stat. §46.15.080(b) (5), (8). See also *Shokal v. Dunn*, 707 P.2d 441 (Idaho, 1985).

[42] *Stempel v. Dept. of Water Resources*, 508 P.2d 116 (Wash. 1973); *Collins Bros. v. Dunn*, 759 P.2d 891 (Idaho, 1988).

[43] *In the Matter of Howard Sleeper*, Dist. Ct. N. M., 1st Jud. Dist., No. RA 84–53C (1985), *rev'd. on other grounds, Enseneda Land and Water Ass'n v. Sleeper*, 760 P.2d 787 (1988).

[44] *Marks v. Whitney*, 6 Cal.3d 251, 491 P.2d 394 (1971).

[45] *Boone v. Kingsbury*, 206 Cal. 148 (1929).

A more recent California case (the so-called *Mono Lake* decision)[46] applied that principle when it found in 1983 that an existing diversion of water from mountain streams by the City of Los Angeles, dating from 1940 that carried water down to the City for urban use was having an adverse effect on bird habitat and aquatic life in the lake into which the streams drained and that it had decimated fish life in the streams themselves. In light of those findings, and although Los Angeles' use permit had been in effect for more than forty years, the Court issued an order that resulted in a significantly reduced diversion designed to restore the lake to nearly its natural level and fish life in the stream to a healthy and sustaining condition. In that case, the court imposed its duty on the state at the behest of a private environmental plaintiff, The National Audubon Society. Moreover, the case produced a highly desirable outcome, as it generated a water conservation program in Los Angeles designed to diminish demand rather than simply encouraging the city to look elsewhere in natural areas for diversions to substitute for the Mono Lake supply.

In many states, the concept of waters being owned by the people is expressed as a public trust, which imports a positive duty on government to act to protect the entitlements of the public. One of the most recent statements of public trust responsibility was put forward by the Supreme Court of Hawaii in a matter known as the *Waihole Ditch* litigation.[47] That case, like those mentioned earlier, also involved a situation of perpetual oversight. For nearly a century, streams and groundwater on the wet (windward) side of the island of Oahu had been captured in tunnels, and transported to the dry (leeward) side where it was used for the irrigation of sugar plantations. In the 1990s, the sugar industry closed down, and water that had previously been diverted was left in its native streams, where it began to restore long-dormant riparian environments and resuscitate some traditional small-scale agriculture by Native Hawaiians who lived on the windward side.

The plantation owners claimed a property right in the water in perpetuity and a right to use it for future developmental purposes, but the Court rejected those claims, holding that "the public trust, by its very nature, does not remain fixed for all time, but must conform to changing needs and circumstances. ... This authority empowers the state to revisit prior diversions and allocations, even those made with due consideration of their effect on the public trust."[48] It ordered the Water Commission to reallocate the water, employing a presumption in favor of public (such as instream, fish, and wildlife) uses, and Native Hawaiian traditional "purposes protected by the trust."[49]

One of the most interesting aspects of the Hawaii decision is the Court's articulation of the state's duty to protect the legal rights of the public in natural resources, a responsibility founded in significant part[50] on the State Constitution, which provides that "all public natural resources are held in trust by the State for the benefit of the people."[51] In adopting its Constitution, "the delegates explained that they had used 'public trust' to

[46] *National Audubon Soc'y. v. Superior Court of Alpine County*, 658 P.2d, at 709, 723–724 (1983).

[47] In re *Water Use Permit Applications*, 94 Hawai'i 97; 9 P.3d, at 409 (2000).

[48] Ibid. at 447, 453.

[49] Ibid. at 454.

[50] Hawaii also recognizes a common law public trust, as well as public rights founded in traditional Hawaii law.

[51] Hawaii Constitution, Art. XI, Sec. 1, ¶2; see also Art. XI, sec. 7 ("The State has an obligation to protect, control and regulate the use of Hawaii's water resources for the benefit of its people").

describe the duty of the state to actively and affirmatively protect, control and regulate water resources."[52]

Hawaii also has incorporated traditional values into its modern law, holding that its former sovereign had reserved to the people "prerogatives respecting water [which] constituted much more than a restatement of police powers, rather . . . it [the state] retained on behalf of the people an interest in the waters of the kingdom which the State has an obligation to enforce and which necessarily limited the creation of certain private interests in waters."[53] When the Hawaiian kingdom gave way to the settlers from the mainland who had effectively conquered the islands, an act known as the Great Mahele instituted the concept of private property in the kingdom.[54] The Court explained that "despite the transition to a private property regime, water remained a resource reserved to the community."[55] Both as part of the American legal tradition, and in response to its own unique history, the Hawaii Court concluded its opinion by quoting the language of the California Supreme Court in the Mono Lake case: "Thus, the public trust is more than an affirmation of state power to use public property for public purposes. It is an affirmation of the duty of the state to protect the people's common heritage of streams, lakes, marshlands and tidelands, surrendering that right of protection only in rare cases when the abandonment of that right is consistent with the purposes of the trust."[56]

Only when this precept is expanded into a general principle of our domestic law governing all our natural resources will we be able to say we have truly implanted environmental jurisprudence into our legal system.

[52] In re *Water Use Permit Applications*, 9 P.3d, at 444, n. 29.
[53] Ibid. at 441.
[54] For an explanation of this historic event, see *McBryde Sugar Co. v. Robinson*, 504 P.2d 1330, 1337–1338 (1973); John J. Chinen, The Great Mahele (Honolulu: University of Hawaii Press, 1958).
[55] In re *Water Use Permit Applications* 9 P.3d, at 446, n. 32.
[56] *National Audubon Society*, 658 P.2d, at 723–724 (1983).

2 Biodiversity and International Law: Historical Perspectives and Present Challenges: Where Do We Come From, Where Are We Going?

Françoise Burhenne-Guilmin*

> Our remote ancestors were so close to their environment that they would have found it hard to think of it as separate from themselves. When you live as hunters or fisherfolk, snatching your living directly from the wild . . . your dependence on the environment is absolute.
>
> Human history has been one of progressive take-over on the flows of energy within natural systems, permitting ever-increasing human abundance and ubiquity. The impacts on the natural world have been immense. Early hunters altered ecosystems by fire, and their extermination of the largest and slowest-breeding animals. But agriculture – the taking of selected plants and animals into human ownership – had a more profound influence because it established the dichotomy between 'domesticated' and 'wild' and began the familiar struggle between the two. Pastoralists slaughtered the wolves or lions that preyed on their flocks and herds, and killed the deer and antelopes that competed with the beasts for pasture. Agriculturalists attacked the 'weeds' they could not eat and guarded their crops against wild herbivores as best they could. These conflicts remain important today.

So writes Martin Holdgate in *The Green Web*,[1] and he adds: "We call this process of transforming nature 'development.'"

Throughout history, humans have aspired to development, and the definition of the limits of development has been a controversial and conflicting process. Which development? for whom? and how? These are questions that are by no means new. The answers are linked, over space and time, to cultures and cultural values. But they also are linked to nature itself, and to its resilience. Our era is not the first to experience resource depletion, pollution, and human-induced natural catastrophes, but the present scale of human impact is unprecedented.

There is also evidence throughout history of awareness and knowledge of rules to be adhered to in order not to upset the flow of nature's benefits. This is particularly true for living resources for which national regulatory measures have deep roots: rules for the protection of various kinds of wildlife were enacted by the Indian emperor Ashoka in 252 BC. In Europe, rules restricting the taking of game were enacted during the Middle Ages. The Dutch jurist Hugo Grotius invented the freedom of the high seas, which has had long-lasting consequences for marine resources.

Then came the Industrial Revolution, which tipped abruptly and brutally the human/nature relationship. In response, the development of national measures for

[1] Martin Holdgate, *The Green Web: A Union for World Conservation* (London: Earthscan, 1999), 1.

* Dr. Françoise Burhenne-Guilmin is Senior Counsel, IUCN Environmental Law Centre.

the protection of economically important species sped up, and the first MEAs were concluded for things considered useful – protecting birds beneficial to agriculture and destroying those that were not (1902) – or to stem the slaughter of shared exploited species such as seals and whales (1911).

The conservation movement emerged in nineteenth-century Europe and North America in reaction to massive destruction of species as well as a result of the intensive exploration of the natural world. Both led to the creation of learned and conservation societies, the first wave of environmental nongovernmental organizations (NGOs). Conservation played an increasingly decisive role in moving away from utilitarian considerations towards a more balanced view of the man/nature relationship. It also provided the foundation for resource management, first expressed in 1910 by Pinchot, Chief Forester under U.S. President T. Roosevelt, as "the use of existing resources for the present generation, the prevention of waste and the development of natural resources for the many rather than the few."[2]

International action soon followed, as exemplified by the 1933 Convention on the Conservation of Flora and Fauna in their Natural State in Africa, and the Western Hemisphere Convention of 1940. A number of initiatives also were taken in North America for the conservation of migratory birds, recognising the need for joint management measures on the part of range states. The trend, however, was set by protective measures for mainly spectacular species, and by the creation of protected areas "set aside" for conservation.

This approach, reflected in national legislation on nature protection or wildlife conservation, produced important positive results, but surely, even if slowly, was bound to evolve towards more comprehensive goals.

It is against this background that IUCN (The World Conservation Union) was created in 1948 under the auspices of UNESCO, by governments and NGOs convinced of the need to work internationally towards the conservation of nature and natural resources, a subject that President Franklin Roosevelt had identified, a year before the end of World War II, as "a basis of permanent peace."[3]

The first statutes describe the Union's goal, in a surprisingly modern fashion, as "the preservation of the entire world biotic community or Man's natural environment, which includes the earth's renewable natural resources of which it is composed and on which rests the foundation of human civilisation."

Even more surprising is that this 1948 constitution identified the preparation of a worldwide convention as one of the main objectives to achieve, and to which it would contribute.

This happened forty-four years later, when, in May 1992, representatives of a large number of the nations of the world adopted the Convention on Biological Diversity (CBD). This marked the end of hectic and difficult negotiations, as well as efforts by many governments, international and national organisations, and individual experts over several years. Unknown to them, the exhausted negotiators also had presented me with a magnificent birthday present, by completing their tasks just before 22 May, now Biodiversity Day.

[2] Gifford Pinchot, *The Fight for Conservation* (New York: Doubleday, 1910).

[3] "I am more and more convinced that conservation is a basis of permanent peace." Cited by M. Holdgate, *History of the Green Web* (London: Earthscan, 1999), 5.

The adoption of the CBD also marked an exceptionally important step in an ever-continuing evolution in the legal field but generated by a profound evolution in the perception of the problems at hand and of the action required to solve them.

At the heart of these changes is the notion of biological diversity, a concept coined only some twenty years ago by scientists as a way to group ecological, species, and genetic diversity.

The flamboyant term proved immensely helpful: in less than ten years, it had entered everyday language. Why this success? Because, as Cyrille de Klemm put it, "It essentially provides a unifying principle which encompasses all genes, species, habitats and ecosystems on earth, thus covering everything from a wild plant's genes to the high seas and Antarctica. This convenient shorthand not only denotes all components of the living world but also reveals the intricate interdependence between them." This is reflected in the CBD's definition,[4] which, continued de Klemm, "makes no distinction between wild and domesticated animals, wild and cultivated plants, land and sea, or areas under or beyond national sovereignty or jurisdiction. Biological diversity therefore functions as an all-embracing concept providing a common frame of reference for the development of appropriate forms of management by all countries."[5]

But let us not anticipate. How was it, when, in 1980, the idea of a comprehensive worldwide convention emerged? It came from IUCN, and, surprisingly, not from the scientists, but from its legal network – the Commission on Environmental Law. Several of its members had argued for years that the natural environment was not yet sufficiently, let alone comprehensively, addressed in the multiplicity of legal instruments that were being created internationally and nationally as a result of the environmental movement of the day. They criticised the fact that too little was being done regarding conservation outside of protected areas. They also criticised the fact that far more attention was being given to the technical aspects of environmental quality, namely, pollution control, and complained about the artificial divide between pollution and living resources issues.

These concerns had first been raised at the 1968 UNESCO Conference on the Biosphere, which had established an international scientific consensus on the need to systematically address the rational use and conservation of the resources of the biosphere and gave birth to the UNESCO Man And the Biosphere (MAB) Programme.

The years that followed witnessed significant progress in the creation of international treaty law addressing "life on earth."

First came the adoption, in 1971 at Ramsar, of a convention on the conservation of wetlands. Although those who initiated this convention had the foresight to create a global framework for the conservation and wise use of a type of ecosystem, each word in this sentence is, you will notice, still modern today. The authors had little knowledge of the intricacies of creating an international convention. This resulted in, for instance, an NGO representative from Germany signing on behalf of the Federal Republic, and other legal deficiencies, which took two decades to redress. Nevertheless, it was a striking

[4] "Biological diversity" means the variability among living organisms from all sources including, inter alia, terrestrial, marine, and other aquatic ecosystems and the ecological complexes of which they are part; this includes diversity within species, between species, and of ecosystems. Convention on Biological Diversity, Article 2.

[5] Cyrille de Klemm & Clare Shine, "International Environmental Law: Biological Diversity" (United Nations Institute for Training and Research, Programme of Training for the Application of Environmental Law, Course 6, 1998), 1, 2.

demonstration of a budding interest on the part of the international community for degrading natural systems, and the beginning of a success story.

The UNESCO World Heritage Convention followed soon after. Initially conceived as a mechanism to protect cultural sites, it was enlarged, at the last minute, with IUCN's input, to cover exceptional natural sites. This convention marked an important step, not only because it introduced the notion of world heritage for natural areas of global importance but also because it created a mechanism to save those in danger. The principle of the international responsibility of states with sovereignty over such sites vis-à-vis the global community was established, along with the corresponding solidarity of the community to assist in conserving them.

Stockholm '72 followed, which provided the foundation for the environment movement and revolution. Its title, you will remember, was a "Conference on the Human Environment," with the emphasis placed on the problems of the day in the developed world – and thus on a good number of "brown issues." But it also sowed the seeds for important trends on the green side, for instance with the recognition that "Man has a special responsibility to safeguard and wisely, manage the heritage of wildlife and its habitat."[6] It also endorsed the efforts of IUCN, ongoing since 1963, towards the negotiation of a global convention on the import, export, and transit of endangered species, and called for an international treaty to deal with those species that migrate over national boundaries. Above all, with the Stockholm Declaration, the conference established a set of principles that has provided the foundation for modern environmental law.

Ten years after an IUCN General Assembly resolution called for it,[7] CITES[8] was adopted at a diplomatic conference convened by the U.S. government in the State Department building in Washington, DC. Never had I seen corridors long enough to travel with an electric cart from one meeting room to the other – which I thoroughly enjoyed – nor had I known that Department of State translators had to adhere to the rule that a text in one language must be translated into another with the same amount of words. Please laugh, if you wish. I did not – at least at the time. Neither did I laugh at the success of the U.K. delegation in calling for the deletion of the draft convention's provisions on transit – on the ground that transit is a nonexistent event in the world of customs. But I grinned at the reintroduction of transit control by decision of the Conference of the Parties, some time later. What really matters, however, is that CITES took off, and it became the cornerstone of the fight against a major threat to species conservation. Its role has evolved over time, and now CITES increasingly deals with species of great economic importance.

The migratory species convention also took several years to become reality. The idea was to provide a framework for coordinated management by all range states of species that IUCN characterised as "shared resources," a legal status that, at the time, did not meet with acceptance internationally. Nevertheless, the convention was adopted in Bonn in 1979. Its novelty was to provide for the negotiations of further agreements on species or groups of species that would benefit from concerted action between Range States.

[6] Principle 4, Declaration of the United Nations Conference on the Human Environment, Stockholm, 1972. U.N. Doc. A/Conf.48/14/Rev. 1 (1973); 11 I.L.M. 1416 (1972).

[7] IUCN General Assembly, Nairobi, 1963.

[8] *Convention on the International Trade in Endangered Species of Wild Fauna and Flora.* The convention was adopted at a diplomatic conference in Washington, DC, on 3 March 1973, and on 1 July 1975 CITES entered into force. See http://www.cites.org/eng/disc/what.shtml.

Today, thirteen agreements have been concluded, ranging from "mini agreements" on specific populations to a whole migratory route, and the technique of nonbinding governmental Memoranda of Understanding (MOU), not foreseen by the convention, has been introduced.

On the eve of the 1980s, a major step in global treaty law on species and ecosystems had been taken. The new global treaties were restricted to issues, which at that point in time were perceived, and politically accepted, as calling for a global response. This perception was then limited. The results could therefore only be fragmentary, and indeed covered only one type of ecosystems (wetlands), one type of threat (international trade), one category of species (migratory), and sites of extraordinary international importance (World Heritage).

At the regional level, where the approach was more encompassing, a number of conventions were in place. The '68 Algiers Convention, for instance, replacing the 1933 colonial treaty, still focused on species conservation and protected areas, but it also added principles and obligations related to other renewable resources, including soil and water. Others followed, with more or less success. This was the case in Europe, with the Bern Convention (1979),[9] which provided a cornerstone for species and habitat conservation. There were not many conventions in Asia and the Pacific (South Pacific). Antarctica benefited from the 1980 Convention on the Conservation of Antarctic Marine Living Resources.

On the marine scene, the dynamic UNEP Regional Seas Programme initiated an integrated approach, resulting in legal frameworks for the Baltic in 1974 and the Mediterranean in 1976. The technique used then was revolutionary: to protect the riches of those seas by tackling first pollution control, and then move on with additional protocols on living resources and ecosystems conservation. Twelve regional seas agreements followed later on.

Stockholm, as well as spectacular accidents, had generated sectoral global responses to pollution with International Maritime Organisation (IMO) agreements on dumping at sea and on ship-generated and land-based source pollution, answering, at least in part, the need to regulate processes and activities that affect living resources.

All these efforts provided a patchwork, rather than a framework, for action, leaving most species and spaces in a legal vacuum. The deficiencies of the patchwork approach became a powerful argument for more comprehensive global approach.

From the point of view of principles, the evolution encouraged yet a further step. The idea that states have a special responsibility to conserve certain elements of the natural heritage for present and future generations rose to the fore. It culminated in the acceptance of the concept of "common heritage of mankind" applied to the deep-sea bed and outer space. This concept also was embraced, initially, by the 1983 FAO Undertaking on Genetic Resources.

From the conceptual point of view, the IUCN Global Conservation Strategy of 1980, provided a global vision, followed by the adoption of the Charter for Nature,[10] which proclaimed for the first time that "every form of life is unique, warranting respect, regardless of its worth to man." Fundamental global conventions were approved – the

[9] *Convention on the Conservation of European Wildlife and Natural Habitats*, adopted in Bern (Switzerland) in September 1979. It came into force on 1 June 1982.

[10] The World Charter for Nature was adopted by the United Nations General Assembly in 1982 (UN GA RES 37/7).

Law of the Sea (1982), essential for ocean conservation and use, and the Treaty on the Protection of the Ozone Layer (1982), the first to deal with a global threat to life on earth. All of these themes were later woven into *Our Common Future* by the Brundtland report (1987), the first international document to use the concept of biological diversity, to acknowledge the responsibility of states vis-à-vis their own resources, and to call for a global treaty on species and ecosystems with appropriate financial measures.

The idea of such a treaty also was slowly making its way through IUCN since its General Assembly of 1980. IUCN's work to develop elements of a possible future convention concentrated on biological diversity of the wild at genetic, species, and ecosystem levels, conservation (including sustainable use) *in situ* and *ex situ*, and processes affecting biodiversity, such as pollution or the introduction of alien species. A primary element was the creation of a multilateral fund financed by contributions based primarily on the commercial exploitation of "biomaterials." Various aspects of the draft were unacceptable to developing and developed countries, for different reasons. For developing countries, the draft did not take sufficiently into account the socioeconomic aspects of biological diversity, was not addressing agricultural diversity, and, above all, provided for mechanisms (global lists, financing), which, because they were multilateral, were not acceptable. For developed countries, the idea of a fund to which sectors of their industries, for example, pharmaceutical companies, would have to contribute, was considered unrealistic, if not scary. Although many elements of the draft found their way into the CBD, clearly the draft did not cover, and indeed had not been intended to cover, the entire breadth of issues related to biological diversity, when it finally hit the international political scene in 1989.

It was a time when the Rio Conference on Environment and Development preparations were about to start, with the objective of setting the foundation for sustainable development. The stakes were high.

It also was a time when the FAO Undertaking on Plant Genetic Resources,[11] concerned with the genetic resources of importance to food and agriculture, was under attack, in spite of three successive modifications moving it away from a common heritage concept to one that was based on sovereignty. It was a time when biodiversity prospecting – the exploration of biodiversity for commercially valuable genetic and biochemical resources – was making waves. The use of genetic resources – mainly originating in the South – by companies – mainly located in the North – and making considerable profits from this use without any retribution to those husbanding them, inflamed the South and many elsewhere as well. This was because most of the resulting products were patented. Biopiracy became a symbol of North/South inequities. Politically, the common heritage of mankind concept was dead, and gave way to that of "common concern of humanity." That is to say, in a world where sovereign states exercise sovereign rights over their natural resources, they have – some will say in spite, and I am saying because, of that sovereignty – a duty towards the international community to conserve the object of this concern. And so, in spite of drawbacks and difficulties, we have moved to, or towards, an obligation *erga omnes*, and to, or towards, a concurrent

[11] The International Undertaking was adopted by the FAO General Conference in 1983 (Resolution 8/83) as an instrument to promote international harmony in matters regarding access to plant genetic resources for food and agriculture.

responsibility of each member of this community to conserve its own biological diversity.

In parallel, emerged the recognition of "common but differentiated responsibilities among states," incorporated in all global environmental conventions since the end of the 1980s. Although it does not affect the obligations deriving from common concern, it introduces the notion of equity into its implementation.

This tandem of principles is particularly important when tackling biological diversity at the global level.

Let me quote Holdgate[12] again:

> There are anything between two and eighty million species on earth – 10 million is a good guess. Forest, grassland, mountains, deserts and coastal zones support distinctive kinds of plants and animals.... It is obvious that the different regions of the world differ in their biological diversity. To give some statistics: there are approximately 250.000 species of vascular plants in the world. Two thirds of these, around 170.000, occur in the tropics and sub-tropics. Over 40.000 species – about a quarter of the tropical diversity or a sixth of the world's vascular plants diversity – are concentrated in the three northern South American countries of Colombia, Ecuador, and Peru. The whole of tropical and sub-tropical Africa in contrast only supports about 35.000 species. South Africa, a great centre of plant diversity, has a flora of some 23.000 species, which is more than the whole of the continental United States (20.000), or Europe (with only 11.300 species).

Holdgate adds, rightly, "This kind of statistics alone can distract from the main point. Sheer numbers of species should not be equated with importance."

Yet, uneven distribution between the North and the South was, and still is, an important consideration in any discussion of a global response. It is against this background that the Biodiversity Convention negotiations started, and its result is the convergence of all these concerns, as the convention's definition of biological diversity and its objectives demonstrate. The long-awaited framework was finally in place, adopted along two other Rio Conventions, both dealing with processes – climate change and desertification – with immense impacts on biological diversity. Only forests were not provided with a specific legal regime, and the discussion on whether this would be a good idea or not is still raging.

Against this background, let us now consider some current aspects of implementation, pertaining to each of the three CBD objectives. Let us do this, keeping in mind that the CBD's chief merit is to provide a forum within which priorities for action and programme of work are to be set, recommendations for implementation developed, financial support priorities agreed, and further guidance and rules adopted, in a binding or nonbinding form.

Guidance on implementation has been provided by CBD conventions of parties (COPs) on virtually all articles of the Convention dealing with conservation and sustainable use, but some questions, because of their cross-cutting nature, have been singled out for priority treatment.

Perhaps the most fundamental COP decision was the adoption of the ecosystem approach as a framework for analysis and implementation of the convention. Going well beyond paying respect to the concept, the COP endorsed a description of the

[12] Martin Holdgate, keynote address, 1992, unpublished.

ecosystem approach, together with principles and operational guidance for its implementation. Together, these documents provide a first strategy for the integrated or holistic management of resources through modern, scientific, adaptive management practices. Although they will evolve as the theory and practice of the ecosystem approach develops, the set of twelve principles is a first important step in defining the basic components of integrated management of land, water, and living resources.

An important principle is, for instance, that the ecosystem approach should seek the appropriate balance between, and integration of, conservation and use of biological diversity. The rationale notes that "there has been a tendency in the past to manage components of biological diversity either as protected or non-protected. There is a need for a shift to more flexible situations, where conservation and use are seen in context, and the full range of measures is applied in a continuum from strictly protected to human-made ecosystems."[13] At last, the North/South debate on conservation versus sustainable use seems to soften and find common grounds.

Work needs to be done to operationalise the ecosystem approach further. This particularly goes for legal research. What does the approach mean from the legal point of view? How can national legislation internalise the concept and its requirements? Are environmental lawyers going to pay more attention to land-use planning tools than they have so far?

Another basic tenet of the convention is its emphasis on sustainable use, and it is not surprising that the parties considered it essential to develop a common understanding of the concept.

The Addis Ababa Guidelines[14] are doing just that. They are based on the premise that "it is possible to use biodiversity components in a manner in which ecological processes, species and genetic variability remain above thresholds needed for the long-term viability and thus that all resource managers and users have the responsibility to ensure that use does not exceed these capacities."[15]

Importantly, the guidelines also recognise that sustainable use is a valuable tool to promote conservation of biological diversity, as "in many instances it provides incentives for conservation and restoration because of the benefits that people derive from the use."[16] This applies to species populations as well as habitats. What kind of use (consumptive or nonconsumptive) and what kind of incentives (social, cultural, and economic) are dependent on the specific situation considered, and require a continuous iterative process: monitoring, assessment, and adjustment. In turn, sustainable use cannot be achieved if isolated from conservation measures – both must operate in tandem. Overexploitation of resources remains a major driver of biodiversity loss, and examples abound in the forestry and the fisheries sectors, with disastrous consequences for the stocks themselves, the ecosystems of which they are a part, and peoples' livelihoods. And so, the adoption of the guidelines – the first to be adopted at a global level on sustainability of use of all biodiversity components – is an achievement. Now they need implementation. Encouraging is also that they are now being recognised and adopted

[13] Principle 10, CBD Decision VII/11, Ecosystem Approach.

[14] The Addis Ababa Principles and Guidelines for the Sustainable use of Biodiversity, adopted at the seventh meeting of the Conference of the Parties (COP-7) in February 2004. They are available in the *CBD Handbook* and at www.biodiv.org/programmes/socio-eco/use/addis-principles.asp.

[15] Guidelines A 8(a), *CBD Handbook*, 1113.

[16] See Note 14.

in other fora – Ramsar, CMS, and CITES have integrated, or are about to integrate them into their work.

Many, if not all, of the fourteen principles call for further legal research. Again, here, lawyers should dialogue on the consequences of these principles on the design of national legislation. For instance, what does it mean in law that "local users of biodiversity components should be sufficiently empowered and supported by rights, to be responsible and accountable for use of the resources concerned"? We read a lot of case studies on this subject, but too many of them are silent on their legal foundations.

Let us turn to conservation measures, taking protected areas (PAs) as an example.

The convention defines a protected area as "a geographically defined area, which is designated or regulated and managed to achieve conservation objectives."[17] This is a very flexible definition, permitting all shades in the intensity of the protection, and silent on considerations of scale (how small, how big), and of level (local, subnational, national, regional, global), let alone on jurisdictional considerations.

In this field also, significant conceptual changes have taken place in the past decade.

- First and foremost, under the impetus of IUCN, the concept has been enlarged to encompass management categories belonging to the realm of land use planning tools. Although this does not reduce the need for general land use systems to be sensitive to environmental and biological diversity conservation everywhere, it has facilitated understanding that PAs are part of such systems, establishing a continuum between "no-use" and "sustainable use" policies.
- Second, the role of PAs for both conservation and sustainable use of biodiversity has fostered the need for PA *systems*, designed to support national, regional, and international strategies towards conservation and sustainable use of biodiversity.
- Third, the perception of PA governance has evolved, and moved to recognize that natural resources, peoples, and cultures are fundamentally interlinked. How PAs relate to local people, and vice versa, has become a central issue, and work in partnership with local stakeholders, a central theme.

Comanagement of government-designated protected areas is an increasingly used mechanism to share responsibility and accountability between government agencies and other stakeholders, in particular indigenous peoples and local and mobile communities that depend on such an area culturally and for their livelihoods. Not only should PAs be established and managed with due regard to their rights to land and natural resources, but these areas also may become an instrument in the restitution of such rights. In either case, these communities should also benefit from, and be actively involved in, protected areas planning and management.

Other trends are emerging, such as the recognition of the value of Community Conserved Areas – voluntarily conserved by indigenous peoples and local communities through customary laws and other effective means – for a "formal" PA system.

Taken together, these various governance options provide (again) a continuum, from government-managed protected areas, to PAs that are comanaged, and further to full authority and responsibility held by the concerned communities.

[17] Article 2, CBD.

The CBD programme of work on PAs builds on these developments, with two essential goals:

- First, to assist parties with regard to tools and processes needed when designing or assessing their PA systems based on their national priorities and the objectives of the CBD.
- Second, to determine, on the basis of regional and global scientific assessments, what a common global approach should be. And this goes also for marine areas outside national jurisdiction, a subject that has often fallen between the cracks.

Indeed, COP VII agreed that there is an urgent need for international cooperation and action to improve conservation and sustainable use of biodiversity in marine areas beyond the limits of national jurisdiction, including through the establishment of further marine protected areas, in particular to protect seamounts, hydrothermal vents, cold water corals, and other vulnerable ecosystems.[18]

Unfortunately, the recent Montecatini meeting of the Ad-Hoc Open-Ended Working Group on PAs stumbled over the discussion of the role of the CBD regarding PAs on the high seas, in particular vis-à-vis UNCLOS and its Open-Ended Informal Consultative Process.[19] Article 23 of the CBD, however, requires consistency with the provisions of UNCLOS, and the UNCLOS process recognises the need "to co-ordinate and cooperate" with the CBD.[20] The discussion is therefore not one about conflicting mandates but, perhaps, one about the articulation of a joint mandate. The next step, and under which convention to take it, can then be discussed once the debate on the desirable type of action is sufficiently advanced.

Again here, lawyers have a role to play. There has not been one single work devoted to the elements of a "modern" PA legal regime since IUCN ELP's work on this issue in the 1960s. At a time when "toolkits" in this field are being identified, lawyers have little to show.

There is, of course, a vast number of other issues of relevance to conservation and sustainable use, which have generated CBD action. It is impossible to consider them all here, but we will deal with two important ones: biosecurity and the protection of indigenous knowledge and cultures, which I will only address in the context of ABS. Let me here only pay tribute to three outputs of the CBD process:

- the Biosafety Protocol – and its present work on compliance and liability;
- the Alien Species Guidelines – still a subject of dissent, but hopefully are on their way to adoption at COP 8; and
- the AKWÉ: KON Guidelines for the conduct of cultural, environmental, and social impact assessments[21] regarding developments proposed to take place on, or which are likely to have an impact on, sacred sites and on lands and waters traditionally occupied or used by indigenous and local communities.

[18] Decision VII/5, paras. 29 and 30.

[19] See *Earth Negotiations Bulletin*, PAWG-1 Final, IISD, 20 June 2005. Available online at http://www.iisd.ca/biodiv/wgpa.

[20] Advance and unedited text, Part A of the report on the work of the Consultative Process at its sixth meeting, elements to be suggested to the General Assembly for consideration under its agenda item entitled "Oceans and the Law of the Sea." June 2005. Available at http://www.un.org/Depts/los/consultative_process/documents/icp-elements.pdf.

[21] Adopted by CBD COP7, Decision VII/16.

Finally, let us turn to Access and Benefit-Sharing (ABS) and related issues. "Equitable sharing of the benefit arising out of the utilisation of genetic resources" is the third objective of the CBD.

It is intertwined with the question of access to genetic resources. Before the CBD, unrestricted access to genetic resources prevailed. This practice became formalised by the FAO Undertaking on Plant Genetic Resources, which, until the adoption of the CBD, was the sole legal instrument on genetic resources. The CBD changed this thinking in relation to all genetic resources – those used in food and agriculture as well as those found in the wild. This was an important evolution – and even a revolution. By recognising that the authority to determine access to genetic resources "rests with the national governments and is subject to national legislation," the Convention has enabled each provider country to regulate access and to base this access on Prior Informed Consent and Mutually Agreed Terms.

This essentially "bilateral" system – between a provider and a user of biodiversity – presents difficulties of implementation. During the negotiation of the convention itself, it became clear and accepted that a purely bilateral system would not be possible for genetic resources used in food and agriculture, because the plant breeding process calls for a broad range of genetic resources as inputs into any one product. As a result, the International Treaty on Plant Genetic Resources for Food and Agriculture (ITPGRFA) was negotiated in the framework of FAO in the aftermath of the CBD and finally adopted in 2001. It entered into force in 2004.

In addition to general provisions on the conservation and sustainable use of all plant genetic resources for food and agriculture, the treaty essentially establishes a multilateral system to facilitate access to sixty-four major food crops. Benefit-sharing mechanisms include information exchange, access to and transfer of technology, capacity-building, and sharing of benefits arising from commercialisation. But the parties recognise that facilitated access to the multilateral system itself constitute the essential benefit. So, although the ITPGRFA shares, vis-à-vis the genetic resources it covers, the same objectives as the CBD, it seeks to implement these objectives in another manner.

Thus, the access and benefit-sharing provisions of the CBD now concern genetic resources for nonfood and nonagricultural uses, that is, mainly chemical and pharmaceutical purposes. Twelve years after the entry into force of the CBD, results do not yet meet the hopes that many had placed in the ABS system.

A fundamental reason for this slow pace is that, although the CBD provides the foundations of this new system in five basic provisions, implementation is dependent on national legislation, both of provider and user countries. Since the entry into force of the convention, a relatively small number of national instruments (twenty-nine) and regional instruments (three) have been adopted for the specific purpose of implementing the CBD ABS provisions. Most are in providing countries.

The number of ABS agreements concluded is reported not to be negligible, but, on the whole, these agreements have failed to meet the expectations of significant benefits. The national regimes adopted in source countries have been criticised by commercial and other users, who complain about their complexity, the lack of predictability of their results, and the time involved in obtaining a decision on access. Source countries complain about the lack of supportive legislative response in user countries, which, according to Article 15(7), are to take action aimed at fair and equitable sharing of benefits. Often called for is the adjustment of user countries intellectual property rights

(IPRs) regimes to require disclosure of the origin of the genetic resource used in the invention. Denmark, Sweden, Norway, and the European Community have taken action in this direction.[22]

The CBD COP addressed these criticisms in 2002[23] by adopting the Bonn Guidelines. Their chief merit is to provide a nonexhaustive menu of elements to be taken into consideration when developing national legal and regulatory ABS systems. By their nature, however, they cannot resolve differences of views over substance.

This is no doubt the reason why the WSSD has called for the negotiation, within the CBD, of an international regime "to promote and safeguard the fair and equitable sharing of benefits arising out of the utilisation of genetic resources." COP VII decided to go ahead.[24]

This negotiation will be decisive for the future of the ABS system. So far, options[25] regarding the scope, potential objectives, and elements of an international regime have been discussed. The results are sobering. Whether the instrument in question should be legally binding or not is an open question. One option is that the international regime be composed of one or more instruments at different levels of implementation (national, regional, and international) and instruments of various natures (including intergovernmental agreements, codes of conduct, national legislation, contracts, ethics, and commissions) with a set of principles, norms, rules, and decision-making procedures, all within the framework of the CBD.

Options for additional substantive rules are many, for example, import regulations, certification, disclosure of origin of material in patent applications and whether to enlarge the system to include derivatives. A related question is to decide in each case which forum is best placed to take action. WIPO may be best for IPRs related issues. The EU has already presented a proposal to the WIPO Intergovernmental Committee to introduce a mandatory requirement to disclose the country of origin or source of genetic resources in patent applications.[26]

As this process is about to start, it is important to underline that the complex questions that the ABS system raises, and that the negotiation of the international regime will have to consider, can only be resolved if "the Parties are able to develop a legally consistent understanding regarding the nature of genetic resources and of the rights to own and use them."[27] Clarity on these subjects will not only facilitate but is a prerequisite for the successful consideration of the international regime.

[22] See Analysis of Measures to Ensure Compliance with Prior Informed Consent of the Contracting Party Providing Genetic Resources and Mutually Agreed Terms on which Access was granted, and of other approaches, including an international certificate of origin/source/legal provenance. UNEP/CBD/WG-ABS/3/5, 10 December 2004.

[23] Decision VI-4.

[24] CBD COP Decision VII-19 sets the terms of reference for the negotiation of that regime.

[25] See Annex I of the Report of the Ad Hoc Open-Ended Working Group on Access and Benefit Sharing on the Work of its Third Meeting, UNEP/CBD/WG-ABS/3/7, 3 March 2005.

[26] See Disclosure of Origin or Source of Genetic Resources and Associated Traditional Knowledge in Patent Applications, WIPO/GRTKF/IC/8/11. This document was submitted by the European Community and Its Member States to the Intergovernmental Committee on Intellectual Property and Genetic Resources, Traditional Knowledge and Folklore, at its Eighth Session, Geneva, 6–10 June 2005.

[27] Santiago Carrizosa, Stephen B. Brush, Brian D. Wright, & Patrick E. McGuire, "Accessing Biodiversity and Sharing the Benefits: Lessons from Implementing the Convention on Biological Diversity." *IUCN Environmental Policy and Law Paper No. 54* (IUCN Environmental Law Programme, 2004), chapter 12, p. 287.

For instance, the definition of genetic resources is confusing. What distinguishes genetic from biological resources, which naturally also contain functional units of heredity, is unclear. Yet the distinction determines the scope of the ABS regime. The negotiations of the CBD and subsequent usage indicate that it is the genetic information and its use as such that are the heart of the ABS regime. Whether this is right or wrong, it deserves clarification.

A clear understanding of what constitutes "utilisation of genetic resources" for which ABS arrangements are required is needed, to make sure that the sale of bulk goods is not included, but also to ensure that purchase of beans from the market does not confer the right to utilise the genetic material without complying with ABS requirements.

And, finally, we also need a common understanding on ownership. So far, no distinction has been made between ownership of the tangible and ownership of the intangible elements of genetic resources.

Given this background, we are essentially seeking a regime, which:

(a) ensures that genetic information is used in accordance with the law of the source country; and
(b) allows the use of genetic information only if such use was part and parcel of the acquisition, or if the right to use the genetic information was obtained later on.

Such a system cannot, and will not be able to function without an international agreement on the rules of the game. The problem is similar to the one faced before CITES was negotiated; several states, such as the United States under the Lacey Act, subjected imports of wild specimens and products to proof of their acquisition according to the laws of the country of origin. Seeking proof of "lawful access" in source countries by individual states or industries proved frustrating, and this contributed greatly to the recognition of the need for CITES by industry and governments alike.

It is impossible here to consider the myriad of other questions, which will be addressed in the discussion of the international regime. Let me consider only one, namely, genetic resources husbanded by indigenous and local communities, and related traditional knowledge, not only because it has become an important element of the ABS debate but also because it has ramification into many other facets of the convention, including the implementation of Article 8(j).

The FAO 1983 Undertaking was the first international instrument to recognise the critical importance of indigenous and local communities in the conservation and maintenance of plant genetic resources. Article 8(j)[28] expands this recognition and specifically addresses the knowledge of these communities, in relation to the conservation and sustainable use of biological diversity.

From a purely ABS point of view, the main question is one of access to knowledge, usually in addition to access to genetic resources. There are, arguably, two questions to be considered: first, are these communities entitled to provide access to genetic resources; and, second, what are the conditions of access to their knowledge on these resources.

[28] Article 8(j), CBD: "Subject to its national legislation, respect, preserve and maintain knowledge, innovations and practices of indigenous and local communities embodying traditional lifestyles relevant for the conservation and sustainable use of biological diversity and promote their wider application with the approval and involvement of the holders of such knowledge, innovations and practices and encourage the equitable sharing of the benefits arising from the utilisation of such knowledge, innovations and practices."

Both questions, according the CBD, are subject to national legislation. Both have wide implications, and lead to much broader issues, namely, the whole "bundle of rights," which Posey identified as "Traditional Resources Rights."[29] Both share commonalities: the importance of the concept of prior informed consent (PIC) and mutually agreed terms (MAT) and the fair sharing of benefits deriving from access to the continuum that resources and knowledge together constitute for indigenous cultures.

Assuming that national legislation provides the necessary prerequisites, the question is then how to implement the PIC and MAT requirements vis-à-vis indigenous communities. These questions are particularly controversial, not only from a national or international point of view but also from a community standpoint. Who is entitled to give consent among indigenous peoples? and what is the situation of indigenous peoples not directly benefiting from this consent, or who may even be opposed to it? There is no single answer to these questions, and each situation will be different. But there are common threads.[30]

A second question is how to fight misappropriation of traditional knowledge (TK), and its illegal use. Both issues have clear international repercussions in the IPR field.

"Defensive protection of TK" seeks to ensure that TK is recognised in the application of IPRs to products that have benefited from it, and that benefits deriving therefrom are shared. It also seeks to prevent that IPRs be granted for inventions that derive directly or indirectly from traditional knowledge in the public domain and that therefore do not meet fundamental requirements for such rights, in particular patentability. Yet, in practice, rarely is traditional knowledge considered during the examination of patent applications.[31] WIPO has identified several mechanisms that could reduce the practical likelihood that patents incorrectly claim inventions making use of TK in the public domain.[32]

The "positive protection of TK" via the development of a legal regime recognising the rights of indigenous peoples over their knowledge using new types of IPRs is not a new idea. That none of the IPR's "traditional" regimes fits the protection of indigenous knowledge has been recognised for years and the development of a *sui generis* regime, advocated for long. A number of countries have taken steps to develop policy, and some have enacted specific laws (e.g., Peru and Panama). But there are limitations to the effectiveness of national action without the integration of TK protection in the international IPR system because the latter sets basic global standards.

Consideration of these issues within the CBD, including potential elements for a *sui generis* regime, and consistent efforts to pursue mutually supportive approaches between the CBD and trade-related agreements have triggered action elsewhere, most importantly within WIPO, where a committee is concentrating on defining policy objectives and core principles for the protection of TK. In parallel, the review of the

[29] Darrell Posey, *Traditional Resource Rights* (Gland, Switzerland: IUCN, 1996).

[30] See Manuel Ruiz, "Access to Genetic Resources, Intellectual Property Rights and Biodiversity." IUCN Information Paper, February 2004.

[31] See Manuel Ruiz, "The International Debate on Traditional Knowledge as Prior Art in the Patent System: Issues and Options for Developing Countries." Occasional Paper, TRADE, South Centre, October 2002.

[32] These are outlined fully in documents WIPO/GRTKF/IC/5/6 and WIPO/GRTKF/IC/6/8. See also references in WIPO/GRTKF/IC/8/8, report of the Intergovernmental Committee on Intellectual Property and Genetic Resources, Traditional Knowledge and Folklore, Eighth Session, Geneva, 6–10 June 2005 "Recognition of Traditional Knowledge within the Patent System: Interim Draft."

TRIPs Agreement is also ongoing, encouraged by the Doha mandate to examine the relationship with the CBD.[33]

Among indigenous peoples, there is a wide array of views on the desirable content of such a protection regime, but there is a consistently held commonality of opinion that it is needed. Adaptation of the IPR regime, however, also has its limitations. Non-IPR-based policy and legislation for TK protection are equally, if not more important, in particular because knowledge cannot be viewed in isolation from the culture, the land, and biological resources that it needs to evolve and grow.

- In spite of all these efforts, biodiversity loss continues . . . The Millennium Ecosystem Assessment[34] provides sobering facts about the present rate of this loss. Its first finding is as follows:

  Human actions are fundamentally, and to a significant extent irreversibly, changing the diversity of life on Earth, and most of these changes represent a loss of biodiversity. Changes in important components of biological diversity were more rapid in the last 50 years than at any other time in human history. Projections and scenarios indicate that these rates will continue, or accelerate in the future

Furthermore:

- Virtually all of Earth's ecosystems have now been dramatically transformed through human action. More land was converted to croplands in the 30 years after 1950 than in the 150 years between 1700 and 1850.
- Across a range of taxonomic groups, the population size or range (or both) of the majority of species is declining.
- Over the past few hundred years, human have increased species extinction rates by as much as one thousand times background rates that were typical over Earth's history.
- The distribution of species on earth is becoming more homogenous.
- Genetic diversity has declined globally, particularly among domesticated species.
- And all scenarios explored by the MEA project lead to a continuing rapid conversion of ecosystems in the first half of the twenty-first century.

And the direct drivers of loss of biodiversity are:

- Habitat transformation,
- Biotic exchange, with the spread of invasive alien species and disease organisms,
- Nutrient loading, anthropogenic increases in nitrogen, and other nutrient-associated pollutants, and
- Anthropogenic climate change.

[33] The TRIPS Agreement requires a review of Article 27.3(b), which deals with patentability or non-patentability of plant and animal inventions, and the protection of plant varieties. Paragraph 19 of the 2001 Doha Declaration has broadened the discussion in requiring the TRIPS Council to also look at the relationship between the TRIPS Agreement and the UN Convention on Biological Diversity, the protection of traditional knowledge and folklore. See Ministerial Declaration, adopted on 14 November 2001, WT/MIN(01)/DEC/1.

[34] Millennium Ecosystem Assessment: *Ecosystems and Human Well-Being: Biodiversity Synthesis* (Washington, DC: World Resources Institute, 2005).

The MA concludes that unprecedented additional efforts would be needed to achieve, by 2010, a significant reduction in the rate of biodiversity. This is the bad news.

The message of hope, however, is the acknowledgment that action taken so far to conserve biodiversity and promote its sustainable use has been successful in limiting biodiversity loss to rates that otherwise would not have been achievable.

And so, the challenge is in stepping up efforts in building up an efficient global response: global in scope, multilayered in its approach, because, as J. McNeely has said, a world scheme for accomplishing the preservation of the maximum amount of biodiversity possible would be the most important single contribution that the people of our generation could make to the future.

How? Through cooperation and synergy with other organisations, initiatives, and processes, and, of course, other relevant conventions. The CBD has pursued this vigorously, and memoranda of cooperation have been established with some seventy organisations. Privileged relationships have been developed with UNEP, FAO, UNESCO, UNFF, WIPO, and WTO. Partnerships have been initiated with other actors to support the CBD's implementation. In addition, COP VII instructed the Secretariat to look into options for the creation of a "global partnership on biological diversity" to enhance implementation through improved cooperation.

Even more interesting, however, are the relationships with existing conventions with converging goals. The rationale is obvious. Policy coherence is the goal. The web of obligations and commitments deriving from the multiplicity of international accords should be implemented in a mutually supportive manner; overlaps should be detected and remedied, and specific roles, as well as common tasks, clearly identified. Early thoughts on synergy included the coordination of the conventions' reporting process, cooperation between secretariats, and cross-representation at the various COPs. Those are still important today.

Further progress has been achieved, in particular with regard to the four global conventions most related to the CBD's goals, which all have MoUs with the CBD.

- First, the CBD has recognised their role in the implementation of its own programme, for example, the lead role of CMS in all questions related to migratory species.
- Second, joint programmes of work have been adopted, based on the CBD framework on thematic and cross-cutting areas.
- Third, a number of concepts and tools, for which the CBD has now become a primary forum of discussion – such as the guidance on invasives, the ecosystem approach, sustainable use guidelines – play a role in the implementation of all sectoral instruments. By adopting the resulting principles and guidelines in the context of their own work, sectoral conventions have achieved a degree of much desired harmonisation.
- Fourth, a liaison group has been created to enhance coherence and cooperation.

A Joint Liaison group also exists for the Rio Conventions, and other privileged relationships exist with the International Treaty on Plant Genetic Resources and the International Plant Protection Convention (IPCC).

But the way towards synergy is a rocky one. Sectoral and regional conventions have been suspicious of the ambit of the CBD, wary about the attention it commands and the funds it attracts, of the political nature of its process, and the length of time needed to achieve concrete results. In addition, the rules of treaty governance are not conducive of cross-pollination.

And yet, whether we will be able to develop a closely knit operation of biodiversity-related instruments will determine the success or failure of a world scheme. The four global conventions are vital but only the tip of the iceberg. The many relevant regional and restricted conventions have, each in its sphere, a role to play. Conventions on processes that drive biodiversity loss also must be part of the process. The study of instruments playing a role in the possible development of marine protected areas demonstrates the difficulty and the magnitude of the task: no fewer than fifty are involved. How do we, then, tackle this daunting task, and organise this web in a coherent manner?

Can we do this by seeking synergies and harmonisation through issue-based modules, as UNEP is now starting to explore? By relying more on a regional approach to operate more coherence in implementation? By a mixture of the two? Whatever the response is, how do we keep those extra layers light enough not to complicate the present difficulties even more? Lawyers must assist in considering these issues, and searching for innovative ways to establish efficient institutional "corridors." This is the most challenging governance issue of our time.

> In the beginning was Nature. Ever since life appeared on the Earth more than two thousand million years ago, evolution has generated hundreds of millions of species of micro-organisms, flora, and, much later, fauna. As geological eras went by and climate changed, plants and animals had to evolve to adapt to new ecological conditions. Major catastrophes occurred, but each time evolution was able to continue because enough species had been spared. The new catastrophe, which is starting and is entirely caused by human action, will most probably bring about the disappearance within a few decades of several million species if nothing is done to stop it. It will be completely without precedent in the Earth, because of its suddenness, on the scale of evolution, and because it will affect the planet as a whole.

This was written when the negotiations of the Biological Diversity Convention were starting, by Cyrille de Klemm, a lawyer, convinced – as we here all are – that among the array of measures needed to stem the loss of biological diversity, law was essential.

3 Some Observations on the IUCN, the Earth Charter, and Global Governance

Brendan Mackey

1 INTRODUCTION

The Earth Charter is an ethical framework of values and principles for a more just, sustainable, and peaceful world. At the IUCN World Conservation Congress in Bangkok, November 2004, the organisations' membership overwhelmingly voted in support of a resolution to endorse the Earth Charter and use it as an ethical guide to the organisation's policy and programme. In this context, it is useful to consider the contribution world ethics, and in particular the Earth Charter, can make to the work of the IUCN, and through it to international law and global governance.

Over the last decade, there has been a plethora of international ethical statements and commitments in relation to the environment and sustainability. These include the Stockholm Declaration,[1] the World Charter for Nature,[2] the Rio Declaration (UNCED),[3] and the World Summit on Sustainable Development Political Declaration (WSSD).[4] Such documents can be thought of as "paralegal rules" in the form of values, principles, and directives for policies, practices, and outcomes. Also of relevance are the ethical principles (such as the precautionary principle) contained within the introductory sections of legal instruments such as the United Nations Framework Convention on Climate Change (UNFCCC).[5]

Given this rich legacy of international ethical resources, what is the added value to international law of a civil society document such as the Earth Charter? The proposition explored in this paper is that the Earth Charter (and similar documents) contributes to building the global moral community that is the foundation of the next generation

[1] *Declaration of the United Nations Conference on the Human Environment*, Stockholm from 5 to 16 June 1972. United Nations Development Programme. World Wide Web. Available at http://www.unep.org/Documents.multilingual/Default.asp? Document ID=97&ArticleID=1503.

[2] *The World Charter for Nature.* United Nations Organisation. Available at: http://www.un.org/documents/ga/res/37/a37r007.htm.

[3] *The Rio Declaration of the 1992 Rio Earth Summit* – the United Nations Conference on Environment and Development. United Nations Environment Program. 2005. Available at http://www.unep.org/Documents/Default.asp?DocumentID=78&ArticleID=1163.

[4] *Johannesburg Declaration on Sustainable Development*, Articles 14 and 17. World Summit on Sustainable Development, Johannesburgh 2002. United Nations Organisation, 2005. Available at http://ods-dds-ny.un.org/doc/UNDOC/LTD/N02/578/83/PDF/N0257883.pdf?OpenElement.

[5] Intergovernmental Panel on Climate Change. *Climate Change 2001: Synthesis Report.* Available at http://www.ipcc.ch/pub/reports.htm.

* Brendan Mackey is with the Fenner School of Environment and Society, The Australian National University, Canberra ACT 0200 Australia. Email: brendan.mackey@anu.edu.au.

of legal instruments, institutions, and processes on global governance. However, to appreciate the basis of this proposition, it is first necessary to briefly review the genesis of the Earth Charter.

2 THE EARTH CHARTER

Many groups in global civil society advanced the idea for an Earth Charter in the post–World War II years, beginning at least as early as the 1950s when the British scientist Julian Huxley proposed the idea to IUCN. In the 1980s, international civil society groups composed numerous draft "charters." The 1987 report of the UN World Commission on Environment and Development[6] called for the creation of "a universal declaration" in the form of "a new charter" that would "consolidate and extend relevant legal principles" creating "new norms . . . needed to maintain livelihoods and life on our shared planet" and "to guide state behavior in the transition to sustainable development."

Following the failure of national governments at the 1992 Rio Earth Summit to support the drafting of an Earth Charter, a new Earth Charter project was launched as a civil society initiative, with support from the Netherlands and Costa Rican governments, and subsequently by philanthropic donations. A secretariat was established in Costa Rica (now co-located with the University for Peace) and an Earth Charter Commission established to oversee the drafting process.[7]

A drafting team was formed chaired by Steven Rockefeller, then Professor of Religion at Middlebury College. The team included members drawn from the IUCN Commission on Environmental Law Ethics Specialist Group. A key member was Ron Engel, then Professor at Meadville/Lombard Theological School at the University of Chicago. Engel had founded the Ethics Specialist Group which in the late 1980s undertook a worldwide consultative process that led to the preparation of chapter II on "Respecting and caring for the community of life" in "Caring for the Earth," the Second World Conservation Strategy.[8] The chapter included "Elements of a World Ethic for Living Sustainably," and recommended continuing a global dialogue that would elaborate and implement this ethic.

The Earth Charter drafting process involved three main stages. First, a review was made of values and principles articulated in existing international treaties and declarations, including the Stockholm and Rio Declarations, and the pronouncements of the related UN World Summits held during the 1990s. More than two hundred international hard and soft law documents were analysed and from these fourteen core principles were identified that represented a global ethical consensus in that they had been debated and agreed to by the international community. Second, this so-called Benchmark Draft was examined at the Rio+5 NGO meeting in 1997 and the text was extensively revised from these consultations.

The Earth Charter Commission then decided to extend the ambitious global consultation process in order to give the document the broadest civil society exposure.

[6] World Commission on Environment and Development. *Our Common Future*, Oxford University Press, Oxford UK, 1987.

[7] The Earth Charter International Secretariat. *Earth Charter Handbook*. Available at http://www.earthcharter.org/files/resources/Handbook.pdf.

[8] *Caring for the Earth – a Strategy for Sustainable Living*. (Gland, Switzerland: IUCN/UNEP/WWF, 1991). Available at http://coombs.anu.edu.au/~vern/caring/caring.html.

Over the next four years, the document was considered by community groups in over forty countries and regional consultations were held, including major forums in Latin America (Brazil), Africa (Republic of South Africa), Middle East (Jordan), and Russia. In parallel, meetings of various expert groups, including international lawyers, scientists, and philosophers, considered drafts of the document. During this period, the charter was redrafted dozens of times in response to the incoming recommendations and comments. The global consultation process was halted in the year 2000 and the finalised document launched that year in a special event at the Hague Peace Palace.

The Earth Charter comprises sixteen major and sixty-one supporting principles, which are preceded by an introductory section entitled "The Preamble," which summarises the ethic in prose form. The charter concludes with a section called "The Way Forward." The principles are organised around four themes: "Respect and Care for the Community of Life"; "Ecological Integrity"; "Social and Economic Justice"; and "Democracy, Non-Violence and Peace."

Everything about the Earth Charter – its size, format, use of language, the wording of every principle – is a product of the expert reviews, global consultations, and associated drafting process. There is a story behind every sentence. Unlike formal negotiations during the drafting of intergovernmental agreements, the global consultation process led to a strengthening rather than a weakening of meaning and commitment. For once, consensus meant the bar was raised higher rather than lower. Critically, representatives from Christian and Islamic, eastern and western, global northern and southern communities found agreement on shared values for a more just, sustainable and peaceful world. Of course, one of these shared values is respect for the diversity of life and cultures – the foundation of any authentic world ethic.

There was a great deal of discussion during the drafting process as to whether an Earth Charter needed the fourth theme of "Democracy, Non-violence and Peace." Input from Indian civil society leaders building on Ghandian philosophy proved influential in the decision to expand the scope of the Earth Charter in this way. Events post–September 11 have pointed to the essential value of such an integrated approach to a world ethic for the twenty-first century.

From a philosophical perspective, Nigel Downer[9] has argued that the Earth Charter takes the middle road between, on the one hand, what we might call the "dogmatic idealist" who seeks to impose on all others their values as the one true set of values, and, on the other hand, the "neoconservative libertarians" who deny any shared values and global obligations. The Earth Charter ethic sits in between these two extremes and can be usefully described as occupying a "cosmopolitan solidarist" position – it celebrates the diversity of values and world views that arise in different cultures, but at the same time seeks to express the shared values that provide the basis for collaborative action in meeting our global responsibilities.

Note that as a "cosmopolitan solidarist" ethic, the Earth Charter does not seek to replace the diversity of values in different cultures with a new, monoethic. Rather, it articulates shared values and principles that coexist with more culturally specific values.

[9] N. Dower, *World Ethics: The New Agenda.* Edinburgh Studies in World Ethics (Edinburgh: Edinburgh University Press, 1998).

3 GLOBAL GOVERNANCE AND THE EARTH CHARTER

Despite widespread understanding of the need to maintain the ecological integrity of Earth's global and local ecosystems,[10] it is perhaps self-evident even to the casual observer that there is a lack of political will to promote new international legal frameworks and associated institutions and processes. Indeed, as demonstrated by the Kyoto Protocol, it is proving difficult to even implement existing international commitments. At the 2002 World Summit on Sustainable Development, I witnessed the resistance from certain countries to even considering timetables and targets for delivering on long-standing commitments such as the Earth Summit's Agenda 21.[11]

So, on the one hand, we have the Millennium Ecosystem Assessment informing us that global environmental security is critically endangered, and, on the other, we find key national governments not wanting to advance to the next generation of global governance measures – including new, integrated legal frameworks – needed to address these challenges. Rather, there is increasing reliance on advancing economic globalisation as the main instrument of global governance on the basis that only this can generate the economic prosperity needed to alleviate poverty and protect the environment. Economic globalization is resulting in, *inter alia*, effective privatisation of the global commons such as the atmosphere and the commoditisation of renewable natural resources including fresh water. This trend continues even though many aspects of Earth's life support system do not lend themselves to privatisation and are better managed as part of the global commons with access to natural resources and environmental services given through a leasehold system.[12]

Thus, at this very crucial point in human history when we so urgently need the next generation of international legal frameworks and associated institutions and processes, we find ourselves at the best in a stalemate and at worst facing a concerted effort by certain parties to prevent the ongoing evolution of global governance. For convenience, we can consider this resistance as reflecting a so-called neoconservative worldview that argues that we have gone too far down the road of international law. Such a view is now evident in the popular press. Consider this quote from an article (2005) by Janet Albrechsten – a prominent columnist writing in Australia's only national newspaper (prosaically called "The Australian"):

> [it] is wrong to think of the culture wars as the lofty esoteric concerns of those with too much time on their hands. On the contrary, the culture wars go to the core of how we, as Australians, wish to be governed. Do we want to govern ourselves? Or do we want to put our blind faith in institutions such as the UN that are unaccountable, undemocratic and ineffective? The real danger arises if we ever stop thinking about the growing incursion of so-called international law into the domestic business of nation states. It is rather chilling to chart the trajectory of international law in the past 50 years.... As laws become more detached from people they become less legitimate.... The goal is ultimately that liberal democracies built around nation

[10] United Nations Organisation. *Millennium Ecosystem Report*, 2005. Available at http://www.millennium-assessment.org/en/index.aspx.

[11] United Nations Organisation, Division of Sustainable Development. *Agenda 21 of United Nations Conference on Environment and Development (the Rio Earth Summit) 1992.* World Wide Web, accessed 2 December 2005. Available at http://www.un.org/esa/sustdev/documents/agenda21/index.htm.

[12] J. H. Hickel. *Crisis in the Commons – The Alaska Solution* (Oakland: Institute for Contemporary Studies, 2002).

states are replaced with a new form of centralised international power wielded by unelected bureaucrats and activists. Welcome to the post-democratic nation state.

It is informative to consider the philosophical underpinnings of this (i.e., neoconservative) worldview.[13] It reflects, among other things, the concept that the nation-state is the only valid foundation of culture, values, moral responsibility, and law. Thus, it argues that there is no global community, culture, and morality, and therefore no social reality that can be used to justify global ethics. It follows there is no culturally related values on which to base international law and global governance structures. A second key philosophical underpinning of the neoconservative worldview is that national governments need only care about ethical principles in international relations up to the point where it is no longer in their self-interest to do so. From these perspectives, governments must never allow ethical considerations to be the overriding factor: the main reason being that the natural state of international affairs is one of war or at least war-readiness, and to view international relations through any other lens is considered naïve and foolish. As many readers with a philosophical background will appreciate, these ideas reflect a much older worldview as they have their origins in (1) the Westphalia Peace Treaty of 1648 that established the modern international nation-state system and the so-called morality of states, (2) the writings of Italian Statist Niccolo-Machiavelli in his book *Discourses*, published in 1513,[14] and (3) the writings of the British political commentator Thomas Hobbes in *Leviathan*, published in 1651.[15]

4 THE WAY FORWARD

To meet the global challenges of the twenty-first century, it is necessary to cultivate a culture of sustainability that will, in turn, demand a new morality of states and the necessary international legal frameworks and associated institutions and processes. Thus, the kind of value system represented by the Earth Charter must become a social reality. For a world ethic to be a social reality, its life supporting values must be widely held by people and communities in different cultures around the world, and its principles embedded within and guide the behaviour of significant international organisations and institutions.[16]

The IUCN is one such organisation that uniquely brings together civil society and national governments to protect nature and help secure the ecological integrity of Earth's life-support systems for the benefit of people. As such, the IUCN can play a vital role in demonstrating through the practical examples of their policies and programmes how cooperation can occur between sectors and people from different cultures, and how ethically based legal and paralegal rules can be used to promote a more just, sustainable, and peaceful world.

The Earth Charter can be validly claimed to be a social reality to the extent these two preconditions are met. As a social reality, the Earth Charter will have contributed to the cultivation of a strong global moral community whose worldview acknowledges

[13] N. Downer.

[14] N. Machiavelli, 1531. *Discourses.* In P. Bondanelli and M. Musa, eds., *The Portable Machiavelli* (Harmondsworth: Penguin Books, 1979).

[15] R. Tuck, ed., *T. Hobbes, Leviathan (1651)* (Cambridge, UK: Cambridge University Press, 1996).

[16] N. Downer.

universal obligations to promote the flourishing of the entire community of life and the equitable sharing of the good things of life for present and future generations – a global moral community that will logically demand the necessary international legal frameworks and global governance structures needed to protect and advance these shared values and responsibilities.

5 CONCLUSION

The neoconservative worldview argues that we have already gone too far down the road of international law and global governance structures. The core argument of this position is that human culture and values – the basis of law – are grounded within the nation state. But, nation states and global society can and do coexist – along with their associated values. We have the beginnings of a global society and world ethic and thus a strong foundation in support of our existing international law. Indeed, this has been the great work promoted by the United Nations since its formation following World War II. The IUCN Commission on Environmental Law has made significant contributions to this mission by helping to advance international legal frameworks in the field of environment and development.

As a civil society document, the Earth Charter is open to endorsement and use by individuals, communities, organisations, and governments alike. Therefore, the Earth Charter's use is not restricted to intergovernmental relations, it can and hopefully will be drawn on by nation-states as a source of paralegal rules in the formulation of new national and international law. In any case, even if the Earth Charter is not used in this way by nation-states, its inherent long-term value lies in helping to cultivate the growth of a global moral community, which respects diversity and includes all life and future generations in its sphere of moral deliberations. When this new worldview is a demonstrable social reality, we will have the cultural foundation for the next generation of legal frameworks and institutions needed to help secure a more just, sustainable, and peaceful world.

Albrechsten is right on one account – it is wrong to think that the culture wars are the lofty esoteric concerns of those with too much time on their hands. They do indeed go to the heart of how we wish to be governed.

4 The Changing Role of Law in the Pursuit of Sustainability

Paul Martin*

I begin with a claim that is to me self-evident, but that does not seem to reflect legal scholarship: *Law is a behavioural discipline.* Its function is to shape how people act. It shares this with economics, marketing, political science, and psychology (to name but a few). Although the literature of the law is populated with examples of weird, wonderful, and frightening aspects of behaviour, legal mainstream legal literature[1] rarely discusses the causes of (or strategies to alter) behaviour, perhaps with the exception of some arguments about the deterrent value of punishment (particularly the death penalty). The focus of that literature is legal instruments and legal interpretation. It contains very little enlightenment about the behavioural effectiveness of law, or the strategies through which desired outcomes could be more efficiently achieved. Neither legal practice nor legal theory are engaged in a scientific discourse about the mechanisms through which (for example) punishment (or the fear of it) works, its limits, or the ways in which public information about rules or judgments impacts within the general community to shape hopes, fears, and resultant behaviour. The idea that one might trade off policing investment for education, or manage transaction costs better to allow for more effective use of resources, is a discussion that is largely foreign to the mainstream legal literature.

Which leads me to the more challenging statement: *Law is a behavioural discipline, sadly bereft of a behavioural theory.* There are some levels at which this could be debated, but in the main the literature of the law itself is supportive of my case. Standing back from the details of construction, what can one see as the preoccupations of legal literature? In the content of Australian environmental law texts, technical discussion of the content of statute emerges as the dominant interest. This is followed by a preoccupation with statutory interpretation. Issues of institutional integrity get some attention, mainly through administrative law as it relates to environmental statute requirements for decision making. There is some consideration of private rights. It is predominantly in other literatures (notably economics and the social sciences) that the broader questions of behavioural impact and cost efficiency of law are debated. Overall, there is little questioning by legal academics of the unstated paradigm of the behavioural impact of the law, in terms that lawyers might readily understand.

This state of affairs ought be troubling to lawyers and policy workers whose goal is sustainability, or whose interest is the role of law and regulation in the advancement of

[1] I refer in this chapter primarily to the textbooks used to educate lawyers and the professional journals used by practitioners, rather than the more esoteric journals.

* Paul Martin is with the Australian Centre for Agriculture and Law, University of New England, New South Wales.

society. The absence of a behavioural orientation means that the energy and creativity of legal thinkers is primarily focused on the refinements of legal tools, rather than on the strategic constructs of the law as a means to achieve social outcomes. This seems much like a building manual with many pages about the relative advantages of different type of hammers or saws, but hardly a paragraph about the architecture or the engineering that makes operational skills and tools valuable.

If one could extrapolate what seems to be the behavioural wisdom embedded in the environmental law literature, it is that natural resource use is primarily driven by response to regulations. The literature also would seem to reflect a belief that the act of judicial deciding is the nexus between environmental harm and actions to prevent that harm, and that implementation follows judgment as the night follows the day. Yet, in social discussion, environmental lawyers are quick to point out that relatively few issues ever make it before a judge, that most environmental harms are unseen and unpunished, and that the details of the law are largely irrelevant to everyday compliant behaviour, compared to social sanctions, values, and economic incentives.

As a lawyer who believes that the history of law shows jurisprudence can lead social change, and that sustainability is the next frontier where social change is essential, I am not comfortable with the situation that I have described. Environmental law should not be devoid of a behavioural theory to inform its professional and academic preoccupations. What I want to do in this essay is make two suggestions to improve the contributions that jurisprudence can make to the cause of sustainability. The first is to broaden the range of instrumental strategies that are envisaged when looking at environmental law. The second is to look far more critically at the efficiency of regulations themselves, in order to improve their functional effectiveness.

I do not intend to use the convention of supporting every statement with a wealth of references. Two preceding empirical studies of the state of environmental regulation in Australia,[2] and the range of market and regulatory strategies used to support sustainability,[3] provide ample data to support the points I intend to make.

1 DO WE NEED A BEHAVIOURAL JURISPRUDENCE FOR THE ENVIRONMENT?

The law will always be relevant, even if perennially suboptimal, to social advancement but will it be as important and useful as it ought be, given the challenges that society faces? It is this type of concern, rather than word-games and bill paying, that has driven the traditions of jurisprudence. Great thinkers such as Bentham or Rawls were concerned about social justice and the utility of the law when they crafted their astounding ideas. Now, when the challenges of sustainability are as pivotal as the issues of social equity were in earlier centuries, it is time to consider a behavioural jurisprudence in service of sustainability.

[2] P. Martin & M. Verbeek, *Fifty Million Australians: Can This Be Sustainable?* (Land & Water Australia, 2002), and P. Martin & M. Verbeek, *A Cartography for Natural Resource Law: Finding New Paths to Effective Resource Regulation* (Land and Water Australia, 2000).

[3] See D. D. James, (1997). *Environmental Incentives: Australian Experience with Economic Instruments for Environmental Management.* Canberra, Environment Australia; National Centre for Environmental Economics (2001). The U.S. Experience with Economic incentives for Protecting the environment. Office of Policy, Economics, and Innovation. U.S. Environmental Protection Agency; R. N. Stavins (2000). Experience with Market-Based Environmental Policy Instruments. Washington, DC, Resources for the Future and http://iisd.ca/greenbud/MATRIX.htm for details.

What might such a jurisprudence look like? I will attempt to stimulate a discussion with a "straw man." Like all such men, this is not in the expectation that he will be transmuted into a being of flesh, blood, and imagination. Rather, it is in the hope and expectation that others, frustrated by his limitations (or perhaps mine) will propose better and more imaginative alternatives.

2 WHAT SHAPES BEHAVIOUR?

In our earlier studies, Miriam Verbeek and I analysed recurrent themes in how different disciplines explain behaviour. This discussion is a summary. Drawing from a range of disciplines, we distil the two driving forces as flows of information, and flows of resources. Information is processed in making decisions, and decisions are in large part attempts to hold or secure resources (and action in essence means the deployment of resources).

When making decisions, people and groups of people use processes for structuring information and for valuing different types of outcomes. In doing so, a complex array of beliefs and knowledge come together.

Behaviour can be considered at (at least) three levels: individuals within small groups, larger groups or organisations, and society. However, the fundamental considerations remain the same:

- it is the direction strength and duration of resource flows that most powerfully shapes behaviour in society;
- the content and duration of information flows is the secondary shaping force; and
- overlaid on this, the state of beliefs and the decision-making approaches will determine how outcomes are valued, and how information is dealt with.

Additional to the flows and the ordering of these flows there are dynamics, such as delay, or the losses of resources or information that occur within the system.

The law deals with aspects of behaviour in its own idiosyncratic fashion. Information is selected as legally relevant according to agreed rules, specialised decision making and valuation are applied, and particular resource flow consequences arise. There is insufficient opportunity in this paper to explain fully here. What there is space to do is to question whether the focus on regulation and regulatory interpretation is short-changing both society and jurisprudence.

3 IS REGULATION THE "FIRST BEST" CHOICE?

Given the emphasis in environmental law on public regulation and policing ("traditional" regulation), an important question is whether this emphasis is justified in the interests of sustainability. It is clear that contemporary sustainability strategy has moved away from a focus on traditional regulation, towards the use of market instruments, voluntarism, and education. The range of strategies used in addition to traditional regulation spans cap and trade (market) or offsetting development rights instruments, various forms of environmental taxes, voluntary mechanisms, information programs, promotion of environmentally benign product alternatives, and schemes to equip potential consumers with the capacity to move to less harmful approaches. A few examples will serve to illustrate the direction of contemporary policy.

Poland charges fees for emissions of pollutants.[4] They include a "normal fee" levied on emissions below the regulatory standard, and a penalty fee for emissions thereafter. Although "normal fees" have been set too low to expect significant emissions effects, penalty fees appear to have reduced emissions, at least for sulfur dioxide and particulate matter.

In Switzerland,[5] the Zurich Model tries to solve the city traffic problem through the reassignment of road services. Segregated tram tracks, bus lanes, and bus priority at traffic signals, combined with a reduction of parking supply, have resulted in a falling share of private cars going into the city. This results in more space to short-range public passenger transport and pedestrians, and less space to private vehicles.

The European Union Flower[6] is an ecolabelling scheme that uses a life-cycle assessment methodology to evaluate the environmental impacts of products. The cradle to grave assessment is voluntary, and carried out by a competent body within each member state. The EU Flower has generated concerns over trade effects on ecolabels for paper products and textiles and it has been suggested that the EU program favours domestic producers. The environmental effectiveness of this program has yet to be established.

The U.S. Coalbed Methane Outreach Program[7] disseminates information that addresses obstacles to mine methane recovery and development, including the lack of information on recovery technology, difficulties in obtaining financing for recovery investments, the lack of markets for recovered methane, and the uncertainty concerning ownership of mine methane. The EPA also provides assistance to pinpoint sources of loans, grants, and technical assistance for profitable coal mine methane projects, as well as a comprehensive guide for private sector financing of coal mine methane projects. Methane recovery by the coal industry has more than doubled since 1993 equivalent to eliminating the emissions from about 1.5 million cars per year.

The Kwinana scheme, administered by the Department of Environmental Protection in Western Australia,[8] limits emissions from point sources subject to meeting ambient concentration targets for specified air pollutants. It applies to sulphur dioxide and total suspended particulates. Costs for compliance and monitoring is shared between the regulator and regulated. It has reportedly gained general acceptance by industry and led to a sense of joint ownership of the management regime between industry and DEP. Its requirement for monitoring and compliance indicate that it is effective in meeting air quality standards.

These are just random examples. In our earlier work, we identified hundreds of examples of different instruments and evaluated about 120. Many sustainability strategies do not rely on traditional "regulate and police" approaches. Each type of instrument has systemic impacts on society, culture, social equity, and the fiscal state of government. Each instrument type depends in different ways on the support of the law, whether in the form of a traditional regulatory approach, defending the credibility of market transactions, or ensuring honesty in systems of administration. (See Table 4.1.)

The economics literature speaks with much empirical support of the relative inefficiency of traditional regulation in achieving sustainability outcomes, when compared

[4] R. N. Stavins (2000).
[5] http://www.iisd.org/susprod/displaydetails.asp?id=92.
[6] http://www.iisd.org/susprod/displaydetails.asp?id=128.
[7] National Centre for Environmental Economics (2001), p. 179.
[8] D. D. James (1997), S10.5.

Table 4.1. Mechanisms, behaviour, and the role of law

Instrument type	How does the instrument work?	What behaviours are promoted?	Some roles of the law
Markets	Through market transactions the price of scarce resources increases; consumption is therefore curtailed by choice or inability to pay.	Market entrepreneurship trading or improved resource access or value.	Creating artificial scarcity by regulation, which generates trading. Ensuring integrity in the transactions. Enforcement of property rights.
Private Regulation	Through private litigation harmful effects are compensated. Harm to third parties is therefore curtailed by the choice to avoid risk.	Avoidance of third party harm and "neighbourly" negotiation of interests.	Specifying the extent of private rights and responsibilities. Providing/ restricting standing to sue. Enforcement of judgments.
Public Regulation	Through penalisation specified behaviours are made expensive. Consumption is therefore curtailed by choice to avoid risk.	Compliance, focused on least cost to avoid the risk.	Defining legal obligations. Specifying evidence requirements. Policing powers. Enforcement of orders.
Incentives	Through contracts desired behaviours are rewarded. Conserving behaviour is thereby promoted.	Administrative entrepreneurship to win grants to satisfy requirements	Defining contractual relationships. Administrative integrity and independence.
Education	Through communication, attitude or knowledge change leading to conserving behaviour.	Civic responsibility	Liability for content.

with market instruments such as tradeable emission credits, well-targeted taxes, or direct incentives for behavioural change.

What is misleading from the economics discussions is the idea that there are distinct "regulatory" and "nonregulatory" instruments (and typically that the latter are more efficient). This reflects an unduly simplistic understanding of the role of law, but economists could be forgiven this error when lawyers seem to share it. In modern economies a legal framework is fundamental to any type of instrument. Traditional regulatory intervention uses one form of regulation (government-policed controls) whereas market instruments rely on another (government-backed private action). There are different combinations and permutations, but in all the role of the law is pivotal. What is perhaps surprising is that environmental law thinking (as reflected in environment law textbooks) has undersold the importance of an elegant legal strategy, even when the tools of preference are private markets.

4 IS LAW DECLINING IN IMPORTANCE?

If traditional regulation is not the first best tool of behaviour change, does jurisprudence have a declining role in the pursuit of sustainability? Definitely not, though the way in which that role is acted out will have to become more sophisticated and diverse, with the growing sophistication and diversity of the instruments being used. The law is a foundation stone for transacting, government action, and the management of conflict. To confine it to policing transactions is far too limiting its contribution to sustainability.

If environmental jurisprudence were concentrating on behavioural effectiveness, and if it were taking proper account of the proliferation of instruments being used in pursuit of sustainability, the content of environmental law books and journals would undergo some changes. Although traditional regulation would still be important, the content also would address the role of the law in market based and voluntarist approaches. Some topics might be:

a. methods to design secure low transaction cost contractual instruments to give effect to environmental marketplace relationships. Contract law, and related rights and responsibilities of the trading entities, would form part of this.
b. The interactions between "government law" and "private law" in an ever more elegant matrix would deserve consideration. Topics might include consideration of the role and enforcement of privately agreed standards such as industry codes or international standards. This may bring into play examination of how voluntary codes may achieve legal enforcement through trade law, contract, and consumer protection rules.
c. Environmental risk management is a topic of growing importance. The question of who is liable once a diffuse environmental problem (like a new weed or pest species) is "out of the bottle," or how environmental risk-management responsibilities are allocated, are important topics deserving of careful legal scrutiny.
d. The role of private actions for the protection of the environment brings in many issues of tort obligations of wrongdoers, or even the concepts of trust for current or future generations. It also raises matters about standing and damages that could help advance the cause of sustainability.

Other relevant and intellectually challenging legal topics can be identified with little effort. A jurisprudence dealing with the interrelationship between the law and strategies to advance sustainability also may take on the role of integrating the legal considerations with some of the broader aspects of behaviour change strategies. This could encompass:

e. examining the interaction between law and other elements of behaviourally effective strategies (breaking down the disciplinary barriers), particularly economics, sociology, and political economy; and
f. incorporating some lessons of science, such as statistical reliability of data, and the challenges of system thinking about issues such as precaution.

Criticism of the law as narrow and tenuously connected to the wider issues in society has existed (probably) for as long as law itself. However, if your starting point is that you want the law to work in furthering sustainability rather then merely working as a source of lawyer's employment and intellectual satisfaction, one would want our jurisprudence to tackle the issues that limit its effectiveness as an instrument of sustainability strategy.

5 ARE WE OVERBURDENING SUSTAINABILITY WITH REGULATION?

In the first part of this essay, I have argued that there is too much emphasis on regulation in environmental jurisprudence, to the exclusion of proper attention being paid to the range of potential strategies available to advance sustainability. In this second half, I will make the case that the sheer volume of environmental regulation acts counter to the goals of sustainability, introducing excessive transaction costs which fall heavily on those trying to act responsibly, and providing opportunities for technical games to avoid the responsibilities that legislators have intended.

The literature about behavioural effectiveness of different types of market instrument, and regulation, demonstrates that confidence in the rules and institutions behind the rules is a fundamental requirement for instruments to work. It matters little whether one is talking about confidence that the government will be free from corruption in its policing (traditional environmental regulation) or diligent in protecting the rights conferred by market instruments. Security of expectations is a behavioural fundamental regardless of choice of instrument. Where communities lack trust in the "system," they begin to take matters into their own hands, resulting in less predictable social, economic, and environmental outcomes. Where legal systems are slow, costly, and unreliable, confidence in them deteriorates.

A requirement for effectiveness is transacting efficiency. If an instrument (traditional regulatory or market) is either too resource-hungry, or essential information is too difficult to secure, then the instrument will not achieve its behavioural purpose (and may well distort outcomes in perverse ways). The economic term "transaction costs" is shorthand for costs that surround a transaction, including information gathering, processing, creating security, and administering. The extent of transaction costs, and on whom they fall, are significant in the effects that an instrument has.[9] Thus, if it is very expensive to carry out a transaction and all of the costs fall on the seller, a likely outcome is to suppress sellers and increase costs (and vice versa, if buyers bear the cost). The imperative to reduce transaction costs as a means of both lowering prices and increasing competitive behaviour in markets is well understood.

I would suggest that the transaction costs that we have introduced with our environmental regulatory system are a source of diminution in confidence in environmental law. The defence of institutional integrity is a matter in which a modern environmental jurisprudence would join hands with both traditional jurisprudence and modern economic writers on managerial efficiency.

It is easy to discern transaction costs in the case of market instruments, but what is less obvious is the impact of transaction costs on traditional regulation. A poorly designed law (from a transaction costs perspective) would be one where the relevant incidents are isolated and difficult to detect without substantial policing investment, costly to prosecute because of evidentiary requirements or rules of proof, difficult to enforce because of a fugitive or asset-poor subject group, and where the "payoff" from enforcement is small relative to the costs of enforcement because of low penalties or no financial return from successful prosecution to the policing agents. If all transaction costs are borne by the policing agency, then this is a law with an inbuilt bias against

[9] For an insightful examination of these issues, see D. W. Bromley, *Environment and Economy* (Oxford: Blackwell, 1991).

Table 4.2. Cost-inefficient regulatory design

Transaction cost	Adverse design conditions
Detection cost	Diffuse, physically obscure offences. Lack of physical "trace" over time, or to the offender. Limited ability to use detection technology.
Proof cost	Detailed proof data required. Potential for evidence destruction or loss. Highly contestable fact issues.
Prosecution cost	Complex prosecution cases. Full onus on policing agency.
Enforcement cost	Fugitive or impecunious offenders. Complex orders.
Funding	Adverse penalty/policing cost relationship. All prosecution and proof costs fall on policing agency. Weak economic incentive to prosecute.

active enforcement, because the drain on agency budgets would be poorly compensated by policing results or financial compensation. There are many environmental laws that fit such a perverse design specification. (See Table 4.2.) One has only to think of hunting or fishing controls to protect particular species, or waste discharge controls, to see that some laws operate at a disadvantage, and that a low level of policing effectiveness is more likely than not. One can contrast these types of environmental regulation with traffic laws, in which the fact of breach is sufficient proof, the penalties are high, and policing is aided by substantial use of technology such as speed cameras and breath-testing devices. What is often surprising is how well some environmental agencies cope under difficult regulatory regimes. What is disappointing is that they are so often "saddled" with these poorly planned regulatory instruments.

These observations lead to the conclusion that at least part of a behavioural jurisprudence for environmental law would be concerned with:

- the confidence that the community might have in the regulations that are passed, and whether these instruments can be consistently and effectively enforced;
- the capacity of these instruments to be communicated to and understood by those whose behaviours are meant to be altered; and
- the extent and the incidence of transaction costs associated with these.

Naturally, the greater the number of regulations, the more potential there is for confusion, high transaction costs, and diminished confidence in the regulatory regime.

6 THE PRACTICAL IMPACT OF AN EXPLOSION OF ENVIRONMENTAL REGULATIONS

As at 2000, there were more than 250 federal and state natural resource management laws in existence[10] in Australia. In addition, there is a myriad of interpretative regulations at all three levels of government, quasi-laws (policies, plans, and codes[11]) and administrative

[10] P. Martin and M. Verbeek (2000).

[11] See Attachment 1 for an example of the policies applicable in just one NSW estuary.

rulings that support this law. More laws mean more interpretation, more opportunities for legal uncertainties that need to be resolved, and therefore more compliance and transaction costs. This point recently has been made strongly by the Business Council of Australia[12], and can be supported from a jurisprudential and philosophic perspective, but it may be equally questionable from a behavioural effectiveness perspective.[13]

The development and implementation of these many rules is carried out by a myriad of bodies. In an earlier study in a mixed farming/urban coastal catchment area with about six hundred thousand residents, a series of workshops was conducted involving community and agency stakeholders. They were asked to identify what administrative or advisory bodies were involved in natural resource management in their region. They identified around fifty, of which perhaps twenty-five had a formal administering or interpretation role. This implies a large number of interactions (transactions) being necessary in the implementation of these rules. Some of these transactions would involve affected citizens seeking information or engaged in compliance transactions, others would be for the purposes of cross-agency coordination, and still others in seeking to resolve who is responsible for what. What does this complexity mean in terms of behavioural impact? This question can be divided into two aspects: on whom do the transaction costs of compliance fall, and what does this structure do to policing effectiveness?

In relation to the first, the experience of those who actively seek voluntary compliance is informative. From the discussions that I have had with people pursuing voluntary environment management system certification,[14] the costs of self-assessment of compliance are very high, and act as a barrier to the adoption of ISO 1401[15] or other environment management systems. Anecdotal comments suggest that self-assessment can cost thousands of dollars, and that the results can be equivocal because of the condition of the rules and the potential for changes in content or administrative application. It is my hypothesis that the costs of a dishevelled state of resource rules falls heavily on those who voluntarily comply, or those with the job of understanding and applying these rules. For those who are unconcerned with compliance, detailed evaluation of the rules is not necessary. They avoid the transaction costs and bear only the (contingent) costs of being caught, prosecuted, convicted and effectively penalised. This issue of complexity and regulatory efficiency is one that would benefit from careful comparative analysis, with regard to both the correlation between particular regulatory frameworks and efficient implementation, and the more challenging questions of causation.

Does the amount of law have an effect on the effectiveness of policing? My hypothesis is that it has a negative effect. I base this on my experience with one estuary, Port Hacking, where for almost twenty years I have seen the ever-growing set of rules alongside ever-declining environmental values.[16] I have observed agency jurisdiction-shopping, with some agents selecting which rule sets they are to administer and ignoring those that are outside their preferred subset, and frequent arguments arising as one agency sought to implement a strategy that clashed with the rules ostensibly being implemented by

[12] *Business Regulation Action Plan for Future Prosperity*, Business Council of Australia, 2005.

[13] A simple Google search on "red tape reduction" returned over 1.92 million "hits," from a wide range of countries, suggesting that this type of concern is not unique to this jurisdiction.

[14] Attachment 2 provides details of such schemes.

[15] ISO 1401, International Organisation for Standardisation, 1999 International Organization for Standardization (ISO) 1, rue de Varembé, Case postale 56 CH-1211 Geneva 20, Switzerland.

[16] This included a period as an environmental activist and as Chair of a regional Catchment Management Board responsible for integrated environmental management.

another.[17] These conflicts and issues are well documented, and I suspect that the situation is far from unique. Again, this is an important issue for comparative jurisprudence.

Complaints about the costs and complexity of law and its administration are loudest from business, in part because they bear the direct economic costs and can reliably measure their costs. These complaints are often dismissed by social justice advocates as "special pleading" of peripheral concern to justice. However, a behaviourally focused environmental jurisprudence would more properly focus on the extent to which excessive regulation and clumsy administration are barriers to the effectiveness of law in achieving sustainability goals.

A behavioural jurisprudence in the service of sustainability would of necessity lift its eyes from the casebooks and statutes, and grapple with the behaviours that it is trying to stimulate. This would be a challenge for law, as it has traditionally been focused more on the prevention of outlier behaviour than with encouragement of a desirable mainstream. Sustainability is necessarily concerned with both the control of the outliers, and mechanisms to make it possible for resource conservation to become the norm.

One outcome of a behavioural focus is a realisation that to achieve sustainability, the law must stimulate significant innovation both in the economically productive efficiency of resource use and in the protection of those resources that are not essential to efficient and profitable production. Unless we can wring more economic value from the resources that are used, we will not have the capacity to protect the other environments that we value. Such a jurisprudence would have to internalise concerns about the economics and "user-friendliness" of regulation and litigation. It would have to develop the capacity to think about systems, and about different types of instrument working in concert to change outcomes of systems.

This type of enquiry would flag some of the issues that are begging for reform within the present system. It would highlight first of all the need to invest more effort into the underlying integrity and efficiency of the system that we have today. Some directions for this investment would include:

a. improving the ability of the harmed and the less powerful to have a voice in the system, and to increase accountability for harm that is done to the less empowered.
b. design of regulation with regard to transaction costs reduction and rational cost allocation to support those who seek sustainability. This would require that we reduce and rationalise the regulations that are in place, and the administrative arrangements for their implementation.
c. finding ways to better integrate regulation with other strategies, including incentive systems and markets.
d. administrative law reform including transparent performance review of the regulatory performance of agencies, the outcomes that they achieve, and the cost-effectiveness of the instruments and strategies that they are using.

7 A REGULATORY TRIPLE BOTTOM LINE?

Sustainability advocates have realised that it is not enough to have a unidimensional focus on the environment because a narrow perspective works contrary to their

[17] The presentation of this essay will involve photographs and other documents to illustrate some of these matters.

objectives. The "triple bottom line" has been received as a way of recognising that environmental, economic, and social goals have to be pursued simultaneously if ecological sustainability is to be more than a vain hope.

It is time that we in the legal profession and academies took this lesson to heart, and broadened our view about what it will take to ensure that the legal system is energetic in pursuit of sustainability. Less regulation, more efficient regulation, and a broadening of the approaches that we are prepared to consider, may be a path to greater effectiveness and an accelerated shift towards sustainability.

Environmental lawyers have, in my view, become camp followers rather than pioneers in the pursuit of sustainability. This passivity is not consistent with the historical role of the law. A creative and open-minded perspective on the role of environmental law would be one way of putting jurisprudential thought back alongside economics and the other social sciences in leading society to a better and fairer future.

Attachment 1. ILLUSTRATION OF INSTRUMENTS

The following is a listing of regulatory, administrative, or advisory instruments which apply to Port Hacking in New South Wales, in addition to statutes identified under the inventory of natural resource management laws noted earlier in this chapter. The list is derived from a survey commissioned by the Southern Catchment Management Board and Sutherland Shire Council, as part of a compliance review. It is illustrative of the scale and nature of instruments that in theory ought to be considered in managing natural resources and use activities in an area. In practice, whether a particular instrument is considered seems to be often a "hit or miss" event.[18]

State Environmental Planning Policy No. 1 Development Standards
State Environmental Planning Policy No. 14 Coastal Wetlands
State Environmental Planning Policy No. 19 Bushland In Urban Areas
State Environmental Planning Policy No. 26 Littoral Rainforests
State Environmental Planning Policy No. 33 Hazardous and Offensive Development
State Environment Planning Policy No. 35 Maintenance Dredging of Tidal Waterways
State Planning Policy No. 60 Exempt and Complying Development
State Environmental Planning Policy No. 62 Sustainable Aquaculture
Navigation in Port Hacking (draft Plan)
State Environment Planning Policy No. 65 Design Quality of Residential Flat
State Environmental Planning Policy No. 71 Coastal Protection
NSW Estuary Management Policy
The NSW Wetlands Management Policy
Southern Catchment Blueprint
Global Programme of Action for the Protection of the Marine Environment from Land-Based Activities
The Australian Marine Project Guide

[18] An observation based on agency selectivity in preparing regional estuary or waterway management instruments.

Policy Guidelines for Aquatic Habitat Management and Fish Conservation
Fish Habitat Protection Plan No. 1: General
Fish Habitat Protection Plan No 2: Seagrasses
Fishnote: Saltmarsh
Corporate Plan 2002–2207: NSW Fisheries
State Environmental Planning Policy No. 32 Urban Consolidation (Redevelopment of Urban Land)
State Environmental Planning Policy No. 37 Continued Mines and Extractive Industries
Sutherland Shire Local Environmental Plan (SSLEP2000)
Blueprint for Action (Sutherland Shire Council)
Swimming Pools Development Control Plan
Residential Subdivision DCP
Residential Subdivision Development Control Plan 2001
Landscape Development Control Plan
Dredging Waterways Development Control Plan
Bushfire Development Control Plan
Dwelling Houses in 2(e) Residential Zones and Kurnell
Duration of Development Consents Development Control Plan
Waterfront Development Development Control Plan
Environment Site Management Development Control Plan
Sutherland Shire Contribution Plan Open Space (2002)
Water Traffic Regulations NSW
United Nations Framework Convention On Climate Change
United Nations Convention on the Law of the Sea
Agenda 21
Convention on Biological Diversity
Convention on Wetlands of International Importance Especially as Waterfowl Habitat
JAMBA
CAMBA
The Burra Charter
International Convention on the Prevention of Marine Pollution by Dumping of Wastes and Other Material
Australia's Ocean Policy
Australia's Ocean Policy – Specific Sectoral Measures
The National Greenhouse Strategy
National Strategy for the Conservation of Australia's Biological Diversity
National Strategy for Ecologically Sustainable Development
The Commonwealth Coastal Policy
NSW Biodiversity Strategy
Aquatic Habitat Management and Fish Conservation Policy and Guidelines
NSW Coastal Policy
NSW Bitou Bush Strategy
The NSW State Groundwater Policy Framework Document
Port Hacking Interim Boating Management Plan

Attachment 2. RESOURCES LIST

- Robert C. Anderson, The United States Experience with Economic Incentives for Protecting the Environment (National Center for Environmental Economics, 2001) http://yosemite1.epa.gov/ee/epa/eermfile.nsf/vwAN/EE-0216B-13.pdf/$File/EE-0216B-13.pdf.

  Documents hundreds of examples of economic incentives at all levels of government in the United States.
- Australian Law Reform Commission, Securing Compliance: Civil and Administrative Penalties in Australian Federal Regulation, ALRC Discussion Paper 65 (Australian Government, 2002) http://www.austlii.edu.au/au/other/alrc/publications/dp/65/.

  Looks at alternative forms of penalties and their likely effectiveness for different uses.
- Ian Ayres and John Braithwaite, *Responsive Regulation: Transcending the Deregulation Debate* (New York: Oxford University Press, 1992).

  Authors draw on empirical studies of regulation from around the world and modern game theory to illustrate innovative solutions to regulatory overburden and limited effectiveness.
- Robert Baldwin and Martin Cave, *Understanding Regulation: Theory, Strategy, and Practice* (Oxford: Oxford University Press, 1999).

  Focuses on British utilities regulation, but contains a broader examination of regulatory theory.
- Eugene Bardach and Robert A. Kagan, *Going by the Book: The Problem of Regulatory Unreasonableness*, 2nd ed. (New Brunswick, NJ: Transaction Books, 2002).

  In this second edition, twenty years after the original issue, the authors argue for flexible rather than a legalistic implementation but highlight the practical difficulties associated with pursuing this ideal.
- John Cary, Trevor Webb, and Neil Barr, *Understanding Landholders' Capacity to Change to Sustainable Practices: Insights About Practice Adoption and Social Capacity for Change* (Bureau of Rural Sciences, Canberra A.C.T. 2002) http://affashop.gov.au/product.asp?prodid=12921.

  Looks at causes for adoption or nonadoption of sustainable practices.
- J. Anthony Cassils, "Exploring Incentives: An Introduction to Incentives and Economic Instruments for Sustainable Development," Working Paper 13 (National Round Table on the environment and the Economy, 1991) http://www.nrtee-trnee.ca/Publications/PDF/Working-Paper_13_E.PDF.

  Discusses the range of instruments and approaches used in Canada, and comments on their use in other jurisdictions.
- Cary Coglianese, Jennifer Nash, and Todd Olmstead, "Performance-Based Regulation: Prospects and Limitations in Health, Safety and Environmental Protection," Regulatory Policy Program Report RPP-03 (Harvard University, 2002) http://papers.ssrn.com/sol3/papers.cfm?abstract_id=392400.

  Report from a workshop convened by the Regulatory Policy Program (US) intended to examine the use of regulated outcome standards rather then process controls.

- Bonnie C. Colby, "Regulation, Imperfect Markets and Transaction Costs: The Elusive Quest for Efficiency in Water Allocation," in Daniel W. Bromley, ed., *Handbook of Environmental Economics* (Oxford: Blackwell Publishers, 1995), 475–502.
  Provides insights into the nature and effect of transaction costs in a regulated context.
- Alastair Davidson and Lisa Elliston, "Regulation and Farm Viability: A Case Study In North West New South Wales." 12 *Australian Commodities* (2005), 1:200–207.
  Uses a "Vulnerability Index" as a basis for evaluation of the impact of regulation on farming.
- David M. Driessen, *The Economic Dynamics of Environmental Law* (Cambridge, MA: MIT Press, 2003).
  Provides a critique of processes of CBA as used by the U.S. EPA. Considers regulation and innovation systems, including path-dependence and new institutional economics.
- Pearl Eliadis, Margaret M. Hill, and Michael Howlett, eds, *Designing Government: From Instruments to Governance* (Montreal: McGill-Queen's University Press, 2005).
  Examines the political and strategic aspects of the choice of market, regulatory, or other instruments from a range of disciplinary perspectives.
- Frederick Edmund Emery and O. A. Oeser, *Information, Decision and Action: A Study of the Psychological Determinants of Changes in Farming Techniques* (Carlton: Melbourne University Press, 1958).
  This seminal study provides insights into differences in farmer patterns of adoption of new ideas, and their response to regulation.
- Jonathan Golub, *New Instruments for Environmental Policy in the EU* (London: Routledge, 1998).
  Examines a range of regulatory and market instruments and strategies used in the EU.
- Lawrence H. Goulder, Ian W. H. Parry, Robertson C. Williams, III, & Dallas Burtraw, "The Cost-Effectiveness of Alternative Instruments for Environmental Protection in a Second Best Setting," Discussion Paper 98–22 (Resources for the Future, 1998) http://www.rff.org/Documents/RFF-DP-98-22.pdf.
  Highlights the importance of context issues such as taxation regimes in determining whether a regulatory or a market instrument is likely to be most effective.
- Neil Gunningham and Peter N. Grabosky, *Smart Regulation: Designing Environmental Policy* (Oxford: Clarendon, 1998).
  Provides detailed guidance on the integration of state regulation with other instruments and strategies.
- Fiona Haines, *Corporate Regulation: Beyond "Punish or Persuade"* (Oxford: Clarendon Press, 1997).
  Considers the economic and political conditions under which compliance with regulation can be achieved.
- Jay Kassirer, Susan Koswan, Kit Spence, Suzanne Morphet, Chris Wolnik, Stephanie Goom, and Tania Del Matto, *The Impact of By-Laws and Public Education Programs on Reducing the Cosmetic/Non-Essential, Residential Use of Pesticides: A Best Practices Review* (Canadian Centre for Pollution Prevention, 2004) http://www.greenventure.ca/hcpi/campaign/BestPracticeReviewC2P2.pdf.

This study of nine communities in Canada, the United States, and Europe that were leaders in reducing their pesticide use evaluates the impact of the various legislative and educational approaches.

- Paul Martin and Miriam Verbeek, *Sustainability Strategy* (Sydney: Federation Press, 2006).

  Provides an approach to designing integrated natural resource management strategy combining regulation, market instruments, and other tools.
- Paul Martin and Miriam Verbeek, *Cartography for Environmental Law: Finding New Paths to Effective Resource Use Regulation* (Land and Water Research and Development Corporation, 2000) http://www.une.edu.au/aglaw/research/cartography_paper.pdf.

  Provides a detailed examination of contemporary Australian environmental laws.
- Steven M. Maser and Douglas D. Heckathorn, "Bargaining and the Sources of Transaction Costs: The Case of Government Regulation." 3 *Journal of Law, Economics and Organisation* (1987), 1:69–98.

  Considers the fundamentals of transaction costs and the role of government as regulator.
- Thea Mech, K. Lowe, and A. Cole, *Land Stewardship and Environmental Management Systems, Land Stewardship* (Victorian Department of Sustainability and Environment, 2003) http:/www.nre.vic.gov.au/DSE/nrenlwm.nsf/9e58661e880ba9e44a256c640023eb2e/74724a6fbc4ed789ca2572510014e04f/-FILE/DSE-EMS-final.pdf.

  Looks at voluntary EMS and the potential of its application as a property-level environmental management tool by agricultural businesses.
- Erling Moxnes, "Not Only the Tragedy of the Commons: Misperceptions of Feedback and Policies for Sustainable Development." 16 *System Dynamics Review* (2000), 4:325–348.

  Summarizes laboratory experiments showing the effects of misperception, timing lags, perceptual filters and self-interest, short-term incentives, and capital investment effects on resource use decisions.
- Earl Finbar Murphy, *Nature, Bureaucracy and the Rules of Property* (New York: North Holland Publishing Company, 1977).

  Considers linkages between regulation and the environment, looking at the development of regulation and the protection of the renewing environment, rules structure, environmental costs, regulation, and property, and the future of regulation.
- National Centre for Environmental Economics, *The United States Experience with Economic Incentives for Protecting the Environment* (U.S. Environmental Protection Agency, 2001) http://yosemite1.epa.gov/ee/epa/eermfile.nsf/vwAN/EE-0216B-13.pdf/$File/EE-0216B-13.pdf.

  An in-depth look at a variety of incentive-based environmental protection measures in the United States.
- Organisation for Economic Co-operation and Development/EEA database on instruments used in environmental policy, available at http://www2.oecd.org/ecoinst/queries/index.htm.

  A useful contemporary guide.

- Organisation for Economic Co-operation and Development, "OECD Guiding Principles for Regulatory Quality and Performance" (Organisation for Economic Co-operation and Development, 2005) http://www.oecd.org/dataoecd/24/6/3497-6533.pdf.
  Following an intensive process conducted in policy committees and in the Special Group on Regulatory Policy, the Guiding Principles for Regulatory Quality and Performance were adopted by the OECD Council in April 2005.
- David J. Pannell, *Public Benefits, Private Benefits: The Final Framework*, Pannell Discussions 80 (University of Western Australia, 2006) http://cyllene.uwa.edu.au/~dpannell/pd/pd0080.htm.
  Final instalment of a series that examines a simple framework for choosing environmental policy instruments, based on levels of public and private net benefits.
- Richard A. Posner and Eric B. Rasmusen, "Creating and Enforcing Norms, with Special Reference to Sanctions." 19 *International Review of Law and Economics* (1999), 369–382.
  Examines the creation, modification, and enforcement of norms as a basis for discussing the limits of feasible government action.
- Margot Priest, "The Privatization of Regulation: Five Models of Self-Regulation." 29 *Ottawa Law Review* (1997–1998), 233–302.
  Concludes that self-regulation is most likely to work only when specific conditions are present.
- Queensland Department of State Development, Guidelines on Alternatives to Prescriptive Regulation (Queensland Government, 2000) http://www.sdi.qld.gov.au/dsdweb/v3/documents/objdirctrled/nonsecure/pdf/2457.pdf.
  Provides an overview of information on alternatives to prescriptive regulation and processes, and case study examples of effective outcomes.
- Barak D. Richman and Jeffrey T. Macher, "Transaction Cost Economics: An Assessment of Empirical Research in the Social Sciences," Duke Law School Legal Studies Research Paper 115 (Duke Law School, 2006) http://ssrn.com/abstract=924192.
  Provides a comprehensive review of the empirical literature in transaction cost economics (TCE) across social science disciplines and business.
- Jackie Robinson and Sean Ryan, *A Review of Economic Instruments for Environmental Management in Queensland* (CRC for Coastal Zone, Estuary and Waterway Management, 2002) http://www.coastal.crc.org.au/pdf/economic_instruments.pdf.
  Reviews the economic instruments to support environmental management currently available in Queensland and provides some guidance for their application. Provides a list of considerations when choosing instruments.
- Kathleen Segerson, "Liability and Penalty Structures in Policy Design," in Daniel W. Bromley, ed., *Handbook of Environmental Economics* (Oxford, Blackwell, 1995), 272–294.
  Identifies behavioural effects of different regimes, and highlights that liability penalties are a potential alternative to other market solutions.
- Kathleen Segerson and Thomas J. Miceli, "Voluntary Environmental Agreements: Good or Bad News for Environmental Protection?" 36 *Journal of Environmental Economics and Management* (1998), 2:109–130.
  Uses a simple model to determine whether VEAs are likely to lead to efficient environmental protection.

- Malcolm K. Sparrow, *The Regulatory Craft: Controlling Risks, Solving Problems, and Managing Compliance* (Washington, DC: Brookings Institution, 2000).
  Concerned with the policing/enforcement/implementation end of regulation. Discusses environmental regulatory and strategy processes.
- Robert N. Stavins, "Experience with Market-based Environmental Policy Instruments," Discussion Paper 01–58 (Resources for the Future, 2001) http://www.rff.org/Documents/RFF-DP-01-58.pdf.
  Considers experience around the world with economic-incentive or market-based policy instruments.
- Matthias Weber and Jens Hemmelskamp, eds., *Towards Environmental Innovation Systems* (Berlin: Springer, 2005).
  Draws together research into innovation, regulation, and sustainability.
- M. D. Young, Neil Gunningham, Jane Elix, Judy Lambert, B. Howard, P. Grabosky, and E. McCrone, "Reimbursing the Future: An Evaluation of Motivational, Voluntary, Price-Based, Property-Right, and Regulatory Incentives for the Conservation of Biodiversity," Biodiversity Series 9 (CSIRO, 1996) http://www.deh.gov.au/biodiversity/publications/series/paper9/index.html.
  Canvasses solutions for biodiversity protection within Australia. Also considers regulatory processes.

PART TWO

BIODIVERSITY: ITS CONSERVATION

SECTION A. NEEDS, PROBLEMS, PREREQUISITES

5 Biodiversity Conservation in the Context of Sustainable Human Development: A Call to Action

Michael I. Jeffery

1 INTRODUCTION

Unguided (unregulated) individual and collective use of natural resources has threatened the sustainability of the environment and biodiversity. Intensive use of resources has been encouraged by policies and strategies primarily concerned with enhancing growth rates and economic development and many countries have benefited from the conversion of natural ecosystems to human-dominated ones and the exploitation of biodiversity.[1] However, such policies have been neither efficient nor equitable in addressing poverty and its manifestations, and have resulted in unequal development between the North and the South, as well as within nation-states. Furthermore, the continued erosion of the resource base, on which development depends, proceeds unabated. With an increasing population in the midst of poverty, urbanization, and industrialization, the path to development for the South is beset by powerful drivers causing and contributing to the persistence of major environmental issues.[2] The poor often depend directly on natural resources and functioning ecosystem services for their livelihoods. At the same time, they are particularly vulnerable to environmental hazards, such as floods, droughts, and landslides. Poverty-environment linkages need to be addressed in efforts to eradicate this situation and effective conservation and use of biodiversity cannot avoid this.[3]

Improving environmental governance[4] to create an enabling environment for resolving poverty-environment concerns and enhancing the asset base of the poor can expand sustainable livelihoods and reduce vulnerability. A solution is improving the quality of growth through the encouragement of sound environmental management, protection

[1] Millennium Ecosystem Assessment, 2005. *Ecosystems and Human Well-being: Biodiversity Synthesis* (Washington, DC: World Resources Institute, 4).

[2] Op. cit. More than eight hundred million people live in absolute poverty in this region.

[3] Department for International Development, Directorate General for Development European Commission, United Nations Development Programme, World Bank; *Linking Poverty Reduction and Environmental Management: Policy Challenges and Opportunities* 2002, 2.

[4] The concept of environmental governance encompasses the relationships and interactions among government and nongovernment structures, procedures, and conventions, where power and responsibility are exercised in making environmental decisions. Jeffery, M. I., *Environmental Governance Issues In The Context Of International Environmental Law: An Australian Perspective*, 2005, 1.

* Michael I. Jeffery, QC is Professor of Law and Director of the Centre for Environmental Law, Macquarie University, Sydney Australia and Chair of Coordinating Committee of IUCN Academy of Environmental Law 2005 Colloquium. The author is indebted to his graduate student research assistant, Jane Steel, for her dedicated and enthusiastic assistance in the preparation of this paper.

of environmental assets, promotion of better livelihood opportunities and reform of international and developed-country policies to address the poverty and environment concerns of the people.[5] *How* decisions are made is equally essential to the task of determining solutions.[6] Particular emphasis should be placed on the need for citizens, interest groups, and communities *in general*, to participate and to define their own actions.[7] The concept of *environmental governance* incorporates this ethic.[8] As an extension of the concept of environmental governance, *good environmental governance* is measured by the effectiveness of the strategies and initiatives implemented to achieve environmental goals. Outcomes of such goals, capacity building, increased access to environmental information, participation, and justice are essential to the effective implementation of biodiversity management and to resolving the poverty-environment nexus.[9]

2 THE DEVELOPMENT PARADIGM

Although the contemporary global development paradigm or consumptive development path of the North has resulted in loss of biodiversity, the South's race to access the same opportunities is contributing to rapidly increasing losses in biodiversity and changes in ecosystem services.[10] Policies that have economic development of central relevance for livelihood development and the alleviation of poverty need serious rethinking. Sustainable human development should be prioritized to ensure that the resource base is conserved and equitably shared. This way, resource dependent development can be enhanced and enjoyed among current and future generations. Internationally guiding policies for the conservation and sustainable development of biodiversity therefore must be underpinned by an environmental ethic cognizant of and responsive to such concerns.

3 THE IMPORTANCE OF BIODIVERSITY

Biodiversity contributes directly (through provisioning and regulating ecosystem services) and indirectly (through supporting ecosystem services) to many aspects of human well-being, including security, provision of essential goods and resources, employment, health, social and cultural relations, and "freedom of choice and action."[11]

[5] Note 3, at 2.

[6] Note 4.

[7] J. Graham, B. Amos, & T. Plumptre, *Governance Principles for Protected Areas in the 21st Century, 2003* (Durban: World Parks Congress, 2003), iii.

[8] *The Earth Charter Initiative, The Earth Charter* (2000) The Earth Charter Initiative, http://www.earthcharter.org/files/charter/charter.pdf at 29 April 2005[8] expresses this sense of environmental responsibility by stating that the improvement of democratic practices, transparency, and accountability of government institutions, along with civil participation in decision making, are strongly related factors to the objectives of the protection of the environment and social and economic justice.

[9] M. I. Jeffery, "An International Regime for Protected Areas," in John Scanlon & Francoise Burhenne-Guilmin, eds., *International Environmental Governance – An International Regime for Protected Areas*, 2004, 11. International environmental law instruments, such as The Earth Charter Initiative, Agenda 21, and the World Conservation Union's (IUCN) Draft International Covenant on Environment and Development, set out the framework for achieving environmental goals such as these. (1992) United Nations Department of Economic and Social Affairs, Division for Sustainable Development, http://www.un.org/esa/sustdev/documents/agenda21/english/agenda21toc.htm at 28 April 2005 and (2004) 3rd ed., IUCN The World Conservation Union.

[10] Note 1, at 4.

[11] Note 1, at 2.

If conservation of biodiversity is to occur, the poverty-environment paradigm must be considered and Multilateral Environmental Agreements (MEAs) need to be reflective of broad-based strategies. Integrating biodiversity issues into national sustainable development and poverty reduction strategies,[12] strengthening decentralization and civil society involvement in environmental management, focusing on vulnerable groups and improving environmental regulation and policy enforcement are merely some of the overriding improvements needed for better governance of biological resources.[13]

4 THE NECESSITY OF RIGHTS-BASED POLICIES

Essential to the implementation of conservation and sustainable use of biodiversity is that policies include action to strengthen resource rights both locally and globally. Increased access, ownership, control, and benefit-sharing of resources are required to enhance the asset base of the poor, as well as to protect the forgotten commons, such as the High Seas.

Locally, the promotion of participatory, transparent management arrangements, capacity development, and access to environmentally sound and appropriate technology supports such efforts. Improving protection of and access to Indigenous and traditional environmental knowledge and technologies, assisting pro-poor technology development and utilizing participatory research techniques are equally important factors in the same endeavour. Fostering private-sector participation and improving the capacity of both government and communities can facilitate local enterprise development related to the sustainable use of biodiversity.[14] Promoting appropriate environmental practice and sustainable use of biodiversity, as well as more effectively allocating resource revenues, also can act to ensure pro-poor environment outcomes.[15] Of greatest priority should be the assurance that environmental safeguards and appropriate regulations protect the interests of both the poor and the environment.[16]

Globally, international cooperation through multilateral environmental agreements requires increased commitment to implementation of activities that effectively conserve biodiversity and promote the sustainable use of biological resources. A plethora of MEAs contribute to conserving biodiversity.[17] Their impacts at policy and practical levels depend on the will of the contracting parties both in implementation and support provided for such agreements.[18] Convention reporting requirements as well as the measures required under the framework of MEAs place much pressure on developing countries.[19] Effective support should be provided financially, through technology transfer and through adequate framework guidance, for the development

[12] Op. cit.

[13] Note 3, at 3–4.

[14] Op. cit. Including community based ecotourism and sustainable harvesting of natural products.

[15] Note 3, at 5.

[16] Note 3, at 4.

[17] Note 1, at 77. The Convention on Biological Diversity is the most comprehensive, but numerous others are also relevant, including the World Heritage Convention, the Convention on International Trade in Endangered Species of Wild Fauna and Flora, the Ramsar Convention on Wetlands, the Convention on Migratory Species, the U.N. Convenation to Combat Desertification, the U.N. Framework Convention on Climate Change, and numerous regional agreements.

[18] Op. cit.

[19] GEF-UNDP, Capacity Development Initiative, "Country Capacity Development Needs and Priorities: A Synthesis," October 2000, 7.

and integration of effective instruments, such as incentives, to assist countries to achieve compliance.[20]

Creating synergies between conventions also should be promoted and further research on dispute resolution mechanisms is required to strengthen the international environmental law framework. Negative impacts related to indirect drivers of biodiversity loss, particularly globalization and international decisions related to trade and economics, should be resolved through greater international negotiation, including capacity development of developing countries to enhance participation and strengthen links between biodiversity conventions and other international legal institutions which impact on these, including the Agreement on Trade Related Aspects of Intellectual Property (TRIPs) and the UN Convention on the Law of the Sea (UNCLOS) agreements.[21] These international agreements must be realigned to ensure they promote sustainable human development, rather than impinge on it.

5 THE ROLE OF LAW

In order to achieve 2010 targets and significantly reduce the current rate of biodiversity loss at the global, regional, and national levels and to contribute to poverty alleviation and to benefit all forms of life,[22] law can play a critical role. It should provide the enabling environment and implementation directive required to ensure sustainable development. A closer examination of the status of relevant frameworks and MEAs is required in order to examine whether such are, or may be effective in achieving and overcoming the poverty-environment nexus. Furthermore, an examination is required to promote good environmental governance as outlined earlier and to identify which gaps still exist and require urgent action.

6 ACHIEVING CONSENSUS

The *Stockholm Declaration*,[23] and later *Agenda 21*, both characterized as "soft law" because of their broad principles and largely nonbinding nature, provide the benchmarks for international environmental policy. Developed within the context of broad-based international conferences, both documents have been heralded as valuable instruments for achieving consensus related to sustainable development and in achieving the "middle ground." As developed and developing nations arguably experience international environmental law in two different paradigms of environment and development respectively, their different views need to be reconciled.[24] "Soft law" is frequently explained as being able to broker international consensus and thus legitimise

[20] Note 1, at 77.

[21] Op. cit.

[22] CBD Decision VI/26. The Conference of the Parties of the Convention on Biological Diversity adopted the target, subsequently endorsed in the Johannesburg Plan of Implementation adopted at the World Summit on Sustainable Development, in April 2002. In 2004, the Conference of the Parties adopted a framework for evaluation, including a small number of global 2010 subtargets, and a set of indicators that will be used in assessing progress.

[23] Adopted by the United Nations Conference on the Human Environment held in Stockholm in 1972.

[24] C. Stone, "Treaties as Antidotes," in *The Gnat is Older than Man: Global Environment and Human Agenda* (Princeton University Press, 1993), 96–121 and D. G. Craig, N. A. Robinson, & Koh Kheng-Lian, *Capacity Building for Environmental Law in the Asian and Pacific Region: Approaches and Resources* (Asian Development Bank, 2002), 387.

international environmental concern in areas of previously exclusive national jurisdiction.[25] For example, Stockholm incorporated international law principles[26] in the environmental context, establishing henceforth the consistent application of provisions relating to the sovereign right of nation-states to exploit their own resources pursuant to their own environmental and developmental policies. Corollary to this, the responsibility to ensure that activities within state jurisdiction or control did not cause damage to the environment of other States or of areas beyond the limits of national jurisdiction, established the general principle underlying more recent transboundary pollution provisions.[27] Moreover, Agenda 21 further elicited principles of prevention and the precautionary principle,[28] and provided considerable support for the application of sustainable development and intergenerational equity.[29]

7 THE FRAMEWORK FOR BIODIVERSITY

The *Convention on Biodiversity (1993)* (CBD) and its *Cartagena Protocol (2000)* provide an overarching framework for sustainable development and the management of "the biodiversity issue."[30] Recognized widely for its innovative, comprehensive rather than sectoral, approach to the conservation of biodiversity and sustainable use of biological resources,[31] the CBD has added to the increasing body of progressive international environmental law developed since Rio in 1992.[32] Characteristic of any such MEAs or convention seeking to institute and regulate sustainable development, the CBD has necessarily engaged both developed and developing nation-parties.[33] Widely recognized

[25] G. Handl, "Environmental Security and Global Change: The Challenge to International Law," in W. Lang et al., eds., *Environmental Protection and International Law*, Graham and Trotman, 1991, 60–83 and Craig et al., 394.

[26] Particularly, the principle of *Sic Utere Tuo Ut Alienum Non Laedas*, Abuse of Rights, Principle 21 of the Stockholm Declaration and further echoed in Agenda 21 on Environment and Development, Rio de Janeiro, 1992.

[27] The *Trail Smelter Case* (United States v. Canada) Arbitral Tribunal, 1941, 3 UN Rep. Int'l Arb. Awards 1941, extended the obligation not to cause harm to other states to environmental damage. D. Hunter, J. Salzman, and D. Zaelke, *International Environmental Law and Policy* (University Case Book Series, 1998), 346. It is regarded as the basis for Principle 21 of the Stockholm Declaration, which is widely viewed to reflect customary law, regarding a State's sovereign right to use their natural resources with the responsibility not to allow activities within their jurisdiction and control to harm the environment of other countries, *ibid.* Hunter et al., 512.

[28] Principle 15 of the Rio Declaration, Agenda 21.

[29] Agenda 21, UN Conference on Environment and Development (UNCED, 1992).

[30] It concerns all aspects of biodiversity (genes, species and ecosystems); with wild and domesticated species; with conservation *in-situ* and *ex-situ*; and with biodiversity components within and outside national jurisdictions. L. Glowka, F. Burhenne-Guilmin, & H. Synge, in collaboration with J. McNeely, L. Guendling, *A Guide to the Convention on Biological Diversity* (IUCN, 1994), 1–7, 645, and Craig et al . and note 24, at 647.

[31] Op. cit.

[32] Article 2(1) of the 1969 *Vienna Convention on the Law of Treaties (VCLT)*, defines a treaty or international law as "an international agreement concluded between States in written form and governed by international law . . ." The CBD necessarily deals with relationships between States and persons or entities in different states, and encompasses the three primary sources of international law: treaties, custom, and general principles. Similarly Article 2 of the Cartagena Protocol also reflects this principle.

[33] "International environmental law and parties thereto can be characterized by the act of nation states voluntarily expressing and accepting obligations between and among themselves, which may reflect consistent practice of states accompanied by *opinion juris* (the conviction of states that the practice set is required by law), general principles of commonly recognized or agreements in any form that the contracting parties agree upon." Available at: Wikipedia, http://en.wikipedia.org.

as now biologically poorer countries, developed nations have largely depleted territorial biodiversity reserves in the process of development. Conversely, the remaining reserves found in developing nations and beyond national boundaries present future and current development opportunities for both the North and the South. It is from this basis that the CBD was negotiated.

In requiring developing nations to forego or restrict the previous consumptive development paradigm, albeit unsustainable, significant trade-offs continue to be faced. Immediate concerns of developing countries relate to loss of short-term income and food production relevant for poverty and hunger alleviation. Hence, in bringing both sides and all considerations to the table, the adoption of the CBD constituted an effort of paramount global significance. In doing so, the CBD has also been effective in forging and integrating, more concertedly and on a global scale, principles of sustainable development, intergenerational equity[34] and the precautionary principle,[35] establishing more distinct and binding principles such as the common concern of humankind, global partnerships, common but differentiated responsibilities and, most important, placing a value on biodiversity.[36]

8 ENVIRONMENT VERSUS SUSTAINABLE DEVELOPMENT

Challenges continue to lie, however, in balancing the environmental management concerns of the North with the sustainable development needs of the South. Environmental management principles alone have been shown to be inadequate, with developing countries requiring practical methods and means by which to implement the CBD.

Although the CBD established a new form of proactive rather than reactive international law, because of the nature of the negotiations, it provided a mixed framework of "soft and hard law." It successfully established more detailed provisions covering biodiversity aspects comprehensively,[37] although the explicit means by which to ensure compliance, enforcement, and definite standards in biodiversity conservation have only gradually been included in the convention through subsequent meetings of the Conference of the Parties (COPs). These have resulted in more binding obligations and detailed arrangements in protocols and annexes, such as the *Cartagena Protocol on Biosafety*. Arguably though, twelve years postinception, many provisions still remain vague or absent seriously affecting implementation of the CBD.

9 CBD OBJECTIVES

In offering its three objectives: the conservation of biodiversity, the sustainable use of biological resources and the fair and equitable sharing of benefits arising out of the

[34] United Nations Conference on Environment and Development (UNCED) 1992, Agenda 21.

[35] United Nations Conference on Environment and Development (UNCED) 1992, Rio Declaration, Agenda 21, Principle 15.

[36] UNEP, "Introduction to International Law Relating to the Environment," Environmental Law Training Manual, 1997 in Craig et al., note 24 at 368.

[37] It identifies a common problem, sets overall goals and policies and general obligations and organizes technical and financial cooperation. "Sustaining Life on Earth," Secretariat of the Convention on Biodiversity. Available at http://www.unep.org.

utilization of genetic resources,[38] the CBD established an equitable approach, compensating the loss of development with express provision for additional contributions from developed nations and increased partnership between the developed and developing ones.[39] By delegating the principal decision-making responsibilities to the national level for provisions on conservation and sustainable use[40] and through provisions, such as Articles 8 and 9, that outline major policies for effective in-situ[41] and ex-situ conservation of biological diversity, respectively, the CBD sought to institute effective decentralization and national sovereignty over biodiversity.[42]

10 SUSTAINABLE USE AND ADAPTIVE AND ECOSYSTEM MANAGEMENT

In seeking to ensure sustainability and conservation principles, the Convention includes provisions on the sustainable use of resources and environmental impact assessment,[43] as well as other monitoring provisions.[44] Arguably, the CBD provides greater use of science then previous MEAs and has more "teeth" in terms of regulating environmental management.[45] Principles subsequently developed[46] enhance the comprehensive coverage of the CBD. An ecosystems approach to biodiversity management reflects the need to control other environmental impacts on ecosystems, rather than biological resources alone, as a means of mitigating the loss of biodiversity.

11 THE ECOSYSTEM APPROACH

The ecosystem approach under the CBD, provides a strategy that promotes conservation and sustainable use through the integrated management of land, water, and living resources. It is reflective of the trade-offs between environment and development that exist in the management of ecosystems and incorporates the need for coordination across sectors and throughout hierarchies of management. This way, it provides a framework for designing and implementing a range of responses, from those directly addressing the needs for conservation and sustainable use of biodiversity to those necessary to address other indirect and direct drivers, such as poverty, that influence ecosystems.[47]

Uniquely, the ecosystem approach focuses on the interaction of species and processes within the ecosystem. Benefits from ecosystem services are analysed, adaptive management practices encouraged, and multilayer, multisectoral management and cooperation

[38] Mackenzie, R., Burhenne-Guilmin, F., La Vina, A. G. M. and Werksman, J. D., "An Explanatory Guide to the Cartagena Protocol on Biosafety, IUCN Environmental Policy and Law Paper No. 46, 2003.

[39] Articles 20, 21, and 39 outline the Financial Mechanism. Articles 15 and 16 outline access to genetic resources and access to and transfer of technology, respectively.

[40] Article 1 of the CBD sets out the convention's objectives, including the conservation of biological diversity and the sustainable use of its components. Article 6 requires each party to develop national strategies, plans, or programs for conservation of biodiversity and sustainable use of biological resources.

[41] It provides parties a set of goals against which to match their own laws and policies.

[42] Craig, D. Introduction, Volume 1 in Craig, et al., note 24, at 3.

[43] Articles 10 and 14.

[44] Article 10 outlines the sustainable use of biological resources, Article 14 dictates environmental impact assessment, and Article 7 uses science as the basis for detailed monitoring.

[45] Articles 7, 12, 14, 17, 18, and 25 deal with science, research, and monitoring aspects of biodiversity management.

[46] Developed at the fourth open-ended workshop on sustainable use, 6–8 May 2003, held as a result of decision VI/13 COP 6 and reiterated under VII (12).

[47] Note 1, at 14.

required.[48] A number of other established approaches, such as sustainable forest management, integrated river basin management, and integrated marine and coastal area management, are consistent with the ecosystem approach and support its application. Cultural relativism, geographical differences, and wealth disparities are challenges to the development of good environmental governance schemes in ecosystems, but these factors must not be seen as complete hindrances to success. Instead, they are factors that require more focused and concerted attention. A common, yet differentiated approach between countries is recognized by the ecosystem approach. The means of achieving better environmental protection may be different, yet the goals of sustainability and conservation can be shared.[49]

12 SUSTAINABLE USE

The Addis Ababa Principles, 2004,[50] provide more comprehensive guidance for the sustainable use of resources within the ecosystem approach,[51] and focus on providing effective tools to combat poverty, and, consequently, to achieve sustainable development.[52] The practical principles in most instances apply to both consumptive and non-consumptive uses of biodiversity components[53] and highlight the requirement of better governance locally, recognizing that policies, laws, and regulations, management of biological diversity, socioeconomic conditions and information, research, and education are all essential components of managing biodiversity.[54]

Moreover, the introduction of the concept of sustainable use acknowledges the poverty-environment nexus, emphasizing that basic necessities, such as food and shelter, are produced either directly or indirectly from using biological diversity.[55] Therefore, the Addis Abeba principles, 2004,[56] may be interpreted as facilitative of the aforementioned balance between environment and development and better environmental governance, particularly in their reference to the World Summit on Sustainable Development and partnerships for attaining sustainable development. They further recognize the incentive importance of sustainable development and sustainable use in developing countries as the basis for conservation and restoration because of the social, cultural, and economic benefits that people derive from the use of biodiversity.

The Sixth Conference Of the Parties (COP 6),[57]reiterated the need to identify underlying causes and threats to biodiversity as a prerequisite for defining appropriate measures and the need for policy studies to be undertaken. The principles of precaution and equity as well as distribution impacts, a participatory and ecosystems approach, awareness, and the need to capture value from biodiversity use for Indigenous and local communities were among many requirements prescribed to develop effective incentives.[58]

[48] Op. cit.
[49] Note 4, at 5.
[50] Principle 6.
[51] Subsidiary Body On Scientific, Technical And Technological Advice, Ninth Meeting Montreal, 10–14 November 2003, Item 5.2 of the Provisional Agenda, Sustainable Use: Development of Practical Principles, Operational Guidance and Associated Instruments, UNEP/CBD/SBSTTA/9/9, 31 July 2003, paragraph 4, 9
[52] Note 51, paragraph 2, 9.
[53] Note 51, paragraph 3, 9.
[54] Op. cit.
[55] Note 51, at 10.
[56] Principle 6.
[57] The Hague 2002.
[58] Decision VII/12, section 3 Associated Instruments.

13 ADAPTIVE MANAGEMENT

The CBD recommends an adaptive approach to interventions and management also in view of the inherent uncertainties related to biodiversity management, the array of managed uses of biodiversity and local context in which they are used, and dynamic communities where circumstances are constantly changing.[59] This requires the establishment of indicators to monitor the effects of new measures, so that the need to make adjustments can be effected [60] Hence, adaptive management deals with the complex nature of ecosystems and their uses and utilizes a precautionary approach in response to the absence of complete knowledge of functioning [61] It also presents the opportunities to respond to uncertainties and to incorporate a "learning-by-doing" approach, which emphasizes the requirement for further locally based research.[62]

14 LOCAL IMPLEMENTATION OF GUIDELINES

Some developing countries are integrating such concepts, through the management of biodiversity corridors. In the Philippines, the Northern Sierra Madre area constitutes one of the country's thirteen biogeographic regions. Biodiversity corridor implementation in this area is mentioned in the Philippines' National Biodiversity Strategy and Action Plan, as a conservation priority. Although the impacts and sustainability of such an approach are not yet clear because of the large area covered and short implementation time, many partnerships among donors, NGOs, and government have been established, such that the practice and principle of adaptive and ecosystem management[63] have been adopted nationally.[64]

15 EFFECTIVENESS OF GUIDELINES

The Millennium Ecosystems Assessment has provided detailed findings on the effectiveness of protected areas,[65] the hallmark of the ecosystem approach for biodiversity conservation and improved human well-being. Protected areas are emphasized as extremely important programs to conserve biodiversity and ecosystems.[66] However, the report's findings illustrated several capacity issues. It highlighted that PAs need to be better located, designed, and managed in order to deal with issues of lack of representativeness, impacts of human settlement within protected areas, illegal harvesting of plants and animals, unsustainable tourism, impacts of invasive alien species, and vulnerability to global change.[67] More implementation guidance is required to ensure sustainable development, solutions to the poverty–environment nexus and incentives to maintain such.

[59] Note 51, at 12.

[60] Hamilton, Alan C, Medicinal Plants and the Ecosystem Approach, *Biodiversity and Conservation* 13: 1477–1517, 2004. Kluwer Academic Publishers, The Netherlands, 1487.

[61] Note 51, at 6.

[62] Op. cit.

[63] Decision VII/ 28 includes very detailed guidelines and plans of action recommended for Protected Areas article 8 (a) to (e) of the CBD, 7th COP Feb 2004.

[64] *Philippine Biodiversity Conservation Priorities, A Second Iteration of the National Biodiversity Strategy and Action Plan*, Department of Environment and Natural Resources 2002.

[65] Note 1, at 69.

[66] Op. cit.

[67] Op. cit.

16 MARINE PROTECTED AREAS

Efforts to expand marine protected areas are also based on findings related to the positive relationship between conservation within PAs and sustainable use immediately outside them.[68] However, management of Marine protected areas magnifies the challenges faced by many land-based PAs but their enforcement is difficult because many marine areas lie outside national jurisdictions. Provisions on in-situ conservation do not apply outside national jurisdiction. Moreover, the CBD does not refer specifically to marine or terrestrial ecosystems. During the 1995 Conference of the Parties, the Jakarta Mandate was issued, which outlined a programme of action for implementing the Convention with respect to marine and coastal biodiversity.[69] Decisions pursuant to the Jakarta Mandate identify five areas in which Party States can take practical steps to apply the Convention to marine habitats.[70] MPAs are one of the five areas.

With regard to implementation of the Convention on the high seas, although Article 4 of the CBD emphasizes national sovereignty over resources, it allows for regulation of biodiversity "beyond the limits of national jurisdiction for processes and activities carried out by a member State, regardless of where their effects occur." Furthermore, Article 5 requires parties' cooperation, "as far as possible and as appropriate, in respect of areas beyond national jurisdiction." Article 8 also requires States to, "establish a system of protected areas or areas where special measures need to be taken to conserve biological diversity."

MPAs on the high seas are a conceivable means of conservation, constrained only by political will; the need for Parties to negotiate in areas beyond national jurisdiction.[71] The possibility of MPA establishment is not so remote with a similar regime incorporating trade-offs, being established by the International Maritime Organisation. Particularly sensitive sea areas (PSSAs), defined as "areas which need special protection through action by the IMO because of their significance for recognised ecological, socio-economic or scientific reasons, and which may be vulnerable to damage by maritime activities," are being established to increase the international shipping community's responsibility to limit the adverse environmental impacts of shipping.[72] Guidelines were recently adopted that list ecological, social, cultural, and economic or scientific criteria that must be met for an area to be designated as PSSA. Once a PSSA is designated, special protective measures can be adopted, which must be respected by the vessels of all IMO member countries.[73]

[68] Op. cit.

[69] A. C. De Fontaubert, "Legal and Political Considerations," in *The Status Of Natural Resources On The High-Seas* (Gland, Switzerland: WWF/IUCN, 2001), 80.

[70] They include: implementing integrated coastal area management; ensuring the sustainable use of coastal and marine living resources; implementing environmentally sustainable mariculture practices; preventing the introduction of alien species; and establishing marine and coastal protected areas.

[71] Note 69, at 80.

[72] A member State or group of States of the IMO may submit an area for designation as a PSSA. This application is reviewed by the Marine Environment Protection Committee (MEPC), the IMO's arm of the organisation that reviews measures designed to limit the impacts of shipping on the marine environment.

[73] Such measures may include traffic separation schemes, pilotage, vessel traffic services and no discharge areas and are designed to avoid the risk of collision, grounding, and other adverse impacts resulting from shipping.

The measures are legally binding and constitute hard law.[74] PSSAs reflect the international community's willingness to restrict some uses in order to protect special protection areas.[75] The designation of MPAs on the high seas is a similar, perhaps more difficult political exercise. The absence of a centralised, overarching jurisdictional authority for environmental law, means that if parties do not wish to be guided by newer international law principles, such as the possible extension of MPAs to the high seas, it would be very difficult to take action and impose such measures on States. Global political will and stronger global regimes may be required to establish governance over the global commons, in particular, the high seas.

17 BARRIERS TO CONSERVATION

In the management of all protected areas, management planning, monitoring and evaluation, financial resources, and the provisions for security and law enforcement are generally weak.[76] Where guidance and technology is not provided to meet capacity deficits, the "paper park" phenomenon has been identified, whereby geographic areas are designated protected areas but fail to achieve the promised form of management.[77]

The establishment of protected areas are no guarantee of poverty alleviation. Good environmental governance is required to ensure that rural people are included and provided with access to resources that have traditionally supported their well-being. PAs can contribute to improve livelihoods when they are managed to benefit local people. Effective governance and meaningful participatory consultation and planning with local people can result in effective management arrangements.[78] Globally, better governance is required to ensure collective will and commitment to the protection of the high seas.

Success of PA management depends on adequate legislation and management, sufficient resources, better integration with the wider region surrounding the protected area, and expanded stakeholder engagement.[79] Moreover, better indicators are required. It is necessary to measure beyond the total area protected as required under the Millennium Development Goals and other targets.

The Millennium Ecosystem Assessment illustrates that these only provide a broad indication of the actual extent of protection afforded by PA systems, and do not reflect targets that consider trade-offs and synergies among other ecosystem services at the regional and national-level planning.[80] Similarly, closer synergy between other regimes, drawing from the initial success of the PSSA, can be fostered to consider the impacts of climate change. Protected area design could maximize joint benefits.[81] The impacts of climate change will increase the risk of extinctions of certain species and may alter biomes through species diversification related to temperature change.[82] Although the CBD fosters conservation based on maximizing biodiversity, the Framework Convention on Climate Change (FCCC) supports measures aimed at mitigating climate change, which might include awarding carbon credits in proportion to standing forests.[83] Recent GEF

[74] Note 69, at 83.
[75] Op. cit.
[76] Note 1, at 69.
[77] Op. cit.
[78] Note 1, at 70.
[79] Note 19, at 10.
[80] Note 1, at 70.
[81] Christopher D. Stone, "Land Use and Biodiversity. 27 *Ecology Law Quarterly* (2001), 4:978.
[82] Note 1, at 70.
[83] Note 81, at 978.

proposals authorize the GEF to support programs of "integrated ecosystem and natural resource management," that is, plans that could, among other things, demonstrate "multiple global benefits." This idea recognizes the potential synergies and even cost-saving opportunities, in a multiple-use strategy. Adding to the biodiversity value, is the value of carbon storage benefits, providing more incentive to conserve ecosystems. However, Stone[84] highlights that, until now, no international agency is assigned to administer such a joint product approach on a systematic basis. Therefore, "efforts to maximize the public good benefits of conservation operate independently, even when there may be overlapping benefits."[85]

18 BARRIERS TO LOCAL CAPTURE OF BIODIVERSITY BENEFITS

Although the type of incentives for financing ecosystem management have generally been widely documented, how these incentives should be implemented in developing nations with the variety of governance and poverty constraints has not yet been successfully demonstrated [86] and more precise guidelines are necessary.[87] Although the CBD principles provide a framework for advising governments and other stakeholders, including Indigenous and local communities and the private sector, about *how* to ensure that their use of biodiversity resources will not lead to the long-term decline of biological diversity, more is required, particularly innovative ways in which to fund such initiatives. In many countries, there is complete or substantial dependence on harvested plants and animals, often among the poorest, for their livelihoods.[88] Increasingly, other uses such as pharmaceuticals for disease prevention and cure are becoming evident and are also being met from using biological diversity. Finally, Indigenous and local communities and their cultures often depend directly on the uses of biological diversity for their livelihoods. In all of these instances, the CBD states that governments should have adequate policies and capacities in place to ensure that such uses are sustainable,[89] but the translation of "*should*" into "*have*" requires more from the regime established under the CBD.

Transferring rights to own and manage ecosystem services to private individuals in the area of watershed management and other resource conservation, has provided owners with a stake in conserving those services. These measures though have been shown to require adequate levels of institutional support and have rarely been transferred to conservation practices,[90] possibly because of the lack of tenure over, or access to resources experienced by many local communities within biodiversity rich areas. In summary, long-term success for response strategies must meet the economic and social needs of communities whose human well-being already depends on the use of biodiversity products and the ecosystem services that biodiversity supports.[91]

[84] Op. cit.

[85] Op. cit.

[86] COP 7 Decision IV/10 "encourages" guidelines for incentives to implement the convention on Biological Diversity to be developed.

[87] Phillipines Environment Monitor, "Interconnected Lives – The Second Philippine National Report to the Convention on Biological Diversity," August 2004, 43. Available at http://www.worldbank.org.

[88] "Addis Abeba Principles and Guidelines for the Sustainable Use of Biodiversity" as adopted in Addis Abeba, Ethiopia, from 6 to 8 May 2003, 10, annex.

[89] Op. cit.

[90] Note 1, at 71.

[91] Op. cit.

Short-term improvements can be made to mitigate biodiversity loss and ecosystem changes by removing or redirecting economic subsidies of a global nature that cause unsustainable practices. As mainly raw-resources exporting nations, developing countries practices are affected by agricultural subsidies in developed countries which reduce global market prices for many commodities. Lower prices encourage developing countries to adopt unsustainable agricultural activities that destroy ecosystems and increase rural poverty in order to compete in the market.[92]

Thus, the removal of developed country agricultural subsidies can immediately alter competition barriers and decrease the need for unsustainable practices that would improve ecosystem services and restrict the rate of biodiversity loss in developing countries. Political will and a balancing act are required to establish positive incentives for conservation and sustainable use, and local participation is therefore critical to successful and transparent biodiversity conservation.[93]

The implementation of the CBD management principles foresees a greater need for technology transfer and greater assistance for capacity development related to management, planning, and research in developing countries. Similarly, environmental management does not exist in a vacuum, and the sustainable development needs of such nations in addressing for example issues of poverty and trade-offs also must be met.

Under this paradigm then, the imbalance between developed and developing nations in respect to MEAs becomes more evident, as does the effectiveness of certain provisions. Environmental protection is clearly outlined, but the mode of achieving sustainable development, which includes social and economic development and behavioural change has been deliberately left vague to be adaptable to different contexts. However, this also has been translated into less detailed commitments to research, training,[94] education, and awareness[95] by parties under the convention. The articles on access to genetic resources and access to and transfer of technology[96] have been largely left to contracting parties and established institutions to decide. Moreover, the financing articles[97] were purposely left vague for the Conference of the Parties to later clarification. In fairness, the inclusion of a financial mechanism was in fact innovative[98] and the first of its kind within MEAs. However, a clear agreement on the "teeth" of sustainable development could not be reached during negotiations. This highlights a deficit in the CBD's "bottom up" approach to environmental management because of the limited "implementation guidance"[99] and concrete incentives provided to address the underlying causes of poverty and concerns of developing nations[100] and also shows the apparent imbalance of power between developed and developing countries during and after treaty negotiation.[101] More commitment from developed parties needs to be gained if developing countries are to cope with the poverty–environment nexus and implement better governance of biological resources.

[92] Op. cit.
[93] Note 1, at 84
[94] Article 12.
[95] Article 13.
[96] Articles 15 and 16.
[97] Articles 20, 21, and 39.
[98] Above note 30 in Craig et al., at 647.
[99] Decision VII/12 Annex II.
[100] J. Gupta, "Global Sustainable Development Governance: Institutional Challenges from a Theoretical Perspective." 2 *International Environmental Agreements: Politics, Law and Economics* (2002), 2:361–388, 369.
[101] Note 24 in Craig et al., 389–390.

19 FINANCING

Previously, the Global Environment Facility (designated by the Convention to administer the financial mechanism[102] of the CBD) guidelines did not allow funding to be used for alternative livelihood options under Biodiversity Projects. This made more difficult to change the communities' behaviour. Without presenting alternative solutions, it is hard to argue for the protection of a resource and its removal from unsustainable resource practices when such use is related to income or food generation and more importantly to the need for daily survival. Consequently, this has restricted effective implementation of the CBD.[103] Such guidelines are generally related to the CBD's definition of additionality and the inherent difficulties of valuing biodiversity.[104]

Developed nations argue that the nature of biodiversity and its present use are largely "intangible" values; the loss of biodiversity resource development potential of nation states cannot easily be calculated as these potentials may not have been discovered or previously valued yet, particularly when many developing nations have not pursued this type of development path previously. Therefore, financing alternative livelihoods under GEF, which are not directly related to the use of biodiversity resources, has not been permitted. However, it is anticipated that the GEF will soon release revised guidelines that will attempt to redress this issue.

20 ACCESS AND BENEFIT-SHARING

As part of the consensus-building approach, developing nations premised their participation in the CBD negotiations on the inclusion in the Convention of obligations and measures related to three types of access: access to genetic resources as part of national jurisdiction; access to relevant technology, including biotechnology; and access to benefits for nation-states ultimately gained from the use of their genetic material in the development of biotechnology.[105]

Previously, free access to genetic resources was commonly practiced and understood with such resources considered, in effect, as part of the global commons. This had enabled developed nations to produce resulting goods that were subsequently protected through intellectual property rights.[106] During the negotiation of the *Convention on Biological Diversity*, the position of developing nations prevailed, in compensation for the developed nations' calls for sustainable environmental management of remaining biological resources.[107] Supposed sovereign control over access to genetic resources would afford more opportunities to many developing nations. Previously the case was to

[102] Article 21.

[103] It could be argued, though, that the presence of a GEF project brings new resources to an area, and potential for resource mobilization for alternative livelihoods.

[104] Article 20 (2) defines additional measures as those "new financing sources required to enable developing country parties to meet the agreed full incremental costs to them of implementing measures which fulfil the obligations of this convention . . ."

[105] Note 30 in Craig et al., 647.

[106] FAO Undertaking on Plant Genetic Resources of 1983 adopts this principle, although it has remained a nonbinding instrument, in Craig et al., note 24, at 649.

[107] Article 15 recognizes that the authority to determine access to genetic resources rests with the national governments and is subject to national legislation.

negotiate mutually agreed terms for fair and equitable sharing of benefits in accordance with Article 15.[108] This remains one of the inherent weaknesses of the CBD.

21 IPR AND TRADE ISSUES

In practices, the failure of the CBD to effectively regulate ex situ genetic resources coupled with the ability of developed countries to secure intellectual property rights, particularly with respect to genetic resources located outside of the countries of origin, seriously compromise sovereign control over access.[109]

This access to genetic resources and benefit-sharing from their use, inevitably entered the realm of intellectual property rights (IPRs), despite provision under the CBD for sovereignty over such resources. Once resources are sold, traded, and developed, the global trade regime inevitably intervenes. Universal patents[110] for the privatization of ideas and goods derived from the WTO's multitrack negotiations[111] and subsequent TRIPs agreement. Many argue that the ability to transform knowledge into private property reflects the relative power of the global economy, although the development of IPR regimes has gone on for centuries and is hardly a new phenomenon.[112] TRIPs was, in large part, the response to continued unauthorized and illegal use of IPRs in many developing countries. Its principal objectives were to reduce market distortions and impediments to international aid arising from different standards of protection as well as to establish minimum levels of protection and enforcement.

Thus, all members of the WTO must provide fair, equitable, and inexpensive enforcement mechanisms[113] against infringement, [114] and developing countries cannot offer special treatment to domestic innovators, without offering it to foreign ones.[115]

22 EFFECTIVENESS OF IPR FOR BIODIVERSITY CONSERVATION

Implications of TRIPs are therefore far reaching for the national sovereignty of biodiversity resources and IPRs are perceived to overlap with access to and benefit-sharing of such. It is feared that the appropriation of biological resources and knowledge pertaining to them, for the purpose of asserting exclusive rights over these resources and the products they generate, will perpetuate inequities. Genetic biological resources are composed of tangible and intangible aspects; the physical component and knowledge related to its cultivation, the latter being more easily undervalued or stolen.[116]

Knowledge regarding the use and properties of various biological resources[117] generally vests in local and Indigenous communities and the CBD has sought to rectify the

108 Article 15(7).

109 Large quantities of genetic resources are held in seed banks and museums around the world.

110 Article 33 of the WTO TRIPS agreement gives one universal time limit for all patents, twenty years.

111 N. Zerbe, "Contested Ownership: TRIPs, CBD and Implications for Southern African Biodiversity." 1 *Perspectives on Global Development and Technology* 302 (Koninklijke, NV: Leiden, 2002).

112 A. T. Mushita & C. B. Thompson, "Patenting Biodiversity? Rejecting WTO TRIPS in South Africa," 2 *Global Environmental Politics* (2002), 1:68.

113 Article 41.

114 Note 112, at 69–70.

115 All members of the WTO are automatically bound to accept and become Parties to WTO administered agreements such as TRIPs.

116 Note 60, at 1486.

117 R. V. Anuradha, "IPRs: Implications for Biodiversity and Local and Indigenous Communities." 10 *RECIEL* (2001), 1:26.

history of misappropriation of knowledge from such groups.[118] The CBD has attempted to restrain the global application of the TRIPs agreement by providing control over access to biological resources and information within national sovereignty, the removal of which is intended to be contingent on the approval and involvement of local and communal owners,.[119]

Similarly, although the TRIPs Agreement intends to ensure greater control over technological innovations in the formal sector, it lacks provisions on the issue of appropriation of knowledge and resources for developing innovations. All this form the basis of IPRs as well as aspects of risk assessment, regulation and control over products and processes relating toGMOs.[120] The interface between both agreements is still lacking and provides an array of issues if sustainable use and conservation of biodiversity are to be effectively implemented. Article 22 of the CBD that outlines the CBD's relationship with other international laws does not provide much clarification.[121] It will restrain other laws depending on interpretation of the phrase "serious damage or threat to biological diversity."[122] Member States to the CBD, at the latest meeting of the Ad Hoc Open-ended Working Group on Access and Benefit-Sharing,[123] expressed diverse opinions regarding the merging of the two agreements.[124] Some countries believe that the TRIPs Agreement should prohibit the patenting of all life forms. No consensus has been reached until now on this issue or of the merger between agreements. These issues also were raised at the latest TRIPs Council meeting,[125] as well as the consequences of noncompliance, although, similarly, no substantive progress was made at that meeting.[126]

IPRs reward innovation in the development of resources or products have been gradually expanded in many industrialized countries to grant private ownership and monopoly over the use of genetic and biochemical products.[127] Currently, the effectiveness of IPR as an incentive for developing countries' sustainable use and conservation of biodiversity is questionable. It can be assumed that IPR implications for the use of biodiversity, require that any application of the knowledge, innovations, and practices of local and Indigenous communities shall take place only with their approval and involvement[128] and that benefits arising from the utilization of knowledge, innovations, and

[118] Article 8(j) of the CBD.

[119] Note 117, at 14–15. It should be noted, however, that the prior informed consent necessary as a condition of permitting access is up to the State, which under its national laws may or may not recognize the rights of its indigenous population.

[120] Note 117, at 27–28.

[121] It provides that the CBD: "shall not affect the rights and obligations of any Contracting Party deriving from any existing international agreement, except where the exercise of those rights and obligations would cause a serious damage or threat to biological diversity."

[122] Note 117, at 24.

[123] Third meeting, Bangkok, 14–18 February 2005, Analysis Of Existing National, Regional And International Legal Instruments Relating To Access And Benefit-Sharing And Experience Gained In Their Implementation, Including Identification Of Gaps. UNEP/CBD/WG-ABS/3/2, 10 November 2004.

[124] The positions reflected the following; that the TRIPs Agreement and the Convention on Biological Diversity are already compatible, that the TRIPs Agreement should be amended in order to ensure its compatibility with the Convention on Biological Diversity and that the TRIPs Agreement should be amended so that patent applicants are required to disclose the origin of genetic resources and associated traditional knowledge and to include evidence of prior informed consent and benefit-sharing. Ibid. note 121, at para. 2–3.

[125] 21 September 2004.

[126] Note 123, at para. 3.

[127] Note 117, at 24.

[128] Op. cit.

practices of local and Indigenous communities shall be shared with them in an equitable way.[129] However, definition over rights to the created product, including residuals, is needed, because the innovator should not have exclusive rights to the product created after merely paying fees for access to the local communities' resource or traditional environmental knowledge vested in the development of the resource itself.[130]

The concept of benefit-sharing with respect to knowledge subject to intellectual property rights faces further criticism, in attempts to assess the commercial value and benefits derived from the use of local knowledge and to quantify these as a percentage of the profits derived from the final product.[131] With the establishment of the Bonn Guidelines, considerable attention has been focused on the elaboration of a model Material Transfer Agreement (MTA) to assist governments and others in regulating access to genetic resources and benefit-sharing.[132]

Experience has shown, however, that the capacity of developing countries and local and Indigenous communities to bargain is critically linked to the issue of "fairness" in negotiations between private corporations and communities.[133] Recently, important proposals have emerged in connection with the use of the existing international customs regime[134] and creation of an international certification system.[135] *Sui generis* systems, recognized under Article 27.3b of TRIPs also have been utilized by some countries, as alternatives for regulation of plant species.[136]

From the biodiversity side however, particularly when IPRs or similar regimes extend to compounds and where genes may be extracted, depletion in richness of genetic

[129] Note 117, at 25.

[130] Note 117, at 31.

[131] Note 60, at 1487.

[132] Ad Hoc Open-Ended Working Group On Access And Benefit-Sharing, Third Meeting, Bangkok, 14–18 February 2005, Global Status And Trends In Intellectual Property Claims: Genomics, Proteomics And Biotechnology Submission by the European Community, Distr. GENERAL, UNEP/CBD/WG-ABS/3/INF/4, 11 January 2005, Global Status and Trends in Intellectual Property Claims: Genomics, Proteomics and Biotechnology – Submission to the Executive Secretary of the Convention on Biological Diversity by Dr. Paul Oldham from the ESRC Centre for Economic and Social Aspects of Genomics (CESAGen), United Kingdom, 16.a) Decision VI/24 "Access and benefit-sharing as related to genetic resources." Available at: http://www.biodiv.org/decisions/default.asp?lg=0&dec=VI/24; b); Decision VII/19 "Access and benefit-sharing as related to genetic resources." Available at http://www.biodiv.org/decisions/default.aspx?m=COP-07&id=7756&lg=0.

[133] Note 117, at 32.

[134] Note 132, at 60. During the Seventh Conference of the Parties, in Kuala Lumpur, Malaysia between the 9th to the 20th of February 2004, Parties established the terms of reference for the negotiation of an international regime by the Working Group on Access and Benefit-Sharing in collaboration with the Working Group on Article 8(j) and related provisions. The terms of reference for the negotiation of an international regime set out in COP7 Decision VII/19 include a wide range of elements relating to, inter alia; research, ethics, benefit-sharing, transboundary genetic resources, respect for the human rights of indigenous peoples and local communities, consent, certification and development goals, that form a well-balanced foundation for the development of an international regime. Decision VII/19 also breaks new ground by promoting a deliberative and participatory process for the elaboration of an international regime, involving Parties, delegates of indigenous peoples and local communities, the scientific community, industry, and civil society organizations.

[135] Op. cit.

[136] Note 117, at 41. A further possible exception under the TRIPs agreement is that members may choose to exclude from patentability plant varieties; however, they are obligated to provide for the protection of plant varieties by an effective sui generis system or by a combination of patenting and a sui generis system. "The basic concerns with the interpretation of Article 27(3)(b) are that there are no guidelines or parameters mentioned for the interpretation of what would amount to an 'effective' and a 'sui generis' system of plant variety protection."

variation may occur.[137] This can be linked to an increase in a vulnerability of species to disease, and the accidental release of unsafe organisms.[138] Biotechnology also may present opportunities in curing disease; however, such may become unaffordable to the poor, with patents making the product exclusive and the cost becoming prohibitive to developing countries.[139] This has further implications for food security.

Loss of diversity can be a loss of plant resource by which to improve varieties and may increase the instability of ecological systems, on which many poorer communities often rely, particularly during times of food shortage. Although the results of corporate research are increasingly protected through strong IPRs, the benefits have rarely been returned to the community.[140] Much then is yet to be considered if the benefits related to access are to compensate the possible negative effectives related to human well being in countries experiencing the poverty–environment nexus.

Trends in the genomics sector suggest that discussions should focus less on physical transfers of biological material, as electronic transfers of genetic material can be readily expressed as information.[141] Technological innovation may eventually permit the in situ extraction of genetic material and the transfer of data into electronic form. This may present potential local environmental governance opportunities for governments, the scientific community, Indigenous peoples and local communities, and civil society organizations.[142] Such measures could complement existing IPR proposals for certification and enhanced disclosure and may potentially provide a possible solution to regulation of the problem of "biopiracy."[143]

On a wider level, bioinformatics and genomics may provide more information related to the biology of species, relationships between species, and processes within particular environments, which could assist biodiversity conservation and sustainable use. Similarly, an alternative form of benefit-sharing directed towards local conservation, human well-being, sustainable use, and development needs could be supported.

These issues, however, need urgent resolution because trends towards the patenting of genetic components and regulatory mechanisms of organisms may result in existing intellectual property claims before access and benefit-sharing arrangements are established. This is certainly not preferable when the objective of sustainable use and access and benefit-sharing is related to sustainable human development. It has been asserted that intellectual property protection may promote trade in goods and services and that foreign direct investment (FDI) and technology transfer will flow to developing countries, yet in practice it is not clear whether such positive benefits exist.[144]

TRIPs has been widely criticized as impeding the recognition of human rights, particularly those of the poor. Universal access to knowledge and technology is necessary to realise human rights. Preserving biodiversity and access rights is also necessary for ensuring daily food supply for the poor and to ensure ecological sustainability to increase the poor's resilience to drought, environmental changes, and war.[145] It has been observed that the attempt to create a global market in property rights imposes one conception of ownership and innovation on a culturally diverse reality, benefiting private industrial research but not public institutes or local communities.[146]

[137] Note 112, at 72.
[138] Op. cit.
[139] Note 112, at 74.
[140] Note 111, at 297.
[141] Note 132, at 16.
[142] Op. cit.
[143] Note 132, at 18–19.
[144] Note 132, at 49.
[145] Note 112, at 80.
[146] Note 117, at 6.

It is also becoming evident that the resources concerned may be too important, in terms of the present and future public good, to be subject to strong intellectual property protection. The recent report of the Ad Hoc Open-Ended Working Group On Access And Benefit-Sharing, recommends that an international regime on access to genetic resources and benefit-sharing directed towards conservation, health, agriculture, and related goals needs to be developed in a more equitable way than the patent system.[147] The development of alternative *sui generis* models such as "open source" style models, which also recognise the existence and rights of Indigenous peoples and local communities, the legitimate rights and interests of states, and the need to foster research and innovation, directed towards the objectives of the Convention on Biological Diversity and international objectives in relation to health, agriculture, development, and human rights needs to be resolved.[148]

Developing nations would do well to consolidate around this issue to solidify their stance on IPR and to protect and pursue the concept of sustainable human development of their citizens. Although the proposed development of an international regime has understandably been met with resistance or uncertainty within certain sectors, the aforementioned working group review of trends in genomics, proteomics, and biotechnology suggested that the Convention on Biological Diversity is the multilateral arena that is best placed to confront these challenges and opportunities of global commons issues related to biodiversity.[149]

23 THE GLOBAL COMMONS AND THE HIGH SEAS

A similar call for a stronger international regime is required for the issue of accessing genetic resources of the deep sea bed, located in areas outside of national jurisdiction. The recent report to the Ad-hoc Open ended working group on access and benefit-sharing[150] concludes that both the UNCLOS and the CBD contain useful principles, concepts, measures, and mechanisms that could assist development of a specific legal regime, focusing on the conservation and sustainable use of marine genetic resources in the deep seabed, beyond the limits of national jurisdiction. It illustrates that the common-heritage-of-mankind principle under UNCLOS could provide an important conceptual basis for use of genetic resources of the deep seabed. It also suggests that the conventions work mutually as they share certain principles and concepts, such as the responsibility of States for activities under their jurisdiction and control; the ecosystem approach; the establishment of marine protected areas; information exchange, consultation and notification regarding activities; environmental impact assessment; sustainable use; and fair and equitable sharing of benefits.[151] The Conference of the

[147] Note 132, at 55.

[148] Note 132, at 60. See also the Plan of Implementation of the World Summit on Sustainable Development. Available at: http://www.johannesburgsummit.org/html/documents/summit˙docs/2309˙planfinal.htm.

[149] Op. cit.

[150] Ad Hoc Open-Ended Working Group On Access And Benefit-Sharing, Third meeting, Bangkok, 14–18 February 2005, Item 4 of the provisional agenda* Analysis Of Existing National, Regional And International Legal Instruments Relating To Access And Benefit-Sharing And Experience Gained In Their Implementation, Including Identification Of Gaps. Distr. GENERAL UNEP/CBD/WG-ABS/3/2 10 November 2004.

[151] Note 150, paragraph 8.

Parties recognized that further work was needed on this issue[152] and requested the Executive Secretary in consultation with Parties and relevant organizations to compile information, for consideration by SBSTTA.[153]

Currently, more detailed provision on the sustainable use and access and benefit-sharing of marine biological resources is necessary for the benefit of all.[154] Not only are marine biological resources threatened by various factors and anthropogenic alterations, which may change or destroy ecosystems, such as pollution[155] and land-based conservation. Incentives could be provided (with sustainable use and added community value of resources), to prevent such practice and encourage conservation.

However, because of the nature of their location, very little is known about the characteristics of organisms or the potential of such resources for future use. As a result of the need for appropriate equipment and specific technical and technological requirements the cost for exploration is much higher and because of its nature, potentially damaging. Not all states will have access and the ability to benefit from such use of resources if the current IPR regime and gap between UNCLOS and CBD provisions on such resources should prevail. As the exploitation of genetic resources often corresponds with practices of bio-prospecting, such activities and other extractive deep seabed mining activities may threaten biodiversity.[156]

Land-based extraction of organisms, and components for pharmaceutical compounds can lead to the significant decline of species' populations, especially where commercial use requires harvesting and exploitation of resources. Although the sampling of micro-organisms may not present a similar serious threat, exploration activities may be destructive to the ecosystem and surrounding community of organisms.[157] If the commercial potential of resources is realized, there will be a need to provide for legal regulations on the protection of biological resources as a growing number of states and entities would engage in bioprospecting activities in deep sea areas, which are currently "free."[158]

The regulation of marine scientific research as well as other regulations concerning marine biological resources depend on the legal regimes established by the UN Convention on the Law of the Sea,[159] the Convention on Biological Diversity[160] and regional

[152] The Conference of the Parties considered issues arising from the study of the relationship between the Convention on Biological Diversity and the UNCLOS in decision VII/5 on marine and coastal biodiversity. The relevant sections of decision VII/5 are included in paragraphs 54 to 56.

[153] Related to: information on the methods for the identification, assessment and monitoring of genetic resources of the seabed and ocean floor and subsoil thereof, in areas beyond the limits of national jurisdiction; information on the status and trends of these genetic resources including identification of threats and the technical options for their protection, Ibid. note 100 at paragraph 9.

[154] Nele Matz, Marine Biological Resources: Some Reflections On Concepts For The Protection And Sustainable Use of Biological Resources in the Deep Sea, (2002) 2:3 *Non-State Actors and International Law* 279–300, 280 (Netherlands: Kluwer Law International).

[155] Note 154, at 281.

[156] Note 154, at 282.

[157] Op. cit.

[158] Note 154, at 253.

[159] UN Convention on the Law of the Sea in Article 118 CLOS only knows a duty to co-operate to protect living resources. As far as the ocean floor beyond the continental shelves is concerned, the UN Convention on the Law of the Sea has established a unique management regime on mineral resources.

[160] In regard to the high seas and the deep seabed, the Convention on Biological Diversity is not applicable to components of biodiversity but only to activities and processes under a state's control. According to Article 4 CBD the Convention is applicable to components within areas of national jurisdiction (Article 4 lit. (a) CBD) but only to activities and processes under a state's control concerning resources outside national jurisdiction (Article 4 lit. (b) CBD), 289.

international agreements as well as national legislation.[161] As a consequence, gaps in such laws allow activities related to the exploration and exploitation of marine biological resources, such as marine scientific research and bio-prospecting, to be performed on the high seas without specific regulation.[162]

One of the most urgent issues is how and to what extent marine scientific research should be regulated and what activities should be considered marine scientific research.[163] Because the issue of the protection and sustainable use of genetic resources in the High Seas is not dealt with by the UN Convention on the Law of the Sea or the CBD, arguably the current international rules do not provide for sufficient regulation of the issue to safeguard the equitable and sustainable use of genetic resources.

24 THE ISSUE OF TECHNOLOGY

The resulting provisions on access to resources of the CBD are said to reflect the importance that developed countries place on intellectual property rights, but nevertheless create a basic obligation to provide or facilitate access to and transfer of, technology, including biotechnology. Yet this provision has not been adequately implemented. Recognising this, decision VII/29 on technology transfer and technology cooperation outlined more guidelines and the Subsidiary Body on Scientific Technical and Technological Advice and also the Ad hoc Open Ended Working Group on Access and Benefit-sharing have encouraged "Type 2 WSSD" partnerships[164] to encourage further South–South cooperation and South–South development of technology. Clearly, this is not sufficient.

Without such biotechnology, developing nations cannot develop their own products from such resources or derive "value-added" income from these and can merely use the resources to either sell them to developed nations or to continue traditional, but now more restricted, resource use practices. Moreover, a recent article on genetically modified caffeine trees growing in Japan, depicts that developed countries have invested heavily in industries that manually achieve what some GMOs potentiality and this creates a tension in the market.[165] Large investors may not be inclined to switch markets.

[161] Note 154, at 286.

[162] See Matz, note 154, 290. He illustrates that "one has to distinguish between the protection and sustainable use of marine living resources harvested for human consumption and genetic resources in the deep sea and the deep seabed. Part XI of the UN Convention on the Law of the Sea dealing with the Area and its resources does not contain provisions concerning marine biological resources. In fact, Article 133 lit. (a) CLOS defines "resources" to include only mineral resources. Accordingly the marine biological resources of the deep seabed are covered by the high seas regime on management and conservation of marine living resources and by the general principles of Part XII CLOS, however, it is doubtful whether the said legal rules are appropriate. Although the scope of the regime can be broadened, since Article 162 para. 2 lit. (o)(ii) Convention on the Law of the Sea provides for the respective institutional competence to establish rules on other than polimetallic nodules, this would not necessarily cover biological resources. The reference to "resources" in this provision has to be understood in the light of the legal definition in Article 133 lit. (a) CLOS, which limits the scope of Part XI, and, consequently, the jurisdictional power of the International Sea-bed Authority to the management of mineral resources."

[163] Note 154, at 286.

[164] Additional agreements should be nonnegotiated and complementary to the commitment by governments in Johannesburg Declaration on Sustainable Development and the Plan of Implementation of the WSSD and shall contribute to translating those political commitments into actions of a voluntary self-organizing nature, thus enabling all stakeholders to make a concrete contribution.

[165] Helen R. Pilcher, "CM Decaf Coffee Grown on Trees." 19 June 2003, *Nature News Service*/Macmillan Magazines Ltd., 2003.

Therefore, presumably, developing nations also may need assistance in market identification and development in order to even attract investment in their biodiversity resources or "compensation" from their altered development practices. Moreover, the lack of a clear benefit-sharing for such resources may be driving investment away from what is perceived as a risky venture.[166] In general terms, technology transfer has occurred under the CBD, particularly in Protected Area projects, in terms of skills development, science exchanges, and social aspects of environmental management.[167] However, this has not occurred in terms of creative utilization of the resource base for economic benefit.

For now, therefore, developing nations seem constrained to be suppliers of resources, but just how much compensation and in which way can be derived from products utilizing such genetic resources needs clarification.[168] Traditional environmental knowledge presents a similar challenge, as the means by which to value Indigenous or local cultivation of such resources has not yet been clarified. Article 8(j) acknowledges Indigenous and local peoples' knowledge, innovations, and practices, yet no method for valuing or protecting such has been outlined[169] and it is questionable whether existing IPR systems are suitable for protection and valuation of such "resources."[170] Arrangements are to be decided bilaterally in each individual situation according to mutually agreed terms. Arguably developing nations have little experience in these types of negotiations. COP 7 discussed new instruments and specific rules on how the origins of valuable samples should be recorded and their benefits shared between nation-states, prospectors, and commercial interests.[171]

These, however, faced developed nation opponents (with the exception of the European Union) who claim that proposed rules run counter to existing patent systems.[172] Thus the challenge exists to create better guidelines. Despite this, some bio-prospecting projects are working, through the transfer of "know-how." In Panama, for example, capacity of local scientists is being increased in relation to the bio-prospecting of young plant leaves and their alkaloid compounds in a collaborative partnership between the University of Utah and the Panama National Authority on Environment.[173] Similarly, the Philippines has enacted a national ordinance for bio-prospecting, ensuring prior informed consent of Indigenous peoples.[174] However, in the Philippines and in many developing nations, biopiracy and a weak enforcement further constrain the full implementation of such access rights and benefits. In 2000, three French scientists were caught trying to smuggle medicinal plants from the Philippines, but this is a rare case of success.[175] Pertinent to this point is the current issue of locating the origin of a

[166] R. Dalton, "Natural Resources: Bioprospects Less than Golden." *Nature Magazine*, August 2004.

[167] Although arguably in the application of "on-the-ground" incentives in terms of park fee implementation, direction is still lacking.

[168] The obligations under Articles 15(7), 16(3) and 19(2) leave considerable discretion with the Party.

[169] B. R. Upreti & Y. G. Upreti, "Factors Leading to Agro-Biodiversity Loss in Developing Countries: The Case of Nepal." 11 *Biodiversity and Conservation* (2002), 1607–1621, 1613, and 1615.

[170] A. G. M. La Vina, "Intellectual Property Rights and Indigenous Knowledge of Biodiversity in Asia," 2 *Asia Pacific Journal of Environmental Law* (1997), 3–4:227–252. Indonesian Country Study on Biological Diversity, UNEP, 1993, 687 cited in Craig note 24.

[171] Such a benefit-sharing framework will be discussed in Brazil in 2006.

[172] Note 112, at 70.

[173] Note 166.

[174] Article 2, Executive Order 247, Prescribing Guidelines and Establishing a Regulatory Framework for the Prospecting of Biological and Genetic Resources, Their By Products and Derivatives; For Scientific and Commercial Purposes; and Other Purposes, 1995.

[175] Op. cit. and Note 169, at 1619.

particular resource, especially in relation to resources collected prior to the CBD. Moreover, it may take years to derive any benefit from a resource, which may have come from several sources and investment also may be lacking, because of the nature of the resource and lack of guidelines.

The current issue between Brazil and Ethiopia highlights some of these points. The discovery of coffee plants with naturally low caffeine and high sales potential has highlighted the vagueness of ownership of biodiversity resources that still exists twelve years after the CBD came into force. Brazil utilized Ethiopian genetic resources to develop the product but had obtained the resources from collections in Costa Rica. No clear guidelines exist under the CBD on how to resolve this issue so is left for diplomatic negotiations.[176]

25 BIOSAFETY ISSUES

The aforementioned examples also raise the important issue of biosafety and Living Modified Organisms (LMOs). In the developing nation context, in which regulation and enforcement is weak, significant guidance is required from the Cartagena Protocol on Biosafety (2000) for the management of these resources. While assisting to promote discussion and information-sharing on the issue of LMOs and issues generally under the CBD, the Biodiversity Clearing House is an essential mechanism to assist parties to implement provisions under Cartagena.[177]

Moreover, the Cartagena Protocol[178] obligates parties, including developing nations to develop a preventive framework[179] in preparation for dealing with such resources, which is something they might not have ordinarily done. However, particularly on issues of liability and access to technology.[180] Guidance for implementation of the Protocol unfortunately does not exist.[181] It is probably significant that the most detailed regulations exist for the transportation and handling of LMOs, particularly those for food or feed or for processing (LMO-FFPs). At best, this is a reflection of current trade experiences in this area, or perhaps relates to health fears and concerns if contamination or unexpected results occur. At worst, it reflects again the relative ease with which environmental concerns are regulated in international environmental law, and sustainable development concerns are not remaining vague provisions and particularly affecting developing nations. An example of the latter would be the financing provisions of the Protocol.[182]

[176] Reuters, "Decaf Coffee Find Brews into Ownership Spat," July 14, 2004.

[177] Article 20 under the Cartagena Protocol, created from Article 18(3) of the CBD.

[178] Developed from Article 19 of the CBD.

[179] Art 2(2) reflects the preventive approach of treaties. Legal rules should prevent damage rather than remedy it after. Article 16(1) and 2(2) both relate to Article 8(g) in CBD, which requires parties to undertake risk management.

[180] Capacity development is encouraged Article 22, and, although vague, financial resources should be devoted by the GEF to the implementation of Article 28.

[181] Article 27 of the protocol requires the COP to the CBD as its MOP to adopt a process for the elaboration of international rules and procedures in the field of liability and redress for damage resulting from the transboundary movements of LMOs, analyzing and taking due account of the ongoing processes in international law on these matters.

[182] Article 28(1) under the Biosafety Protocol requires Developed nations to "take into account" provisions of Article 20, of the CBD. This reflects a softening of the financial mechanism as they are not obliged to provide financial resources, but merely to consider the issue of financial resources and second the provisions of Art 20 are not declared to be directly applicable to the protocol but are taken into account.

26 AGRO-BIODIVERSITY

In relation to developing nations, significant issues relating to the loss of agro-biodiversity arise. Nepal, for example, has no means to regulate nor prevent alien species threatening indigenous ones, or any act to control biopiracy.[183] Studies undertaken suggest that different development projects have introduced exotic species, which now threaten indigenous species. In view of the human health and socioeconomic aspects related to LMOs, clear guidelines need to be established. Damage to biological diversity, appropriate redress, and compensation mechanisms need to be studied further,[184] to consider many situations in which restoration and reinstatement is not possible. Loss of endemic species and ecosystems are difficult to value, especially if these played an important role in the socioeconomic life of the people of the affected nation.[185]

27 INTRAGENERATIONAL EQUITY

The CBD needs to consider and integrate more fully the concepts of intragenerational equity and sustainable development. In developing nations, local capacity building, funding, and implementation strategies are needed to protect the environment. Environmental legislation will not work well unless the causes of environmental degradation, particularly poverty, are understood and legislative responses are tailored to this situation and integrated into the broader sphere of sustainable development. To achieve this, a transfer of wealth and technology from higher to lower income countries may be necessary in many cases.[186] The concept of intragenerational equity is not merely a legal one, but a political, economic, social, and practical one. A dilution of the international environmental standards is required for developing countries and local environmental protection. (This should not be the case.) The principles established by international environmental law are well-founded and established; it is their implementation that affects the effectiveness of laws such as the CBD and its Cartagena Protocol. What is needed, particularly related to the issue of biodiversity, is the acquisition of technological know-how relating to the access of resources. This and strengthened institutions is what "sustainable development" locally requires.[187]

28 CONCLUDING COMMENTS

Undeniably then, international implementing institutions, such as UNEP, UNDP, World Bank and special bodies created under the CBD, such as the GEF, and various

Perhaps after action taken under Decision VII/32, which establishes guidelines for the third review of GEF, stricter guidelines may be formulated.

[183] Note 169, at 1613.

[184] The intergovernmental committee for the Cartagena protocol (ICCP) adopted by decision V/1 of the fifth COP lists liability and redress as one of the issues to be considered by it at its second meeting. Draft recommendations on the process for elaboration of such international rules and procedures including inter alia the review of existing relevant instruments and identification of elements for liability and redress.

[185] Workshop Proceedings from the workshop on liability and redress in the context of the convention on biological diversity, Paris, 18–20 June 2001, UNEP/CBD/WS-L&R/3, 29 June 2001.

[186] B. Boer, "Institutionalising Ecologically Sustainable Development: The Roles of National, State, and Local Governments in Translating Grand Strategy into Action." 31 *Willamette Law Review* (1995), 312–333, as cited in Craig note 24, at 412.

[187] Note 25, at 406.

other working groups and fora and the Conference of the Parties,[188] have been effective in gaining treaty consensus and in formulating more detailed guidelines for implementation. But subsequent compliance to and implementation of the CBD is a different thing. The CBD is comprehensive and consensus-based[189] and presents additional opportunities for developing states to participate in technology transfer, additional financing, as well as presenting new potential trade and capacity development initiatives. However, the adequacy of such provisions to enable actual implementation of environmental protection and sustainable human development in developing nations is currently dubious.[190] Therefore, in conclusion, the CBD's effectiveness needs to be further assessed and enhanced.

[188] Articles 21, 25, 15, and 23, respectively.

[189] As of August 20, 2002, 185 parties have ratified the CBD.

[190] Hughes et al., *Environmental Law and Policy*, 2nd ed. (Toronto: Edmund Montgomery Publications, 1998), 331–335, as cited in Craig note 24, at 383.

6 Legal and Paralegal Rules for Biodiversity Conservation: A Sequence of Conceptual, Linguistic, and Legal Challenges

D. E. Fisher*

1 INTRODUCTION

The enforceability and hence effectiveness of environmental law depends to some extent on the language used to express its rules. Apart from environment itself, such words include protection, conservation, enhancement, improvement, utilisation, precaution, sustainability, equity, heritage, nature, and, of course, biological diversity (hereafter biodiversity). Words such as these perform different functions. Some are descriptive; a few state objectives; a number describe processes and procedures; some state values. Perhaps the function of some is unclear. Often, however, the way in which words are used, their relationship with other words and the context of their use illuminate their meaning and the part they play in the system that comprises the rules of environmental law. So it is with the conservation of biodiversity.

The conservation of biodiversity – which is part of the natural and cultural environment – together with the protection of the environment from harm are merely two of the essential elements of the concept of sustainability. Although sustainable development drives much of contemporary environmental law, it is by no means certain what are its functions and its status within the legal system. As we shall see, sustainable development is in some respects an outcome to be achieved by the detailed methodology of decision making prescribed by the legal system. How this is incorporated within the legal system is an ongoing challenge.[1] Despite a significant number of responses to this

[1] The growing literature on sustainable development includes Alan Boyle & David Freestone, eds., *International Law and Sustainable Development* (Oxford: Oxford University Press, 1999); Nico Schrijver & Friedl Weiss, eds., *International Law and Sustainable Development: Principles and Practice* (Leiden: Martinus Nijhoff, 2004); M. C. Segger & C. G. Weeramantry, eds., *Sustainable Justice: Reconciling Economic, Social and Environmental Law* (Leiden: Martinus Nijhoff, 2005); and Duncan French, *International Law and Policy of Sustainable Development* (Manchester: Manchester University Press, 2005). For the evolution of the concept of conservation and the current function of sustainable development in Australia, see D. E. Fisher, *Natural Resources Law in Australia* (Sydney: Lawbook Company, 1987), chapters 20, 22, and 23 and D. E. Fisher, *Australian Environmental Law* (Sydney: Lawbook Company, 2003), chapter 10.

* D. E. Fisher, MA, LLB, PhD (University of Edinburgh), is Professor of Law, Queensland University of Technology: Consultant, Phillips Fox Lawyers. This chapter is the published version of a presentation given at the Third Colloquium of the IUCN Academy of Environmental Law in Sydney in Australia on 11 July 2005.

challenge, there is no clear or consistent doctrinal approach from the perspective of the law.[2]

But let us now return specifically to an analysis of the conservation of biodiversity as an aspect of sustainability. These are two complex concepts: conservation and biodiversity. The meaning of conservation is, on the face of it, quite clear. Its dictionary meaning equates it with preservation. But its meaning in legal instruments is far less clear, to the point of ambiguity in some cases. Is it, for example, an outcome of a process or is it the process itself? Then there is the expression biological diversity or more colloquially now biodiversity. Is it, for example, a statement describing the present and future state of elements of nature? Or is it a value that underlies how the society in question perceives nature? The combination of the two concepts as the conservation of biodiversity compounds the difficulties faced by the legal system. Biodiversity is one of those concepts that does not fit comfortably within the legal system. If it is assumed that biodiversity is in certain contexts a value, then the function described as the conservation of biodiversity seeks to protect a value that is as elusive as other values that are said to underlie the legal system such as freedom, liberty, democracy, or property.

2 THE VALUES OF THE NATURAL ENVIRONMENT

2.1 Their Nature

It is trite to observe that the values recognised and protected by the environmental legal system over the years have reflected the religious, spiritual, economic, and political philosophies accepted at the time by the society in question. For example, according to Ian McHarg, "the implicit attitude of western man to nature and the environment" is clear enough:

[2] See, for example, Alan Boyle and David Freestone "Introduction," in Alan Boyle & David Freestone, eds., *International Law and Sustainable Development* (Oxford: Oxford University Press, 1999), 16–18; Vaughan Lowe, "Sustainable Development and Unsustainable Arguments," in Alan Boyle & David Freestone, eds., *International Law and Sustainable Development* (Oxford: Oxford University Press, 1999), 31–35; Nicolas de Sadeleer, *Environmental Principles: From Political Slogans to Legal Rules* (Oxford: Oxford University Press, 2005), chapter 6; Ximena Fuentes, "International Law-making in the Field of Sustainable Development: The Unequal Competition between Development and the Environment," in Nico Schrijver & Friedl Weiss, eds., *International Law and Sustainable Development: Principles and Practice* (Leiden, Martinus Nijhoff, 2004), 19–36; Judge C. G. Weeramantry, "Achieving Sustainable Justice through International law," in M. C. Segger & C. G. Weeramantry, eds., *Sustainable Justice: Reconciling Economic, Social and Environmental Law* (Leiden: Martinus Nijhoff, 2005), 24–36; and Justice U. C. Banerjee, "The Doctrine of Sustainable Development – A Discussion," in M. C. Segger & C. G. Weeramantry, eds., *Sustainable Justice: Reconciling Economic, Social and Environmental Law* (Leiden: Martinus Nijhoff, 2005), chapter 4; and M. Segger, "Governing and Reconciling Economic, Social and Environmental Regimes," in M. C. Segger & C. G. Weeramantry, eds., *Sustainable Justice: Reconciling Economic, Social and Environmental Law* (Leiden: Martinus Nijhoff, 2005), 584–592. For an analysis of the development of legal doctrine in Australia, see D. E. Fisher, "Considerations, Principles and Objectives in Environmental Management in Australia" (2000) 17 *Environmental and Planning Law Journal* 487; D. E. Fisher, "Sustainability – The principle, its implementation and its enforcement; (2001) 18 *Environmental and Planning Law Journal 361*; D. E. Fisher, "The Achievement of Sustainability – An Australian Perspective" (2002) 14 *Environmental Law and Management* 145; D. E. Fisher, *Australian Environmental Law* (Sydney: Lawbook Company, 2003), chapter 6.

> Man is exclusively divine, all other creatures and things occupy lower and generally inconsequential status; man is given dominion over all creatures and things; he is enjoined to subdue the earth.[3]

The oriental approach is in many respects different. Humans do not dominate nature. Respect for nature is part of this philosophy. Judge Weeramantry of the International Court of Justice has recalled that a sermon on Buddhism preached to King Devanampiya Tissa around 223 BC included these words:

> O great King, the birds of the air and the beasts have as equal a right to live and move about in any part of the land as thou. The land belongs to the people and all living things; thou art only the guardian of it.[4]

Judge Weeramantry himself commented that this sermon "contained the first principle of modern environmental law – the principle of trusteeship of earth resources."[5]

In any event, this notion of trusteeship or stewardship coupled with an ethic of conservation has over recent years permeated aspects of the environmental legal system. Thus, again according to Ian McHarg:

> We must see nature as process within which man exists, splendidly equipped to become the manager of the biosphere; and give form to that symbiosis which is his greatest role, man the world's steward.[6]

This encapsulates three critical points:

- the relationship between humans and nature is symbiotic;
- humans are part of nature;
- humans have the capacity to manage the biosphere.

So humans manage nature, including biodiversity, not only for the sake of themselves but also for the sake of nature itself. This idea is beginning slowly to emerge through the legal system. But the evolution of the law in this direction is a painful and challenging process.

Why is this so? Put simply but perhaps unhelpfully: it is because of the characteristics of the legal system and the relationship between nature, conservation and law. The environment, nature, and biodiversity exist only as the subject matter of rules of law. They have no independent existence or status themselves. Equally important, even although there may be private rights in relation to the environment, nature, and biodiversity, they derive from and are perhaps conditional on the much wider public or collective interest in them. In the absence of personality or status, this collective interest can be protected only by the application of socially constructed rules of law. In other words, the recommendation of Justice Douglas in the *Sierra Club* case that "contemporary public

[3] Ian McHarg, "Values, process and form," in *The fitness of man's environment* (Washington, DC: Smithsonian Institution Press, 1968), 213.

[4] *Judgement in the Case Concerning the Gabcikovo-Nagymaros Project* (1998) 37 *International Legal Materials* 162 at 210.

[5] Ibid. at 210.

[6] Ian McHarg, "Values process and form," in *The Fitness of Man's Environment* (Washington, DC: Smithsonian Institution Press, 1968), 227.

concern for protecting nature's ecological equilibrium should lead to the conferral of standing upon environmental objects to sue for their own preservation"[7] has not been followed.

3 THEIR RELATIONSHIP WITH LAW

Although humans have an interest in nature – reflective of their own cultural backgrounds – it is nature as a whole and how it is or should be managed that is now one of the objects of the legal system. Recognising and protecting this collective interest in nature is one of the problems for the legal system. One commentator, Karl-Heinz Ladeur, has said this:

> The collective element of the environment as a subject of a right poses particular problems for constitutional doctrine because "environment" forms a complex "network of networks" of partially social and partially natural interrelationships which are difficult to describe and even more difficult to reduce to attributable and individualised "parcels." Since traditional doctrine is not adapted to a normative area which is so difficult to structure, making the protection of such a complex structure of effects the subject of a fundamental right requires that new meta-rules of argumentation and decision-making be created.[8]

This approach may be taken further: toward the creation not only of new methodologies for decision making, but also of a set of rules that link the methodology of decision making to its substance and its outcomes. The legal system has for the most part been comfortable with setting standards for behaviour that are applied *ex post facto* to circumstances that have arisen and with setting procedures for future behaviour, actions, and decision making. It is most uncomfortable with ensuring *a priori* that the intended outcomes of decision-making – their substance – are achieved. The reasons are clear enough:

- intended outcomes are a prediction of a consequence;
- intended outcomes are usually expressed as a matter of law in relatively general terms;
- intended outcomes are thus taken usually to be unenforceable as a matter of law.

Is this necessarily so? Can the legal system be structured so that the achievement of intended outcomes can be assured? To some extent is a question of language. Language is such a subtle and often perplexing medium. Although words are themselves fascinating, great care must be taken in their use because they represent the medium through which rights, obligations, and the outcomes of the performance of functions become effective and, hence, potentially enforceable. In this sense, nature including biodiversity is a point of reference for the rights and duties of persons. According to traditional legal doctrine, nature does not, indeed cannot, sustain rights and duties: hence the reference by Karl-Heinz Ladeur to what he described as meta-rules of decision making. Let us extend this concept to rules governing the achievement of outcomes of decision making.

[7] *Sierra Club v. Morton* (1972) 405 United States 727 at 741 and 742.

[8] Karl-Heinz Ladeur, "Environmental Constitutional Law," in Gerd Winter, *European Environmental Law – A Comparative Perspective* (Dartmouth: Dartmouth Publishing, 1996), 18 and 19.

Rules of law – whatever their source is – reflect and implement the values and aspirations of the society from which they emerge. These rules are recognised or created and enforced through the institutional structures established by the society in question, that is, by their legislative, executive and judicial organs. These values and aspirations have not for the most part been incorporated within these structures so as to be directly recognised or enforced. Increasingly, however, particularly at the international level, these values and aspirations are being incorporated within this institutional framework in ways that impact on the enforceable rules of law. This is apparent in the context of environmental protection and biodiversity conservation. These are expressions of values and aspirations that are becoming part of the environmental legal system as much as traditional rules of law. What is important is the relationship between enforceable rules of law and these statements of values and aspirations: namely legal rules and paralegal rules respectively. Paralegal rules assume a wide range of forms, for example, purposes, objects, principles, strategies, policies, plans, guidelines, and codes of practice – In other words, something like the *acquis communautaire* of the legal system of the European Union. Are there any such paralegal rules existing side by side with legal rules about biodiversity conservation?

4 THE CONSERVATION OF THE NATURAL ENVIRONMENT

4.1 The Functions of Conservation

What emerges from this rather metaphysical and metalegal analysis is the range of interests that the law may recognise in nature. The first is the interest that nature has in itself. The second is the interest that the community has in nature. The third is the interest that persons have in nature, whatever their function is. Let us now add to nature and biodiversity the concept of conservation. Three different functions are often performed in relation to the environment and nature: protection, preservation, and, of course, conservation. These words may have subtly different meanings if they are used as nouns or as verbs. Let us consider them as verbs first of all. To protect is to keep safe from harm or danger. To preserve and to conserve have the same meaning as to protect. But each has an additional connotation. Thus, to preserve means not only to protect but also to maintain a state or circumstance or to retain a certain condition. To conserve means not only to protect but also to do so particularly with an intent of later use. So the emphasis in relation to protection is keeping safe from some external event or activity. However, the focus of preservation and conservation includes not only that but also the maintenance of the existing state of affairs. In the case of preservation, it is to keep it as it is, but in the case of conservation it is with a possible view to future use.

Traditionally, the legal system has been reasonably comfortable with the function of protection. This is simply because it involves the regulation or prohibition of activities impacting on the subject matter of protection. This may be in relation to preservation and conservation but not necessarily so. These expressions contemplate an element of sustainability. In other words, leave things as they are or do not interfere with things as they are. Or, if you do interfere with things as they are, limit the way in which you do it so as not to destroy or damage forever the thing to be preserved or conserved.

On one occasion, the Court of Appeal of England had to resolve a dispute as to the meaning of the desirability of preserving or enhancing the character or appearance of a conservation area for the purposes of the planning legislation. It was stated:

> The word "preserving" is used in the subsection in conjunction but in contrast with the word "enhancing," which itself imports the notion of a positive improvement. In my judgment, on the ordinary meaning of words, the character or appearance of an area can properly said to be "preserved" by development where they are not harmed, even though the word would be no less apt to include preservation by restoration or reinstatement.[9]

Clearly, therefore, any activity or proposed activity that would bring harm would constitute neither preservation nor enhancement of the conservation values in question. Although preservation may be either negative or positive, enhancement in this sense is positive. In this case, preservation received its meaning not only from its wider context but also from the words associated with it.

Although conservation values were protected in these circumstances by the processes of preservation and enhancement, the word conservation was not itself used for this purpose. It has already been suggested that conservation may be either an outcome or a process. The conservation of nature, for example, may be stated to be a consideration in a decision-making process or an outcome, or perhaps even the sole outcome of a decision-making process. In these circumstances, conservation is the present and future state of affairs that is intended to be the result of current and future decision making and activity. Thus, the law may create a duty to take measures – sometimes described as conservation measures – to conserve nature or biodiversity. In this case, the outcome of the implementation of the duty is conservation. By contrast, conservation may refer to the ways and means by which an outcome may be or is to be achieved. In this case, conservation or conservation measures are how the values of nature are to be recognised and assured. This is a subtle difference, perhaps, but one that may affect considerably the nature and subject matter of the duty imposed by the legal system. This is an issue that affects effectiveness and enforceability. This is simply because a duty explaining how an outcome is to be achieved is much easier to enforce then a duty to achieve an outcome. In other words, the difference is between a duty to take prescribed measures that are expected to conserve and a duty to conserve.

4.2 Conservation and the Law

These are matters of language. However, the meaning of nature, biodiversity, and conservation is critical for the legal system. It is clear that neither nature nor biodiversity is granted status within the legal system: at least, status in the sense of *locus standi*. Even if nature or biodiversity did have such status, this would be of little consequence in the absence of enforceable rights and duties. The traditional approach of the common law has been to enforce rights only to the extent that there are reciprocal duties. For example, the duty to take reasonable care in the circumstances and the duty not to engage in an activity that constitutes a nuisance. This approach essentially protects private interests:

[9] *South Lakeland District Council v. Secretary of State for the Environment* (1992) 1 *All England Reports* 45, at 52.

particularly those in relation to land rather than in nature and biodiversity. In other words, the common law for the most part does not protect the collective interest in nature and it certainly does not protect the interest of nature in itself.

The restricted scope of the common law is even more apparent because of the essential characteristics of nature and biodiversity. The focus of the common law has been on land owned by the state or the Crown and land in private ownership. Nature and biodiversity do not recognise such cadastral limitations. Fauna is essentially mobile. Although flora is attached to the surface of the land, certain aspects of flora are just as mobile as fauna. The physical and biological connections between land and nature may be obvious. But the focus of the law on land and the ownership and use of land within identifiable boundaries – particularly over the last three or four hundred years – led to the dramatic conclusion reached by Aldo Leopold in 1948:

> Conservation is getting nowhere because it is incompatible with our Abrahamic concept of land. We abuse land because we regard it as a commodity belonging to us. When we see land as a commodity to which we belong, we may begin to use it with love and respect.[10]

So the law had to move from the recognition of private interests in land to a recognition – enforceable in some ways – of the collective interest in nature and even a recognition of the interest of nature in itself. Private interests are recognised and protected by a system of correlated rights and duties that are enforceable: a system of legal rules. The collective interest is more likely to be recognised and protected by a system that includes paralegal rules.

How this is done requires an analysis of a number of international, regional and national legal instruments that deal with the conservation of biodiversity. The questions for review include these:

- what is the meaning of conservation;
- what function does conservation play in the system;
- what is the meaning of biodiversity;
- what is the nature of the interest to be conserved;
- what outcomes is the legal instrument seeking to achieve;
- what duties does the legal instrument impose;
- what is the nature of these duties;
- are these duties enforceable;
- what rights are associated with these duties;
- who is entitled to enforce these rights and duties;
- what is the relationship between these rights and duties and the mechanisms by which biodiversity conservation is achieved.

[10] Aldo Leopold, *A Sand County Almanac with Other Essays on Conservation from Round River* (New York: Oxford University Press, 1966), x. For a more detailed analysis of the evolution of rights of property in the context of the environment, see Sean Coyle & Karen Morrow, *The Philosophical Foundations of Environmental Law: Property, Rights and Nature* (Oxford and Portland: Hart Publishing, 2004), chapter 2. For an Australian perspective, see D. E. Fisher, *Natural Resources Law in Australia* (Sydney: Lawbook Company, 1987) part II; D. E. Fisher, *Environmental Law: Text and Materials* (Sydney: Lawbook Company, 1993), chapter 3; and D. E. Fisher, *Australian Environmental Law* (Sydney: Lawbook Company, 2003), at 26–31 and 138–151.

5 INTERNATIONAL LEGAL AND PARALEGAL RULES

5.1 Introduction

The management of natural resources from various perspectives has been on the international agenda for many years now. However, it has only been in the last thirty or so years that the focus has moved to conservation and more particularly the conservation of nature and biodiversity. According to the dictionary, as we have seen, conservation involves the twin elements of protection and maintenance. There is no doubt that sustainable use is an element of this concept. Indeed, the introduction to the conservation of biological diversity in *Agenda 21* makes this clear:

> Our planet's essential goods and services depend on the variety and variability of genes, species, populations and ecosystems. Biological resources feed and clothe us and provide housing, medicines and spiritual nourishment. The natural ecosystems of forests, savannahs, pastures and rangelands, deserts, tundras, rivers, lakes and seas contain most of the Earth's biodiversity.[11]

And it concludes that "the current decline in biodiversity is largely the result of human activity and represents a serious threat to human development."[12] The related functions of sustainable use of biodiversity and its protection from harm clearly underlie these comments.

Philippe Sands has described the functions of biodiversity conservation in more general terms in a way that points to some of the legal challenges facing its achievement. In his view:

> The reasons for conserving nature and biodiversity are essentially threefold. First, biodiversity provides an actual and potential source of biological resources (including food, pharmaceutical, and other material values which support fisheries, soil conditions, and parks). Secondly, biodiversity contributes to the maintenance of the biosphere in a condition which supports human and other life. Thirdly, biodiversity is worth maintaining for non-scientific reasons of ethical and aesthetic values.[13]

The first is anthropocentric. The second is ecocentric. The third is closer to a recognition of the intrinsic value of biodiversity. Loss of biodiversity needs to be addressed, he argues, not only by focussing on the species and habitat in question but also by eliminating the deficiencies of the legal system, such as the failure of property arrangements to address conservation. Thus, "the international legal order does not lend itself to an approach which allows the totality of the earth's resources to be managed and used in a manner which is sustainable over the long term."[14]

Although the Convention on Biological Diversity 1992 represents the current approach at international level, it is the culmination of the evolution of legal concepts and instruments that had been taking place for a number of years before 1992. According to Patricia Birnie and Alan Boyle, "the Convention on Biodiversity is therefore the first attempt to deal with the lacunae arising from the old system by establishing a more comprehensive and inclusive regime for conservation of biodiversity as such. While

[11] *Agenda 21*, para. 15.2.

[12] Ibid., para. 15.2.

[13] Philippe Sands, *Principles of International Environmental Law* (New York: Cambridge University Press, 2003), 499 and 500.

[14] Ibid., at 501.

recognising the intrinsic value of biodiversity to humankind and its future survival, at the same time it also allows a sustainable use of biological resources and incorporates many of the new conservatory principles and strategies that have developed in contemporary environmental law."[15] These principles and strategies are examples of what have been described as paralegal rules.

International environmental law has, over recent years, attempted to address the tensions between the exercise by states of their sovereign rights to manage their natural resources as they see fit, and the limitations to be placed on the exercise of these rights, so to achieve the sustainable development of their natural resources. A tension reflected, of course, in national systems of law by the exercise of individual rights of ownership of natural resources – particularly land – and the regulation of the exercise of these rights in the interests of the environment. The analogy between international and national systems is incomplete: simply because States cannot be deprived compulsorily of their sovereign rights, whereas individual rights of ownership can be expropriated. Moreover, the international community has yet to embrace the notion that biodiversity is part of the common heritage of mankind or even a type of common property. The reluctance of the international community to adopt a fundamental change of approach has led almost inevitably to the incorporation of more traditional regulatory techniques within the system. Let us consider some examples.

5.2 The Approach of Two Early Conventions

The preamble to the Convention on Wetlands of International Importance 1971 went no further than to declare that "the conservation of wetlands and their flora and fauna can be ensured by combining far-sighted national policies with coordinated international action."[16] This is achieved to some extent by compliance with the obligation to designate suitable wetlands for inclusion in the list of wetlands of international importance.[17] Significantly, selection for inclusion in the list is to be determined by the application of ecological, botanical, zoological, limnological, or hydrological criteria.[18] Even more important, the inclusion of a wetland in the list does not prejudice the exclusive sovereign rights of the State in whose territory the wetland is situated.[19] The convention thus includes one legal rule – the obligation to designate – and little else of substance.

The preamble to the Convention for the Protection of the World Cultural and Natural Heritage 1972 went somewhat further. It acknowledges that parts of the cultural or natural heritage are of outstanding interest and therefore need to be preserved as part of the world heritage of mankind as a whole.[20] In addition, it notes the need to adopt a new approach. This includes the establishment of an effective system of collective protection of the cultural and natural heritage of outstanding universal value.[21] Moreover, the interpretation of natural heritage includes items of outstanding universal value from

[15] P. W. Birnie & A. E. Boyle, *International law and the environment*, 2nd ed. (Oxford: Oxford University Press, 2002), 568, 569.

[16] *Convention on Wetlands of International Importance* 1971, preamble, recital 6.

[17] Ibid., Article 2 (1).

[18] Ibid., Article 2 (2).

[19] Ibid., Article 2 (3).

[20] *Convention for the Protection of the World Cultural and Natural Heritage* 1972, preamble, recital 6.

[21] Ibid., preamble, recital 8.

the point of view of conservation, including the habitat of threatened species.[22] There are therefore three points of significance in this context:

- the need to preserve natural heritage as part of the world heritage of mankind;
- the creation of collective responsibility for its protection;
- the recognition of conservation as a value.

The convention goes on to create duties – albeit of a limited nature – to take appropriate legal measures necessary for the identification, protection, conservation, presentation and rehabilitation of this heritage.[23] In this respect, these five functions, including conservation, may be seen to be the way in which these elements of the world heritage of mankind are preserved. To this extent, these are part of the effective system of collective protection contemplated by the convention. The legal rules – these limited duties – are complemented by statements in the nature of paralegal rules.

5.3 The Declarations of 1972, 1982, and 1992

The next stage in the evolution of rules comprises the statements in the Stockholm Declaration 1972, the World Charter for Nature 1982, and the Rio Declaration 1992. The structure of language in some of these statements is in some respects different from its structure in international agreements. Although the rights and responsibilities of human beings are stated in relatively general terms, there is increasing reference to the ways in which the environment, its resources, and its nature should be treated. Human beings are not left out of the picture, but at the same time they are not the focus of the statement.

For example, the Stockholm Declaration places a special responsibility on man to safeguard and wisely manage the heritage of wildlife and its habitat. So human beings are the focus of this statement.[24] By contrast, the World Charter for Nature declares that nature shall be respected and its essential processes shall not be impaired.[25] In this case, the emphasis is on nature and its processes. There is no reference to human beings. Human beings nevertheless are either the totality or a part of the arrangements by which nature shall be respected.

The focus of the Rio Declaration is again somewhat different. Many of its statements are directed at States. However, it declares that human beings are at the centre of concerns for sustainable development and that they are entitled to a healthy and productive life in harmony with nature.[26] Human beings and nature are thus seen to be interdependent but their relationship is expected to be harmonious. Although in this way sustainable development is a concern, it is supported by two statements formulated passively without direct reference to human beings. First, the right to development must be fulfilled so as to equitably meet developmental and environmental needs of present and future generations.[27] Second, in order to achieve sustainable development, environmental protection shall constitute an integral part of the development process.[28] Once again,

[22] Ibid., Article 2.
[23] Ibid., Article 5 (d).
[24] *Stockholm Declaration* 1972, principle 4.
[25] *World Charter for Nature* 1982, Article 1(1).
[26] *Rio Declaration* 1992, principle 1.
[27] Ibid., principle 3.
[28] Ibid., principle 4.

the choice of words and the grammatical and syntactical structure of the sentences are critical in constructing the message that the statement is transmitting to the international community. The passive rather than the active nature of these propositions suggests that they are paralegal, not legal, rules.

The substantive meaning of the words, of course, is just as important as the way in which they relate to each other. The focus of the Stockholm Declaration is the environment and the protection of the environment from harmful human activity. But clearly the protective function extends to natural resources. More specifically, flora and fauna and especially representative samples of natural ecosystems must be safeguarded.[29] However, the maintenance as well as the protection of such natural resources is also contemplated. Thus, the capacity of the earth to produce vital renewable resources must be maintained and, wherever practicable, restored or improved.[30] This is a concept very much like that of conservation but is not described as such.

However, there is a further statement:

> Man has a special responsibility to safeguard and wisely manage the heritage of wildlife and its habitat which are now gravely imperilled by a combination of adverse factors.[31]

The reference to responsibility suggests a limited form of duty. The juxtaposition of safeguarding and managing in relation to wildlife and its habitat implies the strict concept of conservation. Then a rather cryptic statement follows:

> Nature conservation including wildlife must therefore receive importance in planning for economic development.[32]

This is the only reference in the Stockholm Declaration to conservation. On the face of it, it seems to be a reference to a value. If this is so, then the statement seems to mean this: while engaging in the process of planning for economic development, important consideration must be given to the desirability of conserving nature. If this is so, then conservation includes the functions of safeguarding and maintaining. This would be consistent with the notion that – to paraphrase rather than restate the text – nature must be safeguarded and its capacity to renew itself maintained.

The World Charter for Nature similarly contemplates the conservation of nature in similar terms. However, from the way in which the general principles are constructed, the Charter puts the emphasis on nature, its protection and its maintenance. Thus the first principle is respect for nature.[33] The second is directed at maintaining and safeguarding genetic viability.[34] Next, these "principles of conservation" are applied to all areas of the earth.[35] Finally, ecosystems and organisms shall be managed to achieve and maintain optimum sustainable productivity, but not in such a way as to endanger the integrity of those other ecosystems or species with which they coexist.[36] So all of the elements of conservation as a value and as a function are present in the charter. Again, it is very much an example of how paralegal rules are constructed.

[29] *Stockholm Declaration* 1972, principle 2.
[30] Ibid., principle 3.
[31] Ibid., principle 4.
[32] Ibid., principle 4.
[33] *World Charter for Nature* 1982, Article 1 (1).
[34] Ibid., Article 1 (2).
[35] Ibid., Article 1 (3).
[36] Ibid., Article 1 (4).

5.4 The Convention of 1992

Biodiversity as an element of nature was addressed directly and comprehensively, of course, by the Convention on Biological Diversity 1992. Its preamble recognises not only the range of values traditionally associated with biodiversity but also the intrinsic value of biodiversity itself.[37] The conservation of biodiversity is regarded as a common concern of human kind but nothing more. The conceptual approach to biodiversity emerges clearly from the statement of objectives:[38]

- the conservation of biodiversity;
- the sustainable use of its components;
- the fair and equitable sharing of the benefits arising out of the utilisation of genetic resources.[39]

Significantly, conservation is treated differently from sustainable use. This distinction, moreover, appears throughout the convention, including the provisions imposing obligations on states. This is interesting because one meaning of conservation – perhaps its traditional meaning – includes the functions of protection and maintenance. Conservation is not given an interpretation by the convention, but sustainable use is interpreted. It means, in effect, a use such that it does not destroy the resource and at the same time maintains its potential for future use.[40] The concept of maintenance is thus built into the interpretation of sustainable use. But does this mean that conservation includes protection but excludes maintenance? There is no obvious answer to this question.

Biodiversity is interpreted to mean the variability among living organisms from all sources and this specifically includes diversity within species, between species, and of ecosystems.[41] The principal mechanism for achieving conservation is the set of obligations associated with in-situ conservation and to a lesser extent ex-situ conservation. These two expressions are interpreted. Ex-situ conservation means the conservation of components of biological diversity outside their natural habitats.[42] In-situ conservation is the conservation of ecosystems and natural habitats and the maintenance and recovery of viable populations of species in their natural surroundings.[43] The interpretation given to ecosystem indicates that it is the complex relationship between biotic communities and their nonbiotic environment.[44]

So in-situ conservation means, first of all, the protection of these relationships and of natural habitats. It may include – because of the traditional meaning of the word conservation – the maintenance of these relationships and natural habitats on an ongoing basis. However, the interpretation in the Convention states that in-situ conservation also means the maintenance and recovery of viable populations of species in their natural surroundings. Clearly the concepts of maintenance and recovery contemplate the long-term future of these species. This distinctive treatment of ecosystems and natural habitats, on the one hand, and viable populations of species in their natural surroundings, on the other, is interesting. It suggests that the long-term future survival

[37] *Convention on Biological Diversity* 1992, preamble, recital 1.
[38] Ibid., preamble, recital 3.
[39] Ibid., Article 1.
[40] Ibid., Article 2 "sustainable use."
[41] Ibid., Article 2 "biological diversity."
[42] Ibid., Article 2 "ex-situ conservation."
[43] Ibid., Article 2 "in-situ conservation."
[44] Ibid., Article 2 "ecosystem."

of biodiversity is just as important as or perhaps more important than the long-term future survival of ecosystems and natural habitats. Clearly, the two are interrelated.

But this analysis may be reading more into the interpretation provisions than is perhaps justified. What is important, however, is that both in-situ conservation and ex-situ conservation are related directly to the conservation of biodiversity, both inside and outside natural habitats. The sustainable use of biodiversity is treated differently. In some respects, therefore, the notions of sustainability and sustainable development that underlie the Rio Declaration complement the approach adopted by the Convention on Biological Diversity. The Convention clearly imposes obligations on States: many are relatively specific. It does so, however, in the context of significant statements in the lengthy preamble, in the objectives, in the interpretation of critical expressions and in the principle itself. This is clearly an example of combination of legal and paralegal rules that relate to and interact with each other.

Each of these legal instruments – whether in the form of agreements or declarations – has evolved out of their own historical and political context. There have been, and no doubt always will be, different perspectives on all of these issues. The differences may be subtle, but nevertheless they are real. The most recent international pronouncement on these issues – the Johannesburg Declaration 2002 – recognised these differences. It reaffirmed global commitment to sustainable development.[45] The different perceptions and values over the thirty years from 1972 to 2002 emerge from its language:

> Thirty years ago, in Stockholm, we agreed on the urgent need to respond to the problem of environmental deterioration. Ten years ago, at the United Nations Conference on Environment and Development, held in Rio de Janeiro we agreed that the protection of the environment and social and economic development are fundamental to sustainable development based on the Rio Principles.[46]

The focus of the Johannesburg Declaration was on the indivisibility of human dignity. This requires action to satisfy the basic requirements of the community such as clean water, shelter, and food. It also refers to the protection rather than the conservation of biodiversity,[47] which is a subtle but perhaps important change of language. From the legal perspective, of course, it is the language that is used in these instruments that represents either the opportunity or the challenge to address the issues raised by the deterioration of biodiversity.

5.5 The Draft Covenant

The draft International Covenant on Environment and Development proposed by the International Union for the Conservation of Nature represents what many see as a considered statement of the principles of international law governing the management of natural resources and the environment. It deals, of course, with biodiversity. Two critical concepts are stated in the preamble:

- the unity of the biosphere, a unique and indivisible ecosystem, and the interdependence of all its components;

[45] *Johannesburg Declaration* 2002, Article 1.
[46] Ibid., Article 8.
[47] Ibid., Article 18.

- humanity is a part of nature and all life depends on the functioning of natural systems that ensure the supply of energy and nutrients.[48]

The objective significantly highlights the relationship between the substantive outcomes of the management of natural resources and the environment and the legal mechanisms by which they are achieved. Thus, its aim is "to achieve environmental conservation and sustainable development by establishing integrated rights and obligations."[49] Although there is no interpretation of terms, the fundamental concepts are clear enough. The first is that the global environment is a common concern – but no more than that – of humanity.[50] Then there is the general reference to respect for all life forms. It is encapsulated in three sentences:

- nature as a whole warrants respect;
- the integrity of the Earth's ecological systems shall be maintained and restored;
- every form of life is unique and is to be safeguarded independently from its value for humanity.[51]

The last sentence is important. It establishes the intrinsic value of every form of life. So biodiversity is conserved for its own sake. In addition, the critical functions – apart from their associated and potentially enforceable obligations – are these:

- respect;
- maintenance;
- restoration;
- safeguarding.

These are all elements of conservation in its widest sense.

Not only does the draft covenant contemplate the integration of rights and obligations; it also contemplates the integration of environmental conservation and sustainable development. Thus, sustainable development policies are aimed at a number of more specific outcomes.[52] One is the conservation of biological diversity and another is the maintenance of essential ecological processes and life-support systems. These are supported by a number of more specific obligations. One is to take appropriate measures to conserve and, where necessary and possible, restore natural systems that support life on earth in all of its diversity including biological diversity.[53] Another is to take all appropriate measures to conserve biological diversity and ecosystem diversity especially through in-situ conservation.[54]

The verb "conserve" is fundamental to each of these obligations. The commentary to the draft covenant states that in this context conserve means "to manage human-induced processes and activities which may be damaging natural systems in such a way that the essential functions of these systems are maintained."[55] Thus, conservation in this sense is a management process leading to ongoing maintenance of the capacities of the natural systems. It is contemplated that this obligation may be discharged in a number

[48] Commission on Environmental Law of the International Union for the Conservation of Nature, *Draft International Covenant on Environment and Development*, 2nd ed. (Gland and Cambridge: International Union for the Conservation of Nature, 2000), preamble, recitals 1 and 2.

[49] Ibid., Article 1.

[50] Ibid., Article 3.

[51] Ibid., Article 2.

[52] Ibid., Article 13(1).

[53] Ibid., Article 20(1).

[54] Ibid., Article 21(1).

[55] Ibid. at 70.

of ways including through the processes of physical planning and environmental impact assessment.[56] The commentary goes on to state that restore means reestablishment of lost or impaired ecological functions.[57]

Although protection is not stated to be part of these processes, protecting the environment, safeguarding every form of life and, by implication, protecting nature from damaging activities are mechanisms appropriate to the conservation of natural systems and biodiversity. Although there is no obligation to conserve biodiversity, there is a clear obligation to take appropriate measures to do so. The draft covenant makes clear the mechanisms that may be appropriate. These are paralegal rules in the sense under discussion.

5.6 Summary

Each of these legal instruments – Conventions, Charters, Declarations, and including the draft covenant – discloses a set of consistent but by no means identical concepts, language, and structures. Although the Declarations are formulated differently from Conventions and perform different functions within the international legal system, a relatively clear structure for conserving biodiversity as an element of nature which is by itself an element of the environment is emerging. This involves the concepts of protection, preservation, maintenance, enhancement, restoration and, of course, conservation itself. These may be seen as outcomes of processes, the processes themselves, the values associated with these processes, or mere descriptions of circumstances. These concepts, which go to the heart of the system, are linked to their subject matter by the use of expressions such as life, forms of life, nature, natural systems, and biodiversity.

All of these elements are linked together in various ways as part of a legal structure. A legal structure comprises a set of rights, duties and instrumental techniques. All of these different elements are bound together by a set of rules and a set of paralegal rules. So we have a set of concepts that gives the whole system substance and two sets of rules which give it validity, coherence and possibly enforceability. It is language that binds these components of the whole system together. If this is the system with which the international community is expected to conform, is it replicated in the systems for conserving biodiversity that States within the international community have imposed on themselves and on their citizens?

6 REGIONAL LEGAL AND PARALEGAL RULES

6.1 Introduction

Let us consider the approach adopted by the European Union as an example of regional arrangements. One of its tasks is to promote a high level of protection and improvement of the quality of the environment.[58] The promotion of sustainable development is clearly an element of this.[59] Although biodiversity is not specifically mentioned in this respect, there can be no doubt that nature and biodiversity are elements of the environment

[56] Ibid., Articles 36 and 37.
[57] Ibid. at 70.
[58] Treaty establishing the European Union, Article 2.
[59] Ibid., Article 6.

which is to be protected and improved. The four principles according to which this is to be achieved are:

- the precautionary principle;
- the principle of preventive action;
- the principle of rectifying environmental damage at source;
- the polluter pays principle.[60]

There are two Directives of particular relevance to biodiversity: the Directive on the Conservation of Wild Birds 1979 and the Directive on the Conservation of Natural Habitats and of Wild Fauna and Flora 1992. The preamble to the 1979 Directive recognises immediately that migratory species of wild birds in particular "constitute a common heritage" and that their transfrontier mobility entails "common responsibilities."[61] The use of these three words – common, heritage, and responsibilities – creates the conceptual framework for the directive. In addition, it is stated that the preservation, maintenance, or restoration of a sufficient diversity and area of habitat is essential to the conservation of all species of birds.[62] Indeed, some species require special conservation measures. A notion of biodiversity, therefore, underlies this Directive and its conservation contemplates the three functions of preservation, maintenance and restoration. The Directive acknowledges the possibility of the exploitation of all species.[63] The critical question then is the relationship between the exploitation of the species and its protection, management, and control.

This relationship is described in considerable and subtle detail. A general obligation is placed on all member States to take the requisite measures to maintain or adapt the population of all relevant species at an appropriate level.[64] This is the level that corresponds in particular to ecological, scientific, and cultural requirements while taking account of economic and recreational requirements. This is complemented by an obligation related to the preservation, maintenance, or reestablishment of a sufficient diversity and area of habitats.[65] This is achieved among other things with the creation of protected areas; the upkeep and management of habitats both inside and outside protected zones in accordance with the ecological needs of these habitats; the reestablishment of destroyed biotopes; and the creation of biotopes.[66] Even more particularly, there is an obligation to take special conservation measures concerning the habitat of species identified to be at particular risk.[67] These special measures assume the form of special protection areas for the conservation of these species. In relation to these special protection areas there is a further obligation to take appropriate steps to avoid pollution or deterioration of habitats or any disturbances affecting the birds.[68]

6.2 The Nature of the Obligations

The meaning and effect of these rules have been discussed on a number of occasions by the Court of Justice of the European Union. In one case, for example, one of the issues

[60] Ibid., Article 174(2).
[61] Directive on the Conservation of Wild Birds 1979, preamble, recital 8.
[62] Ibid., preamble, recital 14.
[63] Ibid., preamble, recitals 15 and 16.
[64] Ibid., Article 2.
[65] Ibid., Article 3(1).
[66] Ibid., Article 3(2).
[67] Ibid., Article 4(1).
[68] Ibid., Article 4(4).

was whether Articles 3 and 4 of the directive "merely impose an obligation to achieve a result, namely to secure the conservation of wild birds" or whether they required "specific measures" to be "taken to conserve the habitats of wild birds."[69] The court concluded:

> Articles 3 and 4 of the directive require member states to preserve, maintain and re-establish habitats as such, because of their ecological value. Moreover, it follows from the ninth recital in the preamble to the directive that the preservation, maintenance or restoration of a sufficient diversity and area of habitats is essential to the conservation of all species of birds. The obligations on member States under articles 3 and 4 of the directive therefore exist before any reduction is observed in the number of birds or any risk of a protected species becoming extinct has materialised.[70]

The obligation in the directive, therefore, is not only to achieve the conservation of wild birds but also to conserve the habitats of wild birds. The reason for this interpretation is not only the language and grammar of the directive but also the ecological value of habitats.

One of the issues in another case was the relationship between Articles 2 and 4 of the directive.[71] Article 2, it will be recalled, imposes a general obligation to take requisite measures to maintain the population of species at appropriate levels "while taking account of economic and recreational requirements." Article 4(4) requires States to take appropriate steps in relation to special protection areas to avoid pollution or deterioration of habitats or of any disturbances affecting the birds. The issue arose in the context of a proposal to reduce the area of a Special Protection Area (SPA) that had already been created. The reason for the proposed reduction of the area was the protection of an overriding component of public interest. As the court itself indicated, "It must be determined whether – and if so, under what conditions – the member states are authorised to reduce the size of a SPA and to what extent other interests may be taken into account."[72] On that occasion, it was decided that the selection of areas suitable for classification as SPAs involves certain discretion. But there is no such discretion in relation to the modification or reduction of the extent of the areas. Otherwise, "member states could unilaterally escape from the obligations imposed on them by article 4(4) of the directive with regard to special protection areas."[73]

In reaching this conclusion, the court analysed not only the form and structure of the Directive but also the relevant recital in the Preamble highlighting the special importance of SPAs. The focus of Article 4(4) – and indeed of the whole directive – is thus on conservation as a value, as an objective of a process and as a process. The court concluded in very clear terms:

> It follows that the power of the member states to reduce the extent of a special protection area can be justified only on exceptional grounds. Those grounds must correspond to a general interest which is superior to the general interest represented by the ecological objective of the directive. In that context the interests referred to in article 2 of the directive, namely economic and recreational requirements, do not enter into consideration. As the Court pointed out in [other judgments], this

[69] *Commission v. Spain* [1993] European Court Reports I–4221 at 4276.
[70] Ibid. at 4276.
[71] *Commission v. Federal Republic of Germany* [1991] European Court Reports I–883.
[72] Ibid. at 930.
[73] Ibid. at 931.

provision does not constitute an autonomous derogation from the general system of protection established by the Directive.[74]

Conservation in all of its manifestations is the paramount consideration driving the implementation of this Directive. Economic considerations are irrelevant, and the ecological imperative of the directive can be overridden only in the most exceptional circumstances.

6.3 The Scope of the Discretions

The Directive of 1992 is more detailed in its approach to the conservation of natural habitats and of wild fauna and flora than the Directive of 1979. But the approach and the essential values that it seeks to protect remain essentially the same. It states, clearly enough, that the aim of the directive is to contribute to ensure biodiversity through the conservation of natural habitats and of wild fauna and flora.[75] Measures taken are designed to maintain or restore, at favourable conservation status, natural habitats, and species of wild fauna and flora.[76] In addition – and of some significance – account is to be taken of economic, social, and cultural requirements.[77]

One of the ways of doing this is the establishment of a coherent European ecological network of special areas of conservation called Natura 2000. This network includes SPAs set up in accordance with the Directive of 1979.[78] Provision is also made for the designation of sites as special areas of conservation (SACS).[79] Conservation measures in these areas include appropriate management plans and other procedures for avoiding the deterioration of natural habitats including the appropriate assessment of any impacts on these special conservation areas of other plans or projects.[80] It is, however, provided that if, despite a negative assessment of such an impact, the plan or the project must nevertheless be carried out "for imperative reasons of overriding public interest, including those of a social or economic nature," all necessary compensatory measures must be taken to ensure that the overall coherence of Natura 2000 is protected.[81]

In the case of a proposed development negatively impacting on an area proposed to be classified as a SPA the court was invited to analyse the relationship between Articles 2 and 4 of the 1979 directive and Articles 6 and 7 of the 1992 Directive.[82] The court first of all confirmed:

- the economic requirements mentioned in Article 2 of the 1979 Directive cannot be taken into account when designating a SPA and defining its boundaries in accordance with Article 4(1) or (2);
- any economic requirements do not constitute a general interest superior to the interest represented by the ecological objective of the directive in designating a special protection area and defining its boundaries under Article 4(1) or (2).

The novel question, however, was whether the reference to imperative reasons of overriding public interest of the kind referred to in Article 6(4) of the 1992 Directive

[74] Ibid. at 931.
[75] Directive on the Conservation of Natural Habitats and of Wild Fauna and Flora 1992, Article 2(1).
[76] Ibid., Article 2(2).
[77] Ibid., Article 2(3).
[78] Ibid., Article 3(1).
[79] Ibid., Article 4(1).
[80] Ibid., Article 6(1) to (3).
[81] Ibid., Article 6(4).
[82] *R v. Secretary of State for the Environment, Ex parte Royal Society for the Protection of Birds* [1997] Queen's Bench Reports 206.

extended the matters authorised to be taken into account when designating a special protection area and defining its boundaries. The court concluded that it did not do so. Article 6 of the 1992 Directive was directed at a different stage of the conservation process than Article 4 of the 1979 Directive. Economic requirements, in other words, may be relevant for the purposes of Article 6(4) of the 1992 Directive but not for the purposes of Article 4(1) or (2) of the 1979 Directive. In this particular case, the issue was the relevance of economic considerations when designating a SPA and defining its boundaries under Article 4 of the 1979 Directive. Economic considerations were therefore irrelevant.[83]

6.4 Summary

These two Directives were concerned with conservation of biodiversity. Each contains a number of obligations linked to outcomes clearly identifiable in the interpretation statements. The overall direction of the Directives is emphasised by the detailed statements in the Preamble. The mechanisms for achieving these outcomes include the Natura 2000 network, special areas of conservation and special protection areas. The methodology of decision making prescribed by the directives is complex. In interpreting and applying the Directives, the court has achieved an overall coherence between the various elements of the whole structure: some methodological, others procedural, some substantive. There is no doubt that some are enforceable legal rules. Several assume the nature of paralegal rules. Together, a coherent structure has emerged to which the court has given effect.

7 LEGAL AND PARALEGAL RULES IN CONSTITUTIONS

7.1 Introduction

The language, form, and structure of international agreements and regional agreements – including those relating to the environment, nature and biodiversity – are sometimes reflected in the language, form, and structure of the Constitutions of individual States within the international community. The problems associated with the incorporation within constitutions of rights and obligations in relation to the environment and nature have been addressed by a number of commentators. There is nevertheless an increasing number of examples of constitutional rights and obligations in relation to these values: for example, a number of the states in the United States, a number of states in continental Europe, several states in South America and Africa, and a number in Asia. Although the way in which Constitutions are interpreted and applied by courts varies, there are a number of examples of a very dynamic and proactive approach on the part of several courts. Let us consider three examples.

7.2 Tropical Rain Forests in the Philippines

The Supreme Court of the Philippines in the *Minors Oposa* case[84] was confronted formally with two of the most fundamental issues related to the enforceability of rights

[83] Ibid. at 256–258.

[84] *Minors Oposa v. Secretary of the Department of Environment and Natural Resources* (1994) 33 *International Legal Materials* 173.

and duties: *locus standi*, on the one hand, and justiciability, on the other. The issue for the court was in general terms the existence and the nature of "the right of Filipinos to a balanced and healthful ecology"[85] associated with intergenerational responsibility and justice. "Specifically," as the court said, "it touches on the issue of whether the said petitioners have a cause of action to 'prevent the misappropriation or impairment' of Philippine rainforests and 'arrest the unabated haemorrhage of the country's vital life-support systems and continued rape of Mother Earth.'"[86] More specifically, it was about the conservation of tropical rain forests in the Philippines.

In effect, the petition sought cancellation of timber licensing agreements and prohibition of the approval of new timber licensing agreements. The values affected by destruction of tropical rain forests included:

- the rich, lush, and verdant rain forests in which varied, rare, and unique species of flora and fauna may be found;
- the irreplaceable genetic, biological, and chemical pool contained in these rain forests;
- these rain forests as the habitat of indigenous Philippine cultures since time immemorial.[87]

The legal instruments providing support for the petition included these:

- provisions of the civil code relating to human relations;
- provisions of the executive order establishing the Department of Environment and Natural Resources;
- provisions of the presidential decree stating Philippine environmental policy;
- section 16 of Article II of the Constitution of the Philippines;
- the concept of generational genocide in the criminal law;
- the concept of man's inalienable right to self-preservation and self-perpetuation embodied in natural law.[88]

Clearly, support was coming from a wide range of sources, but for present purposes it is the Constitution that is most important. Relevantly, the Constitution states: "The state shall protect and advance the right of the people to a balanced and healthful ecology in accord with the rhythm and harmony of nature."

This right appears under the Declaration of Principles and State Policies and not under the Bill of Rights. According to the court, this did not in any respect reduce its importance, "for it concerns nothing less than self-preservation and self-perpetuation."[89] Formally, the provision in the constitution is a duty imposed on the State. The subject matter of the duty is to protect and advance the right in question. The right contains a number of elements:

- it is a right of the people at large;
- it is a right for the people to have a balanced ecology;
- it is a right for the people to have a healthful ecology;
- it is linked to nature through rhythm and harmony.

[85] Ibid. at 175 and 176.
[86] Ibid. at 176.
[87] Ibid. at 177.
[88] Ibid. at 183.
[89] Ibid. at 187.

So, although there is a reference to nature, it remains on the face of it essentially a human right and perhaps a collective right.

Although the duty may be placed on the State, the right of the people – certainly in this generic sense – is unlikely to be protected in the absence of further explicit or implied provisions. The court thus added, largely by implication, the existence of a "correlative duty to refrain from impairing the environment."[90] This correlative duty can be imposed on only one institution and that is the State. There is, therefore, a right, a duty on the State to protect this right and the implied duty not to damage the environment or, in this case, nature including biodiversity. This gives rise to a cause of action if there has been a violation of the right or a failure to comply with the duty.[91] The right of the people in this case had been violated by the approval of the timber licensing agreements. There was, therefore, a justiciable issue.

One of the arguments suggesting the absence of justiciability was the nature of the right. Particularly, it raised issues that were political rather than legal. Not only that: the subject matter of the right was sufficiently vague and indefinite so as to conceal a justiciable issue. This was rejected by the court. Thus, "what is principally involved is the enforcement of a right *vis-à-vis* policies already formulated and expressed in legislation."[92] In other words, the right in the Constitution received support and substance from other elements of the legal system even though these other elements of the legal system were couched in terms of policy. Moreover, such an expansive approach to this issue was supported by a paragraph in section 1 of Article VIII of the Constitution, namely:

> Judicial power includes the duty of the courts of justice to settle actual controversies involving rights which are legally demandable and enforceable, and to determine whether or not there has been a grave abuse of discretion amounting to lack or excess of jurisdiction on the part of any branch or instrumentality of the government.

It is no surprise that for these reasons the court decided that *locus standi* had been established and justiciable issues raised. Just as important, although the issues were not couched in terms of conservation of nature and biodiversity, conservation of biodiversity as an outcome was undoubtedly a component of the concepts scrutinised in detail by the court. Significantly, the court gave substance to the right in the Constitution by reference to a range of legal concepts and instruments probably not enforceable by themselves. In other words, in this case, the court adopted a set of legal and paralegal rules to give coherence to the approach.

7.3 Traditional Lifestyles in India

Many of the decisions of the Supreme Court of India have been concerned with pollution brought about by industrial, commercial, and related activities. One was concerned with the values of nature and biodiversity[93] and how they are protected by the Constitution. The Constitution of India has a number of relevant provisions:

- according to Article 32(1) the right to move the Supreme Court by appropriate proceedings for the enforcement of the rights conferred by Part III is guaranteed;

[90] Ibid. at 188.
[91] Ibid. at 191.
[92] Ibid. at 193.
[93] *Animal and Environment Legal Defence Fund v. Union of India* (1997) 3 *Supreme Court Cases* 549.

- according to Article 37 the provisions contained in Part IV shall not be enforceable by any court, but the principles therein laid down are nevertheless fundamental in the governance of the country and it shall be the duty of the state to apply these principles in making laws;
- according to Article 48-A in part IV (the directive principles of state policy), the state shall endeavour to protect and improve the environment and to safeguard the forests and wildlife of the country;

According to Article 51-A in part IV – A (fundamental duties) it shall be the duty of every citizen of India to protect and improve the natural environment including forests, lakes, rivers, and wildlife, and to have compassion for living creatures.

The Supreme Court of India has taken advantage of these provisions to create a legal framework within which to recognise and protect ecological values and at the same time recognise the capacity of any person to come to the court to seek a remedy if the rights contained within this framework have been violated.

This case involved a conflict between the values of biodiversity and the values associated with the lifestyle of the local tribal – villagers. The petition presented to the court in the public interest challenged an order of an official of the government of Madhya Pradesh. The decision in question was the grant of a large number of fishing permits to members of the tribes who formerly resided within the Pench National Park for fishing in a reservoir situated in the heart of the Pench National Park Tiger Reserve. It was argued that if fishing were to be permitted in the heart of the national park, then "the biodiversity and ecology of the area" would be seriously affected.[94] Not only that: the fishing activity might well lead to a degradation of the values of the national park itself. By contrast, before the national park had been established, it was a reserved forest area where the tribal – villagers resided. Fishing was their main source of livelihood. These tribal – villagers had effectively been displaced. "No agricultural land has been made available to them, no work has been made available to them and they do not have any means of livelihood except catching fish which is their traditional occupation." In the absence of fishing permits, "a serious problem of feeding and supporting their families will arise."[95] What then has priority? The conservation of nature or the protection of traditional lifestyles.

In this particular case, the court was faced with a conflict of values. It reviewed the relevant laws including the legislation about forests, wildlife, and national parks. There was no legislation, it would seem, protecting the traditional lifestyle of tribal-villagers. Moreover, in the course of referring to Articles 48-A and 51-A of the Constitution the court pointed out that "on the promulgation of the Constitution, the right to safeguard forests and wildlife has received constitutional sanction."[96] But it concluded that, "while every attempt must be made to preserve the fragile ecology of the forest area, and protect the Tiger Reserve, the right of the tribals formerly living in the area to keep body and soul together must also receive proper consideration."[97] The ecological objectives were sanctioned by the Constitution. However, the source of the right of the tribal-villagers to their livelihood was unstated, nevertheless it existed.

[94] Ibid. at 552.
[95] Ibid. at 553.
[96] Ibid. at 550.
[97] Ibid. at 553.

The court took the opportunity to comment that other arrangements for ensuring the livelihood of the tribal-villagers "would have been far more desirable."[98] But arguably that was a matter for the executive rather than for the judiciary. Indeed, the court commented:

> We are not in a position to say whether these outlying parts of the reservoir are accessible or whether they are suitable for fishing, in the absence of any material being placed before us by the State of Madhya Pradesh or by the petitioner. Some attempts, however, seem to have been made by the State of Madhya Pradesh to contain the damage by imposing conditions on these fishing permits.[99]

Significantly, however, the court did go further. In a sense, it achieved a compromise between the competing interests. A set of additional conditions was attached to the fishing permits. The court found it necessary to clear up some doubts and to give some additional directions in relation to implementing the conditions of the permits. So the judicial organ of government engaged in the process of giving fairly detailed and fairly specific directions, such as how the rights associated with the fishing permit should be exercised and how the conditions attached to these permits should be implemented. In other words, these directives were one among a number of examples of fairly detailed and specific judicial involvement in the management process. The inspiration for these initiatives, of course, was the Constitution.

7.4 Cultural Values in Japan

Cultural issues similarly lay at the heart of the decision of the Sapporo District Court in Japan in the *Nibutani Dam* case in 1997.[100] Land in a region of Hokkaido had been confiscated to enable the construction of a dam and the flooding of a substantial area of land for the purposes of flood control and the rational use of water resources. The land belonged to members of the Ainu people. They owned, occupied, and used it in accordance with their own distinctive culture. It was argued that the confiscation was unlawful because there had been a failure to consider the impact that the construction of the dam and the flooding of the area were likely to have on the Ainu people and on their culture. The court had little doubt in concluding that "accomplishment of the project plan will impose hardship on the Ainu people living in the Nibutani area or, even if that is not the case, it will greatly impact their lifestyle and culture."[101]

Their lifestyle and culture comprised a range of elements. The Ainu people inhabit riverside areas in village groupings. Their culture is based on hunting, gathering, and fishing. The Ainu have their own language and their traditions are based on a respect for natural things including wild animals and fish. The court emphasised that "their values rested in nature worship, i.e. in living together with the gods who gave human kind this bounty of nature."[102] So the area that the Ainu inhabited not only provided their lifestyle and their livelihood but also were a place of spiritual, archaeological, and ceremonial significance.

Although the court acknowledged that the process of expropriation involved a balance between the public benefits and the public and private disadvantages of the project,

[98] Ibid. at 553.
[99] Ibid. at 557.
[100] *Kayano v. Hokkaido Expropriation Committee* (1999) 38 *International Legal Materials* 394.
[101] Ibid. at 410.
[102] Ibid. at 411.

it exercised a supervisory jurisdiction over the way the decision was reached. The analysis of the court focussed on two legal instruments:

- Article 27 of the International Covenant on Civil and Political Rights 1969 to which Japan is a party and has given effect;
- Article 13 of the Constitution of Japan.

Article 27 of the covenant states:

> In those states in which ethnic, religious or linguistic minorities exist, persons belonging to such minorities shall not be denied the right, in community with the other members of their group, to enjoy their own culture, to profess and practise their own religion, or to use their own language.[103]

Article 13 of the Constitution states:

> All of the people shall be respected as individuals. Their right to life, liberty, and the pursuit of happiness shall, to the extent that it does not interfere with the public welfare, be the supreme consideration in legislation and in other governmental affairs.[104]

The court analysed and interpreted the provisions of these two instruments with reference to each other. Neither set of rights was regarded as unlimited. Nevertheless, in each case, any limits on the rights had to be confined as much as possible. In effect, therefore, Article 13 of the Constitution guaranteed to the plaintiffs the right to enjoy the distinct ethnic culture of the Ainu people. But the court added this comment:

> Of course, in speaking of this right, we understand it to be subject to the public welfare limitation included expressly within the provisions of [article 13], but in consideration of the character of the human right involved, that limitation must be kept to the narrowest degree necessary.[105]

It was against this background that the process of comparative balancing required by the expropriation legislation should have been carried out. In the event:

> We find that the Minister of Construction, who was the authorising agency and the agent for the enterprise authority in the instant matter, neglected the investigative and research procedures that were necessary to judge the priority of the competing interests accompanying the accomplishment of the project plan. He unreasonably made little of and ignored various factors and values that should have been given the highest regard. Furthermore, despite being unable to make a proper judgment, he recognised only the smallest possible impact on Ainu culture and left any damages thereon unremedied.
>
> After all of this, the Minister of Construction determined to give precedence to the public benefits of the project over losing interests and associated values, and consequently issued the project authorisation. Nothing more can be said except that such action exceeded the administrative discretion given to the authorising agency pursuant to Land Expropriation Law article 20(3) and was illegal.[106]

[103] Ibid. at 417.
[104] Ibid. at 418.
[105] Ibid. at 419.
[106] Ibid. at 427.

It is clear from this that the rules governing the administrative decision-making process were contained in the expropriation legislation. However, these processes were reviewed in the context of the paralegal rules contained in the Constitution of Japan and the International Covenant on Civil and Political Rights. So the rights in these two instruments are guaranteed not so much in themselves but through the impact and the influence that they have on the application of other elements of the legal system; hence the reference to them as paralegal rules. Although neither the covenant nor the constitution had anything to say about nature and biodiversity, it was the importance of nature and biodiversity to the culture of the Ainu that rendered these elements of the environment relevant for the purposes of their recognition and protection indirectly by the covenant and the constitution. So, although it was the lifestyle of the Ainu that lay at the heart of this decision, it was the relationship between that lifestyle and nature in that culture that is particularly significant for present purposes.

8 LEGAL AND PARALEGAL RULES IN AUSTRALIA

8.1 Introduction

The constitutional framework within which Australia as a federation operates is remarkably different to the arrangements in the Philippines, India, and Japan. There is nothing in the constitutional framework of the Commonwealth of Australia or of the States and Territories within the Commonwealth regarding the environment, nature, or biodiversity. This is not to say that these constitutional arrangements are not relevant. Indeed they are. They comprise rules that distribute the power to legislate rather than rules that prescribe the substantive merits of the legislation enacted in accordance with these powers.

Although the Commonwealth is able to influence the management of the environment through its capacity to control fiscal and budgetary matters, four areas in particular of legislative competence of the Commonwealth enable the Commonwealth to validly regulate aspects of the environment, nature, and biodiversity. These are:

- the overseas and interstate trade and commerce power;
- the trading corporations power;
- the race power;
- the external affairs power.

So far, it has been largely the external affairs power that has been used by the Parliament of the Commonwealth to become involved in managing Australia's environment. Otherwise, it is a matter for the States and Territories to legislate on these matters.[107]

The Commonwealth and each of the States and Territories has enacted legislation for protection of the environment and for conservation of the natural environment.[108] Although the legislation in each of the jurisdictions in Australia is similar, it is by no means the same. There are differences of structure, form, and language. In particular

[107] For the constitutional position in Australia, see, generally, D. E. Fisher, *Australian Environmental Law* (Sydney: Lawbook Company, 2003), chapter 4.

[108] Ibid., chapters 8 and 9.

sets of circumstances, these differences could prove to be critical. Typically in each jurisdiction there are three approaches:

- legislation for the protection of the environment;
- legislation for the establishment and management of protected areas such as national parks;
- legislation for the conservation of nature.

Biodiversity is one of the values able to be protected either directly or indirectly by these statutory arrangements. Despite its limited legislative capacity, the parliament of the Commonwealth has chosen to adopt an integrated rather than a fragmented approach by incorporating these three functions in the *Environment Protection and Biodiversity Conservation Act* 1999 (Cth). The states and territories, by contrast, have retained a more fragmented approach. Let us consider the legislation of the Commonwealth first and then examine the approach in Queensland as an example of how the States and Territories have confronted the challenge of biodiversity conservation.

8.2 The Approach of the Commonwealth

8.2.1 The Structure of the Legislation

The objects of the *Environment Protection and Biodiversity Conservation* Act 1999 (Cth) include these three:

- the protection of the environment;
- the conservation of biodiversity;
- ecologically sustainable development through the conservation and ecologically sustainable use of natural resources.[109]

Although these are interlinked purposes, they are stated separately. In this sense, protection of the environment involves the conservation of biodiversity and the conservation of biodiversity likewise involves the protection of the environment. One of the principles of ecologically sustainable development is the precautionary principle[110] and the precautionary principle is in addition required to be taken into account quite specifically in the decision-making processes about protecting the environment and conserving biodiversity.[111] One of the other principles of ecologically sustainable development is that the conservation of biological diversity and ecological integrity should be a fundamental consideration in decision-making.[112] The conservation of biodiversity is thus a critical factor in decision making, but also one of the fundamental principles underpinning the legislation. For practical purposes, the conservation of biodiversity is addressed in two ways in the legislation; first, in accordance with chapter 2 about protecting the environment and, second, in accordance with chapter 5 about conserving biodiversity and heritage.

[109] *Environment Protection and Biodiversity Conservation Act* 1999 (Cth), section 3(1)(a) to (c).
[110] Ibid., section 3A(b).
[111] Ibid., section 391.
[112] Ibid., section 3A(d).

8.2.2 Protection under Chapter 2

Let us consider first how biodiversity is protected as an element of the environment. Biodiversity may be one of the values of a declared world heritage property, that is, an item on the world heritage list kept for the purposes of the Convention for the Protection of the World Cultural and Natural Heritage 1972. Similarly, biodiversity may be one of the values of a specified wetland for the purposes of the Convention on Wetlands of International Importance 1971. Alternatively, biodiversity may be protected as a listed threatened species, a listed threatened ecological community or a listed migratory species. The constitutional validity of these approaches depends, in the context of the external affairs power, on the nature and extent of Australia's obligations under a number of international arrangements, including the Convention on Biological Diversity 1992. Significantly, the Act confers a power to make regulations for the specific purpose of giving effect within Australia to this convention.[113] It seems reasonably clear that the Commonwealth, if it wishes, can protect and conserve the various components of biological diversity wherever they occur in Australia, provided the Parliament of the Commonwealth is doing so in accordance with the external affairs power.[114] This might even include the prohibition of the clearance of vegetation, if that would destroy the habitat of a listed threatened species.

There are in effect two mechanisms for protecting biodiversity as an element of the environment. One is proactive and the other is reactive. First, any action that is likely to have a significant impact on the values protected by the Act, including those relating to biodiversity, is unlawful, unless authorised in a number of different ways including the grant of approval of the taking of the action.[115] This procedure involves an application, an assessment of the likelihood of significant impacts and a decision whether or not to approve the action. In this way proposed activities impacting significantly on biodiversity values are either prohibited or regulated if approval is given. Second, if an action has already taken place that has had or is likely to have a significant impact on protected values, then an application may be made to the Federal Court for a remedy.[116] An applicant for a remedy must have an interest. This may be either that the interests of the applicant have been or would be affected or that the applicant has been engaged in a series of activities for protection or conservation of the environment, including research, at any time during the preceding two years.[117] There is therefore almost no impediment to the making of an application. We shall consider an example of this approach in later paragraphs.

8.2.3 Protection under Chapter 5

Biodiversity is in addition conserved by chapter 5 of the *Environment Protection and Biodiversity Conservation Act* 1999 (Cth). This part of the Act provides for the establishment and management of protected areas, where biological diversity is protected and conserved. For this purpose, a protected area is either an area such as a world heritage area for which Australia has international responsibilities, or a Commonwealth area for which a reserve has been created. A Commonwealth area includes an area owned

[113] Ibid., section 520(3)(i).

[114] *Tasmania v. Commonwealth* (1983) 158 Commonwealth Law Reports 1.

[115] *Environment Protection and Biodiversity Conservation Act* 1999 (Cth), section 12.

[116] Ibid., sections 15A and 475.

[117] Ibid., section 475(6).

or leased by the Commonwealth or a Commonwealth marine area. A protected area is created as a reserve and the reserves must fall into one of the categories created by the International Union for the Conservation of Nature.[118] Each area is managed in accordance with the relevant management principles and in accordance with a management plan if one has been prepared. There are a number of principles that apply to the management of all reserves. These are:

- community participation;
- effective and adaptive management;
- precautionary principle;
- minimum impact;
- ecologically sustainable use;
- transparency of decision making;
- joint management with aboriginal people.[119]

The principles relevant to a particular reserve reflect the purpose for which the reserve has been created. For example, in relation to strict nature reserves:

- habitats, ecosystems and native species should be preserved in as undisturbed a state as possible;
- genetic resources should be maintained in a dynamic and evolutionary state;
- established ecological processes should be maintained.[120]

Conservation of biodiversity includes, as we have seen, not only protection of the values of biodiversity but also their maintenance with a view to future use. Hence the restrictions in the Act are linked to the conservation and ecologically sustainable use of natural resources. It is thus generally unlawful to interfere with listed threatened species, listed threatened ecological communities or listed migratory species without a relevant permit.[121] These arrangements have effect within a framework of plans for the conservation of biodiversity; such as recovery plans, threat abatement plans and wildlife conservation plans. The grant of a permit is linked to the provisions of these kinds of plans. For example, a permit must not be granted unless the taking of the action that would be permitted by the permit is not inconsistent with the recovery plan in force for the species or the ecological community in question.[122]

8.2.4 The Management of Biodiversity

The complexity of the regime created by the *Environment Protection and Biodiversity Conservation Act* 1999 (Cth) is partly a response to the constitutional restrictions on the capacity of the Parliament of the Commonwealth to make laws with the respect to biodiversity. It also a response to the function of conservation and the nature of biodiversity itself. It is no surprise that the Act contains sets of rules able to be enforced directly, such as the prohibition of the taking of an action that is likely to have a significant impact on

[118] Ibid., section 347.
[119] Environment Protection and Biodiversity Conservation Regulations 2000 (Cth), regulation 10.04 and schedule 8, part 1.
[120] Ibid., regulation 10.04 and schedule 8, part 2, paras 1.02 to 1.04.
[121] *Environment Protection and Biodiversity Conservation Act* 1999 (Cth), sections 196, 197, 254, and 255.
[122] Ibid., section 201(3)(b)(ii).

the values of biodiversity that are part of the values protected in a world heritage area.[123] Although such a rule may be difficult to apply in particular sets of circumstances, it is not a prohibitive restriction that is intrinsically unenforceable. Indeed, as we shall see, these rules can be and have been enforced.

Provisions such as these also have an effect within the wider framework of the Act. This includes a number of elements which may not in themselves be capable of direct enforcement. So in this sense they complement the provisions that are directly enforceable. The first element comprises the objects of the Act including environmental protection and biodiversity conservation. Next, there are the principles supporting the achievement of these objects, and these include the principles of ecologically sustainable development in general and the precautionary principle in particular. Then there is the regulatory system, already discussed, comprising enforceable rules, that require Commonwealth approval for actions that are likely to have a significant impact on the values of the natural environment protected by the Act. Then there are protected areas – in this case, Commonwealth areas – set aside to be managed for the purposes of biodiversity conservation in accordance with a wide range of interconnected mechanisms. These include:

- identifying biodiversity;
- listing species;
- listing threatened species;
- formulating recovery plans, threat abatement plans, and wildlife conservation plans;
- establishing reserves;
- formulating management plans for reserves.

This analysis of the *Environment Protection and Biodiversity Conservation Act* 1999 (Cth) indicates that there are two quite distinct functions involved in the conservation of biodiversity: management and regulation. Significantly, it is the Act itself that creates the foundations for these two functions. The Act not only states the procedures for establishing reserves, but it also states the principles according to which these areas are to be managed. These management principles themselves acknowledge the three critical elements of protection, preservation and conservation of biodiversity. Regulation is achieved by the enactment of a set of rules prescribing relevant standards of behaviour in relation to activities supported by rules that create criminal, civil, and administrative liability for failure to comply. These management principles assume the form of paralegal rules, whereas regulation comprises a set of legal rules. However, it is the concurrent application of both sets of rules that is likely to assure the conservation of biodiversity.

8.2.5 The *Flying Foxes* Case

The relatively open approach to *locus standi* in the Act has given the Federal Court the opportunity to analyse these arrangements in some detail. The decision of the court in the *Flying Foxes* case is instructive.[124] A large lychee orchard was located in close proximity to a world heritage area whose values are protected by the *Environment Protection and Biodiversity Conservation Act* 1999 (Cth). The world heritage area is the habitat of the spectacled flying fox. The flying foxes were attracted by the lychees growing

[123] Ibid., sections 12 and 15A.

[124] *Booth v. Bosworth* [2001] Federal Court of Australia 1453 and 117 *Local Government and Environmental Reports of Australia* 168.

in the orchard. For the purpose of protecting the fruit the orchardist had constructed a series of aerial electric fences in a grid pattern. The purpose was to electrocute the flying foxes as they flew over the orchard. The applicant for an injunction complained that the actions of the orchardist had or were likely to have a significant impact on the world heritage values of the world heritage area in question. The court agreed and favoured the grant of an injunction.

The evidence presented to the court was extensive. It included information about the number of flying foxes injured and killed; information about the habitat of the flying foxes; information about where the flying foxes electrocuted by the grid had come from. Then there was evidence about the implications of this information for the species of flying fox whose habitat was in the world heritage area. The methodology for determination of the issue adopted by the court involved three questions after it had been established how many flying foxes had been injured and killed by the grid. These were:

- do the flying foxes killed by the grid reside in the world heritage area?[125]
- do the flying foxes contribute to the world heritage values of the world heritage area?[126]
- is the operation of the grid an action that has or will have or is likely to have a significant impact on a world heritage value of the world heritage area?[127]

The first two issues are matters of fact and the third is the application of the legal rule prescribed by the Act. The application of the rule itself required an answer to two questions. The first was whether the disappearance of flying foxes from the world heritage area or an appreciable reduction in their numbers would impact on the world heritage values of the area. The second was, if so, whether this impact was likely to be significant.

The court noted that this species of flying fox is "part of the record of the mixing of the faunas of the Australian and Asian continental plates and that the species constitutes part of the biological diversity"[128] of the world heritage area in question. It was concluded that the disappearance of flying foxes or an appreciable reduction in their numbers would impact on the world heritage values of the area. The reason was stated to be this:

> Either such event would tend to detract from the biological diversity of the area and from the importance and significance of the habitats contained within it for in-situ conservation of biological diversity. Further, I am satisfied that the disappearance of the spectacled flying fox from the Wet Tropics World Heritage Area or a dramatic reduction in its numbers in the area, would detract from the record contained in that area of the mixing of the faunas of the Australian and Asian continental plates.[129]

Attention then turned to the second question: that is, whether this impact was likely to be significant. The response of the court is so important that it justifies lengthy quotation:

> This is an issue on which virtually no authoritative guidance appears to be available. Having regard to the objects of the Act, which include the conservation of biodiversity, and the terms of the World Heritage Convention, which include a recital which emphasises the international recognition of the significance of the "deterioration" of natural heritage, I have concluded that in the circumstances of the

[125] Ibid. at 180.
[126] Ibid. at 181.
[127] Ibid. at 185.
[128] Ibid. at 194.
[129] Ibid. at 194.

> present case it is. In this context, in my view, a dramatic decline in the population of a species, so as to render the species endangered, where that species forms a part (other than an inconsequential part) of the record of the Earth's evolutionary history or of the biological diversity of a most important and significant habitat for in-situ conservation of biological diversity, is to be understood as having an impact that is important, notable or of consequence. I reject the submission of the respondents that before this conclusion can properly be reached it would have to be established that the spectacled flying fox is itself, when compared with other species, a species of outstanding universal value. In any event, I note that outside of Australia the spectacled flying fox is found only in Papua New Guinea and there only in less than ten locations. In this context, the loss of the spectacled flying fox from the Wet Tropics World Heritage Area and from Australia would, in my view, be a matter of considerable consequence. I find that the continued operation of the grid is likely to have a significant impact on the world heritage values of the Wet Tropics World Heritage Area.[130]

This rationalisation is critical for a number of reasons. The court was concerned in the first instance with a rule of law – a legal rule – stated in the Act: namely, whether the action in question was likely to have a significant impact on the values protected by the legislation. In doing so, the court specifically had regard to the objects of the Act and this particularly included the conservation of biodiversity. Consideration also was given quite specifically to the terms of the Convention for the Protection of the World Cultural and Natural Heritage 1972. In particular, the court accepted for the purposes of the Act the interpretation given to biological diversity and to natural heritage by the Convention. Not only that but also the expressions used by the court clearly reflected the concepts and language of the Convention. In effect, therefore, the application of the legal rule stated in the Act was supported in detail and substance by the Convention itself. The Convention – like any other convention – is not part of the law of Australia. Nevertheless, it is accepted that the rules and principles of international law are relevant in interpreting and applying the law of Australia. In this sense, therefore, the provisions of the Convention comprised a set of paralegal rules in support of the legal rules applied by the court.

8.3 The Approach in Queensland

8.3.1 Introduction

Let us turn now to the approach in Queensland as an example of biodiversity conservation in the States and Territories of Australia. The conservation of biodiversity may be a relevant value or process in most – perhaps even all – sets of legal arrangements that impact on the use, development, and conservation of natural resources (e.g., the regimes for planning the use of land and other natural resources, for granting interests in land, for determining issues in relation to native title, for managing forestry resources, for managing threatened native vegetation, and for managing water resources). Let us, however, focus on:

- the *Nature Conservation Act* 1992 (Qld);
- the *Environmental Protection Act* 1994 (Qld).

[130] Ibid. at 194 and 195.

8.3.2 The Nature Conservation Act

The object of the *Nature Conservation Act* 1992 (Qld) is stated as simply and as widely as the conservation of nature.[131] This is achieved by a management system supported by elements of regulation. It is, however, the concepts of conservation and nature that are critical. For this purpose, conservation is the protection and maintenance of nature allowing for its ecologically sustainable use.[132] Protection includes rehabilitation.[133] Conservation, then, in this comprehensive and integrated sense includes protection, maintenance, rehabilitation and use. All of these functions relate to nature. Nature is interpreted quite specifically to include biodiversity.[134] In this sense, the reference to biodiversity incorporates one of the qualities or values of nature as distinct from nature itself. Nature may be seen to be simply the descriptive reference to the subject matter of conservation. The incorporation of biodiversity, however, includes this additional element of quality or value.

The interpretation given to biodiversity for this purpose reflects its meaning for the purposes of international law. This interpretation is the natural diversity of native wildlife together with the environmental conditions necessary for their survival.[135] However, it specifically includes, consistently with the Convention on Biological Diversity 1992, regional diversity, ecosystem diversity, species diversity, and genetic diversity.[136] It is the word diversity itself, which describes not only existing values of biota but also the values that are to be maintained for the future.

Although it is the conservation of nature as a whole that is the object of the Act, much of the focus is on wildlife, native wildlife, and protected wildlife. Wildlife is any taxon or species of an animal, plant, protista, prokaryote, or virus.[137] Protection, however, is given to native wildlife prescribed according to various categories, such as presumed extinct, endangered, vulnerable, rare, or common. This is divided further into protected animals and protected plants. It is specifically stated that all protected animals and all protected plants are property of the State[138] except protected plants on private land.[139] The investment of the state with these rights of property underpins the regulatory regime for protecting these species and for enabling their ecologically sustainable use.

Let us turn to the critical function of the management of protected wildlife and of their habitats. Protected wildlife is managed in accordance with the relevant management principles and in accordance with any conservation plan prepared for it.[140] Protected areas are similarly managed in accordance with the relevant management principles and in accordance with the management plan prepared for them.[141] The management principles for protected wildlife include these:

- conservation of wildlife and the values of wildlife;
- the survival and natural development of wildlife in the wild;
- conservation of their biological diversity to the greatest possible extent;
- reduction or removal of the effects of threatening processes;
- conservation of their critical habitat to the greatest possible extent.[142]

131 *Nature Conservation Act* 1992 (Qld), section 4.
132 Ibid., section 9.
133 Ibid., schedule "protect."
134 Ibid., section 8(2)(d)(i).
135 Ibid., section 10(1).
136 Ibid., section 10(a) to (d).
137 Ibid., schedule "wildlife."
138 Ibid., section 83(1).
139 Ibid., section 84(1).
140 Ibid., sections 72(1) and 73.
141 Ibid., section 15.
142 Ibid., section 73(a).

The management principles in relation to protected areas vary in accordance with the purpose for which the area is declared a protected area. Let us take two examples: national parks and nature refuges. Although these management principles are principles in the sense that they incorporate values, they contain elements of objects or objectives, but not only that: in some respects, they are expressed as outcomes of a process. Thus, a national park is to be managed:

- to provide to the greatest possible extent for the permanent preservation of the area's natural condition and the protection of the area's cultural resources and values;
- to present the area's cultural and natural resources and their values;
- to ensure that the only use of the area is nature-based and ecologically sustainable.[143]

It is, however, specifically provided that it is the first of these three that is taken to be "the cardinal principle" for the management of national parks. This gives it significance over and above the other two, but clearly it does not render the other two irrelevant.[144]

Nature refuges are particularly important because they may include within them private land. Although the creation of a nature refuge involving private land may be achieved with the agreement of the owner of the land,[145] there is nevertheless provision for compulsory declaration of a nature refuge.[146] This may be done only if the opinion is formed that the area is, or includes, an area of major interest or a critical habitat.[147] An area of major interest is one that contains natural resources of significant nature conservation value[148] and critical habitat is a habitat essential for the conservation of a viable population of protected wildlife or a community of native wildlife.[149] A provision is made in any case for the payment of compensation for any injurious affection suffered by the owner of the land.[150] Once a nature refuge has been established, it is managed in accordance with these principles:

- to conserve the area's significant natural resources;
- to provide for the controlled use of the area's natural resources;
- to provide for the interests of landholders to be taken into account.[151]

The management of protected areas and protected wildlife is supported by the regulatory regime that allows for its enforcement. This system of regulation is based on a series of prohibitions. It is thus unlawful:

- to take, use, keep, or interfere with a cultural or natural resource of a protected area;[152]
- to take, use, or keep a protected animal;[153]
- to take a protected plant.[154]

These restrictions do not apply if the activity is authorised in one way or another, for example, in accordance with any conservation agreement, a relevant conservation plan, a lease, a permit or some other kind of authority. Failure to comply with this set of rules opens the way for administrative, civil or criminal proceedings. Thus, an

143 Ibid., section 17(1).
144 Ibid., section 17(2).
145 Ibid., section 45.
146 Ibid., section 49.
147 Ibid., section 49(1) (b).
148 Ibid., schedule "area of major interest."
149 Ibid., section 13(1).
150 Ibid., section 67.
151 Ibid., section 22.
152 Ibid., section 62.
153 Ibid., section 88.
154 Ibid., section 89.

interim conservation order may be made by the relevant minister,[155] an enforcement order granted by the court on the application of any person,[156] or a prosecution brought for the commission of a criminal offence.[157]

8.3.3 The *Lizard Island* Case

These enforcement proceedings seek to ensure compliance by those responsible for unlawful activities affecting nature and biodiversity. Are those responsible for administering and implementing the regime for the conservation of nature subject to judicial supervision? In principle, administrative decisions are subject to judicial review in the normal way. It is essential, of course, to identify an issue that is for this purpose justiciable. The issue in the *Lizard Island* case[158] was whether there had been compliance with the principles for managing a national park. It involved the cardinal principle stated in the set of statutory arrangements for managing national parks which have now been replaced by those in the *Nature Conservation Act* 1992 (Qld). The relevant provision stated:

> The cardinal principle to be observed in the management of national parks shall be the permanent preservation, to the greatest possible extent, of their natural condition and the director shall exercise his powers under this Act in such manner as appears to him most appropriate to achieve this objective.

The second part of this provision places a duty on the director to exercise powers in a particular way. Although there is an element of discretion in how these powers are to be exercised, actually they are clearly linked to the achievement of the objective of the Act. This presumably is the permanent preservation to the greatest possible extent of the natural condition of national parks.

In this case, the director had granted an application for approval to construct buildings on land in a national park. The applicant already held a lease of the land, which authorised the construction of buildings. The question for the court was whether the director had adopted the methodology of decision making indicated by this provision. The director had approached the application by asking the question whether permission could be reasonably withheld. The implication of this methodology was the existence of a presumption in favour of granting the application. The court decided that the director had adopted the wrong approach. It was indicated what the appropriate approach should have been:

> The correct question was what was the most appropriate way of achieving the objective of the permanent preservation, to the greatest possible extent, of the natural condition of the park having regard to all the circumstances including the existence of the sublease for tourist and recreational facilities; whether it was by refusing permission to construct the buildings or to grant it subject to conditions or, as seems most unlikely, to grant it unconditionally.[159]

In this case, the court did little more than state the terms of the enactment without further explication of its meaning. In other words, the court did not discuss the principles to be observed, a duty to exercise powers in a particular way, the achievement of the

[155] Ibid., section 102.
[156] Ibid., sections 173D and 173F.
[157] Ibid., sections 164 and 165.
[158] *Cape York Land Council Aboriginal Corporation v. Boyland* (2000) Queensland Court of Appeal 202.
[159] Ibid. at para 16.

objective of the Act or, indeed, the status of a cardinal principle compared with any other kind of principle. Nevertheless, the approach of the court is important. On the face of it, the provision in question could be taken to have conferred on the director considerable discretion – perhaps unlimited discretion – in responding to an application. Arguably words such as principle, power, and objective would have supported this conclusion. The court, however, did not do so. The court identified a justiciable issue and then an enforceable duty out of the textual language of the relevant provision of the Act. So, on the face of it, what might have been perceived to be a paralegal rule incorporated in the legislation turned out to be something much more in the nature of a legal rule and, hence, enforceable.

8.3.4 The Environmental Protection Act

Let us turn now to the contribution that the *Environmental Protection Act* 1994 (Qld) may make to the conservation of biodiversity. The object of the Act is to protect Queensland's environment while allowing for development that improves the total quality of life, both now and in the future, in a way that maintains the ecological processes on which life depends.[160] In other words, it is a form of ecologically sustainable development. It is, however, the concept of environment that makes biodiversity as a value relevant to the purpose of this Act. The interpretation of environment includes not only ecosystems and their constituent parts but, more particularly, the quality and characteristics of locations, places, and areas that contribute to their biological diversity and integrity.[161] The focus of the Act is the protection of the environment in accordance with the system of regulation created by it. Although there are management functions created by the Act, it is the function of regulation that dominates. This requires an approval in one form or another of an environmentally relevant activity.[162] In other words, the principal regulatory technique for protecting the environment is the prevention of environmental harm.

Environmental harm is any adverse effect or potential adverse effect on an environmental value.[163] An environmental value is a quality or physical characteristic of the environment that is conducive – among others – to ecological health.[164] The environment includes – certainly by implication – nature and biodiversity of nature. When this is translated into an environmental value, it is biodiversity as a value that emerges as a quality or physical characteristic of the environment conducive to ecological health. It would be therefore difficult to deny that biological diversity, as a component of the environment, is a value that the legislation protects from activities that constitute unlawful environmental harm.

Environmental harm becomes unlawful when an act or omission, for which a person is responsible, causes serious or material environmental harm or an environmental nuisance.[165] There are, therefore, two elements that comprise the concept of unlawful environmental harm. There must be an act or an omission for which a person is responsible and there must be harm to the environment that is serious, material, or an environmental nuisance within the meanings given to these words.[166] The focus of the

160 *Environmental Protection Act* 1994 (Qld), section 3.
161 Ibid., section 8.
162 Ibid., sections 426 and 427.
163 Ibid., section 14(1).
164 Ibid., section 8(a).
165 Ibid., section 436.
166 Ibid., sections 15 to 17.

Act is on the effect or the consequence – the harm to the environment – brought about by the activity of the person in question.

The Act contains a range of mechanisms for ensuring compliance with these obligations. These are, as one would expect, a range of administrative, civil and criminal proceedings. Significantly, civil proceedings for an order to remedy or restrain an offence or a threatened offence may be brought not only by someone whose interests are affected but also by someone else with the leave of the court, even although the person does not have a proprietary, material, financial, or special interest in the subject matter of the proceedings.[167]

The *Environmental Protection Act* 1994 (Qld) contains two potentially significant sets of obligations. Unlike the negative duty, already discussed, not to engage in activities that bring about unlawful environmental harm, there are two much more positive duties contained in the Act. One is the general environmental duty.[168] Thus, a person is under a duty to take all reasonable and practicable measures to prevent or minimise environmental harm caused by, or likely to be caused by, any activity for which this person is responsible. Although a breach of this duty does not give rise to a civil right or remedy,[169] it may give rise to the making of an environmental protection order.[170] This duty is directed at those actually engaging in activities that are likely to cause environmental harm. For this purpose, the outcome does not necessarily have to be unlawful environmental harm in the sense already discussed. In addition, from the reverse point of view, compliance with this general environmental duty is a defence to a claim that an activity has caused unlawful environmental harm.

Then there is the obligation created by section 5 of the Act that provides:

> If, under this Act, a function or power is conferred on a person, the person must perform the function or exercise the power in the way that best achieves the object of this Act.

This is a duty of a rather unusual type. Although it relates to the performance of functions and the exercise of powers under the Act, this does not necessarily exclude any impact on the way which activities regulated by the Act are undertaken. For example, if a person holds an environmental authority to engage in an activity which would otherwise cause unlawful environmental harm, a failure to exercise this power in accordance either with the Act or with the environmental authority itself might either amount to a breach of this duty or perhaps even a breach of the duty not to engage in an activity that causes unlawful environmental harm.

8.3.5 The *Maroochy* Case

The decision in the *Maroochy Shire Council* case[171] demonstrates some of these points. An application was made for an order to restrain an offence against the Act. Timber was allegedly being harvested without a development permit and in a way that caused unlawful environmental harm. The relationship between the duty not to cause unlawful environmental harm and the general environmental duty to take reasonable and

[167] Ibid., section 505.
[168] Ibid., section 319.
[169] Ibid., section 24(3).
[170] Ibid., section 358(d).
[171] *Maroochy Shire Council v. Barnes* (2001) Queensland Planning and Environmental Law Reports 475.

practicable measures to prevent it was explained as simply and clearly as possible in these words:

> An activity which causes serious or a material environmental harm does not constitute an offence of unlawfully causing that harm provided the activity was otherwise lawful and the person engaged in the activity took all reasonable and practicable measures to prevent or minimise the harm.[172]

In this case, the harvesting of the timber was not lawful in the absence of a development permit. But, in addition, all reasonable and practicable measures to prevent or minimise the harm had not been taken. Consequently, if the harvesting of the timber caused serious or material environmental harm, then this activity might be unlawful. Was it unlawful in the circumstances of this case? The court concluded that there was ample evidence that material environmental harm had been done.[173] But was it unlawful material environmental harm? Even if the harvesting of the timber was a lawful activity – which it was not – then it was argued:

> The only aspects of activity which may amount to a failure to take all reasonable and practicable measures to prevent or minimise environmental harm is the felling of trees in an unnecessarily criss-cross manner thereby failing to minimise unnecessary damage to smaller vegetation and the evident intention to not leave sufficient habitat and recruitment time for wildlife.[174]

In effect, therefore, the way in which the timber was harvested constituted unlawful environmental harm. The unacceptable and therefore illegal aspect of the activity was not the activity itself but the unnecessary damage to small vegetation and insufficient habitat and recruitment time for wildlife.

In this case, the court did not rely on the obligation in section 5, linked to the achievement of the object of the Act. However, it is suggested that this duty would have supported the methodology adopted by the court in this case. The reason is simply this: the duty is placed on all persons performing functions or exercising powers under the Act. On the face of it, this includes the court. This then renders relevant, if not mandatory, a consideration of the ways and means by which the object of the Act is best achieved. At the very least, this paralegal rule supports an interpretation of the relevant provisions in a way that achieves, rather than thwarts, the achievement of the object of the Act. Because the object of the Act is the protection of the environment, an interpretation and application of the Act that is at least consistent rather than inconsistent with that object, is to be preferred.

9 CONCLUSION

The enforcement of duties imposed by the law has traditionally been the means by which correlative rights are recognised and assured. For the most part, duties such as these have been imposed on individuals or organisations endowed with what may loosely be described as a private right or interest. The public right or interest, on the other hand, has traditionally been assured by the performance of functions rather than the discharge of duties. However, the performance of functions in the public interest has

[172] Ibid. at 478.
[173] Ibid. at 483.
[174] Ibid. at 483.

been increasingly constrained within the legal system by statements about purposes, objects, and principles.

The approach of the legal system to the conservation of biodiversity reflects this emerging approach. Individuals and organisations seek protection of their private rights and interests. The collective interest in the conservation of biodiversity is assured by the performance of functions in the public or collective interest, in accordance with these relevant statements about purposes, objects, and principles. The emphasis of the international legal regime tends to be on these statements, while the emphasis in national legal regimes continues to be for the most part on the enforcement of duties. In other words, the balance set by the legal system between legal rules and paralegal rules has increasingly attracted the attention not only of the international community and of national legislatures but also of the courts at international, regional, and national levels. The examples considered in the foregoing paragraphs suggest an increasingly close relationship between these two sets of rules.

This is perhaps one way to address the fundamental issue identified by Judge Weeramantry:

> An important conceptual problem arises when, in such a dispute *inter partes*, an issue arises regarding an alleged violation of rights or duties in relation to the rest of the world. The court, in the discharge of its traditional duty of deciding *between the parties*, makes the decision which is in accordance with justice and fairness *between the parties*. The procedure it follows is largely adversarial. Yet this scarcely does justice to rights and obligations of an *erga omnes* character – least of all in cases involving environmental damage of a far-reaching and irreversible nature.[175]

His Honour concluded with remarks applicable to national as well as international systems:

> We have entered an era of international law in which international law subserves not only the interests of individual states, but looks beyond them and their parochial concerns to the greater interests of humanity and planetary welfare. In addressing such problems, which transcend the individual rights and obligations of the litigating States, international law will need to look beyond procedural rules fashioned for purely *inter partes* litigation.[176]

[175] *Judgment in the case concerning the Gabcikovo-Nagymaros Project* (1998) 37 *International Legal Materials 162*, at 216.
[176] Ibid. at 216.

7 Future Directions in Conservation of Biological Diversity: An Interdisciplinary Approach

Abdul Haseeb Ansari*

1 INTRODUCTION

The biodiversity of the world is a precious gift from God to humans. All living and nonliving constituents of it have been created by Him for our benefits. They are a continuous source of knowledge and immensely valuable, especially in maintaining ecological balance, in fulfilling the food and medicinal needs of humankind, and in generating plentiful financial resources.[1] Such benefits can be sustained for all generations to come only when they are used moderately and in a sustainable way. On the contrary, relentless egotistical and wasteful use of various components of biological diversity and unwarranted transboundary movements of plant and animal species have contributed to virtual ecological destruction, with many plant and animal species having already vanished. If the prevailing activities are not reversed, many more that are at the verge of extinction will go into oblivion in the near future.[2] In addition to the economic and social loss to humanity, depletion of various plant and animal species has caused a long-lasting and in certain areas, irreversible loss to biodiversity and to scientific endeavors based on it. This depletion is also responsible for ecological imbalance.[3]

These problems began to be addressed in 1992 at the United Nations Conference on Environment and Development (UNCED), popularly known as the Rio Conference. The 1992 UN Convention on Biological Diversity (CBD)[4] was signed by a large number of states that had participated at the UNCED, including Malaysia. The CBD is an umbrella convention having some basic treaty norms that provides for conservation of biodiversity by member states. This convention is operative along with conservation strategies stated in Agenda 21, the rules of sustainable management of forests developed by the International Tropical Timber Organization (ITTO), the treaty norms of the Convention on Wetlands of International Importance especially as Waterfowl Habitat

[1] See UNDP, *Conserving Indigenous Knowledge: Integrating Two Systems of Innovation* (New York, 1994), 5–9.

[2] See T. Dobson, "The Loss of Biodiversity: An International Environmental Policy Perspective" (1992) 17 *North Carolina Journal of International Law and Commercial Regulations* 34; Esther Tan, "Dire Need to Conserve Natural Resources," *New Sunday Times*, 27 December 1998.

[3] See M. Chandler, "The Biodiversity Convention: Selected Issues of Interest to the International Lawyer" (1993) 4 *Columbian Journal of International Environmental Law and Policy* 142; A. H. Ansari & Parveen Jamal, "The Convention on Biological Diversity: A Critical Appraisal with Special Reference to Malaysia" (2000) 40 *Indian Journal of International Law* 138–177.

[4] See the text at http://www.biodiversity.org/convention/articles.asp.

* Abdul Haseeb Ansari, B. Sc., LL. M., PhD, is Professor, AIKOL, International Islamic University, Malaysia. ahaseeb@iiu.edu.my.

(Ramsar Convention)[5] made for conservation of wetlands of the world, the treaty norms of the Convention on International Trade in Endangered Species (CITES),[6] rules contained in the Forest Principles, the Precautionary Principle, and other international legal rules. In order to achieve effective conservation of biodiversity there has to be meaningful and relevant international cooperation. From the CBD, many sociolegal and scientific questions have arisen that are agitating intellectuals in relevant disciplines, who are making concerted and relentless efforts to meet the social, environmental, and scientific challenges posed by these issues.

Conservation of biological diversity is the basic requirement for biotechnological research, because biological diversity provides the necessary genetic material.[7] Loss of biodiversity means loss of genetic materials. At this point, we have three important tasks: first, conserving biological diversity, second, conducting biotechnological research that provides the food and medicinal needs of the growing population; and third, achieving safe biotechnology outcomes. To deal with the later, the Biosafety Protocol, commonly known as the Cartagena Protocol, was negotiated.[8] Unfortunately, this protocol can serve only a limited purpose. Although the six-year-long moratorium by the European Union on the import of genetically modified food has been lifted,[9] a large number of people in Europe and elsewhere, including the United States,[10] do not have confidence in the use of genetically modified living organisms (GMOs) and food containing genetically modified stuffs (GM food).[11] They are demanding the application of the "precautionary principle"[12] in this matter and proper labelling

[5] See the text at http://www.ramsar.org/key˙conv˙e.htm.

[6] See the text at http://www.cites.org/eng/disc/text.shtml.

[7] The phenomenon that is bothering scientists is fast depletion of plants and animal species. Their depletion means erosion of genetic materials. According to a conservative estimate, by the year 2100, twelve hundred species of birds will disappear. This will affect cross-pollination and many plant species will vanish. For example, with the decline of vultures in India, the populations of dogs and rats have exploded; with the result of that, thirty thousand of the world's thirty-five thousand rabies deaths took place in India. See *New Straits Times*, 15 December 2004.

[8] Cartagena Protocol on Biosafety. It has come into force on 11 September 2003. As of 8 June 2005, it has received 119 members, including Malaysia. See the full text at http://www.biodiv.org/biosafety/protocol.asp.

[9] It can be noted that the EU has lifted the import ban from the genetically modified corn.

[10] See, for the contrary view, Harry Cline, "U. S. consumers unconcerned about biotech crops' food." Available at: http://www.KeepMedia.com. Accessed on 16 April 2005.

[11] People in the European Union, G-77 countries, and some international NGOs have voiced concern about the known and unknown impacts of GMOs on human health and on the environment. Some of these concerns include the following: (1) corruption of the natural gene pool through unintended cross-pollination and gene transfer; (2) harm to biodiversity and the possibility of a negative impact on the susceptibility of crops to pest or disease outbreaks from increased gene uniformity; (3) disruption of the ecosystem balance by excessive population growth and altered competition patterns; (4) unintended toxicity to animals or insects, which may in turn induce the evolution of "super-pests" that develop a resistance to the genetically engineered toxicity; and (5) health risks to consumers. Unfortunately, these are given more importance over the following beneficial aspects of GM Food: (1) increased crop yield and nutritional value of crops, which in turn improves food supply and food security; (2) a reduction in amount of pesticides; and (3) a multitude of benefits to the mankind and development of pharmaceuticals. See The World Bank Group's Environment and International Law, "Biosafety" at http://www.4.worldbank.org/legal/legen/legen-biosafety.html.

[12] Principle 15 of the Rio Declaration 1992 defines it as: "where there are threats of serious or irreversible damage, lack of full scientific certainty shall not be used as reason for postponing cost-effective measures to prevent environmental degradation." For other definitions, see Abdul Haseeb Ansari & Parveen Jamal, "Meaning, Scope and Implementation of Precautionary Principle: A Critical Appraisal" (2003), *Indian Journal of International Law*, 43, at. 625. People do not have confidence about the genetically modified food because there is no guarantee that its use will be safe.

under their right to information.[13] The Trade Related Intellectual Property Rights (TRIPS)[14] has been negotiated to protect all kinds of scientific inventions, including breakthroughs in the area of biotechnology.[15] But this international legal instrument serves the purposes of the developed countries that generally conduct research. The vested interests of developing countries and underdeveloped countries, along with poor residents of these countries, which supply genetic materials for research, are deprived of the benefits and will remain deprived unless there is equitable distribution of scientific and financial benefits from scientific research conducted on the genetic materials obtained from developing countries, and unless developing countries reform their existing patenting legislations and make appropriate laws to give effect to "geographical indications."[16]

This chapter examines some of the issues and problem areas stated here so that our future conservation strategies and biotechnology research serve humanity in the best possible way.

2 CONSERVATION IMPERATIVES AND BIODIVERSITY

The CBD does not define the word "conservation," but it generally means preventing the species from loss, waste, or change. Conservation of biodiversity also demands preventing habitats from destruction or degradation. In practice, the conservation of allelic diversity cannot succeed unless the geneticist knows which individual animal/plant belongs to what species or to which population within species; and who, within each population, is related to whom. So as to have an easily accessible record, there should be a database of plant and animal species. This will help modern conservation geneticists know who is related to whom, who belongs to what population and species just by looking at the plants and animals that exist in a particular area. It is for this reason that the convention requires member states to conduct the basic research first, and puts an obligation on them to adopt sufficient strategies towards conservation of the existing biodiversity of the world.[17]

Conservation options range over a wide array of techniques, from species management programmes in the wild to offside protection in biotic gardens, zoos, genebanks, and aquaria. An integrated approach to conservation – one that utilizes the

[13] For this reason, the biotechnology research in the area of "biotech food" is slow. Biotech companies are scared that in case of nonacceptance of certain genetically modified food by the public around the world, the money invested on the research will be sheer wastage. Many countries, for this reason, are also scared. They do not want to invest in this area of biotechnology. Thus, some 99 percent of genetically modified crops are grown in six countries – the United States, Canada, Brazil, China, Mexico, and South Africa; and virtually all the worldwide acreage is devoted to only four crops: soybean, corn, cotton, and canola. See Andrew Pollack, "Narrow range for new biotech food crop," *New York Times*, 22 May 2004. Reprinted in *New Sunday Times*, 23 May 2004.

[14] See the text at http://www.wto.org/english/tratap_e/trips_e.htm.

[15] This is notable here that Article 16(5) of the Convention imposes an obligation on the parties to cooperate in ensuring that intellectual property rights are supportive of and not run counter to the objective of the Convention.

[16] We know the stories of patenting *Basmati* rice and pesticide manufactured from *Neem* tree. Indian efforts are notable. This may be noted here that in order to bring the state patenting laws in line with international law, countries are amending their domestic legislation. India is one of the examples. This also may be noted here that many are opposing this trend. They believe that the changes will hinder providing cheap medicines and vaccines to poor countries.

[17] This can be inferred on the basis of Articles 7 and 12 of the CBD. See Note 4.

entire range of techniques – is a cornerstone of diversity conservation. *Ex-situ* conservation is required where a species has suffered badly. This would apply to tigers in India, orangutans in Malaysia, and pandas in China. This kind of conservation technique may not yield the desired results where the provided habitat is not congenial and conservationists lack knowledge or are negligent.[18] The best example of a successful conservation exercise is the rice gene bank established by the International Rice Research Institute (IRRI) of the Philippines. A host of gene banks of medicinal plants in China and India are yet other examples. The IRRI provided indigenous varieties of rice when needed by Cambodian scientists and were not locally available.[19]

Biodiversity refers to the variability among living organisms from all sources, including terrestrial, marine, and other aquatic ecosystems, and the ecological complexes of which they are part. This includes diversity within species (genetic diversity), between species, and of ecosystems. It is estimated that there are about fourteen million plant and animal species of which only 1,750,000 are known to science.[20] Along with social and economic services, these diverse species contribute to a wide array of environmental services. These services, in turn, are socially and economically beneficial. Human health and well-being is directly dependent on biodiversity, as 10 percent of top-selling drugs are derived from natural resources.[21] Likewise, biodiversity also provides genetic resources[22] for genetic research in the area of agriculture and medicine.[23]

Among all kinds of ecosystems, tropical forest ecosystems and ecosystems of wetlands and mangrove forests[24] are the most species-rich. These are known as hot spots of biodiversity. Although they cover less than 10 percent of the world's land area, they have about 90 percent of the world's species. Thus, from the point of view of conservation of biodiversity, it is crucial to conserve the forests of the world, including tropical forests. As an umbrella convention, the CBD discusses conservation generally and emphasizes identification and monitoring of biological diversity, and its sustainable use. In order to achieve this, the convention emphasizes technology transfer between, and enhancing the conservation capabilities of, all states. It should be noted that one of the main purposes of conservation of forests and the animal species that inhabit them is to prepare a strategy that helps in conserving all kinds of plant and animal species together. Conservationists must know all the species of an area that are to be conserved. To achieve this objective, scientists must prepare an exhaustive inventory of all the species, plants, and animals.

[18] It is said on the basis of the deaths of rhinos in Malaysia and tigers in India at conservation centers. See Loretta Ann Soosayraj, "Rhinos in Peril," *New Straits Times*, 13 November 2003; *Times of India*, 23 March 2004.

[19] The IRRI acts as a custodian of genes. Without the consent of the state to which varieties belong, there cannot be exports. Once some of the Thai rice species were exported to the United States, the Thai government objected to it on this ground and the IRRI had to ensure the safe use of the exported rice species. See *New Straits Times*, 14 December 2004.

[20] See UNEP – WCMC (2000) 34–65; M. K. Tolba, "Conserving Species, Population and Genetic Diversity," in M. K. Tolba, ed., *Global Diversity* (WRI, IUCN and UNEP, 1992), 133–36.

[21] See 2002 Global Environmental Outlook – 3. See the full text at http://www.unep.org/GEP/geo3/english/pd.htm-14.

[22] It can be a single living cell or a group of cells or body part.

[23] Genetic materials are generally obtained form the biodiversity-rich areas, for example, hot spots of tropical forests.

[24] Mangrove forests have rich plants and animal species because they are congenial breeding places for many aquatic and amphibian animal species.

This job is comparatively easier in a country such as Singapore, which is small in area, or in the Gulf States, which do not have rich terrestrial biodiversity. But the task for a country such as Malaysia[25] is arduous, intricate, and time-consuming. The job can be more easily accomplished if we take into consideration the following:

1. Inventories should be prepared by area. For this purpose, scientists, according to scientific expediency, should divide the whole forest area into various sectors.
2. Sufficient experts and support staff are needed.
3. Sufficient availability of equipment is required.
4. More competent states should extend help to less capable states in terms of providing expertise, transfer of technology, transfer of financial resources, and training of local people.
5. The local government should extend all kinds of support.

Once an inventory is prepared, priority areas have to be determined. Once the priority areas are known, we can proceed further for conservation strategies, *ex-situ* and *in-situ*. Having a complete inventory is also crucial from the point of view of ecological balance.

Conservation of forests as such has been a matter of great concern because forests of the world are being depleted relentlessly. There is no global convention on forests. At the Rio Conference, Forest Principles were adopted. The Forest Principles read with the relevant provisions of Agenda 21 and the CBD, provide that conservation of forests and animal species inhabiting them should be a priority area.[26]

For obvious reasons, the global community has given special attention to conserving tropical forests.[27] Towards this end, the International Tropical Timber Organization (ITTO), which has been established under the International Tropical Timber Agreement (ITTA), is making constructive endeavors. It has developed certain principles for sustainable management of tropical forests and provides logistical and financial support to the tropical timber producing member countries to adopt them. December 2000 was the target, but only Malaysia is very close to the target.[28]

Conserving mangrove forests also should be a priority area. Efforts are being made around the world to save them and to enhance the mangrove forest areas by various means, including plantations.[29] Countries are striving hard to protect them.

[25] This is because Malaysia is one of the twelve megabiodiversity countries of the world. It is estimated that it has 15,000 species of plants and 4,000 of fish species and 150,000 different insects and invertebrates. This has been revealed by the Secretary General of the Ministry of Natural Resources and Environment at the Five-Day International Conference on Biodiversity: Science and Governance, 25–30 January 2005, Kuala Lumpur, Malaysia, has decided to prepare a complete inventory of all plants and animal species of the country and the job has been entrusted by the National Biodiversity Council, which is headed by the prime minister of the country, to the Forest Research Institute Malaysia (FRIM). See *The Star*, 25 January 2005.

[26] It is notable here that at the Rio Conference, developing forest-rich countries opposed the proposal to have a global convention on forest for sovereignty reasons. Now those developing countries, including Malaysia, support the idea of a global convention on all forests of the world, but developed countries are opposing it for unknown reasons.

[27] Among other environmental services rendered by forests, it is significant that forests are sinks for absorbing CO_2.

[28] See Abdul Haseeb Ansari, "Legal Issues in Forest Management in India and Malaysia: A Critical Appraisal," *Malayan Law Journal*, (2004) 2 MLJ i–xcvi.

[29] Although plantation mangrove forests, like other plantation forests, cannot have a rich biodiversity, it will render many environmental services and will protect the area from harsh sea currents.

International bodies are also playing a constructive role in this area. A United Nations link initiative to fund projects on conservation and sustainable use of mangroves is significant among them. The Global Environment Facility (GEF) under its Small Grants Programme (SGP) is calling on local nongovernmental organizations (NGOs) and community-based bodies in various countries to undertake mangrove conservation programmes.[30] The work of the SGP towards conservation of mangroves is significantly positive. The author feels that, in view of the recent tsunami, its efforts towards conservation of mangrove forests should be intensified because they can act as a shield to protect coastlines. The programme should diversify its efforts in conserving coral reefs, too.[31] This suggestion gets strength in the aftermath of the recent tsunami.[32] In fact, resuscitation of coral reefs in seriously devastated areas should be given priority. Transplantation is one of the viable choices to bring the destroyed coral reefs back, but only a few coral reefs can be transplanted; sensitive corals such as brain corals grow very slowly. They take hundreds of years to take their normal shape. Another hurdle in coral transplantation is that they cannot survive in different environmental conditions. So, while transplanting a type of coral, it has to be determined whether that type of coral is found in that particular area or not.[33] Artificial corals can be used for beautifying the place or to provide a breeding place for some animal species, but they cannot be a replacement for the natural coral reefs. Joint and concerted efforts of international bodies, NGOs, and states could restore coral reefs, if not fully, at least partially. Scientists also can play a constructive role in the conservation of mangrove forests and coral reefs by making innovations in the area of developing better quality of trees and reefs that grow faster and are able to face adverse environmental conditions.[34] It is advisable here that an integrated approach would be more useful. Community-based strategies are also appropriate, provided communities are involved with conservation activities and benefit from them.[35]

[30] It is notable that since 1992, SGP financially supports activities of nongovernmental organizations and community-based organizations in developing countries towards climate change abatement, conservation of biodiversity, and protection of international waters. Other projects include reduction of the impact of persistent organic pollutants and prevention of land degradation while generating sustainable livelihood. Funded by the GEF as a corporate programme, SGP is implemented by the United Nations Development Programme (UNDP), the World Bank and the United Nations Environment Programme (UNEP). For the activities of the SGP towards protecting the mangrove forests see, Marina Emmanuel, "Funding to Save Mangroves," *New Straits Times*, 14 January 2005.

[31] If seashores are densely covered with mangrove forests, the thrust of sea waves will ease, however strong they are. In the areas where mangroves could put strong barriers to the recent tsunami waves, the water could not cause serious damage. It is, therefore, unfortunate that mangrove forests are depleting fast. See Marina Emmanuel and Elizabeth John, "More than Mere Trees," *New Straits Times*, 16 January 2005. Also see "Mangroves Can Help Reduce Damage Greatly," *New Straits Times*, 8 January 2005.

[32] Tsunami has badly affected coral reefs of the affected areas. In some areas, their destruction seems to be irreversible. However, a concerted and combined effort could reverse the situation.

[33] See Deborah Loh, "Expert: Coral Transplant Not Viable," *New Straits Times*, 30 September 2004.

[34] This should be noted here that coral reefs have some kind of protective quoting on them. Slight rise of temperature and abnormal waves can easily erode them. This becomes a means of destruction to them. Efforts, therefore, should be made by scientists to develop varieties that could withstand rises of temperature and abnormally fast currents.

[35] The examples of community-based programmes of South Africa pertaining to certain animal species are notable. Likewise, community-based reforestation programme in the Himalayas have proved to be very successful. If communities are involved in growing trees that grows fast and provide useful timber, or in growing fruit trees or trees of medicinal or commercial importance, like eucalyptus trees, sandal wood tree, and agar wood tree, they will take an interest in conservation efforts. For that matter, scientists can develop certain varieties of trees that are more productive with less effort in growing them.

It is worth noticing here that most states do not have specific legislation to protect these two valuable natural resources. It is, therefore, suggested that coastal states should enact, on a priority basis, appropriate central legislation that aptly protects them and helps in conserving them. If there is any constitutional hurdle in enacting the law, it should be cleared.[36] The law should reflect the basic conservation principles specified in a national plan for conservation in general, and protecting sensitive areas of biodiversity specifically. Malaysia, for example, has prepared under the auspices of the National Physical Council, headed by the prime minister of the country, a National Physical Plan in the wake of findings that mangroves and wetland have shrunk by 23 percent. The plan protects certain mangrove forests and swamp areas in various states that are environmentally sensitive and important from the point of view of biodiversity. The plan provides a macro-framework for systematic and balanced development and protection of the environment. It is now high time for Malaysia to have central legislation for conservation of mangroves, swamps, and coral reefs.[37]

In addition to what governments are doing for conservation of forests, in these countries, scientists should make efforts to develop certain species of trees that can grow faster even in adverse weather conditions. Some species, including those developed by the Forest Research Institute Malaysia, for example, have proved to be very useful in reforestation, but there is a need to do more in this area.[38] Scientists in developed countries, through collaboration, could play a significant role. For this purpose, scientists in the developed world should collaborate with developing countries in order to test these new species in the climatic conditions of the developing countries. It is now easier because this kind of biotechnology research is among the priorities of developing countries, especially of tropical countries as they have rich genetic resources and are hopeful to be among the front-runners in the biotechnology era. It should be noted that although plantation forests cannot be as rich in respect to biodiversity as virgin forests, they can serve environmental purposes to a certain extent.

Research has identified logging activities that are carried out with the least wastage of biodiversity and with rapid reforestation. It is necessary to do further research in this area. Almost all forest-rich countries have the requirement of mandatory environmental

Community-based programmes can be helpful in conservation also, because in that case, local inhabitants consider themselves as one of the beneficiaries. In South Africa, forest inhabitants because of benefit-sharing of commercialization of certain animal species, help fight against poachers.

[36] It should be noted here that for enacting a central law, forests should be made a central subject. For example, in India, initially, forest was a state subject. It created problems in enforcing central policies on forests of the country. Forest was made a subject of the concurrent list of the seventh schedule of the constitution. Thus, the central government enacted a law, which could put a control on the act of deforestation done on logging permits issued by the state governments and the relentless acts of the states converting forests to nonforest uses. Now, such conversions can take place only on the permission of the central government. In Malaysia, the federal government can legislate in state matters for sake of uniformity of law, but the law will be operative only when the states ratify it in state assemblies. If law made by the federal government is not acceptable to states, the law will have no effect. The country has experience difficulties in acceptance of the amendment of the National Forestry Act 1984, which enhanced penalties for illegal logging from two years' imprisonment to twenty years' imprisonment. States found it very stringent measure and showed hesitation in accepting it. Stets accepted it only on persuasion by the federal government. See Abdul Haseeb Ansari, Note 28 in this chapter, at xxx–xxxv.

[37] See Zubaidah Abu Baker, "Green Muscle (National Physical Plan Will Protect Environmental Sensitive Areas), *New Straits Times*, 26 January 2005.

[38] Similar efforts in other countries are also being made, but the efforts are not praiseworthy.

impact assessments (EIA) carried out when forest areas are to be cleared. The mechanism seems to be workable, but most of the countries have enforcement problems. It is, therefore, suggested that the area for which the EIA is mandatory should be small enough so as to be manageable for the enforcement officers. All EIAs should be done honestly by a group of experts and there should be public consultation. This has to be followed by a competent and honestly carried out auditing process, both internal and external.[39]

So as to ensure that the timber has been extracted from an area that can bear the adverse effects of logging, certification/labelling, has to be done by a competent agency with enough experts. In the process of certification/labelling the help of indigenous experts is critical. Presently, most of the tropical countries, including Malaysia, are taking help from foreign experts so that the credibility of certified timber exported from these countries is not doubted. For the time being it is fine, but in the long term these countries should have their own experts. Developed countries should properly train them if possible. The process of certification/labelling in tropical countries should be carried out under the supervision of the ITTO. This is necessary for meeting the demand for tropical timber in timber-importing countries.[40]

For conservation and sustainable use and utilization of all kinds of biological resources, biotechnology research must stick to the following:

1. Growing and breeding more on a sustainable basis within the available facilities.
2. Producing species that can withstand adverse weather conditions.
3. Producing species that are not easily affected by pests or prone to common diseases.
4. Using technologies that do not generate unemployment.
5. Conserving plant and animal species of a particular area and enhancing other components of the ecosystem so that balance is not disturbed.
6. Rejecting genetically modified species that might prove harmful to the environment in general and human health specifically.[41]
7. Conducting research on genetically modified living organisms so that their harmful effects on plant, animal, and human health can be minimized.
8. Avoiding cloning even among animals unless critical for saving the animal species from becoming extinct.[42]

3 MOVEMENT OF GENETIC MATERIALS AND SCIENTIFIC RESEARCH BASED ON THEM

We have noted earlier that the countries of the southern hemisphere have very rich biodiversity. Generally speaking, genetic materials, whose mystery has not yet been fully revealed to local scientists, are taken by multinationals based in developed countries.

[39] On EIA in Malaysia, see Abdul Haseeb Ansari, Note 28 in this chapter, at xxxv–xlviii.

[40] Note 24 in this chapter, at xlix–li.

[41] We are aware of scientific research of *termination seeds*, plants that themselves produce pesticides, like genetically modified cotton. These and other similar research has caused more harm than benefit.

[42] Scientists have to keep themselves away from human cloning, both therapeutic and reproductive for various reasons, scientific and religious.

Based on them, valuable research is conducted, but monetary benefits derived from them are not equitably shared with the countries of origin of genetic materials and biopiracy is prevalent. To solve this problem, Article 15 of the CBD recognises sovereign rights of states to their natural resources, and their right to determine access of other states to them on a mutually agreed basis (informed consent). Hence, natural resources, including biological resources, cannot be viewed as a common heritage of mankind. The importance of sovereignty over biological resources has also been emphasized in the Forest Principles declared at the UNCED. It is important to mention here that Article 15 of the CBD and Principle 8 of the Forest Principles require the states to take measures with the aim of sharing, in a fair and equitable manner, the results of research and the benefits arising from commercial and other such utilization of the research outcome. This is such an important aspect of genetic research that in Agenda 21 it was conspicuously emphasized. In view of these provisions, what is initially required is to put a control on the exodus of genetic materials from biodiversity-rich countries. For this purpose, appropriate legislation on access and benefit-sharing (ABS) should fast be developed by the member states of the CBD so that the international norms may be given effect through local legislation. In the presence of such legislation, genetic materials can be taken out of the country only on the basis of a bilateral agreement or informed consent basis, and all kinds of biopiracy can be checked. The local legislation should be designed in such a manner that it becomes a potent instrument to regulate and protect biological resources from any kind of biopiracy, intellectual property rights, and ensures fair and equitable sharing of benefits from the use of the genetic resources taken out of the country.[43] Some experts predict that such a selfish attitude of biologically diverse countries will encourage smuggling of genetic materials.[44] Nevertheless, this possibility will be reduced if the importing country has political will and is ready to have transparency in the outcome of the research and its potential to generate money. In addition, an altruistic attitude is necessary on the part of biotechnology companies and individual scientists so that the scientific and financial benefits of biotechnology research are equitably shared. In the whole process, transparency of the research conducted on or with the help of imported genetic materials is the grey area. The author is of the opinion that to ensure benefit-sharing, the genetic material should move on a government-to-government basis under an appropriate locally legislated law. Any interested private sector should get the required material through the government where the company or firm, as the case may be, is registered, and the benefit-sharing should also be on this basis. The money received by the country that had supplied the genetic materials should be spent on conservation and enhancing such plants and animals specifically and other plants and animals in general. This will maintain the supply of genetic materials and will save the plant and animal species from becoming extinct. However, in the whole scenario, the importance of fair play in international biodiversity governance through the principle of access and benefit-sharing of the use of biological resources is of paramount importance.[45]

[43] See Santha Oorjitham, "Getting Biotech Off Ground," *New Straits Times*, 16 July 2004.

[44] Abdul Haseeb Ansari, "Free Trade Law and Environmental Law," (2001) 41 *Indian Journal of International Law* 1–43.

[45] The Prime Minister of Malaysia, while delivering his speech at the International Conference of Biodiversity: Science and Governance, Organized by the French Government and Sponsored by the UNESCO, 24–29 January 2005, Paris.

4 TECHNOLOGY PROBLEMS

The age of information and computer technology is reaching saturation. After this, comes the age of biotechnology. In the area of medicine, biotechnology has already yielded millions of dollars. It has tremendous potential in agricultural, medical, chemical, and other areas. Scientists are already venturing into these areas and have achieved notable success. Biotechnology is being considered as a necessity for the future world. For example, in developed countries in the coming decades the population will be stabilized; but it will continue to grow at the rate of 4 percent annually in developing and underdeveloped countries. The ever-growing population will need food and healthcare. Only biotechnology can ensure these. So, all countries, developed and developing, have to be ready, jointly and severally, to face the challenge. In the area of conservation of biodiversity and in order to fulfill the aspirations of the member states of the CBD, new species of plants will have to be developed, which can grow faster, even in adverse weather conditions, and cater to their financial, food, timber and environmental needs. Biotechnology has already shown some remarkable inventions in this area and there is tremendous potential to further develop this area of research. Developed countries lead developing countries in all the above-mentioned areas.[46] It is their responsibility to make their counterparts capable of facing the challenges.

Article 16 of the CBD *inter alia* provides for transfer of technology because conservation of biodiversity requires the application of technology, especially in the area of reproduction, remote sensing, and producing newer and newer species. Nevertheless, the fate of technology transfer for conserving the fast-dwindling species and in the area of biotechnology is not different than in other areas. This is because of the lack of sufficient political will on the part of developed countries. It becomes imperative to developing and less developed countries to progress in the relevant areas of technology as fast as they can and become self-sufficient. There should be a national biotechnology policy and enough financial and technological support for augmenting biotechnology in each country. Some such countries, including Singapore, India, China, and Malaysia, have realized this fact.[47] What is required for the scientists in these countries is to double their effort to acquire and apply knowledge. They should make all possible effort to acquire the latest knowledge independently or in collaboration with scientists and scientific institutions of developed countries. There is an appalling tendency that many scientists go to developed countries for higher studies and become part of the work force of that country. Such experts have revealed that their country cannot make use of their expertise; and even if there is such a possibility, facilities are not so lucrative. This type of attitude can be changed only if in addition to material benefit, scientists look at their moral responsibility and commitment towards their respective countries. States also should make efforts to entice them. Transfer of technology also has to be demanded. Developing states should press their demands and try to get as much as possible. They also should make an effort in collaborative research.

[46] See M. S. Swaminathan, "Biotechnology and Better Common Present: A Synthesis," in I. P. Getubig, V. L. Chopra, & M. S. Swaminathan, eds., *Biotechnology for Asian Agriculture* (Kuala Lumpur: Asia and Pacific Development Centre, 1991), 95.

[47] They have a biotechnology policy, and, to give effect to the policy, they are providing all kinds of support to biotechnology research. They are also making efforts to get back their scientists working overseas. India and China are ahead of many countries because they are growing genetically modified cotton and rice at a large scale. Other countries are trying to emulate them.

For Muslim countries, biotechnology research is no longer a taboo. The declaration of the 1998 Kuwait Conference, which was attended by a large number of Muslim scientists, has categorically affirmed that all kinds of genetic research excluding cloning are in conformity with Quran and *Sunnah* (*the practices of the messenger Mohammad*),[48] because all plants and animals have been created for the beneficial use of man. Better varieties of plants and animals will serve the human mass, present and future, in a better way. It will be in the interest of the general public (*maslaha*), provided they are safe and good (*halal* and *tayeb*). It was requested, therefore, by Muslim countries to provide all kinds of encouragement to this branch of knowledge. In view of this, in the United Nations, when a resolution to ban all kinds of cloning was introduced, Muslim countries took two years to decide on this issue. The author is of the opinion that gene manipulation for creating better quality of plants and animals will serve humanity in a better way and for a longer period. Gene manipulation should be a complement to the techniques of improving genes by cross-breeding. Presently, efforts should be made to make maximum use of existing genetic resources in conducting research in the area of pharmaceuticals and creating high-quality subsistence farming.[49] Because most of the Muslim countries are developing countries, scientists in these countries should also double their efforts in these areas. These areas have tremendous scope in tropical countries such as Malaysia, where a lot of plant species are yet to be explored and classified. The second priority should be to develop vaccines. This area is also within the reach of scientists in developing countries. This can easily be fostered in countries such as Malaysia, China, India, South Africa, the Philippines, and Brazil, which have sufficient resources and capable expertise. In this area, if possible, joint ventures among developing countries and developing and developed countries should be preferred.

What is required from all developing and less developed countries is to venture strongly into the area of biotechnology research and other areas that are important for the conservation of biodiversity with a priority in the area of agricultural biotechnology. Otherwise, they will have to depend on the West. This might become a kind of neocolonialism. We have the example of termination seeds scientifically developed by some companies in the West. It might happen that farmers in a country are enticed into using this kind of seed, because it gives more crops. This will have the result of wiping out indigenous species. Farmers will be forced to buy seeds from the company that has developed the termination seed. It will lead to total dependency on the West. We also know the story of cottonseeds. They have the ability to produce a kind of protein that kills pests. If, suppose in Pakistan, farmers totally depend on this variety of cotton because it does not require them to resort to spraying pesticides, then local varieties of cotton might vanish, and the farmers will become totally dependent on these GMOs. This might result in the loss of valuable biodiversity. This might also result in exploitation. So scientists in the developing world must caution local farmers about such danger

[48] The Fiqh Academy, Jeddah and Islamic Education, Science and Culture Organization, Kuwait jointly held the seminar on 13–15 October 1998. See http://www.Islamset.com. This is notable here that the traditional view that no change can be done in Allah's handiwork, which was pleaded on the basis of a Quranic verse (*ayah*), was considered to be a narrow interpretation of that *ayah*. According to the majority of participants of the seminar, genetic modifications for public interest can be made.

[49] There is notable research in the area of subsistence farming. One significant breakthrough of the British Scientists in March 2005 is the innovation of a variety of rice that contains vitamin A. This will protect a large number of children of poor countries who become blind because of a lack of vitamin A.

and must concentrate their research to develop similar plant and animal varieties locally so that new varieties are developed along with the preservation of local varieties. India, Thailand and China are practicing this. This also requires maintaining gene banks of locally grown varieties.

5 CLONING

The task before scientists is how to countenance the social, economic, ethical, and moral, religious and legal ramifications of cloning. We are hearing about producing duplicates of animals.[50] We also have heard about claims of successful human cloning.[51] Many people are against all kinds of cloning because, according to them, cloning is not going to serve, in any way, human and other environmental processes. These people have gotten encouragement from the UN General Assembly's March 2005 nonbinding declaration that calls on states to "prohibit all kinds of human cloning in as much as they are compatible with human dignity and the protection of human life."[52] Many of those who are involved in cloning are doing it for the sake of fame. They started with animals. When they saw that it is no longer considered to be a big scientific endeavor, they started to attempt human cloning. We have heard of it, but we are yet to see a cloned baby. We have not even heard of cloning of animals that are genetically close to human. The South Korean cloning pioneer Hwang Woo Suk has successfully performed stem cell research via cloning, which is known as therapeutic cloning suited to male and female persons suffering diseases such as Parkinson's disease, Alzheimer's disease, or diabetes. He is of the opinion that reproductive human cloning is not possible in the next hundred years.[53] We might see it in the future, but this kind of research will only be for the sake of research. It is not going to serve humanity in any way. Rather, the conducting of cloning research wastes a lot of genetic materials (lives) because the scientific process has to be repeated innumerable times. Taking lives for giving a life is not approved by any religion, nor can it be supported on moral grounds. Many cloned animals have been born ill or deformed. Even Dolly, the first cloned sheep, died mysteriously. In view of this, many do not support cloning as a beneficial scientific endeavor. They argue that we can produce a better quality of animal species by a variety of methods, such as gene manipulation and cross breeding, which have proved to be easy, convenient, less expensive, and abundantly fruitful. Why should we resort to cloning then? Scientifically speaking, in view of the cloning endeavors around the world so far, cloning is not a solution for conservation of animal species.

Apart from scientific inhibitions, reproductive human cloning poses the following sociolegal questions: Will society accept cloned men/women? What will be the parentage of the cloned person? Will he be considered a son or brother of whose duplicate he/she is? Will the government grant registration to a cloned baby in the birth register of the country? Naturally, the cloned baby will move around with such a stigma that present day society will never accept him. He might remain an outcaste. If all these questions are

[50] Dolly is its first example.

[51] See *New Straits Times*, 21 May 2005.

[52] The General Assembly of the United Nations Declaration on the human cloning, by which member states were called on to adopt all measures necessary to prohibit all forms of human cloning inasmuch as they are incompatible with human dignity and protection of human life. GA/10333, dated 8 March 2005.

[53] See *New Straits Times*, 8 June 2005.

not resolved amicably in favor of the cloned person, he will be the real sufferer; and in that case he might sue the person who had produced him by cloning.[54] These questions are not relevant to therapeutic cloning.

From the moral and ethical point of view the act of reproductive human cloning is objectionable. An act of cloning is a socially deviant behavior. All socially deviant behaviors that are in no way beneficial to the society, if practiced, will erode social values. For this reason, they are considered to be immoral. Thus, on the part of scientists, human cloning will be an unethical act. Nature has an established system of procuring offspring. Deviating from that is sailing against nature and challenging a system that has divine wisdom. From this point of view also, all kinds of cloning is a deviant behavior. These arguments also are not relevant to therapeutic cloning.

According to Islam, the act of cloning is interference in the domain of God, because giving birth and taking life is the job of Almighty. Thus, all kinds of cloning will be interference in the domain of God. Life, according to Islam, is an *amanah* (trust) to man, which comes from God and ultimately returns to Him on His will. Man has no authority to create this *amanah* by himself. Other religions have similar views. No religion allows taking lives for making or saving a life.[55] The theory that aliens cloned man for the first time is absurd and is based on mere surmise.[56]

For these reasons, reproductive human cloning has been opposed. In Britain, it is banned[57] and in the United States the Human Cloning Prohibition Act 2003 was passed by the House of Representatives but was not acted on by the Senate.[58] The Act makes it a federal crime to perform human cloning to create a pregnancy or for medical research purposes, as well as to import a cloned human embryo or any product derived from one. However, scientific research on human stem cells, or cloning techniques to produce molecules, DNA, or cells from nonhuman embryos, tissues, organs, plants, or animals would be permitted. The main reason for banning human cloning, as stated in the Act, is that it permits human embryos to be created and then destroyed to enable embryonic stem cell research.

This deviant act is not permitted even for experimental purposes. The author is of the opinion that scientists should not be involved in any kind of human cloning activities. They should abstain even if they feel tempted. The author further feels that states that have not yet legislated to ban cloning should legislate without further delay. The law should have sufficient penal sanction. It should ensure transparency in biotechnology research so that undesired results could be checked and averted. It is very difficult to answer questions pertaining to stem cell research for therapeutic purposes. Many argue in favour of this.[59] However, as noted earlier, religious authorities go against it for two

[54] See Parveen Jamal & Hamzah M. Salleh, "Problems in Biotechnology Research" (2002) 3 *IIUM Engineering Journal* 32, 35.

[55] Note that in both kinds of cloning, therapeutic and reproductive, premature fetuses have to be used.

[56] See Abdul Haseeb Ansari & Parveen Jamal, "Towards an Islamic Jurisprudence of Environment: An Expository Study" (2001–2002) 11–12 *Religion and Law Review* 79–103.

[57] *New Straits Times*, 21 May 2005.

[58] See http://www.lib.msu.edu/skendall/cloning/laws.htm.

[59] See Emma Bonino & Marco Cappato, "The Debate over Therapeutic Cloning," *New Straits Times*, 8 June 2005. In May 2005, seventy-eight Noble Laureates demanded legalized therapeutic cloning. Luca Cocioni Association, an NGO devoted to the freedom of scientific research, called on governments to reject the demand of prohibition in favour of "rules that protect the right to life and health by ensuring

reasons: taking lives for protecting a life in no case is allowable; and cloning as such is interference in the domain of God. Probably, for these reasons, the United Kingdom has taken a cautious approach and the United States has banned federal funding for it.

So far as cloning in animals is concerned, there are contradictory opinions among scientists. Some boast by conducting cloning in some animal species, and justify such activities by arguing that they are helping to increase the number of those animals that are on the verge of extinction, like the panda in China. Some others regret the results of their cloned animals because 95 percent of the cloned embryos have so far been dead or deformed and the live ones suffer from incurable diseases. Euthanizing the first cloned sheep, "Dolly," because of incurable rheumatisms and complicated lung infection, have provided support to those who oppose cloning in animals. The author is of the opinion that all kinds of cloning among animals also should be banned for three reasons: first, it interferes in the reproductive system given to man by God; second, it is not going to render any significant service to mankind, thus it cannot be justified on the basis of public interest; third, it cannot be considered as a conservation strategy. There are successfully practiced methods of improving animal species, including *exsitu* conservation. These should be exploited and efforts should be made to augment them.

The CBD is silent about cloning. It will be better to ban all kinds of cloning through a global convention under the auspices of the United Nations. The matter also has been discussed in the General Assembly for two years. Although a large number of states were in favour of such a legal instrument, they wanted more time to think about it. It has been noted earlier in this chapter that the UN General Assembly issued in March 2005 a nonbinding ruling against the human cloning. It does not fulfill the demand to have a global convention banning all kinds of cloning.

6 DREAM TO CONQUER MORTALITY

We know that every human being has between thirty thousand and forty thousand genes, and different genes are responsible for different DNA patterns.[60] The completion of the human genome project has revealed that there may be about four thousand kinds of diseases for which faulty genes are responsible. Thus, via suitable tests, we can know some diseases in advance. To prevent them, suitable gene therapy could be used. But such treatment might not be suitable to all, and many others cannot bear its high cost.[61] Regarding stem cell research, Aileen Anderson of the University of California says that, much more research must be done before safely testing stem cells in people.[62] Nevertheless, the United States has not shown much interest in it. President Bush has severely restricted Federal financing of such research.[63] Another means to prevent such diseases is to remove bad genes from the body of the child in the womb. This might make sure that the baby will not inherit genetic diseases; but many people criticize

freedom of research, choice, and knowledge," and note the recent Italian referendum, held on 13 and 14 June 2005, which is against therapeutic cloning.

[60] D. A. Razak, "Exciting Discoveries from DNA Structure," *New Sunday Times*, 2 March, 2003.

[61] See *New Straits Times*, 18 March 2006.

[62] See *New Straits Times*, 25 September 2005.

[63] See at http://www.wsws.org/articles/2003/jan2003/clon-j08.shtml.

such tampering on ethical and moral grounds. Currently, ethical issues pertaining to "saviour siblings" – embryos fertilized *in vitro* and tested for suitability as a donor match – have agitated minds in the West. Many consider it as interference in the natural reproductive process. For many others, it is a life-saving device. For example, a boy is suffering from anemia. His brother in utero is tested to see whether his cells can be used for curing the elder brother. After his birth, blood is removed from the placenta and umbilical cord and transplanted in the elder brother's body. Research can make this process absolutely safe for the donor. Laws may need to be changed because, for example, in one case, a British High court rejected the application seeking the right to use embryo screening.[64]

The author is of the opinion that the above-mentioned scientific breakthrough is notable in genetic science. But the techniques should be free from any adverse effects, and they should be performed only by licensed clinics/laboratories. They seem to be in conformity with morality and religion as well. However, it will be better to take juristic opinions (*fatawa*) on this matter. They also might conform with conservation imperatives when performed in animals. This will be in conformity with the Islamic view on life, and provisions of life and death. Juristic opinions also should be taken in other religions.

On the basis of gene splicing, a sibling of one's choice can be produced. This dream has partially come true. Now, people are thinking of achieving a total success by overcoming the genes that make a man old and take him ultimately to death. Some are aspiring for this and augmenting their endeavors in this direction. But the question is: If it comes true, what would be the fate of the human mass? Truly speaking, if this comes within the ambit of possibility, man will become devoid of emotions, good or bad feelings, because joy and woe go together. Their separate existence is unconceivable. The conservation of biodiversity does not warrant such kinds of efforts. It will result in the condition of man being like a machine made up of flesh. The author has no hesitation in saying that such efforts are unethical, immoral, and against religious norms. It is, therefore, suggested that the smorgasbord of human alteration, which is based on gene splicing, nanotechnology, and cybernetics should be brought under legal control.

7 BIOSAFETY, BIOTECHNOLOGY RESEARCH, AND CONSERVATION OF BIODIVERSITY

We have noted that genetically modified soybean, maize, and cotton seeds and canola are gradually becoming popular, because their producer countries – the United States, Brazil, China, and South Africa – are making all efforts to make them popular, so that they become a permanent and good source of income.[65] The United States is promoting these by all means in the United States and overseas. American producers and authorities argue that 70 to 80 percent of Americans are eating foods containing GM substances in them. This argument has failed to convince people around the world, especially in the EU

[64] In fact, the High Court opposed the method of screening test tube embryos to determine the tissue type of couple's baby. See Chris Talbot, "Britain: High Court Decision Attacks Embryo-Based Medical Science," at http://www.wsws.org/article/2003/jan2003/clon-j08.shtml.

[65] See *New Straits Times*, 21 June 2005.

countries. Because of the lack of enough evidence of safety[66] and counterpublicity, people are scared of consuming any products containing them. The problem is that U.S. scientists do not give a guarantee of safety for these genetically modified Living Modified Organisms (LMOs) and food containing them (GM food). In spite of the fact that international guidelines for assessing the risk of GM food, which are governed by the World Health Organization (WHO) and the Food and Agriculture Organization (FAO), are adequate, according to a recent report published by the WHO for measuring the safety of current GM products,[67] Margaret Mellon of the Union of Concerned Scientists said that there was no system to track health problems caused by GM foods.[68] Overall, food control systems in many developing countries are underfunded and suffer from lack of capable technology. For this reason, one of the three African countries, where genetically modified corn was supplied under a food aid package, refused to accept it. On March 6, 2003, on the basis of the adverse report of the Genetic Engineering Approval Committee (GEAC), the apex technical body for allowing GMOs in the country, the Indian Government also refused to accept twenty-three thousand tonnes of Corn Soya Blend (CSB), which was offered to it under the U.S. Food Aid Programme. Recently, a genetically modified variety of rice has been created.[69] This kind of rice can withstand drought and saline water. But it does not have a guarantee of safety. Likewise, genetically modified cotton and rice, commonly known as BT Cotton and BT Rice, have the capacity to produce a kind of toxin that can kill pests. The problem is that the effects of consumption of their oil on the human body are not known. This is also the case with animal feed produced from them.

To meet such challenges, Article 19 of the CBD states that the member states will establish and maintain the means to regulate, manage, or control the risk associated with the use or release of LMOs that are likely to have adverse environmental effects also taking into account the risk to human health. So as to enforce this, the Biosafety Protocol has been made under the CBD,[70] but the problem with this Protocol is that it deals with movements of LMOs only.[71] It does not deal with products containing

[66] There is a strong perception that GM food can cause allergy or toxic reactions or harm the environment. Worries include the mixing of crops with regular ones either by handlers or by pollen.

[67] See *New Straits Times*, 24 June 2005.

[68] Currently, companies engaged in developing GM foods voluntarily send their data to the SDA, but there is no official approval before products go on sale. See "Genetically Modified Foods Eaten Regularly," *American Post*, 2 April 2005. This has been reproduced in *New Sunday Times*, 3 April 2005.

[69] See Ducan French, "The International Regulation of Genetically Modified Organisms: Synergies and Tensions in the World" (2001) 3 *Environmental Liability* 127, 130; Heike Baumuller, "The Cartagena protocol on Biosafety – Environmental Perspective" (2003) 18 *Environmental and Planning Law Journal* 36, 37.

[70] The Protocol has the provision about advance informed agreement procedure (AIA) under Articles 7 to 12. Article 15 stipulates that risk assessment should be carried out in a scientifically sound manner and taking into account the existing recognized risk assessment techniques. Article 16 establishes an appropriate domestic mechanism to regulate, manage, and control risks associated with LMOs. Article 22 strives for capacity building in among the member states. This Article in turn strives for meaningful cooperation in the area of biotechnology so that importing countries that are mainly developing or less developed could be competent to assess the safety imperatives of LMOs. See B. C. Nirmal, "Overview of the Biosafety Protocol" (2004) 46 *Journal of Indian Law Institute* 373–392.

[71] In continuation of note 54, the following points are notable: (1) Advance Informed agreement (AIA) procedure for transport and trade in LMOs and Cleaning-House mechanism to share and advance scientific, technical, environmental, and legal research and to keep account of actual experiences in LMOs transport and use. (2) LMOs that are destined for release into the environment are distinguished from LMOs that are destined for food, feed, or processing. (3) Domestic regulations have to be complied

LMOs. The author is of the opinion that the scope of the Protocol should be widened to cover all kinds of products containing LMOs.

Another problem is that people around the world want to know about the products containing LMOs, so that if they do not want to consume them, they may refrain from doing so.[72] They want this type of information from restaurants also. Some countries have legislated to protect the right to information. The author is of the opinion that such information can easily be given by a mandatory provision for labelling. So, to facilitate this, suitable legislation should be enacted.

In view of this, it is warranted that scientists, when developing any kind of GMO, must make substantial efforts to ensure its safety. If LMOs are unsafe, they might yield devastating results. If they do so, in the long run, it might benefit the scientist. With respect to introducing LMOs and food containing them, it is argued that the "precautionary principle" should be applied.[73] The author is also of this opinion that if the safety of any product cannot be ensured, it should simply not be introduced. It is, therefore, necessary for scientists to carry out extensive and repeat testing on the safety of genetically modified products based on the international guidelines governed by the WHO and FAO. If they do so with transparency, it will develop confidence among people around the world with respect to genetically modified food. In effect, this will help the biotechnology sector. Agricultural biotechnology should not be limited to cotton, soybean, maize, and canola. It should be diversified. The biotechnology research on rice is not so encouraging. It is warranted that in view of the average rise of the world's population, production of rice should rise 1 percent annually over the next twenty to thirty years. It is also warranted that new varieties of rice also should be developed that are safe and fulfill the needs of the people.[74] The task should not be difficult, as the IRRI of Manila has a gene bank of more than one hundred thousand rice varieties and the sequencing of the rice genome has opened up the largely untapped commercial possibilities of the tiny cereal. For developing new varieties of rice that cater to the need of the ever-growing population of the world, the efforts should not only be made by the private sector; the public sector also should be involved through the financial backing of respective governments. It should be noted here that the importance of the development of BT Rice is different than developing BT Cotton. BT Cotton has its basic use in textile industries and animal feed, except for the oil produced by it. It is also an export item in India and China. Conversly, BT Rice has to be GM food. BT Rice, therefore, cannot become popular unless the safety aspects are guaranteed beyond a doubt. In view of this, it is suggested that new varieties of rice should be developed that achieve higher yield even in adverse weather conditions.

We have noted earlier that from the Islamic point of view food has to be safe (*tayeb*).[75] Development of safe food stuff is the religious mandate. It is also in the interest of the general public (*maslaha*). It is, therefore, warranted that the safety aspects of agricultural biotechnology is quite important in Islam. The safety issue is not limited only to human heath. It has to be understood in its wider sense, so that the plants and animal species

with. (4) The importing country can accept, or accept on conditions, or ban the shipment. (5) It may ask the exporting country to follow the AIA requirements for subsequent exports also. (6) Absence of response will not amount to consent.

72 See Z. P. Lu Song & J. K. Chen, "Pollen Flow of Cultivated Rice Measured under Experimental Conditions" (2004) 13 (3) *Biodiversity and Conservation* 579–90.

73 It is in line with Articles 10(6) and 11(8) of the Biosafety Protocol.

74 See *New Straits Times*, "Patents Worry in Rice Research," 8 December 2003.

75 Supra, at p. 12.

are also protected. This is because animals also will consume genetically modified food stuffs. If a species or plant is developed that withstands all kinds of adverse weather conditions and is not affected by insects, will it overwhelm other similar species?[76] If this happens, it goes against the whole idea of conservation of biodiversity enshrined in the CBD.

8 TRADE-RELATED INTELLECTUAL PROPERTY RIGHTS (TRIPS)

Intellectual property rights protect the right of an inventor to benefit from his inventions. In view of globalization and the use of computers in sale and purchase transactions, the value of trade-related intellectual property rights have become more important. To meet the challenges of international trade, along with other international legal instruments, there are the Berne Convention for the Protection of Literary and Artistic Works 1971[77] and the Paris Convention for the Protection of Industrial Property 1983.[78] But the legal regime is not considered to protect rights of inventors. This resulted in the creation of the World Trade Organisations trade-related aspects of intellectual property rights (TRIPS) council. It is said that TRIPS[79] is against the CBD and does not protect trade-related interests of developing and less developed countries. It is said that the CBD is for the conservation of natural resources, it grants ownership to the country where they are situated, and allows their movements only on an informed consent basis. But TRIPS protects the right of inventors and those who have patented any plant or animal or any products related to or containing them, no matter how the genetic materials were procured and the patenting will affect the rights of indigenous people. This has created a lot of problems in the preceding decade. We know the story of the patenting of the *neem* tree by some multinationals in Europe. Every part, including its fruits and seeds, of a *neem* tree has antiseptic effects. Thus, local farmers had used the tree parts as a natural pesticide for centuries. They also were used for natural healing by indigenous people. The patenting violated their rights. India, where the tree is found in abandance, protested against such patenting and filed a formal case. The decision came in favor of the local people. The claim of the company was rejected because it had not done any innovations. An American company patented Basmati rice widely grown in India and Pakistan. In a case against it, the panel decided that the patenting was wrong because the American company had not done any innovation. The variety of *basmati* rice that was developed by the company was protected. This decision was welcomed in India and Pakistan also.[80] In view of this, it is suggested that patenting

[76] In the context of genetically engineered rice that is bacterial blight-resistant and BT cotton, many scientists have expressed their concern about human health and risk to the environment. See GREENPEACE Briefing on them, based on scientific writings, issued in April 2005 at its Web site. It can be noted here that there are naturally produced insecticides. The most trusted one is the insecticide produced with body parts of the *neem* tree. This tree can easily be grown in tropical and subtropical climates. This has to be promoted by all means.

[77] See the full text at http://www.law.cornell.edu/treaties/berne/overview.html.

[78] See the full text at http://www.wipo.int/treaties/en/ip/paris.

[79] For the text, see Note 14.

[80] The sequencing of the rice genome recently not only opened up the largely untapped commercial possibilities of the tiny cereal but also set the pace for potential property rights disputes between corporate entities and governments. The advent of biotechnology has caused a spurt in patents on gene products associated with rice. Other staple foods might also face the same problem. But if we strictly adhere to the legal position that only innovations can be patented, there will not be any dispute, and if there is any, it can be resolved on the basis of this.

should protect all medicinal plants, including the bintangor tree of Sarawak, Malaysia, that has bright prospects of curing HIV/AIDS. So to facilitate this, states, including Malaysia, are amending their existing patent laws to widen their scope. In order to protect plants or animals found in a particular region and that benefit people of the area, there are provisions in the international patenting scheme that prevent them from being patented in other countries. For this purpose, states rich in biodiversity, including Malaysia, have legislated Geographical Indications Acts. The object of these Acts is to facilitate the registration of plants and animals found in that country. In Malaysia, such plants and animals can be registered under the Geographical Indications Act 2000 (amended in 2002), or the products made using them can be patented. It is suggested here that in case one tree is found in more than one country, there should be a regional agreement so that its illegal exodus could be checked, and all countries should register it under each Geographical Indications Act, or patent products based on them under the patenting laws, as the case may be. Here the role of scientists becomes crucial; they will have to work hard and do research so that the outcome, along with the source, could be protected in developing countries. Likewise, if there is anything used by a class of people in any area for a long period, it cannot be patented on the basis of the rule of "geographical indication." Scientists should identify and help governments to register such plants and animals as geographical indications.

We have discussed the terminator seed and some other genetically modified food varieties.[81] In connection to this, it is reiterated that scientists should continue to conduct research on all indigenous food varieties and animals by gene manipulation or otherwise, so that farmers and animal breeders have alternative options.[82] Dependency on genetically modified imported varieties would be suicidal. For this purpose, it is necessary to maintain gene banks and sperm banks. It is also necessary to patent all useful innovations. There is a tendency among some scientists to keep their research secret. They keep improving on it, so that they can bring it to the public in a perfect form. If they do so, they are taking a risk. After research has reached an interim presentable stage, it should be patented; otherwise there will be chances of piracy. There is a bad tendency to patent genes. This tendency should be prohibited. If we allow patenting of genes of plants and animals, no other scientist can legally do further research on them. For this reason, in most of the countries, animals, or plants, or their body parts cannot be patented. Initially, some countries allowed such patenting. With the result of that, a large number of applications came for patenting various genes and tissues, including human genes and tissues. The author is of the opinion that it is appropriate to allow patenting of products made of human and plant tissues, but not the plant or animal as such.

9 CONCLUSION

The latest international legal instruments pertaining to conservation of biological diversity will help stem the depletion of plant and animal species. These legal instruments require facilitating conservation of existing biodiversity by all means, *ex-situ* and *in-situ.*

[81] Supra at p. 12.

[82] See J. R. Kloppenberg, *First the Seed: the Political Economy of Plant Biotechnology* (Cambridge UK, 1998), 132–143.

This task can be achieved only when all countries have the political will to cooperate to achieve total success. Towards this end, it is necessary to have an inventory of all plant and animal species throughout each country. Conservation of biodiversity does not mean making efforts to have better quality plant and animal species by genetic modifications that can withstand adverse weather conditions and can grow faster and produce more. Rather, this type of research is essential to conserve the biodiversity of the world and fulfill the food needs of the ever-growing population of the world.[83] Some notable breakthroughs, including the new varieties of rice, cotton, maize, soybean, canola, and trees that can be used for replanting the forests are already there. Developing countries, such as Malaysia, should enhance their efforts to learn more from their developed counterparts. Towards this end, collaborative efforts can be useful. All scientific research should be done on the condition that new varieties of crops should be safe to human health and compatible to conservation strategies. BT Cotton and BT Rice are not welcome from this point of view. Research predominantly based on economic lust or mere earning fame should be discouraged. This kind of research is also against ethics and religion.

The conservation of forests is important for biodiversity conservation because it provides habitat to animal species. In addition to other measures and help from the ITTO, Malaysia is imposing a levy, in addition to the normal fee paid by logging concession holders, for reforestation activities. This has helped to quickly reforest the logged areas. Other forest-rich countries should follow this initiative. In view of the recent tsunami, efforts should be doubled for conservation of mangrove forests along the coasts and coral reefs.

South Africa has commercialized conservation of animal species by providing hunting licences for high fees and investing the fees in increasing the populations of the hunted species and giving a part of the fees to the local inhabitants. This has proved to be successful in alleviating poaching activities; local people now have vested interests and thus fight against poachers along with forest rangers. Other countries should investigate the possibility of emulating this practice.

The new varieties of subsistent food grains will be of no use unless they are guaranteed as safe. There needs to be research to ensure the safety of genetically modified LMOs and GM food. They should be introduced only when it is certain that they are safe. It will be appropriate to apply the "precautionary principle" with respect to LMOs and GM food. It should be followed by repeated scientific research. If we do so, we will be enforcing the true spirit of the Biosafety Protocol. States should also legislate to make labelling of GM food a necessary requirement. The EU is supportive of this. It has allocated money to sponsor research projects on GM food.[84] Many people are consuming GM food without knowing it. All countries should have a body for approval of imports of GM food. There should be a set and transparent mechanism of ascertaining the safety aspects of such foods. The job of the safety determination can be entrusted to

[83] This may be noted here that the population in developed countries will be stabilized, but developing and less-developed countries will experience population growth at the rate of 4 percent per year.

[84] The European Commission wants to know how GMO crops might affect human and animal health in the longer term. The Commission through its Web site has advertised, seeking applications for conducting research on GMO crops. For this, it has earmarked 50,000 euros. Although the EU has lifted the moratorium on GM food effective from May 2004, it has not granted approval for any for planting since then. See *New Straits Times*, 31 March 2005.

respective public sector institutions such as the Indian Council of Medical Research (ICMR) of India. The basis of approval should be a long-term exposure to the GM food proposed to be imported. This will be in conformity with ethics and religion, because no religion, including Islam, likes to consume food that is unsafe. It has been a common practice of some multinational companies based in the West to collect genetic materials from developing and underdeveloped countries and commercialise them. But they are reluctant to share the monetary and technological gains resulting from this commercialisation. To avert this exploitative situation, the CBD provides for enforcement of the movement of genetic materials only on an informed consent basis, which is based on bilateral agreements. The CBD also provides for the sharing of such benefits. To make the biotechnological achievements pervasive and beneficial to all, it is necessary that the transfer of technology and financial resources from developed countries to developing and less developed countries should be smoother and faster. At the same time, less resourceful countries have to work harder, so that they become self-sufficient. This demands the following strategies:

1. Increase the number of properly trained scientists in developing and less-developed countries.
2. Provide these countries with facilities to venture into useful areas of biotechnology and conservation techniques. For this purpose, states should increase financial allocations in these areas.
3. Establish biotechnology centres in universities and other institutions of higher learning. These centres should have experts in all related disciplines and necessary sophisticated equipments. These institutions should emphasize collaborative research.
4. Make efforts to have gene banks of known varieties of plants, especially of those that are essential for the survival of humans, including medicinal plants.
5. Make enough efforts to conserve those animal species that are important for the survival of humankind.
6. Make efforts to augment research in the area of indigenous medicinal plants.
7. Optimize collaboration between biotechnology scientists of developed and developing countries. States should take initiatives for this.
8. Protect habitats and water resources by all means.
9. Prepare area-wide inventories of plant and animal species.
10. Develop new varieties of trees to be used in enhancing forests around the world.
11. Double the efforts for conserving mangrove forests in coastal areas.
12. Protect coral reefs by all means.

For all of these reasons, all kinds of cloning should be prohibited. This should be done by a global convention under the auspices of the United Nations followed by local legislation. Banning cloning is in line with religions, especially Islam and Christianity.

The processes of gene splicing, gene therapy, nanotechnology, and cybernetics in the human body should be brought under strict legal control. They should be allowed to be performed only by licensed clinics or laboratories and there should be total transparency in the verification process. Developing and underdeveloped countries, including Malaysia, should follow the efforts made in this direction in the West. The Human Fertility and Embryology Act 1990 of the United Kingdom is a good piece of legislation to be emulated.

The TRIPS, in operation, has been unfavorable to developing and underdeveloped countries. Thus, developed countries should have an altruistic attitude towards developing and underdeveloped countries. They should patent only innovations. They should be liberal in the area of life-saving medicines. They should respect the species that are considered geographical indications. Developing and underdeveloped countries also should make efforts through appropriate legislation to protect their valuable plant and animal species. Towards this end, if need be, the existing patenting law should be changed and laws for geographical indications should be made. There should be a total prohibition of patenting of all kinds of genes. In no circumstance should the patenting of genes be allowed.[85]

[85] For problems pertaining to allowing patenting genes, see Sarah Sbaratnam, "Gene Monopoly," *New Straits Times*, 28 February 2001.

8 Experience, Mistakes, and Challenges: The Implementation of the Convention on Biological Diversity in Brazil

José Rubens Morato-Leite*, Heline Sivini Ferreira**, and Patryck de Araújo Ayala***

1 A BRIEF SUMMARY ABOUT THE MAIN ENVIRONMENTAL FACTS THAT HAVE INFLUENCED THE NEGOTIATIONS AND ADOPTION PROCESSES OF THE CONVENTION ON BIOLOGICAL DIVERSITY (CBD)

The necessity to conserve biological diversity and to use its elements in a sustainable way has recently been put onto diplomatic agendas. The relationship between conservation and sustainability was first emphasized at the United Nations Conference of the Human Environment (Stockholm) in 1972. This conference assembled emergent and developed countries and gave environmental issues international relevance. Although many regional and international agreements were signed at the conference and the United Nations Environmental Programme (UNEP) was established as an expression of the environmental consciousness of the United Nations (UN), the experience of the following years have demonstrated that many other challenges need to be faced.

The integration between environment and development has emerged as an extremely important problem in the 1980s. Considering the interdependence between these two elements, in 1982, the General Assembly of the United Nations adopted the World Charter for Nature, which emphasizes the intrinsic value of specimens and ecosystems. In 1983, the World Commission on Environment and Development was established to study the topic worldwide and write a formal report with its conclusions. In this report – *Our Common Future* – the commission has stated that economic development should become environmentally less destructive and, considering this, the *sustainable*

*José Rubens Morato Leite: Visiting Fellow, Macquarie University, Centre for Environmental Law (MU-CEL), supported by CAPES/Brazil; Professor of Environmental Law, *Universidade Federal de Santa Catarina* (UFSC/Brazil); Member of the Law for a Green Planet Institute (NGO/Brazil) and the IUCN Commission on Environmental Law; Coordinator of the Researching Group about Environmental Law and Political Ecology in the Risk Society, registered on CNPq/Brazil; Author of books and papers on the Environmental Law Area.

**Heline Sivini Ferreira: PhD Candidate in Law, *Universidade Federal de Santa Catarina* (UFSC/Brazil); Visiting Scholar, Macquarie University – Centre for Environmental Law (MU-CEL, Australia), supported by CAPES/Brazil; Master in Law, UFSC/Brazil; Researcher of the Researching Group about Environmental Law and Political Ecology in the Risk Society, registered on CNPq/Brazil; Member of the Law for a Green Planet Institute (NGO/Brazil); Author of books and papers on the Environmental Law Area.

***Patryck de Araujo Ayala: PhD Candidate in Law, *Universidade Federal de Santa Catarina* (UFSC/Brazil); Attorney of Mato Grosso State; Master in Law, UFSC/Brazil; Researcher of the Researching Group about Environmental Law and Political Ecology in the Risk Society, registered on CNPq/Brazil; Member of the Law for a Green Planet Institute (NGO/Brazil); author of books and papers in the area of environmental law.

development concept was introduced. Despite some progress, the increasing loss of biological diversity has continued to be a problem globally.

In the 1990s, the certainty about the growing number of environmental problems that demanded international solutions became stronger. In 1992, an unprecedented number of nations, civil society, and economic sector representatives went to Rio de Janeiro in order to attend the United Nations Conference on Environment and Development. An historic set of agreements was signed at the Conference, including two binding agreements: the Convention on Climate Change[1] and the Convention on Biological Diversity[2] (CBD), the first global agreement on the conservation and sustainable use of biological diversity.

The CBD was negotiated under the auspices of the United Nations Environment Programme (UNEP). In 1988, UNEP convened to the Ad Hoc Working Group of Experts on Biological Diversity to explore the need for an international convention on biodiversity. In 1989, the Ad Hoc Working Group of Technical and Legal Experts was established to prepare an international legal instrument for the conservation and sustainable use of biological diversity. Two years later, the Ad Hoc Working Group had become known as the Intergovernmental Negotiating Committee and its works culminated, in 1992, with the Nairobi Conference for the Adoption of the Agreed Text on the Convention on Biological Diversity.[3] Soon after, in June 1992, the CBD was opened for signature and it entered into force on 29 December 1993, ninety days after the thirtieth ratification.

2 BRAZIL AS A CONTRACTING PART OF THE CBD

The CBD was signed by 150 government leaders at the United Nations Conference on Environment and Development. Although Brazil joined this group, it only ratified the Treaty in 1994, when it entered into force.[4] Since then, Brazil has undertaken its commitments to conserve biodiversity, to use its components in a sustainable way and to share fairly and equitably the benefits from genetic resources exploitation.[5]

The CBD was opened for signatures until 4 June 1993. The nations that signed the treaty most recently were South Africa, Czech Republic, and the United States, which has never ratified, accepted, or approved the document. After that, twenty other nations have accessed to the CBD. Up to the present moment, 188 nations have consented to be bound by the Convention.

3 THE ESSENTIAL CHARACTER OF THE CBD

The CBD has particular significance for global protection in the environment and development area. It is structured as a framework agreement. The CBD goes beyond the conservation of biodiversity and sustainable use and addresses issues such as access to genetic resources, benefit sharing from biotechnology, biosafety, and use of genetic

[1] *Convention on Climate Change.* Available at http://unfccc.int/2860.php.
[2] *Convention on Biological Diversity.* Available at http://www.biodiv.org.
[3] European Community Clearing-House Mechanism. Available at: http://biodiversity-chm.eea.eu.int/.
[4] The Convention on Biological Diversity was approved by Legislative Decree 2, of 3 February 1994 and promulgated by Decree 2.519 of 16 March 1998.
[5] *Convention on Biological Diversity* – About CBD. Available at http://www.biodiv.org.

material. Nevertheless, its provisions represent overall goals and policies, instead of hard obligations.

The CBD was enacted to reverse biodiversity loss and to ensure biodiversity sustainability. This treaty was the first international document dealing with genetic diversity specifically covered in a binding global proposal.[6] The CBD was unique on matters such as conservation of biodiversity, by recognizing the common concerns of humankind. By including issues such as access to use of genetic resources, as well as technology transfer and biosafety, the CBD has introduced several innovations in the environmental field. The CBD emphasizes the sovereign rights of states over biological resources, while at the same time it establishes that the conservation of biological diversity is of common concern. This reflects the common responsibility of the international community as a whole. Article 3 and the preamble of the CBD establish national sovereignty and common concern.

The CBD affirms the responsibility and obligation of states on the following matters:

1. general measures for conservation and sustainable use (Article 6);
2. in situ conservation (Article 8); and
3. sustainable use of components of biological diversity (Article 10).

Concerning access of genetic resources, Article 15 of the CBD stresses that the authority belongs with national governments and should be subject to national legislation.

Some of the many issues dealt with under the Convention include: measures and incentives for the conservation and sustainable use of biological diversity; regulated access to genetic resources; access to and transfer of technology, including biotechnology; technical and scientific cooperation; impact assessment; education and public awareness; provision of financial resources; and national reporting on efforts to implement treaty commitments.

The CBD (Article 20) creates a financial mechanism to be assisted by the contribution of developed country parties for the exclusive use of developing countries. The funds are to be new and additional funds should be applied to enable developing country parties to meet the agreed incremental costs of implementation. The agreement on what exactly these costs are is to be made bilaterally between each developing country party and the institution chosen to handle the financial mechanism. This financial mechanism (Article 21) provides financial resources to developing countries on a grant or concession basis, under the authority of the Conference of the Parties (COP) to which it is directly accountable. The Global Environment Facility[7] (GEF) was created as an institutional structure operating the financial mechanism on an interim basis and conditional on restructuring. According to the Global Biodiversity Outlook (GBO),[8] the national reports from many parties in Latin America, Asia, and Africa identify a common need for additional financial and human resources in order to help implement the Convention, lack of these being a major constraint to implementation.

The COP, its subsidiary body on scientific, technical, and technological advice, and the secretariat have key roles for implementation of the CBD. The COP is the

[6] Dona Craig et al., eds., *Capacity Building for Environmental Law in the Asian and Pacific Region: Approaches and Resources* (Asian Development Bank, 2002).

[7] *Convention on Biological Diversity*, Article 39.

[8] *Convention on Biological Diversity* – Global Biodiversity Outlook. Available at http://www.biodiv.org/gbo/chap-04/chap-04-01.asp.

governing body of the Convention, and advances implementation of the Convention through the decisions it takes at its periodic meetings. The last meeting of the Conference of the Parties to the Convention on Biological Diversity was held in Brazil from 20 to 31 March 2006. The COP has set out a series of standing items for the provisional agenda of its meetings, namely: organizational matters; reports from subsidiary bodies, the financial mechanism, and the Executive Secretary; review of the implementation of the program of work; priority issues for review and guidance; and other matters.[9]

Article 25 of the treaty establishes an open-ended intergovernmental scientific advisory body known as the Subsidiary Body on Scientific, Technical and Technological Advice (SBSTTA). SBSTTA is a subsidiary body of the Conference of the Parties (COP) and is to report regularly to the COP on all aspects of its work. Its functions include providing assessments of the status of biological diversity and assessments of the types of measures taken in accordance with the provisions of the Convention, and it responds to questions that the COP may put to the body.[10] The COP also has undertaken to prepare and develop a Strategic Plan for the Convention, which was adopted at its sixth meeting. The plan will initially cover the period 2002–2010. It will be based on the longer-term programs of work of the COP and SBSTTA and is intended to provide strategic and operational guidance for the implementation of these programs. It will contain a set of operational goals that the Conference of the Parties wishes to be achieved in the period covered by the plan, relating to the three main areas of work, these being the thematic programs, cross-cutting issues and initiatives, and the implementation of the provisions of the Convention.

The COP adopted a Strategic Plan for the Convention on Biological Diversity. The Conference of the Parties urged parties, states, intergovernmental organizations, and other organizations to review their activities, in particular, their national biodiversity strategies and action plans in the light of the Strategic Plan for the Convention on Biological Diversity. The full text of the Strategic Plan was established by Decision VI/26 of COP.[11]

Many others tasks remain to be addressed by the CBD, such as considering the need for further negotiation of certain issues through the preparation of protocols. CBD (Article 19) requires consideration to be given to a protocol on the safe transfer, handling, and use of any living modified organism resulting from biotechnology that may have an adverse effect on the conservation and sustainable use of biological diversity. Other protocols may be needed as implementation efforts proceed.

4 AN OVERVIEW OF THE CBD IMPLEMENTATION STRATEGY

The CBD, as an international treaty, identifies a common problem, sets overall goals and policies and general obligations, and organizes technical and financial cooperation. However, the responsibility for achieving its goals rests largely with the countries

[9] *Convention on Biological Diversity* – Conference of the Parties (COP) background and status. Available at http://www.biodiv.org/convention/cops.asp.

[10] *Convention on Biological Diversity* – Subsidiary Body on Scientific, Technical and Technological Advice (SBSTTA). Available at http://www.biodiv.org/convention/sbstta.asp.

[11] *Convention on Biological Diversity* – Strategic Plan. Available at http://www.biodiv.org/sp/default.asp.

themselves.[12] Development and adoption of a national biodiversity strategy is the foundation for implementation of the Convention by Parties.[13] Therefore, the political issue is a key for implementation because it depends on the contracting parties to put into place a legislative regime consistent with the requirements of the CBD.[14]

The general overview of obstacles to the implementation of CBD are reported in the Global Biodiversity Outlook (GBO), including the following:[15]

1. ***Political***: political/societal obstacles; lack of political will and support to implement the Convention on Biological Diversity; limited public participation and stakeholder involvement; lack of mainstreaming and integration of biodiversity issues into other sectors, including the use of tools such as environmental impact assessments; political instability; lack of precautionary and proactive measures, causing reactive policies.
2. ***Institutional***: institutional, technical and capacity-related obstacles; inadequate capacity to act, caused by institutional weaknesses; lack of human resources; lack of transfer of technology and expertise; loss of traditional knowledge; lack of adequate scientific research capacities to support all the objectives.
3. ***Access of information***: lack of accessible knowledge/information; loss of biodiversity and the corresponding goods and services it provides not properly understood and documented; existing scientific and traditional knowledge not fully utilized; dissemination of information on international and national level not efficient; lack of public education and awareness at all levels.
4. ***Economic issues***: economic policy and financial resources; lack of financial and human resources; fragmentation of GEF financing; lack of economic incentive measures; lack of benefit-sharing.
5. ***Exchange and collaboration***: collaboration/cooperation; lack of synergies at the national and international levels; lack of horizontal cooperation among stakeholders; lack of effective partnerships; lack of engagement of scientific community.
6. ***Social factors and others***: socioeconomic factors; poverty; population pressure; legal/juridical impediments; lack of appropriate policies and laws; unsustainable consumption and production patterns; lack of capacities for local communities; natural phenomena and environmental change; climate change; natural disasters.

Moreover, private companies, landowners, fishermen, and farmers take most of the actions that affect biodiversity. Governments need to provide the critical role of leadership, particularly by setting rules that guide the use of natural resources, and by protecting biodiversity where they have direct control over the land and water.

Under the Convention, governments undertake to conserve and sustainably use biodiversity. They are required to develop national biodiversity strategies and action plans, and to integrate these into broader national plans for environment and development. This is particularly important for such sectors such as forestry, agriculture, fisheries,

[12] *Convention on Biological Diversity* – Global Biodiversity Outlook. Available at http://www.biodiv.org/gbo/chap-04/chap-04-01.asp.

[13] *Convention on Biological Diversity* – Global Biodiversity Outlook. Available at http://www.biodiv.org/gbo/chap-04/chap-04-01.asp.

[14] Michael Jeffrey, "Bioprospecting: Access to Genetic Resources and Benefits – Sharing under the Convention on Biodiversity. Bonn Guidelines" (2002) *Singapore Journal of International & Comparative Law*, 747, 808.

[15] Convention on Biological Diversity – Strategic Plan. Available at http://www.biodiv.org/sp/default.asp.

energy, transportation, and urban planning. Other treaty commitments include identifying and monitoring the important components of biological diversity that need to be conserved and used sustainably; establishing protected areas to conserve biological diversity while promoting environmentally sound development around these areas; rehabilitating and restoring degraded ecosystems and promoting the recovery of threatened species in collaboration with local residents; respecting, preserving, and maintaining traditional knowledge of the sustainable use of biological diversity with the involvement of indigenous peoples and local communities; preventing the introduction of, controlling, and eradicating alien species that could threaten ecosystems, habitats, or species; controlling the risks posed by organisms modified by biotechnology; promoting public participation, particularly when it comes to assessing the environmental impacts of development projects that threaten biological diversity; educating people and raising awareness about the importance of biological diversity and the need to conserve it; reporting on how each country is meeting its biodiversity goals.

Specific problems identified at the start of the biodiversity planning process include: inadequate political support for crucial aspects of the planning process and for approval of action; weak legislative base; inadequate information; lack of appropriate scientific and technical expertise and experience in biodiversity planning; lack of institutional coordination within governments, and between governments and stakeholders; difficulties in access to and availability of funding; direct economic pressure on ecosystems and a lack of national budget allocations; the need for increased public education and awareness; the need for recognition of the long-term nature of the NBSAP process; complexity of translating a biodiversity strategy into a prioritized action plan; scarcity of examples of the effective integration of biodiversity considerations into sectoral or cross-sectoral plans.

4.1 The Brazilian Strategy Concerning the CBD

The Brazilian Government established in 1994 the National Biodiversity Programme (PRONABIO), in order to plan, coordinate, monitor, and evaluate measures relating to the conservation and sustainable use of Brazilian biodiversity, especially those in the ambit of the CBD. The PRONABIO was created to promote partnerships between government and society in the conservation of biodiversity, the sustainable use of its resources, and the sharing of the benefits derived. Funding comes from the Treasury and overseas, meeting the priorities defined by a coordinating commission with parity between government and society. The PRONABIO's specific tasks included the definition of methodologies, mechanisms and processes; the promotion of international cooperation; the encouragement of research; the production and dissemination of information; training of personnel; institutional support; raising public awareness; and the development of concrete, demonstrative actions for the conservation of biodiversity and its sustainable use.

In 2003, the Commission National of Biodiversity (CONABIO) assumed the PRONABIO obligations and it is now in charge of putting into force the Brazilian strategy concerning the CBD, as well as the priorities to be taken according to the National Policy of Biodiversity.[16] The United Nations Development Programme (UNDP) has

[16] Brazilian Ministry of the Environment. Available at www.mma.gov.br.

provided technical and administrative support to PRONABIO through its project, Brazilian Biodiversity Management. Financial and technical support for the implementation of PRONABIO has come also from two complementary projects funded by the Brazilian government, and by GEF (through the International Bank for Reconstruction and Development [IBRD]).

Support for biodiversity research and conservation also has been made available through other government programs, including the National Environment Fund (FNMA), the National Environment Programme (PNMA), and the Pilot Program for the Conservation of Tropical Rain Forests (PPG-7). As a result, some progress has been achieved in such areas as the establishment of information networks and databases, administrative infrastructure in the implementation and consolidation of protected areas, in geographic and diagnostic research for the principal biomes, in setting up germ plasma banks, in testing new models, and in increasing incentives for the sustainable use of biodiversity. The last ten years have seen a major government-financed project concerning the monitoring of fires and deforestation in the Amazon. This program has now been consolidated into the Surveillance System for the Amazon (SIVAM), with the major participation of the National Institute for Space Research (INPE).

With regard to legislation, the Public Attorney's Office has been an important ally, with its powers to open inquiries and take legal action for the enforcement of environmental laws. The Brazilian program for conservation of biodiversity and its sustainable use, and the commitments undertaken by Brazil in relation to the CBD, are legally underpinned by the Federal Constitution of the Republic of Brazil (1988), which devotes an entire chapter (Article 225) to the environment. Brazilian legislation makes provision for a National Environmental Policy, a National Council for the Environment (CONAMA), a National Policy for Water Resources, a Land Statute, a Forest Code, an Act for the Protection of the Fauna, a Decree-Law for the Protection and Promotion of Fisheries, an Act of Biosafety, an Act for the Protection of Cultivars, an Act of Industrial Property, and an Act of Environmental Crime, which defines liability and civic–public action to be taken in the event of damage caused to the environment. The Act of the National System of Conservation Units (SNUC) was put in force in 2000, concerning protected areas.[17]

4.1.1 National Reports on CBD

In 1998, Brazil presented its first National Report on the CBD. Recently, between 1999 and 2002, the country took charge of establishing a National Strategy for Biodiversity. In essence, this strategy supports the organization of synthesis on biodiversity knowledge, identifying priority areas and action for conservation of Brazilian biodiversity, and creating legal instruments for biodiversity management. In 2002, the Second National Report was concluded.[18]

In 2003, Brazil defined the national biodiversity strategy, which presupposes the implementation of a legal precedent. Moreover, it established a need for consultation with Brazilian society. Additionally, the implementation of these policies under the

[17] Brazilian Ministry of the Environment – Biodiversity and Forests. Available at http://www.mma.gov.br/port/sbf/index.cfm.

[18] Brazilian Ministry of the Environment – Biodiversity and Forests – Convention on Biological Diversity. Available at http://www.mma.gov.br/biodiversidade.

National Biological Programme must be integrated with all other South American countries. These integrated efforts are essential for the fulfillment of obligations under the CBD and to establish cooperative planning and the interchange of ideas between these bodies. In this context, it would be remarkable to actualize the knowledge of the National Biological Diversity Strategies (NBS) of all South American countries in such a way as to involve each nation's compromised perspectives on biodiversity conservation and sustainable use. Moreover, the identification of common interest themes would be of great value for defining an agenda of cooperative action. Some subjects, such as protected areas, exotic species, desertification, and cross-border issues, can already be identified as of great interest for this discussion.

It is important to contemplate and discuss the methodologies used by South American countries that signed the CBD in the actual process of drafting national biodiversity strategies. The main outcome of the process was the creation of a foundation for future proposals that would be focused primarily on cross-sector strategies.

The Brazilian Ministry of the Environment promoted a South American regional meeting for the identification of issues on biodiversity for the cooperation and interchange amongst the countries.[19] This meeting was held on 15–17 December 2003, in Rio de Janeiro, and the representatives of the following countries were present: Argentina, Bolivia, Brazil, Colombia, Ecuador, Paraguay, Peru, Suriname, and Uruguay. Representatives from French Guiana also attended. The participants discussed the possibilities of exchange and cooperation in the region, in order to facilitate compliance with the commitments undertaken under the Convention. Nineteen priority themes were defined.[20]

5 CHALLENGES IN THE BRAZILIAN BIOLOGICAL DIVERSITY

Brazil is considered the biggest country in biological diversity around the world comprising between 10 percent and 20 percent of the mondial flora and fauna species. Its ground biota has the richest flora worldwide, with approximately 56,000 of the 250,000 superior plants species already known. Brazil has approximately 517 of the 4,000 species of amphibians; 1,677 of the 9,700 species of birds; 518 of the 4,550 species of mammals; 550 of the 6,000 species of reptiles; more than 3,000 species of freshwater fish; and 5 to 10 million insect species. It also has 12.7 percent of the world's river water (5,190 cubic kilometers per year) and a very rich social and cultural diversity.[21]

With an area of approximately 8.5 million square kilometers, Brazil covers almost half of South America. The distinct climatic zones[22] contribute to the ecological variations, which are responsible for the creation of biomes. According to the Brazilian Institute of Environment and Renewable Natural Resources (IBAMA),[23] as shown in Figure 8.1,

[19] Brazilian Ministry of the Environment – Meeting for identification of issues in biodiversity for cooperation and interchanging among South America Countries. Available at http://www.mma.gov.br/ingles/sbf/chm/estrateg/apringl.html.

[20] Brazilian Ministry of the Environment – Priority themes on biodiversity for cooperation and interchanging among South America Countries. Available at http://www.mma.gov.br/port/sbf/chm/doc/guiaing.pdf.

[21] IBAMA – Brazilian Ecosystems – Amazônia. Available at http://www.ibama.gov.br.

[22] Brazil has three distinct climatic zones: the tropical, which is the main one, the equatorial, and the subtropical (Brazilian Ministry of the Environment). Available at http://www.mma.gov.br>

[23] IBAMA – Brazilian Biomes. Available at http://www.ibama.gov.br.

Figure 8.1. Brazilian's Biomes Share.
Source: IBAMA (http://www.ibama.gov.br).

Brazil has seven distinct biomes: *Amazônia*, *Caatinga*, *Cerrado*, *Pantanal*, *Mata Atlântica*, *Campos Sulinos*, and *Costeiros*.

The *Amazônia* is the biggest reserve in biological diversity around the world. It is also the largest Brazilian biome, encompassing approximately 3.7 million square kilometers. The diversity of trees in *Amazônia* varies from between forty and three hundred distinct species by hectare. Although only 30 percent of the fauna species is known, there is a large diversity of animals in this region. This percentage comprises an amount of 163 species of amphibians, approximately 4 percent of the species registered around the world and 27 percent of those identified in Brazil; 465 species of reptiles, approximately 7.7 percent of the species known worldwide and 84.5 percent of those registered in Brazil; and 311 species of mammals, equivalent to 6.68 percent of the species already identified around the world and 61.9 percent of those known in Brazil. The *Amazônia* concentrates one-fifth of the mondial fresh water volume, 98 percent of the indigenous lands, and 49.2 percent of the natives[24] who live in Brazil.[25]

The *Cerrado* is the second largest Brazilian biome. It has an area of approximately two million square kilometers, which corresponds to 23 percent of the national territory.

[24] Nowadays, there are in Brazil about 345,000 indigenous people, down from approximately 5 million who used to live in the country before it was discovered by Pedro Álvares Cabral. They are distributed in 250 indigenous communities. It is important to emphasize that this indicator has considered only those natives who live in indigenous communities. In addition to these people, there is an estimated 100 to 190 thousand indigenous people living outside the indigenous areas. (FUNAI/BRAZIL – http://www.funai.gov.br).

[25] AmbienteBrasil – Amazônia Forest. Available at http://www.ambientebrasil.com.br/composer.php3?base=./natural/index.html&conteudo=./natural/biomas/amazonia.html.

With a diversified flora, the Brazilian *Cerrado* is known as the richest savanna in biodiversity around the world, comprising many distinct ecosystems and more than ten thousand species of plants. This wealthy environment also comprises a wide variety of fauna species. In this biome, about 1,575 species of animals are already known, which creates the second largest concentration of animals worldwide.[26]

The *Caatinga*, which means White Forest in *tupi guarani* (indigenous language), is the main ecosystem in the northeast of Brazil. It is a unique biome because, even located in a semiarid area, it has very diversified vegetation. According to the IBAMA, at least 932 species of plants were already registered in this region. In spite of having a small number of animals when compared to environments with a higher rainfall level, this biome comprises a considerable number of endemic species. The *Caatinga* is home to the biggest reserve of prehistoric sites from America – the National Park of the *Serra da Capivara*. There are more than four hundred archaeological sites, with thirty thousand rock paintings in 260 of them.[27]

The *Mata Atlântica* is considered the fifth richest area in endemic species worldwide. This biome comprises a diversified mosaic of ecosystems, each one with a particular characteristic. In accordance with the IBAMA, the *Mata Atlântica* is the most diversified forest around the world, comprising more than twenty-five thousand species of plants. The great rainfall level during the year creates rich and dense vegetation, including trees with a height of thirty meters. This region also comprises a large diversity of animals. Up to the present, approximately 1,361 species of fauna have been catalogued. Among those, about 567 are endemic species.[28]

The *Pantanal* is considered one of the largest wetland areas around the world and the most important wetland region of South America. This biome is located on the River Paraguay Basin. Its geographic location has a particular relevance in as much as it connects the *Cerrado* (Brazil), the *Chaco* (Bolivia), and the *Amazônia* (Brazil). Because it is a transition area, the *Pantanal* comprises a mosaic of terrestrial ecosystems that has affinity, especially, with the *Cerrado* and the *Amazônia*. This ecological heritage has an exuberant vegetation and a very rich and diversified fauna.

The *Campos Sulinos* biome is also known as *Pampas*, a name of indigenous origin that means Plane Land (grassland). This denomination, however, characterizes only one of the biome's typical vegetation. In addition to the grasslands, this area comprises tropical and subtropical forests. The subtropical forest is mainly compounded by the *Araucárias* Forests, in which the *Paraná* Pine tree predominates. The flora also includes a variety of some 515 species. This biome comprises diversified fauna, which includes endemic, rare, endangered, and migratory species.[29]

The *Costeiros* biome includes the Brazilian coastal and marine zones. It has approximately 3.5 million square kilometers with cold waters off the south and southeastern coasts (Argentinean zone) and warm waters off the eastern, northeastern, and northern coasts (Caribbean zone). This biome supports a wide range of coastal and offshore ecosystems, which include coral reefs, dunes, wetlands, lagoons, estuaries, and mangroves.[30]

[26] IBAMA – Brazilian Ecosystems – Cerrado. Available at http://www.ibama.gov.br.

[27] IBAMA – Brazilian Ecosystems – Caatinga. Available at http://www.ibama.gov.br.

[28] IBAMA – Brazilian Ecosystems. Available at http://www.ibama.gov.br.

[29] IBAMA – Brazilian Ecosystems. Available at http://www.ibama.gov.br.

[30] Brazilian Ministry of the Environment – Coastal and marine management. Available at http://www.mma.gov.br/port/sqa.

The conservation of such huge biological diversity for present and future generations[31] is not easy, particularly in an emergent country as Brazil. Among the many difficulties that Brazil has been facing through the last years, one of the most crucial is the relationship between development and environmental conservation and sustainable use. Box 8.1 addresses some of the challenges in each biome.

As mentioned earlier, the integration between environment and development has emerged as an extremely important problem in the 1980s. Almost twenty years after the publication of *Our Common Future*,[32] which stated that economic development should be environmentally less destructive, sustainable development is still a big challenge to Brazil, as well as to many others countries.

When development is limited to economic growth, it usually is harmful to the environment. This is because environmental conservation is not observed as it should be, and because, sometimes, the environment is considered itself to be an economically profitable option to the economic integration process. As an example, there is frequent internal migration of people engaged in placer-mining or predatory logging in Brazil, particularly in the *Amazônia* area. These activities are carried out even within indigenous areas. Action has been taken by the Government to prohibit invasion of indigenous lands, as witnessed by the recent removal of goldminers from the *Yanomami* reserve. Nonetheless, this is one of the main causes of the loss of biodiversity, along with the advance of the agricultural frontiers in biomes like *Cerrado* and the *Amazônia.* This restricted view about development also affects other areas that, directly or indirectly, interfere with the environmental balance. Poverty, for example, seriously damages natural resources and biodiversity conservation. Although Brazil has the ninth highest per capita income among the emergent countries, it occupies the twenty-fifth position considering the poverty indicators. It means that Brazil has a high income and, at the same time, a high poverty level. According to the Research Institute of Applied Economic,[33] Brazil tops the list of countries with the biggest gap between the rich and the poor.

Since the 1980s, the state has gone through successive phases of harsh policies regarding fiscal adjustment. Under a restricted development process view, these policies are not conducive to the allocation of funds for research or the establishment of programs for environmental issues. However, a suitable standard of biodiversity conservation depends on these funds to be successful. Many instruments, such as a consistent legal regime, an effective environmental policy and a qualified group of professionals, are essential to make environmental protection possible, and it demands financial support. Unfortunately, without an integrated, harmonious, and consistent protection/conservation structure, Brazilian biodiversity becomes extremely vulnerable to exploitation.

In short, a realistic view of the conservation and sustainable use of biodiversity must take into account numerous factors. The problems are many, complex, delicate, and difficult to separate. However, after overtaking the invisible frontier of the twenty-first century, all the societies around the world face the challenge of implementing sustainable development, which must be able to conciliate ecological prudence, economical feasibility, and social justice. If Brazil doesn't face this challenge seriously, the Brazilian environment will continue to be destroyed and the results could be worse than those

[31] Article 225, Brazilian Constitution.

[32] The Bruntland Report (1987).

[33] Research Institute of Applied Economic. Available at http://www.ipea.gov.br/.

Box 8.1. Current ecological status of the brazilian biomes

According to the IBAMA,[1] 15 percent to 18 percent of the *Amazônia* area has been devastated. Most part of the pristine forests are still intact but, according to the National Institute for Research of *Amazônia* (INPA) and the Smithsonian Institute,[2] it could be only 4.7 in 2020.[3] In addition to this, almost 84 percent of the indigenous delimitated areas suffer any kind of external interference. In this biome, there are forty-one endangered species of fauna.*

Until the 1950's, the *Cerrado* was very well preserved. Between the 1960s and 1980s, many ecosystems were destroyed and replaced by agriculture and livestock. As a result, 67 percent of the biome's area was seriously damaged. Nowadays, only 20 percent of the *Cerrado* is still preserved. In this region, there are sixty-five endangered species of fauna.*

The *Caatinga* biome is extremely modified. Agriculture and livestock has been causing damage to the native vegetation. Deforestation and the practice of burning the land to prepare the soil for agriculture and livestock (*queimadas*) are ordinary activities. Unfortunately, these practices not only damage the flora but also affect the fauna, climate stability, and water quality. About 80 percent of the *Caatinga* original ecosystems were already modified. There are twenty-eight endangered specimens of fauna* in this biome.

Nowadays, about eighty million inhabitants – approximately 50 percent of the Brazilian population – live in the *Mata Atlântica* area. Only 7.3 percent of its native ecosystems remain. Because of this, the *Mata Atlântica* is considered the fifth most endangered area in the world. Unfortunately, there are approximately 268 endangered species of fauna.*

Many activities that cause direct impacts to the *Pantanal* biome, such as gold and diamond digging, hunting, fishing, tourism, predatory agriculture, livestock raising, and highway and hydroelectric plant construction, have developed without any environmental consideration. The extensive activities in the surrounding plateaus are one of the main sources of environmental impacts to this biome. Contamination of several rivers with fertilizes and quicksilver is becoming worse. Around seventeen species of fauna* are under risk of extinction in this area.

Agriculture, livestock, and industrialization have caused many environmental problems to the *Campos Sulinos*. Many pine trees areas, for example, were replaced by corn, wheat, rice, and soy cultivations. In addition, a desertification process was triggered by poor management of some ecosystems. Nowadays, this biome has a restricted number of protected areas with its original ecosystems and twenty-three endangered specimens of fauna.*

Nowadays, almost half of the Brazilian population lives within two hundred square kilometers of the sea. This means that more than seventy million people have a direct impact on the *Costeiros* biome. The coastal zone is the biggest source of contamination of the Brazilian marine ecosystem.

Coastal cities comprise a huge number of industrial complexes, including harmful sectors such as chemical, petrochemical, and cellulose industries. In the *Costeiros* biome, there are about thirty endangered species of fauna.*

* Some species can be found in more than one biome.
Source: MMA (http://www.mma.gov.br/port/sbf/index.cfm); IBAMA (http://www.ibama.gov.br).
1 IBAMA – Brazilian Ecosystems.
Available at http://www.ibama.gov.br.
2 National Institute of Research about Amazônia.
Available at http:/www.inpa.gov.br.
3 About the devastation of the *Amazônia* biome, see item 7.

presented below. The current indicators are not good and they point out how hard Brazil has to work in order to reach an environmental protection standard compatible with its huge biodiversity.

Unfortunately, a high level of destruction can be observed in these scenarios of huge wealth. There are numerous subsystems and ecosystems within all of these biomes, each with unique characteristics, and the conservation of all of them is vital for the preservation of their biodiversity.

6 LEGAL REGIME FOR BIODIVERSITY CONSERVATION IN BRAZIL

6.1 Instruments for Biodiversity Protection and Management

6.1.1 Instruments and Objectives of the National Environment Policy

The first initiative for the systematization of rules, objectives and instruments for the protection of biodiversity in the Brazilian Environmental Law has its origin in the Act that established the National Policy of Environment (Act 6938/81). Before the definition of this National Policy, the Brazilian Legislation had already important protection instruments for natural spaces (permanent preservation areas and legal reserve areas), as seen in the Forest Code (Act 4771/65).[34] However, these instruments established limited protection to the prohibition or control of human intervention in some natural spaces with the goal of protecting its ecological functions.

The National Policy of Environment defines environmental protection actions, proposing principles, goals, and a set of instruments with different management approaches in order to solve problems related to the need of conciliating economic development and protection of natural resources. This is the first goal of the National Policy, which can be recognized by the need of "adjusting the social and economic development to environmental preservation and ecological balance."[35]

Another relevant feature deals with the modification of protection instruments, concerning not only the traditional measures of control but also measures for the rational use of natural resources. This point is important to the consolidation of the current approach of biodiversity protection by law, which prioritizes the access to resources

[34] The Act n. 4771/65 will be analyzed later in this paper.
[35] Article 4th, incise I.

and knowledge. In this aspect, three goals could be emphasized: (1) soil, underground, water, and air use rationalization;[36] (2) ecosystem protection with preservation of representative areas;[37] and (3) control and zoning of potential or effectively polluting activities.[38]

The same management approach of natural resources and spaces was reproduced through its goals. Among these goals, the most important are: (1) defining priority areas of government action on environmental quality and ecological balance;[39] (2) environmental quality standards on the use and handling of natural resources;[40] and (3) preservation and restoration of environmental resources, for its rational use and permanent availability.[41]

The main contribution of the National Policy of Environment to the regime of biodiversity protection is the establishment of instruments to implementing actions that give effect to its principles and goals. These instruments still constitute the central point to the management and control of the activities with the potential to cause environmental impacts, focusing on: (1) the environmental zoning; (2) the environmental impact assessment; (3) the environmental licensing; and (4) the definition of protected spaces.

6.1.2 Environmental Impact Licensing and Environmental Impact Assessment

Environmental licensing is one of the most important environmental risk management instruments. It also constitutes a decision-making process that aims at identifying and evaluating potential risks that may be produced by some activities and making decisions about its admissibility. It is mandatory and constitutes a basic condition to the installation or development of any activity. This issue is regulated by the National Council of Environment (CONAMA), which has established obligations in relation to many potentially polluting activities[42] and established general rules about its procedure.[43] The CONAMA's Resolution 01/86 defines environmental impacts and establishes the need for an environmental impact evaluation if the activity can cause significant environmental degradation. This instrument, which had already been foreseen by the National Policy of Environment,[44] was recognized by the Brazilian Constitution,[45] creating fundamental innovations to the current biodiversity protection regime: (1) its mandatory previous making and (2) the obligatory publicity of its conclusions.

6.1.3 Ecologic–Economic Zoning

The ecologic–economic zoning is also a mechanism of the National Policy of Environment.[46] However, it was only regulated in 2002 by the Act 4297/02, filling a federal blank

[36] Article 2nd, incise II.
[37] Article 2nd, incise IV.
[38] Article 2nd, incise V.
[39] Article 4th, incise II.
[40] Article 4th, incise III.
[41] Article 4th, incise VI.
[42] These activities include Resolutions 312/2002 (fresh water prawn culture); 305/2002 (genetically modified organisms); 396/2004 and 289/2001 (land reform settlements); 284/2001 (irrigation); 279/2001 and 06/87 (electric sector); 16/93 (fuels); 8/90, 9/90 and 10/90 (mining); 6/88 (dangerous industrial residue); and 5/88 (basic sewage).
[43] Resolution 01/86, which has instituted the mandatory of the environmental impact study for activities that could cause strong damage to the environment, and proposed the concept of environmental damage, and Resolution 237/97, which concerns conceptual aspects and general rules of the administrative process, should be mentioned in this context.
[44] Article 9th, incise III.
[45] Article 225, §1, incise VI.
[46] Article 9th, incise II.

of more than twenty years. This Act defines zoning as an instrument of the territory organization, which aims at managing public and private decisions about activities that consume natural resources. So, it supports the conservation of biodiversity and ecosystems.[47] The Act 4297/02 must be understood as a part of a set of actions for implementing biodiversity conservation measures in situ, mainly those related to the Ecologic–Economic Zoning Program (ZEE). This program's main goal was the identification of priority vulnerable areas to conservation and areas with potential use to biodiversity.[48] The identification process of these areas originated from five studies carried out from 1998 to 2000 in each of the Brazilian biomes (*Amazônia, Cerrado/Pantanal, Caatinga, Mata Atlantica/Campos Sulinos, Costeiros*). Up to the moment of the presentation of the Second National Report on the CBD, it had identified nine hundred priority areas, 43 percent in the *Amazônia*, 9 percent in the *Caatinga*, 20 percent in the *Mata Atlantica* and *Campos Sulinos*, approximately 10 percent in *Cerrado* and *Pantanal*, and 18 percent in the *Costeiros*.[49]

6.1.4 Protected Areas

The fourth instrument is related to protected territorial spaces, which are defined by the Brazilian Constitution[50] and complemented by legislation.[51] According to the Act, these protected natural spaces are submitted to the rules of a National System of Conservation Units (SNUC).

The Act defines conservation units as areas of special natural interest, legally recognized by the state as being protected with defined objectives and boundaries,[52] which can be classified into two groups: strict use units and sustainable use.[53] The first ones (strict use) have the main objective of preserving the nature, being admitted only for the indirect use of its natural resources.[54] The second ones (sustainable use) aim at "[. . .] making the conservation of nature with the sustainable use of part of its natural resources possible."[55]

In spite of establishing a national system, the Constitution also granted protection to five large ecosystems, which the SNUC have not considered, because of its importance to the protection of the Brazilian biodiversity. These ecosystems are: *Amazônia, Mata Atlântica, Pantanal, Serra do Mar* and *Costeiros*,[56] The establishment of these territorial

[47] Articles 2nd and 3rd, *caput.*

[48] The criteria for identification of these areas were established by Federal Decree 5092, of 21 May 2004.

[49] Ministry of the Environment; *Second National Report on the Convention about Biologic Diversity* (MMA) (2004) 215–216.

[50] Article 225, §§2 and 4, Brazilian Constitution.

[51] Act n.9985/00, which has defined the National System of Conservation Units (SNUC). Ruled by Federal Decree n.4340/02.

[52] The Article 2nd, incise I, defines them as those "[. . .] land areas together with the environmental resources within them, including the waters, with special natural characteristics, legally established in Public Law, for the purposes of conservation and with defined geographical limits, managed under a special administrative structure to guarantee their protection."

[53] The types of conservation units are enumerated in detail in the Attachment A of this work, distributed according to the respective classification group.

[54] Art. 7, §1, of the Act 9.985/00. The units of strict protection are the following: Biological Station, Biological Reserve, National Park, Natural Monument, and Wild Life Refugee (Art. 8, including I to V).

[55] Article 7, §2, Act 9985/00. The units are the following: Environmental Protection Areas (APAs), Relevant Ecological Interest Areas, National Forests, Extractive Reserve, Fauna Reserves, Sustainable Development Reserves and e, Private Reserves of the Natural Heritage (RPPNs). (Art. 14, including I to VII).

[56] Article 225, §4, Brazilian Constitution.

spaces is an important move towards the maintenance of their essential natural conditions as well as to the concretization of the fundamental right to an ecologically balanced environment.

It is important to observe that this kind of protection was already stated in Brazilian legislation. Even before the establishment of the SNUC, the exclusion of some spaces and areas from the possibility of economic exploitation was foreseen by law. These areas were classified in the Forest Code[57] as permanent preservation areas. The reason for the establishment of these areas is the protection of the resources necessary for the reproduction of essential ecological processes in these spaces. The vegetation located in these areas is under protection because its permanence was considered indispensable for soil protection, for sensitive ecosystems such as the *manguezais*, and for the water resources or other natural formations. An important characteristic of the protection system of these areas is the way that they are placed under special protection. This protection does not depend exclusively on a government act (as it was proposed by the SNUC). The Forest Code foresees two ways of creating protected areas: in the first one, the vegetation and the forests of some spaces were declared by an Act as unavailable for economic appropriation and exploitation, as not only the vegetation but also the spaces where they are located are under permanent preservation.[58] In this case, the special protection does not come from any government initiative, but from the Act. The second way demands a declaration by a government act, just like the SNUC pattern. But even in this modality, the protected spaces are not susceptible to economic exploitation or private appropriation either. As permanent preservation areas, they are only there for the protection of ecological functions.[59]

If the protection of private property requires that its owner accomplishes the social function of the space, the rule is more restrictive considering conservation units. In this case, there are specific and previously defined actions that have to be carried out by the owner as a condition for the permanence of the rights that he has over the space.

The ecosystems under constitutional protection are also not excluded from the exercise of economic activities on their resources or spaces. The Brazilian Constitution expressly stated the possibility of such use, which must be legally defined, as it allows for the preservation of those elements.[60] The Constitution did not prohibit the private appropriation of protected areas, but only their predatory and degrading use. In this way, either human activity was excluded or their activities were limited and conditioned.

The Brazilian pattern contemplates both alternatives. The first encompasses strict protection units, which do not allow the exercise of individual functions in these areas. The second involves sustainable use units, in which private activity is allowed because some conditions and uses are respected. Such accomplishment implies the achievement of the social function. No less important is the democratic focus proposed by SNUC for the management of the spaces of ecological interest. An important instrument established by this Act is public consultation, which has the objective of defining the main physical-natural space components, requiring the social participation not only to

[57] Act 4771/65.

[58] Article 2, "a" to "h," Act 4771/65.

[59] In comparison to the Forest Code system, the SNUC presents a different pattern in this matter (appropriation rules). It admits, for some modalities of conservation units (sustainable use units), the partial or total private appropriation of the protected areas, *conditioning* the exercise of the economic exploitation rights to the permanent exercise of only sustainable activities.

[60] Article 225, §4[t], Brazilian Constitution.

hear the local affected population but also to inform them about the main effects and results expected.[61]

Despite previewing this important instrument, the Brazilian pattern does not contemplate a system of management attributed directly to the population that had already been using the spaces and their natural resources (typical case of the traditional populations). The proposed solution was the creation of councils, composed by the members of the communities, but they don't always have the power to decide the destination of the conservation units.[62]

6.1.5 The National Policy of Biodiversity

An important contribution for implementing the CBD's goals in Brazilian law was carried out with the elaboration of the National Policy of Biodiversity by the Decree 4399/02, which establishes principles and guidelines for implementing the policy of biodiversity protection. Its enforcement is attributed both to the government and to society at large,[63] mimicking the constitutional rule for sharing responsibilities. Its elaboration is guided by twenty principles and nine directives, which consider: (1) the principles of precaution and prevention; (2) the participation of society in decisions about the management of natural resources; (3) the integration of sector and cross-sector programs and plans in the management of the resources; (4) the approach of decentralization in its management; and (5) the emphasis on the need to consider the causes of sensitive reduction or loss of biological diversity.

6.1.6 Biosafety and Access Instruments to Genetic Heritage and Associated Traditional Knowledge

The Act 11.105/05 is the legislative benchmark for biosafety in the Brazilian Legislation, which replaced Act 8974/95 that governed the subject to that point.[64] The new Biosafety Act establishes some safety and control systems related to activities that involve genetically modified organisms.[65]

The access to genetic resources, however, is still ruled by Provisional Act 2186–16/01, which deals with the access to genetic heritage, the protection of and access to associated traditional knowledge, the sharing of benefits, the access to technology, and the transfer of technology. Among the main aspects of the Provisional Act, two are mentioned: (1) the recognition of the right to decide the use of the traditional knowledge associated with the indigenous people;[66] and (2) the definition of an alternative of sharing benefits through contract, which also works as an instrument for accessing the genetic heritage benefits.[67] However, the proposed alternative to access and share benefits as well as the exclusion of the mandatory prior informed consent for accessing the knowledge of other traditional communities reveal the document's fragility.

[61] Article 5, §2, Federal Decree 4320/02.
[62] This is so in the case of the national forests, about which the council has only the consultation function (article 17, §5, Act 9.985/00).
[63] Article 1.
[64] The administrative infractions foreseen in the law were recently regulated by Decree n.5459/05.
[65] Article 1, *caput*.
[66] Article 8, §1.
[67] Article 19, §1.

6.2 The Implementation of the Convention on Biological Diversity

6.2.1 Sharing of Administrative Competence in Biodiversity Management and the Implementation of the CBD

The responsibility for planning, coordinating, controlling, and assessing measures for biological diversity conservation was shared between three bodies: the General Coordination for Biological Diversity (COBIO), the Environmental Issues Coordination Office (SMA), and the Department of Formulation of Environmental Policies and Programs (DEPAM).

The execution of those measures and the possibility to propose rules on this issue also was attributed to the Forests and Biodiversity Office, a special office that compounds the structure of the Ministry of the Environment.[68]

This structure concentrates a large part of the attributions concerning biodiversity protection. It comprehends the concentration of the prerogative of proposing rules, definition of policies and strategies and the execution and implementation of programs and projects related to managing, knowing, conserving, and the sustainable use of biological diversity,[69] actions that include the theme of access to genetic resources,[70] and the management of the National System of Conservation Units.[71]

6.2.2 National Biodiversity Commission (CONABIO)

As mentioned earlier, the National Biodiversity Commission was established by Decree 1354/94 and was further fixed by Decree 4703/03. Included is the implementation of the PRONABIO, the elaboration of National Biodiversity Policy, and the implementation of the commitments assumed by the Convention on Biological Diversity.

6.2.3 Sharing of Legislative and Administrative Competences Concerning Biosafety

6.2.3.1 Legislative Competence

The Brazilian Constitution establishes a system of shared legislative competences on environmental issues. It has stated that the federal government and the states have the competence to legislate on environmental subjects.[72] It also grants the federal government the right to deal with general rules[73] and gives states the power to specify federal rules.[74]

In this way, it could be argued that every state could aggregate and specify federal rules on biosafety in order to regulate aspects of specific interest of each state. However, the Brazilian Supreme Court has severely restricted this guideline, when considered on two occasions – before the new Act of Biosafety. In this case, the states could not rule in different ways as the rules were already defined by the federal government.

[68] Article 9, incise I *usque* VIII, Decree 2972/99.
[69] Article 1, incises I and II.
[70] Article 1, incise III.
[71] Article 1, incise IV.
[72] Article 24, incise IV, Brazilian Constitution.
[73] Article 24, §1, Brazilian Constitution.
[74] Article 24, §2, Brazilian Constitution.

This was because the rules would be considered general and, therefore, only the federal government would be able to produce them.[75]

6.2.3.2 The Genetic Heritage Management Council (CGEN)

The specific management of the genetic heritage and biosafety has been attributed to the CGEN – an office affiliated to the Ministry of the Environment, which was created by Provisional Act 2186–16/01[76] with the fundamental goal of coordinating the implementation of policies to manage the genetic heritage.[77]

This office concentrates important deliberative functions, such as to authorize the access to the genetic heritage and traditional associated knowledge as well as to establish criterion for elaborating the contracts for the use of genetic heritage and benefit-sharing.[78] The council has been strongly criticized because of the lack of instruments of social participation and, in this particular case, instruments of direct participation of indigenous people.

In the terms of Decree 3945/01, the CGEN is formed exclusively by members of nineteen federal public administration entities, and does not consider the possibility of the participation of any member of the society for the practice of its attributions.[79]

It is important to stress that, regarding indigenous people, the Constitution establishes two conditions for any use and access to natural resources in their lands: (1) the justification of relevant interest of the federal government; and (2) the definition of its relevant interest in complementary law.[80]

By contrast, the implementation of the CBD demands that the authorization for access or use of natural resources or associated traditional knowledge must be preceded by the consent of the interested indigenous people (stakeholders).[81]

Neither of these conditions was implemented by the federal government. For this reason, any act of exploitation and access of natural resources in the indigenous land, carried out by third parties must be considered invalid.[82]

6.2.3.3 The Decision Makers in the New Act of Biosafety

The biotechnology management and biosafety regulations have received new shape with a new legislative benchmark: Act 11.105/05.

This Act has created an institutionalized approach to manage the GMO's risks. One of the problems is that the decisions about the potential dangers has been attributed to a specialized institution made up of members of the scientific community and government represented by actors not necessarily involved in any activities or representing any interests related to these matters.[83]

The Act also established a new structure of administration on this subject, in a system that is now structured in two decisions levels and one control level. There is a higher

[75] ADIMC 2303/RS. *Rio Grande do Sul Governor v. Rio Grande do Sul Parliement* (2003) In http://www.stf.gov.br.
[76] Its composition was organized by Decree 3945/01.
[77] Article 11, incise I, Provisional Act 2186–16/01.
[78] Article 11, incise IV, "a" *usque* "d," Provisional Act 2186–16/01.
[79] Article 2, incise I, I *usque* XIX.
[80] Article 231, §6, Brazilian Constitution.
[81] Article 8, CDB.
[82] Ibid.
[83] The National Technical Commission on Biosafety (CTNBio), in Article 11, §10, admits the participation of society only under invitation and without the right to vote.

level, represented by the National Council of Biosafety (CNBs) made up exclusively by members of the government. At this level, there is no public participation. There is also a technical advising and supporting level with deliberative and consultative participation: the National Technical Commission of Biosafety (CTNBio), which is under the responsibility of the Ministry of Science and Technology.

The CNBs has to formulate and implement the National Biosafety Policy (PNB) and decide about the authorization and liberation of the GMOs for commercial use.[84]

With this new Act, the CTNBio, which is the second decision level, has became the original decision maker in the biosafety matter of modified organisms, not only in relation to researching activities but also regarding their commercial use.[85] Its decision has a binding effect in relation to any public offices.

In addition to the power to decide about the biosafety of GMOs, the Act has given to the CTNBio the power to access and decide about the demand or discharge of a previous environmental impact assessment, according to the evaluation of the activity's potential impact.[86]

Finally, there is a controlling and monitoring level with attributions shared among several ministries.[87]

Another relevant aspect of the new Act is related to the creation of an Information System for Biosafety (SIB), which is administrated by the Ministry of Science and Technology.[88]

As if the democratic deficit created in the decision-making bodies was not enough, it is still possible to see identical arbitrariness present in the texts of Acts 10688/03 and 10814/03,[89] which have authorized the planting of genetically modified soy in the 2004/2005 harvest, before the publication of the Act of Biosafety. This authorization can be postponed by exclusive decisions of the president of the republic.[90]

7 BRAZILIAN ILLUSTRATIVE CASES: THE *AMAZÔNIA* FOREST AND THE MONSANTO'S SOY BEANS

7.1 The Deforestation in the *Amazônia* Biome

In May 2005, the Brazilian Ministry of the Environment (MMA) published the 2004 annual deforestation rate in *Amazônia*. The measurement, which was made by the Institute of Spatial Research (INPE) based on 103 satellite images, revealed that approximately twenty-six thousand square kilometers of forests were put down between August 2003 and August 2004. As can be observed in Figure 8.2, this indicator is the second highest since 1989, when the INPE begun to analyze the biome's deforestation indicators.

In the 1990s, deforestation amounted to the 16.5 thousand square kilometers yearly. The indicator was considered extravagant worldwide and, since then, Brazil has been a focus of concern regarding the future of the tropical forests of the world. Despite this, the beginning of the new century has seen an exacerbation of this. In 2003, when

84 Article 8, incises II and III.

85 Article 15, incise XII.

86 Article 16, §§2 and 3.

87 Ministry of Health, Ministry of Agriculture, Cattle and Fueling; Ministry of the Environment; and Presidency of Republic's Special Office for Agriculture and Fishing (article 17, *caput*).

88 Article 19.

89 This issue will be analyzed in the next section.

90 Article 36 and paragraph.

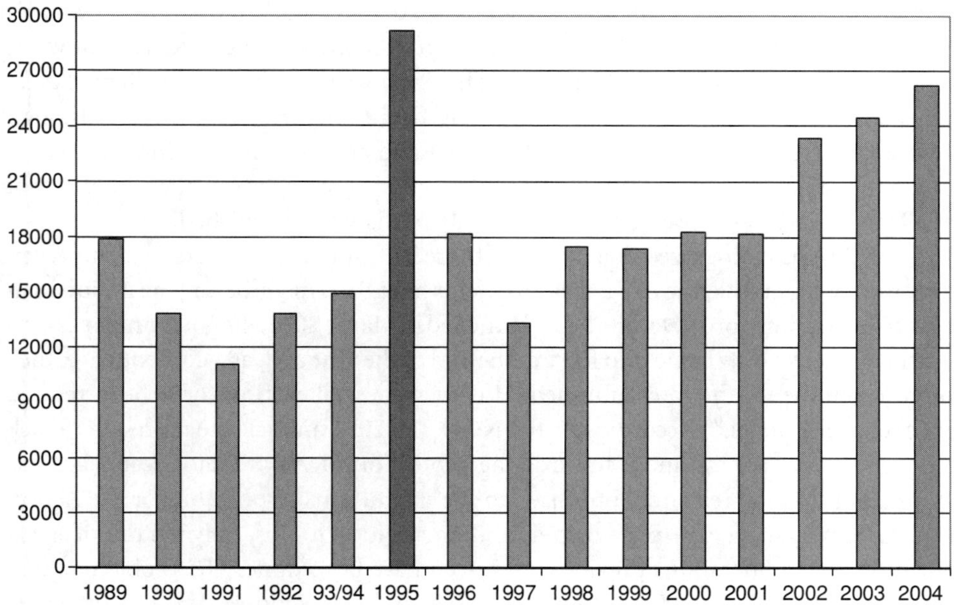

Figure 8.2. Deforestation in *Amazônia* – Annual Rates (Square Km)
Source: INPE (http://www.obt.inpe.br/prodes/index.html)

the INPE data was published, there was a general impression that the second historical deforestation rate had been reached. Nevertheless, the rate published in 2004 outranked the previous one by 6.5 percent, and the situation appeared to be out of control.

The *Mato Grosso* State, which is presently governed by the biggest individual producer of soy beans worldwide (Blairo Maggi), was responsible for almost half of the total area deforested in this biome (58.1 percent). According to Greenpeace Brazil,[91] 67 percent of the 12.586 square kilometers were illegally deforested. After the publication of that data, Blairo Maggi has accused the federal government of improperly managing the areas with less than three hundred hectares.[92] The MMA, however, asserts that the state has received high investments from the government and has today the best monitoring system in the country. At the same time, the Ministry has guaranteed that the monitoring operations in this region would be intensified. Concerning the deforestation percentages, the *Mato Grosso* is succeeded by the following Brazilian states: *Pará* (25.7 percent), *Rondônia* (15.8 percent), *Amazonas* (4 percent), *Acre* (3.1 percent), *Maranhão* (2.8 percent), *Tocantins* (0.4 percent) and *Roraima* (0.0 percent).

Considering some previous statistics about the deforestation in the *Amazônia* biome, which could reach twenty-three thousand square kilometers, in March 2004 the government launched an ambitious plan in order to minimize the problem. The Action Plan to Prevent and Control the Deforestation in *Amazônia* has overseen the installation of nineteen monitoring and controlling bases in the biome. In the same year, the government announced that 82 million *reais* would be driven to the workgroup responsible for looking after the human pressure on this area, under the IBAMA's coordination. A value three times bigger than that would be allocated to the workgroup responsible for

[91] Greenpeace Brasil – Amazônia. Available at http://www.greenpeace.org.br/amazonia/?conteudo_id=2064&sub_campanha=0.

[92] The government of the state has the duty to inspect the areas with more than three hundred hectares.

the region's land management. Furthermore, the Surveillance System for the *Amazônia* (SIVAN), one of the most modern aerospace and ground monitoring systems worldwide, was activated by the government in 2002. There is also a suitable legal system (Forest Code, Brazilian Constitution and Act of SNUC) regarding protected areas. Although there was a structured plan, an available budget and an apparent governmental commitment, the publication of the new deforestation rate is evidence that, whether or not the Plan's targets were observed, they were only partially accomplished.[93]

The MMA has recognized that the indicator recently published is very high, however, the Ministry claims that the INPE measurements have been made before the Action Plan measures came into force. Despite being launched in March 2004, the government asserts that the measures only came into force at the end of the year and, as a consequence, they could not influence the rate published. However, these allegations have been refuted by Greenpeace Brazil.[94] According to the NGO, the 2004 annual rate represents a lack of governmental commitment towards the protection of *Amazônia*. Greenpeace has pointed out that the resources promised to the institutions responsible for the Action Plan implementation were not fully released. In addition to this, only ten out of sixty-four monitoring operations previously foreseen have been done. The problem is that the IBAMA has only forty-three engineers and eight hundred inspectors to a total area of five millions square kilometers. In other words, there is just one inspector to each 6.5 thousand square km and one engineer to each 120 thousand square kilometers. This is clearly not enough.

Although accusations have been exchanged trying to find out who has failed, the lack of integration among all the institutions that should protect the forest becomes evident. Actually, all of them are guilty in the limits of their competencies. And the private sector, the international community, and the civil society must also be considered as part of the problem. There is no possibility of conservation without planning. The Acts are insufficient without a clear and viable environmental policy. The success of an environmental policy requires a multidisciplinary and qualified group working together. In the accomplishment of their attributions, these professionals depend on modern and effective equipment and control/monitoring systems. Finally, in order to formalize this, political interest and financial support are indispensable elements.

Unfortunately, the problem is still not considered in its whole complexity and, as a consequence, the *Amazônia* biome continues to be deforested. According to INPA and Smithsonian Institute (EUA) estimate, if the deforestation trend continues increasing for the next years, in 2020 the total area destroyed could be from 28 percent to 42 percent of the forest. The research done also indicates that infrastructure and highway project investments could overlap the conservation initiatives in the region. Furthermore, few ecosystems would comprise intact forests, barring those located in the western side of *Amazônia*.[95]

The high level of destruction of the *Amazônia* biome during the last ten years causes loss of several species of fauna and flora. It happens not only because the areas where they live are reduced but also because they are isolated from their original habitats. In addition

[93] Manoel Francisco Brito, "Relatório sobre o fracasso" (2005). Available at http://www.oeco.org.br.

[94] Greenpeace Brazil – Amazônia. Available at http://www.greenpeace.org.br/amazonia/?conteudo_id=2064&sub_campanha=0.

[95] Philip Ferarnside et al., "O futuro da Amazônia: os impactos do Programa Avança Brasil," (2002) *Revista Ciência Hoje* 61, 65.

to this, it is important to consider all the harm that these modifications have been causing to the indigenous population. These communities have been increasingly acculturated and confined into small reserves, which usually suffer any external interference. Finally, because the *Amazônia* is one of the greatest ecosystems in the world, it can be directly associated to climate changes problems. Until some years ago, Brazil was responsible for a negligible percentage of the greenhouse gas effect. Nevertheless, in the last few years, Brazilian emissions have increased considerably, reaching measures that are of great concern because of the uncontrolled deforestation rates. The consequences of this, in both global and local terms, are extremely serious.[96]

7.2 Biosafety and Soy Beans: The Monsanto Case

Just as in European law, genetically modified organisms have been at the center of a complex legislative and judicial controversy in Brazil. However, some peculiarities distinguish the Brazilian and European conflicts.

Despite the fact that there is already a minimum set of rules that has defined and regulated GMOs since 1995 (Act 8974/95), the main reason concerning the mentioned controversy only gained public visibility in recent times. It has been motivated by a specific set of facts that ended up in a unilateral decision by the Brazilian government about the destiny of transgenic soy harvests all over Brazil.

In 2003, the beginning of the public controversy, it was observed that the Brazilian State of Rio Grande do Sul had its harvest almost exclusively constituted by the genetically modified seeds "Roundup Ready." These seeds were illegally introduced through Argentina without paying any royalties to the multinational companies that owned the rights of the technology use for developing these seeds (Monsanto and Monsoy).

It has happened in a moment that this use was under severe juridical censure because the decision that has authorized it was taken by a body constituted exclusively by scientists (CTNBio), who allowed for very little democratic participation. Additionally, the decision was not based on conclusions obtained though an environmental impact study.

It is important to emphasize that the Brazilian Constitution imposes the obligation of previous investigation and demonstration of the inexistence of risks on any activity able to produce significant environmental damage. The instrument to carry out this previous investigation is the environment impact study (EIA).[97]

Considering this, genetically modified soy was prohibited. It happened firstly by a decision of the Sixth Court of Brasilia City in as a preparatory safeguard measure of a public civil action.[98] It has expressively recognized the obligation of Monsanto and Monsoy to undertake the EIA as a condition for use of the genetic modified soy.

This decision was confirmed by the First Region's Regional Federal Court on the trial for appealing 2000.01.00.014661-1/DF.[99] Considering the GMOs risks, the fundamental importance of the application of the precautionary principle was recognized.

[96] Israel Klabin et al., "O futuro da Amazônia é o nosso futuro," (2005) *Folha de São Paulo* A3.
[97] Article 225 §1, incise IV.
[98] The public civil action is similar to a class action in the United States.
[99] Civil Appeal 2000.01.00.014661-1/DF, *The Federal Government and Monsanto do Brasil v. Greenpeace* [2001]. Available at http://www.trf1.gov.br.

Some time later, this decision was reviewed. In a long decision (of 719 pages),[100] execution of it was suspended until the motion was judged, under the argument that the agrobusiness sector would suffer intolerable damage, facing the uncertainty on the possibility of the use of biotechnology. This decision was suspended by the Fifth Circuit of the same Regional Federal Court,[101] but its effects were very limited.

Under intense influence of economic interests, the Brazilian federal government edited the Provisional Acts 113 and 131 (unilateral decisions by the president). Later, these Provisional Acts were converted into Acts 10688/03 and 108414/03, which has established the possibility of commercialization of the genetically modified soy harvests of 2003 and 2004. It was considered a direct and frontal contrast to the Brazilian Constitution, and also contrary to valid court orders that continue to impose the EIA obligation.

The constitutionality of these legal measures is under a decision of the Brazilian Constitutional Court (Federal Supreme Court) in four actions proposed by different authors.[102] At this moment, this undoubtedly opposes Executive and Legislative Powers and the productive sector to the Brazilian Constitution and national courts in a tense balancing definition relationship, which exposes the environmental protection to a dangerous condition of institutional uncertainty.[103]

8 CONCLUSIONS

- The CBD has particular significance for global protection in environment and development areas. The main purpose is a framework agreement. The CBD was unique on matters such as conservation of biodiversity, by recognizing the common concerns of humankind. Its provision represented overall goals and policies, instead of hard obligations.
- The national reports from many parties in Latin America, Asia, and Africa identified a common need for additional financial and human resources in order to help implement the Convention. The lack of these was quoted as a major constraint to implementation of the CBD.
- The COP adopted a Strategic Plan for the Convention on Biological Diversity. The plan will initially cover the period 2002–2010. It will be based on the longer-term programs of work of the COP and SBSTTA and is intended to provide strategic and operational guidance for the implementation of these programs. The COP urged

[100] Suspensive effect on the Civil Appeal n.1998.34.00.027602-0/DF, *Monsanto do Brasil and another v. the Federal Government and IDEC* [2003]. Available at http://www.trf1.gov.br.

[101] This suspended decision has led to the commercialization of transgenic soy. Available at http://www.trf1.gov.br/Trf/Setorial/Ascon?AbreNoticia.pp?id=165 & count=&email=.

[102] In chronologic sequence, we have the Direct Actions of Unconstitutionality 3011, 3014, 3017, respectively, proposal by the Green Party, the Confederation of Agriculture Workers (CONTAG) and by the General – Prosecutor of the Republic facing the Provisional Measure 131. Recently (9 January 2004) the general prosecutor of the republic also proposed a new action (3109), this time, with regard to law 10814, resulted in the conversion of the Provisional Measure. In all these actions, two violations can be observed: the first one to the constitutional obligation to implement the Previous Environmental Impact Assessment; and the second one to the principles of independence and harmony among powers.

[103] This tense relationship has recently converted itself in relation to the lack of balance favoring the productive sector. The advance of agrofrontiers, especially to the soy craps towards the legal Amazon, has converted itself into expressive degradation sceneries, expressed in the recent divulgation of the tree-cutting rates of 2004, with international knowledge.

parties, states, intergovernmental organizations, and other organizations to review their activities, especially their national biodiversity strategies and action plans in the light of the Strategic Plan for the CBD.

- The general overview of obstacles to the implementation of the CBD was reported in the Global Biodiversity Outlook (GBO), including the following; political as well as lack of political will and support or political instability; institutional as well as lack of transfer of technology or loss of traditional knowledge; access of information as well as lack of accessible social factors; and others such as poverty, lack of appropriate policies and laws, and unsustainable consumption and production patterns.
- The Brazilian government has established the National Biodiversity Program (PRONABIO/CONABIO) since 1994. The environmental legislation in Brazil is almost updated, but the lack of enforcement has played a key issue in implementation matters.
- Brazil is an extremely diverse country. However, the conservation of such huge biological diversity to the present and future generations has been considered insufficient. Among the many difficulties Brazil has been facing, the controversial relationship between development and environmental conservation is a big challenge that still remains. And, when the development view is limited to economic growth, it usually becomes very harmful to the environment.
- In general, the problems regarding the conservation and sustainable use of biodiversity are many, complex, delicate and difficult to separate. However, after overtaking the invisible frontier of the twenty-first century, all of the societies around the world should face the challenge of implementing the sustainable development, which must be able to conciliate ecological prudence, economical feasibility, and social justice.
- The 2004 annual deforestation rate published by the Brazilian Ministry of the Environment has revealed that approximately twenty-six thousand square kilometers of forests were destroyed between August 2003 and August 2004. This rate is the second highest in the last fifteen years, which suggests that the situation seems to be out of control.
- The lack of integration among all the institutions that should protect the forest has become evident. All of them have failed in the limits of their competencies. And the private sector, the international community, and the civil society also must be considered as a part of the problem. There is no possibility of conservation without planning. The Acts are insufficient without a clear and viable environmental policy. The success of an environmental policy requires a multidisciplinary and qualified group working together. In order to accomplish their goals, these professionals depend on modern and effective equipment and control/monitoring systems. Finally, in order to concretize all of this, political interest and financial support are indispensable elements.
- The beginning of the controversy in the matter of GMOs in Brazil was not a normative controversy but a judicial and political one. It was related to the absence of the Previous Environmental Impact Assessment, required by the Law, that were not carried out by the multinational companies when they introduced the GMOs into the Brazilian market.
- The new Brazilian Biosafety Act has been met with a lot of criticism. This is mainly because the Act has proposed a decision-making process based on an institutionalized

approach to manage the GMOs risks (introduction or its use). Among other problems, it has attributed the decision-making power to a specialized organ formed mostly by members of the scientific community and government, without public participations, which has produced a hard and serious democratic *deficit* in the Brazilian Biosafety Policy.

SECTION C. NATIONAL AND REGIONAL LEGAL AND INSTITUTIONAL TOOLS AND REGIMES

9 EC Law and Biodiversity

Nicolas de Sadeleer*

1 INTRODUCTION

The term "biodiversity" was not coined until the 1980s, when it was popularised by the eminent Harvard biologist E. O. Wilson.[1] The most tangible manifestations of biodiversity are the species of plants, animals and micro-organisms that surround us. Yet biodiversity means more than just species diversity. At the micro level, it includes the genetic material that makes up the species, whereas at the macro level, it covers natural communities, ecosystems and landscapes. Biodiversity essentially relates to the full array of life on Earth.[2]

In an apparently continuous movement, biodiversity emerged over the course of the geological eras, wending its way through both biological evolution and periods of mass extinction. Such diversification of the living world is made possible by the genetic adaptation of species to environmental changes, whether natural or human caused. Communities themselves evolve on the basis of fluctuations in their environment, according to complex historical processes that explain the present state of the biosphere. The first living beings appeared in the oceans roughly 3.5 billion years ago in the form of primitive bacteria, which subsequently diversified into the multitude of organisms of every shape and size and are now classified under five kingdoms (animal, plant, fungi, bacteria, and protists), each of which is divided into systematic classifications that emerged following the branching out of the particular species. Humankind has still a long way to go before acquiring a complete knowledge of the species that populate the Earth. Although about 1,320,000 animal species have been catalogued, scientists estimate the total number of species on Earth at more than ten million.[3] This biodiversity is not distributed evenly across the planet. Generally speaking, on the continents, it increases from the poles toward the equator, whereas in the oceans the increase is much less pronounced, and sometimes operates in reverse. Such an unequal distribution can be explained by climatic, historic, and geomorphologic factors.

[1] E. O. Wilson & F. M. Petter, eds., *Biodiversity* (Washington, DC: National Academy Press, 1988), 521.

[2] The 1992 CBD defines it in terms of three conceptual levels. According to the CBD, "biological diversity" means "the variability among living organisms from all sources including, inter alia, terrestrial, marine and other aquatic ecosystems and the ecological complexes of which they are part; this includes diversity within species, between species and of ecosystems."

[3] UNEP/WCMC, *Global Biodiversity. Earth's living Resources in the 21st century* (Cambridge, UK: Cambridge University Press, Aventis Foundation, 2000) tableaux 3(1)(1) and 3(1)(2).

* Nicholas de Sadeleer is Professor of Law at the University of Oslo, Norway.

Biodiversity today is passing through a period of major crisis. Most natural or seminatural, continental, and costal ecosystems are now subject to significant modifications as a result of human activity. Scientists expect that these disruptions will cause an unprecedented drop in the wealth of specific and genetic diversity.

Having said this, however, legal regulation has not taken a back seat, especially at the international level. Over the past four decades, international law has been enriched by a raft of conventions and agreements intended to put a stop to this deterioration of the living world. Although highly diverse in nature, these rules may be classified under three broad categories, the first covering the exploitation of biological resources, where necessary limiting exploitation to guarantee its continuity, the second aiming at protecting the elements of biodiversity, and the third intended to curb processes that affect the biosphere, whether or not on a global scale.

Moreover, the adoption in 1992 of the Convention on Biodiversity (CBD) represented a watershed in the development of the international law on biodiversity. Although it does not codify the existing international law on the conservation of species and ecosystems, it does, as a framework convention, establish the foundations that must underpin both national legislation and subsequent international agreements on the conservation and sustainable use of biodiversity. In addition, it also would constitute an ideal basis for the future regulation of the access to genetic resources and the equitable sharing of benefits flowing from their exploitation. In spite of the criticisms that have frequently been brought against it – in particular, in relation to its utilitarian character and the weak binding force of its arrangements – the CBD constitutes a reference point that, for the first time, covers biodiversity in its entirety. Its dynamic character means that it can preside over the evolution both of international law and the various national laws on biodiversity.

International rules on the conservation of biodiversity are by no means lacking in Europe. An impressive array of international agreements have been adopted both by the Council of Europe and the UN.[4] However, the existence of so many agreements should not lull us into thinking that all areas of biodiversity are now well protected. Conservation objectives vary from one agreement to the next, such that no harmonisation, even on a geographical level, is assured. Although particular areas of biodiversity (such as migratory or the most endangered vertebrate species, international watercourses, and semiinland seas) are covered well at a continental scale, others (such as landscapes) have only recently been brought under international law, and still others (such as micro-organisms or fungi, fundamental ecological processes, animal genetic resources) are practically ignored. Finally, only rarely do conventions require the conservation of all wild species, or of all species of the same group (such as birds or marine mammals).

Finally, some significant geographical disparities are also apparent. Although the Bern Convention on the Conservation of European Wildlife and Natural Habitats covers the entire continent, it does not, extend to the whole spectrum of biodiversity. Moreover, some regions such as the Mediterranean Sea, Black Sea, North East Atlantic, Alps, Carpathians, and the Benelux area, are well covered, the protection of other areas is markedly lower.

One might then wonder whether the implementation of a biodiversity policy under the auspices of Community law might offer better protection of ecosystems and species

[4] For a comprehensive analysis of the agreements in force in Europe, see N. de Sadeleer & C.-H. Born, *Le Droit international et communautaire de la biodiversité* (Paris: Dalloz, 2004), 780.

than a highly variegated international law. Indeed, Community law today extends to twenty-five Member States and will probably extend to more in the years to come. The Commission enjoys specific powers to require Member States to apply the rules of European Community (EC) law and environmental policy has already cut its teeth in this area.

It should therefore be noted at the outset that, unlike international law, the Community legal order is not equivalent to either the Convention on Biological Diversity, or the Montego Bay Convention on the Law of the Sea, agreements that laid the basis for conservation regimes covering both inland and marine biodiversity. Moreover, as will be argued later in this chapter, biodiversity in Community law is covered by relatively heterogeneous legislation, adopted at different times without any general overview and coming in the form of both regulations and directives. Although these rules were normally passed within the context of the Community's environmental policy, they also have resulted from other policies, such as the common agricultural policy, common trade policy, or that of the internal market.

The purpose of this chapter is to take stock of the contribution of Community law to the conservation of biodiversity in Europe. It will start with a brief overview of the present state of biodiversity on our continent and go on to address particular problems.

2 THE STATE OF BIODIVERSITY IN EUROPE

On the European continent, biodiversity can be distributed into eleven biogeographical regions, namely, the Arctic, Boreal, Continental, Atlantic, Mediterranean, Macaronesian (Madeira, Azores, and Canaries), Anatolian (continental Turkey), Pannonian (Caucasus), Steppe, and Alpine.

3 LEGAL BASIS OF THE EC DIRECTIVES AND REGULATIONS ON THE CONSERVATION OF BIODIVERSITY

According to a line of cases of the Court of Justice relating to the competence of Community lawmakers, the choice of the legal basis of an act must be founded on objective elements, which can be subject to judicial review. In particular, such elements include the aim (e.g., the conservation of natural habitats) and content (e.g., the obligation to classify land according to scientific criteria) of the act.[5]

It is therefore appropriate to distinguish between the criteria that will allow for the enactment of a Community regulation on biodiversity either under Article 175 of the EC Treaty (environmental matters), Article 37 (CAP), Article 95 (internal market), or Article 133 (common trade policy).

3.1 Biodiversity and the Internal Market

It is not the case that every provision remotely relating to biological diversity has been passed under the only chapter of the EC Treaty dedicated to environmental policy. Article 95 (formerly Article 100A) – which extends horizontally to all measures affecting the establishment and the functioning of the internal market, including those relating

[5] C-45/86 *Commission v. Council* (1987) ECR 1493, paragraph 11; C-269/97 *Commission v. Council* (2000) ECR I-2257, paragraph 43; C-36/98 *Spain v. Council* (2001) ECR I-779, paragraph 58.

to environmental protection (Article 95(3)) – was the basis for the harmonisation of the rules relating to products (e.g., GMOs, biocides) that represent a danger to the environment. The fact that some of these harmonising directives also pursued environmental goals did not prevent them from being passed under Article 95 as this provision expressly refers, in the first, third, and fourth paragraphs, to the protection of the environment. Naturally, this provision does not give Community lawmakers any general competence to harmonise national rules in health or environmental matters.[6] However, in the "Biotechnology Patents" case, the Court interpreted the use of Article 95 as a legal basis in a broad sense to cover instances even when the regulation was not exclusively intended to remove obstacles to the internal market.[7]

3.2 Biodiversity and Common Trade Policy

The scope of this policy has been interpreted in a broad sense and any acts founded on Article 133 of the Treaty can cover environmental aspects on account of the principle of integration. In the "Greek Chernobyl" case, the Court of Justice upheld the use of Article 113 to adopt a regulation on the conditions for the importation of agricultural products from outside the Community following the Chernobyl nuclear disaster.[8] Although the incorporation of the Carthage Protocol on biotechnological risk prevention into the common trade policy (Article 133) could have brought this agreement under the exclusive Community competence relating to common trade policy, recourse to Article 175 implied Member State competence alongside that of the Community, as the former have retained competence in this area (shared Community competence). Referring to its consistent findings on the objective elements that must found the choice of legal instrument, and that can be subject to judicial review, the Court of Justice indicated in its judgment that the Carthagena Protocol is essentially intended to prevent biotechnological risks and not, as the Commission had argued, to facilitate or regulate commercial exchanges. The Court laid particular emphasis on the context within which the protocol had been negotiated, namely, the Convention on Biological Diversity, going through the Protocol's preamble and provisions with a fine-tooth comb in order to establish its basic aim and content. The Commission's argument focussing on the practical difficulties stemming from the implementation of the mixed agreement was not deemed sufficient to tip the balance in favour of Article 113 of the Treaty. Finally, the Court held that the Protocol would have to have been founded on a single legal basis specific to environmental policy, that is, Article 175.

3.3 Biodiversity and the Common Agricultural Policy

It is important to briefly note that the Court's case law has not furnished any legal test for determining which legal regime takes priority when a measure falls more specifically under the Common Agricultural Policy (Article 37) or under Community Environmental Policy (Article 175). It is by no means easy to trace the dividing line between the two. Although rules limiting the use of drift nets and promoting agro-environmental

[6] C-300/89 *Commission v. Council* (1991) ECR I-2867; C-155/91 *Commission v. Council*, (1993) ECR I-939.

[7] C-377/98 *Netherlands v. Parliament & Council* (2001) ECR I-7079.

[8] C-62/88 *Greece v. Council* (1990) ECR 1527.

measures are clearly founded solely on the provisions governing the CAP, even where environmental protection concerns may have contributed to their adoption,[9] provisions specifically relating to environmental policy must be founded on Article 175 of the Treaty (which falls under Title XIX on the environment), even if among their objectives is the improvement of agricultural production. This would for instance be the case for a directive on phyto-pharmaceutical products whose legal basis was Article 37 EC Treaty, the provision endowing the Community with specific competences as regards agriculture.[10] In contrast, the European Court of Justice took the view that measures to defend forests against risks of destruction and deterioration caused by fires and atmospheric pollution fall squarely within the class of environmental actions for which Community competence is founded on Article 175 of the Treaty.[11] As a result, such measures have to be based on Article 175 and not Article 37 EC Treaty.

4 POLICY DEVELOPMENT

4.1 Core Issues

A real policy of conserving biological diversity is gradually coming to light in a series of nonbinding acts adopted by Community institutions. These acts can be classified within a pyramid-shaped hierarchy. At the pinnacle lie the various proposals formulated by the European Commission together with the decisions taken by the various "environmental" Councils and European Councils relating to sustainable development and the integration of the environment into other Community policies. At an intermediate level are initiatives relating to biodiversity envisaged under the sixth Community action program for the environment. The pyramid rests on more precise action programs adopted by the Commission to promote biological diversity and on the numerous sectoral strategies provided for by the sixth action program, which should contribute to the preservation of ecosystems in the European Union.

4.2 Instruments Dedicated to Sustainable Development

By inviting the different incarnations of the Council of Ministers (agriculture, transport, energy) to develop their own strategy for environmental integration, the European Council (meeting at Cardiff on 15–16 June 1998) paved the way for coordinated Community-level action on the integration of environmental requirements into the various sectoral policies. It was, however, necessary to await the European Council's meeting in Göteborg on 15–16 June 2001 for the adoption of a Community-wide strategy on sustainable development, by adding an environmental dimension to the existing social and economic considerations (cf. Lisbon strategy). Finally, the European Council, meeting in Brussels on 20–21 March 2003 reiterated that sustained growth constituted one of the priorities of the Union. Particular "environmental indicators," including

[9] C-405/92 *Mondiet* (1993) ECR I-6133, paragraphs 25–27; C-366/00 *Huber* (2002) ECR I-1749, paragraph 33.

[10] C-303/94 *Parliament v. Council* (1996) ECR I-2943.

[11] Joined Cases C-164/97 and C-165/97 *European Parliament v. Council* (1999) ECR I-1139.

the state of biological diversity, should allow for the evaluation of progress made on sustainable development.[12]

4.3 Sixth Environmental Action Programme

Among the main priorities of the Sixth Community action program[13] is a declaration aspiring to put an end to the depletion of biodiversity by 2010 in accordance with international commitments (no. 79) as well as "protecting, conserving, restoring and developing the functioning of natural systems, natural habitats, wild flora and fauna with the aim of halting desertification and the loss of biodiversity, including diversity of genetic resources, both in the European Union and on a global scale" (Article 2(2)(ii)). Specific action is announced "on nature and biodiversity," including research, implementation of the Community Biodiversity Strategy, establishment of the Natura 2000 network, fair and equitable division of benefits generated from the use of genetic resources, invasive alien species prevention (Article 6(2)(a)). Further action is also foreseen relating to the sustainable use of the sea and the conservation of marine ecosystems (integrated management of costal areas, Natura 2000) (Article 6(2)(g)), forest ecosystems (certification of sustainable forest management, criminalisation of frauds, climate change) (Article 6(2)(h)) and GMOs (ratification of the Carthage Protocol) (Article 6(2)(g)). It should, however, be noted that the objectives are formulated in a relatively vague manner (absence of precise and dated regulatory proposals),[14] and they will therefore have to be interpreted in the light of other types of documents.

4.4 Programming Specific to Biodiversity

In order to implement the Convention on Biological Diversity, to which the European Community is party[15] and, more specifically, Article 6 which deals with the development of strategies, plans, and programs designed to ensure the conservation and the sustainable use of biological diversity and the integration of conservation and sustainable use of biodiversity into the sectoral programmes, plans, and policies, the European Commission adopted, in February 1998, a communication on a community biodiversity strategy,[16] which was approved by the Council in June 1998 and by the European Parliament in October of the same year.[17] "Aiming to anticipate, prevent and combat at source the marked reduction or loss of biodiversity," this strategy is structured around four principal themes: the conservation and sustainable use of biological diversity; the sharing of the benefits flowing from the exploitation of genetic resources; research into, and identification, monitoring, and exchange of biodiversity; and finally education, training, and sensitisation. In accordance with the CBD, this document stresses the need to integrate biodiversity concerns into sectoral policies relating to the conservation

[12] Commission's report to the Council of 20 September 2002, Analysis of the open list of environment-related headline indicators (COM) 2002, 524 final.

[13] European Parliament and Council Decision 1600/2002/EC of 22 July 2002 laying down the Sixth Community Environment Action Programme (OJEC, L 242, 10 September 2002, p. 1).

[14] L. Krämer, "Thirty Years of European Community Environmental Law: Perspectives and Prospectives" 2 *Yb. Eur. Env.L* (2002), 164.

[15] Council Decision of 25 October 1993 (OJEC, L 309, 13 December 1993).

[16] Communication from the Commission to the Council and to the European Parliament, on a European Community Biodiversity Strategy (COM (1998) 42).

[17] Council conclusions of 21 June 1998 and Parliament resolution (A4-0347/98).

of natural resources, agriculture, fishing, regional development, forests, energy, transport, tourism, and developmental aid. Finally, the strategy envisages the development of action programs for the relevant sectoral activities, which in turn must set out specific measures in each sector for fulfilling the particular objectives.

The first action program, which promoted biological diversity in the area of natural resource conservation, passed on 27 March 2001.[18] This plan was designed for the protection of wild flora and fauna as well as of ecosystems and habitats on the basis of existing legal arrangements (Birds and Habitats directives, CITES regulation). Subsequently, an action program for biological biodiversity in agriculture[19] identified several priorities including agro-environmental measures, the establishment of an ecological infrastructure over the whole territory, the diversification of agricultural genetic capital, the marketing of the landraces and the plant varieties, and the fight against nonindigenous species. An action program to promote biological diversity in fishing[20] seeks to preserve and reinvigorate biological diversity where it is threatened by fishing and agriculture activities. Finally, an action program to promote biological diversity in the area of economic cooperation and developmental aid[21] is under consideration. Such a plan would make significant inroads in the fight against poverty and the reversal trend towards environmental deterioration.

4.5 Other Programs

Other communications and recommendations of the Commission are likely to contribute to the taking of specific action formulated within the framework of the Community Biodiversity Strategy. Such instruments include the Commission communication on integrated costal zone management (COM (2000) 547) intended to contribute to the protection of coastal wetlands (no. 760), the 1998 communication "Sustainable Urban Development: a Framework for Action in the European Union" (COM (605) 98) designed to encourage the conservation of biodiversity in urban areas as well as the Commission's communication of 16 April 2002, "Towards a Thematic Strategy for Soil Protection" ((COM 2002) 179 final), which provides for the implementation of a Community soil strategy, including promotion of organic farming, reforestation, and limits on the use of pesticides, during the course of 2004. Another initiative, set out in the Commission communication of 2 October 2002 on "A Strategy to Protect and Conserve the Marine Environment," also provides for the sixth action program, and includes a review of the numerous threats that endanger marine environments such as reduction of biological diversity, elimination of habitats, and contamination by dangerous substances. The aim of this instrument is to promote the sustainable use of the sea and the conservation of marine ecosystems, in particular in areas of significant value for biological diversity. The communication to the Council and European Parliament on "A Forest Strategy for the European Union" (COM (1998) 649 final) also covers the conservation of biodiversity.

[18] Communication from the Commission to the Council and the European Parliament of 27 March 2001, COM (2001) 162 final, vol. 2.

[19] Communication from the Commission to the Council and the European Parliament of 27 March 2001, COM (2001) 162 final, vol. III.

[20] Communication from the Commission to the Council and the European Parliament of 27 March 2001, COM (2001) 162 final, vol. IV.

[21] Communication from the Commission to the Council and the European Parliament of 27 March 2001, COM (2001) 162 final, vol. V.

Last but not least, the fifteen ministers responsible for territorial management in the Member States, in an informal meeting at Potsdam on 11 May 1999, adopted the European Spatial Development Perspective (ESDP). The objective of this document is to promote a balanced and sustainable development of the Union's territory through inclusion into the mainstream of European policymaking, without, however, expanding Community competence in this area. This nonbinding document, examines the impact of Community policies and their contribution to a balanced and sustainable territorial development, also formulating guidelines on natural heritage.

5 SPECIES AND ECOSYSTEM APPROACH

As a result of the high level of interdependence of the rules on the conservation of habitats and wild species contained in two separate instruments (the Habitats and Birds directives), this section will discuss the two approaches in tandem.

5.1 EC Obligations under International Law

As well as being a party to the CBD[22]– a treaty promoting the implementation of conservation measures in situ – the Community also has several international and regional conventions that are specifically targeted at protecting the habitats of numerous animal and plant species. The Community is a signatory to:

- the Bern Convention on the conservation of European wildlife and natural habitat;[23]
- the 1982 Geneva Protocol concerning specially protected areas in the Mediterranean;[24]
- the 1991 Salzburg Convention on the protection of the Alps;[25]
- the 1995 Barcelona Protocol concerning specially protected areas and biological diversity in the Mediterranean;[26] and
- the 1994 Convention to combat desertification[27]

It is not, however, party to the European Landscape Convention and the Ramsar Convention, although the Habitats and Birds directives guarantee the conservation by national authorities of a very large number of marine habitats similar to the Ramsar sites.

5.2 Indigenous Species Approach

Generally speaking, the Birds directive lays down a general prohibition on the killing, capture, (deliberate) disturbance, retention, and commercialisation of bird species, the keeping of protected species as well as the destruction, damage or collection of their nests and eggs (Articles 5 and 6(1)). Furthermore, Article 8 outlaws the use of all means, arrangements or methods to capture or kill on a large or nonselective scale. This regime

[22] Council Decision 93/626/EEC, 25 October 1993 (OJEC, L 309, 13 December 1993; corrigendum L 82, 25 March 1994).

[23] Council Decision 82/72/EEC of 3 December 1981 (OJEC, L 38 of 10 February 1982, p. 1; Council Decision, 21 December 1998 (OJEC, L 358, 31 December 1998).

[24] Council Decision 84/132/EEC of 1 March 1984 (OJEC, L 68, 10 March 1984).

[25] Council Decision 96/191/EC of 26 February 1996 (OJEC, L 61, 12 March 1996).

[26] Council Decision 1999/800/EC of 22 October 1999 (OJEC, L 322, 14 December 1999).

[27] Council Decision 1998/216/EC of 1998 (OJEC, L83, 1998).

is, however, not absolute as important exceptions are allowed, in particular relating to marketing (Article 6), hunting (Article 7), and capture (Article 9).

As a result of often passionate reactions from the hunting lobby, the transposition of the Birds directive into internal law and its subsequent application was dogged by its share of difficulties. The Commission has had to take action against several foot-dragging Member States by instigating default proceedings. In the vast majority of judgments handed down by the Court, the Commission's position has been vindicated. Moreover, numerous national courts have invoked the direct effect of particular provisions of the directive in order to rule on disputes, especially those concerning hunted species and hunting seasons.

Unlike the Birds directive, the Habitats directive does not set up a general protection regime for wild animal and plant species living within the Community territory, as the protective measures only apply to a limited number of species of Community interest. Two regimes are provided for, one covering species in need of strict protection (Annex IV) and whose capture can only be allowed in exceptional circumstances, and the other covering species whose capture may be subject to management measures (Annex V). However, the transposition of this directive's provisions on species protection has subsequently given rise to numerous difficulties. Of particular concern is that, as for the Birds directive, this directive has run into resistance on the part of certain States members. Both birds and Habitats Directives call upon Member States to designate and to protect huge tracts of land as EC protected areas with the aim of preserving various threatened species and habitats. In restricting activities endangering wildlife, these EC obligations impinge upon national and regional development and land planning policies.

5.3 Exotic Species Approach

Alongside the United States and Japan, the European Community represents one of the three largest markets for the international trade in wild species. Although the first pillar of Community policy on nature conservation consisted of guaranteeing protection to species indigenous to the European Community together with their habitats, a second pillar covers the trade in exotic species imported into the Community. The Community has first of all applied the CITES Convention without however having being able to ratify it; it has as well as this forbidden of its own accord the trade in particular large mammal species well-known by the general public (whales, baby seals, major fur-bearing predators), all the time subject to intense pressure from the hunting lobby.

It is in this context important to stress the role of the CITES (EC) regulation 338/97, which considerably broadened the scope of application of the CITES Convention within the Community legal order. The regulation classified wild animal and vegetable species under four annexes, while subjecting other species that are not necessarily included in the CITES annexes to control regimes.

6 GENETIC APPROACH

6.1 The Conservation of Genetic Resources

Because it did not become a member of the FAO until 1991, the European Community was not party to the International Agreement on Phytogenetic Resources (1983). By contrast, it participated in the development of Bonn guidelines of the CBD on the access to and division of benefits as well as signing on 6 June 2002 the recent international Treaty on Phytogenetic Resources for Food and Agriculture. Parties to the Convention on Biological Diversity, are also required to take the necessary measures at the Community level regarding the access to genetic resources and the sharing of benefits.

On a political level, the European Community has only recently broached the issue of genetic resources. Accordingly, the fight against the impoverishment of genetic resource diversity constitutes one of the objectives of the Sixth Action Program (2002).[28]

The first measures promoting actions in favour of genetic resources in agriculture and forestry were taken in 1992, within the framework of the agro-environmental regime. The new regulation 1257/1999/EC provides that support may be granted "ways of using agricultural land which are compatible with the protection and improvement of... genetic diversity" (Article 22(2)). More specifically, support may now benefit farmers involved in the breeding of local animal races native to the particular area and that are in danger of dying out (according to the Annex I criteria of regulation 445/2002), or in the preservation of genetic plant resources "naturellement adapted to the local and regional conditions and threatened by erosion génétique" (applying where appropriate also to forests).

Moreover, a legal framework was established in 1994 to promote specially tailored projects for the conservation, characterisation, collection, and use of genetic resources. Stressing the importance of preserving genetic resources in order to preserve the "irreplaceable fund" represented by biological diversity in agriculture, the Council adopted on 20 June 1994 regulation 1467/94 on the conservation, characterisation, collection, and utilisation of genetic resources in agriculture.[29] The general objective of this regulation is to "promote the aims of the common agricultural policy and safeguard biological diversity in line with the Convention on Biological Diversity" (first paragraph of the preamble; Article 1 of regulation 1467/94), as confirmed by the stated legal basis, namely, Article 37 of the Treaty (agricultural policy).

6.2 Management of GMOs

A lively debate has been raging across Europe regarding the risks related to the dispersal into the environment of genetically modified organisms (GMO), both in relation to ecosystems as well as the integrity of the nonmodified or wild stock of the parent species, as well as for neighbouring species. Moreover, the Council of Ministers of the environment, meeting on 24 June 1999, imposed a *de facto* moratorium on the marketing of new GMOs (following the approach of several Member States: Denmark, France, Greece, Italy, Luxemburg, and, since 2001, Austria) in the absence of clear rules on the traceability and labelling of GMOs placed on the market, as well as on environmental responsibility.

The Community did not neglect to invoke the threat to biodiversity in its Sixth Action programme, as well as in its strategy in favour of biological diversity and its action programmes on the protection of natural resources and on agriculture.

Distinguishing itself by a recourse founded to the precautionary principle, Community law on GMOs has not stopped expanding, aiming both at ensuring the functioning of the internal market in relation to this type of product as well as responding to

[28] Article 2(2), of Decision 1600/2002/EC.

[29] OJEC, L 159, 28 June 1994.

the expectations of the environmental protection circles and consumers alike. Directive 2001/18/EC on the deliberate release into the environment of genetically modified organisms is the mainstay in the prevention of the appearance of these risks. This directive is founded on a core principle according to which no GMO may be released into the environment on an experimental basis (part B of the directive) or subsequently be placed on the market (part C of the directive) without having been previously authorised by the competent authorities following a scientific assessment designed to establish the absence of risks for the environment and human health.

Finally, taking care to abide by its international commitments undertaken in 2000 in Carthagena, the European Community was quick to investigate means for implementing the Protocol on Biosafety into the heart of the EU. Against this background, the European Commission presented a draft regulation to the European Parliament and the Council on the transfrontier movements of genetically modified organisms.[30] The draft was based on Article 175(1) of the EC Treaty and, according to an opinion handed down by the Court, was designed to implement, "in accordance with the precautionary principle," a system of notifications and exchange of information relating to the export of GMOs outside European Community, in order to "contribute to the assurance of an adequate level of protection" for the transfrontier movements of GMOs, which constitute a risk for biodiversity or health.

7 CONCLUSION

Four observations flow from the foregoing analysis, the first in relation to the international legal order, the second to the development of a legal framework specifically tailored to the problems touched on, the third to the integration of biodiversity issues into the Community legal order, and the last to the implementation of this law by the Member States.

As far as the international scene is concerned, all biodiversity watchers recognise that the European Community has become the linchpin of international environmental policy. Without the active engagement of the Community, agreements such as the Carthage Protocol, the Stockholm Convention on Persistent Organic Pollutants, or the Kyoto Protocol would not have been concluded or would not have entered into force. Without the efforts of the Community institutions, the precautionary principle would never have come to the forefront of international policy making. Yet the picture is not as idyllic as one might be led to think. As for the sharing of benefits derived from the exploitation of genetic resources and the transfer of technologies, Europe still lags behind its purported aspirations.

As far as the Community legal order itself is concerned, large gaps remain in the structure from the point of view of biodiversity conservation. In the absence of a framework directive on biological diversity, it has found itself forced to fall back upon legislative acts stemming from diverse areas of policy making, each adopted according to its own specific procedures, pursuing different goals, and elaborated without any general overview. Disputes over the choice of legal basis have led to interminable turf wars. There is significant overlap in the application of legislative acts; for instance, the

[30] Commission proposal 2002/0046 for a regulation of the European Parliament and Council on the transboundary movement of genetically modified organisms, COM (2002) 85 final, 18 February 2002.

various directives providing for impact studies apply in a cumulative manner, special protection and conservation areas end up being subject to complementary yet distinct classification and protection arrangements, and the coexistence of multiples "zonings" each answering to different directives pursuing multifarious objectives is to say the least problematic. The recent Community drive to promote biological biodiversity and the action programmes ensuing from it have been barely able to infuse a minimum of coherence into the law.

On the integration score, an issue that has been left aside here for reasons of space, the challenges remain considerable. One at a time, policies that had for more than five decades pursued a frenetic obsession with productivity *se mettent à la page*. However, the road to the reconciliation of economic development with the conservation of natural resources under the aegis of the principle of sustainable development remains strewn with pitfalls.

Finally, the acid test for this law lies in its application, which, it is important to reiterate, is incumbent on the Member States. The numerous findings against Member States by the Court of Justice make up only the tip of the iceberg. The absence of political will, the lack of financial resources, the predominance of traditional interests over ecological interests, outdated systems of criminal law, the inability of environmental associations in many Member States to bring court actions, and the ambiguity of the applicable legal provisions are just a few of the factors undermining the application of harmonised Community rules.

And yet, thanks to proactive theories on compliance obligations, the useful effect, direct effect, Community law presents a clear advantage over public international law in terms of efficiency. It can, at the very least, because of the doctrine of direct effect and the prejudicial question mechanism, come to the forefront of disputes brought before the national courts. Recent developments could, however, dash the hopes that conservationists today place in Community law. Following its incorporation into the EC treaty, the principle of subsidiarity has led to the production of fuzzy and soft law to the detriment of precise and unconditional rights, which can be invoked by private persons against state organs. Though subsidiarity has had the merit of offering, in areas as complex as the granting of agro-environmental aid or the management of drainage areas, indispensable room for Member States to manoeuvre, this principle could well sound the death knell for a truly common policy. Many authoritative commentators, including my colleague Ludwig Krämer, have argued that an approach based on an over-responsibilisation of state authorities and a corresponding weakening of Community control could lead to a race to the bottom in terms of environmental protection.

10 Community-Based Biodiversity Conservation in the Pacific: Cautionary Lessons in "Regionalising" Environmental Governance

Justin Rose*

1 INTRODUCTION

This chapter investigates the legal and institutional aspects of the region-wide promotion of "community-based conservation and natural resource management" as an environmental governance mechanism in the Pacific Island Region.[1] There is a clear consensus among stakeholders that community-based approaches should now form the core of in situ biodiversity conservation efforts in Pacific Island Countries (PICs).[2] Justifications for adopting this approach are broadly consistent with those applied in other regions of the world where rural communities are collaboratively engaged in conservation and natural resource management initiatives. These justifications may be grouped into two broad categories. First, the responsible government agencies have limited technical and other capacity to coercively regulate citizens' everyday resource uses. Second, various economic, geographic, cultural and historical factors, including prevalence of subsistence livelihoods, highly valued and contested communal land tenure arrangements, and the widespread persistence of customary authority and institutions combine to indicate that in Pacific jurisdictions participatory and collaborative conservation and natural resource management approaches are likely to be more successful than either centralised regulation or individual actors negotiating within a market.[3]

During the past two decades, community-based conservation and natural resource management has been the focus of much regional, national, and subnational programmatic activity in Pacific island countries, but legal and institutional reform has in general

[1] A discussion of the term "community-based" is presented in the following section. "Environmental governance" herein defined as the manner in which debate is held, decisions are made and authority exercised over an area's environment and natural resources, whether effectual or ineffectual, formal or informal, or intentional or unintentional. J. Dore, "Environmental Governance in the Greater Mekong Sub-Region," in M. Badenoch et al., *Mekong Regional Environmental Governance: Perspective on Opportunities and Challenges* (Chiang Mai: World Resources Institute, 2001), 1.

[2] For present purposes, PICs are Cook Islands, Federated States of Micronesia, Fiji, Kiribati, Marshall Islands, Nauru, Nuie, Palau, Papua New Guinea, Samoa, Solomon Islands, Tonga, Tuvalu, and Vanuatu. A good example of stakeholder consensus is regional nature conservation strategies. Signed by all SPREP members and key NGOs, the current strategy calls for 5 percent of land and inshore marine areas to be under effective community-based management by 2007. SPREP, *Action Strategy for Nature Conservation in the Pacific Islands Region 1999–2002* (Apia: SPREP, 1999); SPREP, *Action Strategy for Nature Conservation in the Pacific Islands Region 2003–2007* (Apia: SPREP, 2002).

[3] P. Hunnam, *Lessons in Conservation for People and Projects in the Pacific Islands Region* (New York: United Nations Development Program, 2002), 3.

* Justin Rose is a PhD Candidate at the Centre for Environmental Law, Macquarie University, Sydney.

not accompanied this paradigm shift in island conservation practice. The result is that although policy commitments and program rhetoric locates traditional communities of resource users at the decision-making and operational centre of biodiversity management, the relevant legal and administrative structures continue to relegate them to the periphery of conservation concerns, as ungrouped individuals whose resource-using actions must be regulated by the state.

The same regional and national plans and strategies that advocate community-based methods as the primary conservation approach in Pacific island jurisdictions also include broad commitments to an enhanced regional coordination of environmental management efforts.[4] It is argued that although these objectives are not necessarily opposed, careful planning and analysis is required to ensure that implementing activities in one sphere (particularly those involving legal reform) do not preclude opportunities for gains in the other. The most significant identified risk is that the design of certain regional activities and programs may skew or inhibit opportunities for mainstream community-based conservation initiatives and genuinely prioritise local participation and decision making. The South Pacific Biodiversity Conservation Programme (SPBCP) (1992–2001) is illustrative of both the contradictions inherent in a "regional bottom-up approach" and of lost opportunities to learn valuable lessons about institutional adjustment in support of community-based biodiversity conservation in the Pacific Island Region.

Literature and theory from the fields of legal pluralism and common property governance is drawn on in support of the argument. Following Griffiths, legal pluralism herein refers to a societal characteristic of multiple legal orders observable in a given society.[5] Some authors regard legal pluralism to be a "sensitising concept," others describe it as an "ethos," whereas some find within literature on legal pluralism "theories" or even "meta-theories."[6] Legal anthropological studies situated in colonial and postcolonial situations provided the core of the literature on legal pluralism until, and to some degree since, the 1970s. From that time, authors also have applied the notion of legal plurality in analyses of noncolonised jurisdictions, and more recently there have emerged arguments suggesting recognition of legal pluralism implies a shifting of perspective that could potentially displace and reorient all legal theoretical bases.[7] Although remaining mindful of these newer domains of legal pluralism, the present subject, rural Pacific island communities, are within legal pluralism's most established realm: postcolonial situations wherein state governance institutions coexist with customary or traditional authority structures. In these contexts, the plurality of the legal constellations are clearly apparent and expressly acknowledged.

The concern uniting common property governance scholars is showing that variations in forms of property rights influence resource management outcomes, having

[4] For example, SPREP note 2 (1999 and 2002).

[5] J. Griffiths, "What is Legal Pluralism?" (1986) 24 *Journal of Legal Pluralism* 1–55, 38.

[6] Sensitising concept – Max Planck Institute for Social Anthropology *Outline of Research Programme on Legal Pluralism* (Halle, Max Planck Institute for Social Anthropology, 2002), 2. Ethos – M. Davies, "The Ethos of Pluralism" (2005) 27 *Sydney Law Review* 87–112. Theories and meta-theories – E. Melissaris, "The More the Merrier? A New Take on Legal Pluralism" 13 *Social and Legal Studies* (2004), 57–79, 58.

[7] Melissaris, note 6: "legal pluralism must be approached not as another legal theory but as *a radicalization of the way we think about the law, which must permeate and inform all theorizing of the law*" (emphasis in original), 58. Davies, note 6: "'the ethos of pluralism' . . . is to be found wherever there is a critique of the autonomy and separateness of law, and, wherever the coherence of law as a neutral system of norms derived simply from state authority is challenged," 110.

repeatedly demonstrated that market mechanisms and state management do not exhaust the range of institutional responses available.[8] Elinor Ostrom defines a common pool (property) resource (CPR) thus:

> A common-pool resource, such as a lake or ocean, an irrigation system, a fishing ground, a forest, the internet or the atmosphere, is a natural or man-made resource from which it is difficult to exclude or limit users . . . , and one person's consumption of resource units removes those units from those available to others.[9]

Common property scholarship is a broad multidisciplinary field involving economists, sociologists, policy practitioners, and scientists addressing a diverse range of topics including community-based and collaborative natural resource management, intellectual property governance, and management of the oceans and atmosphere. The study of CPR management is centrally relevant to the legal and institutional aspects of community-based conservation and natural resource management in PICs wherein customary land tenure and nonstate authority permeates political, social, and economic activity. For more than thirty years, CPR scholars have examined questions surrounding the capacity of groups to successfully manage shared resources. The combined contributions of the best of this research has resulted in the identification of indicative factors useful in assessing whether communities or groups may be able to successfully manage their CPRs, as well as consideration of what "success" means in these contexts.[10] This material also addresses the causes of centralised regulatory failure in relation to CPRs, especially in the many situations in which a "deep-rooted 'culture of distrust' permeates relationships between the State and local resource users."[11] Research on CPRs usually focuses on some aspect of the relation between the physical resource and human institutions involved in the use and maintenance of that resource.

The material is presented in five sections. The first outlines the international and regional policy context of community-based biodiversity conservation and management. The second introduces scholarship on legal pluralism and common property governance. The topic addressed in the third section is the United Nations Development Programme (UNDP)–sponsored evaluation of the SPBCP, and the lessons for institutional reform in support of community-based biodiversity conservation revealed by the evaluation process. The fourth sectiondraws onthe preceding material in suggesting that maintaining an aim of a "regional model" for institutional frameworks in support of community-based conservation is likely to be counterproductive. The fifth section summarises two recent developments of institutional innovation in this area: passage of Vanuatu's *Environmental Management and Conservation Act 2003* and the formation of the Micronesian Conservation Trust.

[8] A. Agrawal, "Sustainable Governance of Common Pool Resources: Context, Methods and Politics." *Annual Review of Anthropology* (2003), 244.

[9] E. Ostrom, "Coping with Tragedies of the Commons." 2 *Annual Review of Political Science* (1999), 493–535, 497.

[10] J. M. Baland & J. P. Platteau, *Halting Degradation of Natural Resources: Is There a Role for Local Communities?* (Rome: FAO, 1996), 284–345. E. Ostrom, *Governing the Commons: The Evolution of Institutions for Collective Action* (Cambridge, UK: Cambridge University Press, 1990); Ostrom note 9. A. Pagdee, Y. Kim, & P. Daugherty, "What Makes Community Forest Management Successful: A Meta-Study from Community Forests Throughout the World" 19 *Society and Natural Resources* (2006), 33–52.

[11] Baland & Platteau, note 10, at 385.

2 THE INTERNATIONAL AND REGIONAL POLICY CONTEXT OF COMMUNITY-BASED BIODIVERSITY CONSERVATION AND MANAGEMENT

In recent decades, an international transformation has been occurring in conservation and natural resource management. "From standardized policies and programmes initiated by centralized and urban-based agencies, a slow but definite shift is taking place towards decentralized, site-specific, community-based activities."[12] Although it is well documented in community development and conservation practice-oriented literature, academic legal scholarship has been slow to take full account of this fundamental transformation, which is particularly evident in relation to the conservation and management of natural resources in rural areas of many developing countries. Before expanding on some of the features and implications of this paradigm shift, and its manifestation in the Pacific Island Region, it is necessary to comment on some key terms commonly used within the discourse.

2.1 Terminology

"*Collaborative management*" was defined by the World Conservation Union's (IUCN) 1996 World Conservation Congress as:

> a partnership in which government agencies, local communities and resource users, non-governmental organizations and other stakeholders negotiate, as appropriate to each context, the authority and responsibility for the management of a specific area or set of resources.[13]

The IUCN included the terms "comanagement," "joint management," "participatory management" and "multi-stakeholder management" as being synonymous with "collaborative management," and others have added to this list terms such as "shared-management" and "round-table agreement."[14] Although the IUCN's formulation of "collaborative management" is only one among many, it clearly indicates the issues generally accepted as being central to the concept. These are *partnerships between stakeholders* accompanied by the *sharing of authority* over resource management. Another key factor recognised in the literature is that there are no blueprints or universally applicable mechanisms by which collaborative management may be applied; on the contrary, there is an enormous variety of options among which a choice can be made to suit a specific context.[15]

"*Community-based management*" was excluded by the IUCN from the listed synonyms of "collaborative management," and to many its use indicates situations in which

[12] A. Kothari, R. V. Anurandha, & N. Pathak, "Community-Based Conservation: Issues and Prospects," in A Kothari et al., eds., *Communities and Conservation: Natural Resource Management in South and Central Asia* (New Delhi: Sage, 1998), 25–57, esp. 25.

[13] World Conservation Congress *Resolution for Collaborative Management for Conservation* IUCN Resolution No. 1.42, adopted at Montreal, Canada, 14–23 October 1996.

[14] G. Borrini-Feyerabend, *Collaborative Management of Protected Areas: Tailoring the Approach to the Context* (Gland: IUCN, 1996), 12.

[15] This is a central theme within the collaborative management discourse. See, for example, Borrini-Feyerabend, note 14; and J. E. M. Arnold, *Managing Forests as Common Property*. Community Forestry paper no. 136 (Rome: FAO, 1998), 39–40.

community-level institutions exercise primary decision-making powers over natural resources, independent from government authorities.[16] It is clear, however, that some researchers and practitioners use the term "community-based" to refer to the same broad range of situations termed "collaborative" by others. In the introduction to *Communities and Conservation: Natural Resource Management in South and Central Asia*, Kothari, Anuradna, and Pathak emphasise that community-based conservation:

> includes a whole range of situations from one extreme in which official/private agencies predominantly retain control but consult with local communities in planning or implementation; to the other extreme in which communities are completely in control.[17]

It is noted that in the Pacific Island Region, stakeholders typically, but not always, use "community-based management" as a generic term inclusive of the full range of circumstances described by Kothari et al.[18]

The term "*comanagement*" (an abbreviation of "cooperative management," listed by IUCN as a synonym of "collaborative management") is frequently used in publications to describe situations in which the collaborative arrangements between government agencies and community-level institutions have been formalised in legislation or contract.[19] It is important to note that whereas a fully implemented comanagement system typically necessitates a process of legal and administrative reform, it:

> is not tantamount to asking for a drastic retrenchment of state responsibilities in resource management. The basic concern is actually with reshaping state interventions so as to institutionalise collaboration between the administration and resource users and end those unproductive situations where they are pitted against one another as antagonistic actors in the process of resource regulation.[20]

Two terms often used in close connection with "collaborative management" and "community-based management" are "*customary management*" and "*indigenous peoples management.*" These terms necessarily imply that the role of local stakeholders in natural resource management strategies are undertaken by traditional institutions, usually in conformity with applicable customary rules and practices. Situations of "customary management" may reside within the restrictive definition of "community-based management" (i.e., undertaken independently by community-level institutions), or be developed within a "comanagement" model. Although the terms "customary" or "traditional management" are commonly used in Pacific island contexts, "indigenous peoples

[16] See, for example, O. Lynch & K. Talbott, *Balancing Acts: Community-Based Forest Management and National Law in Asia and the Pacific* (Washington, DC: World Resources Institute, 1995), 25. See also M. King & L. Lambeth, *Fisheries Management by Communities* (Noumea: Secretariat of the Pacific Community, 2000), 79.

[17] Kothari, Anuradna, & Pathak, note 12, 1.

[18] A prime illustration of this usage is the *Action Strategy for Nature Conservation in the Pacific Islands Region 1999–2002* (Apia: SPREP, 1999) wherein the term "community-based" is used extensively to describe programs that are collaborative in nature. See also King & Lambeth, note 16, for a Pacific formulation that distinguishes between "community-based" and "comanagement."

[19] See, for example, the definition of "co-management" provided in J. Whyte, *A Review of Lessons Learned and Best Practice in Integrated Watershed Conservation and Management Initiatives in the Pacific Island Region*, Pacific Island International Waters Programme Technical Report 2002/06 (Apia: SPREP, 2002), 70.

[20] Baland & Platteau, note 10, at 347.

management" is more often used in jurisdictions where indigenous resource users are minority groups within societies dominated by nonindigenous majorities, such as Australia, New Zealand, Canada, and the United States.[21]

It is apparent from the above that although there is much agreement among contributors to the discourse on some of the core elements of "collaborative management," little effort has been afforded to precise definition of key terms, many of which are used interchangeably in both academic and practice-oriented literature. Although some commentators regard this as a significant problem, this author is content to accept that the flexibility of the language applied in different regions and situations mirrors the need for flexibility in management systems accounting for specific local circumstances.[22]

2.2 An International Paradigm Shift

Over the past three decades, the use of community-based and collaborative approaches to conservation and natural resource management has steadily become more prominent and popular, and is now well established. Today, a key element of the environmental programmes of many governments, in both developed and developing countries, is substantial community involvement in planning, design, and implementation. With environmental law becoming globalised, a commitment to some level of community involvement can be recognised within international benchmarks models.[23] This is especially true in rural development, in which collaborative approaches now form the entry point for understanding local cultures and their construction of local reality, with the aim of tailoring interventions with the greatest possibility of success. Where these initiatives have led to improved outcomes, it often has been because of the commitment and mutual trust of the individuals, communities, and agencies involved. Their combined efforts have drawn into question the long-held policy assumption that the incentives created by private ownership, or coercive state regulation, are the only forces capable of curbing destructive self-interested resource use.

Much has been and is being learned by the communities and professionals involved in these processes, and the lessons are fairly well documented.[24] Despite the increasing

[21] See the definition of "indigenous peoples" applied by the United Nations ECOSOC Sub-Commission on the Prevention of Discrimination and Protection of Minorities, quoted in Section 1.3.3. Uluru and Kakadu National Parks are Australian examples of comanaged conservation areas, wherein the state and the indigenous traditional landowners share control. Von Benda-Beckmann notes that in these situations "conditionalities" are often linked to state recognition of indigenous people's rights: F. Von Benda-Beckmann, "Legal Pluralism and Social Justice in Economic and Political Development." Paper presented to the IDS International Workshop on the Rule of Law and Development, London, 1–3 June 2000, 4–5.

[22] An argument in support of strict and limited usage of terms such as "community-based" can be found in Lynch & Talbott, note 16.

[23] Yet there exists a tension between the homogenizing effects of international environmental governance on national environmental law, and the growing global commitment of stakeholders at all levels to promoting diverse, locally designed community-based natural resource management. These conflicting global pressures are experienced most acutely in small, underresourced developing countries. The issues addressed in this chapter focuses on a small aspect of this tension. This phenomenon is illustrated well in the "four scenarios" of the UN's *Millenium Ecosystem Assessment Synthesis Report* (New York: United Nations, 2005), 28.

[24] Examples of publications of this kind include: R. McCallum & N. Sekhran, *Race for the Rainforest: Evaluating Lessons from an Integrated Conservation and Development "Experiment" in New Ireland, Papua*

numbers of community-based and collaborative initiatives in different parts of the world, it is evident that when success has been achieved it is very often limited to small areas or "project sites." Importantly, it must be noted that much of what is billed as "collaborative" is so in name only. To claim success, collaborative strategies must build local skills, interests, and capacities that remain effective and resilient long after any catalysing "project" ends.[25]

National and provincial governments in Asia have made efforts in the collaborative management sphere.[26] Government agencies in India, Nepal, China, and the Philippines are participating with networks of citizens' organizations in collaborative forestry programmes supported by legislation or contracts.[27] Currently, in India it is estimated that 10.24 million hectares of forest lands are being managed under the Joint Forest Management programme through 36,075 committees in twenty-two states.[28] The potential of collaborative approaches for natural resource management in rural regions of Thailand, Vietnam, Cambodia, Indonesia, and Laos also has been explored.[29] Legal endorsement of collaborative management in these latter countries is sparse, with the primary organisational and financial impetus provided by international NGOs, United Nations–affiliated agencies, and the Asian Development Bank (ADB).[30]

New Guinea (Waigani: PNG Department of Environment and Conservation & UNDP-GEF, 1997). J. Ellis, *Race for the Rainforest II: Applying Lessons Learned from Lak to the Bismarck-Ramu Integrated Conservation and Development Initiative in Papua New Guinea* (Waigani: PNG Department of Environment and Conservation & UNDP-GEF, 1997). World Bank, *Voices from the Village: A Comparative Study of Coastal Resource Management in the Pacific Islands* (Washington, DC: World Bank, 1999). A. White et al., eds., *Collaborative and Community Based Management of Coral Reefs: Lessons from Experience* (Bloomfield, CT: Kumarian, 1994).

25 G. Baines, P. Hunnam, M. Rivers, & B. Watson, *South Pacific Biodiversity Conservation Programme Terminal Evaluation* (New York: United Nations Development Programme, 2002), 27–28.

26 A. Kothari et al., eds., note 12. Lynch & Talbott, note 16.

27 India: 73rd and 74th amendments to the *National Constitution of India* (guaranteeing aspects of village self-rule). Article 51A(g) of the *National Constitution of India*: *Panchayats (Extension to the Scheduled Areas) Act* (Act 24 of 1996). Nepal: *Forest Act 2049* (1993). Forest Regulation 1995 (No. 2051 of 1995). Community Forestry Directives 1995 (No. 2052 of 1995). China: see J. Bruce, *Legal Bases for the Management of Forest Resources as Common Property* (Rome: FAO, 1999), 103–107. *Land administration law of the People's Republic of China*, adopted at the sixteenth meeting of the standing committee of the sixth National People's Congress and promulgated by order 41 of the President on June 25, 1986, effective 1 January 1987. Philippines: *Revised Forestry Code 1975*: *LOI 1260* of 1986 sanctioning the Integrated Social Forestry Program under which stewardship contracts and community forestry leases are issued. These methods are not restricted to forestry, as they are applied to coastal fisheries, irrigation, and water supply.

28 See http://www.teriin.org/jfm/jfm.htm.

29 For Laos, Cambodia, and Vietnam, see material collected at "Mekonginfo – Regional Information System On Participatory Natural Resource Management," http://www.mekonginfo.org/. For Thailand: C. Wittayapak & P. Dearden, "Decision-Making Arrangements in Community-Based Watershed Management in Northern Thailand" 12 *Society & Natural Resources* (1999), 673–691, 676. Also Lynch & Talbott, note 16, 67–109. For Indonesia, see S. Yuniati, "The Challenges of Developing Community-Based Forest Management in a New Indonesia" 13:1 *Asia-Pacific Community Forestry Newsletter* (2000), 21, also *Government Regulation Relative to Forest Exploitation and Collection of Forest Products in Production Forests* (No. 6), 27 January 1999.

30 Lynch & Talbott, note 16, 92–95, 98–100. C. Wittayapak & P. Dearden, "Decision-Making Arrangements in Community-Based Watershed Management in Northern Thailand" 12 *Society & Natural Resources* (1999), 673–691, esp. 676. A review of community forestry activities in Cambodia identified nine pilot projects, and the involvement of four UN agencies, three international NGOs, two ADB project teams, and one international research and training institute: K. Rotha & D. Henderson, "Cambodia Country Update" 1 *Asia-Pacific Community Forestry Newsletter* (2000), 22.

Programmes and activities comparable to those in Asia are also taking place in Africa and South America. A global survey of them is unnecessary in the present context. The need for information clearinghouses on community-based and collaborative management is being met both globally and regionally by organisations such as the World Conservation Union, the Food and Agriculture Organization of the United Nations, and the International Association for the Study of Common Property.[31]

Community-based and collaborative management is not a panacea for the world's biodiversity conservation problems. Its widespread adoption in the past few decades has in part caused, and has in part been caused by, an explosion of published material declaring its benefits, defining its limitations, and decrying its pitfalls.[32] Community-based and collaborative management, in its many forms, has been both praised for protecting and rehabilitating forests, reefs, and fish stocks and criticised for failing to do so. It has been linked to a wider democratisation of the societies in which it is adopted, yet in many cases it perpetuates institutionalised inequality and disenfranchisement.[33] Politically, it represents a rare example of broad policy consensus among international agencies, multilateral financial institutions, and conservation NGOs of all descriptions.[34] Collaborative projects often seek to integrate conservation and economic development objectives, which is a practical prerequisite to achieving sufficient levels of community involvement and compliance.[35]

2.3 The Pacific Island Regional Context of Community-Based Biodiversity Conservation

> The underlying rationale for community-based biodiversity management... is, in fact, of fundamental importance for the future of Pacific Island countries in that it is the only effective and lasting approach to poverty avoidance and alleviation.[36]

In Pacific island countries, community-based and collaborative management has been strongly promoted by multilateral agencies, such as the South Pacific Regional

[31] See the IUCN's "hub": http://www.iucn.org/themes/pmns/. FAOLEX contains the most substantial electronic collection of conservation and natural resource management legislation from developing countries, including many relating to collaborative and community-based management: http://faolex.fao.org/faolex/. See also IASCP's "Digital Library of the Commons": http://dlc.dlib.indiana.edu/.

[32] Baland & Platteau, note 10, is a seminal work in this area, and its bibliography provides an extensive listing of relevant sources, as does the "recent publications" section of the *Common Property Digest*, a quarterly publication of the International Association for the Study of Common Property (IASCP). However, only a small percentage of these publications address the issues from a legal perspective.

[33] D. Hill, "Assessing the Promise and Limitations of Joint Forest Management in an Era of Globalisation: the Case of West Bengal." Paper presented at *Constituting the Commons: Crafting Sustainable Commons in the New Millennium, the Eighth Conference of the International Association for the Study of Common Property*, Bloomington, Indiana, 31 May–4 June 2000, 6–7, 11.

[34] Evidenced by the many collaborative projects funded by ADB in Asia, the in-country facilitation of which is undertaken by NGOs, a key example of which is the Asian Development Bank's support of the *Nature Conservancy's* efforts in Pohnpei, FSM, as reported and discussed in Chapter 4 of this book. Also Hill, note 33, 10–11. See also documents related to the World Bank Workshop on Community-Based Natural Resource Management, Washington, DC, 10–14 May 1998 at http://www.worldbank.org/wbi/conatrem/index.htm.

[35] For example, R. Connor et al., "Local Conservation Area Ownership and Traditional Management," in SPREP, *Fifth South Pacific Conference on Nature Conservation and Protected Areas. Volume 2: Conference Papers* (Apia: SPREP, 1993), 90–95. Also R. Margoluis & N. Salafsy, *Measures of Success – Designing, Managing and Monitoring Conservation and Development Projects* (Washington, DC: Island Press, 1998).

[36] Baines, Hunnam, Rivers, & Watson, note 25, at 4.

Environment Programme (SPREP) and international NGOs, such as the World-Wide Fund for Nature and The Nature Conservancy (TNC). For example, the *Action Strategy for Nature Conservation in the Pacific Islands Region 2003–2007* adopted by all SPREP member countries and major regional NGOs, includes a commitment to place "at least 5 percent of coastal and terrestrial areas under effective community-based conservation management in all Pacific Island Countries and Territories."[37] Also, the previous regional strategy had as its second and third major objectives:

- Policy, Planning and Legal Frameworks.
  To integrate nature conservation and natural resource management into development polices, plans, legislation and budget processes *at all levels.*
- Local Communities and Custom.
  To involve and support local communities, resource owners and resource users in cooperative and sustainable natural resource management that recognises and strengthens the rights and customs of local people as a basis for promoting environmentally sustainable and equitable development.[38]

To date, although there has been much regional, national, and subnational activity in furtherance of these objectives, coordination between strategies in the two spheres appears lacking. For example, although the 1999 Action Strategy reported the establishment of thirty-four community-based conservation areas since 1994, the formal legal status of many of these remains ambiguous.[39] SPREP member countries enacted a substantial volume of environmental law during the same five-year period, but instances of management responsibilities being allocated to communities are rare. In this regard, the Samoan community-based inshore fisheries management program provides an operational example of co-management of natural resources in the Pacific islands region, and the Vanuatu *Environmental Management and Conservation Act 2003* represents the formalisation of a comanaged protected area approach.[40]

An issue closely linked to the legal adoption of collaborative initiatives in the Pacific island region is the role to be played by traditional laws and institutions. Many Pacific island communities maintain customary institutions exercise some authority over natural resources within their locality. In many remote locations (typically "outer-islands," where government control over citizens actions may be all but nonexistent), these customary resource management systems still operate effectively. Traditional Pacific island fisheries expert Bob Johannes reported in 2002 that over the past quarter century there has been a renaissance in community-based marine resource management in

[37] SPREP 2002, note 2, at 8.

[38] SPREP 1999 note 2, at 9–10. Emphasis added.

[39] Many of these conservation areas were established under the South Pacific Biodiversity Conservation Program (SPBCP). Reporting of related legal development during the project was scarce; see discussion at SPBCP *Report of the Fifth Meeting of the Technical and Management Advisory Group* (Apia: SPREP, 1997) 4. Baines, Hunnam, Rivers, & Watson, note 25, reported that this lack of legal development was a significant problem for the SPBCP.

[40] For Samoa: U. Fa'asili, *The Use of Village By-Laws in Marine Conservation and Fisheries Management.* Secretariat of the Pacific Community Information Paper No. 17 (Noumea: SPC, 1999). M. King & U. Fa'asili, "A Network of Small, Community-Owned Village Fish Reserves in Samoa" 11 *Traditional Marine Resource Management and Knowledge* (1999), 2–6. For Vanuatu: R. Nari, "Merging Traditional Resource Management Approaches and Practices with the Formal Legal System in Vanuatu" 17 *Traditional Marine Resource Management and Knowledge* (2004), 15–16.

Pacific island countries.[41] Johannes and Kenneth Ruddle agree that the "Pacific island region probably contains the world's greatest concentration of still-functioning traditional community-based systems for managing coastal-marine fisheries and other resources."[42] Even when traditional rules controlling natural resource use are no longer regularly applied, local institutions remain interested and influential in determining the nature of resource use, development, and regulation because of land tenure arrangements deriving from customary common property systems.[43]

3 INTRODUCING LEGAL PLURALISM AND COMMON PROPERTY GOVERNANCE

3.1 Legal Pluralism

This chapter is underpinned by two separate, but related, branches of scholarship. The first is the study of "legal pluralism," a societal characteristic that has been described as "more than one legal order observable in a given society."[44] There are many who deny the logical possibility of legal pluralism, in the Hobbesian tradition coupling "law" inexorably to the sovereignty of the state and its monopoly on legitimate sanctioning power.[45] John Griffiths's construction of "the ideology of legal centralism," which he presents in contrast to legal pluralism, typifies such attitudes:

> Law is, and should be, the law of the state, uniform for all persons, exclusive of all other law, and administered by a single set of state institutions. To the extent that other, lesser normative orderings, such as the church, the family, the voluntary association and economic organization exist, they ought to be and in fact are hierarchically subordinate to the law and institutions of the state.[46]

For those willing to entertain a less restrictive conception of what may constitute "law," the works of legal pluralists provide useful reference points in understanding and analysing governance dynamics in jurisdictions with significant nonstate legal sources.

Although legal plurality, broadly defined, is recognisable everywhere, it is very often found in analyses associated with colonial and postcolonial situations.[47] This is the case with the Pacific Island Region, wherein institutions of formal governance transplanted from the former metropolitan powers coexist with ancient, community, and village-based systems. The operation of these customary authority systems "entails a fundamentally different comprehension of the nature and exercising of power and authority than that understood in the modern Western intellectual tradition."[48] Brian Tamanaha commented in the Micronesian context:

[41] B. Johannes, "The Renaissance of Community-Based Marine Resource Management in Oceania" 33 *Annual Review of Ecological Systems* (2002), 317–340.

[42] K. Ruddle, "The Context of Policy Design for Existing Community-Based Fisheries Management Systems in the Pacific Islands" 40 *Ocean & Coastal Management* (1998), 105–126, 105. Johannes, note 41, makes essentially the same comment at 318.

[43] Baines, Hunnam, Rivers, & Watson, note 25, at 45. [44] J. Griffiths, note 5, at 38.

[45] Von Benda-Beckmann, note 21, at 5–6. [46] Griffiths, note 5, at 3.

[47] Two examples are C. McLachlan, *State Recognition of Customary Law in the South Pacific* (University College London, PhD diss., 1988) and von Benda-Beckmann, note 21.

[48] G. Petersen, "Ponape's Body Politic: Island and Nation." Paper presented at *Evolving Political Structures in the Pacific Islands*, Institute for Polynesian Studies, Brigham Young University, Hawaii, 1982, 3–7 November, 10.

> Any lawyer would master the law in Micronesia following a quick perusal of their constitutions and legal codes. They would master the law, but they would not understand it. Law in Micronesia is an extraordinary flux and flow of contrasting thought and meaning, inside and outside the legal system.[49]

For Peter Sack, "[l]egal pluralism is more than the acceptance of the plurality of law; it sees this plurality as a positive force to be utilised – and controlled – rather than eliminated. Legal pluralism thus involves an ideological commitment."[50] Others reject Sack's suggestion that the study of legal plurality cannot be decoupled from the processes and decisions involved in "use" and "control."[51] Nevertheless, Sack's construction, as expanded in the passage quoted here, accurately describes the current posture towards the ideas and observations of scholars of legal pluralism:

> It is not blind to the strengths of state law and the weakness of people's law. It merely insists that all forms of law have their limitations and that none has advantages which are so overwhelming that it would be justified to grant it a monopoly or a position of hegemony. The aim of legal pluralism is not the elimination of some forms of law and the fostering of others but a situation where different forms of law cooperate, each performing the task or tasks for which it is best suited and in a way which maximises potential.[52]

With regard to Pacific island environmental governance, the current situation is one in which culturally isolated state institutions are ineffectively applying (or not applying) centralised legal mechanisms to local resource users which retain strong attachments to alternative sources of authority.[53] Thus, three fundamental questions continually arise:

- In what ways are existing systems of customary authority affecting biodiversity conservation in PICs?
- Would enhanced collaboration between the traditional and formal authority systems result in improved environmental governance outcomes? and
- Under what conditions would reform facilitating this collaboration be both socially and ethically sound, and most likely to succeed?

Observers recognising legal pluralism in Pacific islands attain a degree of insight into the shortcomings of the region's existing environmental governance that is beyond the reach of a "standard" regulatory theory approach, which by habit assumes the existence of an indomitable state, a Hobbesian Leviathan. In contrast, the practical situation facing both natural resource users and managers in many Pacific islands is that "both the state and the customary system have an independent capacity to act and react."[54]

[49] B. Tamanaha, *Understanding Law in Micronesia: An Interpretive Approach to Transplanted Law* (Leiden: Centre of Non-Western Studies, 1993), 1.

[50] P. Sack, "Legal Pluralism: Introductory Comments," in P. Sack & E. Minchin, *Legal Pluralism: Proceedings of the Canberra Law Workshop VII* (Canberra: Australian National University, 1986), 1.

[51] See, for example, von Benda-Beckmann, note 21, at 7: "[L]egal pluralism . . . does not suggest any moral or political preference for or against any specific plural legal constellation or their components or how it would relate to 'social justice.'" Also McLachlan, note 47, at 43.

[52] Sack, note 50, at 3.

[53] For nonenforcement, see N. Wendt, *Welcome Address to Pacific Island Judges Symposium on Environmental Law and Sustainable Development* (Apia: SPREP, 2002): "Pacific island states . . . have, to varying degrees, institutionalised environmental planning and management with some supporting legislation and regulations, little of which is actually enforced."

[54] McLachlan, note 47, at 20.

Thus, any accurate legal appraisal of the issue must be undertaken from a perspective that seeks to understand and respond to both of these spheres of authority; their actions, reactions, and interactions.

Once the assumption that "law" must of necessity have a basis in the institutions of a sovereign state is set aside, the eternal question "what is 'law'?" comes again into focus. Literature endorsing legal pluralist perspectives has been criticised for expanding the domain of "law" to include all forms of social ordering, a construction so broad that the terms "law" and "legal" lose significance.[55] Conversely, even the most persistent critics of legal pluralism's ambiguities recognise that it has succeeded in exposing deeply-embedded Eurocentric assumptions equating "law" with "state law," as well as the falseness of claims to universality of theories based on those assumptions.[56] This tension is acknowledged while judging the benefits of the latter as outweighing the perceived shortcomings of the former.

An issue to be emphasised regarding a pluralist reconceptualisation of "law" is that praxis is privileged: "Law, is not what the lawyers say about it, it is what the actors make out of it. It is what the citizens make out of it. It is the practices of the citizens which permit us to measure the efficacy of law. Law is not in the texts, it is in the practices."[57] It is perhaps the case that the integrity of "bottom-up environmental governance," as community-based methods are sometimes described, will over time require the development of "bottom-up jurisprudence," which ensures that issues of authority and legitimacy as they are understood in villages are taken into account by scholars and decision makers.

Legal pluralism also endorses the questioning of common assumptions about notions of "governance," "accountability," and even "land," thus providing analytical breathing space for Pacific conceptions of "good governance" that are beginning to emerge as a reaction to international pressures associated with globalisation.[58] Indeed, before the recent surge in the globalisation of environmental law, it seemed to some almost inevitable that environmental law in Pacific island jurisdictions would in time be an integrated system combining customary and state authority, as indicated by the 1986 statement of senior Pacific island legal scholar Mere Pulea:[59]

> In spite of the changes brought about by colonial and post-colonial legislation, the complex traditional systems of environmental management continue to operate in practice.... [T]he recognition of custom in the Pacific – in this field as in others – is not a matter of ideological preference but of political necessity.[60]

[55] B. A. Tamanaha, *General Jurisprudence of Law and Society* (Oxford: Oxford University Press, 2001), 174.

[56] Ibid. at 175. Tamanaha advocates what he terms a nonessentialist legal pluralism.

[57] Etienne Le Roy, quoted and translated in Christoph Eberhard, *Common Humanities and Human Community: Towards A Dianthropological Praxis of Human Rights.* (European Academy of Legal Theory, Brussels, Master of Legal Theory thesis, 1997), 4.

[58] For a range of examples of the ongoing public debate regarding the notion of "governance" drawn from across the region, see the Australian Broadcasting Corporation's thirteen-part *Time to Talk* radio series, which examines the evolution of Pacific societies and systems of government: http://www.abc.net.au/timetotalk/. For an academic analysis of these issues, see P., Larmour, ed., *Governance in the South Pacific* (Canberra: National Centre for Development Studies, Australian National University, 1998) and W. Sutherland, "Global Imperatives and Economic Reform in the Pacific Island States" 31 *Development and Change* (2000), 459–480.

[59] M. Pulea, "Customary Law and the Management of the Environment in the Pacific Islands," in P. Sack & E. Minchin, *Legal Pluralism: Proceedings of the Canberra Law Workshop VII* (Canberra: Australian National University, 1986), 171–172.

[60] Ibid.

In this regard, the past two decades have resulted in many policy statements and donor-funded projects in support of customary and community-based natural resource management in PICs, but as indicated in Section 1, to date legal recognition of the role of nonstate institutions is sparse.

3.2 Common Property Resource Governance

The stream of common property scholarship receiving the greatest attention focuses upon the management of common-pool natural resources by local communities, the studied communities very often being situated in rural regions of developing countries. Bonnie McKay, in her Presidential Address to the 2000 Conference of the International Association for the Study of Common Property, characterised this branch of CPR scholarship as providing "post-modern" analyses and solutions, distinguished from the "modern" or "traditional" form of natural resource management currently dominant in policy, law, and economics.[61] McKay justifies these labels by identifying features and components of each approach, providing the following characterisations of modernist natural resource management:

- It is guided by utilitarianism and the allocation of commodified "human use-values";
- It tends to rely on single species data sets and models;
- Decision making regarding natural resource management is organised hierarchically from the top down by centralised bureaucracies;
- Management decisions are based exclusively on scientific data with models applying "deterministic" notions such as equilibria, stability, and maximum sustainable yield;
- "Modern resource management has little to say about people except as constraints and demands on the system."[62]

McKay, relying on Rudel and Gerson, also provides contrasting "components of post-modernism" in natural resource management. The first is the rejection of "meta-narratives or grand theories," a theme that has occupied much CPR scholarship, particularly as a reaction to the almost universal, and often inappropriate, application of the reasoning used by Garrett Hardin in his 1968 *Science* article, "Tragedy of the Commons."[63] The second postmodern characteristic is a recognition of social fluidity and indeterminacy, because changing conditions necessarily place ecosystems, institutions, and individuals in a state of constant flux. The third component is the emphasis on local communities and their role, both actual and potential, in the management of natural resources.

> [P]ost-modernism places greater primacy on the local. If multiple truths are important, then local perspectives – and knowledge – must be attended to. If indeterminacy and uncertainty are general features, then we must question generalizations about society and ecology, devoting ourselves to understanding the specifics of particular places and times – the local – in relation to their histories and larger contexts.[64]

[61] B. McKay, "Post-Modernism and the Management of Natural and Common Resources" 54 *Common Property Resource Digest* (2000), 1–8.

[62] Ibid., 2.

[63] G. Hardin, "The Tragedy of the Commons" 162 *Science* (1968), 1243–1248.

[64] B. McKay, note 61, at 4. Similar analytical approach advocated by others using different terms, for example, R. Mearns, M. Leach, & I. Scoones, "The Institutional Dynamics of Community-Based Natural Resource Management: An Entitlement Approach" Proceedings of the Biannual Conference International Association for Common Property (Indiana: IASCP, 1998).

The dichotomy in approaches to natural resource management and biodiversity conservation presented here is best explained as representing two extremes between which most existing natural resource management programs would fall. Much existing "modern" management is being incrementally transformed by embracing concepts such as integrated ecosystem management and social impact assessment, whereas many reportedly collaborative (i.e., postmodern) initiatives are simply business as usual with a window dressing of extra consultation. McKay's is nevertheless a useful summary of the themes focused on by CPR scholars, and their points of departure from other analyses and solutions.

The study of CPR management is centrally relevant to the issues here addressed. For more than thirty years, CPR scholars have examined questions surrounding the capacity of groups to successfully manage shared resources. The combined contributions of the best of this research has resulted in the identification of indicative factors useful in assessing whether communities or groups may be able to successfully manage their CPRs.[65] This material also addresses the causes of centralised regulatory failure in relation to CPRs, especially in the many situations in which a "deep-rooted 'culture of distrust' permeates relationships between the State and local resource users."[66]

4 REVIEWING THE SOUTH PACIFIC BIODIVERSITY CONSERVATION PROGRAMME

4.1 Design and Delivery

In the early 1990s, one of the outcomes of a series of workshops initiated by the IUCN's Traditional Ecological Knowledge Working Group was the financing by the Global Environment Facility (GEF) of the South Pacific Biodiversity Conservation Programme (SPBCP).[67]The SPBCP was designed in view of a growing consensus among stakeholders that community-based methods were the most appropriate form of in-situ biodiversity conservation to be pursued in PICs. The rationale underlying the SPBCP was supporting community management of natural resources "as a basis for sustainable livelihoods and economic development, and to avoid the costly environmental and economic mistakes that have occurred in many of the world's other tropical island regions."[68] The SPBCP project document gave the following justifications for piloting a community-based approach to biodiversity conservation in PICs:

- Virtually all of the land and inshore sea resources of the Pacific Islands region were once held under customary tenure. In some countries this is strongly supported in policy and law. Even where the State has introduced legislation to override customary tenure *there is little the State can do without the cooperation of those who have customary land and sea rights.*
- Experience in the islands region and elsewhere has shown that the use, management and protection of biodiversity cannot succeed unless local communities are at the centre, in control of the process and empowered to make decisions.

[65] Baland & Platteau, note 10, at 284–345. E. Ostrom, notes 9 and 10.
[66] Baland & Platteau, note 10, at 385.
[67] Baines, Hunnam, Rivers, & Watson, note 25, at 7.
[68] Ibid.

- Pacific Islands communities and cultures and their livelihoods are intimately connected with their natural environment, biodiversity, and resources.
- Government schemes to conserve nature have generally been ineffective. *The role of governments and regional agencies should be to facilitate and promote an enabling environment that supports local initiatives.*[69]

The SPBCP project document stated that "a regionally coordinated programme for biodiversity conservation and sustainable resource management is the most effective strategy" but provided only weak justifications for this statement, referring to successful regional programmes that had no community component.[70]

The executing agency for the SPBCP was SPREP, wherein a small project management unit was established for SPBCP implementation. The project design stipulated that for each project site there would be a designated a Lead Agency (usually a government office) and a locally representative Conservation Area Coordinating Committee (CACC). The establishment of each project site included the appointment of a Conservation Area Support Officer (CASO) to facilitate most of the local organisational functions. The CASOs also were the recipients of most of the capacity-building included in the programme.[71] Administratively, the SPREP-based management unit maintained more of a micro-management role than described in the project document.[72]

Although the overall conclusion from the UNDP's terminal evaluation is that the SPBCP did not achieve these objectives, the evaluators emphasised that "the concept underlying the SPBCP was, and remains, highly relevant.... The need for the type of result intended through the SPBCP intervention is now pressing."[73] It is thus appropriate that the achievements and failures of the SPBCP, the most significant biodiversity project undertaken in the Pacific island region to date, be more fully assessed and considered in order to improve future programs. This chapter is a limited contribution towards that assessment.

4.2 Evaluation Findings and Lessons

The terminal evaluation of the SPBCP, undertaken on behalf of the UNDP by a team of four specialists, is both a critical appraisal of the region's largest biodiversity conservation project and a substantial contribution to the nascent discourse on institutional reform for biodiversity conservation and management in the Pacific Island Region. This discourse is yet to fully develop but will do so if there is to be a reconciliation of law and practice in Pacific island conservation; an outcome that is by no means inevitable.

Boxes 10.1 and 10.2 present the summarised evaluation "lessons," first from the full report, and second as formulated by one of the evaluation team members in a digested report. Some of these lessons suggest or imply a need for fundamental changes in the way that problems of biodiversity conservation are conceived and addressed throughout the region by institutional stakeholders at all levels.[74] It is not the current intention to consider all of the findings of the evaluation but instead to focus on a single,

[69] Ibid., 8. Italics added.

[70] Ibid. at 41.

[71] Baines, Hunnam, Rivers, & Watson, note 25, at 43. P. Hunnam, *Lessons in Conservation for People and Projects in the Pacific Islands Region* (New York: United Nations Development Programme, 2002), 3, 5.

[72] Hunnam, note 71, at 11–12.

[73] Baines, Hunnam, Rivers, & Watson, note 25, at 4.

[74] Examples are lessons 4, 5, and 8 from Box 10.1, and lessons 1, 2, 3, 6, and 8 from Box 10.2.

Box 10.1. Lessons from the SPBCP final evaluation report

1. The protection of ecosystems and of their native species in the Pacific Islands region can be achieved only through an applied approach that addresses natural resource management in its widest sense and that adequately encompasses the social basis for resource management.
2. The need for proven approaches to community-based biodiversity conservation (meaning use and protection of biological resources and of associated biodiversity) remains, and has become more pressing as Pacific islander populations have grown and their natural resources have degraded.
3. Programme designs for biodiversity conservation at a community level must adequately address community approaches and participation, prescribe realistic social parameters for activities, and provide for some project personnel to have expertise in these areas. Without this emphasis too much is left to "interpretation" and there is a high risk of failure.
4. It is difficult to redress the imbalance in "power" between governments, development assistance agencies and NGOs providing support for community-based conservation, and the communities themselves. Greater attention is needed in programme design and execution to effectively transfer of some of that "power," through more meaningful participation, capacity building and management responsibility – and over a lengthy period, not in a final flurry of "hand-over."
5. External support should be through a framework approach that provides for the community to design its own project and in the context that it views as important. Pacific islander communities do not see a biodiversity context in itself as sufficiently important to engage and sustain their interest.
6. A comprehensive analysis of a community's social structure and decision making procedures and the relationship of these to other levels of administration (village, local government, national government) should be an essential pre-requisite to finalisation of a community-level programme design.
7. An appreciation of the importance of biodiversity and of its management requirements cannot be achieved by simplistic biodiversity-focused awareness raising. Education on these matters must be placed in a livelihoods context and, to be truly effective, must be undertaken as a partnership, with outsider experts exchanging knowledge with insider experts.
8. Community-based conservation initiatives, even where firmly based on recognised customary tenure, cannot be sustained in the absence of supporting national policy and legislation. Programmes should make provision for support activities for policy and legislation development where needed, and should also provide for support for communities to engage in the process of gaining legal sanction for their biodiversity management initiatives.
9. Conservation and development programmes at a community scale cannot be successfully implemented across several levels of government. Regional or subregional programmes need to be split into a series of devolved projects.
10. A preparatory phase, as provided for in the SPBCP Project Document, was good practice, but to make use of this opportunity to fine-tune the approach and the project design the Programme management needed much more specific guidance.
11. A training needs assessment is an essential precursor to the identification of training needs, and the nature of the training need must determine the context in which it is provided. On-site training, supported by long-term mentoring, is more effective

than the regionally aggregated classroom mode of training adopted for some SPBCP training.

12. It is critical, at the outset, to establish a system for collecting, recording, analysing, storing and sharing information acquired.
13. Collaboration between organisations with shared interests and experience in biodiversity use and protection is essential – to bring the best knowledge to bear on community support interventions, and so that Pacific islanders can get the best results from the institutions set up to serve their needs.

Source: Baines, Hunnam, Rivers, & Watson, UNDP, 2002

yet very important and perhaps underemphasised, issue revealed by it: the ability of regional projects to encourage or inhibit diversity and experimentation of institutional approaches to community-based biodiversity conservation.

The issue of present concern, the role of regional programmes in encouraging homogeneity or diversity of institutional approaches to community-based biodiversity conservation in PICs, cuts across many of the lessons presented in the boxes above. Most specifically, Lessons 4 and 8 from Box 10.1 identify both the need to share authority with community institutions and the need for supportive policy and legislation to enable this; even when customary institutions exercise effective authority at a local level, it remains necessary for governments to review their legal and organisational frameworks to ensure complementarity with local efforts. Regarded in isolation, these propositions provide no indication of whether such frameworks could be delivered as regional models, or alternately whether the range of unique cultural, political, and legal contexts would necessitate each PIC devising their institutional frameworks internally.

The thirty-six "findings" of the SPBCP evaluation were constructed as a direct response to the performance of the SPBCP in relation to the measures identified in its original project document, providing greater critical detail than the "lessons."[75] Finding number 19 states:

> There has been much talk of an SPBCP "model" of community-based conservation but apart from defining this as allegedly being "community-based," it is unclear what else it was. Had the SPBCP really been seeking to develop a "model," then a systematic approach would have been used, differing approaches tested, the results monitored from the outset, and a careful analysis of the results undertaken. This could have been a major contribution to conservation and to sustainable development in the Pacific Islands region. The need for carefully explained approaches and "models" is yet to be satisfied.[76]

We may speculate on why the evaluators placed "model" in inverted commas. Nowhere in the evaluation is the desirability of a regional model addressed directly, but taken as a whole the document identifies many contradictions for "regional bottom-up conservation."[77] The foundation of many of these contradictions is that accepting

[75] Baines, Hunnam, Rivers, & Watson, note 25, at 41–44.
[76] Ibid., at 43.
[77] See lessons 8 from Box 10.1 and 9 from Box 10.2.

Box 10.2. Lessons from the SPBCP summary report

Biodiversity Conservation as Part of Sustainable Development

1. Biodiversity conservation in the Pacific Island countries requires wider strategic thinking and planning, to get beyond preconceived and conventional approaches. Narrow, protectionist approaches are of marginal interest or relevance to Pacific islanders. The most appropriate and effective strategy is through the management of resource uses.
2. Biodiversity conservation must be designed and promoted as an integral component of ecologically sustainable development. Conservation projects cannot be carried out effectively in isolation of mainstream social and economic programs, either at the level of local communities or nationally. Conservation efforts must understand and work with the economic, social, and political interests which surround them.

Local Communities at the Centre

3. Conservation of the biodiversity of a place must be meaningfully integrated with the lives and economies of local people. In the Pacific Island countries, this means centring conservation efforts strongly on local communities, whose survival, culture, and prosperity depend on local resources being used sustainably.
4. Biodiversity conservation would be significantly strengthened by Pacific Island governments and national and regional institutions recognising and making more systematic use of customary tenure, local culture, community institutions and traditional ecological knowledge and management practices in their policies, development planning and programmes.
5. A "local community" is not necessarily a simple, homogenous, or harmonious social unit. A Pacific Island village community is likely to be made up of a number of "lineage communities," each sharing a common ancestry and tenure of a portion of land.

Improving Programme Delivery

6. Governments, aid agencies, and NGOs interested in conservation of Pacific Islands natural resources have considerable capacity and power – through money, education, skills, knowledge, ideas, opportunities, confidence, and political access – to achieve their objectives. For resource conservation to be effective in the long-term, a good measure of this capacity and power needs to be transferred to the local community.
7. An outside assistance programme must become transformed into the local community's own project. The community must be able to self select to participate in the project, with ownership and control vested in the local community, to determine its own plans, activities, The ways in which programmes are designed and carried out reduce their effectiveness. Biodiversity conservation programmes are not achieving their objectives.
8. Conservation and development programmes in developing countries have become increasingly large and complex over the past decade and cannot be managed as simple, singular projects. Rather than being introduced across multiple jurisdictions and layers of government, such complex initiatives must be split into a series of devolved projects.
9. More time and care needs to be spent on programme preparation and design. The starting point must be a comprehensive analysis of the problem to be tackled.

Source: Hunnam, UNDP 2002.

community-based approaches as the principle method of biodiversity conservation also involves accepting that the interests and voices of local communities should be paramount, yet almost unavoidably a regional donor-funded initiative will prioritise the interests, processes, and "imperatives" of contributing donors and facilitating intergovernmental agencies.[78]

Two propositions drawn from the SPBCP evaluation are thus identified as being of central concern here: first, that law and policy requires adjusting, in order to better support community-based conservation; and, second, that no proven "models" for this exist (the aim of a "model" is itself questionable), and so there is a need to test and learn from differing approaches.

While acknowledging that hindsight is a convenient perspective, we may find it useful to consider choices made in designing the SPBCP when applying a single institutional model as described earlier in Section 4.1 Design and Delivery.[79] This decision and approach was criticized indirectly in the evaluation in a combination of findings: the evaluators found that communities should be able to "self-select" and that "external support should be through a framework approach that provides for the community to design its own project in the context that it views as important."[80] Also "[c]onservation and development programmes at a small community scale cannot be successfully implemented across several levels of government. Regional or subregional programmes need to be split into a series of devolved projects."[81]

The SPBCP's externally imposed framework meant that local stakeholders invested little in establishing the institutions responsible for the conservation areas, the CASOs were perceived as employees of the SPBCP and little effort was devoted to building the capacity of local stakeholders, other than CASOs, to sustain the project areas. The evaluation reports that towards the end of the SPBCP, many of the Lead Agencies had largely disengaged themselves from it.[82] The SPBCP evaluation presents a vision that future programmes directed towards promoting community-based environmental governance, should be responsive to the institutional imperatives of communities, rather than those of external agencies.

In the course of designing the SPBCP, at least two alternatives were possible to the universal model selected. The first was to develop two or more pre-packaged institutional frameworks for the various Conservation Area sites; the second was to relinquish the regional uniformity goal and place the responsibility for institutional design

[78] This is a theme evidenced in many statements made in the evaluation regarding specific aspects of programme delivery. Lesson 4 of Box 10.1 and lesson 6 of Box 10.2 also indicate imbalances of interests and power between stakeholders. Also on the theme of power relations in this area, J. Turnbull, "South Pacific Agendas in the Quest to Protect Natural Areas" 34 *Development and Change* (2003), 1–24 presents a highly critical perspective, suspicious of all foreign involvement in Pacific environmental governance as a conduit for the entrenchment of the capitalist ideology of outsiders. The assumptions afflicting Turnbull's argument are closely allied to those it critiques; for example, disparagingly writing-off community conservation areas as "mechanisms to draw rural communities further into the cash economy" (p. 13) ignores both the complex web of incentives, beliefs, ideals, goals, and perspectives that the participants bring to these initiatives, and underestimates the ability of local stakeholders to behave strategically in their own (short- or long-term) interests. Nevertheless, Turnbull's is a useful reminder that conservation and development in PICs is caught up in a wider agenda, often constrained by structural forces of an international or global nature (p. 19).

[79] For each of the seventeen SPBCP Conservation Areas, there was a Lead Agency, a Conservation Area Support Officer, and a specially created Conservation Area Coordinating Committee.

[80] Baines, Hunnam, Rivers, & Watson, note 25, at 45.

[81] Ibid.

[82] Ibid. at 10.

on local stakeholders, with SPBCP management requiring only broad parameters of accountability for funds and activities. To those familiar with the design of large regional projects it is immediately understandable, given the two alternatives outlined earlier, why programme designers may have chosen their universal option: to do otherwise would risk increasing by degrees of magnitude the complexity, uncertainty, and cost of an already complex, uncertain, and costly exercise.

Issues of regional programme design in this area are systemic as well as operational. SPREP as the facilitating agency of the SPBCP was accountable for more than $USD10 million of GEF funds, distributed over a nine-year period by UNDP. The design of multilateral funding processes ensures that programmes are not supported without grantees detailing accountability for their procedures, essentially stating who will be spending the money and on what. Under these circumstances, it is difficult to see how the SPBCP project document could have been drafted without fairly concrete preconceptions of the institutional framework for the programme's activities. The outcome is that, regardless of any operational arguments in favour of local control of institutional design, the imposition of a single regional model would probably have been an inevitable result of the funding allocation process.

It is noted that even with the advantage of a uniform set of institutions around the region the SPBCP still encountered problems in resolving the interests of donors and communities with regard to complex accountability procedures. The SPBCP evaluation stated:

> The multi-level financial and administrative reporting system adopted for the Programme's management was a major hindrance to effective action, especially at the community level. The rigidity with which UNDP required its National Execution (NEX) guidelines to be applied contributed to this problem.[83]

In summary, the core lessons of the SPBCP evaluation suggest that a key to successful community-based biodiversity conservation in Pacific island jurisdictions is to recognise the positive nexus between the vitality of ecosystems and the vitality of local communities who may have the potential to flexibly construct (or retain) their economic, social, and political arrangements in a way that maintains sustainable human-biodiversity relationships. In a specifically institutional sense, the SPBCP evaluation recognises the need for reform in this area, confirms that the SPBCP model was not successful, and adds that, by failing to experiment with different approaches, the programme contributed little towards the developing of knowledge to help find legal and policy solutions. It also was noted that although the evaluation may have advised flexibility and experimentation, depending on one's location in a regional planning hierarchy, flexibility may appear as unpredictability and diversity may be understood as inefficiency.

The following sections draw on common property governance studies and legal pluralism, as well as national examples from within the region, in adding weight to the argument that the search for a regional model in this area may be illusory and that regional programme design needs to guard against promoting homogeneity in institutional structures.

[83] Baines, Hunnam, Rivers, & Watson, note 25, at 42.

5 LESSONS FROM COMMON PROPERTY GOVERNANCE AND LEGAL PLURALISM

This chapter is not the first to link common property governance studies and legal pluralism, as the fields are naturally complementary, especially when considering postindependence rural development and related topics, such as land reform, biodiversity conservation, and natural resource management.[84] An issue worthy of initial emphasis is that these two areas of scholarship are closely linked because each takes as its starting point the perspectives and experiences of community members or resource users in answering key questions such as: What rules or laws apply to uses of our land and water? Who should make them and how? Who should enforce them? Why should we take notice of the rules?

Elinor Ostrom, an important contributor to the common property field, provides the following justifications for the devolution to local polities of rule-setting for natural resource governance:

1. *Local knowledge.* Appropriators who have lived and appropriated from a resource system over a long period of time have developed relatively accurate mental models of how the biophysical system itself operates, as the very success of their appropriation efforts depends on such knowledge. They also know others living in the area well and know what norms of behaviour are considered appropriate by this community.
2. *Inclusion of trustworthy participants.* Appropriators can devise rules that increase the probability that others are trustworthy and will use reciprocity. This lowers the cost of relying entirely on formal sanctions and paying for extensive guarding.
3. *Reliance on disaggregated knowledge.* Feedback about how the resource system responds to changes in actions of appropriators is generated in a disaggregated way. Fishers are quite aware, for example, when the size and species distribution of their catch changes over time.
4. *Better adapted rules.* Given this, appropriators are more likely to craft rules that are better adapted to each of the local common-pool resources than any general system of rules.
5. *Lower enforcement costs.* Because local appropriators have to bear the cost of monitoring, they are apt to craft rules that make infractions highly obvious so that monitoring costs are lower. Furthermore, by creating rules that are seen as legitimate, appropriators encourage higher conformance.
6. *Redundancy.* Multiple units are experimenting with rules simultaneously, thereby reducing the probability of failure for an entire region.[85]

When this can be shown to operate effectively, common property literature has revealed that community-based approaches are likely to be more successful than either centralised regulation or individual actors negotiating within a market.[86] Ostrom also

[84] See, for example, von Benda Beckman, note 21, and R. Meinzen-Dick & P. Rajendra, *Legal Pluralism and Dynamic Property Rights.* CAPRi Working Paper no. 22 (Washington, DC: International Food Policy Research Institute, 2002).

[85] E. Ostrom, note 9, at 526.

[86] A. Agrawal, "Sustainable Governance of Common Pool Resources: Context, Methods and Politics," *Annual Review of Anthropology* (2003), 243–262, esp. 244–245.

identifies potential disadvantages and pitfalls of devolved rule-setting: including failure to organise, local tyrannies, stagnation of process, lack of access to scientific information, unresolved conflicts, and an inability to deal with external factors.[87] These erode existing common property systems and often, perhaps usually, defeat attempts by external actors to catalyse a reinstigation of common property governance in situations in which it has lapsed.

Among the most insightful of Ostrom's theoretical observations is the conceptualisation of natural resource policy as an ongoing experimental process.[88]That is, as environmental governance represents the mediation of interactivity between two sets of highly complex and dynamic systems (social and ecological), all policy proposals affecting natural resource governance should be considered as experiments, and it should be acknowledged that all resulting policy experiments have a positive probability of failing. "Policy changes are experiments based on more or less informed expectations about potential outcomes and the distribution of these outcomes for participants across time and space."[89]

Conceptualising environmental governance as an experimental process leads to a very different type of analysis than assuming that central planning and regulatory agencies are always perfectly informed and adequately empowered with legitimate authority.[90]When planning and programme design occurs in an intercultural setting, such as with the SPBCP, one also can predict that cultural differences will impact on the relative performance of governance arrangements between jurisdictions. "[T]here is no axiom more basic to the study of law and society than that a legal rule (a command to act or refrain from acting in a certain way) will produce different behaviour on the part of individuals differently situated."[91] Hobbe's Leviathan may be a serviceable philosophical narrative for a modern state, but the on-the-ground reality of natural resource governance in most developing countries reveals no omnipresence available to enforce environmental commandments. Much literature now suggests that, when improved environmental governance outcomes are sought in situations of common property governance, policy and law must take account of the full suite of social, economic, and environmental factors contributing to the behavioural incentives of resource users, rather than assuming that modifying behaviour is a straightforward legal and administrative process.[92]

As evidenced in Ostrom's sixth and final justification for devolved rule-setting, reconceptualising environmental governance as an experimental process supports the logic of applying participatory and community-based resource governance wherever feasible, including high degrees of local autonomy in rule-setting. The reason for this is that when governing authority is centralised, policies tend to experiment simultaneously with all of the common-pool resources within their jurisdiction. This is a process that takes a long time to produce data and lessons to feed back into governance planning, and because comparative data is lacking, multiple interpretations of the results are likely to be contradictory. As noted by Ostrom, and arguably as shown in the SPBCP, "An experiment that is based on erroneous data about one key structural

[87] E. Ostrom, note 9, at 526–527.
[88] Ibid. at 520.
[89] Ibid.
[90] Ibid. at 507.
[91] J. Bruce, *Legal Bases for the Management of Forest Resources as Common Property* (Rome, 1999), 21.
[92] See, for example, the sources in Notes 105–110.

variable or one false assumption about how actors will react can lead to a very large disaster."[93]

A notion of "community" whether expressed or implied, is a necessary part of any common property governance analysis; as outlined in Chapter 1, in many contexts "communities are now the locus of conservation thinking."[94] As noted, however, by Agrawal and Gibson in a 1999 *World Development* article, "the greatest danger of using the term 'community' is that it may give a misleading suggestion of the potential of the group of stakeholders to come together to manage a resource in common."[95] The danger they identify is that authors often use of the concept of "community" in participatory and community-based natural resource governance literature without due regard given to whether the group or groups of people so described possess the characteristics that the term is meant to imply. Agrawal and Gibson compellingly justify the deconstruction of this "mythic community" in research and policy, to be replaced by more rigorous examination of the multiple interests and actors operating within and on local groups, the processes by which these actors interrelate, and the various institutions that structure the interactions.

Participatory governance literature often seeks to justify the focus on "communities" by reference to group characteristics of size, interactions, composition, activities, and interests.[96] These authors tend to view "community in three ways: as a spatial unit, as a social structure, and as a set of shared norms."[97]Small groups, located near to the resource in question, are presented in theory as interacting often with both the resource and each other. They are thereby well placed to efficiently make collective decisions regarding management of the resource that coincide with their shared incentives to ensure sustainable use.[98] These groups display in theory homogenous social characteristics in such matters as ethnicity, religion, language and political beliefs, and assets and incomes are fairly evenly distributed. "[H]omogeneity is assumed to further cooperative solutions, reduce hierarchical and conflictual interactions, and promote better resource management. Outside the community conflicts prevail; within, harmony reigns."[99] People living in small, spatially defined homogenous groups are in theory also possessors of common interests (real or perceived) and shared internalised norms that direct their behaviour. These shared norms can beneficially guide resource management behaviour in two ways; first by specifically prohibiting or limiting some activities that would damage the resource, and second by promoting cooperative decision making within the group.[100]

[93] Ibid. at 520. Ostrom also lists disadvantages of devolved rule-setting, including failure to organize, local tyrannies, stagnation of process, lack of access to scientific information, unresolved conflicts, and inability to deal with external factors.

[94] A. Agrawal & C. Gibson, "Enchantment and Disenchantment: The Role of Community in Natural Resource Conservation" 27:4 *World Development* (1999), 629–649, 631. The authors provide a sound justification for this comment, noting the numerous international agencies that have 'found' community conservation, and referring to the "flood" of publications on it. On this theme, see also Section 1.2 of this chapter.

[95] P. DeCosse & S. Jayawickrama, "Issues and Opportunities in Co-management: Lessons from Sri Lanka," in A. Kothari et al., eds., *Communities and Conservation: Natural Resource Management in South and Central Asia* (New Delhi: Sage, 1998), 193.

[96] Agrawal & Gibson, note 94, at 633.

[97] Ibid.

[98] Baland & Platteau, note 10, at 298–302.

[99] Agrawal & Gibson, note 94, at 634; Baland & Platteau, note 10, at 302–303.

[100] Agrawal & Gibson, note 94, at 635; Baland & Platteau, note 10, at 116–127.

The preceding paragraph presents features of the "mythic community" common in the literature. The myth arises not because small size, shared social characteristics, and internalised norms are unimportant in assessing the capacity of groups to collectively manage natural resources, but because the reality of most "communities" is more complex and less insular. Unequal power relations and conflict are not uncommon within and between small spatially discrete groups, and social homogeneity and the existence of shared norms must be shown, rather than assumed, to exist. Even when evidence is presented in support of these features, there is also a need to recognise the specific dimensions that are relevant to natural resource conservation and management. Numerous "studies show that there is no easy correspondence between social homogeneity and sustainable resource use."[101] Shared internalised norms, when they in fact exist, are powerful determinants of behaviour not easily amenable to external regulatory intervention, but there is no guarantee, or perhaps even likelihood, that these norms will lead to behaviour more consistent with sustainable management of natural resources.[102]

A significant proportion of common property governance literature has been focused on identifying measures of success for common property governance, and factors that indicate a particular common property resource may be amendable to successful management by the community or communities that regard themselves as owning it. Elinor Ostrom is among the founders of the contemporary common property discourse and her work is very influential.[103] Baland and Platteau's *Halting Degradation of Natural Resources: Is There a Role for Local Communities?* is a seminal text, considering in detail a broad range of case studies, as well as relevant economic and social theory and analysis.[104] Arun Agrawal combined the findings contained in "landmark works" of these contributors, as well as that of Wade.[105] In his 2003 article-length summation of the status of knowledge in common property governance,[106] Agrawal identified thirty-five variables reported in the in the literature as relevant to the success of common property governance.[107] The most recent composite study of this kind is that of Pagdee, Kim, and Daugherty, which reports on their review of sixty-nine case studies of community forest management from around the world. These authors identified ten measures of success applied to community forest governance initiatives, and forty-three variables indicating the likelihood of success.[108] Pagdee, Kim, and Daugherty's measures of success are summarized in Table 10.1, whereas Table 10.2 lists Agrawal's "enabling conditions for sustainability on the commons."

It is unnecessary here to explore in detail the implications of each of these measures and success indicators, or their interactions, but a few issues do require emphasis. The

[101] Agrawal & Gibson, note 94, at 635.

[102] Agrawal & Gibson, note 94, at 635–636, 640; Baland & Platteau, note 10, at 333–334, 340–341.

[103] E. Ostrom, notes 9 and 10. E. Ostrom et al., eds., *The Drama of the Commons* (Washington, DC: National Academies Press, 2002).

[104] J. M. Baland & J. P. Platteau, note 10.

[105] R. Wade, *Village Republics: Economic Conditions for Collective Action in South India* (Cambridge, UK: Cambridge University Press, 1988).

[106] A. Agrawal, "Sustainable Governance of Common Pool Resources: Context, Methods and Politics." *Annual Review of Anthropology* (2003), 243–262.

[107] See also A. Agrawal, "Common Resources and Institutional Sustainability," in E. Ostrom et al., Note 103, at 41–72.

[108] A. Pagdee, Y. Kim, & Daugherty, "What Makes Community Forest Management Successful: A Meta-Study From Community Forests Throughout the World" 19 *Society and Natural Resources* (2006), 33–52.

Table 10.1. Measures of success in commmunity forest management

Ecological sustainability includes:
- Improving forest conditions (e.g., increase of forest area, species diversity, forest productivity, and number of valuable species).
- Addressing environmental degradation (e.g., reforestation, soil erosion protection, and watershed management).

Equity refers to:
- Enhancing equitable sharing of the management function (right to manage), entitlement (right to access and control), and responsibility for a given territory or set of natural resources.
- Improving equitable benefit distribution among community members.
- Increasing investment in the future productivity of the forests.

Efficiency includes:
- Meeting a range of local needs, improve local living standard, and alleviate poverty.
- Reducing conflicts between local communities and authorities.
- Controlling corruption.
- Resolving mismanagement (e.g., imbalance of administrative power, and imbalance between ecological and socioeconomic dimension).

Reduce individual misuse of the forest (e.g., timber smuggling)

Source: This list is summarized from Sixty-Nine cases of community forest management in Y. Kim & P. Daugherty, "What Makes Community Forest Management Successful: A Meta-Study from Community Forests Throughout the World." 19 *Society and Natural Resources* (2006), 33–52, at 43.

success indicators in Table 10.1 reveal that community governance initiatives, while seeking ecological sustainability, also maintain a strong focus on improving the quality of life of resource-reliant communities, and in strengthening governance institutions. The second issue to emphasize is that, although gaps and uncertainties remain, there is also much agreement on the core aspects of the common property governance literature; comparable results have been reported on enough occasions for researchers to be confident that the data is sound. Nevertheless, the sheer number of factors now considered of relevance for the success of common property governance makes analysis difficult. "As soon as we concede the possibility that somewhere between thirty and forty variables affect the management of common-pool resources, and that some of these variables may have important inter-actional effects, we confront tremendous analytical problems."[109]

The many factors relevant to the success of common property governance indicate the complexity of designing legal or other interventions in support of it. In the field, site-specific investigation of these variables is in itself complex and will inevitably give rise to further questions. Yet, it is only on attaining a good understanding of the social, economic, and institutional landscape that one can begin to confidently assess the prospects of choices between various comanaged, community-based, or other participatory approaches to (in?) natural resource governance.[110] From the perspective of centralised planners, such as the SPBCP implementers, undertaking these investigations for every watershed-scale location, digesting the data and designing a

[109] A. Agrawal, note 111, at 243–262, 254.

[110] Recall evaluation lesson 6 (Box 10.1): "A comprehensive analysis of a community's social structure and decision making procedures and the relationship of these to other levels of administration (village, local government, national government) should be an essential pre-requisite to finalisation of a community-level programme design."

Table 10.2. Enabling conditions for sustainability of the commons

Resource system characteristics
- Small-size
- Well-defined boundaries
- Low levels of mobility
- Possibilities of storage of benefits from the resource
- Predictability

Group characteristics
- Small-size
- Clearly defined boundaries
- Shared norms
- Past successful experiences – social capital
- Appropriate leadership – young, familiar with changing external environments, connected to local traditional elite
- Interdependence among group members
- Heterogeneity of endowments, homogeneity of identities and interests
- Low levels of poverty

Relationship between resource system characteristics and group characteristics
- Overlap between user-group residential location and resource location
- High levels of dependence by group members on resource system
- Fairness in allocation of benefits from common resources
- Low levels of user demand
- Gradual change in levels of demand

Institutional arrangements
- Rules are simple and easy to understand
- Locally devised access and management rules
- Ease in enforcement of rules
- Graduated sanctions
- Availability of low-cost adjudication
- Accountability of monitors and other officials to users

Relationship between resource systems and institutional arrangements
- Match restrictions on harvests to regeneration of resources

External environment
- Technology
  - Low-cost exclusion technology
  - Time for adaptation to new technologies related to the commons
- Low levels of articulation with external markets
- Gradual change in articulation with external markets
- State
- Central governments should not undermine local authority
- Supportive external sanctioning institutions
- Appropriate levels of external aid to compensate local users for conservation activities
- Nested levels of appropriation, provision, enforcement, governance

Source: Adapted from A. Agrawal, "Sustainable Governance of Common Pool Resources: Context, Methods and Politics." *Annual Review of Anthropology* (2003), 243–262, at 253. Table titled "Critical enabling conditions for sustainability on the commons."

programme accordingly, is an unwieldy and unrealistic prospect. However, there are groups of people, that is, local resource users, who can rapidly provide answers to all the questions. This suggests that legal adjustments in this field should be genuinely "bottom-up," able to take a detailed view of the situation accounting for local factors, because "[t]he same institutional rules can have different effects on resource governance depending on variables in the biophysical, social, economic and cultural contexts."[111]

Returning to legal pluralism, in a 1988 doctoral thesis Campbell McLachlan thoroughly examined the "persistent fact" of legal pluralism in the Pacific Island Region.[112] McLachlan argued that legal pluralism is neither an attribute of state law, nor of society, but a characteristic of the operation of law within society. "It consists of a recognition that... state law is not the only form of regulation or dispute resolution in society and that many groups within society have a capacity to create their own rules and dispute resolution processes."[113] McLachlan's research highlights a key feature of the environmental governance paradigm in the Pacific, where both the state and the customary systems of authority have an independent capacity to act and react, an issue reacknowledged in the SPBCP evaluation.[114]

Recognising this central facet of Pacific island legal pluralism (that operates regardless of whether or not state law recognises and accounts for it) is a simple yet fundamental step in considering legal reform for community-based biodiversity conservation. In most PICs, both state and community-level institutions have a stake in controlling land and natural resources, although each may question the legitimacy of the other's claim to authority. Given this overlapping authority, it can be expected that if there is no cooperation or integration of decision making between the two spheres, there is likely to be conflict.

There is also a second, more technical lesson of relevance to institutional reform for community-based or comanagement in PICs to be drawn from studies of legal pluralism, borne out by research into postcolonial legal development in many regions of the world. The lesson is that the more customary institutions are incorporated into state law, and the more they are so defined, the more their fundamental nature is altered from what it was before the legal recognition.[115] Moreover, the changes so wrought generally reduce the effectiveness of the customary institution empowered by the state. The issue thus becomes "how to recognise a group without converting it into something else."[116] Succeeding in this is among the most difficult challenges facing stakeholders seeking institutional reform for community-based biodiversity management in PICs. Whatever the specific responses to this challenge will be or are, they will almost certainly vary markedly between jurisdictions.

6 TWO RECENT DEVELOPMENTS: VANUATU ENVIRONMENTAL MANAGEMENT AND CONSERVATION ACT 2003 AND THE MICRONESIA CONSERVATION TRUST

This section outlines two recent developments that may assist in guiding future directions in environmental governance. The first is the achievement of the Vanuatu government in enacting the *Environmental Management and Conservation Act 2003* providing a framework for community-based conservation in that country; the second is the establishment of the Micronesia Conservation Trust in the Federated States of Micronesia.

[111] A. Agrawal, note 112, at 41–72, 45.

[112] McLachlan, note 47.

[113] Ibid. at 53.

[114] McLachlan, note 47, at 20.

[115] J. Fingleton, *Legal Recognition of Indigenous Groups* (Rome: Food and Agriculture Organisation of the United Nations, 1998), 1–7. Also ibid. at 347–348.

[116] Ibid. at 7.

Vanuatu's *Environmental Management and Conservation Act 2003* implements the Convention on Biological Diversity in Vanuatu. Its substantive provisions are divided into three subject areas; environmental impact assessment, bio-prospecting, and conservation areas. The law was developed over a period of seven years including extensive consultation with a broad range of stakeholders.[117] Sections 35–40 of the Act deal conservation areas, focusing exclusively on community-based management. The Act provides that customary landowners are able to register their land or site as a Community Conservation Area, in negotiation with the Vanuatu Environment Unit, if the site is shown to possess special characteristics. These may be unique genetic, cultural, geological, or biological resources or it may contain "good habitat for species of wild fauna or flora."[118] The benefits to landowners of registering their land under the Act include:

- Formal recognition of the importance of their area;
- Identification and evaluation of conservation, protection, and management options;
- Possible technical assistance to implement an appropriate conservation and management plan;
- Strengthened ability to enforce local conservation rules; and
- Assistance in identifying potential financial assistance where necessary to support conservation management activities.[119]

It is emphasised that the purpose of summarising the Vanuatu law here is neither to suggest that it should be adopted as a model for other jurisdictions or even to suggest that it has solved the institutional issue for Vanuatu. With regard to the latter, that will be seen over coming years as areas of land are registered and managed under the Act's provisions. As regards its usefulness as a regional model, the opposite lesson is intended: that to the extent the Vanuatu law is successful in its objective of providing an institutional framework for community-based conservation, this will be because stakeholders in Vanuatu have invested their own time, effort, and intellect to its design. In essence, if Vanuatu's *Environmental Management and Conservation Act 2003* succeeds, it will be in large part because it is *owned* by ni-Vanuatu.

The *Environmental Management and Conservation Act 2003*, while refocusing Vanuatu's in-situ biodiversity conservation on community-based management, could be said to maintain a "conservation protectionist" approach, as compared to the "people in a biodiversity context" methods suggested in the SPBCP evaluation.[120] That is, the Act does not aim to develop sustainable human–ecosystem interactions across all of Vanuatu in a way that maximises ecosystem services, but rather prioritises site-specific conservation values. There is no information to assess why this might be the case; one can only speculate as to whether the *Environmental Management and Conservation Act 2003* may have created a people-oriented framework for community-based biodiversity

[117] R. Nari, "Linking Traditional Resource Management Approaches and Practices into the Formal Legal System In Vanuatu." Paper prepared for the *IMPAC Law and Environment Workshop*, Townsville, Australia, 29 March–2 April 2004, 8.

[118] *Environmental Management and Conservation Act 2003*, section 35.

[119] Government of Vanuatu, *Information Brochure on the Environmental Management and Conservation Act 2003.*

[120] Baines, Hunnam, Rivers, & Watson, note 25, at 3.

management if it had been de-coupled from the process of ensuring national compliance with the global *Convention on Biological Diversity*.

Other observations regarding the Vanuatu *Environmental Management and Conservation Act 2003* that can be made at this stage, include noting its clear focus on community-based conservation approaches. The law is as significant both for what is omitted than for what is included; that is, the legal provisions are themselves merely a framework for the future negotiation of conservation areas between partnerships of local and government stakeholders. The law sensibly places no constraints on customary decision-making processes, and authority over the establishment of conservation areas is shared between the Vanuatu Environment Unit and local customary institutions. Finally, the *Environmental Management and Conservation Act 2003* promises very little other than the government's support for local stakeholders seeking to sustainably manage their biological resource, in this sense it represents realist posture with regard to environmental law and governance.

The Micronesia Conservation Trust (MCT) is an example of an institutional innovation providing an effective funding mechanism for community-based biodiversity conservation in the Federated States of Micronesia (FSM). The formation of the MCT was guided by a broad-based steering committee in 2001, who met with representatives of two other trust funds in the Asia-Pacific – the Foundation for the Philippine Environment, and the Papua New Guinea Mama Graun Conservation Trust Fund. Following a public nomination process, the founding board of MCT was appointed in April 2002.

> The MCT is set up as a private non-profit corporation with a governing board that Includes members from national, state, and municipal governments, NGOs, business, and academic institutions. It works to mobilize funding from a variety of sources to build an endowment from which to provide long-term support for sustainable natural resource management in FSM. Recently, interest in the trust has been expressed by a number of donors, including the European Union, the US Department of the Interior, and several private foundations. The Trust places special emphasis on building the capacity of Micronesian organizations to design and manage conservation programs. In addition, the MCT will provide a forum to bring together the national, state, and local governments with private enterprises and non-government organizations to collectively address the challenges of natural resource management in FSM, form public-private partnerships, and share experiences and best practices.[121]

The MCT is described here for two reasons. The first is because it is an example of an institution devoted to biodiversity conservation playing what could be described as a "funding mediator" role. From a community perspective, the MCT is in touch with the economic, cultural, political, and ecological landscape in the FSM and is thus well placed to decide which initiatives warrant funding, to efficiently monitor projects and to provide guidance and mentoring to grantees. From the perspective of donors such as those mentioned earlier, the MCT is managed in light of donors' needs for transparency and accountability for the spending of funds provided, and MCT is in the process of developing a track record of success that will in time enhance donor confidence in projects supported by it.

[121] FSM Government, *Sustainable Development Plan* (Palikir: FSM Government, 2005).

The second reason for noting the successful establishment of the MCT is that this is an example of an institutional change that could be a useful and productive regional model. The suggestion here is not for a regional trust fund (this has already been suggested and abandoned by SPREP), but for a regional strategy that facilitates the development of a network of national biodiversity trust funds in PICs.

7 CONCLUSION

Regional models and model laws have legitimate roles to play in Pacific island environmental governance, but providing the institutional basis for community-based biodiversity conservation and natural resource management may not be among them. The SPBCP evaluation confirmed the need for stakeholders in each Pacific jurisdiction to back policy commitments to community-based biodiversity conservation with administrative and legal frameworks that are complementary with this objective. In some jurisdictions, it is likely that no new laws will be required but, with the adoption of genuinely participatory processes, the necessary changes can be accommodated within existing provisions. Conversely, even if the "perfect" institutional framework were discoverable, application of it would not assure success in the context of poor leadership or high levels of antagonism between stakeholders.

If regional co-management or community-based biodiversity conservation succeeds in Pacific jurisdictions it will be via a complex adaptive process involving hundreds of communities, many partnering with government and nongovernment agencies, experimenting with rules, monitoring, sanctions, and regulatory processes over time; all sharing knowledge. It is likely that the most effective institutional solutions will be those carefully adjusted to specific local circumstances, and so other jurisdictions should be cautious in adopting them as "models." What undoubtedly can and should be shared throughout the Pacific Island Region by all concerned are the lessons drawn from the experience of engaging in the process of institutional reform.

Institutional reform for community-based biodiversity conservation is not something that can be delivered in a book or a box or a project – it is a path that participants can travel either willingly or not at all. The SPBCP emphasised that the key to conserving biodiversity in the Pacific Island Region is engaging local rural communities, and identified the key to engaging Pacific communities to be *assisting in the construction of development processes that enhance economic security and retain cultural integrity while ensuring sustainability in human-ecosystem interactions.* In this area of governance, the strongest incentives for sustainable behavioural choices may be those derived from the self-interest and communal identity of individual resource users.

A realist perspective acknowledges that there will be many instances, perhaps a majority, where competing interests, local tyrannies, lack of vital data, evolving markets or various other factors, undermine the success of community-based biodiversity conservation initiatives in PICs. The same perspective also acknowledges the proven failure of centralist alternatives. Given this evidence, a further conclusion is expressed as a broad design principle for institutional reform for community-based and co-management in PICs: *build on the respective strengths, and shore up the weaknesses, of both the community-based (customary and civil society) and governmental institutions.*

Was the ten-year, $USD10 million regional SPBCP a failure? The programme's terminal evaluation answered this question with a firm "yes." Although the evaluators found some benefit accrued "at the margins," and presented sound reasons for their criticisms, the report's rarely compromising tone could be considered somewhat harsh given the tremendously difficult challenge that the SPBCP presented its implementers. If we accept that environmental governance policy initiatives are experiments, and the higher the number of variables the less likelihood of success, we can see that "failure" of the SPBCP was all but inevitable. Perhaps a more productive question at this stage of the process is; was the SPBCP a beneficial use of time, effort, and money? The answer to this question cannot yet be provided with honest clarity. Nevertheless, optimists among us can validly respond, "Yes, but only if the wealth of experiences it represents, and the resulting knowledge and wisdom are put to good use in the future."

PART THREE

CONSERVATION MEASURES

SECTION A. AREA-BASED MEASURES

11 The Recent NSW Experience, from Regional Forest Agreements to Brigalow and the Introduction of the Community Conservation Area

R. J. Debus

1 INTRODUCTION

When I last spoke on Monday during the opening ceremony, I talked briefly about the many magnificent national parks we have so close to Sydney. While I'm particularly proud of those parks, today I want to talk about what's been happening in the rest of New South Wales. I especially want to focus on one part of the State, as it provides an excellent and very contemporary example of our experience in implementing biodiversity conservation.

First, let me place my remarks in context.

The current NSW government, under the leadership of Premier Bob Carr, was first elected in 1995. It was reelected in 1999 – at which time I became the Minister for the Environment with responsibility for national parks and biodiversity conservation – and again in 2003. Over that time, there has been a significant expansion of the conservation reserve system in New South Wales (NSW).

For example:

- In 1995, there were 4 million hectares of national parks in NSW. There's now nearly 6.5 million hectares. That's almost 8 percent of the State's land mass, a 63 percent increase;
- In 1995, there were *no* marine parks in NSW whatsoever. There's now four, covering more than 160,000 hectares of our coastal waters;
- Since 1995, the area of wilderness in NSW – the very highest conservation reserve category – has more than tripled;
- We now have more than 1.7 million hectares of private land included in what are known as Wildlife Refuges or Voluntary Conservation Agreements. This land is owned by conservation-minded citizens and is managed and protected accordingly.

There cannot be many, if indeed there are, *any* jurisdictions that have so enlarged their network of conservation reserves – by nearly two-thirds in just a decade – in such a short period of time. Conserving these landscapes is generally achieved in one of two ways. First, the government simply buys private land, voluntarily offered by landowners.

Some of our most important national parks have been formed like this: the 320,000-hectare Paroo Darling National Park in the far West of NSW that was formerly half a dozen pastoral properties, each around 50,000 hectares in size, or the very recently

* R. J. Debus is Attorney-General and Minister for the Environment, New South Wales, Australia.

announced Yanga National Park, 80,000 hectares in size, that has a 150 kilometer frontage to the great Murrumbidgee River and snakes across southern and southwestern NSW. Second, new parks have been created as one of the outcomes of what are known as comprehensive regional assessments. These assessments focus on one or more of the State's bioregions and address all the various, and often competing, conservation and natural resource management interests. They have typically occurred in regions with significant areas of remaining native forest, where, almost always, productive State Forests logging activity was underway.

2 THE BRIGALOW

Today, I want to talk about one such area of Western NSW – comprising two areas known as the Brigalow Belt South and the Nandewar Bioregions, a total of 77,000 square kilometres or 10 percent of the entire State. This is an area where, until now, few national parks existed.

This area, like much of Australia, has experienced high species extinction rates, a massive rate of vegetation clearance (about 70 percent in this area's case) and strong community pressure to preserve employment. The region was also complicated by the fact that a number of small country towns had become virtually dependent on one industry – logging the white cypress pine and ironbark forests.

In this region, the government was faced with difficult choices: complex social and economic interactions, industry-dependent communities, and an obvious and compelling argument for a strong conservation outcome.

This particular assessment forced us as a government to think of new ways to deliver conservation outcomes, ways that were suited to this particular region. We decided to create a new category of land tenure – known as a Community Conservation Area.

3 THE COMMUNITY CONSERVATION AREA CONCEPT

Deciding the new approach of a Community Conservation Area followed a journey through five major comprehensive regional assessments.

The NSW forestry reform process – which we commenced in 1995 – has been one of the most participatory ever undertaken by government, with representation and extensive involvement of key government agencies, nongovernmental organisations and the general community.

It is based on implementing the National Forest Policy Statement (signed in 1992) of which a key element is the completion of full assessments of environmental, heritage, resource, economic, and social values of forests in a particular region.

These comprehensive regional assessments form the basis for negotiating Regional Forest Agreements between the federal and the various state governments.

The agreements set out a set of principles and a framework for the cooperative management of all forests, whether managed by government agencies or by private owners. They are supported by NSW legislation known as the *Forestry and National Park Estate Act 1998*.

As I mentioned earlier, these assessments are the second means by which we have managed to expand our network of national parks. Well over one million hectares of Crown land (including tate orest) has been transferred to national parks and reserves as part of this process.

This has made a significant contribution to the achievement of the Comprehensive, adequate and representative reserve system, one of the goals of the 1992 National Forestry Policy Statement.

In essence, this means that our reserve system must be:

- comprehensive – sampling the full range of ecosystems;
- adequate – large enough to be viable in the longest term; and
- representative – including good examples of the diversity of animal and plant communities.

Historic regional forest agreements have been produced in the four major coastal regions of NSW. They set a national benchmark for the involvement of all stakeholders and community groups. However, in the latest assessment of the Brigalow region, we did something quite innovative.

The Community Conservation Area concept – or the CCA as I will call it – has combined a broad approach to community-based involvement and participation in management with more specific conservation and forestry-based management. It very much sets a new direction for NSW and, indeed, for all of Australia.

The CCA had its origins in IUCN Reserve Category 5 – multiple use reserves created in the often highly modified landscapes of Europe, where "wilderness," at least in the sense that we use the word here, simply does not exist.

Multiple-use reserves are widely used throughout the world to allow for the improved conservation of land with economic, historical, and cultural association to industries and practices that are based on the sustainable use of resources. Parks such as the Yorkshire Dales and Lakes District in Britain and the Appenines in Italy are good examples of such reserves.

The CCA is all about adapting the IUCN Category 5 reserve to the sort of circumstances we face in NSW. Consistent with international best practice in conservation, the CCA includes large core areas for conservation with buffers and links, which allow remnants to be managed for conservation across the landscape.

In NSW we have traditionally managed land for conservation by including it in national parks and nature reserves – as I've said, more than six million hectares are currently protected this way.

4 VALUE OF BRIGALOW

Before I explain what led us to this decision and why we think it will deliver the highest conservation outcome for this region, I should explain why it needed saving.

The Brigalow and Nandewar regions in the northwest of NSW have experienced more than one hundred years of intensive development. They are in the centre of what's known as the sheep-wheat belt. The vegetation has been cleared and the land continually cropped and grazed to produce strong economic development – but at a cost to our environment.

Approximately 70 percent of the original vegetation is gone. Species decline in the region is amongst the worst in Australia. Our national government declared the Brigalow region one of fifteen Biodiversity Hotspots in Australia. These National Biodiversity Hotspots were identified by the Australian Government's Threatened Species Scientific Committee, with input from recognised experts in the field of biodiversity conservation from each Australian state and territory.

Almost half of the Brigalow Belt South's ecosystems meet national thresholds for being rare, endangered, or vulnerable. This includes a total of twenty-eight endangered ecosystems, thirteen vulnerable ecosystems, and nine rare ecosystems.

Although few in number, formal national parks do dot this landscape, the volcanic formations of the Warrumbungle and Mt. Kaputar national parks being the most dominant. But although picturesque and extremely important today, they have been saved almost by accident rather than planning. They became part of the reserve system as they were not of the fertile productive agricultural soils which surround them. They were the steep, craggy remnants and leftovers after the ring barking teams had moved in.

The Brigalow assessment focused on what else was left after a century of agriculture and timber harvesting that had cleared 70 percent of the original vegetation.

The assessment showed that there were still high conservation forests remaining; there were threatened species just holding on; there were areas of important Aboriginal cultural significance. It also showed that without a public lands decision in this part of the world, it would not be possible to build a representative reserve system.

What we needed was an approach that would give permanent conservation outcomes as well as maintaining a sustainable value to timber industry and appropriate mineral extraction.

The public lands that form the fundamental building block for a representative reserve system in this region contain the highest quality habitat for the most endangered species and the best of the region's remaining vegetation and biodiversity.

The Community Conservation Area is the single most important one-off addition to the reserve system in western NSW – conserving 352,000 hectares of land. This land protects habitat for a wide range of animals, from koalas and squirrel gliders, to turquoise parrots, glossy black cockatoos, and significant remnant colonies of Malleefowl. Also conserved are black-striped wallabies, regent and painted honeyeaters, swift parrots, barking owls, and several endangered bats.

The Community Conservation Area is divided into four zones, three of which will be statutorily defined conservation zones, with no timber extraction.

Zone 1 will be managed in accordance with the management objectives of a national park, under the National Parks and Wildlife Act 1974.

Zone 2 is based around Aboriginal cultural heritage and creates Aboriginal areas, under the National Parks and Wildlife Act 1974.

Zone 3 allows for conservation, recreation and mineral extraction, in accordance with the objectives of a state conservation area and will also be governed by the National Parks and Wildlife Act 1974.

Zone 4 will provide for timber extraction and mining and exists under the statutory responsibility of the Minister for Primary Industries.

In terms of reserve design, this allows us to manage the whole of the habitat, not just parts of it.

This approach provides both benefits and challenges.

One of the key benefits is integration. Although individual government agencies will be responsible for managing each of the four zones, the coordination of management across the entire area rests with a newly formed Community Conservation Council.

The Council will consist of the Directors-General of the Departments of the four Government agencies involved in land management and will be responsible for developing what will be known as a Community Conservation Agreement.

The Agreement will provide a coordinated framework for the management of the entire area. The management of the big common issues, such as pests, weeds, and fire will be efficient and most effective.

And it is in this integrated approach that the Community Conservation Area provides a better conservation outcome than a scattered collection of national parks, nature reserves, state conservation areas, and state forests.

While working collectively with other land managers has always been a good management practice, now it is compulsory. Feral animals cannot read maps and so do not know whether they're in a national park or a state forest. Similarly, fires occur irrespective of land tenure. Managing the fire hazards will be looked at on a map without boundary lines – a tenure-blind approach.

Land management objectives are clearly set out in the legislation. The Department of Environment and Conservation will have different objectives than the department that manages the timber and mineral resources – the Department of Primary Industries. The challenge will be to work together on common principles for the CCA, without compromising respective management objectives.

We know that this can work.

In NSW we already have in existence the Marine Parks Authority – a multiagency group that oversees the management of important marine areas. This authority has established four marine parks, which carefully balance the needs of conservation, recreational, and commercial activities.

The CCA concept was borne out of necessity in the Brigalow and Nandewar areas. Here we were faced with fragmented woodlands under extreme pressure and species dependant on these lands under threat.

One aspect on which I have only touched is perhaps the ingredient that made a conservation outcome very complex. Communities throughout the Brigalow area have long established ties with the timber industry.

Industry support, development, and exit packages are tied into the deal. Eighty million dollars has been allocated to manage the conservation areas, provide mills with options and allow communities to continue to prosper. In detail:

- $A15 million over five years has been provided for industry to invest in value adding, new timber products and export markets.
- $A12 million over five years will be allocated to a timber industry job creation fund.
- $A29 million will be provided to a conservation jobs fund to employ staff to manage new conservation areas.
- $A10 million will be allocated to capital investment projects in the area.
- $A14 million will be provided to a business exit fund to assist mills and their workers that will cease production as a result of the creation of the CCA.

5 COMMUNITY PARTICIPATION

The CCA concept also has a built in component of community participation that is central to the decision.

The Community Conservation Council will be advised by three Community Conservation Advisory Committees, which will play a fundamental part in the process. These Advisory Committees will include representatives of local communities as well as links to existing formal reserves and other land tenures though the involvement of key positions on existing committees.

Catchment Management Authorities will have a seat on each of the Community Advisory committees, linking private land into the equation. The community-based committees will act as a constant reminder to the management authorities that they are part of a living landscape that includes not just trees and birds but also communities that have needs and expectations beyond the boundaries of the conservation zones.

The CCA has been specifically designed to allow communities to have a broader say and greater input into the recreational use of high biodiversity areas of conservation. It is about community input and community access. A key part of the community participation in the CCA will come from local Aboriginal communities.

More than 20,000 hectares of the CCA will be zoned for management consistent with an Aboriginal Area under the National Parks and Wildlife Act. Indeed the assessment process itself enabled many people to reengage with their past and their culture. The assessment of the Aboriginal cultural heritage values within Brigalow was the largest ever undertaken in NSW and documented for all time that cultural values have a real human element.

In many respects, the extent of Aboriginal involvement and guidance resulted in the project becoming an Aboriginal community-based project, through which Aboriginal people articulated a strong sense of cultural, historical, and contemporary attachment to the region.

The Aboriginal heritage projects brought together the memories of Aboriginal people and their ancestry lives to illustrate the constant and considerable role that Aboriginal communities have had as a source of labour and knowledge in the economic life of the bioregion.

Aboriginal people have had a central, although largely unacknowledged, role in the economic development of the bioregion. The changing labour patterns of recent years have led to a marked decline in Aboriginal involvement in the paid labour force. This is a source of considerable concern to communities for a number of reasons, including loss of economic independence, loss of pride, and reduced access to country.

Today, the field of resource conservation recognises a landscape approach and the importance of working with Aboriginal people, their knowledge of the local ecology, their history, and their culture, in developing conservation strategies, as well as socioeconomic opportunities. These concurrent developments have set the stage for a rethinking of landscape conservation and an unprecedented opportunity for collaboration.

As a result, the CCA decision provides at least twenty Aboriginal identified jobs and potentially up to thirty-five, phased in over several years – an exceptional outcome. These positions will be real, long-term, and will be involved directly in various roles.

The development of partnerships with Aboriginal people will be an integral part of the process and positions are being designated to this important function. For example, three positions will be responsible for establishing and nurturing partnerships with the local Aboriginal communities, including the culturally highly significant areas of Goonoo and Terry Hie Hie. These areas can cater for traditional usages such as ceremonies, wild resource gathering, and culture camps for young people.

The amount of land zoned in the CCA for Aboriginal culture is twice the total area of all current Aboriginal Areas in NSW. Managing that much land is something that we want to get right.

12 Local People's Perceptions and Attitudes towards the Management of Nech-Sar National Park, Ethiopia

Desalegn Wana*

1 INTRODUCTION

Most of the economies of developing countries are heavily dependent on biodiversity resources.[1] This is evidenced by the facts that agriculture produces the lion's share of GDP (greater than 30 percent) in most African countries and more than 60 percent of the employment for the rural population. The importance of biodiversity for socio-economic development is even more critical in the Ethiopian context. For instance, about 85 percent of the rural population of Ethiopia depends directly on agriculture, which again contributes 85 percent of exports mainly generated from coffee, skin, and hides.[2] It is also reported that 45 percent of the country's GDP is contributed by the agricultural sector. The overwhelming majority of the rural population of Ethiopia, about 80 percent, depends on herbal medicine.[3] The noneconomic aspects of biodiversity use, such as global climate regulation, hydrological regime, oxygen production, and so on, are vital components of biodiversity.[4] However, these resources are being lost at an unprecedented level and would put the life-support systems of these nations at stake.

Despite their multiple ecological functions and immense uses for socioeconomic development, the country's biodiversity resources are being destroyed in critical proportions. The large-scale destruction of the forest resources is clear evidence. Nearly 40 percent of the country's total area was covered with forests at the beginning of the twentieth century.[5] This was reduced to 16 percent in the 1950s and to roughly 3 percent in the 1990s.[6] Presently, the area coverage of forests is less than 3 percent, and deforestation is estimated to proceed at the rate of 150,000 to 200,000 hectares per annum.[7] The loss of biodiversity resources may have serious consequences in Ethiopia because the majority of the rural population depends directly on those resources for food, medicine, clothing, and shelter.

[1] John Mugabe, "Biodiversity and Sustainable Development in Africa," in John Mugabe & Norman Clark, eds., *Managing Biodiversity: National Systems of Conservation and Innovation in Africa* (Nairobi: Acts Press, 1998).

[2] Shibru Tedla & Martha Gebre, "Biodiversity Management in Ethiopia," in John Mugabe & Norman Clark, eds., 1998.

[3] John Mugabe, Note 1.

[4] WCMC, *Global Biodiversity: Status of the Earth's Living Resources* (London: Chapman and Hall, 1992).

[5] EFAP, *Ethiopian Forestry Action Program.* EFAP Secretariat, Addis Ababa, Ethiopia, 1994.

[6] Ibid. [7] Ibid.

* Lecturer (MA in Biogeography): Department of Geography and Environmental Studies, Addis Ababa University, P.O. Box 150178, Addis Ababa, Ethiopia; e-mail: deswana2002@yahoo.com.

In view of the continuing destruction of the biological resources, and in an attempt to curb the problem of biodiversity destruction, efforts have been made to conserve and manage the biodiversity resources of the country over the past three decades. These efforts include the establishment of national parks, wildlife sanctuaries, game reserves, and controlled hunting areas.[8] Presently, there are nine national parks, three sanctuaries, eleven game reserves, and eighteen controlled hunting areas.[9] The national parks and sanctuaries cover a total area of 32,000 square kilometers, whereas 161,600 square kilometers are allocated for game reserves and controlled hunting; these constitute 2.7 percent and 13.5 percent of the land surface area of the country, respectively.[10]

The Nech-Sar National Park, which is one among the nine national parks of the country, is one of the richest biodiversity centers in Ethiopia. It is believed to contain 800 to 1,000 species of higher plants (12 percent of 6,500–7,000 species), 91 species of mammals (32 percent of the country's mammals), 351 species of birds (40 percent of the country's bird species), and many other animals and insects. Of the thirty-one endemic species of mammals of Ethiopia, five are found in the Nech-Sar National Park. Moreover, some bird species are found only within this park (e.g., the Nech-Sar Nightjar).[11]

The Nech-Sar National Park was established in 1975 with the stated major objectives of conserving the endemic *Swayne's Heartbeest* and also the scenic landscapes of the area, thereby generating economic benefits through provision of tourism services to the country.[12] Presently, however, it is not meeting these objectives.[13] This is mainly because the management strategy pursued has not considered the livelihoods of the local people. Moreover, local people have been excluded from the management processes and their perceptions, knowledge, and practices have been undervalued.

The main aim of this study is, therefore, to examine the local people's perceptions and attitudes towards management of the Nech-Sar National Park and articulate sustainable management strategies for the park. The specific objectives are (1) to discuss the importance of a participatory approach for the conservation of biodiversity; (2) to describe the local people's perceptions and attitudes about the management of the park; and (3) to study the level of exploitation of park resources by the local community to support their livelihoods.

2 NATURAL RESOURCE MANAGEMENT PERSPECTIVES

In the early decades of the twentieth century nature was seen as separate from human experience and, therefore, human beings were able to exploit it without limit or consequences.[14] In this view, "nature is inert and passive so that humans can mange it, use it

[8] TGE, Transitional Government of Ethiopia, National Report on Environment and Development: A report prepared for the United Nations Conference on Environment and Development, held in Rio de Janero, Brazil Addis Ababa, 1992.

[9] Ibid.

[10] Tedla & Gebre, Note 2.

[11] EWNHS, "Important Bird Areas of Ethiopia: A First Inventory, Ethiopian Wildlife and Natural History Society," Addis Ababa, 1996.

[12] G. H. H. Brown, "The Conservation Situation of Ethiopia," 2 *Biological Conservation* (1970), 293–298; EWNHS, Note 11.

[13] Ibid. See also Tedla & Gebre, Note 2.

[14] Ian Kapoor, "Towards Participatory Environmental Management?" 63 *Journal of Environmental Management* (2001), 269–279.

as a resource or degrade it without fearing the after effects. This approach has fostered the creation of a top-down managerial approach in which decisions are taken at the top and implemented by the lower ranks."[15]

That approach, however, generated negative socioeconomic and political consequences especially in developing countries. First, certain natural resources with unique beauty and ecological significance were excluded from human use, and, in the process, endangered the livelihoods of rural populations.[16] Second, environmental policy makers have tended to subscribe to the neo-Malthusian argument that exploding population growth in the developing countries is the main cause for the destruction of natural resources.[17] According to this school of thought, people may exploit resources selfishly and without restraint; therefore, they are considered direct threats to biodiversity. Thus, the government and other external bodies are justified as "objective" in their approach to management of natural resources and in their disregard of indigenous knowledge in resource management including biodiversity.[18]

The management and conservation of biodiversity has followed the same trend. The traditional top-down approach has prevailed since the colonial period in many developing African countries.[19] This approach has resulted in the establishment of protected areas such as national parks.

However, experience has shown that traditional top-down exclusionary approaches, which involve the creation of protected areas, sometimes called "fortress conservation" or "fences and fines," are not effective in reaching conservation objectives.[20] These approaches have failed to achieve their initial objectives because they disregarded local resource users and negatively influenced the livelihoods of the local communities.[21]

The continuing challenge of survival and the negative perception of local people towards protected areas have led many to question the objectives of protected areas management approaches. Development was assumed to cause biodiversity loss before 1980s when the notion of sustainable development began to hold sway.[22] Conservation thinking shifted from a preservationist paradigm, which aimed to shield nature from the surrounding human influence,[23] to incorporation of local human needs and socioeconomic development as one of the central planks of the conservationist agenda.

Blaike and Jeanrenaud[24] have identified three conservation paradigms, namely, the classical, populist, and neoliberal approaches. The classical approach considers people as a direct threat to biodiversity loss; the populist approach sees the participation and empowerment of local people as a necessary aspect for the conservation and management

[15] Ibid. at 270.

[16] Uday Sharma, "An Overview of Park-People Interactions in Royal Chitawan Park, Nepal." 19 *Landscape and Urban Planning* (2001), 133–144; Kapoor, Note 14.

[17] Katrina Brown, "Innovations for Conservation and Development" 168 *Geographical Journal* (2002), 6.

[18] A. Gbadegesin & O. Ayileka, "Avoiding the Mistakes of the Past: Towards a Community Oriented Management for the Proposed National Parks in Abuja, Nigeria." 17 *Land Use Policy* (2000), 89–100.

[19] Ibid.; K. Brown, Note 17.

[20] Susanne Stoll-Kleeman & Timothy O'Riordian, "From Participation to Partnership in Biodiversiy Protection: Experiences from Germany and South Africa." 15 *Society and Natural Resources* (2002), 161–177.

[21] K. Brown, Note 17, and Susanne Stoll-Kleeman & T. O'Riordian, Note 20.

[22] K. Brown, Note 17.

[23] Uday Sharma, Note 16.

[24] P. Blaike & S. Jeanrenaud, "Biodiversity and Human Welfare," in K. Ghimire & M. P. Pimbert, eds., *Social Change and Conservation* (London: Earthscan, 1997), 61, cited in K. Brown, Note 17, at 7.

of biodiversity resources; and the neoliberal approach considers institutional, market, and policy aspects as important components of biodiversity conservation.[25]

The classical approach promotes the establishment of core protected areas where the use of biological resources is prohibited, but as noted earlier, it did not work out as expected. The neoliberal approach emphasizes that the lack of clear biodiversity policy, market failures, and institutional problems are underlying causes of biodiversity degradation in many African countries. To address these issues, the federal government of Ethiopia has recently crafted the biodiversity policy of 1997.[26]

The populist approach, by contrast, emphasizes the participation and empowerment of local people in the conservation and management of biodiversity; hence, it is a bottom-top approach as opposed to the classical top-down approach. The need for such an approach was long overdue because of the inherent problem of livelihood security and the subsequent failures of top-down approaches to address the objectives of biodiversity conservation. In addition, local knowledge, attitudes, and management skills are essential to attain biodiversity conservation. Through the genuine involvement and participation of local people, these skills and knowledge can be put to use.

Protected areas can coexist with local people, provided that local people support the conservation of biodiversity through integration of their livelihood needs and the development aspirations of the community. This may require provision of alternatives that can offset direct dependence on park resources. Alternatives may include skills training, education and health services, or enhancing and enriching the park resources through increased market value.[27] The study reported here underscores factors such as local community participation, local livelihood security, local perception, and local support for protected areas as important components of biodiversity conservation.

3 THE STUDY AREA

The Nech-Sar National Park is located between 5°52′N and 6°N and 37°30′E and 37°45′E (Figure. 12.1 shows the approximate location of the park). The Nech-Sar National Park covers a total area of 514 square kilometers and is characterized by diverse topographic conditions. Elevation ranges from 1108 meters to 1650 Meters above sea level.[28] The park is named after the white grass that is found in the extensive undulating plains of the area. The park is contained by the Amaro mountain chain in the east, the Chencha highlands in the west and northwest, extensive plains of the Rift Valley at the center, and the country's two important fishing areas – portions of Lakes Abaya and Chamo (Figure. 12.1). The two lakes constitute about 15 percent of the park area.

The study area exhibits a semiarid climate and receives a bimodal rainfall pattern,[29] with the two wet seasons interrupted by two dry seasons. The main rainy season occurs during April and May, while a less significant rainy season is in September and October. The total annual amount of rainfall recorded around Arbaminch is 800 millimeters at 1,200 meters. The vegetation of the area consists mainly of savanna grassland, bush

[25] K. Brown, Note 17.

[26] J. Mugabe, Note 1.

[27] J. Abbot, D. Thomas, A. Gardner, S. Neba, & M. Khen, "Understanding the Links between Conservation and Development in the Bamenda Highlands, Cameroon." 29 *World Development* (2001), 1115–1136.

[28] EWNHS, Note 11.

[29] EMA, *National Atlas of Ethiopia* (Ethiopian Mapping Authority, Addis Ababa, 1988).

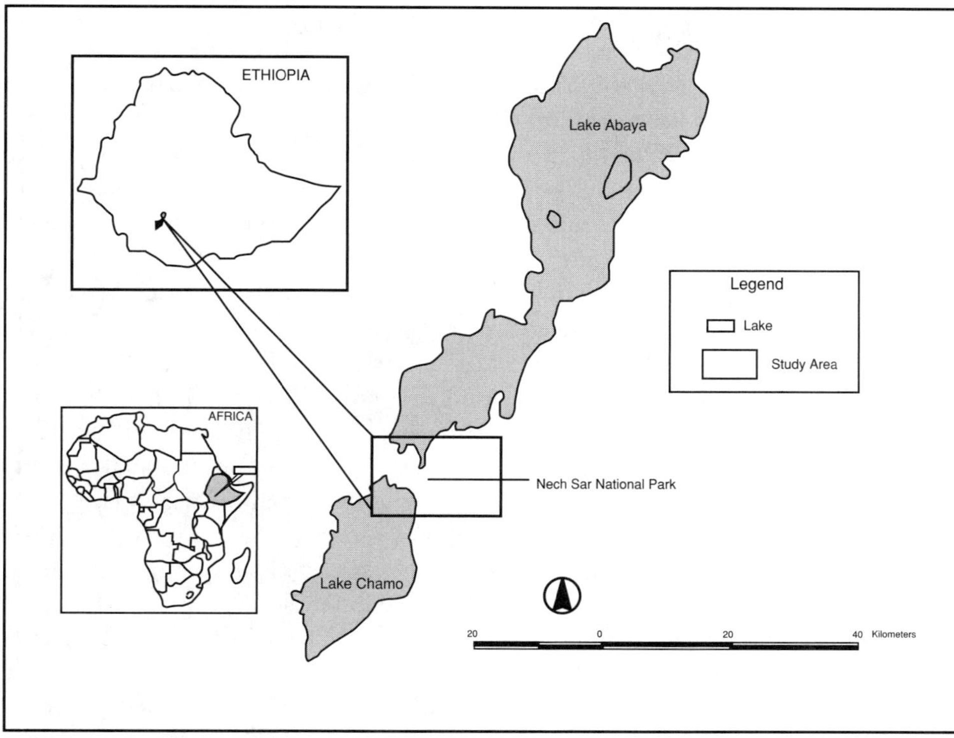

Figure 12.1. Location Map of the Study Area.

land, dense thickets, and riverine and groundwater forests.[30] Generally, the study area belongs to the Somali-Masai regional center of endemism.[31]

The Nech-Sar National Park contains a variety of mammals, avifauna, and fish. The endemic Swayne's hartebeest is found in large number in the Nech-Sar National Park. Some of the conspicuous mammals observed in the Nech-Sar include Burchell's zebra, Grant's gazelle, leopard, Greater kudu, and hippopotamus. The Nech-Sar National Park also hosts about 40 percent of the country's bird species.[32] Some of the bird species include the lesser kestrel, kesser flamingo, pallied harrier, black-billed wood hoopoe, and the endemic Nechisar nightjar, to mention but a few.[33] Lakes Abaya and Chamo host a great variety of fish species, including Nile perch and catfish.

4 METHODS

The methods used to collect data in this study include questionnaire survey, informal interviews, and focus group discussions. The questionnaire was designed mainly to generate data on socioeconomic characteristics, local people's involvement and participation, perception of the communities towards the park and wildlife, and the stream of

[30] EWNHS, Note 11.

[31] F. White, The Vegetation of Africa. A Descriptive Memoir to Accompany the UNESCO/AETFAT/UNSO Vegetation Map of Africa (1983). UNESCO, Paris.

[32] Chemere Zewde, *Nech-Sar National Park: Yesterday, Today and Tomorrow (in Amaharic)*. A paper presented at the Forest and Wildlife Biodiversity Conference, Addis Ababa, 6–7 May 2003.

[33] EWNHS, Note 11.

benefits drawn from the park. The survey was conducted in August 2004. The sampling was carried out from two villages: Chamo Letto and Tsalke. Chamo Letto village is located roughly 10 kilometers south of Arbaminch town and adjacent to the park. Most of the people in Chamo Letto are Guji-Ormo, who were relocated from the Nech-Sar plain and resettled there. Tsalke village is found within the park about 46 kilometers east of the park office. The majority of people in Tsalke village are also Guji-Oromo. Thus, very few respondents from Gamo and Kore ethnic groups were encountered during the questionnaire survey.

There was no official list of households in the two villages. Zewdu and Yemesrach (2003)[34] reported that there were fifteen hundred households of Guji-Oromos settled in the park. However, some of them have recently been relocated. The Kebelle officials from two villages provided an estimate of five hundred households in the Tsalke village and three hundred households in the Chamo-Letto village. A random sample of 10 percent of the estimated population from each village was interviewed, yielding a total of eighty households, fifty households from Tsalke, and thirty from Chamo-Letto Village.

Informal interviews and focus group discussions were conducted with local elders and individuals who have adequate knowledge of the park. The issues discussed included the relationship between the park management office and the local people, local people's participation in the management process of the park, the benefits they could generate from wildlife and other aspects of the park, their perception towards the existence of the park, and their views as to how they can coexist with the wildlife and the park. For focus group discussions, ten individuals from different age groups were selected to represent different views in the two sampled villages.

The data collected through questionnaire survey were analyzed using SPSS 10 for Windows. Cross-tabulation and the chi-square test (χ^2_{df}) was used to find out the association/relationship between local people's perception (dependent variable) and socioeconomic variables such as age, length of residency near the park, and knowledge of the park boundaries (independent variables). Multiple response questions are presented in multiple response tables, considering both total number of people and total responses percentages.

5 RESULTS AND DISCUSSIONS

5.1 Livelihood and Economic Orientation

The major economic activities in the study area were mixed farming and livestock rearing. All of the respondents interviewed reported that they combine cattle rearing with crop farming. The Kore and Ganta (Gamo) ethnic groups mainly depend on crop cultivation, whereas livestock serve as an integral part of their production and livelihood systems. The dominant way of making a living for the Guji-Oromo community is pastoral nomadism, although recently they have begun to shift to crop farming.

The Guji-Oromo and other ethnic groups currently practice farming activities and produce different crops for household consumption and the market. As shown in

[34] Belete Zewdu & A. Yemesrach, "Willingness to Pay for Protecting Endangered Environments: The Case of Nech-Sar National Park." *Social Science Research Report Series No. 31*, Organization for Social Sciences Research in Eastern and Southern Africa (2003).

Table 12.1. Important crops produced by the community

Crops	No. of responses	%
Maize	80	100
Banana	65	81.3
Cotton	46	57.5
Sugar cane, mango, & avocado	30	37.5
Sweet potato	4	5.0
Total responses	225	281.3

Source: Survey Results, August 2004.

Table 12.1, all of the respondents produce maize as a staple food crop, whereas banana, cotton, sugar cane, and other fruit trees are mainly grown for sale. Cotton, banana, sugar cane, and fruit-tree crops such as mango and avocado augment household income and also have value as clothing and as food stuffs.

Additionally, about 5 percent of the respondents, all from the Chamo Letto peasant association, reported that they produce sweet potato for household consumption.

Some focus group participants pointed out that until a few decades ago they depended mainly on cattle for their livelihood. They mentioned that they would prefer to pursue such a lifestyle today, but circumstances, such as lack of grazing land, prevalence of drought, and tsetse infestations, had forced them to shift their way of life from purely pastoral to semipastoral and nearly settled agriculture. Ayalew Gebre[35] also has observed this kind of economic reorientation in the pastoral communities of the Karrayu-Oromo in the Awash National Park. He noted that the Karrayu-Oromo transhumance had recently, mainly after the 1980s, started combining rainfed/irrigated agriculture with their pastoral life mainly in response to the expropriation of their pastoral land and the subsequent weakening of their pastoral livelihood.

5.2 Local People's Involvement and Participation

If a protected area is to succeed in its conservation objectives, it must win support from the local communities.[36] The local communities living around protected areas such as national parks bear significant costs in a number of ways. First, they are denied their customary rights to use the resources for grazing, cultivation, or hunting. Second, they are vulnerable to being termed as poachers and illegal land users. Third, they are evicted from their homelands.[37] For these and a number of other reasons, local communities have developed resentment towards protected areas such as the national parks. This was apparent in Ethiopia, particularly in the Nech-Sar National Park, during the collapse of *derg* government in 1991.[38] After 1991, parks and reserve areas were handed over to

[35] Ayalew Gebre, "The Effects of Development on Karrayu of Methara Area, in People, Space and the State." Proceedings of the workshop held by ESSSWA, 28–30 January 2003, (2004), 245.

[36] William M. Adams, *Against Extinction: The Story of Conservation* (Earthscan, 2004).

[37] William M. Adams & David Hulme, "If Community Conservation is the Answer in Africa, What is the Question?" (2001) *Oryx* 193–200. See also Adams, *Against Extinction*, Note 36.

[38] EWNHS, Note 11.

Table 12.2. Who occupied the area before the establishment of the park?

Ethnic groups	No. of responses	% responses
Guji-Oromo	77	62.1
Kore	29	23.4
Gamo	18	14.5
Total responses	124	100

Source: Survey Results, August 2004.

new regional governments, which lacked financial resources, administrative skills, and human resources to effectively manage them.[39]

When asked who administers Nech-Sar National Park, respondents varied in their answers, indicating a lack of knowledge as to who administers the park. About 43.8 percent responded that it was the federal government; 31.3 percent indicated that the regional government, that is, Southern Nations, Nationalities and People's Region (SNNPR), was in charge. By contrast, about 19 percent responded that the park is administered by the Woreda Bureau of Agriculture (Gamo Gofa Zone); and the remaining 5.9 percent had no clear idea.

Some focus group discussants raised the issue of federalism on the basis of ethnicity and language. To the extent that the present government follows ethnic federalism, they argued that the Oromia regional state should administer the Nech-Sar National Park. This is clearly articulated by Ato Gemeda Bako, eighty years old, of the Tsalke village:

> Oromiya is a regional state as SNNPR does. This land does not belong to Gamo Gofa people. It does not belong to the Koiyra [Kore] people either. It belongs to Guji-Oromo. Therefore, if we follow justice the park and the people should be administered by the Oromiya regional state.[40]

Interregional resource conflicts pose potentially difficult situations for the management of natural resources and biodiversity. Contrary to the viewpoint expressed by Ato Gemeda Bako, claims over the park come from the three ethnic groups that belong to two regional states. The interview result is summarized in Table 12.2, in which a given individual can provide one or more responses to the question,[41] "Who occupied the area before the establishment of the park?"

Three ethnic groups seem to have claims over the park resources. From the total responses, 62.1 percent indicated that the park belonged to Guji-Oromo, whereas 23.4 and 14.5 percent indicated that it belonged to Kore and Gamo, respectively. The practical challenge of managing biodiversity, particularly when it is a cross-border resource, is more complicated if different ethnic groups belonging to their respective regional governments have claims over such resources. Local people's involvement and participation in the conservation activities requires devolution of authorities and power as is

[39] Chemere Zewde, Note 32.

[40] Mr. Gemeda Bako, eighty years old, was interviewed in the environs of Tsalke inside the Nech-Sar National Park, 13 August 2004.

[41] Three individuals were unwilling to respond to this question, so they were omitted from computation (total respondents equal 77).

Table 12.3. Have you ever participated in the management process of the park?

			Reasons for not participating		
Response	Frequency	Percent	Reasons	Frequency	Percent
Yes	19	23.8	I was not requested	57	93.4
No	61	76.3	I do not support it	4	6.6
Total	80	100	Total	61	100

Source: Survey Results, August 2004.

the case elsewhere.[42] The lack of clear knowledge on the issue of who currently administers the park may reflect the knowledge that different authorities from federal and regional levels play a part in such activities.

When asked whether they have participated in the management process of the park (Table 12.3), most of the respondents (76.3 percent) reported they had not participated at any stage of park management decisions, whereas the remaining 23.8 percent replied that they had participated in the process of park management. Even those who have been "involved" did not participate in a true participatory sense because typically they were forced by the *Kebelle* administration to attend meetings.

When respondents were asked why they failed to participate, almost all (93.4 percent of those who had not participated) reported that no one had requested their participation, and the rest (6.6 percent) replied that they did not support the ideas that park officers brought for discussion. The local communities were sometimes contacted by the park officers and the message usually conveyed either involved concerns over evictions from the park or allegations that the communities are bad neighbors to wildlife.

The local people distrust the park officers because of their past experiences. As one of the eloquent speakers of the Guji-Oromo, Ato Koronel Jarso, in Tsalke village succinctly put it: "Some came up with their pens while others with their matches (to burn our houses and destroy properties) and still others came up with rifles. This was the whole story of participation in the Nech-Sar." He further elaborated, "those who came with the pens/pencils recorded our views and came back with a decision against what the local people expressed." Everybody in the villages of Chamo-Letto and Tsalke knew and spoke about the burning of their houses and destruction of properties during the *derg* regime. They remember being chased away by the military force of three successive governments including the Ethiopian People's Revolutionary Democratic Front (EPRDF). These type of actions still prevail there today, as the author has observed a police station inside the park (near Nech-Sar plain) where officers check out the movements of local people and fence them off from any use of the resources in spite of the inclusion of the phrase "community participation in park management" in policy documents.[43]

Consequently, local people have developed hatred and resentment towards the park officers. Even if the park officers were to come up with some new measures to enhance community participation, the likelihood of success seems minimal. In this regard, Adams and Hulme[44] have discussed the failure of true community participation in

[42] Susanne Stoll-Kleeman & Timothy O'Riordian, Note 20.
[43] EWNHS, Note 11.
[44] William M. Adams & David Hulme, Note 37, at 196.

Table 12.4. The reasons for liking the presence of the Nech-Sar Park

Resources	No. of responses	% responses
Source of springs and rivers	28	34.6
Grazing land	26	32.1
Scenic beauty or tourist	14	17.3
Source of livelihood	11	13.6
Protect desertification/soil moisture	2	2.5
Total response	81	100.0

Source: Survey Results, August 2004.

Africa as a result of lack of trust by the communities: "Local people have long memories, and are often acute (and cynical) political analysts. Men in uniform who yesterday held guns are not credible agents for participatory approaches to conservation."

5.3 Local People's Perception towards the Park and Wildlife

5.3.1 Perception towards the Park

A protected area cannot coexist with people hostile to its existence living around it. As the involvement and participation of the local communities is an essential and important component for the conservation of biodiversity in the protected area systems, so are perceptions of the neighbors and the local people around protected areas. Any management plans regarding protected areas should carefully examine the perception of local communities in order to win their support of conservation activities. In the following section, a brief account of the local perceptions towards the Nech-Sar National Park and wildlife of the park are provided.

The question: "Do you like the presence of the Nech-Sar National Park" was answered "yes" by 58.2 percent of the respondents implying that they like the presence of the park, whereas 41.8 percent of the respondents indicated their dislike. Those who liked the presence of the park mentioned a number of reasons (Table 12.4).[45] For instance, 34.6 percent of the total respondents indicated that they like the park because of its service as source of springs and rivers, whereas 32.1 percent expressed liking the park because of grazing land.

About 17.3 percent of respondents indicated that they like the park because of its scenic beauty or its ability to attract tourists, while 13.6 percent appreciate the park because it serves as a source of the resources they need for livelihood such as food, fuel, wood, and income. The local people also appreciated the presence of the park for the indirect services it provides (serving as a buffer against desertification and helping the soil to retain moisture).

Liking/disliking of the park does not have significant association with the age of the respondents ($\chi_2^2 = 3.94$, $P < 0.139$). The weak association between age groups (<30, 30–50 and >50) and overall attitude toward the park may be result of exposure in terms of education, discussion with the park management office, or any outlet toward ideas

[45] Respondents could identify more than one reason for liking the presence of the park.

such as are considered to be important in changing conservation attitudes. However, the length of residency in the vicinity of the park or duration of the stay of the respondents has a significant association ($\chi_2^2 = 6.27$, $P < 0.04$) with attitude towards the park. All of the individuals, who have lived for ten to fifteen years near the park, responded that they like the presence of the park. Of those who had lived for fifteen to twenty years in the vicinity, very few (1.3 percent) disliked the presence of the park. In contrast, the majority of the respondents (40.5 percent of the respondents) who have lived inside or near the park for more than twenty years expressed a negative attitude towards the presence of the park.

The two main reasons expressed by those who did not like (41.8 percent) the presence of the Nech-Sar National Park were anticipated eviction from the park area and lack of benefits from income generated from the park. Restrictions to resource use and movement also were mentioned as a main reason that they disliked the park. During focus group discussions, they expressed their grievances regarding the lack of benefit from the park. Some of them remembered the promise made by the imperial government to provide them with compensation for the lands they lost to the park in terms of schools, health posts, and employment. Ato Gemeda Bako, in the Tsalke village, expressed that during the time that Haile Selassie was emperor:

> We were promised to provide 30 individuals from our community who would be given opportunities for education and employment but none has been realized. Even today there are some of our children who have completed secondary education yet they (three of them) were employed as gate keepers for the sake of telling us that our community benefited from such employment activities.[46]

A similar story of unfulfilled promises was made by the imperial government of Ethiopia to the Karrayu-Oromo when the Awash National Park was established. The promises ranged from paying money as compensation for lost grazing land[47] to other benefits such as employment and education.

The question "What is your opinion on the size of the park?," which provided respondents with a range of possible responses from "too big" to "right size" to "too small" to "no opinion" was answered "too big" by a large majority of respondents (89.9 percent), whereas just 10.1 percent answered the "right size." No one replied that the park is too small in size or indicated that they had no opinion regarding this issue. There was no significant association between age groups regarding opinions on the size of the park ($\chi_2^2 = 3.44$, $P < 0.179$). People who have lived longer in the area (82.3 percent of the respondents) in and around the park felt that it is too big relative to other potential uses that the land could be put to. The people who have stayed longer in the area pointed out that the park has gradually increased in size since its establishment. They also claimed that the steady increase of the park area had led to tension and conflict with the local communities.

When the respondents were asked the question, "Do you know the boundary of the park?," a majority of them (68.4. percent) responded they knew the boundary, whereas 31.5 percent answered that they did not know the boundary. Cross-tabulation was made to find out whether there was any association between the knowledge of the park boundary and impression on the size of the park (Table 12.5). Of those who

46 Mr. Gemeda Bako, Tsalke; see also Note 40.

47 Ayalew Gebre, Note 35.

Table 12.5. Cross tabulation of park knowledge with the size of the park

	Do you know the park boundary?		
	Yes	No	Total
Is the park too large?	51	20	71
% of total	64.6	25.3	89.9
Is the park the right size?	3	5	8
% of total	3.8	6.3	10.1
Total count	54	25	79
Percent	68.4	31.5	100

Source: Survey Results, August 2004.

responded that they knew the boundary, the vast majority (fifty-one of the fifty-four respondents) indicated that the park is too big. Only three respondents, who claimed to know the park boundary, believed that the park was the right size. The knowledge of the park boundary and impression of the size have significant association ($\chi_1^2 = 3.918$, $P < 0.048$).

Focus group discussions confirmed the views expressed in Table 12.5. Most of the discussants indicated that the park is too large. This could be an acceptable reaction from the perspective of the local communities who have continuously been pushed away from their ancestral lands. The fact that no one regarded the park as too small might be related to the obvious problems of eviction or because of a lack of benefits/compensations for lost agricultural or grazing lands.

The local people know clearly the duties of the scouts/game guards. Most of them reported that the scouts protect wildlife from "illegal hunters," protect forests from fire, and keep wood cutters and charcoal makers out of the park. About 9 percent of the respondents reported that they do not know the duties of the scouts and refrained from responding to the question. When asked the question, "What is your opinion on the duties of scouts/game guards in the park?" with possible answers of "good," "bad," "no opinion," or "various reasons," the majority of respondents (70 percent) indicated that the duties of scouts were good. Those who said the duties of game guards were "bad" or had "no opinion" accounted for 30 percent. The response of "no opinion" could be interpreted as "bad" because local people had daily contact with the game guards and usually perceive the scouts negatively for a number of reasons.

Those who perceived the duties of the game guards as "bad," were asked to explain their answer. Almost all of them pointed out that "the scouts do not do their duties honestly." Their responses also indicated that the game guards "disgrace the local communities as if the people were there to encroach on the park and the guards were very suspicious about poaching by the local communities." One respondent pointed out that the game guards usually make a deal with charcoal makers and wood cutters for some sort of concessions.

5.3.2 Perception towards Wild Animals

The perception of local communities toward wildlife is as important as their perception towards the park itself. When asked "Do you think wildlife creates problems to the local people?" the majority of respondents (60 percent) said yes, 37.5 percent said no, and 2.5 percent refrained from responding the question.

All of the respondents who indicated that wildlife creates problems for local communities mentioned crop depredation as a common phenomenon. A few respondents (12.5 percent) reported that wild animals attack their livestock. Apes and monkeys were identified by the local communities as the worst crop depredators, whereas lions and leopards were considered the species that damage/kill livestock, identified by 50 percent and 10 percent of the respondents, respectively. However, the incidence of livestock damage by the top carnivores such as lions and leopards was a rare phenomenon as compared to crop depredation by apes and monkeys. Some respondents (5 percent) reported that in addition to apes and monkeys, hippos trample and damage their crops.

Different studies[48] have indicated that crop damage caused by the big mammals or apes and monkeys can be expected to yield negative attitudes towards a park. Bauer[49] reported that the local people living around the Waza National Park in Cameron identified the baboon as the most notorious crop depredator. The present study, however, does not show a significant relationship between crop depredation and perception towards the park ($\chi_1^2 = 0.4$, $P < 0.52$, not significant). The lack of significant association between crop depredation and perception towards the Nech-Sar National Park may partly be attributed to the desire of respondents to conceal their true feelings because they fear that they would be relocated if found to be in conflict with the wild animals.

A number of measures were taken by the local communities to manage/control crop depredation and livestock damage caused by wild animals. Of those who saw wild animals as a threat to their crops or livestock, about half (46 percent) mentioned that they either kill or trap nuisance wild animals in response to the damage they inflict on the communities crops or livestock. They also mentioned that there was no compensation for their losses from the park management. During focus group discussions, community elders confirmed that often they kill wild animals if the damage caused is too large for them to bear. However, this was a measure that they opted to take only if other efforts to protect crops and livestock from wild animals had become difficult or was unsuccessful.

5.4 Resource Use Patterns and Benefits from the Park

Local communities depend directly on the natural resources of the park for their livelihoods. Traditionally, protected areas prohibit resource uses and shield off nature from any kind of human uses.[50] Recently, however, the prohibition of resource uses in protected area systems has been strongly debated both from a pragmatic point of view and a humanitarian approach.[51] The situation is becoming more problematic in view of the growing population and arduous level of poverty in developing countries, such as Ethiopia, which could undermine conservation objectives. The following paragraphs

[48] W. de Boer & D. S. Baquete, "Natural Resource Use, Crop Damage and Attitudes of Rural People in the Vicinity of the Maputo Elephant Reserve, Mozambique." 25 *Environmental Conservation* (1998), 208–218.

[49] Hans Bauer, "Local Perceptions of Waza National Park, Northern Cameroon." 30 *Environmental Conservation* (2003), 175–181.

[50] Sharma, Note 16.

[51] Ervin H. Zube & Miriam L. Busch, "Park-People Relationships: An International Review." 19 *Landscape and Urban Planning* (2003), 117–131; W. de Boer & D. S. Baquete, Note 48. See also Abbot et al., Note 27.

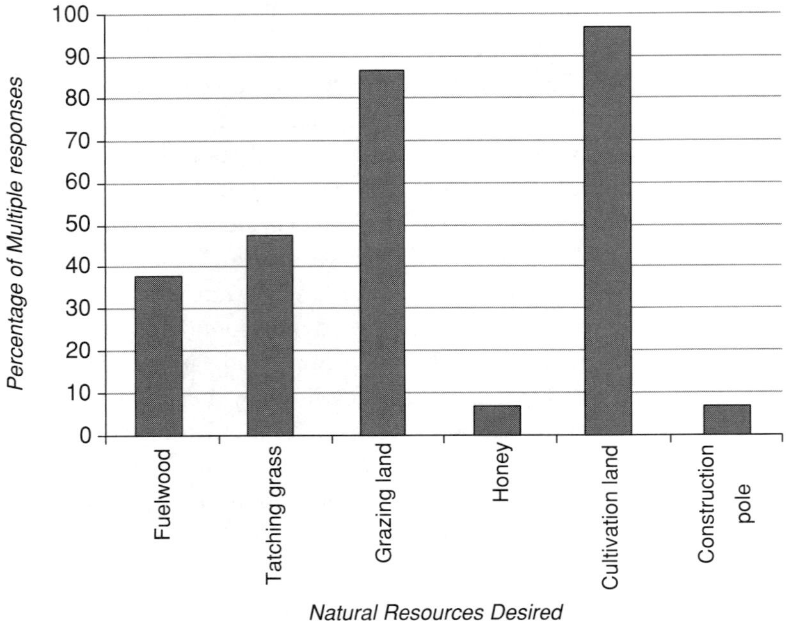

Figure 12.2. Natural Resources Harvested from the Nech-Sar National Park.

provide a short account of natural resource use and benefits of the Nech-Sar Park to the local communities.

When asked, "Do the local communities have traditional/customary rights to use the park resources?," a large majority (95 percent) answered yes, whereas only 5 percent of the respondents answered no. Those few people who answered no provided reasons why they have no such rights and one expressed with humor that "the reality shows that the land and the people belong to the government so when the government needs a given piece of land, it can take it away or do whatever." This expression is an indication of local people's experience of being pushed out of the park during the past two successive governments. By contrast, those who have expressed that the local communities do have the traditional/customary rights to use natural resources of the park have pointed out that they were born inside the park and it is the land of their ancestors.

When asked the question "Who should decide on individuals or households access to the park resources?" diverse responses were provided. Some of the respondents (15.3 percent) indicated that they want free access to the park resources, referring to the ancestral claims to the land. Over half of the respondents (51 percent), however, preferred that the local elders' council/Geda system officials decide on the individuals/households access to the park resources, whereas 12 percent of the respondents suggested a dual management scheme that would involve the local elders committee and park officers. Only three individuals preferred that park officers decide on individual/household access to resources of the park.

Local people depend on the natural park resources of the park for their livelihoods in many ways. In order to understand the exploitation of natural resources of the park and dependency on such resources, the respondents were asked to list important resources they harvest legally or illegally from the park (Figure 12.2). The two most important resources of the park were cultivation land (96.3 percent) and pasture/grazing land (86.3 percent). Almost all of the respondents indicated that they exploit these resources

Table 12.6. Weighted rank values of Natural resources exploited from the Nech-Sar National Park

Natural resources	Weighted value ranks 1st	2nd	3rd	4th	Weighted value rank sum	%
Fuelwood	4	6	50	2	62	9.68
Thatching grass	8	24	10	13	55	8.6
Grazing land	32	162	8	1	203	31.7
Cultivation land	276	21	2	0	299	46.7
Construction pole	0	9	8	0	17	2.6
Honey production	0	0	2	2	4	0.6
Weighted value rank sum	320	222	80	18	640	100
Percent	50	34.7	12.5	2.8	100	

Source: Survey Results, August 2004.
The first rank has a weight value of 4, whereas the fourth rank has a weight value of 1.

from the park everyday. Zewdu and Yemesrach[52] reported that large majority of the respondents (86 percent) visited the Nech-Sar National Park for the purpose of grazing, followed by farming (48.7 percent), water sources (29.9 percent), hunting (20 percent), and fishing (2 percent).

Thatching grass and fuel wood are also considered as important resources because the local people depend on the grass and woody biomass for house building and repair, and energy demands, respectively. A number of studies conducted elsewhere[53] (Sharma, 1990; Stræde & Helles, 2000) have indicated that thatching grass and fuel wood provision from a park has a direct influence on the local people's perception towards the protected areas. For instance, in the Chitawan National Park in Nepal, Stræde, and Helles[54] reported that the grass-cutting program was the backbone of people-park relationships because it contributed positively towards fulfilling some of the livelihood questions of the communities. However, challenges existed as to how to execute the program in the face of increasing population pressure in the vicinity of the park. A study undertaken in the Maputo Elephant Reserve in Mozambique[55] also indicated that most local people use thatching grass for house building purposes.

The local people did not appreciate the importance of construction wood, probably because it is readily available. Honey production within the park is limited and, thus, few people (2.2 percent) appreciated its importance as a resource for the community (Figure 12.2). The local people harvest honey from the forest while grazing the domestic animals in the park. There were no beehives made for these purposes within the park, with the exception of one individual who was an urban dweller working on honey production for market. Honey production by the local community for market purposes could be a way of enhancing local income, thereby encouraging conservation rather than negative attitudes towards the park.

Respondents were asked to rank the natural resources they extract from the park in order of importance (Table 12.6). When considering only the most important resources,

[52] Zewdu & Yemesrach, note 34, at 25.

[53] S. Stræde & F. Helles, "Park-People Conflict Resolution in Royal Chitawan National Park, Nepal: Buying Time at High Cost?" 27 *Environmental Conservation* (2000), 368–381; Sharma, note 16; W. de Boer & D. S. Baquete, Note 48.

[54] Ibid.

[55] W. de Boer & D. S. Baquete, Note 48.

land for cultivation accounted for 86.25 percent of the responses, followed by grazing land (10 percent), and thatching grass and fuel wood (3.75 percent).

Cultivation land (46.7 percent) and pasture/grazing land (31.7 percent) were identified as the two most conspicuously needed resources. About 18.3 percent of the respondents' resource needs can be satisfied by the provision of fuel wood and thatching grass, whereas a very small proportion (3.2 percent) of the respondents needed construction poles and honey.

Officially, fuel wood collection from the Nech-Sar National Park is prohibited, but a number of people collect fuel wood either for household energy demand or for sale. Most of the wood collectors are urban dwellers. Park scouts chase away those individuals who are involved in collection of dry woods from the park; yet it is difficult to stop them from such activities.

Identifying the relative importance of the park's natural resources is essential for any intervention activities. The pattern of resource use in the Nech-Sar National Park indicates the overall use of the resources follows the main livelihood activities of the people residing within or around the park. The large majority of the respondents chose land as the first most important resource of the park; this could be taken as a dynamic tendency of livelihood orientation occurring in the study area and elsewhere in the pastoral communities in the Rift Valley regions of Ethiopia. For instance, Ayalew Gebre[56] indicated that with response to the changing circumstances (adaptation mechanism) and alienation of the land for different land uses (park, agro-, and state farms), the nomadic Karrayu-Oromo have started to build permanent settlements in the middle section of the Awash river over the last fifty years.

The relatively low rank (0.6 percent) of the value of honey production can be taken as a future potential area for intervention in the Nech-Sar National Park. Enriching park resources by providing a market for them and enhancing the quantity and quality of the existing resources would assist park management in winning the support of local communities through provision of some of the local people's livelihood demands. Enhancing and enriching park resources and their respective values to the community are widely worked practices in conservation and development projects in many parts of Africa.[57] These are important options when the park management cannot be in a position to provide alternatives, such as schools, clinics or veterinary services, for the local communities to reduce their direct dependence on park resources or to compensate them for lost access to park resources.

The park management office has currently proposed to relocate the Guji-Oromo communities from park area to Tore village near Dilla. The people, as discussed in earlier sections, developed negative attitudes towards the park because of the anticipated resettlement program. Some of the informants pointed out that they need a compensation payment if they are to be removed from the park area. As discussed in Section 4.1, the local communities produce perennial and annual crops and hence require compensation for their investment in the land they owned.

6 CONCLUSION

Protected area systems, such as national parks, are the last resort to conserve the remaining biological diversity of a country. Nonetheless, they are not effectively serving this

[56] Ayalew Gebre, Note 35.

[57] J. Abbot et al., Note 27.

function and often exist at the expense of the livelihoods of the local people who are residing near them. The Nech-Sar National Park is not immune from these problems. It was established in 1975 with the intention of conserving the immense natural resource of the area and generating economic benefits from tourism to the country. Presently, however, it is not serving these objectives to the desired extent and remains a burden rather than contributing to local development needs and livelihood security of the local communities. This is mainly because the "fortress" management approach pursued in the Nech-Sar National Park has yielded a number of socioeconomic and conservation challenges. The park management office still strives to protect nature from local people through eviction, resettlement, or paramilitary force. These actions, in turn, result in resentment and negative attitudes towards the park and wildlife.

The results of the study show that the local communities have not participated in park planning and management activities. Genuine involvement and participation are essential tools for conservation because local people could then prioritize their development aspirations and it would help to build their cooperation for conservation. If the Nech-Sar National Park is to survive for future generations, inclusion of the local people as partners for conservation and appreciating their development needs and livelihood security is essential.

Not only have the local people been excluded from the management processes, but also their perceptions, knowledge, and practices have been undervalued. The Nech-Sar National Park cannot coexist with people hostile to it living around it. The results of this study also indicate that most of the people (58.2 percent of respondents) appreciate the presence of the park primarily because it provides sources of water and grazing land for the communities. The remaining 41.8 percent of the respondents disliked the presence of the Nech-Sar National Park because of anticipated relocation from the park area and restrictions on resource uses. Different schemes of arrangements for resource uses could be made, for instance seasonal grass cutting and fuel wood collection, and other similar schemes could provide access to the natural resources of the park. These types of schemes would of great help to develop positive attitudes towards the park and its wildlife and, in turn, to foster community support for the conservation objectives of the Nech-Sar Park.

Generally, it can be argued that the existence of the Nech-Sar National Park will not be ensured by fencing off nature and wildlife. Rather, sustainable solutions for better management strategies for the park are required. For example, the creation of alternatives for the local communities such as schools, health centers, and veterinary services will eventually reduce pressure on the park. Equally important, increasing the local communities' livelihood security through enhancing and enriching the existing park resources is important. For instance, developing apiculture in the area could provide an important source of income for the community. It is fitting to conclude with a quote from UNEP Executive Director Achim Steiner:[58]

> In the past they [protected areas] have been seen as islands of protection in an ocean of destruction. We need to learn to look on them as the building blocks of biodiversity in an ocean of sustainable human development, with their benefits extending far beyond their physical boundaries.

[58] Achim Steiner, "Trouble in Paradise." *New Scientist* (2003), 180:2417, 21; cited in William M. Adams, Note 36, at 123.

7 ACKNOWLEDGMENTS

I am very grateful to UNEP for providing funds to attend the 3rd Colloquium of IUCN Academy of Environmental Law, Sydney. I thank David Leary for organizing my travel to Sydney. Dr. Jeremy Firestone deserves special thanks for his critical comments and improving the language. This research is funded by the Organization for Social Sciences Research in Eastern and Southern Africa (OSSREA).

13 Japanese MPAs at a Turning Point: Nomination of Shiretoko for World Heritage Status

Yasuhiko Kagami*

1 INTRODUCTION

This study explores recent trends in Japanese Marine Protected Areas (MPAs). The most common definition of a Marine Protected Area is:

> Any area of intertidal or subtidal terrain, together with its overlying waters and associated flora, fauna, historical and cultural features, which has been reserved by law or other effective means to protect part or all of the enclosed environment. (Resolution by 17th General Assembly of the World Conservation Union [IUCN], 17.38, 1994)

As Graeme Kelleher has correctly pointed out in the *Guidelines for Marine Protected Areas*, this definition of MPA "does not state that an MPA should keep people out."[1] An MPA is not a "fence" in the sea but a marine management tool to help preserve ecosystems/biodiversity and sustainable development (in particular, fishery). It is vital to keep in mind that establishing an MPA never blocks fishery.

However, Japanese fishers often misinterpret MPAs as no-take zones, causing them to object strongly to their establishment. This is also the case with the Japanese government; in Japanese fishery diplomacy, the fishery agency considered an MPA that expanded into the Exclusive Economic Zone (EEZ) or even into the high seas to be an area that could prevent fishing operations.[2]

An MPA is not a no-take zone; the broad spectrum of MPA management approaches (which can include no-take areas) is key to sustaining resources, safeguarding ecosystem functions and biodiversity, or providing a framework to support the use of resources and space with minimal conflict.[3] Following the adoption of the Convention of Biological Diversity in 1992, there has been increasing awareness of the results of MPAs.

The nomination of the Shiretoko Peninsula as a World Heritage Site is forcing a change in the negative Japanese attitude toward MPAs. This study explores the change that Japan must negotiate as a result of this nomination, following an examination of the current Japanese coastal fishery regime and MPA systems.

[1] Graeme Kelleher, *Guidelines for Marine Protected Areas*. IUCN, 1999: xviii–xix.
[2] Fishery Agency, *Japanese Fishery Diplomacy*. 2003:14.
[3] T. Agardy et al., "Dangerous Targets? Unresolved Issues and Ideological Clashes around Marine Protected Areas." 13 *Aquatic Conservation: Marine and Freshwater Ecosystems* (2003), 63.

* Thanks are due to Dr. Mitsutaku Makino and Professor Hiroyuki Matsuda for their valuable input. All views expressed in this chapter are the sole responsibility of the author.

2 JAPANESE COASTAL FISHERIES REGIME

2.1 Community-Based Fisheries Management System

Japanese coastal fisheries[4] are governed by the 1949 Fisheries Law, the primary objectives of which are to ensure fishery production and to provide holistic use of the sea surface by means of fishery adjustment commissions that have fishers as principal constituents (Art. 1). Under this law, those with a right to fish may engage in the fishery, which has been divided into three categories: large scale set-net fishing, aquaculture (demarcated) fishing, and common fishing.

In coastal areas, the common fishing right is at the center of these fishing rights. The prefecture governor grants fishing rights to individual local fishing communities.[5] In this case, the term "local fishing communities" refers to fishing cooperative associations (FCAs). Common fishing rights are granted only to local FCAs, composed of local fishers; most fishing communities have an FCA, and there are about fifteen hundred FCAs along the coast. In order to coordinate holistic fisheries in local fishing grounds, FCAs must establish operational regulations (FCA regulations) that stipulate gear, catch restrictions, and fishing ground closures.

Compared to the management systems of Japan's distant water and offshore fishing, which are strictly regulated by the government, FCAs have broad discretionary powers over the coastal fishery. In fact, FCAs perform almost all aspects of fishery management (planning, organizing, implementation, and enforcement), which consist of practices that have been established throughout a long history of trial and error.[6]

The advantage of this system is that experienced local fishers can take the initiative, instituting regulations that apply to local conditions. Unlike agencies in the United States, Canada, and much of Europe, the Japanese fishery agency does not have a bureau or division responsible for fishery management;[7] this means that there is no cost to national and local governments. Fisheries economists call this sort of system "community-based management," meaning that fishers (users) manage fisheries on their own.[8]

[4] Coastal fishery refers to capture fishery, normally performed by family members of a fishing household to sustain their livelihood with either no boat, a nonpowered boat, or a powered boat under ten gross tons. Coastal fishery includes aquaculture (freshwater and saltwater). Japan International Fisheries Research Society (JIFRS), *Japan and Her Fisheries.* 2004:13.

[5] About 80 percent of Japanese fishers engage in coastal fisheries and there are about fifteen hundred fishing cooperative associations (FCAs) in the nation.

[6] For a detailed analysis of legislative history and a case study of Japanese coastal fisheries, see Mitsutaku Makino & Hiroyuki Matsuda, "Co-Management in Japanese Coastal Fisheries: Institutional Features and Transactional Costs." 29 *Marine Policy* (2005), 441–450.

[7] Tadashi Yamamoto, "Community-Based Coastal Fisheries Management Developed in Japan." Available at http://www.arc-corp.co.jp/JIFRS/English/CBFMinJapanFinal.htm.

[8] See, in general, Tadashi Yamamoto, "Development of a Community-Based Fisheries Management System in Japan." 10 *Marine Resources Economics* (1995), 21–34. As Yamamoto has pointed out, the term "community-based coastal fishery management" was first used during the FAO/Japan Expert Consultation on the Development of Community-Based Coastal Fishery Management Systems for Asia and the Pacific, held in Kobe, Japan, 8–12 June 1992. The proceedings from that conference are available in the FAO report of the FAO/Japan expert consultation on the development of community-based coastal fishery management systems for Asia and the Pacific. *FAO Fisheries Report 474*, FAO, 1993.

2.2 Regulation without Environmental Perspective

The community-based management system has a number of problems. First, the "community" is composed solely of fishers and their employees, which results in fishery regulations giving explicit priority to increased fishery productivity, with possible concomitant neglect of ecosystem/biodiversity preservation. This means that FCA regulations may not correspond to public values; indeed, Japanese fisheries-related legislation often neglects environmental considerations. The Basic Law on Fisheries Policy (2001) was the first Japanese fisheries–related legislation to explicitly use the term "ecosystem"; but even this law does not make ecosystem/biodiversity preservation a legal obligation.

The concept of "community" has led to increasing problems because it does not include recreational fishers, who may use highly developed fish-finders and catch large numbers of fish without restriction. The fact that the fish that they catch are not registered in official statistics makes fishery management more difficult. FCAs imply self-restrictions, and these constraints do not apply to those who do not rely on fishing for a living.

Second, the government is reluctant to establish protected areas because the right to fish is vested on the basis of sea areas. If a government decides to establish protected areas (which may include fishing bans), it may have to pay substantial compensation for fishery-related losses.[9] Consequently, fishery based on the right to fish makes it difficult for a government to designate and operate MPAs, which FCAs consider irrelevant to fishery production.

3 JAPANESE MPA SYSTEMS

3.1 Types of Japanese MPA Systems

Are there any MPAs in Japan? There are, but the term "marine protected area" is not used in national legislation and the term is unfamiliar to the public. However, coastal areas have many MPA-like areas, as noted in *A Global Representative System of Marine Protected Area.*[10] These are classified into four systems: Ordinary Zones in National Parks, Marine Parks, Nature Conservation Areas, and Fishery Resources Protection Areas.

3.1.1 Ordinary Zones in National Parks

Marine areas included in National Parks, Quasi-National Parks, and Prefectural Nature Parks are based on the Nature Parks Law (1957) and are classified as Ordinary Zones.[11]

The objective of a National Park is given in the Nature Parks Law: "This Law shall aim at the protection of places of natural scenic beauty and also, through the promoted utilization thereof, at the contribution to the health, recreation and culture of the

[9] Guidelines on Public Expropriation (Cabinet Decision) in 1962, Section 5, Arts. 38–40.

[10] Graeme Kelleher, Richard Kenchington, & Sue Wells, eds., *A Global Representative System of Marine Protected Area*, Vol. IV (Great Barrier Reef Marine Park Authority, The World Bank and the World Conservation Union, 1995), 116–118 (this section was written by François Simard).

[11] See, in general, Japanese National Parks, Ministry of Environment (Japan), Nature Conservation Bureau Environment Agency 1995 (4th ed.). Available at http://www.env.go.jp/en/pol/ncj/section5.html.

people" (Art. 10. In light of this objective, Japanese parks generally would be properly classified as Category V of the IUCN Protected Area Management Categories (Protected Landscape/Seascape), rather than Category II (National Park: protected area managed mainly for ecosystem protection and recreation). Even though an area may have inherent biodiversity, without scenic beauty it will not be designated as a National Park.[12] Despite the fact that, in 2002, there was a revision to the Nature Parks Law creating, as an additional state responsibility, "the aim to ensure diversity in the ecosystem and creatures in Natural Parks" (Art. 3 (2)), the designated criteria remained unchanged.

A place designated as a National Park is not necessarily owned by the government; of the total National Park area (2,061,040 hectares), 30 percent (520,805 hectares) is owned by private citizens. This "mosaic" ownership system prevents effective creation and enforcement of regulations.

There are few restrictions in an Ordinary Zone (terrestrial or marine), and an Ordinary Zone is a de facto buffer. Development is not prohibited; only prior notification to the Minister of the Environment is required for the following activities (Art. 26):

1. Constructing, reconstructing, or extending large-scale structures;
2. Causing an increase or decrease in the water level or quantity of water in rivers, lakes, marshes, swamps, wetlands, and so on;
3. Putting up or setting up advertisements, and so on;
4. Reclaiming water surface or reclaiming by drainage;
5. Mining minerals or extracting soil and stones;*
6. Changing features of the land; and
7. Changing features of the seabed.*

*Apply only around Marine Park areas (see Section 3.1.2 of this chapter).

As of 2005, many Ordinary Zones had been designated in coastal areas along shorelines. However, as noted earlier, the regulations are powerless even to protect scenery. For example, Setonaikai National Park, the largest National Park in Japan, contains a large Ordinary Zone (terrestrial areas were designated in 1934 and marine areas were included in 1956). After designation, development of the coastal areas progressed and changed the scenery. In the 1970s, water pollution became a serious issue, and now little natural beach remains.

Section 4 of this chapter discusses the marine areas of Shiretoko, which was nominated as a World Heritage Site and categorized as an Ordinary Zone.

3.1.2 Marine Parks

The Marine Parks (MPs)[13] system was introduced by a revision to the Nature Parks Law in 1970 (Art. 24). Because this system is also based on the Nature Parks Law, its goal is also to preserve scenery (in this case, "beautiful underseascapes," Art. 24). Again, even though some marine areas may have inherent biodiversity, no site will be

[12] In general, Japanese people traditionally tend to interpret "nature" as "scenery"; when taking a photograph or drawing a picture of nature, animals tend to be eliminated. So, for Japanese people, "scenery" means "greenery." The nature protection regulation reflected in the Nature Parks Law therefore corresponds with a common viewpoint, which is now gradually changing.

[13] See, in general, Marine Parks Center of Japan, *Protecting Nature of the Sea: Roles and Activities of Marine Parks* (Marine Parks Center of Japan, 2001).

designated as a MP without a beautiful underseascape. The old but still effective "Policy for Designation of Marine Park Zones" (Guideline of Designation of MPs issued by the Director-General, Parks Department, Ministry of Welfare, 1970) provides the following criteria for designation:

1. Both land and sea areas surrounding the Marine Park Zone are designated as National or Quasi-National Park, and nature conservation on land can be fully ensured;
2. The seabed topography is characteristic and undersea fauna and flora are also abundant;
3. Sea water is transparent and unlikely to become dirty or polluted;
4. Water has a maximum depth of twenty meters;
5. The current is not overly rapid nor are waves overly violent;
6. There should be enough space on nearby land to construct connected facilities such as a landing pier, rest-house, visitor center, parking lot, and so on;
7. Coordination with fisheries should be possible, through cooperation with local fisheries in particular, concerning Marine Park Zones; and
8. In addition to all of this, there should be little risk of destruction as a result of industrial development.

The result ensuing from these criteria is that most designated MPs are small areas of coral reef and seaweed, and MPs are designated only within sea areas of National or Quasi-National Parks.

The regulation of MPs is relatively tight. In particular, Nature Parks Law restricts "capturing, killing or wounding, gathering, or damaging tropical fish, coral, seaweed, or plants and animal life similar to those that have been designated . . . by the Minister of the Environment with the consent of the Minister of Agriculture, Forestry and Fisheries" (Art. 24, para. 3 (2)). However, this article is a product of compromise, and it does not designate the target species of fishers.

This regulation may be the strictest restriction in Japan's protected area system, but it is not without problems. First, a 2003 report on the Kushimoto MP sharply criticized a number of operational items,[14] indicating that current criteria designating species are unclear and that the designated species are totally incompatible with the current situation; under Article 24, fifty-four species are currently designated, but these species were first designated thirty years ago, and the designations have remained unchanged.[15] The report concluded that current regulation is unlikely to preserve species, and that significant revision of designated species and criteria is needed.[16]

Second, Nature Parks Law does not regulate fishing at all. When the MP system started, FCAs voluntarily abstained from fishing in those areas to promote resource conservation. However, in early 1990s, only 26 percent of MP areas were under voluntary abstention.[17] Current legislation does not provide a way to alter this situation.

[14] Ministry of Environment, Nature Conservation Bureau, *Project Report on the Preserving Activities in Marine Park Areas.* 2002 (in Japanese). Kushimoto Marine Park was one of the first Marine Parks, designated in 1975. Surprisingly, this Project Report was the *first* comprehensive assessment report since designation.

[15] Keiichi Nomura, "Review of the Designated Species in the Marine Park Areas," in *Project Report of the Preserving Activities in the Marine Park Areas*, note 14, at 92.

[16] Ibid.

[17] Toshio Torii, "Research on the Current Situation of Marine Parks in 1991." 98 *Marine Parks Journal* (1993), 9 (in Japanese).

Third, the MP area is relatively small; as of March 2004, there were 64 zones in 139 units (total 2,664.2 hectares). An average Unit has an area of only 18.8 hectares, which is not large enough to allow effective management.

As François Simard has correctly pointed out, "[i]n most cases, Japanese MPs cannot play the role of protecting a natural sea area. They only play an educational and tourism role, because they are not large enough to provide for effective management."[18] An interesting divergence in motivation emerged during the first MPA conference held in Japan, the "International Conference on Marine Parks and Reserves" cosponsored by the IUCN and the Marine Parks Center of Japan, which was held in Tokyo in 1975.[19] Participants discussed criteria and guidelines for describing and managing MPs and reserves, and demanded the establishment of a well-monitored MPA system that represented the world's marine ecosystem.[20] However, although IUCN participants promoted MPAs for environmental reasons, Japanese participants were most interested in using MPs as tourism resources.[21]

3.1.3 Nature Conservation Areas

The Nature Conservation Law was adopted in 1972 to mitigate the shortcomings of the scenery-focused Nature Parks Law. Under this law, Nature Conservation Areas (NCAs) are designated to comprehensively promote conservation of natural environments (Art. 1). Unlike the Nature Parks Law, the word "scenery" is deliberately left out of the designation's objective; NCAs can include places that do not necessarily have scenic beauty. This means that of the IUCN Protected Area Management Categories, NCAs would be classified under Category I, III, or IV, but not V.

However, because a Nature Park cannot simultaneously be a Nature Conservation Area, only one marine area is currently designated as an NCA (Art. 22). Sakiyama Bay on Iriomote Island, which covers 128 hectares and supports large *Galaxea fascicularis*, was designated as an NCA in June 1983.[22] Even though areas like this are highly protected, fishing is not restricted, even in NCAs.

3.1.4 Fishery Resources Protection Areas

The Fishery Resources Protection Area (FRPA)[23] system is based on the Fishery Resources Protection Law, which was adopted in 1951. It differs from other protected areas described earlier in this chapter, in that its objective is to sustain the reproduction of commercial species (Art. 1). The Ministry of Agriculture, Forestry, and Fisheries designates FRPAs based on advice from the Central Council for Fisheries Regulation, and

[18] François Simard, "MARINE REGION 16 Northwest Pacific," in *A Global Representative System of Marine Protected Area*, Vol. IV, supra note 10, at 117.

[19] National Research Council, *Marine Protected Areas: Tools for Sustaining Ocean Ecosystems.* (National Academy Press, 2001), 146. The Marine Parks Center of Japan was dissolved in March 2002.

[20] Ibid. See also Proceedings of the Conference, *Bulletin of the Marine Park Research Stations* 1, No. 2 (1977).

[21] One participant of the first MPA Conference recalled that there was a fundamental ideological gap between the English title ("International Conference on Marine Parks and Reserves") and the Japanese title ("International Conference on Marine Parks"). Shun Inano, "Marine Parks and Fishery." 42 *Marine Parks Journal* (1977), 13 (in Japanese).

[22] *Protecting Nature of the Sea*, Note 13, at 22.

[23] See, especially, Simard, Note 18, at 117–118.

FRPAs are managed by Prefecture Governors (Art. 14). In contrast to other protected areas, the Minister of Environment cannot intervene in this designation process.

FRPA management usually includes a complete ban on fishing, strict regulations on fishing gear, and seasonal closure of fishing grounds within breeding, spawning, and nursery sites. In general, FRPAs are small spots located in river mouths or inland waters. The system is based on fishing production and does not consider ecosystem or biodiversity conservation (the Fishery Resources Protection Law does not refer to these terms). This type of protected area would be classified under Category VI of the IUCN Protected Area Management Categories (Managed Resource Protected Area). As of August 2002, there were 120 FRPAs, totaling 2,303 kilometers of rivers, 214 hectares of lakes, and 2,948 hectares of ocean.

3.2 Common Shortcomings of the Japanese MPA System

Common shortcomings of this system include:

1. The laws regulating such systems are very old; because these laws are rarely revised, the goal of preserving marine ecosystems/biodiversity (which has been gathering strength since the 1990s) is not appropriately articulated.
2. Each designated area is too small to protect marine species and related ecosystems, and in these MPAs there are no fisheries restrictions (except in Fishery Resources Protection Areas). During the designation of Japanese MPAs, officials carefully avoid any connection with fisheries.
3. No scientific committees or monitoring systems have been established for these protected areas; it is no exaggeration to say that Japanese MPAs are neglected after designation. This is somewhat ironic, given that the first MPA conference held in Japan recommended the establishment of a well-monitored MPA system.
4. Systems are isolated from legislation relating to, for example, coastal management; they lack relationships with other MPA systems and coastal management related legislation. One author wrote that an MP is "oil in the water."[24]

In summary, the Japanese MPA system is based on a three-decades-old balance of interests and is not in line with the current requirements of marine environmental protection. The Japanese marine management system seems to lack vision when it comes to achieving a balance between the preservation of ecosystems/biodiversity and a sustainable fishery.

4 BIRTH OF SHIRETOKO MPA

4.1 Description of Shiretoko, Nominated as a World Heritage Site

The nomination process of Shiretoko as a World Heritage Site constitutes a major turning point for the Japanese marine management system, and it provides an opportunity to discuss MPAs at a national level.

Although there are already two World Natural Heritage Sites in Japan (Yaku Island and the Shirakami Mountain Range), the Shiretoko Peninsula and its surrounding sea

[24] Inano, Note 21, at 12.

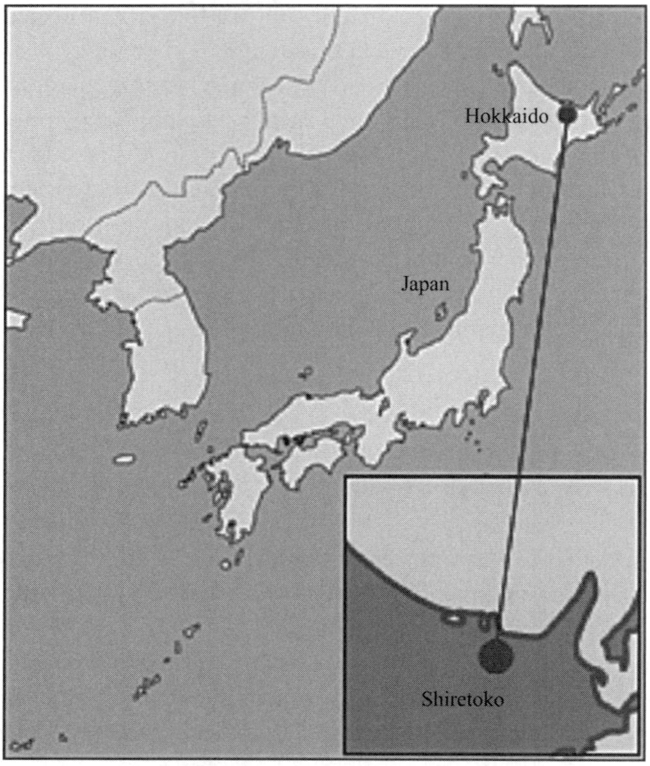

Figure 13.1. Location of Shiretoko World Heritage Site.

areas (hereafter simply referred to as "Shiretoko") is the first nominated World Heritage Site in Japan that contains sea areas. (see Figure 13.1.)

The peninsula is located in northeast Hokkaido, which is Japan's northernmost island. Shiretoko is an aboriginal (Ainu) word meaning "the end of the land" or "cape." The nominated site includes the terrestrial area from the peninsula's central part to its tip and the surrounding marine area. Shiretoko is an outstanding example of an integrated ecosystem, displaying the interrelationship between a terrestrial ecosystem and a contiguous marine ecosystem with unique seasonal sea ice characteristics.[25]

Because of the plankton nurtured by sea ice, Shiretoko's coastal waters have a high level of biological productivity, supporting numerous fish, marine mammals, and birds. The chum salmon and pink salmon that swim upstream to spawn are closely linked with the terrestrial ecosystem; they play an important role as a food source for brown bears, birds of prey, marine mammals, and seabirds. The Walleye Pollock (*Theragra chalcogramma*) is the target species of the local Rausu FCA; it is also an important food resource for the Stellar Sea Lion (*Eumetopias jubata*), which the IUCN Red List of Threatened Species lists as Endangered.

The entire site had already been designated as Shiretoko National Park on 1 June 1964; this marine component of this National Park was designated as an Ordinary Zone.

[25] For more detailed description of the nominated site, see the *Nomination Form under the Terms of the Convention Concerning the Protection of the World Cultural and Natural Heritage*, at http://www.env.go.jp/nature/isan/shiretoko/english_01/index.html.

4.2 Shiretoko Nomination Process

4.2.1 First Round: Management Plan and IUCN First Letter

On 16 January 2004, two weeks before Shiretoko's formal nomination, the Japanese government published the Management Plan for the Shiretoko World Natural Heritage Nominated Site (Management Plan).[26]

The Management Plan included several interesting initiatives to help manage the area as a World Heritage Site., including formation of the Scientific Council, the first council overseeing protected areas in Japan.[27] This council is entrusted with high-level management and ensures detailed zoning plans for all terrestrial areas of the nominated site.

The Management Plan for marine areas, by contrast, remained the same. In contrast to terrestrial areas, marine areas are classified only under a National Park Ordinary Zone. As mentioned earlier, this Ordinary Zone is nothing but a buffer, with few restrictions in place. Furthermore, the designated marine area is only 1 kilometer from the coast; this is based on Nature Parks Law rather than on ecological requirements. As the impetus behind this low-level marine management, additional fisheries restrictions have been a matter of serious concern.

With regard to fishery resource management, the Management Plan states, "[s]upported by the high biological productivity of the sea, the fishery in the coastal waters of Shiretoko has maintained a sustainable yield level. The marine resource will continue to be appropriately managed through requirements that are determined by laws and regulations on fishery as well as the voluntary actions by the fishers (e.g., designation of non-fishing zones and periods, taking back all wastes)."[28]

From 20 to 26 July 2004, an IUCN evaluation panel visited Shiretoko. Although the panel rated the site highly, it sent a letter to the Japanese government about a month later (IUCN First Letter, dated 20 August 2004[29]), expressing several concerns. It focused particularly on the marine component and pointed out the following concerns: the marine component of the nominated site only covers areas under 1 kilometer from the shore and is currently classed as an Ordinary Zone; this site has one of the lowest levels of protection available for protected areas under the National Parks Law; and fishing occurs throughout the nominated site, despite the decline in the population of Walleye Pollock (one of the main food sources of the Stellar Sea Lion, a flagship species of the nominated site).[30] The panel recommended enhanced protection of this site including the marine component:

- In the short term, strengthening the level of protection within the marine component of the nominated site. This should aim to ensure that breeding, spawning, and

[26] See *Management Plan*. Available at http://www.env.go.jp/nature/isan/shiretoko/english_02/Appendix4.pdf.

[27] The Scientific Council is composed of sixteen members who are experts in ecology and so on; the Council was formed to provide scientific advice, with the collaboration and cooperation of the Regional Liaison Committee.

[28] *Management Plan*, Note 26, at 200.

[29] *IUCN First Letter* (sent by David Sheppard, Head of Programme on Protected Areas), dated 20 August 2004. Available at http://www.env.go.jp/nature/isan/shiretoko/iucn_letter/letter_e.pdf. The letter raised two concerns: one about marine and fisheries components of the nominated site and the other about the dam construction on rivers. This chapter focuses on the former.

[30] Ibid.

nursery sites for key fish species within the nominated site, such as the Walleye Pollock, are strictly protected and that no fishing should be allowed in these areas. The life cycle analysis of key species and the identification of no-take areas should be based on the best science available. The fishing industry needs to be involved in this process to ensure that any protection measures are agreed to by all stakeholders and will be implemented.

- In the longer term, using research into the location of breeding and feeding habitats for key fish species in the Sea of Okhotsk and the Nemuro Straits, to establish representative marine protected areas within and surrounding the nominated site. This also would be based on the best available science and could draw on examples from other parts of the world.[31]

Because the IUCN recognized that fishing is a vitally important industry in the region around the nominated site (IUCN First Letter, para. 4 (d)), the recommendation should not be interpreted as denying fishing activities but as enforcing stricter fishing regulations to preserve the ecosystem, particularly in areas important to fish life cycles.

After receiving the recommendations, the Scientific Council formulated an opinion and submitted it to the government (14 October 2004).[32] It advised the government to admit that marine protection in the nominated site is undeveloped. Given that the fundamental issue regarding protection of marine areas is not fishery restriction but, rather, sustainable fisheries, the Council advised:

> A Marine Protected Area is defined as a tool to ensure sustainable fisheries as well as to preserve the environment and biodiversity. In particular, when no precise information is available other than catch statistics, MPAs are an effective alternative way to ensure the sustainability of fishery resources. The government should consider MPA establishment in order to promote the fishery industry.[33]

The Japanese government's response to the IUCN First Letter, however, did not reflect the opinion of the Scientific Council. The response stated that existing FCAs had already voluntarily adopted tight restrictions to adequately manage fishery resources and that, although Walleye Pollock stocks have been declining throughout the Sea of Okhotsk,[34] fishery resource levels in the nominated site had been fairly stable.

The response continued that a Multiple-Use Integrated Marine Management Plan (MUSIMMP) would be developed in five to ten years in order to conserve the marine area within the nominated site. The plan would address fishery resources through the sustainable use of marine resources, as well as the conservation of marine life and ecosystems in the nominated site and its surrounding marine areas.

As such, the MUSIMMP seems to avoid the issue of imposing additional restrictions. According to the response, the plan is to be based on existing fisheries rules and, in place of an MPA, it will address the maintenance of key marine resources, measures to conserve and manage marine life and ecosystems and methods to monitor them, and appropriate

[31] Ibid.

[32] *The opinion of the Scientific Council* (dated 14 Oct. 2004, in Japanese). See http://www.sizenken.biodic.go.jp/park/higashihokkaido/topics/8/advice1014.pdf.

[33] Ibid. (translated by the author).

[34] The total allowable catch (TAC) of Walleye Pollok was set higher than its allowable biological catch (ABC).

marine recreation activities such as recreational fishing. In essence, the MUSIMMP is intended to answer the IUCN's concerns while keeping guidelines the same.[35]

As this chapter has clearly indicated, this strong opposition to MPAs is based on misinterpretation; the government and fishers have considered the IUCN recommendations a way to establish no-take zones, whereas the press has reported that the government has already promised FCAs affected by the nomination that no additional fishery regulations would be imposed.[36]

4.2.2 Second Round: IUCN Second Letter and Japanese Response

The Japanese response was discussed at the IUCN World Heritage Panel (13–17 December 2004). The panel concluded that the marine environment required more protection. In a rare move, the IUCN sent a second letter to the Japanese government (IUCN Second Letter, dated 2 February 2005[37]).

The IUCN Second Letter questioned, in particular, whether the limited marine areas included within the nomination could provide sufficient habitat coverage and protection to ensure the long-term ecological health of marine life and to safeguard terrestrial life (including birds) dependent on marine food sources. It requested that the Japanese government answer whether it would be able to:

(a) expedite the Marine Management Plan, as well as strengthen the provisions within this Plan so as to ensure the protection of marine species; and
(b) substantially extend the marine component of the nominated site.[38]

The IUCN Second Letter was really an ultimatum to the Japanese government, which had a contract with fishers not to impose additional restrictions. However, fishers did not want to make the site fail in its nomination; the issue was therefore difficult for the Scientific Council, which needed to simultaneously satisfy all of the following conditions:

(a) As promised to FCAs, do not add further government fishing restrictions;
(b) Enlarge the marine component of the nominated site;
(c) Strengthen the level of marine ecosystem protection; and
(d) Keep sustainable fishery viable.[39]

In summary, the Council needed to raise the level of protection without imposing additional (governmental) restrictions. It came up with the idea of strengthening the level of protection through FCA self-restriction rather than through governmental restriction.[40]

[35] *Response to the Letter from the World Conservation Union (IUCN)* (sent by Hiroshi Onodera, Director General, Nature Conservation Bureau, Ministry of Environment) dated 5 November 2004. Available at http://www.env.go.jp/nature/isan/shiretoko/iucn_letter/letter_ree.pdf.

[36] Remarks of Professor Hiroyuki Matsuda, a member of the Scientific Council.

[37] *IUCN Second Letter* (sent by William J. Jackson, Director of Global Programme, dated 2 February 2005), at http://www.env.go.jp/nature/isan/shiretoko/iucn_letter/letter2_e.pdf. It is unusual for the panel to send a second letter.

[38] Ibid.

[39] *Minutes of the First Meeting of the Sea Areas Working Group of the Scientific Committee*, p. 2 (in Japanese). Available at http://www.sizenken.biodic.go.jp/park/higashihokkaido/topics/8/01kagakugiji.pdf.

[40] Remarks of Professor Hiroyuki Matsuda, a member of the Scientific Council.

This time, the Japanese government made several decisions based on the advice of the Scientific Council[41] and responded to the UNESCO World Heritage Center one day before the deadline.[42] Its response to the IUCN Second Letter was as follows: First, the MUSIMMP would be developed within three years; based on the advice of the Scientific Council, the plan would be developed through consensus among local fishers and other stakeholders.

Second, existing fishery restrictions and voluntary restrictions enforced by local fishers and fishery organizations would be incorporated into the plan as community-based marine resource management initiatives. Consequently, the MUSIMMP would identify strategies and measures necessary for the sustainable use of fisheries resources, and the conservation and management of marine life and ecosystems. The strategies would be based on scientific verification of research, and findings would be monitored; decisions will require the agreement of local fishers, fisheries organizations, and other stakeholders.[43] This means that the term "community" includes stakeholders other than fishers.

Although the government did not impose additional regulations, the local FCA (Rausu FCA) decided to strengthen the pollock self-regulation (e.g., lengthening the closure by five days and enlarging the closed area to about four times the usual size).[44] The FCAs accepted this decision under the condition that the Ministry of Environment and Prefecture government prepare a (rarely issued) official document stating that it will not impose additional restrictions.[45]

Third, based on scientific and ecological needs, the marine component of the nominated site will be extended from the current area (within one kilometer of the coastline) to an area within three kilometers of the coastline, which includes an underwater shelf that is two hundred meters in depth.

Although the government's response did not include the term "MPA," the marine component of the nominated site clearly seems to be an MPA.

5 CONCLUSION

Compared to existing Japanese MPAs (see Section 3.2), the Shiretoko MPA provides many advantages. Its purpose is to ensure a balance between the sustainable use of fishery resources and the conservation of marine life and ecosystems; fishery regulations (in the context of preserving ecosystems/biodiversity) are available; the Scientific Council, having been established, monitors the effect of protection measures; and a large marine area has been designated, the area of which does not consist of small patches but is a substantial marine area large enough to encompass marine ecosystems and biodiversity.

The UNESCO World Heritage Commission decided to add Shiretoko to the World Heritage List on 14 July 2005 during the twenty-ninth session of the World Heritage Committee in Durban, South Africa. The decision took only eight minutes, and the site was officially added on 17 July 2005.

[41] The opinion of the Scientific Council, dated 14 March 2004 (in Japanese). Available at http://www.sizenken.biodic.go.jp/park/higashihokkaido/topics/8/advice0314.pdf.

[42] *Response to the Letter from the World Conservation Union (IUCN) concerning Shiretoko (Japan)*, at http://www.env.go.jp/nature/isan/shiretoko/iucn_letter/letter2_ree.pdf.

[43] Ibid.

[44] *Mainichi Shinbun* (newspaper), 11 March 2005.

[45] Ibid.

However, an IUCN Technical Evaluation[46] submitted and discussed at the Commission required that Japan host a panel visit to the property, two years from its official addition to the World Heritage List. This will allow the IUCN to assess the progress of the Marine Management Plan's implementation and its effectiveness in protecting the area's marine resources. This means that, for the time being, IUCN is monitoring the Shiretoko World Heritage Site; the site's success depends on the stakeholders' efforts and cooperation.

The Japanese government has been preparing for the nomination of two other sites, the Ryukyu Islands and the Ogasawara Islands; both sites have a substantial marine area. The Shiretoko case will have a huge impact on these nominations; it is likely to result in the further development of MPAs to preserve ecosystems/biodiversity and sustainable fisheries.

[46] *World Heritage Nomination: IUCN Technical Evaluation Shiretoko (Japan)*, ID No.: 1193. Available at http://whc.unesco.org/archive/advisory_body_evaluation/1193.pdf.

14 Ten Years of Threatened Species Legislation in NSW – What Are the Lessons?

Karen Bubna-Litic*

1 INTRODUCTION

From the first days of settlement in Australia until the present time, there has been conflict between private landowners' rights to develop and community interest in sustainable land management and functioning ecosystems. Biodiversity[1] is impacted by a multitude of actions taken daily by individual land managers, industries, communities, and governments. The long-term and cumulative effects of these individual actions in terms of native species and natural systems is difficult to track and manage. Many species at risk do not live in the protected areas of New South Wales (NSW) but on private land, and there are often, and inevitably, conflicts about what should be the appropriate activities carried out on such lands and waters. Are legal mechanisms the best way to resolve this conflict?

NSW has recently introduced comprehensive reforms to try to deal with these conflicts. These reforms cover all aspects of threatened species, native vegetation, and biodiversity planning. This chapter concentrates on the protection and assessment of threatened species and the certification process, leaving out those matters concerning the listing process.

Section 2 describes the background to these issues covering the historical context, the current state of biodiversity in NSW and what has happened in NSW in the past ten years since the introduction of the Threatened Species Conservation Act 1995. Section 3 identifies the challenges that would need to be addressed by the reform process. Section 4 critically analyses the reforms and Section 5 addresses the question as to whether law is the best mechanism to address these challenges.

[1] The Natural Resources Commission (NSW) has defined biodiversity as: "Biodiversity is vital for healthy, functioning landscapes, has intrinsic value, and is part of the indigenous cultural landscape. It supports primary industries and is valued by the community for environmental, social and cultural reasons. Healthy, functioning native vegetation communities are valuable in themselves. They provide ecosystem services and habitat for native species, support Aboriginal cultural values, have extractive uses and have potential to provide other benefits in the future. Native fauna provide essential ecosystem services such as pollination and nutrient cycling; without them there would be widespread system collapse."

* Senior Lecturer in the Faculty of Law, University of Technology, Sydney.

2 BACKGROUND

2.1 Historical Context

Protection of biodiversity began in NSW in the mid- to late nineteenth century, with the protection of a few native birds and mammals from overhunting.[2] Today, biodiversity protection in NSW extends not only to species but also to ecological communities and key threatening processes[3] and is integrated with planning and land-use laws and regional plans. What is the role of legislation in the protection of biodiversity? Is it to react to changes in circumstances, such as new scientific knowledge or community perceptions, or can it play a leadership role in changing these perceptions?

Initially, laws in NSW were of two types, "game laws," which protected a species so that there would be enough of them to hunt, and laws that encouraged the killing of "agricultural pests."[4] Under the gaming laws, which protected both native and nonnative species, the only perceived threat was direct human killing and the community value in relation to these animals was to be able to hunt them for sport, except for the kookaburra, which was the first native animal to be protected for its aesthetic (singing) value.[5] Later,[6] some birds were protected because they were of benefit to agriculture as they ate insects.

Around the late 1800s, bounties were put on many of Australia's native species after strong lobbying by the farmers, which confirmed that agricultural interests took precedence over wildlife on pastoral lands. These included bandicoots, wallabies, bilbies, and wombats. There also was a view that the land could be improved by introducing exotic plants and animals.[7]

Community attitudes began to change in the 1890s when farmers began to experience difficulties with drought and rabbit invasions. There was a recognition of the damage of the clearing of trees and native vegetation, soil erosion, and the saltation of streams and waterbodies.[8] In 1918, a new piece of legislation reversed the protection provisions in relation to hunting. The Birds and Protection Act 1918 (NSW) listed those that could be hunted with all unlisted species being protected.[9]

The first half of the twentieth century saw changes in attitude towards biodiversity evidenced through the need to stop the export of Australian biodiversity and through the setting up of island and school sanctuaries to preserve endangered species. Laws also were introduced to protect NSW wild flowers and native plants from being picked and harvested, although there was no protection of their habitat.[10] For the first time in Australia's history, the interests of sportsmen and farmers were not paramount, but the first real indication of government commitment to conservation was the enactment of the Fauna Protection Act 1948. Under this Act, there was limited protection of habitat.

[2] P. Jarman & M. Brock, "The Evolving Intent and Coverage of Legislation to Protect Biodiversity in New South Wales," in Hutchings, D. Lunney and C. Dickman, eds., *Threatened Species Legislation – Is It Just an Act?* (Royal Zoological Society NSW, 2004).

[3] Threatened Species Conservation Act 1995 (NSW).

[4] Jarman & Brock, Note 3, at 2.

[5] Ibid. at 3.

[6] Birds Protection Act 1881.

[7] This was supported by the establishment of Acclimatisation Societies. See Jarman & Brock, Note 3, at 4–5.

[8] Ibid. at 6.

[9] Although it only included birds and mammals, with rodents, reptiles, frogs, and invertebrates still excluded from protection. They were included in an amending Act in 1922.

[10] Wild Flowers and Native Plants Protection Act 1927.

It was the first time that imprisonment could be imposed as a penalty for killing wildlife in NSW.[11]

The second half of the twentieth century saw the need to establish national parks and other reserves for conservation. It was recognized that conservation of native flora and fauna was not always consistent with other land uses. In 1967, the National Parks and Wildlife Service was established.[12] However, to a large extent, the legislation still did not protect habitat. The question of whether the destruction of habitat threatened endangered species was considered in *Corkill v. Forestry Commission of New South Wales*,[13] which held that the Act could be used to prevent an indirect threat through habitat destruction. In the late twentieth century, states in Australia introduced legislation to conserve threatened biodiversity.

NSW biota is now covered by the Threatened Species Conservation Act 1995 (NSW) (TSC Act) and the Fisheries Management Act 1994 (NSW). At the national level, there is the Environmental Protection and Biodiversity Conservation Act 1999 (Cth) (EPBC Act). The TSC Act lists, in addition to whole species, populations of species and whole ecological communities, and it conserves critical habitat and recognizes key threatening processes. It has recognised that protection from killing and the creation of conservation reserves alone would not necessarily be enough to preserve the ecological integrity of endangered species and that there needs to be a system of cooperative management with private landowners. There also has been a recognition that conservation is affected by many types of land use and so, to this end, many other laws need to be integrated with threatened species legislation, involving cooperation between government departments such as the Department of Infrastructure, Planning and Natural Resources and the Department of Primary Industry. There is cooperation between the Commonwealth and the states, all of which now accept the internationally used definitions of rare and endangered species, as supported by the IUCN. This allows monitoring, auditing, and comparisons with other countries.

So, finally, NSW has established a system that aims to protect biodiversity through cooperative community-based conservation in partnership with all levels of government.

2.2 Current State and Trends

Although there is limited data to describe biodiversity in Australia and NSW, available information suggests it is both declining and degrading in condition.[14] The condition and extent of native vegetation has declined significantly since European settlement, through pressures such as clearing, grazing, the introduction of exotic species, altered fire regimes, and urbanisation. Many introduced exotic species in Australia have become weeds and destructive pests, causing widespread ecological problems at an unprecedented rate and scale. A third of all recorded world extinctions of mammals this century have occurred in Australia.[15] There are more threatened species of amphibians and reptiles in Australia than in any other country.[16]

[11] Jarman & Brock, Note 3, at 8.

[12] National Parks and Wildlife Act 1974.

[13] (1991) 73 LGR 126.

[14] National Biodiversity Decline Working Group, Natural Resources Policy and Programs Committee (NRPPC) (Ministerial Council – Australia) Working Papers unpublished 2005.

[15] Ibid.

[16] Ibid.

The Australian Terrestrial Biodiversity Audit[17] showed that threatened ecosystems occur across much of Australia, with most bioregions (90 percent) having one or more threatened ecosystem. However, more than half of the total are in the central east coast, the Darling Riverine Plains, the Murray Darling Depression, and other parts of NSW. The survey found that the vegetation clearing and increased fragmentation of remaining vegetation are amongst the most common threatening processes for threatened species – both of which occur in NSW.[18]

Key findings included:

1. The condition of nationally important wetlands although good, in many cases, is declining;
2. The condition of riparian zones is degraded across much of southern and eastern Australia;
3. 2,891 threatened ecosystems identified across Australia, and nearly half of these are eucalypt forest and woodland;
4. The highest number of threatened species occurred within subregions from the southern highlands in Victoria and NSW along the coast from Sydney to the north of Brisbane;
5. Mammal extinction has been substantial in the last two hundred years – twenty-two Australian mammals are now extinct – a third of the world's recent extinctions, along with a massive contraction in distribution in arid and semiarid regions;
6. Bird populations are markedly reduced – twenty-nine species show significant decreases in cleared and scapes in the last twenty years, with grassland, woodland, and ground-nesting birds most affected;
7. Vegetation clearing is the most significant threat to species and ecosystems in eastern Australia; and
8. Overgrazing, exotic weeds, feral animals, and changed fire regimes are additional key threats to wetlands, riparian zones, threatened species, and threatened ecosystems across much of Australia. These threats are widespread and pervasive.[19]

In the face of such scales of loss and degradation attention has been focused on the costs of repairing damaged ecosystem services. The 2002 National Land and Water Audit included estimates of the value of lost agricultural production due to degradation ($A1.2 billion) and the costs of repairing natural systems (some $A2–6 billion would be needed annually for full repair).[20]

The NSW 2003 State of the Environment (SoE) Report gives a snapshot, even if somewhat incomplete, of the current state and trends in biodiversity in NSW. Of the sixteen biodiversity indicators, over a third received a red light traffic light[21] in the report. These were:

- extent and condition of vegetation;
- vegetation clearing rate;

[17] The Australian Terrestrial Biodiversity Assessment 2002, National Land & Water Audit, available at http://audit.deh.gov.au/ANRA/vegetation/docs/biodiversity/bio_assess_contents.cfm.

[18] Ibid.

[19] Ibid.

[20] Ibid.

[21] This is where the available data shows that the trend is mostly negative and therefore represents a poor or generally deteriorating environmental condition.

- number of both terrestrial and aquatic extinct, endangered, and vulnerable species, communities, and populations;
- extent and condition of aquatic ecosystem; and
- estimated wild fish stocks.[22]

The report states that the net loss and degradation of native vegetation was continuing, with extensive clearing occurring in the Central Division of NSW in the tablelands and the western slopes that make up the wheat belt of NSW. Significant clearing also has occurred in the Eastern Division as a result of forestry, intensive agriculture, and urban development. Both of these areas have an average of 42 percent of native vegetation. This compares with the Western Division, which has over 97 percent cover remaining. Before the current 2004 reforms, it is estimated that each year between sixty thousand to one hundred thousand hectares of native vegetation had been cleared in NSW.[23] However, the rate of clearing was reducing each year between 1998 and 2002 to approximately fifty-eight thousand hectare/annum. This compares to twelve thousand to fifteen thousand hectare/annum in the late 1990s. Recent National Parks and Wildlife Service studies estimate that in some regions (again the southwestern slopes and New England Tablelands) this loss represents a 50 percent clearing rate.[24] In some subregions, it is known that 100 percent of original native vegetation has been cleared.[25] This loss of native vegetation has an impact on terrestrial habitats and is a major threat to biodiversity. With such high level of clearing, the SoE report points out that even small amounts of additional clearing can have high impacts on biodiversity. The native vegetation remaining is often very heavily modified by for example, grazing, feral animals, and changed fire regimes. It is of interest that the least disturbed ecosystems in NSW are on less productive soils in the eastern escarpment.

> Two more species have been declared extinct in NSW since 2000 and, while numbers of recovery plans for threatened species has increases (now 44), many more species are now listed as threatened (a further 137 listings an increase of 18% on 2000).[26]

Despite this, the SoE report recognized that the scale of the threat to species in NSW is becoming clearer as the processes for recognising species and communities at risk has increased in its sophistication. The diversity of bird populations is a good surrogate indicator of wider potential biodiversity losses. Significant loss of bird habitat and higher than expected numbers of threatened species among ground-nesting and groundfeeding birds have been found with significant falls in population of these and woodland species.

A similar tale of degradation is recorded in the SoE report for wetlands. Wetlands are important habitats in NSW and cover an enormous 4.5 million hectares and 6 percent of the state. One estimate suggests that 50 percent of wetlands could have been lost since European settlement.[27] Whereas one-fifth of coastal wetlands are reserved (18 percent),

[22] NSW Environment Protection Authority, *State of the Environment Report* (2003).

[23] Benson 2001 and Australian Conservation Foundation 2001 in NSW, *State of the Environment Report* (2003).

[24] National Parks and Wildlife data as at November 2002, reported in NSW SoE Report 2003.

[25] Pressey et al., "Terrestrial reserves in NSW – Gaps, Biases and Priorities to Minimize Further Loss of Native Vegetation." 96:11 *Biological Conservation* (2000), 55–82.

[26] NSW Environment Protection Authority, *State of the Environment Report* (2003).

[27] C. M. Finlayson & N. Rea "Reasons for the Loss and Degradation of Australia's Wetlands." 7(1) *Wetland Ecology & Management* 1–11.

inland and riverine ecosystems (16 percent of inland lakes) are underreserved and under pressure from population and settlement growth. One such impact is the diversion of river flows for irrigation, such as in the Murrumbidgee floodplain, where 75 percent of the wetlands have disappeared or have been degraded and, in conjunction, 80 percent of water bird populations have declined by more than 80 percent. This is consistent with worldwide wetland losses.[28]

However, the SoE report indicates that it is not all bad news, as there are now extensive reserves covering approximately 5.8 million hectares or 7.3 percent of the state and extensive reserves across all main ecosystem types on the ranges and the coast. This is a rise on the reported 6.6 percent in the 2000 SoE report. However, the biggest gaps in the state's reserve system are correspondingly in the central and western parts of the state. Nationally, each state in Australia is encouraged to establish a comprehensive, adequate, and representative system of protected areas (known as CAR). The aim is to formally protect 15 percent of land (representing 15 percent of the area of forested ecosystems that existed in 1788). In NSW, only four out of seventeen bioregions achieve the CAR aim of 15 percent protected area. So, although there has been an improvement from 2000 to 2003, more still needs to be done.

The Australian Terrestrial Biodiversity Assessment 2002 found that only 6.6 percent of the Australian continent was protected in the formal conservation reserve system (IUCN management categories I–IV), and 71 of the 384 subregions have no reserves.[29] At the continental scale, it was determined that over fifteen hundred ecosystems Australia-wide required reservation to achieve the accepted 15 percent benchmark. In some instances, where ecosystems are naturally restricted or rare, 100 percent reservation is desirable. Hence, there are significant gaps in both the conservation reserve systems comprehensiveness and representativeness. Furthermore, the assessment also recommended that there is a need to accelerate conservation reserve system establishment to both protect ecosystems under pressures before they disappear, as well as set aside areas that are still in relatively good condition. By way of illustration, currently for private land in NSW there are only 170 Voluntary Conservation Agreements (VCAs) in place (since 1987) and approximately 934 property agreements (covering 90,078 hectares), with only 25 percent of these in secure and long-term management arrangement.[30] This is not an outstanding result. Section 3 of the chapter will consider the effectiveness of the reforms in achieving biodiversity conservation in NSW.

2.3 What Has Happened in the Past 10 Years

The effect of the Threatened Species Conservation Act 1995 (NSW) (TSC Act) needs to be considered in conjunction with the Native Vegetation Conservation Act 1997 (NSW) (NVC Act). Under the TSC Act, listing was used as a trigger for criminalising behavior, which was likely to have an adverse effect on threatened species habitat.[31] This

[28] R. T. Kingsford & R. F. Thomas, *Changing Regimes & Wetland Habitat on the Murrumbidgee Floodplain of the Murrumbidgee River in Arid Australia* (Report to Environment Australia and NSW National Parks and Wildlife Service, 2001).

[29] Australian Terrestrial Biodiversity Assessment 2002, Note 18.

[30] Data from the Department of Infrastructure Planning and Natural Resources (DIPNR), 2004.

[31] D. Farrier & R. J. Whelan, "(Why) Do We Need Threatened Species Legislation?" in P. Hutchings, D. Lunney and C. R. Dickman, eds., *Threatened Species Legislation – Is It Just an Act?* (Royal Zoological Society of NSW, 2004).

command regulation involved directions from government, enforced by government agencies, with sanctions against those in breach. It has been questioned whether this has been the most effective way to achieve desired conservation outcomes.[32] Once an application has been made, the process under the NSW legislation is one of assessment and approval with licensing conditions. There was little scope for refusing applications to develop based on harm to species or harm to habitat. Under sections 118A and 118D *National Parks and Wildlife* Act 1974 (NSW) (NPW Act), it is a defence to an offence to harming endangered or threatened species or endangered ecological communities or threatening habitat of such, if a licence was given under the TCA Act or it was essential under a development proposal under the *Environmental Planning and Assessment* Act 1979 (NSW) or under a conservation agreement.[33] It has been argued that in the former National Parks and Wildlife Service (NPWS), now the Department of Environment and Conservation (DEC), the regulator of the TSC Act had mostly been left out of the process of approving developments where threatened species or their habitats may be an issue.[34] The Director-General would only become involved when a local council or other agency referred it to NPWS/DEC on the grounds that they are likely to significantly affect threatened species or populations or threatened ecological communities,[35] in which case there would need to be a species impact statement.[36] But even this role of NPWS/DEC was limited, with the Land and Environment Court and the Minister for Planning and Natural Resources having final decisions under the NVC Act. However, there were regional variances with NPWS staff in some regions being very active in preapplication processes. Often, decisions stayed with local government; the problem was that many had little expertise in this area. Having local government at the forefront of threatened species decisions has some difficulties attached to it. In addition to their lack of expertise, there are systemic biases in favour of development.[37] The presence of threatened species should be a consideration when land is being zoned. Under this scheme, once land had been zoned to enable some type of development, there was an assumption that this type of development would be allowed. The focus, therefore, on the application was on the details, not whether the development should be allowed to go ahead at all.[38] So, when issues of threatened species arose, the local council wanted to keep the development viable. It was really too late in the process to bring in threatened species issues and the local council would be reluctant to use this for the basis of refusing development consent.[39] This became one of the factors considered in assessing the environmental impact of the development.

The situation in NSW before 2003 was that although there was command regulation,[40] in practice the decision maker's brief was:

> not to protect the interest of threatened species at all costs, but to balance the socio-economic interests of the proponent and the broader community against the community's interest in threatened species conservation.[41]

[32] Data from DIPNR, Note 32.
[33] Sections 118A(3) and 118D(3).
[34] Farrier & Whelan, Note 32.
[35] Environmental Planning and Assessment Act 1979 (NSW) section 79B(3), (8).
[36] Ibid., section 79B(5).
[37] Farrier & Whelan, Note 32, at 35.
[38] Ibid., at 36.
[39] Ibid.
[40] Environmental Planning and Assessment Act 1979 (NSW), sections 118A and 118D.
[41] Farrier & Whelan, Notes 33, 36.

Even DEC has been bound by this.[42] Take, for example, the proposed Mawland Hotel development at the North Head quarantine station. Because of the amount of interest that this proposal generated, a Commission of Inquiry was conducted and their report handed down in July 2002.[43] Two endangered populations, the Little Penguin and the Long-Nosed Bandicoot, were assessed in the species impact statement. North Head was declared a critical habitat for the penguin population in January 2003. The Commission of Inquiry applied the precautionary principle and imposed a dusk to dawn ferry curfew[44] so as to avoid impacts on the population coming ashore to feed their young. However, despite this recommendation, development approval was given allowing ferries to operate until 11 PM each night, which is too late to offer any real protection, as penguins generally come ashore approximately one hour after sunset.[45] With the endangered Long-Nosed Bandicoot, the Joint Determining Authorities report did recognise that road kill was one of the major threats to the bandicoots and this was one of the reasons for not allowing the blanket dusk to dawn curfew of ferries, as this would increase the vehicle traffic. However, trade-offs like this between endangered populations for the sake of approving a development seems to indicate the lack of effectiveness of the Threatened Species Conservation Act.[46]

Another identified problem arising in the past ten years has been that offences are triggered by the fact that a species is listed rather than focusing on development, which impacts on threatened species habitat. In fact, although there is provision to provide for identification of critical habitat,[47] it has only been declared in two instances. Usually the listing is just by species, and there is no requirement to list the habitat of the threatened species, as well. However, protection of habitat is crucial in biodiversity conservation as well. Additional problems exist with sections 118A and 118D of the NPW Act in that, under the latter, proof of knowledge is required, which assumes that some mechanism exists for informing landholders that their land contains protected habitat, and under section 118A, there is uncertainty on the question of knowledge, with some argument that it is a strict liability offence.[48] If threatened species offences were regarded as strict liability, defendants would have to show that they had actually considered whether there were listed species or plants on their property and that their belief was reasonable. In this situation, there would be the opportunity for regulators to educate landholders on what precautionary measures would be reasonable before clearing native vegetation.[49]

The past ten years also has seen the existence of many incentives for private landowners to avoid the identification of threatened species on their land. These include the delay in the approval process; the cost of a species impact statement from between $5,000

[42] Environmental Planning and Assessment Act 1979 (NSW), section 79(5)(h).

[43] Report to the Hon. Andrew Refshauge, Deputy Premier, Minister for Planning, Minister for Aboriginal Affairs, Minister for Housing, "Proposed Conservation and Adaptive Re-Use of the North Head Quarantine Station," July 2002, http://www.coi.nsw.gov.au//inquiry.

[44] Ibid. at 138.

[45] Joint Determination Report by the Determining Authorities: NSW Minister for the Environment, NSW Heritage Council, NSW Waterways Authority on North Head Quarantine Station Conservation and Adaptive Re-Use Proposal.

[46] J. Lambert, "Threatened Species Legislation: Does It Work for Local Communities or Local Government," in P. Hutchings, D. Lunney, and C. R. Dickman, eds., *Threatened Species Legislation – Is It Just an Act?* (Royal Zoological Society of NSW, 2004).

[47] Section 47 TSC Act.

[48] Farrier & Whelan, Note 13, at 41.

[49] Farrier & Whelan, Note 13, at 39.

and $50,000; and the restriction of profit, from say, timber, agriculture, and residential development.

The major lesson of the past decade is that a threatened species decision involves costly disputes – pitting a particular development against a particular threatened species. The present system operates at the micro-level and at the very end of the planning process, with too narrow a focus on individual threatened species or isolated populations and far too little focus on the protection of wider habitat or landscape.

3 THE CHALLENGES

Although progress has been made in the past ten years, the situation in NSW still remains critical.[50] As much of the land is managed by private landholders, one of the challenges is to ensure that landowners see the discovery of a listed species as a blessing rather than a curse.

Other administrative and process challenges include:

1. The ability to protect habitat. It is more cost-effective to target protection and management of existing habitat, rather than attempting to rehabilitate or restore habitats and communities that have been lost or degraded;
2. Integrating threatened species into planning, where trade-offs involve setting threatened species considerations against economic and social considerations, which often dominate;
3. Engaging the community effectively so that their involvement is incorporated into decisions, where community opinion is often polarized and influenced by vested property interests;
4. The difficulties of enforcing a command regulation such as the TSC Act – the reticence to use powers under the Act and transparency of government decisions;
5. Aligning the listing criteria with the IUCN assessment criteria and giving reasons why they haven't been used will improve transparency;
6. Accountability and boundary issues between government department portfolios;
7. The "compensatory habitat" approach. This approach is that where land has been identified as holding threatened species or endangered species or endangered ecological communities, that habitat has been allowed to be lost in exchange for other habitat. The concern is that the replacement habitat may be of lesser quality;
8. The use of unaccredited consultants who are pressurized to give favourable reports;[51]
9. Is local government the appropriate determining authority in relation to developments which encroach on threatened species habitats? Local governments often lack the capacity and expertise to assess likely impacts of development on threatened species and, at the local government level, social and economic reasons often override threatened species considerations.[52];
10. Catchment management authority capacity and capability in biodiversity planning and threatened species management;

[50] Department of Environment and Conservation White Paper, *Threatened Species Conservation: Towards A More Effective Approach*, October 2003, 4.

[51] M. Fowler, "A Review of the Success of the Threatened Species Conservation Act in Protecting Threatened Species Within NSW." Paper prepared for the North Coast Environmental Council, May 2004. Available at http://www.ncec.org.au/thspp_report.

[52] Ibid.

11. The current project by project approach;
12. In some cases, there is a preemptive clearing of threatened species habitat so as to come within the "routine agricultural management activities" exemption before the development application is lodged;
13. Prosecution difficulties where section 118D of the NPW Act says that a person who damages threatened species habitat must "know that the land concerned is habitat of that kind" for a successful prosecution in the Land And Environment Court; and
14. Ability to identify habitat and critical habitat.

These all operate in the context of two other compounding issues. The first is tracking and managing the key threatening processes.[53] Of these, climate change[54] and invasives[55] are emerging as the ones needing most research. The second is the scale and rate of degradation that would suggest that, despite all current efforts, there needs to be a higher magnitude of investment and effort at all levels of government and within the community.

4 THE NSW REFORMS 2004

The Threatened Species Act Amendment Act 2004 (NSW) introduced in 2004 builds on the previous Threatened Species Conservation Act of 1995 and accompanying Fisheries Management Act 1994 (NSW). This important landmark legislative reform aims to slow and reverse the trend of extinctions and species decline by establishing better procedures to resolve conflicts in a way that will better protect threatened species.

The aim is to get more integrated, balanced, and transparent decision-making procedures. The previous regime relied on processes to protect isolated populations with far too little focus on the protection of wider habitats or landscapes. That regime operated at the micro-level and at the very end of the planning process. Threatened species were too often considered very late in the process – often only after an individual development application has been submitted or after all the other consents had been given.

The Threatened Species Reforms are also part of the government's recent significant reforms of the state's natural resource management system arising from the Wentworth Agreement.[56] In December 2003, the NSW government passed three new pieces of legislation intended to overhaul the natural resource management framework in NSW, the Catchment Management Authorities Act 2003, the Natural Resources Commission

[53] Seven key threatening processes have been identified in NSW. They are:
Overgrazing in the inland plains
Ongoing land clearing and fragmentation
Urban expansion on the coast
Overuse of water – river and floodplain
Weeds and feral animals
Altered disturbance regimes (e.g., fire)
Climate change.

[54] There is a need to better understand and predict/model the impacts of climate change on biodiversity – understanding impacts on existing biodiversity conservation programs, incorporate biodiversity conservation in drought policies and programs, assessing likely changes in the extent and distribution of viable/marginal agricultural land and associated pressures on areas of high biodiversity value.

[55] Preventing introduction, establishment, and spread of invasives is a very cost-effective investment, compared with control actions once they have established (through consistent approaches to regulation of trade, and international and internal movement of travellers and goods, as well as research and development of control techniques, and priority setting).

[56] Wentworth Group of Concerned Scientists, *Report to Premier Carr: A New Model for Landscape Conservation in New South Wales* (3 February 2003).

Act 2003, and the Native Vegetation Act 2003. These reforms aimed to halt broad-scale land clearing in NSW and establish fifteen Catchment Management Authorities (CMAs) to make resource management decisions at the local level. It is the intention that an end to broad-scale land clearing also will result in improved protection of threatened species on private land. Part of this reform was the investment of $A406 million over a four-year period into conservation projects. To be eligible, landowners must submit a property vegetation plan (PVP) for approval by the CMAs. CMAs will formulate catchment action plans (CAPs). The Natural Resources Commission is an independent body, which recommends standards and targets and they approve and audit the success of these CAPs. One of the potential problems with this reform is that it is unclear whether the CMAs are required by law to consider the CAPs when approving individual PVPs. The reforms mirror those for native vegetation with a streamlined processes for farmers in relation to routine activities such as fencing, farm roads, and control of noxious plants and animals, so that these can occur without the need for a threatened species assessment or license. This has been possible in part because of the introduction of the property vegetation plans (PVPs) under the native vegetation reforms. Through property vegetation plans, farmers can access funding to manage native vegetation, biodiversity and threatened species. Under a PVP, a farmer is free to undertake activities without the need for a separate threatened species license. The PVP is underpinned by world-class science and methodology that focuses on protecting landscapes, rather than individual plants and animals.[57]

> At present, many farmers consider threatened species to be liabilities. The new system will make them central to their everyday work.[58]

As the CMAs will administer the PVPs, this will empower CMAs as the single interface with farmers in their area.

The threatened species reforms aim to integrate the state's natural resource management and land-use planning system with NSW's biodiversity conservation laws. This is achieved by focusing on strategic planning of NSW's areas experiencing intense development pressure (the Far North Coast, Greater Metropolitan Sydney, Lower Hunter, South Coast/Illawarra, and the Sydney-Canberra corridor). The Act allows the Minister for the Environment (or the Minister for Primary Industries in the case of the Fisheries Management Act) to "certify" an environmental planning instrument that promotes conservation of threatened species and biodiversity more generally. In this way, threatened species conservation consideration is incorporated at the beginning of the planning process when the local environmental plan, regional environmental plan or other planning instrument is being prepared. This biodiversity certification will replace the existing eight-part test as to "significance" and the need for a species impact statement. It is argued that the site specific surveys need to be retained "because of the cryptic nature of many threatened species" but its shortcomings should be supplemented by the landscape planning component.[59] The strengths of the site-specific assessments included the fact that it was based on an objective test of the impacts on threatened species and that it was subject to third-party appeal rights in the Land and Environment Court. Third-party appeal rights have been retained under the reforms.

[57] Minister for the Environment NSW, 2nd Reading Speech, Threatened Species Amendment Act 2004 (NSW).

[58] Ibid.

[59] Fowler, Note 49, at 8.

Biodiversity planning assistance will be provided to councils to ensure the best available science is used in the process. Appropriate safeguards are also being put in place to ensure that the Minister for the Environment may withdraw biodiversity certification in relation to specific catchments if, for example, the Catchment Management Authority fails to act consistently with the native vegetation reforms or otherwise fails to protect threatened species through its core activities.

The Act also includes a number of other reforms that will assist in resolving assessment and licensing problems.[60] There are also provisions for greater flexibility for the reservation of land, entering into conservation agreements, and restoring threatened species habitat.

The reforms more clearly separate two key stages in threatened species conservation: identifying the threats to biodiversity through the state's listing by the Scientific Committee and improved recovery planning. Under the current system, a recovery plan must be prepared for every threatened species. For current listings alone, this could amount to over nine hundred plans. To date, fewer than sixty recovery plans and two threat abatement plans have been approved.[61] Under the reforms, priorities for action are to be identified in a Priorities Action Statement. Finally, the reforms introduce new categories of "critically endangered" ecological communities and species – that is, those that are at an extremely high risk of extinction in the immediate future. It has been suggested that this should be extended to "critical habitat."[62]

The newly created Natural Resource Commission (NRC) and the Standards and Targets framework for natural resources are also an important part of the NSW reforms. "The adoption of statewide standards and targets presents an important opportunity to focus NRM investment on the most important natural assets, and the critical opportunities and threats they face."[63] Ultimately, the achievement of the NRC's statewide targets is expected to result in healthy, functional landscapes in NSW. The NRC has defined a draft set of fifteen aspirational goals or long-term statements, which describes natural resource assets (Biodiversity, Water, Land, and Community) in terms of the desirable functions that they serve.[64] The standards and targets are in development and not yet released by the government. The intent of the statewide resource condition targets and indicators for biodiversity targets is to ensure that biodiversity is retained and enhanced in the long term. The targets are intended to protect a variety of fundamental ecological processes. Promoting the biodiversity targets at the regional level will help CMAs to focus on these key agreed biodiversity outcomes, such as increasing the extent and connectivity of native vegetation, improving vegetation condition of both remnant vegetation and regrowth, identifying invasive species causing most impact and threat to those species and habitats, and a renewed focus on threatened species recovery activities.

5 IS LEGISLATION THE RIGHT MECHANISM?

The intention of the threatened species legislation in NSW is not to criminalise behavior. Instead, the intention is to try to bring the proposed activity that might trigger threatened

[60] These include assessments and surveys guidelines, and an accreditation scheme for consultants.

[61] Minister's speech, Note 59.

[62] Fowler, Note 49.

[63] NRC Statewide Standards and targets Draft Recommendations Report.

[64] Ibid.

species legislation into the application and approvals processes, through licensing of activities and granting of approvals. Generally, the more effective method of enforcement is through civil rather than criminal means, in which the objective is prevention and remediation. In NSW, there is also the philosophy of existing use that allows for an exemption from licensing requirements when "routine agricultural activities"[65] are being carried out. But how is "routine agricultural activities" defined? Another difficulty is that before taking criminal proceedings under section 118D of the National Parks and Wildlife Act 1974, the regulatory authority must be able to prove beyond a reasonable doubt that the landholder knew that the relevant land was the habitat of a threatened species, endangered population or endangered ecological community.[66] This results in an adversarial approach to habitat protection, with those wanting to avoid protecting habitat, simply destroying the habitat, and keeping quiet about it. It has been argued that it may be easier to prosecute under section 118A, where there may be strict liability imposed when protecting a threatened species, endangered population, or endangered ecological community.[67]

The National Biodiversity Decline Working Group (NBDWG) of the Natural Resources Management Ministerial Council (NRPPC) has recently undertaken an evaluation of the effectiveness of the current and past biodiversity programs of each of the jurisdictions.[68] Some critical findings have emerged. The review looked at both regulatory and incentive programs. It covered twenty-five programs across all states and territories and the Australian government. The programs ranged in size from around $A0.03 to $A56 million per annum, addressing biodiversity from a variety of perspectives, including programs targeted at particular threatened or high profile species (such as the Gould's Petrel, the Koala), pest species (foxes, starlings, Phytophthora) or particular geographic areas (NSW Macquarie Marshes and Northern Rivers, WA Wheat belt and Western Shield), and others addressing broader conservation issues. These programs used a range of approaches including direct action, acquisition, grant schemes, incentives, regulation or legislation, capacity-building, and data collection. They found that the lack of effective and affordable monitoring systems has limited the ability to learn from previous actions in some cases as a result of poorly defined conservation goals and objectives, intent not linked to auditable outcomes, or no achievement of outcomes in practice for other reasons.[69]

This report has thrown light on some critical learnings from past approaches to biodiversity conservation in Australia. The review of programs has shown that although much of the work undertaken to date has provided a useful platform for biodiversity conservation – such as putting in place research, planning, capacity-building, public support, and changes in land management – there have been limited on-ground improvements to biodiversity conservation. The assessment has shown that where there have been positive impacts on conservation, these outcomes were very localised. It has been noted that many of the programs aim to avoid or reduce future degradation, such as covenanting or attempts to prevent pest establishment, they may prove to have long-term biodiversity value even though no short-term improvements may be discernable. Many jurisdictions have dealt with or are dealing with broad-scale clearing and this

[65] Threatened Species Conservation Act 1995, section 113A.
[66] Farrier and Whelan, Note 13, at 38.
[67] Ibid.
[68] See Note 15.
[69] Ibid.

is making a very significant contribution to addressing biodiversity decline in those states. By contrast, it also found that national investment in other NRM programs has exacerbated the loss of biodiversity.

The review found that the major constraints to achieving effective delivery of outcomes were:

- lack of transparency in investment decisions between public and private good;
- lack of clarity of objectives and purpose;
- programs being too ambitious;
- lack of early emergent market mechanisms;
- long time frames to achieve outcomes, compared to short-term programs;
- lack of framework for defining success (no common "benchmark" for assessment or agreed quantifiable measures or metrics to monitor);
- inadequate capacity to monitor progress and apply adaptive management;
- lack of coordination/consistency with other policies and programs;
- lack of strategic targeting to priorities (especially reactive grants programs)
- limited engagement with business/industry;
- inadequate investment for the scale of the problem;
- lack of skills and advice directly applicable to biodiversity conservation;
- lack of strategic or adequate research capacity and inadequate information base; and
- external factors (bushfire, drought, pests, development pressures, tourism).

Taking into account that the factors that the Working Group has identified have limited success in biodiversity programs it would suggest that more targeted, informed and innovative approaches will be needed into the future. It could be argued that we have reached the limits of regulation to control environmental impact and loss of biodiversity and that dispersed activities across the landscape do not lend themselves to a command-and-control strategy. The Working Group found that incentive schemes are emerging as a new and effective tool but that they should not be seen as a substitute for environmental regulation. The advantage of legislation is that it provides a basic bottom-line standard for acceptable land use, whereas incentives encourage parties to make positive individual contributions.[70] Our community would be worse off without legislation as, at its minimum, it provides the opportunity for participation by the community.[71] It has been argued that people are starting to disengage with the process at both a federal and state level when they continue to see the lack of political will to effectively enforce this legislation to the benefit of development.[72] The challenge of moving to a more flexible legislative regime is to retain the intent of the underlying legislation, while designing the alternative compliance strategies that give greater flexibility and reduce red tape and conflict.

6 CONCLUSION

The Threatened Species Conservation Act 1995 (NSW) and the Native Vegetation Act 1997 (NSW) were regarded as innovative when they were introduced in the mid-1990s. Ten years later, we can conclude that NSW biodiversity continues to be degraded and

[70] National Biodiversity Decline Working Group Report, Note 16.
[71] Lambert, Note 28, at 162. [72] Ibid. at 163.

to decline with vegetation clearing remaining one of the most serious threats to species and ecosystems. Better knowledge of the science is indicating that protection of habitat, and not just protection of species, is crucial in biodiversity conservation.

The main lesson of the past ten years has been that pitting a particular development against a particular threatened species has resulted in decisions being made to resolve costly disputes rather than decisions being made on the basis of the long term view of biodiversity protection. The system has operated at the micro-level and at the very end of the planning process, with too narrow a focus on individual threatened species or isolated populations and far too little focus on the protection of wider habitat or landscape. These lessons raise a number of challenges, which the latest legislative reforms have tried to tackle. The reforms are trying to move away from the conflict that exists between private landowners' rights to develop and the community interest in sustainable land management and functioning ecosystems to try to achieve a more integrated, balanced, and transparent decision-making process through the establishment of catchment management authorities overseen by the Natural Resources Commission.

This chapter has identified some concerns that come out of these reforms and that still need to be addressed. They include the need to declare areas of critical habitat; the capacity building of catchment management authorities; whether the farmers will actually use the PVPs; the problems of biodiversity certification cutting out site-specific assessments; how to bridge the information and knowledge gaps of both local councils and the catchment management authorities; and whether the catchment action plans are legally enforceable. The 2004 reforms are a move in the right direction, but these real concerns, as identified, will need to be addressed in the process of achieving effective biodiversity conservation.

15 Sanctuaries, Protected Species, and Politics – How Effective Is Australia at Protecting Its Marine Biodiversity under the Environment Protection and Biodiversity Conservation Act 1999?

Ilona Millar and Jessica Wood*

1 INTRODUCTION

Consistent with international obligations,[1] marine biodiversity protection in Australia is achieved primarily through the establishment of protected areas or sanctuaries, the sustainable management of fisheries and the protection of indigenous and endangered marine species. Australia historically has had a multiplicity of legislative regimes at a federal and state level that addressed the protection the marine environment. However, in recent years, with the adoption of Australia's Oceans Policy[2] in 1998 and the passing of the Environment Protection and Biodiversity Conservation Act 1999 (C'th) (EPBC Act), the federal and state governments have begun to develop complementary management approaches for marine ecosystems and to put in place strong legal sanctions to enhance the protection of the marine environment. This essay provides an overview of the current legal and policy framework for the protection of marine biodiversity in Australia, with special reference to the enforcement of that protection through the EPBC Act. It reflects the state of the ongoing legal preceedings as at the time of writing. Using the recent decisions of the Federal Court in *Humane Society International Inc. v. Kyodo Senpaku Kaisha Ltd.*[3] and *Humane Society International v. Minister for Environment and Heritage*[4] as case studies, this chapter explores the effectiveness of the protection afforded by Australian laws in circumstances in which politics and complex international relations can undermine conservation objectives.

[1] Including the Convention on Biological Diversity 1992, the Report of the United Nations Conference on Environment and Development – Agenda 21 1992, the United Nations Convention on the Law of the Sea 1982, the Convention concerning the Protection of the World Cultural and Natural Heritage 1972, and the Convention on Wetlands of International Importance, Especially for Waterfowl Habitat 1971, the International Convention for the Regulation of Whaling 1946, the Convention on the Conservation of Antarctic Marine Living Resources 1980, Convention on the Conservation and Management of Highly Migratory Fish Stocks in the Western and Central Pacific Ocean, 2000, and the United Nations Fish Stocks Agreement 1995.

[2] Commonwealth of Australia, *Australia's Oceans Policy* (Commonwealth of Australia, 1998).

[3] (2004) FCA 1510; (2005) FCA 664.

[4] (2006) AATA 298.

* Environmental Defender's Office (NSW).

2 BACKGROUND TO AUSTRALIA'S COMMITMENT TO MARINE BIODIVERSITY PROTECTION

At an international level, Australia has played a pivotal role in negotiating international agreements for the protection and sustainable management of oceans and marine species. Examples of this leadership include, first, Australia's strong opposition to proposals to lift the ban on commercial whaling and the condemnation of the exploitation of loopholes in the *International Convention on the Regulation of Whaling 1948* (Whaling Convention) relating to scientific whaling by Japan at the forum of the International Whaling Commission (IWC); and, second, Australia's strong support for the establishment of high seas marine protected areas and the adoption of more effective high seas governance in relation to the regulation of fisheries and bioprospecting.[5] Third, Australian delegations have been, for over thirty years, actively involved in negotiations for all the major international agreements dealing with marine pollution promulgated by the International Maritime Organisation and have implemented domestic laws and policies to give effect to those agreements.[6]

Australia also has been closely involved in the development of regional approaches for the protection of the marine environment. In recent years, Australia has joined with states in the South Pacific to adopt the Convention for the Protection of the Natural Resources and Environment of the South-West Pacific Region 1986 and has committed itself to cooperate with South Pacific States in the surveillance and enforcement of fisheries[7] and also the sustainable management of regional fisheries.[8] Importantly, Australia is also viewed as a strong supporter of the establishment of multijurisdictional protected areas, including the Southern Ocean Whale Sanctuary and the proposed South Pacific Whale Sanctuary.[9]

The reasons for Australia's strong engagement in marine biodiversity protection relate most obviously to the vested interest that Australia has in sustainable oceans management because of its vast marine territory. Australia has rights and responsibilities over approximately sixteen million square kilometers of oceans,[10] making Australia the third largest fishing zone in the world. Over 97 percent of that jurisdiction[11] forms what is known as the exclusive economic zone (EEZ), which surrounds mainland Australia and its external territories and extends to two hundred nautical miles seaward of Australia's territorial sea baselines.[12] Pursuant to Article 56 of the United Nations Convention on the Law of the Sea 1982 (UNCLOS), Australia has sovereign rights over its EEZ, which entitles it to explore, exploit, conserve, and manage the natural resources within the area of the EEZ. Statistics from the National Oceans Office indicate that the use of ocean resources, predominantly commercial fishing, is Australia's fifth largest primary industry generating over $A1.6 billion each year for the Australian economy.[13] Moreover,

[5] See, for example, M. Kithell, "Statement of Australian Delegation to United Nations Informal Consultative Process on Oceans and Law of the Sea – Fifth Meeting," New York, 9 June 2004.

[6] D. Rothwell & S. Kaye, "A Legal Framework for Integrated Oceans and Coastal Management in Australia" *EPLJ* (2001), 278, 282.

[7] Nuie Treaty on Cooperation in Fisheries Surveillance and Law Enforcement in the South Pacific 1992.

[8] For example, the Convention for the Conservation of Southern Bluefin Tuna between Australia, New Zealand and Japan 1993 and the Convention on the Conservation and Management of Highly Migratory Fish Stocks in the Western and Central Pacific Ocean, 2000.

[9] Rothwell & Kaye, Note 5, at 282.

[10] Oceans Policy, Note 2, at 7.

[11] *Australia's Oceans Policy*, Note 2, at 6.

[12] United Nations Convention on the Law of the Sea, Article 67.

[13] National Oceans Office, available at http://www.oceans.gov.au/background_paper_1/page_005.jsp.

the Australian Commonwealth Scientific and Research Organisation (CSIRO) have estimated that Australian oceans have more than $A200 billion of undiscovered oil and gas reserves.[14] Accordingly, the sustainable use and management of marine resources is critical to the maintenance of these sectors of the economy.

However, a further reason for Australia's international political stance on marine issues relates to the inherent social and cultural attachment that Australians have with oceans and marine species. Many Australians live in proximity to the coastline and take immense pride in the relatively pristine nature of the country's beaches and oceans. Additionally, there is widespread community awareness about the existence and significance of marine species such as sharks, dolphins, and whales, which live in or migrate through Australia's coastal waters. For example, in a public petition organised by the popular Sydney *Daily Telegraph*, the paper collected more than three hundred e-mails from readers protesting against Japanese whaling in Australian waters. The e-mails were delivered to the Japanese Embassy.[15]

As a result of progressive environmental laws, conservation groups and members of the public who are concerned about actions relating to the marine environment can legally challenge decisions of the government and actions of third parties that may impact on that environment. Therefore, the Australian government faces close scrutiny from the public about the decisions that it makes in relation to marine protection.

Within this context, Australia in 1998 adopted the Ocean Policy, which has as its vision the creation of "healthy oceans cared for, understood and used for wisely for the benefit of all, now and in the future."[16] The goals for the care and wise use of Australia's oceans include:[17]

(a) To exercise and protect Australia's rights and jurisdiction over offshore areas, including offshore resources.
(b) To meet Australia's international obligations under the United Nations Convention on the Law of the Sea and other international treaties.
(c) To understand and protect Australia's marine biological diversity, the ocean environment and its resources, and ensure ocean uses are ecologically sustainable.
(d) To promote ecologically sustainable economic development and job creation.
(e) To establish integrated oceans planning and management arrangements.
(f) To accommodate community needs and aspirations.
(g) To improve our expertise and capabilities in ocean-related management, science, technology, and engineering.
(h) To identify and protect our natural and cultural marine heritage.
(i) To promote public awareness and understanding.

In order to achieve these goals, the Oceans Policy contains a number of principles that relate to decisions and actions affecting the access to any use of Australia's marine jurisdiction and adjacent waters. These principles recognize that ocean ecosystem, health, and integrity are fundamental to ecologically sustainable development. In relation to biodiversity conservation, the principles[18] state that

[14] CSIRO Wealth from Oceans. Available at http://www.csiro.au/index.asp?type=balnk&id=Oceans_Home.

[15] "The Japanese Embassy Collects Your Whale Mail – Then Insults Our Humpbacks: Stop Your Blubbering." *The Daily Telegraph* (Sydney), 19 May 2005.

[16] *Australia's Oceans Policy*, Note 2, at 4.

[17] Ibid.

[18] Ibid. at 26.

- Ocean planning and management decisions should be based on the best available science and other information, recognizing that information regarding ocean resources will often be limited.
- If the potential impact of an action is of concern, priority should be given to maintaining ecosystem health and integrity.
- Incomplete information should not be used as a reason for postponing precautionary measures intended to prevent serious or irreversible degradation of the oceans.

In order to implement the Policy, some of the initial steps taken by the Federal Government involved putting in place new institutional arrangements including the National Oceans Ministerial Board, the National Oceans Science Advisory Group and the National Oceans Office and Regional Marine Plan Steering Committee. In 2003 the Oceans Board of Management was established comprising representatives from seven Australian Government Departments and agencies that provides high-level, whole-of-government advice on operational aspects of the Policy and regional marine planning.[19] As a result of recent Departmental changes, the Minister for the Environment & Heritage (Minister), in conjunction with ministerial consultation when required, now has lead responsibility for Australia's Ocean Policy.[20] The National Oceans Office continues to have lead responsibility for regional marine planning but has been incorporated into the marine division of the Department of the Environment and Heritage (DEH).

In accordance with the Oceans Policy, the government also made a number of commitments to accelerate the development of the national representative system of marine protected areas; to nominate, protect, and implement recovery plans for threatened marine species; to develop a regulatory framework to identify criteria for the assessment of the conservation status of marine biota; to strengthen protection for whales through the continued pursuit of an international ban on commercial whaling and the establishment of whale sanctuaries; and to ensure that marine species are not overfished beyond ecologically sustainable levels. At the heart of the Policy is the adoption of an integrated, ecosystem-based approach to management of ocean resources to be implemented through regional marine plans. Such an approach moves away from the previous sectoral approach to marine issues based on single issues or species.[21] These commitments have been give statutory force through the passing of the EPBC Act.

3 THE ENVIRONMENT PROTECTION AND BIODIVERSITY CONSERVATION ACT 1999 AND THE MANAGEMENT OF MARINE BIODIVERSITY

3.1 Overview

As Rothwell and Kaye note, when the EPBC Act commenced in July 2000, it represented "one of the most substantial adjustments to Australian environmental law in nearly 20 years."[22] The Act sought to consolidate, in a single piece of legislation, Australia's commitment to give effect to its obligations under international environmental

[19] National Oceans Office. Available at http://www.oceans.gov.au.

[20] In 2004, the National Oceans Ministerial Board was dissolved as a result of administrative changes made following announcement of the electoral victory of the fourth Howard Ministry.

[21] P. Burgess, "Biodiversity Conservation and the Marine Environment (Plenary Session)." Paper presented to Third Colloquium of the IUCN International Law Committee, 12 July 2005.

[22] Rothwell & Kaye, Note 5, at 288.

conventions and to establish a comprehensive regime for the environmental impact assessment of actions likely to impact on matters of national environmental significance.[23] The EPBC Act was drafted with the 1992 Rio Declaration firmly in mind, with its objectives including the promotion of ecologically sustainable development and the conservation of biodiversity.[24]

The EPBC Act applies to certain acts, omissions, matters, and things in the Australian jurisdiction.[25] The Australian jurisdiction is defined to mean the land, waters, seabed, and airspace in, under or above Australia; or an external territory; or the EEZ; or the continental shelf.[26] Australia's EEZ is defined in the EPBC Act,[27] the Seas and Submerged Lands Act 1973 (Cth)[28] and the UNCLOS[29] as being the area of sea that stretches up to two hundred nautical miles from the low water basemark of the territorial sea. However, pursuant to the Offshore Constitutional Settlement Act 1980 between the Commonwealth and the States, the States have jurisdiction over coastal waters within three nautical miles from the coastline of each State.[30]

The EPBC Act contains a range of provisions that are directly relevant to the management of Australia's marine environment. Those provisions include:

- the listing of threatened marine species and migratory species and the preparation of recovery plans and threat abatement plans for those species;[31]
- requiring environmental impact assessment for actions that are likely to have a significant impact on a matter of national environmental significance which may include, for example, the world heritage values of the Great Barrier Reef or Shark Bay;[32]
- the protection of cetaceans in the Australian Whale Sanctuary;[33]
- the declaration of Commonwealth reserves and the creation of marine protected areas;[34]
- the permit requirements for actions in Commonwealth marine areas;[35]
- the implementation of wildlife conservation plans for listed marine species;[36]
- the strategic assessment of Commonwealth fisheries;[37] and
- the approval and accreditation of operations involving the international trade of marine species.[38]

For the purposes of this chapter, we will focus on those provisions of the EPBC Act that deal with the assessment and approval regimes for the protection of marine species, in particular cetaceans, the establishment of marine protected areas and the management of fisheries.

[23] Including listed world heritage properties, listed threatened species, Ramsar wetlands, places of national heritage significance, the marine environment, and nuclear actions.
[24] Environment Protection and Biodiversity Conservation Act section 3(1).
[25] Ibid., section 5(1).
[26] Ibid., section 5(5).
[27] Ibid., sections 24 and 528.
[28] Ibid., section 3.
[29] United Nations Convention on the Law of the Sea, Article 57.
[30] Coastal Waters (State Powers) Act 1980.
[31] Environment Protection and Biodiversity Conservation Act; Part 13 Division 1.
[32] Ibid., Part 3 Division 1.
[33] Ibid., Part 13 Division 3.
[34] Ibid., Part 15 Division 4.
[35] Ibid., section 23.
[36] Ibid., Part 13 Division 5.
[37] Ibid., Part 10, Division 2.
[38] Ibid., Part 13A.

Although the Minister is responsible for decisions that affect the marine environment under the EPBC Act, the Act also provides significant opportunities for public involvement in marine protection. Members of the public have the opportunity to:

- Nominate species for listing as threatened;[39]
- Comment on the content of draft recovery plans or threat abatement plans for threatened species;[40]
- Nominate places for protection as Commonwealth heritage places[41] and comment on proposals for such listing;[42]
- Comment on proposals to establish Commonwealth reserves[43] and on the content of draft management plans for those reserves;[44] and
- Comment on the environmental impact assessment for actions that are likely to have a significant effect upon matters of national environmental significance (including listed threatened species and Commonwealth marine areas).[45]

In addition, certain members of the public are recognised as having standing to seek to review decisions of the Minister (for example, to approve a wildlife trade operation) and to bring civil enforcement proceedings to remedy or to restrain breaches of the Act.[46] The broad standing provisions in the EPBC Act have enabled conservation groups to bring two of the cases referred to in Section 3 of this chapter.

3.2 Marine Protected Areas

Marine Protected Areas (MPAs) can be defined as:

> An area of land and/or sea especially dedicated to the protection and maintenance of biological diversity, and of natural and associated cultural resources, and managed through legal or other effective means.[47]

MPAs play a vitally important role in the protection of marine biodiversity. In particular, they operate to:

1. Conserve biodiversity and habitat, especially the habitat of threatened species;
2. Help maintain viable fisheries;
3. Contribute to increased marine knowledge;
4. Protect the genetic diversity of intensely exploited species; and
5. Protect cultural diversity, such as shipwrecks.[48]

Part 15 of the EPBC Act deals with protected areas, including world heritage properties (such as the Great Barrier Reef and Shark Bay),[49] places listed as having national

[39] Ibid., section 191.
[40] Ibid., section 275.
[41] Ibid., section 314E.
[42] Ibid., section 341M.
[43] Ibid., section 351.
[44] Ibid., section 368(2).
[45] Ibid., section 74(3) and sections 93, 98, 103, and 110.
[46] EPBC Act, sections 487 and 475.
[47] *Australia's Oceans Policy*, Note 2, at 45.
[48] *Guidelines for Marine Protected Areas* (IUCN – World Conservation Union, Gland, Switzerland, and Cambridge, UK, 1999), xvii. See http://iucn.org/themes/wcpa/pubs/pdfs/mpa_guidelines.pdf (copy on file with author).
[49] Environment Protection and Biodiversity Conservation Act, Part 15, Division 1.

heritage value,[50] Commonwealth heritage places,[51] and Commonwealth Reserves.[52] Marine areas may be included for protection under any of these designations. However, the thirteen offshore MPAs and five terrestrial protected areas that have marine components have all been established as Commonwealth reserves on the basis of meeting characteristics of the categories for protected areas developed by the IUCN.[53] Those reserves include the Commonwealth waters of the Ningaloo Marine Park in Western Australia, the Solitary Island Marine Reserve in New South Wales and the Great Australian Bight Marine Park. The terrestrial protected areas include national parks such as Kakadu National Park and Christmas Island National Park and also the Heard and McDonald Islands Marine Reserve in the Southern Ocean.[54]

In addition, the Commonwealth manages two MPAs that are not Commonwealth reserves – the Great Barrier Reef Marine Park and the Antarctic Special Protection Area – and has adopted special legislation to protect shipwrecks.[55] Australia also has established an Australian Whale Sanctuary within its EEZ (which includes Australia's EEZ adjacent to its Antarctic territory), which provides for the protection of cetaceans in Australian waters.[56]

Similar to other Commonwealth reserves, MPAs are managed in accordance with management plans that provide for the protection and conservation of the reserve and that identify how the reserve or zones of the reserve and its features are to be managed, the range of operations that may take place in the reserve, and any limitations on those activities.[57] Where management plans are yet to be prepared, the reserve must be managed in a way that is consistent with the IUCN category to which it has been assigned.[58]

As noted earlier, under Australia's Ocean Policy, the Commonwealth Government aims to implement a whole-of-government approach to managing marine resources on a large scale through the establishment of Regional Marine Plans (RMPs). On 1 July 2004, a new Zoning Plan for the Great Barrier Reef Marine Park came into force, which increased the level of high protection zones from 4.5 percent to 33.3 percent, making the Great Barrier Reef Marine Park the largest network of protected marine areas in the world.[59]

[50] Ibid., Part 15, Division 1A.

[51] Ibid., Part 15, Division 3.

[52] Ibid., Part 15, Division 4.

[53] Ibid., sections 344–348.

[54] The Department of Environment and Heritage Web site lists all the Commonwealth Marine Protected Areas. See http://www.deh.gov.au/coasts/mpa/commonwealth/manage/estate.html.

[55] The Great Barrier Reef Marine Park, managed under the Great Barrier Reef Marine Park Act 1975 (Cth); the Antarctic Special Protection Area, managed under the Antarctic Treaty (Environment Protection) Act 1980 (Cth), and fourteen historic shipwrecks, managed under the Historic Shipwrecks Act 1976 (Cth).

[56] Environment Protection and Biodiversity Conservation Act, section 225.

[57] Ibid., section 367.

[58] Commonwealth marine protected areas and any zones established within those areas must be assigned to one of seven internationally recognised management categories. The categories, established by the World Conservation Union (IUCN) and incorporated into the EPBC Act Part 15, provide a convenient means of describing the rationale for selecting a particular area for protection and the actions that are permissible in that area. In principle, the system is not aimed at establishing a hierarchy and one category is no more or less protected than another. An example of a category is a Strict Nature Reserve managed primarily for scientific research and environmental monitoring. Certain zones are commonly referred to as "no-take zones" or green zones, which are areas in which no flora or fauna is allowed to be taken. This is an effective means of conserving biodiversity by not allowing activities, such as fishing, in these areas at all.

[59] D. Brigs, "Great Barrier Reef – Continuing to Set Benchmarks in Marine Conservation." 11(2) *Waves* (2005), 9.

This change was implemented in lieu of recognition that the previous low percentage of high protection zones was inadequate to maintain the function and integrity of the Great Barrier Reef ecosystem. The new zoning implemented the Representative Areas Program, which involved rezoning the Park into bioregions based on distinct habitat types and ensuring that at least 20 percent of each bioregion was adequately protected in a network of Green or "No-Take" Zones.[60] This will allow a much greater level of conservation and protection of ecosystems and species.

The Commonwealth, State, and Territory governments have been working together since the early 1990s to establish the National Representative System of Marine Protected Areas (NRSMPA). The aim of establishing the NRSMPA is to protect representative examples of the full range of marine ecosystems and the communities of plants and animals they contain in order to ensure the conservation of marine biodiversity and ecological processes. As at 2002, the NRSMPA covered approximately 64,600,000 hectares (7 percent of Australia's marine jurisdiction) and 90 marine protected areas have been declared in the period 1992–2003. Although this is a start, a number of conservationists argue that there remains a long way to go. Australia is well behind the World Parks Congress recommendation that between 20 and 30 percent of each marine habitat in the world's oceans be protected and, as Smythe comments, Australia "has not drawn up any roadmap to get there."[61] Andrew McIntosh similarly argues that despite over $A50 million being invested in the program, only one regional plan has been produced and no new marine protected areas have been created.[62]

Although the EPBC Act provides a strong legislative framework for the creation and management of MPAs, a number of major threats to the integrity of those areas remain, even when they are designated as protected. Those threats include:

- The continuation of recreational and commercial fishing in multiuse zones and on the boundaries of MPAs;
- Land-based diffuse-source pollution, such as fertiliser runoff;
- Climate change;
- Invasive marine species;
- Shipping and associated problems, such as the introduction of exotic pests through ballast water;
- Military activities involving sonar, which may adversely impact whales and dolphins;
- Transportation of hazardous substances, such as oil;
- Gas and oil exploration; and
- Bioprospecting.

Many of these threats have not been adequately addressed even where areas of high quality marine biodiversity has been protected through the creation of reserves.

Importantly, the major threat that terrestrial activities pose on the marine environment must be recognised and laws relating to terrestrial activities should have regard to any adverse impacts that those activities may have on the marine environment. Dr. Karen Edyvane contrasts the approach taken by the Commonwealth in developing the South-east Regional Marine Plan based on options proposed by key stakeholders, with

[60] Great Barrier Reef Marine Park Authority. See http://www.gbrmpa.gov.au.

[61] C. Smythe, "Missing the Target on Marine Protection." 11(2) *Waves* (2005), 11.

[62] Quoted in A. Darby, "Ocean Care Plan Sinks without a Trace." *Sydney Morning Herald*, 24 October 2005. See http://www.smh.com.au/text/articles/2005/10/23/1130006005938.html.

the science-driven approach to marine zoning in the GBRMP.[63] In order to address the many threats facing the marine environment, she argues, and the authors agree, that independent, transparent, science-driven approaches to planning are required that are consistent across State and Commonwealth jurisdictions.[64]

3.3 Species Protection

Pursuant to section 248 of the EPBC Act, the Federal Minister is required to maintain a list of endangered marine species. Species can be added to the list if the Minister is satisfied that the species occur naturally in the Commonwealth marine area and listing is necessary to ensure the long-term conservation of the species.[65] To date, more than one hundred marine species have been listed as endangered under the EPBC Act, including thirty-two snakes, five marine turtles, and over fifty seahorses.[66] There are also eleven marine species nominations currently under consideration for listing, including the School Shark and the Southern Dogfish.[67] However, noticeably, none of the commercial species that have been nominated that meet the listing criteria (such as Southern Bluefin Tuna) have been listed.[68] The Humane Society International (HSI) recently nominated the Southern Bluefin Tuna (SBT) for threatened species listing under the EPBC Act. The Threatened Species Scientific Committee found that the species continues to be overfished despite the international management arrangements that have been formally in place since 1994 and that the species is eligible for listing as endangered under the EPBC Act. However, the nomination was unsuccessful because the Minister determined that the listing may be detrimental to the survival of the species, as it may weaken Australia's ability to influence the global conservation of the species, and, by implication, its conservation in Australian waters.

Part 13, Division 5 of the EPBC Act allows the Minister to prepare and implement wildlife conservation plans for listed marine species and cetaceans. These plans should be prepared in consultation with the States and Territories unless the relevant species can only be found in a Commonwealth marine area.[69] Wildlife conservation plans identify habitats important to the survival of the relevant species and set out a process to ensure the continued survival of the species and protection of its habitat.[70]

It is an offence to take an action that results in the death or injury of a listed marine species in or on a Commonwealth area. If the offence is reckless, then the offender may be punished with up to two years' imprisonment and fines of up to $A110,000;[71] otherwise, fines of up to $A55,000 may apply.[72] Similarly, it is an offence to take, trade, keep, or move a member of a listed marine species in or on a Commonwealth area.[73] The EPBC Act, however, provides that certain actions involving the killing, injuring, or taking listed

[63] K. Edyvane, "NRSMPA – Policies, Planning and Science." 11(2) *Waves* (2005), 10.

[64] Ibid.

[65] Environment Protection and Biodiversity Conservation Act, section 250.

[66] For a full list of marine species declared under the EBPC Act, refer to the Department of Environment and Heritage Web site. Available at www.deh.gov.au/coastal/species/marine-species-lit.html.

[67] Department of the Environment and Heritage Web site. Available at http://www.deh.gov.au/biodiversity/threatened.

[68] Australia Institute, "Environment Protection and Biodiversity Conservation Act A Five Year Assessment." Discussion Paper 81, July 2005.

[69] Environment Protection and Biodiversity Conservation Act, section 285.

[70] Ibid., section 287.

[71] Environment Protection and Biodiversity Conservation Act, section 254.

[72] Ibid., section 254A.

[73] Ibid., sections 254B–E.

marine species are not offences. Section 355 of the Act establishes statutory defences when, for example, the action is taken in accordance with a plan or approval; the action is taken in a humane manner and is reasonably necessary to relive or prevent suffering by an animal; the action is reasonably necessary to deal with a risk to human health or an emergency that involves a serious threat to human health or property; or the action occurs as a result of an unavoidable accident that is not reckless or negligent.

The Minister may issue permits for the taking of actions that may kill, injure, take, trade, keep, or move a listed marine species in a Commonwealth area.[74] However, the Minister must be satisfied of a number of matters before a permit can be issued. Those matters include, but are not limited to, being satisfied that the specified action:

- will significantly contribute to the conservation of the species; or that impact on the species is only incidental to, and not the purpose of the action,
- will not adversely affect the conservation of the species,
- will be inconsistent with a wildlife conservation plan for the species, and
- will ensure that all reasonable steps will be taken to minimise impacts on the species.[75]

The only reported decision of a prosecution for an offence against the provisions of the EPBC Act that protect marine species is the case of *Minister for the Environment and Heritage v. Wilson* (2004) FCA 6. This case concerned a civil prosecution for a contravention of section 354(1)(a) of the EPBC Act. That provision prohibits a person from killing, injuring, taking, trading, keeping, or moving a member of a native species in a Commonwealth reserve unless permitted by a management plan. The proceedings were brought against a fisherman who caught a shark just inside the boundary of the Great Australian Bight Marine Park off the coast the South Australian mainland, which is a Commonwealth reserve proclaimed under section 344 of the EPBC Act. The fisherman admitted to committing the offence and was ordered to pay a civil penalty of $A12,500, despite the availability of a maximum penalty of $A55,000 for a breach of section 354 of the EPBC Act. The fisherman's breach of the EPBC Act was found by the Court to be negligent, if not reckless.[76] However, the Court took into account the following undisputed facts in imposing the penalty:

1. The fisherman was an experienced shark fisherman with no prior convictions and he had cooperated with the DEH in relation to the breach;
2. The fisherman's net was set for three to four hours close to the boundary of the Marine Park; during that time, the fisherman was not able to look at the GPS system on the boat. When the net was set the fisherman's boat drifted into the Marine Park; and
3. The total value of fish caught by the fisherman was $A11,500. The fisherman suggested that the value of the fish taken from inside the park was about $A200.[77]

The Court found that the fisherman had taken a risk in setting his net so close to the boundary of the Marine Park and the Court also considered the need to deter others from doing the same given the large area of the park.[78]

The provisions referred to here exclude cetaceans or listed threatened or migratory species, which are provided for separately under the Act. However, the regime that

[74] Ibid., section 258.
[75] Environment Protection and Biodiversity Conservation Act, section 258(3).
[76] (2004) FCA 6, para 7.
[77] Ibid., para 6.
[78] Ibid., para 7.

establishes offence provisions for the killing or injuring listed threatened species and listed migratory species and that exempt certain actions from those provisions are in almost identical terms.[79] These provisions have the potential to be relied on in circumstances in which endangered seabirds, such as albatrosses and petrels, are killed or injured as a result of long line fishing in Australian waters.[80]

3.4 Protection of Cetaceans

Part 13, Division 3 of the EPBC Act[81] deals with the protection of whales and other cetaceans in Commonwealth marine areas. Section 225 of the EPBC Act establishes the Australian Whale Sanctuary (AWS).[82] The purpose of the AWS is "to give formal recognition of the high level of protection and management afforded to cetaceans in Commonwealth marine areas and prescribed waters."[83]

All cetaceans are protected in the AWS, and, in addition to that protection, five species of cetaceans are listed as threatened species under the EPBC Act.[84]

The AWS covers all Commonwealth marine areas and Australia's external territories, including its sub-Antarctic territories of Heard and Macdonald islands and the Australian Antarctic Territory. The AWS does not include the coastal waters of each State and the Northern Territory unless those areas are declared by the Environment Protection and Biodiversity Conservation Regulations 2000 (EPBC Regulations) to be prescribed waters for the purposes of the Act.[85]

Similar to the offence provisions relating to marine species, the EPBC Act creates offences that relate to actions involving cetaceans both within and outside of the AWS. These provisions apply to the activities of all persons, aircraft, and vessels within the AWS, including foreign nationals and foreign vessels and aircraft.[86] Those offences are as follows:

1. Recklessly killing a cetacean;[87]
2. Intentionally taking, trading, keeping, moving, or interfering with a cetacean;[88]
3. Treating a cetacean that has been illegally killed or taken.[89] "Treating" means cutting up or taking any product from the cetacean;[90] and
4. Possessing a cetacean or part of a cetacean or a product of a cetacean that has been illegally killed or taken.[91]

[79] See Environment Protection and Biodiversity Conservation Act, sections 196–207 for threatened species and sections 209–222 for migratory species.

[80] In September–October 2004, a number of seabirds were killed as a result of longline fishing operations. In response to these events, the Department of Fisheries amended the Threat Abatement Plan for the Gillnet Hook and Trap Fishery requiring lines to be weighted in high risk areas to mitigate against further incidents (Nicola Beynon, campaign manager, Humane Society International; personal communication, 22 February 2005).

[81] Ibid., sections 224–247.

[82] Whales were previously protected in Australian waters under the Whale Protection Act 1980 (Cth), which was repealed by the Environment Protection and Biodiversity Conservation Act.

[83] Environment Protection and Biodiversity Conservation Act, section 225(1).

[84] Environment Protection and Biodiversity Conservation Act, List of Threatened Species, viewed at http://www.deh.gov.au/cgi-bin/sprat/public/publicthreatenedlist.pl?wanted=fauna#mammals%20that%20are%20Critically%20Endangered.

[85] Environment Protection and Biodiversity Conservation Act, sections 225(2)(b), 226, 227, and 228.

[86] Ibid., sections 5 and 224.

[87] Ibid., section 229.

[88] Ibid., section 229B.

[89] Ibid., section 229D.

[90] Ibid., section 229D(3).

[91] Ibid., section 230.

Breaches of these provisions are strict liability offences.[92] The maximum penalty for taking actions without a required permit are up to two years' imprisonment or a fine of up to $A110,000 for an individual or $A550,000 for a corporation.[93] Fines of up to $A33,000 also can be imposed if a person contravenes the condition of a permit.[94]

Pursuant to section 236 of the EPBC Act, foreign whaling vessels that are brought into a port in Australia or an external territory are guilty of an offence unless the master of the vessel has obtained the written permission of the Minister to bring the vessel into the port.

The same categories of exemptions as apply to offences relating to marine species apply to cetaceans.[95] Similarly, the Minister may authorise the issue of a permit to kill, injure, take, trade, keep, possess, move, or interfere with a cetacean, but only when he is satisfied that the action will contribute significantly to the conservation of cetaceans and will not adversely affect the conservation status of or population of the species.[96]

3.5 Actions and Approvals

The Commonwealth marine environment is identified as a matter of national environmental significance under the EPBC Act.[97]

It is an offence to take an action that has, will have, or is likely to have a significant impact on the Commonwealth marine environment, unless the person taking the action has approval, is the Commonwealth or a Commonwealth agency, or some other form of ministerial authorisation has been granted.[98] As a result, actions and decisions that may have a significant impact on Commonwealth marine areas, or which take place within Commonwealth marine areas and may have a significant impact on the environment,[99] are subject to the environment protection procedures under the EPBC Act, which include requirements for environmental impact assessment to be carried out before granting any approval for the action.[100]

Examples of recent referrals triggering the protection of marine environment include onshore commercial developments that may impact on adjoining marine reserves such as the redevelopment of accommodation facilities at Horn Island referred by the Australian Fisheries Management Authority and the proposed development of a residential subdivision and golf course near Bowen on the Queensland coast by a company called Whitsunday Shores.[101] Additionally, offshore petroleum exploration and drilling also may trigger environmental impact assessment in accordance with Part 9 of the EPBC Act, as was the case for the proposal by Roc Oil (WA) Pty. Ltd. to drill for oil and gas in the Commonwealth marine area between Kalbarri and Cliff Head in Western Australia.[102]

[92] Ibid., sections 229A, 229C(3), 229D(2), and 230(2).

[93] Ibid., sections 229(2) and 229B(3).

[94] Ibid., section 240.

[95] Ibid., section 231.

[96] Ibid., section 238(3).

[97] Ibid., sections 23–24A.

[98] Ibid., section 23(4).

[99] The term "significant" is not defined in the EPBC Act but has been held to mean "an impact that is important, notable or of consequence having regard to its context or intensity" the case of *Booth v. Bosworth* (2001) FCR 39, at 64.

[100] Environment Protection and Biodiversity Conservation Act, Chapter 4.

[101] Department of Environment and Heritage Web site. See http://www.deh.gov.au/cgi-bin/epbc/epbc_ap.pl?name=current_referral_detail&proposal_id=2195.

[102] Department of Environment and Heritage Web site. See http://www.deh.gov.au/cgiin/epbc/epbc_ap.pl?name=current_referral_detail&proposal_id=2185.

World Heritage properties and national heritage places (which may include marine areas) and listed threatened species and migratory species (which also may include marine species) are also identified as matters of national environmental significance.[103] Accordingly, similar offence provisions relating to the taking of actions that significantly affect those matters apply, as do the requirements for environmental impact assessment before the grant of approval to take such actions.[104]

The extent of the Minister's inquiry in determining the impacts of an action on a matter of national environmental significance was recently considered in *Queensland Conservation Council Inc v. Minister for the Environment & Heritage* (2003) FCA 1463 and the subsequent appeal in *Minister for the Environment and Heritage v. Queensland Conservation Council Inc* (2004) FCAFC 190. In decisions of the Federal Court both at first instance and on appeal, the Court found that the likely impacts of the construction and operation of the proposed Nathan Dam on the Great Barrier Reef World Heritage Area was a matter which the Minister was required to consider when assessing the impacts of the proposal under section 75 of the EPBC Act. The issue in this case was whether the Minister was required to consider all adverse impacts of the construction and operation of a dam on the Dawson River, which flows into the Great Barrier Reef World Heritage Area. In determining whether the construction of the dam was a controlled action under section 75 of the EPBC Act, he did not consider the impacts that the use of the dam for the irrigation of cotton farms would have on the World Heritage values of the Great Barrier Reef – in particular, the impacts of agricultural pollutants, such as endosulfan. The Court found that when assessing the impacts of a referred action under section 75 of the EPBC Act, the Minister is required to consider the cumulative impacts of the action, including the impacts of third parties.

This case is important because it recognises the indirect impacts of land based activities on the marine environment and requires those impacts to be considered as part of the environmental impact assessment process.

3.6 Strategic Assessment of Fisheries

Pursuant to the Oceans Policy, the federal government committed to a number of steps in relation to the management of Australia's domestic fisheries. These steps included:

- Adopting an ecosystem-based approach to fisheries management;
- Implementing a fisheries by-catch policy in relation to environmental impact assessment of fisheries;
- Undertaking strategic environmental impact assessment of all new management plans for Commonwealth fisheries; and
- Removing the blanket exemption of marine species from wildlife export controls, to ensure that exemptions are only available for marine species harvested in accordance with sustainable and ecologically based management arrangements.[105]

The Fisheries Management Act 1994 (Cth) provides the statutory framework for the development of fisheries management plans and the licensing regime for fisheries.

[103] Environment Protection and Biodiversity Conservation Act, sections 12–15C.

[104] Ibid., sections 12–15A for world heritage; sections 15B for national heritage; sections 18–19 for listed threatened species; and sections 20–21 for listed migratory species.

[105] *Australia's Oceans Policy*, Note 2, at 26.

However, the EPBC Act also plays an important role in relation to the strategic assessment of Commonwealth-managed fisheries[106] and the trade in native species.[107]

Part 10 of the EPBC Act deals with strategic assessments of the impact of an action taken under a policy, plan or programme on a matter protected under Part 3 of that Act. In this respect, if there is a policy, plan, or program that deals with Commonwealth marine areas or protected marine species, then the Minister may evaluate the content of the policy, plan, or program, pursuant to a strategic assessment to ensure that relevant environmental issues have been taken into account and appropriate mitigation measures are contained in the policy, plan, or program.

Specifically in relation to Australia's fisheries, the EPBC Act requires the Australian Fisheries Management Authority or the Minister for Agriculture, Fisheries and Forestry to enter into an agreement for the strategic assessment of all management plans and policies for Commonwealth managed fisheries.[108] The assessment of the fishery involves a review of a report assessing the impacts of the adoption of the management plan. The terms of reference for that report are determined by agreement and having regard to public consultation and the EPBC Regulation 2000.[109] DEH has prepared Guidelines for the Ecologically Sustainable Management of Fisheries (the Guidelines), which outline specific principles and objectives designed to ensure a strategic and transparent way of evaluating the ecological sustainability of fishery management arrangements.[110] The two guiding principles for management are, first, that a fishery must be conducted in a manner that does not lead to overfishing, or for those stocks that are overfished, the fishery must be conducted such that there is a high degree of probability that the stock(s) will recover. Second, fishing operations should be managed to minimise their impact on the structure, productivity, function, and biological diversity of the ecosystem (e.g., by avoiding by-catch). There are twenty-one Commonwealth managed fisheries and a number of state and territory fisheries that are undergoing strategic assessment under the EPBC Act with a view to their completion by December 2005.

3.7 Trade in Native Species

Part 13A of the EPBC Act regulates the international movement of wildlife specimens, including the exports of regulated native specimens that are listed pursuant to Appendix I, II, and III of the Convention on International Trade in Endangered Species (CITES) and native specimens. Native species are defined to include species that are indigenous to, or which periodically or occasionally visit Australia or an external territory, which includes the seabed of the coastal sea, the continental shelf and the EEZ. Species that are listed pursuant to CITES and that are therefore subject to Part 13A include the Great White Shark and the Australian Lung Fish. In addition, CITES and EPBC listed marine mammals include, among many cetaceans, the Southern Minke Whale, the Blue Whale, and the Humpback Dolphin.[111]

[106] Environment Protection and Biodiversity Conservation Act, Part 10.
[107] Ibid., Part 13A.
[108] Ibid., section 148.
[109] Ibid., section 146 (2).
[110] Department of Environment and Heritage Web site. Available at http://www.deh.gov.au/coasts/fisheries/guidelines.html.
[111] List of CITES species is available on the Department of Environment and Heritage Web site. Available at http://www.deh.gov.au/biodiversity/trade-use/lists.cites/index.html.

It is a very serious offence to export a CITES specimen or native specimen without lawful authority, attracting penalties of up to ten years imprisonment and $A1,100,000.[112] Before a species regulated by Part 13A may lawfully be exported, the Minister is required to make a series of decisions under the EPBC Act, for example, whether to grant a permit for individual exports[113] or, in relation to commercial purpose exports, whether the export is in accordance with an approved wildlife trade operation or approved wildlife trade management plan.[114]

Relevant to fisheries, the Minister may declare a fishery to be an "approved wildlife trade operation" if the Minister is satisfied that certain legislative criteria have been met on the sustainability of the fishery. Before making such a declaration the Minister is required by the EPBC Act to be satisfied that the operation (among other things) will not be detrimental to the survival or conservation status of the species; will not be likely to threaten any relevant ecosystem including (but not limited to) any habitat or biodiversity; is consistent with certain objectives;[115] and there are effective management regimes in place for the operation.[116]

The effect of determining that a particular export activity is an approved wildlife trade operation is that the activity can take place without the need for further environmental impact assessment under Part 9 of the Act.

In 2005 the Minister determined that the export of SBT was an approved wildlife trade operation. The SBT had been nominated for listing as a threatened species pursuant to the EPBC Act. The decision to approve the wildlife trade operation has attracted criticism from conservation groups on the grounds of the Minister's failure to consider the nomination of the species under the EPBC Act. HSI applied to the Administrative Appeals Tribunal to review the merits of the Minister's decision. This case is analysed in more detail later in this chapter.

4 HOW EFFECTIVE ARE THE PROTECTIONS AFFORDED?

Section 3 of this paper has provided an overview of the key federal laws that exist to protect marine biodiversity and to regulate the sustainable management of marine resources. The EPBC Act has admirable objectives and puts in place legislative mechanisms, such as environmental impact assessment and public participation, consistent with well-established principles for biodiversity conservation and ecologically sustainable development. As Chris McGrath states:

> viewed in the context of other laws and initiatives, the EPBC Act is a major step forward that fundamentally improves the Australian legal system. It has made, and no doubt will continue in the future to make, an important contribution to environmental protection and sustainable development in Australia.[117]

[112] Environment Protection and Biodiversity Conservation Act, sections 303CC and 303DD.

[113] Ibid., sections 303FA–FI.

[114] Ibid., sections 303FJ–303FT.

[115] Ibid., section 303BA(1) Including (a) to protect wildlife that may be adversely affected by trade (b) the precautionary principle; (c) to promote the conservation of biodiversity in Australia and other countries; (d) to ensure that any commercial utilisation of Australian native wildlife for the purposes of export is managed in an ecologically sustainable way; (e) to ensure it is intaken into account in making decisions relating to the utilisation of wildlife.

[116] Ibid., sections 303FN(3) and (4).

[117] C. McGrath, "Key Concepts of the Environment Protection and Biodiversity Conservation Act 1999 (C'th)." 22 *EPLJ* (2004), 20, 39.

It must be noted that the EPBC Act is still in its infancy, operating for just five years, and therefore the body of case-law applying, enforcing, and interpreting the Act is still only small. However, the cases that have been and that still are under consideration by Australian Courts and Tribunals provide an interesting insight into the regulatory approach adopted by the Federal Government.

Of the estimated fourteen reported cases that have been brought pursuant to the EPBC Act, only two have been commenced by the federal government. The balance of cases has been brought by third parties, being individuals or organisations with conservation objectives. In those cases where proceedings have been brought against a non-Governmental party, such as the Japanese company Kyodo Senpaku Kaisha Ltd., (it is arguable that) the proceedings could have been commenced by the Minister himself. Therefore, a question about the political will to enforce the EPBC Act arises. In the remaining cases, where actions have been brought against the Minister himself, claiming procedural errors in the decision-making process or flaws in the merits of a decision, there is a need to consider the effectiveness of the mechanisms in the Act for the protection of the environment and the strength of the political will to achieve this protection. These questions will be considered in the following review of cases brought under the EPBC Act that deal with the marine environment.

4.1 Domestic Regimes – EPBC Act Cases Relating to Marine Protection

There have been very few cases brought under the provisions of the EPBC Act that relate to marine protection. Both civil and criminal sanctions are available to DEH to enforce the provisions of the EPBC Act. However, since the Act came into force in July 2000, only four prosecutions have been commenced by the Minister, three of which relate to offence of harm caused to protected marine species, only one of which has been reported.[118]

The DEH has a compliance and enforcement policy that includes:[119]

- the carrying out of regular and random patrols;
- the conduct of audits and investigations into possible breaches of the EPBC Act;
- random inspections; and
- the requirement for licence and permit holders to regularly report on their compliance with their licence conditions.

In determining the appropriate response to suspected contraventions of the EPBC Act, the DEH will consider certain matters including:[120]

- the seriousness of the harm caused by the alleged contravention;
- whether the contravention is intentional, reckless, negligent, or a mistake;

[118] *Minister for the Environment and Heritage v. Wilson* (2004) FCA 6; *Minister for the Environment & Heritage v. Greentree (No. 2)* (2004) FCA 741 and two unreported decisions from the Magistrates Court in the Northern Territory resulting in the conviction and subsequent imprisonment of Indonesian fishermen who caught dolphins in Commonwealth waters to use for shark bait.

[119] Department of Environment and Heritage Compliance and Enforcement Policy, August 2004. Available at http://www.deh.gov.au/about/compliance/index.html#responding. The Prosecution Policy of the Commonwealth, which is Management by the Commonwealth Department of Public Prosecutions also applies to the DEH. Available at http://www.cdpp.gov.au/Prosecutions/Policy/ProsecutionPolicy.pdf.

[120] Ibid.

- whether the suspect has a history of prior contraventions;
- the cost to the Australian government or general community of the contravention;
- the commercial value of the contravention to the suspect;
- the time which has elapsed since the contravention;
- the extent of the evidence of the contravention;
- the likelihood of the contravention continuing or being repeated;
- the prevalence of the type of contravention;
- the likely public perception of the breach and the manner with which it is dealt; and
- whether the use of the response option in a specific case would create a desirable precedent.

Where the DEH obtains evidence of a serious contravention of the EPBC Act it may commence a civil or criminal prosecution against the offender. Criminal proceedings will only be brought where the elements of the offence can be proved beyond a reasonable doubt. A serious civil or criminal offence involves at least one of the following:

- a blatant disregard for or significant degree of indifference to the law or a significant degree of criminality on the part of the offender; or
- where previous administrative or civil actions have not resulted in compliance; or
- where the Australian government or the community expects the offence to be dealt with prosecution; or
- where the offence had resulted in or had the potential to result in significant harm or detriment to the Australian government, the community, or the environment, including cultural heritage, economy, resources, assets, or the well-being of Australia; or
- where the nature of the crime is such that the prosecution will act as a deterrent.[121]

Where there are breaches of the marine protection provisions of the EPBC Act, the location of the breach and the significance to the community of the marine animals or the environment which is harmed are important factors that will be considered by the DEH in determining whether to prosecute. In the case of two recent unreported judgments of the Magistrates Court in the Northern Territory in which Indonesian fishermen were imprisoned for killing dolphins to use their flesh as shark bait, the decision to bring criminal proceedings would not have been a difficult one to make. The fishermen were fishing illegally in Australian waters, in which they intentionally killed protected cetaceans, namely dolphins, which have special significance to the Australian community, and they used them to catch other species illegally, species that also may be protected.

Australia treats illegal fishing in its waters very seriously. On a number of occasions the Australian Fisheries Management Authority (AFMA) has deployed an armed vessel to patrol the Patagonian toothfishery located in Australia's EEZ around its external territories of Heard and McDonald islands in the sub-Antarctic.[122] This fishery is subject to extensive overfishing and illegal fishing. In January 2004 the AFMA seized an

[121] Ibid.

[122] The Attorney General's Department Oceanic Viking Started patrolling the area December 2004. Available at http://www.ag.gov.au/agd/WWW/justiceministerhome.NSF/Page/Media_Releases_2004_3rd_Quarter_31_August_2004_-_Dedicated_armed_vessel_to_toughen_crackdown_on_fish_poachers and http://www.ag.gov.au/agd/WWW/justiceministerHome.nsf/Page/Media_Releases_2004_4th_Quarter_19_November_2004_-_Warning_to_Fish_Poachers_as_Armed_Patrols_Begin.

Uruguayan vessel and charged the entire crew for illegally fishing in the Australian EEZ off Heard and McDonald islands.[123]

The approach of the Commonwealth government taken to the management of the patagonian toothfishery in the sub-Antarctic is dramatically different to that taken by the government to protect cetaceans from illegal whaling in Australian waters adjacent to the Australian Antarctic Territory, which is also an external territory of Australia.[124] Here, Japanese vessels are permitted to kill protected whales in the Australian Whale Sanctuary without being patrolled, arrested, or even chased out on sighting. As a result of government inaction in relation to illegal Japanese whaling in Antarctica, a nongovernmental organisation, HSI, has used its own resources to bring proceedings against a Japanese whaling company in an attempt to restrain it from continuing to breach the provisions of the EPBC Act that protect whales in Australian waters.[125]

The ability of individuals and conservation groups to bring proceedings to enforce the provisions of the EPBC Act is a matter that the DEH also will consider in determining whether to initiate civil or criminal proceedings.[126] As noted earlier, the majority of civil actions under the EPBC Act have been instituted by individuals and conservation groups. This has been made possible by the broad-standing provisions in section 475 of the EPBC Act, which permits an "interested person"[127] to apply to the Federal Court for an injunction to restrain a breach of the Act.

4.2 Protection of Cetaceans: Law, Politics, and Enforcement – A Case Study of *Humane Society International Inc. v. Kyodo Senpaku Kaisha Ltd.*

Although Australia has a long history of whaling before the closure of the last whaling station in 1978, since the declaration of an international moratorium on commercial whaling under the Whaling Convention in 1982, Australia has been one of the most vocal antiwhaling nations at the IWC.

Australia's antiwhaling stance is reflected in its legislation. As outlined earlier, the EPBC Act contains a very comprehensive and powerful regime for the protection of whales and other cetaceans. However, the gap between the existence of these legislative provisions and the practice of the Australian government in enforcing its laws has recently been demonstrated in the case of *Humane Society International Inc. v. Kyodo Senpaku Kaisha Ltd.*[128] The case has been followed with interest by both academia and

[123] See AFMA media release 12 February 2004. Available at: http://www.afma.gov.au/news/media/2004/mr120204.php. See also *Olbers v. Commonwealth (No. 4)* (2004) 136 FCR 67.

[124] D. Leary, "The Interaction of Domestic and International Law and the Conservation and Sustainable Management of Marine Biodiversity in Australia. Two Case Studies in Conflict and Convergence." (2005). Copy provided by author.

[125] *Humane Society International Inc. v. Kyodo Senpaku Kaisha Ltd.* (2004) FCA 1510.

[126] Department of Environment and Heritage Web site. Available at http://www.deh.gov.au/about/compliance/index.html#responding.

[127] Environment Protection and Biodiversity Conservation Act, section 475(7). An "interested person" is defined as:

an organisation whose interests have been, are, or would be affected by the conduct or proposed conduct to which the injunction relates;

an organisation whose objects or purposes included the protection, or conservation of, or research into the environment during the two years immediately before the conduct; and

the organisation engaged in a series of activities related to the protection, or conservation of, or research into the environment.

[128] (2005) FCA 664; (2005) FCA 678; (2004) FCA 1510.

the popular media both because of the high-profile status of whales and the recent developments at the IWC and because the case gives rise to a number of interesting issues about the interaction of Australian and international law and the role of politics in law enforcement.

Although Australia has been quick to enforce the laws protecting cetaceans in the EEZ surrounding Australia's mainland, as was indicated in the prosecution of the two illegal Indonesian fisherman who killed dolphins in Australian waters, the same level of protection has not been afforded to cetaceans in Australian waters adjacent to Australia's external territories.

In October 2004, HSI, represented by the NSW Environmental Defender's Office, commenced proceedings in against Japanese whaling company, Kyodo Senpaku Kaisha Ltd (Kyodo), for breaching the provisions of the EPBC Act by illegally killing whales in waters adjacent to the Australian Antarctic Territory (AAT), which forms part of Australia's EEZ and the AWS.

Photographic evidence of whaling by Kyodo was collected by Greenpeace, which conducted an expedition to the Antarctic to photograph illegal whaling in Australian waters during 2001 to 2002.[129] Evidence as to the details of the location of the whaling and the numbers of whales caught by Kyodo in Australian waters was obtained from reports coauthored by Kyodo, the Institute for Cetacean Research based in Tokyo and the Obihiro University of Agriculture and Veterinary Medicine. Those reports were presented to the IWC.

The basis of HSI's claim is that between December 2000 and March 2004 Kyodo killed approximately 428 Antarctic minke whales within the AWS adjacent to the AAT. Kyodo did not hold a permit to kill whales under sections 231, 232 or 238 of the EPBC Act allowing it to kill whales in the AWS. Furthermore, Kyodo has indicated in its reports that it intends to continue to return to the AWS to kill whales.[130] HSI is seeking a declaration that the activities of Kyodo are in breach of sections 229–230 of the EPBC Act and an injunction under section 475 of the EPBC Act restraining Kyodo from further unlawful activities.

Although HSI objects to Japan's insistence on killing whales despite the moratorium and in spite of the creation of the Southern Ocean Sanctuary by the IWC in 1994, there is no claim made in the proceedings that Japan does not have authority under the Whaling Convention to issue itself with a permit to kill whales for what Japan claims to be scientific research. The permit that Japan issues to itself for the purpose of killing Antarctic minke whales in the Southern Ocean is known as the Japanese Whale Research Program under Special Permit in the Antarctic (JARPA). This permit is issued in purported compliance with Article VIII of the Whaling Convention that allows parties to conduct scientific research on whales; such research may involve the killing of whales. Japan has been issuing permits to itself under this provision since 1987. The whale meat is sold in Japan.

Kyodo is not a registered company in Australia and it does not have a registered company office in Australia. Accordingly, HSI is required pursuant to the Federal Court

[129] Refer to the Affidavit of Kieran Mulvaney sworn 9 November 2004. Available at http://www.hsi.org.au/news_library_events/Japanese_Whale_Case/Court_Documents.htm.

[130] Refer to the Affidavits of Nicola Beynon sworn 18 October 2004 and Kieran Mulvaney sworn 9 November 2004. Available at http://www.hsi.org.au/news_library_events/Japanese_Whale_Case/Court_Documents.htm.

Rules to seek leave to serve the proceedings on Kyodo in Japan.[131] In order to grant leave to HSI to serve the proceedings outside of Australia, the Court must be satisfied of the following matters:

1. that it has jurisdiction to hear the proceedings;
2. that the proceeding are founded on a breach of an Act committed in the Commonwealth;
3. that HSI has a *prima facie* case on findings of fact; and
4. that the Court is the appropriate forum in which to bring the proceedings.

Although the cause of action in the proceedings is based solely on a breach of the EPBC Act that was relatively straightforward to establish on the facts, a number of international legal issues are raised by the case by virtue of the fact that the EPBC Act implements a number of Australia's international obligations.

The creation of the AWS in the EPBC Act reflects Australia's rights and obligations under both UNCLOS and the Antarctic Treaty System, which includes the Antarctic Treaty 1959, the Convention on the Conservation of Antarctic Marine Living Resources 1982, and the Protocol on Environmental Protection to the Antarctic Treaty 1991 (Madrid Protocol). The claim of an EEZ on the waters adjacent to the AAT is based on Australia's claim to sovereignty in Antarctica pursuant to a transfer of title to the land from the United Kingdom.[132] Although Australian sovereignty over the AAT is only recognised by the United Kingdom, New Zealand, France, and Norway, Australia has established sovereignty over the AAT by virtue of Australia having effective occupation of the coastline surrounding its three permanent Antarctic bases, which are Mawson, Davis, and Casey. It is effective occupation, not sovereignty, which gives rise to the establishment of sovereignty at customary international law.[133] Australia has asserted its sovereign rights over the waters adjacent to its AAT by claiming an EEZ there under UNCLOS.

It is this sovereignty of the AAT that gives rise to the ability of the Australian government to declare a sanctuary for whales in the waters adjacent to the AAT and that allows the government to enforce its laws protecting whales. Specifically, Article 65 of UNCLOS allows States to regulate whaling within the EEZ. It was on the issue of the enforcement of the AWS in Australia's Antarctic EEZ that Justice Allsop of the Federal Court called for submissions from the Commonwealth Attorney-General.

In response to Justice Allsop's invitation, the Commonwealth Attorney-General made written submissions to the Court.[134] In those submissions, the Attorney-General conceded that HSI had established that Kyodo had breached the EPBC Act and acknowledged that the lack of recognition by Japan and other States of Australia's AAT does not preclude the application of the EPBC Act in the EEZ off the AAT. However, the Attorney-General refused to lend support to the leave application on the basis that the

[131] Federal Court Rules, Order 8, Rules 2(2).

[132] The Commonwealth declared the AAT to be a Territory under the authority of the Commonwealth on the commencement of the Australian Antarctic Territory Acceptance Act 1933 in 1936. The Australian Antarctic Territory Act 1954 provides for the government of the AAT.

[133] Professor Gillian Triggs, *International Law and Australian Sovereignty in Antarctica* (Sydney: Legal Books Pty. Ltd., 1986).

[134] *Humane Society International Inc. v. Kyodo Senpaku Kaisha Ltd.* (2005) FCA 664 Outline of Submissions of the Attorney-General of the Commonwealth as Amicus Curiae dated 25 January 2005. Available at http://www.hsi.org.au.

"Commonwealth Government considers that it is generally more appropriate to pursue diplomatic solutions in relation to activities by foreign vessels in the EEZ off the AAT."[135]

Annexed to the Attorney-General's submissions is an extract from instructions to Australian Antarctic Division Voyage Leaders. The instructions direct voyage leaders who sight vessels involved in whaling activities within the Australia's EEZ adjacent to the AAT to advise those vessels that they are within the AWS and to ask them to leave. The instructions state that in the event that Japanese whaling vessels are encountered in those waters, no enforcement action may be taken against them in the event that they refuse to leave. This is an explicit instruction made by an executive body to its employees to ignore a breach of an Australian law by a foreign national. This decision of the executive is directly contrary to section 5(4) of the EPBC Act, which provides that the Act applies to everyone in the Australian EEZ including persons who are not Australian citizens and vessels that are not Australian vessels.

In its reply to the submissions of the Attorney-General,[136] HSI refers to the 1992 House of Representatives Standing Committee on Legal and Constitutional Affairs report to Parliament on Australian law in Antarctica,[137] which stated that:

> 2.31 The Committee is of the view that there exists a strong misconception about the scope of Article 4(2) of the Antarctic Treaty and the degree to which it constrains Australia in applying Australian law to foreign nationals in the Australian Antarctic Territory. The Committee agrees . . . that Australia is not prevented by Article 8(1) or Article 4(2) of the Antarctic Treaty from applying Australian laws to foreign nationals in the Australian Antarctic Territory.
>
> 2.32 It is both in Australia's sovereign interests and consistent with Australia's obligations under the Antarctic Treaty to extend and apply Australian law to foreign nationals in the Australian Antarctic Territory who are not otherwise exempted by Article 8(1) of the Antarctic Treaty.[138]
>
> 2.33 This conclusion is consistent with the stated intention of the Australian Government at the time of implementing the Antarctic Treaty obligations in Australian legislation. In speaking on the second reading of the Antarctic Treaty Bill 1960 the Hon Fredrick Osborne, the then Minister for Air, stated:
>
>> In exercise of her sovereignty Australia has applied a complete code of law to the Australian Antarctic Territory. That law is, in our view, applicable to all persons in the Territory, and a breach of the criminal law, for example, would be punishable in an Australian court.[139]

Recommendation 1

> The Committee recommends that, as a matter of principle, Australian law be extended and applied to those foreign nationals in the Australian Antarctic Territory who are not otherwise exempt under Article 8(1) of the Antarctic Treaty.

[135] Ibid., paras. 20–21.

[136] *Humane Society International Inc. v. Kyodo Senpaku Kaisha Ltd.* (2005) FCA 664 Applicant's Reply to the Submissions of the Attorney-General and to the Court's Questions dated 10 February 2005. Available at http://www.hsi.org.au.

[137] House of Representatives Standing Committee on Legal and Constitutional Affairs, *Australian Law in Antarctica: The Report of the Second Phase of an Inquiry into the Legal Regimes of Australia's External Territories and the Jervis Bay Territory* (AGPS, Canberra, 1992), 15–18.

[138] Article 8(1) of the Antarctic Treaty provides for designated observers and scientific exchange personnel.

[139] House of Representative Debate, 28 September 1960, at 1432.

> 3.10 The Committee is greatly concerned at the practice of not applying to foreign nationals Commonwealth legislation expressly relating to the Australian Antarctic Territory, particularly in relation to legislation which implements Australia's international obligations in Antarctica. Not only is it in contravention of the express intentions of the Parliament but it, as least arguably, sits ill with Australian claims to sovereignty over the Territory...

HSI's submissions also noted that it was significant that the Parliament has provided standing to a class of persons including HSI in section 475 of the EPBC Act to seek an injunction to restrain a breach or other contravention of the Act, thereby bypassing the Attorney-General's traditional discretion to grant his fiat to support a relator action to enforce public laws.[140]

Justice Allsop found, in his interim judgment, that HSI had established a *prima facie* case for the relief sought in that the evidence disclosed a clear breach of the EPBC Act.[141] In his final decision on HSI's leave application, Justice Allsop was swayed by the submissions of the Attorney-General and His Honour declined to grant leave to HSI to serve the proceedings on Kyodo.[142] The basis for the decision was that the enforcement of the prohibition of whaling in the AWS established in the EPBC Act would be likely to give rise to an international disagreement between Australia and Japan. His Honour agreed with the view of the Attorney-General that:

> the attempt to enforce the EPBC Act may upset the diplomatic status quo under the Antarctic Treaty and be contrary to Australia's long term national interests, including its interests connected with its claim to territorial sovereignty to the Antarctic.[143]

Furthermore, His Honour also determined that the proceedings would be futile because the remedy of an injunction could not be enforced by HSI and, furthermore, "the making of a declaration alone a course suggested by the applicant) might be seen as tantamount to an empty assertion of domestic law (by the Court) devoid of utility beyond use (by others) as a political statement."[144]

The EDO lodged an appeal to the Full Federal Court on behalf of HSI on 17 June 2005. The grounds of the appeal include failure to consider the intention of the legislature that the EPBC Act be applied to foreign nationals and the consideration of irrelevant matters, including political and diplomatic issues. Although the Australian government is very vocal in support of a permanent ban on whaling, it refuses to enforce its own laws against foreign nationals in Australian waters in Antarctica, and it does not support the court action by HSI. Swayed by public pressure and a concerted media campaign following the announcement of Japan to overhaul JARPA by doubling the quota of Antarctic minke whales and to begin targeting Humpbacks and Fin whales,[145] both of which are listed as threatened species under the EPBC Act,[146] the Prime Minister Mr.

140 There is no doubt the Attorney-General and the Commonwealth Director of Public Prosecutions retain a discretion whether to prosecute any person for a breach of Commonwealth law that the courts will not normally question: *Hinchcliffe v. Commissioner of Police of the Australian Federal Police* (2001) 118 FCR 308 at [33]–[35] per J. Kenny.

141 (2005) FCA 664 at para 30.

142 (2005) FCA 664.

143 Ibid., para 27.

144 Ibid., para 34.

145 Plan for the Second Phase of the Japanese Whale Research Program under Special Permit in the Antarctic (JARPA II) – Monitoring of the Antarctic Ecosystem and Development of New Management Objectives for Whale Resources released at the 57th Meeting of the IWC during 20–24 June 2005.

146 See the Department of Environment and Heritage Web site. Available at http://www.deh.gov.au/biodiversity/threatened/species/index.html.

John Howard was moved to write a letter to the Japanese Prime Minister Junichiro Koizumi, asking Japan to stop killing whales in the name of science.[147] Mr. Koizumi ignored the letter and during the 2005/2006 whaling season Japan intended to kill 850 Antarctic minke whales as well as 50 Humpback and 50 Fin Whales. Most of this was expected to occur in protected Australian waters.

4.3 Southern Bluefin Tuna Case

HSI also has recently brought proceedings in the Administrative Appeals Tribunal (the Tribunal) in an attempt to protect Southern Bluefin Tuna (SBT) from continued over-exploitation by the Australian fishing industry.

The SBT is listed in Annex I of UNCLOS as a highly migratory species of pelagic fish. The species is found throughout the high seas of the Southern Hemisphere, as well as within the EEZ and territorial seas of Australia the South Pacific. As Sturtz notes, the fish is extremely valuable as a food source, especially in Japan, where it is coveted as a delicacy for sashimi.[148] The SBT is on the IUCN's Red List of Threatened Animals, and conservationists are urging its inclusion as an endangered species internationally under CITES and domestically under the EPBC Act. In July 2005, the Scientific Committee that advises the Federal Minister on applicability for listing of species under the EPBC Act indicated that SBT met the Act's criteria for listing as endangered. However, the Minister has not amended the list of threatened species to include SBT.

The international SBT fishery is managed by the Commission for the Conservation of Southern Bluefin Tuna (CCSBT). Allocations for member nations' SBT take have been set through the CCSBT. Australia's long-standing national allocation is 5,265 tonnes of a current total of 16,113 tonnes in national allocations for CCSBT members (i.e., 32 percent). These figures do not include catches outside the formal control of the Commission. Because of an impasse at the Commission over national allocations, Australia's national allocation has remained unchanged since 1989, over which time the status of the stock and prognosis for its recovery has, in HSI's opinion, worsened.

The proceedings brought by HSI challenge a decision made by the Minister on 10 November 2004 to declare the SBT fishery an approved wildlife trade operation (WTO) pursuant to section 303FN of the EPBC Act (the Decision). HSI considered the Decision to be contrary to Australia's domestic policy and legal obligations to ensure its fisheries are ecologically sustainable.

The Australian government acknowledged that "the stocks are seriously overfished and the stocks are unlikely to rebuild at current fishing levels."[149] Furthermore, the latest Australian Government Fishery Status Report summarises the status of SBT as follows: "Overfished, and overfishing is occurring; spawning stock severely depleted and current catches severely limit probability of rebuilding."[150] Recent assessments by

[147] On 24 May 2005.

[148] L Sturtz, *Southern Bluefin Tuna Case: Australia and New Zealand v. Japan* 28 *Ecology Law Quarterly* (2001) 455, at 460.

[149] Minister's *Statement of Reasons* for Decisions of 10 November 2004 (to declare the Southern Bluefin Tuna Fishery under section 303FN of the Act) and 26 November 2004 (to include Southern Bluefin Tuna on the List of Exempt Native Specimens under section 303DC of the Act) dated 11 February 2005.

[150] 2004 Fishery Status Report by the Australian Government Department of Agriculture, Fisheries, and Forestry, Bureau of Rural Sciences, at 85.

Australian scientists estimate the current parental SBT biomass to be between 4 and 19 percent of its unfished size.[151]

Notwithstanding this evidence, the Minister justified the Decision largely on the basis of the argument that the domestic management regime is effective in controlling, monitoring, and enforcing the level of take from the Australian fishery within the catch quota set by the CCSBT and that the recognised need to reduce catch is best addressed through the CCSBT. In his reasons for the Decision, the Minister stated that:

> "I was satisfied that the management of the stocks, including the rebuilding of the stocks to ecologically sustainable levels, through proactive engagement with the fishing nations taking SBT and within the framework of the CCSBT was most likely to provide for sustainability in the long term."

It is the Australian government's long-standing position that "Any unilateral reduction in take by Australian fishers is unlikely to provide any significant protection to the SBT stock or allow for rebuilding as other nations would almost certainly take up Australia's allocation."[152] The government argues that any unilateral action by Australia to reduce its SBT take would be ineffective in achieving the conservation of the stock because it would allow other nations (who, it is argued, use less sustainable fishing methods than Australia) to catch the fish Australia refrains from taking.

It is interesting to note that Australia and New Zealand have previously instituted arbitral proceedings against Japan in the International Tribunal for the Law of the Sea ("ITLOS") under Part XV of UNCLOS in relation to over fishing SBT in breach of their CCSBT quota on the basis that the overfishing posed serious harm to the environment.[153] In that case, ITLOS ultimately determined that it did not have jurisdiction to hear the case and, therefore, protective measures compelling Japan to act in accordance with the CCSBT could not be imposed. It is perhaps this experience that makes the Australian government wary of taking any action that may impact on the CCSBT regime.

HSI does not dispute the importance of Australia's involvement in the international negotiations regarding the management of SBT, which occur through the CCSBT. However, in the proceedings before the Tribunal challenging the Minister's Decision, it has argued that unilateral action by Australia – namely, a reduction in Australia's SBT catch – is both lawful and would significantly contribute to the conservation of

[151] *Strategic Assessment of the Southern Bluefin Tuna Fishery*, published by the Approval and Wildlife Division of the Australian Commonwealth Government's Department of Environment and Heritage in 2004, at 6.

[152] Department of Environment and Heritage, *Strategic Assessment of the Southern Bluefin Tuna Fishery*, 2004, at 11.

[153] See L. Sturt, note 147. Australia and New Zealand specifically alleged that Japan: (1) neglected to adopt necessary conservation measures to protect the southern bluefin tuna from its nationals fishing on the high seas; (2) carried on unilateral experimental fishing above its TAC; (3) took unilateral actions contrary to the rights of Australia and New Zealand; (4) failed to cooperate with Australia and New Zealand in an effort to protect the southern bluefin tuna; and (5) otherwise fell short of meeting its obligations under UNCLOS to conserve and manage the fish populations.

Pending the formation of the arbitral tribunal, the governments of Australia and New Zealand sought and obtained several provisional measures from ITLOS to protect their rights and the environment, including orders that Japan: (1) refrain from further experimental fishing; (2) negotiate and cooperate with Australia and New Zealand in an effort to agree to future conservation efforts; (3) ensure that its nationals do not take more than the total annual catch that Japan is allotted; and (4) restrict its total southern bluefin tuna catch to its national allocation as last agreed. Unfortunately, when the dispute reach final hearing, ITLOS determined that the dispute resolution procedures under the CCSBT were exhaustive and therefore ITLOS did not have jurisdiction to hear the dispute under Part XV of UNCLOS.

SBT. HSI argued that as a matter of international law it is open to Australia to reduce the amount of SBT it takes and to deny other SBT fishing nations the right to take the remainder of Australia's quota by asserting a claim over the remainder of its allocation for stock conservation purposes.

In addition, HSI asserts the Minister's decision to declare the SBT fishery a WTO was not the correct or preferable decision, principally because the Minister erred in being satisfied that Australia's commercial SBT fishery operation will not be detrimental to the survival and conservation status of the SBT stock, and that the operation is consistent with the objectives of sustainable fisheries management.

This case was heard by Tribunal in late September 2005, during which time the Tribunal heard expert evidence from the leading SBT fisheries scientists that addressed the conservation status of the species, the international and domestic management regimes for the SBT fishery and the likely impacts of the WTO declaration on the species. As a result of the hearing taking place immediately before the twelfth meeting of the CCSBT, final submissions were adjourned pending the outcomes and recommendations of the CCSBT meeting. Those submissions will be presented in early November 2005. In reviewing the Minister's decision, the Tribunal stands in the shoes of the Minister and can make its own decision about whether the SBT fishery should be excluded from the need for further environmental impact assessment before trade in that species takes place.

Similar to the whaling case, HSI's challenge to the approval of the SBT fishery as a WTO raises interesting issues about the political will of the Federal government to take bold steps to protect marine species that are subject to international management regimes. In the SBT case, the government's basis for refusing to take domestic action to reduce the Australian catch is based on an argument that it is uncertain whether unilateral action by Australia would make a positive contribution to stock recovery. However, HSI considers the Government's argument that it should not take unilateral action and reduce Australia's SBT catch to be seriously flawed. This argument demonstrates a lack of political will to take strong action to conserve a species under threat.

The Tribunal delivered its decision on 3 April 2006. The Tribunal found that the approval of the SBT fishery as a WTO would not be detrimental to the survival and conservation of the species and upheld the Minister's decision. This was an extremely disappointing outcome to the proceedings. With all due respect, the Tribunal struggled to deal with the complexities of the scientific evidence stating:

> it is obvious that the Minister . . . and on review, the Tribunal, are required to embark on a decision making process in a field of endeavour which is highly specialized and equally highly uncertain."[154]

As a result of this, the Tribunal relied largely on the strategic assessment report prepared by AFMA in 2002 and revised in 2004. Having regard to the considerable body of more recent scientific evidence provided by the Scientific Committee of the CCSBT and others, the reliance placed on this report was, in HSI's opinion unsatisfactory.

5 CONCLUSION

Australia has adopted one of the most progressive approaches to integrated marine resource conservation and management through its Oceans Policy and the EPBC Act.

[154] (2006) AATA 298, at para 59.

However, although there are sound legal protections for marine species, the application of relevant laws has been limited. Clearly, there are difficulties in policing activities in Australia's vast marine territory. However, where evidence of breaches is readily available, such as in the example of Japanese whaling in Antarctic waters, the failure of the federal government to take legal action is disappointing. The intervention by the Attorney-General in the *HSI v. Kyodo* case is demonstrative of the political complexity of enforcing marine laws in external territories and the EEZ foreshadows the possibility that marine species in those areas may be afforded lesser protection that species in Australian coastal waters. This approach, the authors submit, is not consistent with the provisions and intent of the EPBC Act.

The federal government's approach to the management of the SBT fishery is also, in the authors' opinion, at odds with the intent of the EPBC Act. In that case, again, it appears that the political ramifications of managing the fishery in a manner that involves the reduction of take allocation under the CCSBT have outweighed the requirement for the Minister to be satisfied that the accreditation of the fishery as a WTO is ecologically sustainable.

Marine management is one of the few areas where international and domestic laws intersect. The Australian government takes the view, as demonstrated by the cases discussed in this chapter, that it is in the best interest of marine biodiversity conservation as a whole for disputes relating to species management to be solved diplomatically through fora such as the IWC and the Secretariat of the CCSBT. However, in circumstances in which strong laws with express application to foreign nationals have been promulgated, the failure to rely on those laws sends a message that Australia lacks the political will to address some of the most pressing threats to that environment.

16 Legal Stewardship of Mountain Regions: The Emerging Ecoregime

Nicholas A. Robinson*

Until the end of the twentieth century, mountain areas were primarily the province of national law. An international law of mountains emerged with the negotiation of the Alpine Convention and the Carpathian Convention in Europe and with the developments of the Andean Pact in South America. There were occasional bilateral agreements on mountain issues, such as the early "peace park" combining the Glacier National Park (USA) and Waterton Lakes National Park (Canada) in the upper Rocky Mountains. However, unlike the international agreements that nations developed for international rivers over the past three centuries, mountains did not seem to need treaties. Montane regions were not used in transfrontier commerce or for their water supplies, and thus the law governing human activity in the mountains remained a legal concern only for each nation wherein mountains were found. Until recently, States chose not to consider regional stewardship of mountainous areas that transverse either over more than one State or more than one political subdivision within a State.

Within nations, important steps were taken to develop environmentally sound management systems for mountains, as, for instance, the experiences with New York's Adirondack Mountains illustrate.[1] Mountains were far away from large human settlements, and many nations found it easier to set aside development in mountains, in preference to other uses. A German Länder, such as Bavaria or individual Swiss cantons, had its own rules for human activities in the mountains, and customary rules for natural resource use exist on the volcanic mountains of islands such as Bali, or in the High Himalayan ranges. Some nations took affirmative measures to manage their mountains; for instance, Costa Rica set aside its volcanic mountains as parks and as watershed catchments to supply San Jose, the nation's capitol, with ample pure drinking water.[2] In large part because of their beauty or recreational potential, many nations have established mountain parks, such as Sagamartha (containing Mount Everest) in Nepal, or Mount Kilamajaro in Kenya, or South Africa's Drakenburgs in Kwazi-Natal, or Argentina's Patagonian parks, or Banff and Jasper in the Canadian Rockies and other

[1] For a history of the measures adopted to manage the Adirondack Mountain region in New York, see Frank Graham, Jr., *The Adirondack Park: A Political History* (New York, Knopf, 1978), and the discussion in this chapter, *infra.*

[2] Costa Rica has preserved its volcanic mountains in parks and in protected watershed areas to ensure a pure water supply for its capital city. See the description of legislation in Grethel Aguilar and Alejandro Iza, *Manual de Derecho Ambiental en CentroAmérica* (IUCN 2005).

* Nicholas A. Robinson is Gilbert and Sarah Kerlin Distinguished Professor of Environmental Law, Pace University School of Law, USA.

mountains in various Canadian provinces, or the parks and national forests of the White Mountains in Vermont or Grand Tetons in Wyoming.

Some mountain parks are patchworks of federal, state, and local management regimes; for example, Yosemite, Kings Canyon, and Sequoia national parks in the Sierra Nevada Mountains,[3] with the adjacent California state ecological zones[4] and other adjacent federal National Forest lands.[5] The Sierra Nevada mountains have a sort of loosely coordinated, mixed federal/state management system. The first national park, Yellowstone, was once considered a vast scientific reserve and recreational "pleasuring" ground.[6] Since the 1980s, as development has encroached on Yellowstone, many espouse the concept of a "Greater Yellowstone,"[7] in which the management of buffer areas can be integrated with areas within that national park. The worldwide pattern of establishing parks in mountains rarely addressed how the preserved lands would relate to adjacent development lands or to the livelihoods of the people living in the area. It became evident in every region of the Earth that more would be needed than setting aside parklands if mountain ecology was to be sustained.

In the twenty-first century, mountains have become a common concern. There are sound reasons for this. Mountainous regions cover 26 percent of the Earth and are home today to 12 percent of the human population. About seven hundred million people live in mountains, and many more people outside of the mountains depend on them in some way.[8] With the increase in the number of human beings on Earth has come growth in the size of settlements in some mountain areas, with attendant increases in human impacts.[9] Human developments impact on flora and fauna, including species that are threatened or endangered with extinction, as their habitat is lost and their numbers

[3] These National Parks are in turn surrounded by National Forests, where the National Forest Service regulates natural resources use, and by local authorities operating under California's environmental controls, such as its environmental impact assessment laws, California Environmental Review Act, Public Resources Code.

[4] California as a state has established a special category of Protected Areas for "Ecological Reserves," See Calif. Fish and Game Code, Sections 1580, et seq., The state can acquire lands to include in such Reserves, see Calif Admin. Code Sections 630 et seq. These are discussed in N.A. Robinson, "Critical Area Controls," in *Environmental Regulation of Real Property* (Law Journal Press, NY, 1982).

[5] The National Forests around Yosemite include Stanislaus National Forest and Sierra National Forest, both of which are larger then the National Park and are managed for multiple uses and sustained yield.

[6] For a history of Yellowstone Park, see A. Haines, *The Yellowstone Story: A History of Our First National Park* (1977). Yellowstone National Park was established by an Act of Congress in 1872; in 1891, the first National Forest Reserve in the United States was established adjacent to Yellowstone National Park. Establishing Yellowstone park status by an act of Congress, set the legislative precedent for all later parks (see, e.g. Canyon Lands National Park, 16 U.S.C. 271. Congress enacted an Organic Act for the National Park Service separately, 16 U.S.C. Section 1.

[7] On the proposals to regulate the lands around the Yellowstone Park, as the "Greater Yellowstone," see Robert R. Keiter and Mark S. Boyce, Eds., *The Greater Yellowstone Ecosystems: Redefining America Wilderness Heritage* (Yale University Press, 1991). See also Robert B. Keiter, "On Protecting National Parks from the External Threats Dilemma," 20 *Land & Water Law Review* 355 (1985).

[8] For instance, the Preamble to the Alpine Convention in Europe states: "recognizing that the Alps constitute the living and economic environment for the indigenous population and are also vitally important for extra-Alpine regions, being the site of important transport routes . . . " See "Convention on the Protection of the Alps (Alpine Convention), done in Salzburg, 7 November 1991, in the *Official Journal of the European Communities.* Austria acts as depository, and the official languages are German, French, Italian, and Slovene. English translation available from the International Commission for the Protection of the Alps (CIPRA), Bretscha 22, 9494, Schaan, Liechtenstein [hereinafter "Alpine Convention"].

[9] For instance, the Alpine Convention in Europe provides in its Preamble, "Aware that the ever-growing pressures caused by man are increasingly threatening the Alpine region and its ecological functions, and that the damage is either irreparable or rectifiable only with great effort, at considerable costs and, as a rule, over a long period of time."

dwindle.[10] Climate change has resulted in the melting of glaciers in mountains all over the world and has caused changes in precipitation resulting in mountain floods or droughts, both of which have consequences of human settlements and biodiversity alike. Climate change also shifts the conditions in which ecological communities can thrive at different mountain altitudes. No single nation can ensure that it can manage its own parts of a mountain region well, when other parts are not managed well.[11] The United Nations Conference on Environment and Development (UNCED) in Rio de Janeiro in 1992 adopted a chapter within its action plan "Agenda 21," which sets forth recommendations for "Managing Fragile Ecosystems: Sustainable Mountain Development."[12]

Ten years later, to follow up on these recommendations from the Rio "Earth Summit," nations with significant mountain geography met to share their concerns about the management of human activities in mountains at the Bishkek Global Mountain Summit in 2002, which was the final global event of the International Year of the Mountains ("IYM"). The UN Food and Agricultural Organization (FAO) had been invited by the United Nations General Assembly in 1998 to be the lead international agency in coordinating with national governments to promote "the conservation and sustainable development of mountain regions, thereby ensuring the well-being of mountain and lowland communities."[13] The Bishkek Global Mountain Summit produced recommendations for States to consider in establishing or enhancing their mountain management systems.[14]

Before evaluating how environmental law may best advance the consensus recommendations from the UN International Year of the Mountains (IYM) in 2002, it is useful to examine current State practice on the law of mountain management, with particular reference to biodiversity conservation. A review of the law of mountains enables us to estimate which IYM recommendations have a realistic possibility of finding implementation in law. This chapter examines one of the oldest and most comprehensive systems of mountain stewardship, that of the Adirondack Mountains in the State of New York (USA). It then surveys the systems elaborated in Europe for the Alps and for the Carpathian Mountains. A comparison is made to very different approach taken by the Andean Pact (South America). This chapter suggests that diverse State practice has produced some effective "best management practices," which together with the general principles of international environmental law ought to constitute the core of an international law for mountain stewardship. It is by building on this core of existing practice that the IYM recommendations can best be realized.

[10] The Preamble to the Alpine Convention notes: "recognizing the fact that the Alps constitute an essential habitat and last refuge for many endangered species of plants and animals."

[11] For instance, the Preamble to the Carpathian Convention states: "Being aware of the fact that efforts to protect, maintain, and sustainably manage the natural resources of the Carpathians cannot be achieved by one country alone and require regional cooperation, and the added value of transboundary cooperation in achieving ecological coherence." The "Convention on the Protection and Sustainable Development of the Carpathians," UN Economic Commission for Europe (ECE), the depository is the Ukraine, and the Parties are The Czech Republic, Hungary, Poland, Romania, Serbia and Montenegro, the Slovak Republic, and Ukraine. The English text is available from the UN ECE, www.unece.org

[12] Chapter 13, Agenda 21. See the annotated version in Nicholas A. Robinson, *Agenda 21: Earth's Action Plan* (Oceana Publications, 1993), "Managing Fragile Ecosystems: Sustainable Mountain Development," which stressed (1) generating and strengthening knowledge about the ecology and sustainable development of mountain ecosystems, and (2) promoting integrated watershed development and alternative livelihood opportunities in mountain areas.

[13] UNGA Res. A/RES/53/24 (10 November 1998).

[14] See http://mountains.unep.ch/mtn/home_page.html.

1 THE ADIRONDACKS

When economic development came to the Adirondacks in the late nineteenth century, the politics and commerce of New York were not unlike the conditions of many developing regions around the world today. Developers wanted to exploit natural resources quickly and make a handsome profit. Unsustainable practices were common. Government supervision was weak, and not infrequently corrupt. Civil society was weak, and nongovernmental organizations (NGOs) were inattentive or not yet organized. There was no technical assistance available; in the last quarter of the nineteenth century, there were no international agencies, such as UN FAO or the UN's Development or Environment Programmes, or the UN Educational, Scientific, and Cultural Organization (UNESCO). The concepts derived from scientific forestry or conservation remained to be discovered, and no federal or international financial help was available to the State of New York to shape a sustainable use of the Adirondack Mountains.[15]

Because many of Earth's mountain regions exist within a single nation, and most are located in developing regions where little international aid is provided for building sustainable mountain practices, New York State's historic experience with the Adirondack Mountains can provide insights regarding legal regimes for stewardship of mountain areas. The Adirondack Mountains have been designated as a Park, although only one-half of the "Park" is protected public lands, and the other half is managed for human use and livelihoods. The State of New York holds a portion of the Park, known as the Forest Preserve as public lands. The entire Park is today larger in size than the entire state of New Jersey.

The Adirondack Park is one of the world's most important biological reserves. Its mountains were formed eleven hundred million years ago, and Mount Marcy, now 5,344 feet above sea level, is thought to have once soared as high as 20,000 feet. Writers,[16] artists,[17] and photographers[18] have celebrated the beauty of the Adirondacks. The Adirondacks' wild forests, 250,000 acres of lakes and ponds, and thousands of miles of flowing streams and rivers remain in their natural setting today because the public cares enough to fight to safeguard New York's Forest Preserve as "forever wild forest land."

The mandate to protect the lands in the Forest Preserve as "forever wild forest" appears in Article XIV of the Constitution of the State of New York.[19] These words were

[15] Conservation law was in its infancy. The federal government in Washington, DC had no role in considering this vast region because it was wholly within the State of New York itself. See Article XIV of the N.Y.S. Constitution and the NYS Environmental Conservation Law, Article 9 ("Lands and Forests" and the NYS Executive Law Section 5800 (Adirondack Park Agency, governing non-State lands in the Forest Preserve of the Adirondack Mountains).

[16] In 1858, Ralph Waldo Emerson and others visited the Adirondacks, celebrating his visit o Follansbee Water and the Lake of Loons," in his poem, *Adirondack Journal* (Houghton Mifflin Co., N.Y.) See also the description of the Philosopher Camp in Alfred L. Donaldson, ***A History of the Adirondacks,*** vol. I, chapter XVI, p. 172 (The Century Company, New York 1921). Beyond Emerson, many writers, such as John Burroughs in the 19th century and the contemporary naturalist writer, Bill McKibben, have celebrated the Adirondacks.

[17] Articles such as Thomas Cole, Asher B. Durand, John Frederick Kensett, Winslow Homer and Harold Weston. See Patricia L.F. Mandel, *Fair Wilderness* (Adirondack Museum, 1990), and Rebecca Foster and Caroline M. Welsh, *Wild Exuberance: Harold Weston Adirondack Art* (Syracuse University Press, 2005).

[18] Photography has become an important method of artistic interpretation of the Adirondacks, see for example, the collections of photographs in Nathan Farb, *100 Views of the Adirondacks* (Rizzoli, 1989); Elliott Porter, *Forever Wild: The Adirondacks* (Harper & Rowe, 1970); or Carl Heilman II, *Adirondacks: Views of an American Wilderness* (Rizzoli, 1999).

[19] The people of the State of New York had convened a constitutional convention to rewrite the state's constitution in 1984, and they added the "forever wild" provision to the constitution then. It has withstood

added in a Constitutional Convention, approved by the people of the state in 1894,[20] and reaffirmed against efforts to repeal them in the New York State (NYS) Constitutional Conventions of 1915,[21] 1938,[22] and 1967.[23] The respect for nature in the Forest Preserve runs deep among New Yorkers, and when such values are embodied in the statutes and Constitution of the state, they become and are among the strongest public rights. Even today, newcomers or persons interested in making a "quick buck" may be unaware of how deeply the NYS public shares these values.

The great civil liberties lawyer Louis Marshall (1856–1929), who argued more cases in the U.S. Supreme Court than anyone but the U.S. Solicitor General and who also was a Trustee of the Association for the Preservation of the Adirondacks, helped draft the "forever wild" clause for the New York Constitution in 1894.[24] Marshall fought to secure observance of the public's right to the Forest Preserve for the next thirty years. He said at one point, "Blister rust, cankers and insects are infinitely less dangerous than *homo sapiens*, who, whether he takes the form of a lumberman, or a tax title exploiter, a vandal or a commercial hotel keeper, is the real enemy of the forest."[25]

Marshall knew whereof he spoke. No sooner had New Yorkers discovered the wild bounty of the Adirondacks in the mid-1800s when a titanic struggle emerged for dominion over the region. The Adirondacks were divided into separate townships, each one with responsible local authority for that subpart of the Adirondack region. Into these different townships came sportsmen, naturalists, and vacationers to enjoy the beauty of the Adirondacks. The Revd. William H. H. Murray's book, *Adventures in the Wilderness: Or Camplife in the Adirondacks* (1869), recommended the great hunting and camping, and enthused that "the wilderness provides that perfect relaxation which all jaded minds require."[26] Ralph Waldo Emerson crossed Massachusetts to camp in Adirondacks; writing in his *Adirondack, A Journal* (1858), he rhapsodized, "As water poured through hollows of the hills to feed this wealth of lakes and rivulets, so nature shed all beauty lavishly from her redundant horn."[27] The naturalist John Burroughs went camping in the Adirondacks with Henry Ford, Thomas Edison, and Henry Firestone. Eventually, great "Camps" were built there for the Vanderbilts and Mellons, and modest fishing camps for the likes of the renowned artist Winslow Homer, as well as for many others less well known. Louis Marshall brought his family there each summer, as did hundreds of other New York families. At the same time, lumbermen came to the Adirondacks, felling vast numbers of trees and clear cutting the forest. Over two hundred iron mines also operated there. The Revd. Murray could still observe, in 1877, that "in such a place

several attempts at repeal in 1915, and currently appears at Article XIV of the N.Y.S. Constitution: "The Lands of the state, now owned or hereafter acquired, constituting the forest preserve . . . shall be forever kept as wild forest lands. They shall not be leased, sold, or exchanged, or be taken by any corporation, public or private, nor shall the timber thereon be sold, removed or destroyed."

[20] The constitution was adopted by referendum in 1895, See Frank Graham, Jr., *The Adirondack Park: A Political History* (NY Knopf, 1978), at p. 167.

[21] See Howard Zahniser, "Where Wilderness Preservation Began," in Ed. Zahnizer, *Where Wilderness Preservation Began* (Utica, North Country Books, 1992) at p. 72.

[22] See Frank Graham, Jr., *The Adirondack Park: A Political History*, at p. 211. While a proposed 1967 Constitution had preserved the text, the voters rejected the new constitution in a referendum, leaving intact the 1894 language.

[23] The Constitutional Convention in 1967 kept the "forever wild" provisions in tact, but the voters rejected the entire proposed constitution, leaving the "forever wild" language of 1894 in effect.

[24] See Charles Reznikoff, ed., *Louis Marshall: The Champion of Liberty.*

[25] *Ibidum.*

[26] See the discussion of Murray in Frank Graham, *The Adirondack Park: A Political History, op. cit.*

[27] Emerson, *Adirondacks: A Journal*, supra note 16.

the sense of time passes from you and the sense of eternity is experienced" (*Adirondack Tales*, "The Story Keg Told Me"),[28] but many saw that the exploitative despoliation of the Adirondacks was incompatible with the less intrusive enjoyment of nature there. The horn of nature seen by Emerson did not flow so inexhaustively as he had supposed that it would.

Marshall, and many others like him, had seen the need to instill some sort of effective ethic for land stewardship. With mountain slopes denuded, the spring melt of snow caused great erosion and flooding, as the roots no longer held the land and absorbed the waters. Railways built into the mountains used wood for their steam engines and their sparks ignited vast forest fires. Flood waters in the Hudson River, whose headwaters are in the Adirondacks, inundated downtown Albany, the state capitol. Worse, the steady flow of water appeared inadequate to supply the flow needed in the Erie Canal. Commercial interests outside of the Adirondacks relied on the Erie Canal to transport their goods. The Chamber of Commerce of New York City, the New York Board of Trade and Transport, and others opposed the economic exploiters of the Adirondack's wood and metals.[29]

In 1872, the same year that Yellowstone was established as the world's first national park (where permanent human occupation and resource development would be banned),[30] New York's legislature received the report of a Parks Commission it had established.[31] The report did not favor closing off the Adirondacks entirely, as had just been done with Yellowstone (the U.S. Army had been sent to take possession of the national park area). "We do not favor the creation of an expansive and exclusive parks for mere purpose of recreation, but, condemning such suggestions, recommend the simple preservation of timer as a means of political economy.... Without a steady, constant, supply of water from these streams of the wilderness, our canals would be dry."[32] Grain and western goods could not find cheap transport to markets of the Hudson Valley and New York City, and the manufactured and imported goods from New York City would be cut from their markets to the west. In 1883, the *New York Tribune* editorialized that to allow further clear cutting of timber would be "tampering with the goose that lays the golden egg."[33]

Attentive New Yorkers knew that the Adirondacks was the watershed for the great Hudson and beyond. In 1884, Harvard Professor Charles Sprague Sargent was commissioned to prepare a report on just how endangered the Adirondacks had become.[34] His report criticized the lumber industry, the railroads, and others who mismanaged the natural resources of the region. His report provided the scientific and empirical foundation for setting aside the region. Despoiled areas needed a period of rest, to let nature recover; no new despoliation could be tolerated.

In 1892, the NYS Legislature enacted Laws 1892, Chapter 707, to establish the "Adirondack Park," as "ground open for the free use of all the people for their health and pleasure, and as forestland necessary to the preservation of the headwaters of the chief rivers of the States and as a future supply of timber."[35] Unfortunately, enactment

[28] Frank Graham, *The Adirondack Park: A Political History, op. cit.*

[29] Id., and Alfred L. Donaldson, *A History of the Adirondacks*, (NY The Century Association, 1920).

[30] For a history of Yellowstone National Park, see A. Haines, *The Yellowstone Story: A History of Our First National Park* (1977).

[31] See Frank Graham, *The Adirondack Park: A Political History, op cit.*

[32] *Ibidum.*

[33] *Ibidum.*

[34] *Ibidum*, at pp. 104–5. Alfred L. Donaldson, *A History of the Adirondacks, op. cit.*, vol. II, p. 188.

[35] See Frank Graham, *The Adirondack Park: A Political History, op. cit.*

of a law did not deter those who could continue to exploit the land. New York's Forest Commission lacked the enforcement capacity to ensure observance of the new law. As evidence of graft and corruption and disregard for the law emerged, the public was outraged. One of New York's periodic constitutional conventions was being prepared, and the advocates for protecting the Adirondacks lakes and forests rallied.[36]

The 1892 law was added to the text of the 1894 Constitution, as Article XIV.[37] Everyone knew, by this time, that it would not be enough to have the law, or even a fundamental constitutional right. Constant vigilance was needed to see that the Constitution's "forever wild" clause was understood and observed. The next two decades saw more floods and forest fires and illegal timber rustling; in 1903 alone, fires burned 940 square miles of Adirondack forest. Louis Marshall observed that the destroyer of the forests "was as great an enemy of the public as one guilty of treason."[38]

On 12 December 1901, civic leaders decided to organize to see that the NYS Constitution was observed. Judge Warrant Higley presided over the first meeting of the Association for the Protection of the Adirondacks.[39] Lt. Gov. Timothy Woodruff addressed the gathering, and later became a Trustee of the Association.

Year in, year out, for the next century and through the present day, the Association has struggled to ensure that Article XIV is observed. Volunteers lead the way. It was only in 1987 that the Association could afford to hire its first full-time staff. The extraordinarily talented David Gibson, a graduate of Yale's School of Forestry and Environmental Studies, was hired.[40]

The Association knew full well that neither a statute, nor a constitutional provision, is truly in place until New York's highest court interprets it. The test came when promoters of the 1938 Winter Olympics wanted to construct a bobsled run in the Forest Preserve near Lake Placid. Over two thousand trees would have had to be cut down. There was non–forest preserve land in the town available, but the decision was made to encroach on the preserve. With the powerful sponsors of the Olympic Games, and local commercial interests campaigning for the bobsled run, the defenders of trees appeared. The Association sued the New York State Conservation Commission, Alexander MacDonald, for violating the "Forever Wild" clause of the NYS Constitution that he had sworn to uphold.

In *MacDonald v. Association* (1930),[41] the Association won its definitive interpretation of Article XIV from the courts. Justice Harold Hinman, in the ruling for the Appellate Division of the State Supreme Court, interpreted the "forever wild" clause with the following words:

> Giving the phrase 'forever kept as wild forest land' the significance which the term 'wild forest' bears, we must conclude that the idea intended was a health resort and

[36] *Ibidum.*

[37] See Alfred L. Donaldson, *A History of the Adirondacks, op. cit.*

[38] This attitude was not uncommon among early conservationists. In his "White House Address to the Governors" in 1908, President Theodore Roosevelt referred to conservation as the equivalent of defending the nation against foreign attack. Those who wanted unbridled exploitation of forests belittled Louis Marshall and others as "the forestry bigots." See Alfred L. Donaldson, *A History of the Adirondacks*, vol. II, at p. 188.

[39] The Association for the Protection of the Adirondacks (AfPA) is located in Niskayuna, New York. See http://www.protectadks.org.

[40] See the Annual Reports of the Association for the Protection of the Adirondacks, on line at www.protectadks.org. The Association's archives are available at the Library of the Adirondacks.

[41] Association for the Protection of the Adirondacks v. MacDonald, 278 App. Div. 73 (1929).

> playground with the attributes of a wild forest park as distinguished from other parks so common in our civilization. We must preserve it in its wild state, its trees, its rocks, its streams. It was to be a great resort for the free use of the people, in which nature is given free rein. Its uses for health and pleasure must not be inconsistent with its preservation as forestlands in a wild state. It must always retain the character of wilderness. Hunting, fishing, tramping, mountain climbing, snow shoeing, skiing, or skating find ideal setting in nature's wilderness. It is essentially a quiet and healthful retreat from the turmoils and artificialities of a busy urban life.

Justice Hinman further noted that:

> Sports that require settings which are man-made and unmistakably inconsistent with the preservation of these forest lands in the wild and natural state in which Providence has developed them.... There will be no limits to such encroachments... if such precedent is established.[42]

When the Conservation Department appealed this ruling to the Court of Appeals, Commissioner MacDonald fared no better. In March 1930, Judge Frederick C. Crain wrote for the Court of Appeals,[43] upholding the Appellate Division's ruling. In the words of the Court of Appeals: "This plea on behalf of a sport is a plea for an open door through which abuses as well as benefits may pass. The Constitution intends to take no more chances with abuses, and therefore the door must be kept shut. The timer... can not be cut and removed... simply for the reason that Section 7, Article XIV of the Constitution says it cannot be done."[44]

But the judicial victory favoring a "forever wild" Adirondacks does not mean that the story is over. Repeatedly, countervailing interests have sought to encroach on the Forest Preserve. Robert Moses, as head of the New York State Council of Parks, disliked the *MacDonald* rulings and repeatedly tried to get Article XIV repealed; he favored new development for sports and access through building new roads. Others encroached on the Park illegally.[45] In the 1950s and 1960s, the City of New York for years tried to have dams build in Adirondack Valleys, to ensure a supply of fresh water for the City.[46] In the 1960s and 1970s, excessive second home development on the nonstate lands in hamlets throughout the Adirondack Park threatened to harm the "forever wild" state lands. To counter this, Governor Nelson Rockefeller supported a state commission to examine how to ensure that recreational second home development proceeded on a sustainable manner, respecting the Article XIV lands, and avoiding an urban sprawl into the mountains.[47] On recommendation of the Commission, and with the governor's support, New York's Legislature established the Adirondack Park Agency (APA), to establish regionwide land-use standards and norms for the privately held lands, and to administer these land-use controls until local authorities themselves had developed their capacity to do so directly.[48] This state imposition on "home rule" prerogatives

[42] *Ibidum.*
[43] *Association for the Protection of the Adirondacks v. MacDonald*, 253 N.Y. 234, 170 N.E. 902 (1930).
[44] 253 N.Y. 234 at 240–41.
[45] See, e.g. *Helms v. Diamond*, 76 Misc. 2d 253, 349 N.Y.S. 2d 917 (1973). See the discussion in Barbara McMartin, *Perspectives on the Adirondacks: A Thirty-Year Struggle by People Protecting Their Treasure* (Syracuse, Syracuse University Press, 2002).
[46] See E. Zahniser, Where *Wilderness Preservation Began* (Utica, N.Y., North Country Books, 1992).
[47] N.Y.S. Temporary State Commission on the Future of the Adirondacks, *The Future of the Adirondack Park* (1970), and the Technical Reports, 2 volumes.
[48] See N.Y.S. Executive Law, Article 27, vol. 18 McKinney Consolidated Laws of N.Y.

of local government engendered some opposition to the APA but not to the Forest Preserve. Eventually, the regional land-use planning systems of the APA have taken hold, and local governments increasingly have assumed responsibility for managing their development in ways compatible with the wilderness character of the Adirondack Mountains region. Indeed, as the APA developed land-use methodology to provide sound planning of private and nonstate lands, its example of sound planning also had the effect of persuading the New York State Department of Environmental Conservation (DEC) to begin its "unit management plans" for each part of the Forest Preserve under its jurisdiction.[49] Unit management plans divide the wild forest, lake, and mountain areas according to their biological characteristics, and specific rules for recreational uses, access, and scientific management are established for each specified area.

There are additional statutes that complement and reenforce this system of planning regulations of the APA for private and municipal lands, and the state DEC's rules for the Forest Preserve under the Unit Management Plans. For instance, New York's legislature also passed a Wild and Scenic Rivers law,[50] to safeguard the free-flowing wild rivers of the Adirondacks in their natural state. These rivers weave in and out of the Forest Preserve and now enjoy common stewardship rules along their banks. This law covers riverbanks, whether owned by public or private entities, and prohibits development there.

A statute of wider application, binding both the APA and the DEC as well as all other governmental entities in New York is the State Environmental Quality Review Act (SEQRA).[51] SEQRA requires the preparation of written environmental impact assessments for all actions by any government authority. These include both public and private actions. SEQRA requires the identification of all impacts and the avoidance or mitigation of adverse effects. SEQRA regulations[52] are detailed in requiring public participation, comment by all interested individuals and agencies, and full disclosure. The EIA statute in New York is strong. SEQRA applies, for instance, to the state Department of Transportation (DOT) with respect to actions affecting state roads throughout the Adirondacks. DOT has special regulations for roads in the region, designed to complement the primitive character of the Adirondacks. SEQRA review is needed to assess the aesthetic impact on wild forestlands of proposed installation of cellular communications towers or wind-to-energy turbines.

One of the weaknesses in the SEQRA process is that it is employed in reaction to proposed actions of agencies and is not used in a holistic fashion to guide future actions and remediate past decisions that cumulative can adversely affect the Adirondacks. For instance, neither APA nor DEC use SEQRA to develop systems that could fully protect migratory species across public and private lands. SEQRA provides a mandate for more affirmative action to protect the Adirondacks than is presently recognized; a part of this shortcoming is the lack of sustained funding for local and state agencies, which have neither the personnel nor other resources to use SEQRA in this way. Private developers,

[49] For a critique of the unit management plan process, see Barbara McMartin, *Perspectives on the Adirondacks: A Thirty-Year Struggle by People Protecting Their Treasure* (Syracuse, Syracuse University Press, 2002), chapter 18, case study 6, pp. 264–276.

[50] Wild & Scenic Rivers were regulated by statutes, 1973 N.Y. Laws, Chapter 400.

[51] Article 8, N.Y.S. Environmental Conservation Law, volume 17½ McKinney's Consolidated Laws of N. Y.

[52] 6 NYCRR Part 620.

and some local governments, do not wish to have their discretion affected by SEQRA's requirements.

As a result of repeated enactments of laws and their implementation through regulations, for over a century and a half the citizens of New York, with their legislators and courts and executive branch authorities, have forged a fairly comprehensive stewardship system for the Adirondacks. Nature, and the Adirondacks' rich natural resources, require human nurture. Nature cannot "shed all beauty lavishly from her redundant horn" unless humans ensure that natural systems will operate "naturally."

It may seem strange that a "wild" area requires tending, just as the nature "tamed" within your garden requires tending. Article XIV is more than a public right to find the Adirondack Forest Preserve in a "wild" state. That would be a passive right. Rather, Article XIV also imposed affirmative duties on all levels of government to imbibe the constitutionally mandated wilderness ethic, and become a steward of what the courts in New York recognize as forest lands in a wild state. New York Governor Theodore Roosevelt was a great naturalist. He was later vice president of the United States, and he was enjoying the Adirondacks' fresh air and wild nature on the side of Mount Marcy when he received the news that he had became president of these United States following the assassination of President William McKinley.[53] The "forever wild" provision also inspired enactment of the Wilderness Act in the United States Congress in 1965.[54]

The precedent of establishing and managing a "wild forest" mountain area takes on new importance in the present era of climate change.[55] Such large biomes are places in which natural systems can evolve and adapt. They provide a living laboratory for scientific study of climate change and its impact on nature. The science of ecology can assist society in understanding better the working of natural systems throughout the Adirondacks and comparable regions. Governments and landowners need to understand the body of ecological science that enables society to manage the "wild" systems more effectively and "sustainably," in order to provide water supplies, watersheds, migratory species corridors, and other renewable "natural utilities" benefiting human, as well as for the inherent value that these places hold as untrammeled wild mountains and other habitats.

Even so-called protected areas, such as the Forest Preserve of the Adirondacks, are not in fact secure. Acid rain from industrial emissions in the atmosphere in the middle of North America still falls across the Adirondacks, gradually poisoning the forests and lakes.[56] Today, fish cannot breed in over three hundred lakes because of effects of this. There is still occasional timber rustling. Illegal roads and efforts to impose new pathways into the wilderness must be monitored and removed. Proposed cellular towers for communications and new wind turbines to generate electricity pose threats that can adversely impact the beauty and ridgelines of the mountains.

[53] See Farida A. Wiley, ed., *Theodore Roosevelt's America* (Devin-Adair Co., NY, 1955).

[54] Congress enacted The Wilderness Act in 1964, as Public Law 88–577.

[55] The several reports of the Intergovernmental Panel on Climate Change as available at www.ipcc.org.

[56] Concerns for the adverse effects of "acid" rain were the basis for a report that Sweden submitted to the 1972 UN Conference on the Human Environment in Stockholm, see "Air Pollution Across National Boundaries, Sweden's Case Study for the UN Conference on the Human Environment" (1971). Similar concerns were the basis for Congress amending the Clean Air Act in 1977 to restrict emissions that cause acid rain, see House of Representatives Report No. 95–294, 95th Congress, 1st Session, 105–137 (1977) for the House Committee on Interstate and Foreign Commerce accompanying H.R. 6161.

Despite such threats, there is ample evidence that others have learned this lesson and obey the strictures of Article XIV. For example, to expand a town cemetery into Forest Preserve Lands, the people of the state actually amended the State Constitution to allow a land swap, expanding the Forest Preserve with new additions, while ceding a small area for the expanded burial ground.[57] When the Forest Preserve was established in 1894, it was about the size of the state of Connecticut. Governor George Pataki, during his tenure from 1995 to 2007 was exemplary in his proactive buying of land and easements to add to the Forest Preserve, expanding its size enormously. Governors Mario Cuomo and Hugh Carey and Nelson Rockefeller all bought land to expand the Forest Preserve. Paper companies, including International Paper, have been willing to turn over their private forest holdings to the State, as nontimber paper products and recycling have reduced the need for lumber.

The Adirondack Mountains are now North America's largest continuous wilderness south of Alaska and Canada. UNESCO recognizes the Adirondacks, together with the adjacent Lake Champlain region, as a world Biosphere Reserve.[58] As nations throughout the world try to cope with the effects of climate change, New York is blessed that the headwaters of its rivers are secure, and that it hosts a safe haven for migratory species of sufficiently large habitats that "wild" conditions can evolve gradually along with the climate shifts. This short history of the Adirondacks provides an object lesson about the rule of law. The courts and public are cut from the same cloth. New York's societal values regarding the "forever wild" Forest Preserve are a part of its Constitution. No story of civic responsibility and public leadership illustrates better the how biodiversity conservation and the rule of law are intertwined. This story of the Adirondacks offers another strand in the grand tapestry of how humans and nature interact over time. Human laws can be devised to indicate a respect for the laws of nature, and our social and economic and ecological lives are the better for it.

2 "BEST PRACTICES" FROM THE ADIRONDACK EXPERIENCE

Over the decades, the interactions of the New York State Department of Environmental Conservation, the Adirondack Park Agency, and civic groups, such as the Association for the Protection of the Adirondacks, have led to a number of "best management practices." From these, a select number of legal tools and norms can be identified as environmental law elements that could be studied and applied in comparable situations in other mountain environments. Legal elements of note include the following:

(1) An inventory, or cadastre, of all the natural resources and benefits of the mountain area needs to be made. This is more than a map, although that is required. This inventory needs to include all the human perspectives about the area, including the cultural, spiritual, or religious uses of indigenous people and traditional communities

[57] On amendments to Article XIV, see Frank Graham, *The Adirondack Park: A Political History, op cit*, at p. 211, and N.A. Robinson, "'Forever Wild': New York's Constitutional Mandates to Enhance toe Forest Preserve," the Arthur Crocker Lecture for 2007 (Association for the Protection of the Adirondacks, at p. 17).

[58] As part of its scientific studies, UNESCO established the Man & The Biosphere Programme, and in coordination with the World Heritage Convention, States identified for UNESCO a series of biosphere reserves within their territory. The Adirondacks and the Lake Champlain region of New York and Vermont were identified as one Biosphere Reserve. Such reserves are vast enough to permit scientific study of natural systems relatively separate from the impacts of human activities.

(for instance, those living in or using mountains) communities, the aesthetic or recreation uses of "wild" nature, the "utility" benefits of watersheds and catchments area, of wetlands, and aquifer recharge areas, the biodiversity benefits of habitats for migratory species, as well as the potential development aspects of timber, minerals, resort communities, and the like.

(2) For ecosystems that retain, or can regain, a natural condition that is "wild" or persists without the impact of human development, strong rules can be enacted to protect such areas. Because of their steep slopes and remote locations, mountains particularly are likely to have "wild" areas that can be designated. These rules need to be reviewed and revised periodically to confront new or changed conditions.

(3) Even "wild" areas need design of management plans in order to help them retain their capacity to sustain robust biodiversity and ecosystem integrity.

(4) For natural features such as rivers or migratory species habitats that cross public and private lands, a regulatory scheme should be designed that is consistent for the resource and does not differ in effect depending on the location or ownership of the sites where the features exist.

(5) A regional focus for the entire mountain area, or biome, is required.

(6) Environmental impact assessment (EIA) should be mandated in all instances of land use throughout the region for actions taken outside the region that nonetheless could affect it.

(7) Local authorities, being closest to the land, should develop a comprehensive plan to govern all privately owned lands and other local lands and resources, to ensure sustainable development practices are followed; this usually involves some sort of zoning or town and country planning, as well as education of all land managers regarding the plan, and a licensing procedure before authorizing development, which is to be consistent with the plan. The public should be consulted during preparation of the plan, and the plan should be based on the inventory or cadastre of resources. Plans need to help sustain local economic activities in ways that do not impair the natural environment of the area.

(8) The procedures by which the rules for stewardship of both the "wild" protected lands and the developable lands need to be clear, be applicable equally to all persons or interests without favoritism, be transparent and open, and provide ample public notice and opportunity for public participation.

(9) Access to justice is important, and all affected or interested persons, including civil society, should have access to the courts to secure independent review of whether the biodiversity conservation norms and other land-use rules are being objectively and competently applied.

These legal elements from "best-management practices" in an intrastate mountain regime can be compared to those evolving under international regimes.

3 THE ALPINE CONVENTION

The 1991 Salzburg Alpine Convention is a framework treaty, applied and made specific through a critical a series of specific protocols.[59] The region of the European Alps involves mountains and resources in the Swiss Confederation (with its separate, self-governing

[59] The Convention on the Protection of the Alps is published in an English translation in the *Official Journal of the European Communities*. It was entered into force on 6 March 1995. The official texts of the treaty

cantons), France, Germany (and the State of Bavaria), Italy, Liechtenstein, Austria, Monaco, and Slovenia, and the European Economic Community (now the European Union [EU]). The framework convention provides shared regional norms for the eight nations that are party to the Convention, and binds their political subdivisions as well. Although the Swiss have ratified the framework convention, resistance by some cantons has meant that ratification of protocols that appear to intrude on their traditional home-rule prerogatives has been delayed.

The need for such a Convention was recognized decades before signing of the convention on 7 November 1991. In 1952, an NGO was founded to address the need for an Alpine-wide approach to conservation and development. The International Commission for the Protection of the Alps (CIPRA) was formed by hundreds of other NGOs in the seven nations of the wider Alpine region, including Monaco.[60] CIPRA advocated negotiation of "an international treaty to guarantee the cultural and natural diversity of the Alpine space" and in the 1980s made the case for such a treaty. By 1989, Germany's environment minister, Dr. Klaus Töpfer, convened a meeting of Alpine nations in Berchtesgaden, Germany, for the first Alpine Conference of Ministers of the Environment.

Over the next fourteen years, with CIPRA as an active NGO advocate, observer, and sometime critic, the Alpine nations agreed to treat the Alps as a single region. Although the eight operational protocols are negotiated, and they each are not yet in force, they do offer one of the best examples in state practice under international law for what may be said to constitute the legal aspects of mountain management. The Convention identifies the twelve priority areas for which Protocols[61] will specifically guide implementation of the norms embodied in the framework convention. These twelve areas essentially inventory the main concerns of the Alpine mountain region:

1. Populations and culture.
2. Spatial planning and sustainable development.
3. Prevention of air pollution.
4. Soil conservation.
5. Water management.
6. Conservation of nature and countryside.
7. Mountain farming.
8. Mountain forests.
9. Tourism.
10. Transport.
11. Energy.
12. Waste management.

The Convention includes a map of the wider Alpine area, and makes clear the transnational approach of the treaty.[62] It is the first international Convention to encompass such a large area of both protected wild lands and developed and developing lands. Any State may extend or withdraw the application of the Alpine Convention to additional

exist in the Italian, French, German, and Slovene languages. Austria is the depository state for the Alpine Convention.

[60] CIPRA is located in Liechtenstein at Im Bretscha 22, 9494 Shaan, Principality of Liechtenstein.

[61] These are set forth in Article 2, para. 2, of the Alpine Convention, together with policy objectives for guiding the preparation of each Protocol.

[62] The map is annexed to the Alpine Convention. Article 1, para. 1, provides that "[t]he Convention shall cover the Alpine region, as described and depicted in the Annex."

parts of its national territory by making a declaration to that effect and filing it with the Depository State.[63]

As a framework Convention, the nations ratifying the agreement undertake as a general obligation the duty to "pursue a comprehensive policy for the preservation and protection of the Alps by applying the principles of prevention, payment by the polluter (the "polluter-pays principle") and cooperation, after careful consideration of the interests of all the Alpine States, their Alpine regions, and the European Economic Community, and through the prudent and sustained use of resources."[64] The Convention requires cooperation on research and systematic monitoring,[65] and on the exchange of legal, scientific, and technical information.[66] The States that are party to the Convention established a Conference of the Parties,[67] which meets every two years[68] through which they report their implementation of the Convention[69] and convene working groups to implement the Convention,[70] adopt Protocols,[71] and generally supervise the agreement. Decisions require unanimous consent in the Conference, except that receipt of scientific reports and recommendations on implementation may be made by two-thirds vote.[72] A "Conference Standing Committee" is established as an executive body for the Convention.[73]

The Convention's general obligations require States to "take appropriate measures"[74] in each of the twelve areas. With respect to biological diversity, the following norms are provided as guidance for the subsequent development of more detailed Protocols:

Conservation and Livelihoods: "population and culture – the objective is to respect, preserve and promote the cultural and social independence of the indigenous population and to guarantee the basis for their living standards, in particular environmentally sound settlement and economic development, and promote mutual understanding and cooperation between Alpine and extra-Alpine populations";[75]

Biodiversity Conservation – "conservation of nature and countryside – the objective is to protect, conserve and where necessary, rehabilitate the natural environment and the countryside, so that ecosystems are able to function, animal and plant species, including heir habitats, are preserved, nature's capacity for regeneration and sustained productivity is maintained, and the variety, uniqueness and beauty of nature and the countryside as a whole are preserved on a permanent basis";[76]

Regional Planning – "regional planning – the objective is to ensure the economic and rational use of land and the sound, harmonious development of the whole region, particular emphasis being placed on natural hazards, the avoidance of under- and over-use and the conservation or rehabilitation of natural habitats by means of a thorough clarification and evaluation of land-use requirements, foresighted integral planning and coordination of the measures taken";[77]

Because the Alpine Convention is consensual, the political will of the contracting nations is needed for implementation. The formal duties of the treaty meet the activism of the CIPRA and the other NGOs that seek implementation of the treaty through its Protocols. The treaty does not provide, in itself, for access to justice. However, it can

[63] Alpine Convention, Article 1, paras. 2 (addition) and 3 (withdrawal).
[64] Alpine Convention Article 2, para. 1.
[65] Alpine Convention, Article 3.
[66] Alpine Convention, Aricle 4. States may apply their national laws on confidentiality; ibid., para. 5.
[67] Alpine Convention, Article 5.
[68] Alpine Convention, Article 5, para. 2.
[69] Alpine Convention, Article 5, para. 4.
[70] Alpine Convention, Article 6(e).
[71] Alpine Convention, Article 6(b).
[72] Alpine Convention, Article 7, para.1.
[73] Alpine Convention, Article 8.
[74] Alpine Convention, Article 2, para. 2.
[75] Alpine Convention, Article 2, para. 2(a).
[76] Alpine Convention, Article 2(f).
[77] Alpine Convention, Article 2(b).

be read *in pari materia* with the 1998 Århus Convention on Access to Information, Public Participation in Environmental Decision-making, and Access to Justice in Environmental Matters.[78] Eventually, NGOs should be able to require that a ratifying State undertake EIA for decisions that it takes when implementing the Alpine Convention and to secure judicial review of the adequacy of implementation. It is a weakness of the Alpine Convention that it lacks a dispute settlement mechanism, but the Parties have negotiated a Protocol on settlement of cross-border disputes.[79]

At present, the Alpine Convention's Protocols, with these additional Århus Convention elements, is not fully operational. The duty to protect the Alps as an integrated region remains an aspiration, and not a reality. As the Director of CIPRA, Andreas Götz, has remarked, "The most important aspect now is that the NGOs are also the one to undertake clear and concrete measures for the implementation whereas the states have not been very active so far."[80]

4 "BEST PRACTICES" FROM THE ALPINE CONVENTION

At the international level, treaty negotiation and implementation can seem to move very slowly. Glaciers in the Alps have already retreated as a result of global warming. As a result, the tourist ski industry may be impacted in the future, as may downstream communities experiencing the flow of waters, and, of course, the flora and fauna as well. However, the existence of its Protocols, and the binding general obligations of the Alpine Convention, do guide State conduct. Nations know what they are to be expected to do, and they do gradually conform to those parameters. The norms do have effect, even if not as immediately as in the case of the Adirondacks.

Although not yet fully implemented, there are several potential legal "best-management practices" that may be discerned from the Alpine Convention as a "work in progress":

(1) The shared fate of mountain upland and related lowland areas require a broader definition of mountain region than just the mountains. Region is to be defined in a holistic fashion, based on hydrology and ecology and the relationships of human communities.
(2) Spatial planning and studies are fundamental to developing a sound set of best management practices, and are themselves such a necessary practice.
(3) Activist NGO leadership is essential to implementation and cultivating the political will for governmental action but, without EIA and access to justice provisions, the effectiveness of beneficial NGO facilitation is limited.

[78] Entered into force 30 October 2001; see 38 I.L.M. 512 (1998).

[79] Only Austria, Liechtenstein, and Germany have ratified this Protocol, which is in force between them.

[80] Andreas Götz, "The Alpine Convention: An International Treaty for Sustainable Development in a Large Region." Paper delivered at the "Symposium on Environmental Law for Judges," Rome, 10 May 2003. He notes by way of example: "As one example I would like to mention the network of communities 'alliance in the Alps.' This network of Alpine villages and cities ass founded again by CIPRA, ... The network has as its principal goal the implementation of the Alpine Convention, Around 150 communities from seven Alpine countries try to find out what this relatively abstract treaty called 'Alpine Convention' might mean on their level, for an Alpine town. So they are trying to put the term of 'sustainable development' into practice in their own village and to share their experiences in international meetings and seminars" (p. 4).

(4) A focus on biodiversity and ecosystem management is a key element of a regional mountain approach.
(5) The regional norms can overcome what the preamble to the Alpine Convention calls "the substantial differences existing between national legal systems, natural conditions, population distribution, agriculture and forestry the state and development of the economy, the volume of traffic and the nature and intensity of tourism."
(6) Local authorities are important, and need to be involved; subsidiarity works within nations but is harder to implement under international law where only the State is the recognized entity for decision making.

In addition to these "best practices," additional guidance can be noted in international "soft law" policy recommendations. CIPRA, the FAO, and the UN Environment Programme, headed at the time by the former German Environment Minister Dr. Klaus Töpfer, convened a meeting on "The Alpine Experience – An Approach for Other Mountain Regions?" in Berchtesgaden, Germany, in 2002. Although assembled as a lead-up to the IYM meeting in Bishteck, the meeting took note of the Alpine Convention process, as "the only example worldwide of a legally binding inter-governmental mountain agreement." Although the Andean Pact appears to have been ignored in the Berchtesgaden consultation and its recommendations, some may consider it overstates the uniqueness of the Alpine Convention. The Berchtesgaden Declaration is essentially correct in noting that little transnational mountain range stewardship exists at either international or national levels.

The meeting adopted ten principles for regional cooperation.[81] When applied to the Alpine Convention, they reflect both the strengths and weakness of the Alpine Convention's approach. The ten principles include:

(1) *Hold Government Accountable* – "The primary responsibility for ensuring sustainable and equitable management across mountain ranges at the national and sub-national levels rests with governments. Sustainable mountain policies nationally are a requisite for any broader regional cooperation. . . . "
(2) *Keep a Regional Focus.*
(3) *Foster Equality and Equity* – "Equitable regional cooperation fostering equal opportunities can secure local livelihoods, reduce vulnerability to disasters and lead to a sustainable use and protection of mountain natural resources. Equitable access to resources is a mainstay for peace. . . . "
(4) *Decentralize* – "Local authorities – if delegated the power and the means – can provide for increased responsiveness and transparency in the management of mountain resources and for increases in local participation."
(5) *Set Clear Objectives – Chart a Course Flexibly* – "Clear objectives, quality expectations, and tangible indicators to measure change are a key to Success . . . Due to the great differences in geopolitical, socio-economic and environmental conditions of mountain regions, objectives, priorities, and processes will vary from region to region."
(6) *Participation of Local Communities and Civil Society Organizations* –"They should be engaged throughout, from planning through implementation, to monitoring.

[81] "10 Berchtesgaden Principles for Regional Cooperation." Annexed to the Berchtensgaden Declaration on Mountain Range Regional Cooperation, 28 June 2002.

Participation creates ownership of, and commitment to, sustainable mountain development and it reduces tensions and conflict."

(7) *Networks* – "To become a sustainable process, regional cooperation requires and benefits from multiple transboundary networks. . . . Academic and research institutions have a major role to play in this context."

(8) *Build Capacity – Share Knowledge* – "Shared knowledge, respect for different forms of knowledge and inter-disciplinary approaches are an important ingredient in building regional consensus and resolving disputes. . . . "

(9) *Encourage Partnerships* – "These should include in particular arrangements, such as e.g. environmental service agreements, between upstream and downstream communities and users of transboundary watershed resources."

(10) *Engage the International Community* – "Examples include the Conventions on Climate Change, Biodiversity, Wetlands, Desertification and Migratory Species. . . . "

As State practice evolves under the Alpine Convention, it may be that these ten principles can be used analytically to shed light on how States can advance beyond the realm of general obligations to observing or implementing the negotiated Protocols to the reality of implementing the reforms. They also may be applied to the agreements that may emerge for the Carpathians and other mountain areas.

5 THE CARPATHIAN AGREEMENT

The Alpine Convention inspired negotiations by the Czech Republic, Hungary, Poland, Romania, the Slovak Republic, Ukraine, and the Federal Republic of Yugoslavia to establish a Framework Convention on the Protection and Sustainable Development of the Carpathians. These "economies in transition" faced a legacy of central planning and, after the end of these controls, the emergency of unsustainable exploitation of the natural resources in the Carpathian Mountains. Through the UN Environment Programme, a series of ministerial meetings prepared a draft of the Framework Convention, eventually submitting it to the Fifth Ministerial Conference on the Environment for Europe, held under the auspices of the United Nations Economic Commission for Europe.[82] This culminated a series of meetings of NGOs, governments, and intergovernmental representatives that began in Poland between November 1999 and December 2000. With the World Wildlife Fund (WWF), which had designated the Carpathians as one of the world's top two hundred ecoregions, and NGOs from the region, the Carpathian Ecoregion Initiative (CEI) was launched in Romania in 2001. CEI interacted, not always harmoniously, with the States of the region that were preparing the text of the Framework Convention with the assistance of the UN Environment Programme (Regional Office for Europe's "European Mountain Initiative").[83]

The Carpathian Framework Convention follows the approach of the Alpine Convention, but with even less cohesiveness. The precise legal definition of the Carpathian region has not yet to be defined. The general obligation is to "pursue a comprehensive policy and cooperate for the protection and sustainable development of the Carpathians

[82] UN Economic Commission for Europe, Draft Framework Convention on the Protection and Sustainable Development of the Carpathians," UN DOC. ECE/CEP/14 (21 May 2003).

[83] Yuriy Vasidlov, "Birth of the Carpathian Convention." KYIV-2003 (Information-analytical Bulletin of the "Kyiv-2003" Project, Nos. 3–4, August/December 2002, "MAMA 86" (Ukrainian National Environmental NGO), Kyiv, Ukraine, p. 16. See also http://www.kyiov2003.org. 4, 4 Nf.

with a view to, *inter alia*, improving the quality of life, strengthening local economies and communities, and conservation of nature values and cultural heritage."[84]

The draft Framework Convention incorporates, with definitions to come with the negotiation of subsequent protocols, several general principles of international environmental law and other concepts:

(a) the precaution and prevention principles;
(b) the "polluter-pays" principle;
(c) public participation and stakeholder involvement;
(d) transboundary cooperation;
(e) integrated planning and management of land and water resources;
(f) a programmatic approach; and
(g) the ecosystem approach.

Although the Carpathian Agreement draft incorporates these general principles of international environmental law into a regionwide agreement, it does not focus their application on specific issues of regionwide concern, as does the Alpine Convention. The proposed agreement also does not make provision for EIA, which is surprising because the States involved in the negotiations are parties to the Århus Convention, and EIA can be considered as a legal tool in furtherance of the precautionary principle, and certainly involves public participation and stakeholder interaction. Perhaps more limiting is the absence of a means by which programmatic planning can be accomplished.

6 EMERGING CARPATHIAN "BEST PRACTICES"

Nonetheless, by introducing the "ecosystem management" approach,[85] the draft agreement builds, into each of the States Parties obligations, a fundamental duty to study the ecology of the region as a whole, and to manage each nation's portion in a way that enhances migratory species corridors, preserves forest cover for watershed, and minimizes development impacts on the ecosystem utilities of the region. If taken seriously, the ecosystem management approach can provide fundamental guidance to produce congruent decision making among the States that govern the Carpathians. This comprehensive concept appears in bits and pieces in the other mountain management governance systems, but here it is presented in a straightforward way. Potentially, the inclusion of a fundamental obligation to employ "ecosystem management" will be the most advanced legal innovation that the draft Carpathian Convention provides for the evolving law of ecosystem management.

7 THE ANDEAN PACT

The nations of the Andes mountain range[86] have taken a rather different approach. These nations seek integration of their political and socioeconomic systems, in much the same way as the European Community (now the European Union (EU)). The Andean Pact

[84] Draft Carpathian Framework Convention, Article 2.
[85] The ecosystem approach is advanced through decisions of the Conference of the Parties of the United Nations Convention on Biological Diversity. See www.cbd.int.
[86] States participating are Bolivia, Colombia, Ecuador, Peru, and Venezuela. Beginning as the Andean Integration System, they became the Community of Andean Nations or the Andean Community. Chile, in 1976, withdrew from the group. www.comunidadadandina.org/english/bodies.htm .

would establish a set of regionwide legislative, judicial, and executive bodies.[87] The Andean Pact does not address the environmental stewardship of the Andres expressly. The Pact promotes regional cooperation and integration of government policies at a supranational level.[88]

The Andean Pact approach eventually may permit promulgation of the sort of binding directives that the EU has adopted and implemented.[89] The shortcoming of the Andean Pact approach is that it may take years before the regional intergovernmental organs of the Pact are functioning. In the interim, each nation follows its own approaches to mountain management. The environmental legal regimes of the Andes are characteristic of the traditional, national approach. Ecuador and Peru have established transboundary "peace parks."[90] There are proposals to link cultural heritage and nature protection along the "Ruta Inca," the ancient Inca highway along the Andes. There are rather weak efforts at migratory species conservation across the region.[91] There is a recognition that the Andes are important to the Amazon Basin. There also are cooperation agreements.[92] Most rivers flowing to the Pacific are within each nation will experience a reduction in available waters as glaciers withdraw and melt as a result of climate change and warming. However, to date, there is in fact little regionwide stewardship of the Andes as a shared mountain region.

Because the Andean Pact is not focused on mountain stewardship, one can only speculate about the "best practices" that might emerge. If we draw analogies to the environmental law directives of the EU,[93] stewardship topics such as migratory species habitat identification and management and pollution prevention might be considered.

[87] The Cartegena Agreement, also known as the Andean Pact, began as a free trade area and was codified as Decision 406, "Codification of the Andean Subregional Integration Agreement," June 25, 1997, www.comunidadandina.org/english/andean/ande_trie1.htm. Regional coordindation of environmental measures is through the Andean Committee of Environmental Authorities ("CAAAM") organized in 1998. Decision 435, at www.comunidadandina.org/normative/dec/d435.htm.

[88] The leading commentary on the Andean Pact is Victor Tafur-Dominguez, "International Environmental Harmonization – Emergence and Development of the Andean Community," 12 Pace International Law Review 283 (2000).

[89] See, for instance, the protected area legislation of the European Union (such as E.C Directive 92/43 on conservation of natural habitats and wild fauna and flora) and of its member States (such as the United Kingdom's designations of sites of special scientific interest, "SSSI", NPACA, Section 23), which is often accomplished through protection of nature in situ. Many of these protected areas are in mountains, and they in turn serve wider conservation measures, such as the Convention on the Conservation of European Wildlife and Natural Habitats (Berne, September 19, 1979). On the European Union's protected area law-making in this regard see Alexandra Kiss and Dinah Shelton, *Manual of European Environmental Law* (2d ed., Cambridge University Press, 1997), at pp. 200–207.

[90] IUCN facilitated the establishment of a Peace Park between Ecuador and Peru in South America, and between several African nations. See, generally, www.iucn.org/themes/protectedareas for the work of the World Commission on Protected Areas to establish peace parks across national borders.

[91] See the Washington, D.C., Convention on Nature Protection and Wildlife Preservation in the Western Hemisphere, 12 October 1940, 161 UNTS 193, 56 Stat. 1354, TS 981.

[92] For example, Brazil and Bolivia have established an ecological corridor across their borders, but little beyond the designation is done to manage the shared ecosystems in an integrated fashion. See also the Treaty for Amazonian Cooperation, which brings together Bolivia, Brazil, Colombia, Ecuador, Guyana, Peru, Surinam, and Venezuela, July 3, 1978, to create an Amazon Cooperation Council, and reaches into the Andean and other mountain areas in the Amazon watershed. See Luis Fernando Macias Gomez, Ed., *Introduction al Derecho Ambiental* (1998).

[93] See Alexandre Kiss and Dinah Shelton, *Manual of European Environmental Law* (2d ed., Cambridge University Press, 1997).

On balance, the prospects for the Andean Pact's broad supranational economic integration organization approach may not become operational in time to avert the degradation of the Andes. Individual policies for sustainable development are not likely to approach the Andes in a consistent way. To be sure, each Andean nation could embrace a system, such as that of the Adirondacks, but culturally this appears unlikely because the indigenous and traditional communities of the Andes are not integrated as comprehensively into each of the national systems of governance,[94] and each nation's capacity for environmental management would require substantial enhancement. Although economic resources now invested in the military could be applied to environmental systems development, there is little indication that this is likely to happen any time soon.[95]

8 CONCLUSIONS

Effective conservation of biodiversity and reasonable assurance of human livelihoods within the Earth's mountainous regions requires affirmative stewardship. A regional legal regime for mountains should be guided by careful scientific analysis of the ecological utilities or natural services that mountains provide. Equally, the cultural and social values that mountains provide to human society should be assessed and sustained. To these ends, whether within the mountains are within a single nation or across several nations, a system of common legal elements need to be agreed and implemented.

Successful examples of successful mountain management do exist, and new efforts to fashion management systems have begun. Based on comparative legal analysis of these efforts, one can derive patterns of the legal elements that are most appropriate for best management practices.

It is premature to say that there is as yet an agreed law of mountains, either at the national or international level. As illustrated by the recommendations to governments made by UNCED in Agenda 21 and by the IYM's Bishtek Conference, there is broad consensus in "soft law" on what a law for regional mountain management should contain. If robust biodiversity and human livelihoods are to be sustained in Earth's alpine regions, nations should make adoption and implementation of environmental mountain law into a priority. Only then will an "ecoregime" for Earth's mountains become a reality.

[94] Following the civil stand-off in Bolivia between indigenous communities and urban centers, the indigenous population won the national elections and assumed the responsibilities of government.

[95] Costa Rica abolished its military, and as a result its environmental capacity has been enhanced, as is its educational, public health, and transportation sectors. No other Latin American state has followed this example.

PART FOUR

USES OF COMPONENTS OF BIODIVERSITY

17 Legal Framework for the Ecological and Biodiversity Needs of Soil: Progress towards an International Instrument for the Sustainable Use of Soil

Ian Hannam*

1 INTRODUCTION

It has been forecast that the global human population will increase from the present six billion to eight billion by the year 2020. In order for there to be sufficient food, both for these additional people and to raise the standard of provision for those at present with an inadequate diet, a large increase in food production must take place. This increase in food production must come from approximately the same land area as is at present under agriculture, as the remainder is too dry, too wet, too cold, or too steep and mountainous to make a significant contribution. This inevitably means greater pressure will be put on prime lands, and especially those with the most fertile soils, to provide the extra food required. As demand increases, there will be increasing pressure also on the less productive soils, where the impact of soil degradation is most dramatically seen, and this could possibly result in the displacement of people from their homelands.[1]

The effects of the increase in the human population on the world, especially in terms of the decline in food security, indicates that soil has ecological limits that change according to the variations within different ecosystems and the cultural relationships with the land and soil resources.[2] There is an increasing imbalance in the production of food because of the difference in the rate of deterioration of soils and their functions and the rate of their regeneration. This situation requires an in-depth reconsideration of human attitudes to natural resources in general, and to soil in particular. This challenge has been taken up by the international soil science community,[3] which is attempting

[1] From Bridges, E. M., I. D. Hannam, L. R. Oldeman, F. Penning deVries, S. J. Scherr, & S. Sombatpanit, eds., *Response to Land Degradation* (Enfield, NH: Science Publishers, Inc., 2002), 1; Hurni, H., & K. Meyer, eds., *A World Soils Agenda: Discussing International Actions for the Sustainable Use of Soils*, Prepared with the support of an international group of specialists of the IASUS Working Group of the International Union of Soil Sciences (IUSS) (Centre for Development and Environment, Berne, 2002), 63.

[2] See F. Penning, de Vries, H. Acquay, D. Molden, S.J. Scherr, C. Valentin, & O. Cofie, *Integrated Land and Water Management for Food and Environmental Security*. Comprehensive Assessment Research Paper 1 (Colombo, Sri Lanka, 2002); M. A. Stocking, "Tropical Soils and Food Security: The Next 50 Years." *Science* (2003) 302 1356–1359; R. Lahmar, M. Held, & L. Montanarella, *People Matter: Food Security and Soils* (Torba, Montpellier, France: Soil and Society/Sols and Societies, 2003).

[3] Hurni & Meyer, note 3.

* Dr Ian Hannam is Associate Professor, Australian Centre for Agriculture and Law, University of New England, Armidale 2351 NSW Australia, ian.hannam@ozemail.com.au; a Member IUCN Commission on Environmental Law; and Chair, CEL Specialist Group on Sustainable Use of Soil.

to create an awareness and knowledge of the sustainable use of soil among all humans. The main objectives of this movement are to:

- Change the attitude of humans about the vital importance of soils;
- Remind humans that soil is the foundation of human physical development and has a fundamental role in sustaining societies;
- Raise the "status" of soil by advising governments of the world of the way to manage their soil as a nonrenewable resource; and
- Build an international network of specialists to impede the progress of soil deterioration.

However, to successfully achieve these objectives, national and international frameworks for soil legislation need to be based on a clear understanding of the confusing differences in the use of terminology in the soil science, sociological, and ecological disciplines. A range of concepts and terms used to analyse the issues and risks associated with soil degradation has evolved. These are not always used consistently by scientists in the relevant disciplines, let alone by different jurisdictions.

2 SOIL AND SOIL DEGRADATION

2.1 Soil

The processes involved in soil formation are complex,[4] and definitions of soil reflect this complexity. The Council of Europe defines soil as:

> ... an integral part of the earth's ecosystems and is situated at the interface between the earth's surface and bedrock. It is subdivided into successive horizontal layers with specific physical, chemical and biological characteristics. From the standpoint of history of soil use, and from an ecological and environmental point of view, the concept of soil also embraces porous sedimentary rocks and other permeable materials together with the water that these contain, and the reserves of underground water.[5]

This definition shows that soil has a fundamental role in the terrestrial ecosystem as a three-dimensional body performing a wide range of functions, principally ecological, cultural, and land-use functions.[6] Any alteration of soil processes can lead to changes in the function of ecosystems. It therefore must be realised that many environmental problems, which become apparent in flora and fauna, may originate from changes in the soil on which that flora and fauna is dependent. It is essential that the principal functions of soil must influence the preparation of legal frameworks for soil. The ecological functions, in particular, should be qualitatively and quantitatively safeguarded and preserved in the long term to ensure conservation of biodiversity, in general, and the

[4] See J. M. Gobat, M. Aragno, & W. Matthey, *The Living Soil, Fundamentals of Soil Science and Soil Biology* (Enfield, NH: Science Publishers, Inc., 2003).

[5] Council of Europe, European Conservation Strategy – Recommendations for the 6th European Ministerial Conference on the Environment (Council of Europe, 1990).

[6] See J. G. Sheals, ed., *The Soil Ecosystem: Systematic Aspects of the Environment, Organisms and Communities.* The Systematics Association, Publication No. 8 (London: Staples Printers Ltd. 1969).

maintenance of human life, in particular. The functions of soil have been incorporated within at least one international convention[7] and many parts of domestic legislation refer to various individual soil functions.[8]

2.2 Soil Degradation

Soil degradation is broadly defined as a loss or reduction of soil functions or soil uses,[9] which lowers the potential capability of the soil to produce ecosystem services. Soil degradation includes physical, chemical, and biological deterioration, for example, loss of organic matter, decline in soil fertility, decline in structural condition, erosion, adverse changes in salinity, acidity or alkalinity, and the effects of toxic chemicals, pollutants, or excessive flooding.[10] Six specific processes are recognised as the main contributors to soil degradation: water erosion, wind erosion, waterlogging, and excess salts, chemical degradation, physical degradation, and biological degradation. Soil degradation now affects one-third of the world's soils used for agriculture, particularly the soils that are physically and chemically unsuitable for agriculture, grazing, and other purposes. The dominant process is erosion caused by wind and water, accounting for 83 percent of the area affected by soil degradation in the world. It has been demonstrated that land use systems are affected in all ecoregions and in most countries, although the impacts differ depending on the type, the severity, and the extent of soil degradation. The most important factors contributing to soil degradation must be taken in account within a legal framework.

3 IUCN COMMISSION ON ENVIRONMENTAL LAW

In April 1999, the IUCN Commission on Environmental Law (CEL) initiated the establishment of a Specialist Group for Sustainable Soils (SGSS) to investigate the national and international dimensions of the legal protection of soils.[11] This working group came about as a result of contacts between CEL members and the principal international soil science organizations.

[7] See *Protocol on the Implementation of the Convention concerning the Protection of the Alps of 1991 in the area of Soil Protection* (Salzburg, 1991), Article 1, available at http://fletcher.tufts.edu/multi/texts/bh993a.txt, but not yet in force. Article 1 sets out the multifunctional role of soil in an effective manner. See also The Soil Campaign, *Save Our Soil to Sustain Our Society*, Appendix p. 34, *Sheet One*, "The Functions Fulfilled by Soil" (in summary): According to current knowledge, soils are Biomass production systems; Substance transformation systems; Regulation systems; A gene reserve; A memory. They are a page in the history of nature and of human evolution: Physical supports for all human activities (agriculture, industry, transport, habitat, craftwork, leisure etc.). Available at http://www.alliance21.org/en/proposals/finals/final_sols_en.rtf: See also the draft revised European Soil Charter of 2002. Available at http://www.nature.coe.int/CO-DBP6/codbp02e_02.doc, which includes an explicit description of the functions of soil.

[8] I. D. Hannam with B. W., Boer *Legal and Institutional Frameworks for Sustainable Soils: A Preliminary Report*, Environmental Law and Policy Paper No. 45 (IUCN Gland Switzerland and Cambridge, UK, and Bonn, Germany, 2002), see Section 4, subsection 2.3.

[9] P. E. V. Charman & B. W. Murphy, eds., *Soils: Their Properties and Management* (South Melbourne, Australia: Oxford University Press, 2000), see chapters 2, 3, and 4.

[10] Ibid.

[11] Note: in June 2005 the Steering Committee of the Commission on Environmental Law broadened the responsibility of the Specialist Group to include legal aspects of desertification.

3.1 The Amman Resolution on Soils

In October 2000, the IUCN World Conservation Congress in Amman, Jordan, passed a resolution, committing the IUCN to investigate this issue, and called on members of the Union to support this work. The SGSS had the principal responsibility to develop the guidelines and prepare reports under the resolution. The text of the resolution is as follows:

> Legal Aspects of the Sustainable Use of Soils:
>
> RECALLING that one of the objectives of the International Union for the Conservation of Nature and Natural Resources (IUCN) since its founding in 1948 was the establishment of laws and treaties for the protection of nature;
>
> RECOGNISING the important contributions made by the IUCN since 1965 towards establishing the field of environmental law;
>
> AWARE that environmental law has become a field of law whose scope is exceptionally broad, ranging from the legal systems of local authorities and the customary law of traditional societies and indigenous peoples, through to the laws of States and the international law among States;
>
> NOTING the significant cooperation and support that exists among the soil science community for the improvement of environmental law and policy for the sustainable use of soils, particularly in regard to the ecological functions of soil for the conservation of biodiversity and the maintenance of human life, including:
>
> (a) the production of biomass and the filtering, buffering and transformation activity between the atmosphere, ground water and plant cover;
> (b) soils as a biological habitat and gene reserve;
> (c) soils as a spatial base for technical, industrial and socio-economic structures and their development; and
> (d) soils as a source of raw materials,
>
> CONVINCED that the future ecological benefits of the world's soils will depend on the existence of adequate global, regional and national legal strategies to enable individual nations to make sound land use and land management decisions, and on building capacity to communicate these strategies;
>
> CONCERNED that there is a need to study further and make recommendations concerning the synergy among several international environmental instruments of relevance to soils and the patterns of their implementation through national legislation, and
>
> ACKNOWLEDGING that whilst there is a range of international instruments addressing aspects of soil conservation, there is at present no specific global environmental law instrument for the sustainable use of soils;
>
> The World Conservation Congress, at its 2nd session, in Amman, Jordan, 4–10 October 2000:
>
> WELCOMES the initiative of the Environmental Law Programme to form a Working Group on the Legal Aspects of the Sustainable Use of Soils to prepare guidelines and explanatory material relating to principles and elements of national legislation and policy to assist States to manage their specific soil degradation and land degradation problems, and to investigate the need for and feasibility of further developing international environmental law in this field, in particular through an international instrument for the sustainable use of soils,

> INVITES IUCN members to provide all possible support to the Environmental Law Programme in developing guidelines on the essential elements to include in environmental legislation and policy for the sustainable use of soils, and its investigation of a global instrument for the sustainable use of soils;
>
> REQUESTS the Environmental Law Programme, in its development of legal guidelines and explanatory material, and investigation into a global legal instrument for the sustainable use of soils, to pay particular attention to the ecological needs of soil and their ecological functions for the conservation of biodiversity and the maintenance of human life.[12]

Building on this resolution and further work of the Environmental Law Programme, IUCN adopted a subsequent resolution at the 3d Session of the World Conservation Congress, in Bangkok, Thailand, 17 –25 November 2004. That resolution requested the IUCN Director General to work with IUCN members to outline options for a global legal sustainable-use-of-soils instrument; prepare "further legal guidelines and explanatory material on the ecological needs of soil and their ecological functions" to support such a global instrument for sustainable use of soil; and continue efforts with interested States for the development of national legislation for sustainable use of soil, and in particular to work with developing States, including "contributing to institutional capacity building and assisting in the development of national environmental policy and strategies."[13]

3.2 The Ecosystem-based Approach

The resolutions of the IUCN requires an ecosystem-based approach to the investigation. In this regard, the Convention on Biological Diversity (CBD) defines an ecosystem as a "dynamic complex of plant, animal, and micro-organism communities and their non-living environment interacting as a functional unit."[14] An ecosystem-based approach is an appropriate strategy for the integrated management of land, water, and all living resources. It also promotes conservation and sustainable use in an equitable way, based on the application of appropriate scientific methodologies. At the fifth meeting of the Conference of Parties of the CBD, governments and relevant bodies were urged to apply the ecosystem approach in their environmental law reform. The Conference of the Parties adopted twelve broad principles for the application of the ecosystem approach, with a clear rationale underlying each principle.[15] It is possible that the survival of human society may depend on a conscious effort to slow down the rate of development and the modification of biological diversity; therefore, an ecological approach is required toward law and policy making, in general, and land-use decision making, in particular.[16] This means developing legal mechanisms to enable an ecosystem-based approach to be

[12] The text of the resolution is directed to both the national and international levels of legal protection. In relation to the international level, the use of the term "international instrument" was deliberately chosen to leave the options for investigation of this area as open as possible.

[13] Resolution 3.072 of the Bangkok World Conservation Congress on the legal aspects of the sustainable use of soils. The Department of State, United States, provided the following statement for the record. "State and agency members of the United States voted against this motion." Ibid.

[14] Article 2, Convention on Biological Diversity.

[15] Hannam *et al.* Response to Land Degradation, section II, subsection 8.

[16] See L. Glowka, in collaboration with C. Shine, O. Rey Santos, M. Farooque, & L. Gündling, *A Guide to Undertaking Biodiversity Legal and Institutional Profiles.* Environmental Policy and Law Paper No. 35 (IUCN Environmental Law Centre, 1998); see Article 1 of the *Protocol on the Implementation of the Convention Concerning the Protection of the Alps of 1991 in the Area of Soil Protection.*

applied in all aspects of soil protection and management. Such a process is likely to have a different outcome from a process that relies merely on the application of the conventional, scientific, and objective principles of ecology to protect and manage soil. This is because the ecosystem approach takes into account the *relationship* between soil, as living ecological communities, and the environment.[17] An effective legal system for the protection of soil, therefore, will depend on the selection of appropriate ecological concepts and the development of a legal structure with the appropriate elements to implement these concepts.[18]

The deterioration of ecosystems, both quantitatively and qualitatively, has made the goal of "ecosystem health" more urgent. Economic activity, social organization, and human health maintenance are all tied closely to the viability and health of ecosystems, a relationship that underscores the critical importance to society of fostering ecosystem health.[19] Humans know from personal experience what it means to be physically dysfunctional and are educated about the process of general screening, diagnosis, monitoring of signs, and other aspects of health care. A similar process should be used when evaluating ecosystem health, one that is defined in an operational manner, and assessments of health status can, at least in part, be based on objective criteria. Systematic diagnosis of ecosystem conditions and the careful study of ecosystems under stress can yield early warning indicators of ecosystem degradation. Ecosystem health practice requires not only diagnostic and curative capabilities but also, importantly, monitoring and preventive measures.

4 ECOLOGICAL INTEGRITY AND THE NEED FOR ECOLOGICAL SOIL STANDARDS

Because the land-use demands on soil are determined by social and cultural factors, the values and standards of soil consumption should be defined rigidly by the ecological limits of different forms of land use. These specific *ecological soil standards* should be developed to evaluate the potential for sustainability or for any practice that may seem appropriate to meet the goal of a sustainable use of soil. The standards also can be used as a basis to formulate elements for soil legislation, with the same goal. Although soil is nonrenewable (except in the very long term) and its continued intensive use currently is reducing the stock for future generations, this does not mean that soil cannot be used for agricultural and nonagricultural practices.[20] Rather it means that all forms of soil use should be subject to a rigid application of ecological soil standards to ensure sustainability.[21] Various eco-ethical concepts should form the basis of standards to be applied in the legal and institutional arenas, to maintain or improve the physical

[17] See A. Macfadyen, "The Systematic Study of Ecosystems," in J. G. Sheals, ed., *The Soil Ecosystem: Systematic Aspects of the Environment, Organisms and Communities.* The Systematics Association, Publication No. 8 (London: Staples Printers Ltd., 1969).

[18] The concept of "agrobiodiversity" is now recognized in the biodiversity literature, where it is defined as "the principal biological means of degradation control and, by mixing of species, the main promoter of increased and more diversified (and more food secure) output from farming systems." See A. Tenberg, & M. Stocking, 2001, "Land Degradation, Food Security and Agrobiodiversity – Examining an Old Problem in a New Way," in E. M. Bridges, I. D. Hannam, L. R. Oldeman, F. Penning de Vries, S. J. Scherr, & S. Sombatpanit, eds., *Response to Land Degradation* (Enfield, NH: Science Publishers Inc, 2001).

[19] See D. R. Rapport, P. Constanza, C. Epstein, C. Gaudet, & R. Levins, eds., *Ecosystem Health* (Malden MA: Blackwell Science Inc., 1998).

[20] See Bridges et al., Note 1, at 479.

[21] See, for example, Bodansky, D., "Customary (and Not So Customary) International Environmental Law," 3(1) *Indiana Journal of Global Legal Studies* (1995) 105, in which the use of nonlegal norms in international

and chemical status of soil, that is, the *ecological integrity of the soil*. It is therefore proposed that the concept of an *ecological soil standard*, which derives from these interrelationships, be accepted as:

> Any process that maintains or improves the ecological integrity of soil, where the term "ecological integrity of soil" means:
>
> > Preserving the ecosystems, including the prevention of loss of wholeness, which is the commencement of soil degradation, to control existing soil degradation, and to protect and manage soil for its sustainable use.[22]

A *standard* includes anything taken by general consent as a basis of comparison, where the basis for "comparison" is the ecological benefit that would accrue to soil by the adoption of one or more *ecological standards*, compared with the loss of ecological integrity of the soil (i.e., degradation) if appropriate *ecological soil standards* are not used. Therefore, it is suggested that the definition of an *ecological soil standard* can be applied to:

- Processes of soil policy formulation and preparation of plans or strategies;
- Techniques applied in land-use planning;
- Land-use decision-making processes; and
- Practical soil conservation measures.

In all instances, it is imperative that the application of an *ecological soil standard* be based on suitable criteria (e.g., soil loss tolerance limits) and values (e.g., criteria to achieve ecologically sustainable land use) that will provide ultimate benefit to the soil environment.

5 NATIONAL SOIL REGIMES

Legislation has been used for many years in many countries in a piecemeal fashion to manage specific types of soil problems (e.g., soil erosion), to control land-use activities, which directly cause soil degradation problems (e.g., overgrazing of cattle and sheep), and to indirectly control soil management problems (e.g., through environmental planning and land use allocation).[23] The 1980s and 1990s witnessed growth in environmental laws at the international and national levels to manage the natural environment. However, soil law reform has not seen the same level of attention. Legal and institutional frameworks in most countries still approach soil conservation in a fragmented way. In the past, the main type of legislation aimed at the control of soil degradation has been the "soil conservation law."[24] Legislation had a land-utilization focus, which is no longer adequate to protect and manage the world's soil degradation problems effectively. In the past, as the area of land affected by soil degradation grew, practical soil conservation techniques were developed and applied in conjunction with expanding agricultural

environmental law is discussed; see also "Environmental Quality Norms," in the *Environmental Code of Sweden*.

[22] See I. D. Hannam, "The Concept of Sustainable Land Management and Soil Conservation Law and Policy in Australia," in P. Henriques, ed., Proceedings of International Conference on Sustainable Land Management (Napier New Zealand, 2002), 153.

[23] See Kurucz, M., "Land Protection, Property Rights and Environmental Preferences (Land Use Control and Land Development)" 8(2) *Connecticut Journal of International Law* (1993), 467.

[24] See M. Grossman & W. Brussaard, eds., *Agrarian Land Law in the Western World* (Wallingford, UK: CAB International Publishers, 1992).

activities.[25] The conservation capabilities of the legislation were overshadowed by the objective of agricultural production, price support schemes for domestic and export needs, and land settlement and development schemes. Soil conservation legislation was introduced in the first half of the nineteenth century primarily to control the effects of soil erosion by wind and water. This type of legislation was prominent in colonial Africa, Australia, New Zealand, the United States, and some European and Asian nations.[26] Soil conservation legislation generally was introduced to prevent, mitigate, or manage soil erosion on arable or pastoral land. Some of the legislation had provisions for catchment or watershed land management planning.[27] In the early 1970s, it was stated that: "The general object of soil conservation legislation is to induce those whose activities affect the soil to act in a manner that preserves its desired qualities to a greater extent than their normal manner of operation would do."[28]

By the mid-1990s, in pursuance of a sustainable land management goal, it was acknowledged that a range of land management programs, policies, and educational initiatives, as well as national and local laws, were necessary to successfully change the behavior of land users.[29] An overview of current national legislation directed to soil indicates that States have adopted a wide variety of legislative approaches to deal with specific soil protection and management problems. This is reflected generally in the broad structural features of soil legislation, as well as in the variety of specific mechanisms used to protect and manage soil and land use. The following observations have been made with regard to legislative systems:[30]

- States have been reasonably creative and innovative in the choice and application of individual mechanisms;
- Some States have developed a framework of legislation to manage a number of distinct soil and land use problems but generally lack linking or coordinating mechanisms to ensure that there is an effective institutional implementation of the legislation;

[25] See N. Hudson, *Soil Conservation* (Ames: Iowa State University Press, 1995).

[26] See, for example, Hazara Forest Act 1936, Pakistan; Soil Conservation Act 1938, New South Wales, Australia; Natural Resources Act 1951, Swaziland; Soil Conservation Act 1951, Sri Lanka; Soil Conservation Law 1952, Cyprus.

[27] See, for example, J. R. Bradsen, *Soil Conservation Legislation in Australia*, Report for the National Soil Conservation Program (University of Adelaide, Adelaide, 1988); Huong Tran, Liu-Hsiang Chuang, & C. Guss, *Natural Resources Conservation Laws: A Study of Seventeen States and Their Selected Counties and Townships* (Washington, DC: Natural Resources Conservation Service, United States Department of Agriculture, 1997); I. Krasnova, "Legal Protection of Soils, Russian Federation" *Environmental Policy and Law* (2000) 3076.

[28] Christy, L. C., *Legislative Principles of Soil Conservating*, Food and Agriculture Organization of the United Nations.

[29] See H. Hurni, with the assistance of an international group of contributors, Precious Earth: From Soil and Water Conservation to Sustainable Land management, International Soil Conservation Organization Conference and Centre for Development and Environment (Bern, Switzerland,1999); S. A. El-Swaify, with an international group of contributors, *Sustaining the Global Farm – Strategic Issues, Principles, and Approaches*, International Soil Conservation Organization, Department of Agronomy and Soil Science, University of Hawaii (Manoa, Honolulu, 1999); UNEP and FAO, *The Future of Our Land: Facing the Challenge* (Rome, 1999).

[30] For a comprehensive review and discussion of national soil legislation, see Note 2, I. D. Hannam, with B. W. Boer, 2002, Note 10, at 40–41; and B. W. Boer, & I. D. Hannam, "Legal Aspects of Sustainable Soils; International and National" 12(2) *Review of European Community and International Environmental Law* (2003), 149.

- The majority of legislation does not take into account the inherent ecological characteristics and limitations of soil bodies as the premise for land-use decision making; rather, the legislation related to soil addresses soil problems ex post facto; that is, to try to rectify the problems caused by poor land-use planning or inappropriate land use in the first place;
- The legislation does not acknowledge soil as an ecological element with a central role in terrestrial ecology, the conservation of biodiversity, and maintenance of environmental amenity;
- The primary functions of soil are not well represented in the legislation in most jurisdictions, and only a few laws refer to the ecological features or needs of the soil;
- A dominant characteristic of existing national soil legislation is that it is directed to the physical problems caused by inappropriate land use, mainly in agriculture and forestry (reflecting short-term private interest as opposed to long-term public interest);
- Following from the last point, the structure of some laws indicates that they are a reaction to a political or institutional issue, rather than designed to effectively manage the soil;
- Many individual laws do not have a clear statement of purpose or objectives. Where the intention is clear, it is often poorly reflected in the substance of the legislation;
- Many laws do not include the range of elements necessary to effectively protect or manage the particular soil problem, and where they do, those elements are often not logically developed; there are also many examples where the exact meaning or intention of the element is not apparent; and
- There is a general lack of consistency in the use of standard scientific soil terminology, and often there is an absence of definitions, or inadequate and poorly stated definitions.

6 NATIONAL LEGAL AND INSTITUTIONAL FRAMEWORKS

The development of frameworks for national soil legislation should be approached from a sound conceptual and ethical basis, with the goal of protecting and managing the ecological aspects of soil to enable its use in a sustainable manner. For such a framework to be effective, States must be willing to accept new values in a legal system for the soil.

6.1 Elements

A primary outcome of the ELC program has been the IUCN Guide for *Drafting Legislation for Sustainable Soils*, which contains over one hundred "sample" legal and institutional elements appropriate for national soil legislation.[31] The elements are generic, and individual States need to ensure that adequate background work is undertaken to identify clearly the actual physical, cultural, institutional, and socioeconomic issues that need to be taken into consideration when preparing specific national soil legislation. States have the freedom to clearly and distinctly address an actual domestic soil protection

[31] I. D. Hannam, and B. W. Boer, *Drafting Legislation for Sustainable use of Soils: A Guide* (IUCN, Gland Switzerland and Cambridge, UK, 2004), 100.

or management issue, and specific provisions should be developed to satisfy the local, regional, or State situation. These elements also can be used to assess the capacity of an existing law to meet prescribed standards of performance for the sustainable use of soil.[32]

6.2 A Legal and Institutional System

A legal and institutional system is used to manage the sustainable use of soil. When a State is designing such a regime, it is important that its current organisational system is reviewed, to ensure that a new law can be administered effectively. In some circumstances, an organisation (or several organisations) may have to be partly or completely reorganised.[33]

6.3 Key Principles for the Sustainable Use of Soil

The two principal sources that established the direction for the development of the suggested elements used in the IUCN Guide for *Drafting Legislation* for *Sustainable Soils* include:

- Ecological and scientific principles for the sustainable use of soil; and
- The Resolution of the World Conservation Congress of 2000 on Sustainable Use of Soil.

6.4 Ecological Principles for the Sustainable Use of Soil

Some of the more important principles include:

- Soil degradation affects the global environment because it represents a loss of integral components of the world's ecosystems and global biodiversity;
- Accelerated soil degradation is mostly human-induced and occurs in all ecoregions of the world, irrespective of social, economic, and political conditions;
- A recognition that soil degradation has a significant impact on the total environment in any particular State;
- The extent, type, degree, and severity of soil degradation varies between one soil community and another;
- Agricultural soils are being lost to nonagricultural uses, especially as a result of urbanization;
- Soil degradation causes damage to the soil resource by erosion, contamination, change of physical or chemical state (acidification, compaction, and salinization), and loss of nutrients and organic matter;
- A significant proportion of the degradation of the atmosphere is a result of greenhouse gas emissions, caused by various forms of soil use associated with agriculture;[34]

[32] "Law" in this context means a body of law enacted by a legislature, for example, an act, decree, regulation, code, or other formal legal instrument that is legally enforceable. It can include agreements or covenants that are expressed to be legally binding.

[33] Note 8, Hannam with Boer 2002, Section 4.

[34] See I. D. Hannam, 2004. International and National Aspects of a Legislative Framework to Manage Soil Carbon Sequestration, *Climate Change*, An Interdisciplinary, International Journal Devoted to the

- Loss of biodiversity is generally related to land-use changes, including deforestation, agricultural intensification, and urban expansion, all of which lead to soil degradation; and
- Accelerated soil degradation exacerbates the scarcity of productive lands and is a major threat to global food security and induces poverty.

The general characteristics of the current global situation with land resource use also point to the need for improved international and national soil legal and institutional frameworks, including:[35]

- The uneven spatial and temporal distribution among nations of populations and consumptive needs;
- The links that have been established between the occurrence of soil degradation and poverty;
- The uneven distribution of productive, unutilized, and underutilized or degrading soils;
- The substantial variation in cropping systems, and occurrence of productive soils;
- Areas of surplus production and of food deficit;
- Varied availability of capital for soil protection;
- The opportunities that exist to transfer knowledge on sustainable use of soils, to combat degradation, and to achieve sustainable land management vary between regions and nations; and
- Consideration of the global soil environment should be independent of political boundaries.

7 INTERNATIONAL LEGAL AND INSTITUTIONAL REGIMES FOR SOIL

7.1 Existing Regimes

The SGSS has reviewed many existing international and regional instruments that make reference to soils. It discussed various relationships between different hard and soft law mechanisms that have been developed in international environmental law. Although the problem of soil and land degradation has not gone unnoticed by the world community, there has been little discussion, until recently, on the role of international environmental law and soil degradation. One particular study in 1993 discussed the types of hard and soft law that related to land degradation,[36] but it was not until the IUCN ELP Program commenced in 1999 that any detailed analysis of the law was carried out, and it was only then that suggestions were made regarding improvements or rationalisation of these laws.[37]

A key response to the rapidly changing political and social aspects of the world and the ever-expanding environmental problems has been the accelerated development

Description, Causes and Implications of Climatic Change, 1–23; see also S. Wood, K. Sebastion, & S. J. Scherr., *Pilot Analysis of Global Ecosystems Agroecosystems* (Washington, DC: International Food Policy Research Institute and World Resources Institute, 2000); Hurni & Meyer (2003), Note 4; Boer & Hannam (2003), Note 30.

[35] Hannam and Boer, 2003, Section III.

[36] See R. Khan, "International Law of Land Degradation." 30(3) *International Studies* (1993), Sage Publications, New Delhi, Newbury Park, London.

[37] Note 18 Hannam with Boer (2002); Boer & Hannam (2003), Note 30.

of international and domestic environmental law. Environmental law is an essential component for setting and implementing global, regional, and national policy. There is an increasing recognition of the role of international environmental law to overcome the global problem of soil degradation, including its ability to provide a juridical basis for action by nations and the international community. Global conventions, treaties, and protocols are assuming increased importance. In recent years, the United Nations has paid growing attention to environmental issues, and many countries have signed individual international environmental treaties relating to climate change, biodiversity, desertification, trade in hazardous wastes, endangered species, the ozone layer, and wetlands. These are all issues that relate, in one way or another, to the use of the land and its soil. The increasing number of nations that have become signatories to these treaties reflects the realisation of the need for international cooperation and understanding between respective nations.[38]

Agenda 21, the action plan from the 1992 UN Conference on Environment and Development (UNCED), identified concrete steps to integrate environment and development. However, UNCED further endorsed the role of environmental law in guiding all nations toward integration. *Agenda 21* emphasized the need to integrate "environment and development issues at national, sub-regional, regional and international levels," including:

- Elaborating the balance between environmental and developmental concerns;
- Clarifying the relationships between the various existing treaties; and
- Ensuring national participation in both developing and implementing these legal measures, with particular focus on developing countries.[39]

7.2 Multilateral Environmental Treaties and Other Agreements

Since the early 1900s, over two hundred multilateral environmental treaties, agreements, and protocols have been developed, covering flora and fauna conservation, protection of fisheries, pollution management, regional conservation protection, Antarctic conservation, settling disputes, civil liberties in relation to environmental damage, protection of world cultural and natural heritage, endangered species, and landscape protection.[40] Although a number of these contain elements that can assist in achieving sustainable use of soil, it was realized by the IUCN ELP that none are sufficient in their own right to meet the requirements of international environmental law in relation to soil. Some of the existing instruments assist by managing some of the activities that directly lead to, or can control, soil degradation, but this role is not readily apparent.

7.3 An International Environmental Law Framework for Soil

Reference to key elements of the Montevideo Program III provided a useful guide as to what the elements of an international framework for soil might be, in order to promote

[38] As discussed in Section V. International Legal and Institutional Regimes for Soil, Subsection 1 – Existing Regimes, in Hannam with Boer, 2002, Note 8.

[39] *Agenda 21*, Chapter 39, "International Legal Instruments and Mechanisms," at 39.1.

[40] United Nations Environment Programme, *Handbook of Environmental Law*, (UNEP Nairobi, 1996).

the goal of sustainable use of soil at a national level.[41] Although all of the general actions set out to address the Effectiveness of Environmental Law in section 1 of the Montevideo Program III are relevant to soil, the ELP considered that the following actions were particularly relevant to an immediate process of legislative development:

- Achieving effective implementation of, compliance with, and enforcement of environmental law by promoting the implementation of environmental law through, *inter alia*, the widest possible participation in multilateral environmental agreements and the development of relevant strategies, mechanisms, and national laws;[42]
- Strengthening measures to prevent and mitigate environmental damage when it occurs;[43]
- Strengthening and developing international environmental law, building on the existing foundations;[44] and
- Applying innovative approaches to environmental law to improve its effectiveness. This requires the identification and promotion of innovative approaches, tools and mechanisms, including the promotion of ecosystem management in law and practice, including the environmental benefits of ecosystems.[45]

7.4 The Case for a Specific International Soil Instrument

In its investigation, the IUCN ELP used a number of key global environmental strategies to establish the case for a specific instrument for soil. The goal of intergenerational equity was considered to be the fundamental objective of sustainable use of soil. This principle recognizes that the present generation has a basic obligation to conserve options for future generations by maintaining to the maximum extent possible the diversity of the resource base. This goal was effectively pointed out in the *Brundtland Report*,[46] with regard to nonrenewable resources. This report stated that present generations have an obligation to consume nonrenewable resources in a manner that give future generations an opportunity for an orderly transition to alternative methods that will provide similar benefits. Other key areas of justification determined by the IUCN ELP as essential to apply this principle to formulate the elements for international soil law included:

- Various Articles adopted by the *Experts Group on Environmental Law of the WCED*;[47]
- Various Principles in the *Rio Declaration*;

[41] Montevideo Programme III – the Program for the Development and Periodic Review of Environmental Law for the First Decade of the Twenty-First Century was adopted by the Governing Council of the United Nations Environment Program in February 2001 (Decision 21/23).

[42] Clause 1 of the "Effectiveness of Environmental Law" under the Montevideo Programme III.

[43] Clause 3 of the "Effectiveness of Environmental Law" under the Montevideo Programme III.

[44] Clause 5 of the "Effectiveness of Environmental Law" under the Montevideo Programme III. Note: this element was seen as being particularly important because it encourages international action to address gaps and weaknesses in existing international environmental law and to respond to new environmental challenges.

[45] Clause 9 of the "Effectiveness of Environmental Law" under the Montevideo Programme III.

[46] See "The World Commission on Environment and Development," *Our Common Future* (Oxford University Press, 1987).

[47] The World Commission on Environment and Development, *Environmental Protection and Sustainable Development; Legal Principles and Recommendations*, Experts Group on Environmental Law (Graham and Trotman/Martinus Nijhoff, 1986).

- The goals and objectives of the Montevideo Program III for the review of environmental law; and
- Various reaffirmations made at the World Summit on Sustainable Development in Johannesburg in 2002.

8 OPTIONS

International environmental law instruments for soil can either be legally binding instruments or nonlegally binding instruments.[48] It is essential that the promotion of an international legal framework to protect the soil environment provides an opportunity for the input of all interested parties, including international environmental organizations, States, soil science institutions, private sector interests, and nongovernment organizations. However, a number of the "known" obstacles to the implementation of international instruments should be taken into account when deciding on a process for an international soil instrument.[49]

8.1 Suggested Elements of an International Framework for Soil

Before considering which of the possible two framework approaches may be appropriate to develop for soil, it is essential to discuss the elements that may be applied to achieve the sustainable use of soil. The principal underlying ethic of the international framework for soil recognises the natural aspect of soil as an ecological element, as well as the basic rights of humans with regard to the role and use of soil and the obligations on respective parties to observe these natural rights. Thus, it should convey principles that allow:

- A right to an ecologically healthy soil environment;
- A right of access to judicial and administrative proceedings, including redress and remedy in exercising rights and obligations;
- A right for a State to take legal action against another State for damage to its soil arising from the transboundary effects of unsustainable land use;
- A right for persons to participate in planning and decision-making processes for soil;
- A right of access by all people to accurate soil information, particularly knowledge of the global and regional status of soil degradation; and
- A right to expect the world community as a whole and States in particular to protect and conserve soil for the benefit of present and future generations.

8.2 Key Points

From the examination of the key technical and ecological issues concerning soil, the IUCN ELP SGSS defined the term "sustainable use of soil" as "*the use of soils in a manner*

[48] See discussion on binding and nonbinding instruments in the UN *Treaty Reference Guide*, op. cit. (United Nations, 1999).

[49] See Kelly, M., "Overcoming Obstacles to the Effective Implementation of International Environmental Agreements," in IX *The Georgetown International Environmental Law Review* (1995) 2:447; and J. Cameron, J. Werksman, & P. Roderick, eds., *Improving Compliance with International Environmental Law* (London: Earthscan, 1996).

that preserves the balance between the processes of soil formation and soil degradation, while maintaining the ecological functions and needs of soil." In this context, the phrase "use of soil" means "*the role of soil in the conservation of biodiversity and the maintenance of human life*" (as taken from the Amman resolution).

The dilemma for soil is that, as the basic ecological component of the terrestrial ecosystem, it is also a basic element (along with water and air) on which humans depend for the maintenance of life. Therefore pressure is put on soil. This situation is complicated further by the problems associated with defining the term "sustainability," and the choice of a particular mode of sustainability – for example, social, economic, or ecological – by the community. These factors influenced the manner in which the SGSS approached and presented its findings. The SGSS concluded that the sustainable use of soil is inadequately addressed in national and international environmental law. Many suggestions are made as to how this may be improved. In the fifteen years since UNCED 1992, there has been an increasing realization within the soil science community, and in related groups, that a new ecologically focused international environmental law instrument will be a critical component of the strategic plan for sustainable soil management in the twenty-first century. This goal is confirmed by the fact that from 2005 to 2007 no less than ten international soil conferences were held in which this issue was a major discussion item. It also has appeared on the agendas of regional soil science workshops.[50]

There are some good examples in which individual States have undertaken soil legislation reform in a very innovative way, leading to much more effective soil legislation frameworks, for example, in Hungary, Iceland, Thailand, China, and Australia. This is very encouraging and much has been learned, but these innovations are rare, and many more nations would need to undertake soil legislation reform before any substantial improvement in the ecological condition of soil can be expected. At the international level, there are "pockets" of evidence of soil legal elements, particularly within some of the regional instruments (e.g., ASEAN Convention, African Convention on the Conservation of Nature and Natural Resources[51]), but these are overshadowed by ecological priorities other than the specific ecological needs of soil. However, encouragement can be derived from the existence of the *Protocol for the Implementation of the Alpine Convention of 1991 in the Area of Soil Protection*, which is the only single legal binding instrument for soil in the world as of this writing. This Protocol provides impetus to develop effective soil instruments at the national and regional levels, including a specific international instrument. Despite the complexities of the legal and physical aspects of the soil, there is a good range of opportunities within the scope of binding and non-binding environmental law frameworks, to develop a plan to improve the national and international legal position for soil. The reports prepared by the IUCN ELP SGSS discuss various approaches and frameworks that may be taken to improve the legal mechanisms for soil at both levels.

[50] For example, Workshop on "Soils and the Sustainable Development Strategy of the European Union," held at the Agricultural University of Uppsala, Sweden, 23–24 April 2001; Workshop on Natural and Socio-Economic Effects of Erosion Control in Mountainous Regions, 11–13 December 2002, Belgrade / Banja Vrujci, Serbia/Yugoslavia; 14th International Soil Conservation Organization Congress, 14–19th May 2006, Marrakech, Morocco.

[51] New text adopted by the African Union Assembly on 11 July 2004.

8.3 Specific Conclusions

The path selected by the IUCN ELP to meet the environmental law needs of soil highlights a number of interacting factors, including:

- An awareness of the poor recognition of soil in current international environmental law, and that national soil legislation generally is inadequate to manage the type and severity of soil degradation problems experienced around the world;
- The need to consider the ecological function of soil for the conservation of biodiversity and the maintenance of human life;
- The need to satisfy the high level of recognition amongst the soil science community of the benefits of introducing an international instrument to raise the awareness of the serious situation of soil degradation, and the need to develop suitable legal tools for individual nations to improve the capability of their domestic law to protect and manage soil in a sustainable way. Of particular concern is the continued high rate of expansion of soil degradation globally, the increase in degree and severity of individual soil degradation processes, and the periodic emergence of new forms of soil degradation. Of even more concern is the prediction that this situation will worsen in the twenty-first century.[52] The data clearly shows that in the immediate future the world will place even greater pressure on its soils than it does today;
- A general realization that the world community must take action sooner rather than later to more adequately cater for the ecological functions and needs of soil in the international and national environmental law regimes, as an integral part of the overall framework of environmental law and policy for environmental management;[53]
- A realization that a number of existing multinational agreements that have specific objectives and responsibilities to improve the condition of the terrestrial environment are not being implemented to their full potential and that this situation may influence the choice of a global instrument for soil. Some developed nations that have taken a leadership role in global environmental management are currently displaying an unsatisfactory attitude toward some of their most important domestic responsibilities;
- In the recent past, there have been some positive national soil law reforms; in a few instances, new statutes have been either passed or tabled. These moves have stimulated some other nations, and some regions, to actively seek assistance to develop new national soil law, but they represent a small number and area of the world;[54]
- The decision to develop international and national soil legislation frameworks also should include the provision to develop the accompanying support materials and explanatory guidelines necessary to ensure the effective implementation of the separate frameworks.

[52] See Bridges et al., note 3; and United Nations Environment Programme, *Global Environmental Outlook 2000*, (Earthscan Publications Ltd., London), see "Future Perspectives."

[53] As indicated in the Amman Resolution, the IUCN CEL Sustainable Soils Working Group mandate, under the Soils Objective of Montevideo Programme III, and WSSD 2002.

[54] For example, regions that have recently shown interest include Southeast Asia (particularly Thailand, Vietnam, Cambodia, Lao People's Democratic Republic), Eastern and Central Europe, and the southern "cone" of South America (particularly Brazil, Argentina, and Paraguay).

8.4 Some Options

In summary, some of the options presented by the IUCN ELP include:

8.4.1 National

- Promotion of the generic *Guide*, which consists of a range of general elements that may be drawn on by individual nations when amending an existing law or developing a new law for soil; and
- Preparation of regional legal frameworks for soil, to be used in conjunction with these basic generic legal elements, which should include a range of specific elements to deal with the physical and legal characteristics of the particular region.[55]

8.4.2 International

Binding instrument options include:

- A specific treaty with all of the essential legal elements for soil;
- A framework treaty, which identifies the soil elements in existing treaties[56] and links them through a separate binding instrument. The new instrument would contain additional, specific legal rules for soil; and
- A protocol to an existing treaty that creates specific rules for soil.[57]

Nonbinding options include:

- An international charter for soil; and
- A declaration for soil.

9 RECOMMENDATIONS

To adequately fulfill the terms of the IUCN World Congress Amman Resolution of October 2000 and its Supplementary Resolution of November 2004, the terms of reference of the SGSS, as well as to accommodate the soil objectives of the Montevideo Program III, a number of actions are called for to promote the findings and conclusions of the ELP reports.

9.1 Recommendations

1. The IUCN ELP host a meeting of representatives of the principal bodies that have an interest in the general objectives of the SGSS project. The objective of the meeting would be to seek their formal endorsement of the SGSS project, and to canvass opportunities for these bodies to input to the project in the interest of achieving a better overall legal strategy for the sustainable use of the world's soils. The IUCN ELP should invite representatives of the principal bodies consulted and of other suitable organizations to make substantive inputs to the project;

[55] See Hannam with Boer (2002), Note 10, Section 4.2 for discussion on regional instruments.
[56] For example, in the Convention to Combat Desertification, and the Convention on Biological Diversity.
[57] Ibid.

2. The ELP expand the terms of reference of the SGSS project into a more comprehensive and substantial sustainable soils project within the IUCN as a whole. Formal links will need to be forged with other IUCN Commissions, and with some of the specific program areas of IUCN, including links with the IUCN regions;
3. The ELP propose that the IUCN Council request the Director General to develop a specific soil education campaign to raise the awareness of the national and international legal needs of soil and to promote the need for the community to adopt an ecologically based paradigm for soil. The ELP would be a key component of this campaign. Such an initiative would support existing initiatives of the global soil science community;
4. The ELP actively promote the Guide to *Drafting Legislation for Sustainable Soils* among the particular regions of the world where soil degradation is the most severe;
5. The ELP complete the drafting of the international instrument for the sustainable use of soils, including accompanying support and guideline materials for its effective implementation;
6. The ELP continue to seek financial support to further the development of legal and institutional frameworks for sustainable soils, including the implementation of "generic" soil law and regional models; and
7. The ELP take appropriate steps to ensure that its initiatives for improved legal and institutional frameworks for sustainable soils continue to be addressed at all relevant international and national environmental conferences and meetings.

18 The Ghanaian Forestry Regime: Bridging the Gap between the North and the South

George A. Sarpong*

1 INTRODUCTION

The importance of forests as sources of food, medicine, habitats, and sinks, *inter alia*, cannot be overemphasized: humankind's very existence relies on the continued existence of these vital natural resources. This can be summed up in the adage, "When the last tree dies, the last man dies." Indeed, the phenomenon of climate change has been declared a common concern of humankind; and forests as sinks for carbon have been identified as one of the major means for dealing with the phenomenon. Hence, the existence of forests anywhere in the world must be of concern to the entire global community.

In Ghana, the forestry sector contributes almost 6 percent of the country's Gross Domestic Product (GDP), with the timber industry providing direct employment to over 100,00 people and indirect employment to over 2.5 million others. Wood fuel accounts for 75 percent of Ghanaian domestic and industrial energy sources estimated at $USD200 million per annum. Hunting and the trade in bush meat also account for between $USD270 and $USD350 million annually. Nontimber forest products also contribute to the daily livelihood of forest fringe communities and the national economy by creating employment for a substantial number of people and by generating an annual amount of $USD250 million.[1] The sector is also the backbone of the country's mainly nature-based tourism industry. Because of well-funded protected areas and the diversity of these nature-based attractions, this sector has become the number three foreign exchange earner for Ghana.[2]

The world's forests are reducing at an alarming rate. The problem is more acute in the tropics, where the rate of deforestation is currently estimated at about 17 million hectares per annum. It has been estimated, for example, that a third of Ghana's forests disappeared in the seventeen years between 1955 and 1972, at an annual rate of 750 kilometers per annum. Current estimates are that, of the country's original 8.22 million hectares of forests (34 percent of the total surface area of Ghana), only 1.6 million hectares remain, with a further annual deforestation rate of 65,000 hectares. At the current rate of exploitation, it is estimated that unless drastic and prudent measures are taken

[1] ¢9000 is approximately $USD1.

[2] *Forestry Commission News: Newsletter of the Ghana Forestry Commission Vol. 1* (January–March 2005).

* George A. Sarpong is Senior Lecturer, Faculty of Law, University of Ghana.

immediately to protect, sustain, and improve on what is left, Ghana will become a net importer of timber within ten years.[3]

The causes of the forest decline are many and varied. They include cultivation for economic crops, especially cocoa, mining, logging, animal grazing, desertification, and bushfires.

Despite the rapid rate of destruction of the world's forests, there is no global convention in existence to address the problem. At the United Nations Conference on the Environment and Development 1992 (UNCED), no other issue divided the North and South more intensely or highlighted the conflict between the environment and development more vividly than the exploitation of forests. The European Community (EC), for example, viewed the matter as being at the very core of sustainable development, whereas developing states in general opined that a binding convention on the subject would infringe on their sovereign rights to exploit their economic resources. What was agreed on at Rio was a nonlegally binding statement of principles for the sustainable management of global forests.[4]

UNCED, however, produced two global conventions on the environment – the Convention on Biological Diversity (CBD) and the United Nations Framework Convention on Climate Change (UNFCCC). It also produced the Rio Declaration on Environment and Development designed to embody rules and principles on sustainable development, as well as Agenda 21, a tool designed to address the major environment and development priorities for the realization of sustainable development. Agenda 21 entails 115 specific programs covering socioeconomic issues; conservation and resource management; the role of nongovernmental organizations (NGOs) and other groups; and institutional and financial mechanisms for implementation.

In spite of the absence of a specific global convention on forests, Ghana, post-Rio, has embarked on institutional and legislative initiatives aimed at ensuring the conservation and sustainable utilization of forestry resources in consonance with the concerns of the North. Concerns about forestry in Ghana, however, date from the precolonial era. Both the colonial power – Great Britain – and successive postindependence governments have addressed the problem, albeit through different perspectives.

This chapter examines the legal regime for forestry in Ghana, bridging the gap between the North and South on an issue at the heart of sustainable development. The chapter is in four sections. Section 1 is the introduction. Section 2 examines the various initiatives – precolonial and postcolonial – adopted by Ghana in the forestry sector up to UNCED. Section 3 addresses Ghanaian post-UNCED institutional and legislative forestry measures; unlike the pre-UNCED regime, the focus shifts from a command and control regulatory framework to one of conservation and sustainable use, concerning emerging concepts in contemporary environmental law and the major stakeholders

[3] Interview with officials of the Forestry Commission, 8 June 2005. Ghana covers a land mass of 92,100 square miles or 238,539 square kilometers. Out of this, Lake Volta, reputed to be the largest man-made lake in the world, covers approximately 3,275 square miles or 8,482 square kilometers. See also *Ghana Forestry Commission at a Glance* (January 2003).

[4] For background information on events leading to the Earth Summit, the Conference itself, and the outcomes, see, for example, F. A. Nelissen, "The Mandate of Rio: Preparations and Expectations" 45 (1991), *International Spectator* (11) 674–680; "Rio Conference on Environment and Development" 22 *Environmental Policy and Law Journal* (1992), 4; Earth Summit Press Release 1992 (New York: UN Department of Public Information).

involved in forestry, especially local communities. Section 4 concludes the subject and offers final remarks.

2 THE PRE-UNCED FRAMEWORK FOR FORESTRY IN GHANA

The picture that emerges from the precolonial era is of a people living in close harmony with nature. In the precolonial era, forest conservation took the form of preserving sacred groves, burial graves, and forests left along the courses of rivers and streams.[5] Forests and land, in general, were regarded as communal property. Among the Akans,[6] land was communally owned and held in trust for and on behalf of the entire community by the chiefs. Nana Sir Ofori Atta, a prominent Gold Coast Chief, put it succinctly: "*I conceive that land belongs to a vast family of whom many are dead, a few are living and countless hosts are still unborn.*"[7] This is a classic exposition of the concept of intergenerational equity, an important element of the principle of sustainable development.

2.1 The Colonial Era

Colonial rules[8] altered this picture. The power to regulate forestry was taken from the chiefs and centrally vested in the colonial power. This totally alienated the chiefs and people from the control or management of forestry. A new dimension to the need for forests emerged: the manipulation of trees and soil to produce sustained outputs of timber and other commercial crops, especially during World War II. Furthermore, to maintain climatic quality, to protect watersheds, and to ensure an environment conducive to cocoa production, the colonial power decided that a permanent forest estate must be established through the process of forest reservation. The chiefs could not be easily persuaded to yield some forests for reservation;[9] and when persuasion failed, force was applied through the Forest Ordinance.[10]

This Ordinance gave the governor power to constitute forest reserves from government, tribal, or private land for the purpose of conservation. In the case of private lands, this had to be at the request of the owner. Under Section 22 of the Ordinance, a person found in or from a Forest Reserve would be guilty of an offence and, on conviction, would be liable for a monetary fine or imprisonment if he does any of the following without authority: fells, uproots, taps, or injures by fire, or otherwise damages any tree or timber; makes or cultivates any farm; sets fire to any grass or herbages; or kindles a fire without taking due precaution to prevent its spreading. Thus, by the stroke of a pen, the chiefs and people had been alienated from their forests; furthermore, they required permission from colonial officials to enter these reserves and do anything there, activities that up to that point had been legitimate.

[5] Kotey et al., *Falling into Place: Ghana Country Study* (International Institute for Environment and Development, 1998).

[6] The Akans are the major ethnic group in Ghana, comprising about 60 percent of the Ghanaian population of eighteen million.

[7] Edith Brown Weiss, *In Fairness to Future Generations: International Law, Common Patrimony and Intergenerational Equity* (New York: Transnational Publishers, 1989). The Gold Coast was renamed Ghana following independence in 1957.

[8] From 1874 to 1957.

[9] Kotey et al., note 5, at 9–13.

[10] Cap. 157.

Subsequent enactments sought to tighten the hold of the colonial government over forests. In 1949, for instance, the Trees and Timber Ordinance[11] was passed to regulate the timber trade through the registration and issuing of property marks to concession holders and the provision of licences and permits as preconditions for the felling of trees. Colonial rule thus separated the chiefs and people from their forests.

2.2 The Postcolonial Era before UNCED

Ironically, the picture portrayed here was not altered significantly during the postindependence era, largely because of the socialist stance of the then Nkrumah regime. In 1959, the government enacted the Protected Timber Lands Act.[12] This Act declared off-reserve forest lands to be protected timber lands and gave the Forestry Department the power to regulate and control farm development and expansion in the affected areas. Thus, the regulation of forests was taken a stage further from the reserves to lands that hitherto could otherwise be used for farming and other cultural practices.

The worse was yet to come, however. In 1962, the Administration of Lands Act[13] was enacted. This Act vested the management of all stool lands[14] and the collection of stool land revenues in the government. Under the Act, forests were reckoned as part of land, and stool land revenues were determined to include royalties and rent. Thus, the Act effectively placed the management of stool lands and revenues under the auspices of the government.

Two other pieces of legislation affecting the forestry sector were enacted in the 1970s: The Trees and Timber Decree,[15] as amended, and the Forest Protection Decree.[16] The Trees and Timber Decree enforced the system of property marks originally established under the 1949 Trees and Timber Ordinance by criminalizing the felling of timber for export without valid property marks. The 1983 amendment imposed stiffer penalties for violations. The Forest Protection Decree substantially reenacted the Forest Ordinance. In addition, the Forest Protection Decree provided for the payment of twice the commercial value of each tree or of the timber or forest produced by a person convicted of an offence under the Decree, in addition to any other punishment that may be imposed.

The enforcement of the Forest Protection Decree in these reserves is entrusted to Forest Officers, who are granted wide powers under the decree. In particular, they may arrest, without warrant, any person whom they reasonably suspect to have committed or to have been concerned with any offence under the Decree. Persons arrested are to be prosecuted. In the event of a conviction, all forest products, instruments, vehicles, and other articles in respect of which or by means of which the offence was committed shall be forfeited to the State.

The Decree further provides that any person who has been convicted three times of an offence under the Decree shall be prohibited from owning, operating, or participating in any timber business or timber concession. Furthermore, all permits and property marks held by such a convict under any enactment relating to forests, trees, or timber

[11] No. 20 (Cap. 158). See earlier comment.
[12] Act 34.
[13] Act 123.
[14] Land held in trust by chiefs on behalf of the community.
[15] NRCD 273, as amended by Trees and Timber Amendment Law, 1983 PNDCL 70.
[16] NRCD 243.

shall be deemed to be forfeited to the state. The consequences of a conviction under the law are grave.

The Forest Protection Decree also enjoins any person permitted under the law to be present, or while present in a reserve, to assist in the prevention and spread of bushfires. Closely related to forest reserves are "protected areas" under the Trees and Timber Decree.[17] As a measure aimed at the prevention of wastage of trees or timber, the Minister responsible for Forestry may declare an area lying outside a forest reserve a protected area. Within such an area, it is an offence to fell or damage any tree or timber, to farm or build, to set fires, or to kindle a fire without taking precautions to prevent its spread without the prior written consent of the Minister.

Contravention of the foregoing provisions attracts penal sanctions in the form of imprisonment or fines. Farming operations may be carried out in a protected area only under a Forestry Officer's licence. The conditions necessary to safeguard the protected area may be imposed as a condition for the grant of the licence. Again, contravention of this provision attracts penal sanctions. The main goal of the law then was to place a ban on virtually every human activity in the forest reserves of Ghana without the permission of the Department of Forestry.

However, in spite of the provisions of these and other laws on conservation of forests, the policy of the government, aimed at generating foreign exchange for the economy through logging, appeared to have taken precedence over the spirit and letter of these conservation laws. Indeed, attempts by the government of the day to revive the timber industry under the Economic Recovery Programme in the 1980s resulted in an influx of persons into the timber trade, which caused a lot of devastation to farmlands and forests, and the sheer export of round logs in the timber trade led to overexploitation of Ghanaian forest resources.

3 POST-UNCED INSTITUTIONAL AND LEGISLATIVE REFORMS

If the control of forests was begun by the colonial powers, then the seal was firmly put in place by subsequent governments – civilian and military – after independence. But a wind of change began to blow in the 1990s, especially after UNCED 1992. This change saw the chiefs and people once more becoming involved in forestry after over a century of alienation.

The 1990s was the most significant period in the Ghanaian forestry regime. Several factors account for this change of events, including international and donor influence and support, the 1992 Constitution, and policy initiatives.

3.1 International Influences

As noted, UNCED did not produce a convention on forests. It did, however, produce the Forest Principles as a blueprint on the subject. Ghana is a participant of the Inter-Governmental Panel on Forests established after UNCED as well as a member of the International Tropical Timber Organization (ITTO). Ghanaian policies and programs

[17] NRCD 273, as amended by PNDCL 70.

on forestry have thus been influenced or shaped by the decisions of these international bodies.

Much of the changes or reforms in the sector also have been the result of donor support to the sector, some of which predate UNCED. Indeed, between 1983 and 1986, about $USD140 million was committed to the timber industry through the World Bank's Export Rehabilitation Project.[18]

At the domestic level, the 1992 Constitution, and the Forestry Policy and legislation enacted since then, also have had significant impact on the subject.

3.2 The 1992 Constitutional Dispensation

Certain provisions of the 1992 Constitution address the subject. Article 37(9) of the Constitution enjoins the State to take appropriate measures to protect and safeguard the natural environment for posterity and to seek cooperation with other States and bodies for the purpose of protecting the wider international environment for mankind. An injunction is also placed on every Ghanaian citizen, in Article 41(K), to protect and safeguard the environment.[19] These provisions are, however, contained in chapter 6 of the Constitution under the Directive Principles of State Policy, and are thus widely regarded as not justiciable.

The 1992 Constitution also makes provision for the creation of a Forestry Commission charged with the responsibility for the regulation, management, and utilization of forest and wildlife resources and coordination of policies in relation to them. In a marked departure from the provisions of the State Lands Act 1962, the 1992 Constitution acknowledges the corporate nature of land ownership in Ghana under Article 36(8), which provides that the State shall recognise that ownership and possession of land carry a social obligation to serve the larger community and, in particular, the State shall recognise that the managers of public, stool, skin, and family lands are fiduciaries charged with the obligation to discharge their functions for the benefit of the people of Ghana, of the stool, skin, or family concerned, respectively, and are accountable as fiduciaries in that regard.

Furthermore, Articles 267(1) and (5) of the 1992 Constitution vest all stool lands in the appropriate stools on behalf of, and in trust for, the subjects of the stool in accordance with Ghanaian customary law and usage. Article 267(2) of the 1992 Constitution established the Office of the Administrator of Stool Lands (OAS), charged with the responsibility for:

- The establishment of a stool land account for each stool, into which all rents, dues, royalties, revenues, or other payments, whether in the nature of income or capital from the stool lands, shall be paid;
- The collection of all such rents, dues, royalties, revenue, or other payments, whether in the nature of income or capital and to account for them to the beneficiaries; and
- The disbursement of such revenue as may be determined in accordance with Article 267(6).

[18] Kotey et al., note 5, at 18 .

[19] On the Constitution, generally, and the environment, see G. A. Sarpong, "From Stockholm to Rio: Some Ghanaian Responses to the Problems of the Environment" 19 *U.G.L.J.* (1993–1995), 53–82.

Article 267(6) provides the framework for the disbursement of stool land revenue:

- Ten percent of the revenue accruing from stool lands shall be paid to the Office of the Administrator of Stool Lands to cover administrative expenses; and the remaining revenue shall be disbursed in the following proportions;
- Twenty-five percent to the stool through the traditional authority for the maintenance of the stool in keeping with its status;
- Twenty percent to the traditional authority; and
- Fifty-five percent to the District Assembly, within the area of authority in which the stool lands are situated.

So, for the first time, the chiefs and people had a constitutionally guaranteed basis for the enjoyment of stool land revenue (including revenue from forests) under state management and control. The chiefs and people of Ghana were once more brought closer to their lands and forests under the new constitutional dispensation.

3.2.1 Other Initiatives

The institutional framework for the management of forests is provided for by the Forestry Commission Act 1999.[20] This Act established a Forestry Commission and entrusted it with the responsibility for the regulation of the utilization of forest and wildlife resources, the conservation and management of those resources, and the coordination of policies related to them. Its mandate is to:

- Regulate the utilization of forest and timber resources;[21]
- Manage the nation's forest reserves and protected areas;[22]
- Assist the private sector and the other bodies with the implementation of forest and wildlife policies;[23]
- Undertake the development of forest plantations for the restoration of degraded forests areas, the expansion of the country's forest cover, and the increase in the production of industrial timber; and

[20] Act 571.

[21] By vetting and the registration of contracts to market timber and such other forest and wildlife products as the Commission may determine; the establishment of procedures to tract the movement of timber, wood, and wildlife products; monitoring the harvesting, marketing of forest and wildlife products, and related contracts; promoting the development and dissemination of appropriate industrial standards and trade guidelines for timber, wood, and wildlife products; the conduct of preshipment inspection and examination of timber, wood, and wild products; and advising on approvals to establish new timber industries; and the registration of approved timber processors and traders in forest and wildlife products.

[22] By proper planning for the protection, harvesting, and development of forest and wildlife resources in a sustainable manner; monitoring the condition and extent of the nation's forest and wildlife resources; controlling the harvesting of forest and wildlife products; making recommendations to the Minister on the grant of timber rights and wildlife licences; and advising the Minister on forest and wildlife policy with particular regard to management practices that sustain resources and improve productivity.

[23] By advising and provision of technical services with regard to matters of resources protection, management and development and of market intelligence pertaining to the timber and wildlife industries; cooperating and liaising with national and international bodies and organizations on forestry and wildlife conservation and utilization; supporting the development of forest plantations for the restoration of degraded forest reserves, the increased production of industrial timber and the expansion of the country's protected forest cover; the provision of training the management and technical skills for related industries; and advising the appointing authority on matters concerning employment, discipline, and training of staff.

- Undertake such other functions as are incidental to the foregoing, or as the Minister responsible for forests may direct.

For the performance of its functions, the Commission is divided into four Divisions: Forest Service; Forest Product Inspection; Timber Export Development, and Wildlife. The division with primary responsibility for the maintenance of forests is the Forest Service Division (FSD). Currently, the FSD maintains 279 Forest Reserves, including fuel wood plantations. The total land mass of these reserves is 25,594 square kilometers, spread throughout Ghana, covering approximately 11 percent of the total land area of Ghana.

The forestry sector was given a further boost in 1994 with the adoption of the National Forest and Wildlife Policy, aimed at the "conservation and sustainable development of Ghanaian forest and wildlife resources for maintenance of environmental quality and perpetual flow of optimum benefits to all segments of society." The objectives of the policy are to:

- Manage and enhance Ghana's permanent estate of forest and wildlife resources for preservation of vital soil and water resources, conservation of biodiversity and the environment, and sustainable production of domestic and commercial products;
- Promote the development of viable and efficient forest-based industries, particularly in the secondary and tertiary processing so as to fully utilize timber and other products from forests and wildlife resources and satisfy domestic and international demand for competitively priced quality products;
- Promote public awareness and involvement of rural people in forestry and wildlife conservation so as to maintain life-sustaining systems, preserve scenic areas, and enhance the potential of opportunities;
- Promote research-based and technology-led forestry and wildlife management, utilisation, and development to ensure resource sustainability, socioeconomic growth, and environmental stability; and
- Develop effective capability at national, regional, and district levels for sustainable management of forest and wildlife resources.

The Forest and Wildlife Policy has impacted positively on the forestry sector. Almost all current initiatives within the sector (such as the institutional reform of the Forestry Department; the revision, formulation, and codification of all forestry laws, the elaboration and adoption of a plantation strategy, the elaboration and adoption of a protection strategy; and the experimentation with collaborative management approaches) are inspired by, and explicitly refer to, the 1994 Policy.[24]

In the timber sector, the government has enacted the Timber Resources Management Act[25] as well as the Timber Resources Management Regulations.[26] These both are designed to ensure that the grant of timber rights is done in a manner that secures the sustainable management and utilization of timber resources in Ghana. An element of social responsibility is also built into the legislation. Through the formalization of hitherto informal agreements on community benefits, the harvester of timber is now

[24] Kotey et al., note 5, at 65.
[25] Act 547, as amended by the Timber Resources Management (Amendment) Act 2002.
[26] LI 649, as amended by Timber Resources Management (Amendment) Regulations 2003.

required to ensure that the community benefits from his/her activities in the form of the availability of social amenities, such as roads, schools, and clinics.

The Act provides for Timber Utilisation Contract (TUC) as an instrument for area-based rights allocation. TUCs replace the former concession leases. The Act seeks to establish open competition for timber rights and a process for this, based on bids that detail work programs to be prepared on the basis of guidelines produced by the forest authority. The Act prohibits any person harvesting timber without a TUC, and does not distinguish between forests resources on-reserve and off-reserve.

TUCs are executed between the government, represented by the Minister of Lands and Forestry, and the timber contractor. However, the land belongs to the stools, whose right to be consulted must be respected. This is catered for by contract identification procedures that put the emphasis on the community's wishes, insofar as the area, boundaries, and operational specifications are concerned. Under the TUC system, a prospective holder of timber rights has to submit a Contract Operations Plan (COP), which details the type and scheduling of proposed harvesting operations, environmental concerns, and social responsibility. Accordingly, under section 3 of the Act, an application for a TUC shall be accompanied by:

- A harvesting plan prepared in accordance with sustainable management of timber resources;
- An assessment of the likely environmental effect and proposed program to redress any such effects;
- Evidence of the financial ability of the applicant to operate the area of land subject to his contract;
- Evidence of the capability of the applicant to operate the area of land subject to his contract;
- Proposals to assist in addressing social needs of the communities that have interest in the applicant's proposed area of operations; and
- Other relevant information or documents as the Commission may request.

A recent initiative also has added a boost to the sector. The Presidential Initiative on Forests (PIF) 2001 has, as its objective, a program of reafforestation involving local communities who are provided seedlings free of charge for replanting on their farms. Over ten thousand hectares of land has been replanted annually under this program. Furthermore, under the current Ghana Government (GOG)/Global Environment Facility (GEF) initiative, 16 percent of Ghana's land surface area has been set aside to conserve samples of her natural ecosystems in the form of forest, national parks, and wildlife reserves. Under the project, GEF has provided a grant of USD$8.7 million to the GOG for the protection of biodiversity in Ghana. Through biological surveys, thirty forest reserves located in four regions of the country – namely, the Ashanti, Central, Eastern, and Western – have been identified as hotspots for biodiversity, to be designated as Globally Significant Biodiversity Areas (GSBAs) for conservation purposes.

The establishment of these GSBAs would result in the loss of access to royalties and other livelihood opportunities to forest fringe communities. To this end, USD$2.5million of the total grant has been earmarked for the development of a Community Investment Fund (CIF) aimed to sustain community-based enterprises in the affected communities, and mitigate these losses.

The implementation of the project is yet another initiative by the GOG to address the destruction of biodiversity through reckless activities, such as illegal timber harvesting, excessive exploitation of nontimber forest produce, and encroachment of limited forest estates.[27]

The role of NGOs must not be left out of this account. The Ghanaian NGO community includes a wide spectrum of organisations ranging from single-community welfare groups to lay or church-based multicommunity NGOs with a strong development orientation, as well as foreign NGOs. In recent years, there has been an upsurge in NGO concern for environmental issues, particularly in forestry. Some NGOs, such as the Adventist Development and Relief Agency (ADRA), have been involved in forestry projects for over twenty years; the United States Agency for International Development (USAID) has funded tree-nursery and woodlot projects on a food-for-work-program basis. Other religious groups are also active in tree-planting activities.

International NGOs have been influential with respect to donor policies in the forest sector. The World Bank and ODA (now DFID) were much criticized by the international arms of Friends of the Earth and the World Wide Fund for Nature, respectively, in the late 1980s for the Export Rehabilitation Programme under the Economic Recovery Programme. Subsequently, the World Bank and ODA support to forest inventories, management, and institutional change was, at least in part, stimulated by responses to criticism from these international NGOs.[28]

The net effect of these legislative policy changes and initiatives is the shift away from the pre-UNCED regime of absolute state control and monopoly over forestry resources to one of collaboration or partnership involving traditional authorities, communities, government, and other stakeholders in the forestry sector. Indications are that the system is working for the benefit of the society as a whole. Indeed, current estimates are that the rate of destruction of forests has reduced from the 750 square kilometers per annum during the 1970s to the current rate of 65,000 hectares per annum.

4 CONCLUDING REMARKS

The review of the legal regime on Ghanaian forestry is significant in several respects: it shows that when people are alienated or denied control over resources in favor of the state, such a measure is unlikely to succeed, unless the communities are made to participate in the scheme of things.

Second, it brings home forcefully the fact that international conventions per se do not ensure implementation of treaty norms at the domestic level. There is the need for political will, the necessary incentives, and goodwill on the part of the government and the governed to implement them. Ghana has signed and ratified both the Convention on Biodiversity and the Convention on Climate Change; yet, to date, no specific enactment has been made to incorporate these norms in domestic legislation. By contrast, forestry that is not governed by any treaty has, since UNCED, seen two major enactments, a policy, initiatives, and programs for the sustainable utilization of forests in Ghana.

[27] See, "Conserving Nation's Natural Ecosystems Underway." *The Ghanaian Chronicle*, 10 August 2005, at 3.

[28] Kotey et al., note 5, at 46.

The Ghanaian policy and legislative initiatives are aimed at the enhancement of forests, thereby providing adequate sinks for carbon as a vital contribution to the mitigation of the adverse impacts of climate change on the international community as a whole. Both the North and the South, as members of the global community, stand to benefit. The Ghanaian initiative is thus a bridge between the North and the South on a matter that the two parties could not agree on at Rio, but a matter that is at the heart of sustainable development.

19 Bridging the Dominant-Indigenous Peoples Cultural Divide: Reflections on Makah Whaling

Jeremy Firestone and Jonathan Lilley*

1 INTRODUCTION

> Like the miner's canary, the Indian marks the shift from fresh air to poison gas in our political atmosphere, and our treatment of Indians, even more than our treatment of other minorities, reflects the rise and fall of our democratic faith.

So stated Felix Cohen in his seminal article, *The Erosion of Indian Rights* (1953).[1] It is through Cohen's lens that we examine the domestic and international controversy over the resumption of whaling by the Makah Indian Nation[2] following the recovery of the eastern North Pacific stock of gray whales (*Eschrichtius robustus* or "California gray whale"). The controversy raises issues of considerable significance: treaty obligations, subsistence and cultural rights versus majoritarianism, contested conservation assessments, animal rights, and politics within multilateral environmental institutions.[3]

We explore these issues independently of our personal views about whaling. Although we support the Makah Tribe's right to decide for itself whether to engage in subsistence whaling, we reject the label "pro-whaling." We likewise do not reflexively label all of those who come to a different conclusion than we do with the pejorative label "anti-indigenous" or "anti-Indian." We fully recognize that principled people may weigh the interests at hand and come to different conclusions. The aim of this article is thus broader than the Makah and whales. We look for messages in the Makah whaling controversy to reveal a principled way forward for nation-States and indigenous peoples to bridge their divide and engage cooperatively to fulfill the twin objectives of a sustainable biosphere and sustainable culture.

[1] Felix S. Cohen, "The Erosion of Indian Rights, 1950–1953." 62 *Yale L. J.* (1953) 348, 390.

[2] Ann M. Renker, "Whale Hunting and the Makah Tribe: A Needs Statement" (2002), submitted by the United States to the IWC, IWC/54/AS2, Agenda Item 5.2 (4 December 2002). The Indian reservation is comprised of slightly more than 27,000 acres in the northwestern corner of the Olympic Peninsula, 719 acres in and around the Ozette village, and two offshore islands.

[3] Matthew Dennis, "Makahs and Gray Whales: Not Black and White." 3 *The Ecotone* (1999) 4. Available at http://www.uoregon.edu/~ecostudy/resources/publications/ecotone/Web%20PDF%20Versions/Ecotone%20Fall%20%2799.pdf.

* Associate Professor and Ph.D. Student, College of Marine and Earth Studies, University of Delaware, USA, jf@udel.edu. Earlier versions of this chapter appeared as Jeremy Firestone and Jonathan Lilley, "Aboriginal Subsistence Whaling and the Right to Practice and Revitalise Cultural Traditions and Customs." 8 *J. Int. Wildlife L. & Pol'y* (2005) 1–43 and as Jeremy Firestone and Jonathan Lilley, "An Endangered Species: Aboriginal Whaling and the Right to Self-Determination and Cultural Heritage in a National and International Context" 34 *Envtl L. Rep.* (2004) (Envtl L. Inst.) 10763–10787.

2 MAKAH WHALING CULTURE

Whaling is central to Makah culture and the Makah way of life. Historically, whaling was not only a vital subsistence and commercial activity for the Makah; but also, perhaps more significantly, it "formed one of the most important organising aspects of Makah culture" and was highly ritualized.[4] The historic importance of whaling to the Makah is underscored by the excavation of the ancient Makah village of Ozette, where whaling accounts for the lion's share of the faunal remains in the middens.[5] The fact that the Makah "were respected up and down the [Pacific] coast as the region's most skilled whalers" also reflects the vital role that whaling played in Makah culture.[6] Data from the excavations of the Ozette village in the 1960s and 1970s suggest a continuous use of whale products for fifteen hundred years. Located in a perfect position for intercepting gray whales during their migration, Ozette was a key Makah settlement that was inhabited for over two thousand years. Approximately five hundred years ago, a mudslide buried the village, wiping out the settlement but allowing for the preservation of a large number of Makah artefacts that would otherwise have been lost.[7] Data from the recently excavated Makah village of Waatch suggest that whalebones were present 3,850 ± 75 BP. (before present). Given the history of Makah whaling, and the extent to which the whales were used,[8] it is hard to overstate the importance of whales in the Makah way of life. Indeed, Makah whaling has been equated with the use of the buffalo by the Indian tribes who lived on the plains.[9]

Whaling was not a task to be undertaken lightly. The crew of a whaling canoe prepared for the hunt by going without sleep for days at a time and fasting to condition their bodies for the rigors they might face if a whale was to tow the canoe far offshore.[10] Spiritual preparations also were undertaken before commencing the voyage and the success of the trip was thought to be as much dependent on the proper observance of the various rituals as it was on the actual skill of the whalers.[11] The wives of the whaling crew also had to pay strict attention to the spiritual side of the hunt – particularly the wife of the chief whaler. When the crew was at sea, the failure of the chief's wife to behave in a certain way had the potential to impact adversely on the hunt.[12] These rituals largely stem from the belief that humans are too insignificant to capture any whale that did not wish to be caught. The ceremonies that the whalers undertook before a hunt were intended to obtain the support of spirits or *tamanos*.[13] As the whaler alone did not have

[4] Jennifer Sepez, "Political and Social Ecology of Contemporary Makah Subsistence Hunting, Fishing and Shellfish Collecting Practices" (2001) (unpublished PhD dissertation, University of Washington) (on file with University of Washington and the authors), 69.

[5] Ibid. at 68.

[6] Ibid.; NOAA-NMFS, "Final Environmental Assessment on Issuing a Quota to the Makah Indian Tribe for a Subsistence Hunt on Gray Whales for the Years 2001 and 2002," 46. Available at http://www.nmfs.noaa.gov/pr/PR2/Conservation_and_Recovery_Program/makah_EA.html.

[7] Robert J. Miller, "Exercising Cultural Self-Determination: The Makah Indian Tribe Goes Whaling" 25 *Am. Indian L. Rev.* (2000–2001) 165, 187.

[8] Ibid.

[9] Ibid.

[10] Miller, Note 7, at 177.

[11] Renker, Note 2, at 9.

[12] Edward Curtis, *The North American Indian: Being a Series of Volumes Picturing and Describing Indians of the United States, the Dominion of Canada, and Alaska 20 vols.* (Frederick W. Hodge, ed., 1911), (Reprinted 1970) cited by Renker, supra Note 2, at 8.

[13] Miller, note 7, 185. An alternative spelling – *tumanos* – is provided by Charlotte Cote, "*It's who we are.*" *Makah and Nuu-chah-nulth Whaling – A History* (2002) (unpublished PhD dissertation, University of California, Berkeley) (on file with University of California, Berkeley and the authors), 42.

the strength to take a whale, the *tamanos*' power was vital in conducting a successful hunt. After a whale had been struck, the Makah would pray and sing to the whale pleading with its spirit to turn to face the shore where the members of the village were waiting to praise the whale as an honored guest of the tribe.[14] Indeed, the Makah saw the whale as being the most respected tribal member[15] and an honorable hunt represented the height of Makah admiration for the whale.[16]

In addition to being an axiom of Makah religious beliefs, the whale hunt also provided for a means of social stratification. The chief of the whaling crew was also the head of a certain social group. This social group would reside in one longhouse that was owned, along with the canoe and all the whaling equipment, by the chief whaler. This man also bore the greatest spiritual burden for the crew and it was predominantly his spiritual power that determined the success of the hunt. This combination of material wealth and a strong link with the spiritual world resulted in a large amount of power being accorded to the whaling crew chiefs.[17]

As a result of this power, the chief whalers – or headmen – were situated at the top of the social pyramid, which was established in each longhouse. Each member of the longhouse was then socially linked to the headman in one way or another and the strength of these linkages determined the social hierarchy. A headman who was successful in hunting whales could offer prestige and resources to the members of his longhouse. By contrast, one who consistently failed to land any whales would lose status in this group, which then resulted in a reduction in both his physical wealth and social standing.[18]

The interrelationship between whale hunting and social standing also affected Makah women. The social status of women mirrored that of the men and the women who were married to the headmen sat atop the female social pyramid.[19]

The important whaling positions were generally handed down from father to son. The roles of the harpooner, the steersman, and the diver who sewed the whales' mouths shut were all passed down on a hereditary basis. The knowledge that accompanied these positions also was passed on to one's descendants, and access to this knowledge was strictly controlled.[20] In the same way that a whaler was usually the oldest son of a whaler, so his wife would be the oldest daughter of another whaler. Such a union between two whaling families would improve the standing of both families in the village. The power obtained from such social maneuvering could then be consolidated by the newly married couple and passed down to the next generation, thereby allowing the family to maintain its position of importance in the community.[21]

Despite the strict hierarchical nature of Makah society, whaling was of benefit to all members of the community. Although only a few tribal members actually whaled, the village shared the whale's resources.[22] As with the other aspects of the hunt, a strict set of rules determined how the butchering process should be undertaken. The rules determined which parts of the whale had to be decorated and ceremonially treated, which parts of the whale those involved in the hunt received, and which parts were given to the rest of the village.[23] This process thus had the dual purpose of both strengthening the social hierarchy of the community and providing resources for the entire tribe.

[14] Miller, Note 7, at 186.
[15] Ibid. at 5.
[16] Sepez, Note 4, at 76.
[17] Renker, Note 2, at 9.
[18] Ibid.
[19] Ibid.
[20] Sepez, Note 4, at 69.
[21] Renker, Note 2, at 9.
[22] Cote, Note 13, at 45.
[23] Renker, Note 2, at 9.

A ceremonial feast, known as a potlatch, provided for a second means of wealth distribution. When a tribal headman had accumulated substantial wealth he might hold a potlatch for the rest of the village. During the feast, he would give away many of his possessions to other members of the tribe, gaining a great deal of respect in the process. The potlatch served the dual purpose of enhancing the headman's standing within the tribe and redistributing wealth to those lower down the social hierarchy.

3 THE LEGAL FRAMEWORK FOR MAKAH WHALING

3.1 Treaty of Neah Bay and the Pre-1995 History of Makah Whaling

The Makah Tribe's ancestral lands are located in the State of Washington on the Olympic Peninsula. In 1855, the United States and the Makah entered into the Treaty of Neah Bay. A treaty with an Indian tribe is a negotiated settlement between sovereigns, that is, the United States and the tribe in question. A treaty establishes "not a grant of rights to the Indians, but a grant of rights from them – a reservation of those not granted."[24] Although tribal powers can be qualified over time by express language from Congress, U.S. law recognizes the centrality of tribal sovereignty and that such sovereignty predates the settlement of the United States by the European colonists.[25] The Makah thus have a "measured separatism"[26] from both federal and state governments.

Tribal chiefs negotiating on behalf of the tribe discussed the Makah's relationship with the ocean, expressing the sentiment that the Makah people considered the sea to be more important than the land. A Makah chief made this point eloquently when he said: "I want the sea. That is my country."[27] Governor Stevens, the U.S. representative who negotiated the Treaty of Neah Bay, "found the Makah not much concerned about their land, apart from village sites, burial sites, and certain other locations, but greatly concerned about their marine hunting and fishing rights."[28] The Makah's close relationship with the sea mirrors their traditional dependence on it for subsistence purposes as most of their food supply "came from the sea where they fished for salmon, halibut and other fish, and hunted for whale and seal."[29] As a result of the Makah's intimate relationship with the sea, Governor Stevens "found it necessary to reassure the Makah that the government did not intend to stop them from marine hunting and fishing but in fact would help them to develop these pursuits."[30]

Although the Makah ceded most of their ancestral lands to the United States in the Treaty of Neah Bay, the Makah, in pertinent part, *reserved* a right to hunt whales. Specifically, the treaty provided that the "right of taking fish and of *whaling* and sealing

[24] *United States v. Winans* (1905), 198 U.S. 371, 381.

[25] Felix S. Cohen, *Handbook of Federal Indian Law* (Washington, DC: United States Government Printing Office, 1942) 122–123.

[26] Charles F. Wilkinson, *American Indians, Time and the Law: Native Societies in a Modern Constitutional Democracy* (Yale University Press, 1987), 14.

[27] Renker, note 2, *quoting* George Gibbs, "Treaty of Neah Bay [Transcript of Journal Proceedings]" (1855), U.S. National Archives, Records Relating to the Negotiation of Ratified and Unratified Treaties with Various Tribes of Indians, 1801–1869; microcopy No. T-494, roll 5.

[28] *United States v. Washington,* (W.D. WA 1974) 384 F. Supp. 312, 363, aff'd, (9th Cir. 1975) 520 F.2d 676, cert. denied, (1976) 423 U.S. 1086 (hereinafter, the "*Boldt decision*").

[29] Ibid.

[30] Ibid.

at usual and accustomed grounds and stations is further secured [to the Makah] ... in common with all citizens of the United States ... "[31] The Treaty of Neah Bay is the only treaty between the United States and a Native American tribe in which a tribe explicitly secured a right to whale.[32] Although other tribes could assert a right to whale under more general treaty reservations, such as a right to fish and hunt,[33] the fact that the Treaty of Neah Bay explicitly secures a right to whale "suggests the historic importance of whaling to the Makah."[34]

As discussed earlier, whaling played a vital role in both subsistence practices and social organization. However, "despite the central place of whaling in their lives," the Makah ceased whaling in the 1920s.[35] A number of reasons have been advanced for this, the first and foremost being that widespread commercial exploitation of whales had placed the gray whale on the brink of extinction.[36] Other reasons include a decline in demand for whale oil, the social and economic dislocation of the tribe, and opposition by federal authorities.[37] Indeed, government officials banned cultural and religious practices such as the potlatch and made repeated efforts to convert the Makah lifestyle from one based on hunting and fishing to one premised on agriculture.[38]

3.2 The IWC and Aboriginal Subsistence Whaling (ASW)

The global conservation, management, and harvesting of great whales is governed by the International Convention for the Regulation of Whaling (ICRW) and the commission it established, the International Whaling Commission (IWC or Commission). Each nation that is a party to the ICRW is a member of the IWC.[39] The ICRW empowers the IWC to establish committees to assist it in performing its duties to manage whale stocks through a "Schedule," which is amended, from time to time, usually on an annual basis.[40] It is through the Schedule that the IWC sets the regulations for whaling, by which participating nations must abide. The Schedule is considered to be an "integral part" of the ICRW, and indeed, a reference to the ICRW is "understood as including the ... Schedule either in its present terms or as amended ... "[41] Since 1986, the IWC has maintained a moratorium on all commercial whaling.[42]

The United States hosted the conference that led to the establishment of the ICRW in Washington, DC, and has been a member of the IWC since its inception. To implement the ICRW, the U.S. Congress enacted the Whaling Convention Act of 1949 (WCA).[43] The WCA prohibits whaling in contravention of the ICRW, including the Schedule, the WCA, and regulations promulgated pursuant thereto by the Secretary of Commerce.[44]

[31] 12 Stat. 939, 940 (1855) (emphasis added).

[32] *Anderson v. Evans*, (9th Cir. 2002), 314 F.3d 1006, 1012, rehearing en banc denied and opinion amended, (9th Cir. 2003) 350 F.3d 815, 825, 2nd request for rehearing en banc denied and second amended opinion (9th Cir. 2004) 371 F.3d 475, 483.

[33] See, for example, Treaty with the Yakimas, 12 Stat. 951, 953 (1855) (securing the "right" of fishing and "privilege" of hunting); *Washington v. Washington State Commercial Passenger Fishing Vessel Association* (1979) 443 U.S. 658.

[34] *Anderson v. Evans*, 371 F.3d, at 483.

[35] Ibid.

[36] *Metcalf v. Daley*, (9th Cir. 2000) 214 F.3d 1135, 1137. See also Sepez, Note 4, at 70.

[37] 371 F.3d, at 483.

[38] Sepez, Note 4, at 37–39; Renker, Note 2, at 12–15.

[39] 161 U.N.T.S.72, Dec. 2, 1946, 62 Stat. 1716. See ICRW, art. III.1., http://www.iwcoffice.org/ICRW.

[40] Ibid., Arts. III.4. and V.

[41] Ibid., Art. I.1.

[42] ICRW Schedule, Section III, paragraph 10.

[43] 16 U.S.C. §§916–916l, 64 Stat. 421 (1950).

[44] 16 U.S.C. §916c(a)(1).

The present regulations, consistent with the ICRW moratorium on commercial whaling that has been in place since 1986, prohibit whaling except for authorized aboriginal subsistence whaling (ASW).[45]

The international community has long treated aboriginal hunting of marine mammals differently than commercial hunting. Indeed, Article IV of the 1911 Fur Seals Treaty provided that it would not apply to "Indians, Ainos, Aleuts, or other aborigines" who carried out pelagic sealing in canoes. A special exception for aboriginal whaling likewise has a long history and can be traced back to the 1931 Convention for the Regulation of Whaling (CRW).[46] This exception was not carried over to the text of the 1946 convention, although the ICRW does recognize that whale stocks should not be stabilized so rapidly as to cause "widespread economic and nutritional distress."[47] Instead, aboriginal whaling has been addressed in the ICRW Schedule. As noted earlier, the Schedule is part of the treaty in every meaningful sense.[48] When the ICRW was negotiated and came into force, it is notable that the Schedule explicitly provided an exception for aboriginal hunting of gray whales. And although the Makah Nation was not explicitly mentioned by name in the provision, the Schedule (like the present Schedule's gray whale aboriginal subsistence whaling provision) did not mention any aboriginal group by name. There are nonetheless suggestions that provision was included in the initial Schedule at the behest of the Soviet Union of behalf of the aborigines of Chukotsk and Korjaksk areas.[49] In any event, the Schedule provided that: "It is forbidden to take or kill gray or right whales, except when the meat and products of such whales are to be used exclusively for local consumption by the aborigines."[50] Over the next several decades, subsequent requests for aboriginal subsistence whaling of other whale species or stocks were handled in a similar fashion.[51]

In the early 1980s, the IWC created a special ad hoc workgroup to provide it with guidance on how to handle proposals for ASW. The workgroup reached agreement on a number of definitions to guide decision making.[52] The efforts of the workgroup ultimately led the IWC to adopt a resolution in 1983 on ASW and to establish a more formal Aboriginal Subsistence Whaling Subcommittee. In the resolution, the IWC recognized the "importance and desirability of accommodating, consistent with effective conservation of whale stocks, the needs of aboriginal people who are dependent upon whales for nutritional, subsistence and cultural purposes."[53] The IWC found it "appropriate

[45] 50 C.F.R. §230.1.

[46] I.N.T.S. CLU. No. 3586, Art. 3, 24 September 1931, http://www.oceanlaw.net/texts/whales31.htm.

[47] ICRW Preamble. See also The 1937 International Agreement for the Regulation of Whaling, 8 June 1937, 52 Stat. 1460, Ts No. 933, 190 LNTS 79, Article 4. Available at http://www.oceanlaw.net/texts/whales37.htm.

[48] ICRW, Art. I.1.

[49] Final Act of the International Whaling Conference (2 December 1946), Art. X, reprinted in Patricia Birnie, *International Regulation of Whaling: From Conservation of Whaling to Conservation of Whales and Regulation of Whale-Watching* Vol. 2 (New York: Oceana Publications, 1985), 695, 697.

[50] ICRW Schedule, paragraph 2. See "Proclamation of President Harry S Truman," 62 Stat. 1716 1723 (10 November 1948).

[51] Alexander Gillespie, "Aboriginal Subsistence Whaling: A Critique of the Inter-Relationship between International Law and International Whaling Commission," 12 *Colo. J. Int'l Envtl. L & Pol'y* (2001), 77, 80.

[52] G. P. Donovan, "International Whaling Commission, International Whaling Commission and Aboriginal/Subsistence Whaling: April 1979 to July 1981, Special Issue 4" (1981). Available at http://www.highnorth.no/Library/Culture/de-of-ab.htm.

[53] Report of the Thirty-Fifth Meeting of the International Commission on Whaling 38, app. III, Office of the Commission (1983).

and desirable to establish principles and guidelines for the management of aboriginal subsistence whaling which recognize and seek to accommodate conservation, *nutritional, subsistence and cultural needs.*"[54] The terms of reference (jurisdiction) of the Subcommittee are to "consider relevant information and documentation from the Scientific Committee," to "consider nutritional, subsistence and cultural needs relating to aboriginal subsistence whaling" and to "*provide advice on the dependence of aboriginal communities on specific whale stocks* to the Commission for its consideration and determination of appropriate management measures."[55] It is apparent that for at least ninety years the international community has recognized the special relationship between aboriginal peoples and marine mammals, with increasing attention over time dedicated to ensuring that the needs of aboriginal peoples and the conservation and proper management of whale stocks are ensured and accommodated.

3.3 The Makah ASW Quota

In the United States, marine mammals that are threatened or in danger of extinction receive protection under two legal regimes: The Endangered Species Act of 1973, as amended (ESA),[56] and the Marine Mammal Protection Act (MMPA).[57] In 1970, the federal government designated the gray whale as an endangered species under a predecessor to the ESA.[58] However, because the population of eastern North Pacific stock of gray whales had recovered to almost its estimated original size, the National Marine Fisheries Service ("NMFS" or "NOAA Fisheries") removed that stock from the ESA list in 1994 and began a five-year monitoring program of the stock's viability.[59] The stock was so healthy that in the 1999 Status Review, twenty-eight large-whale biology experts agreed that, "the stock was nearing its environmental carrying capacity."[60] In 2001, NMFS received a petition requesting it to relist the eastern North Pacific gray whale as threatened or endangered. NMFS rejected the petition because it did "not present substantial scientific or commercial information" sufficient to warrant the listing.[61]

In response to the removal of the gray whale from the ESA list, the Makah Nation approached the United States government – the Department of Commerce (DOC), National Oceanic and Atmospheric Administration (NOAA), which is housed in DOC, and NMFS, which is also part of NOAA – and requested the U.S. government seek on its behalf an annual aboriginal subsistence whaling quota from the IWC of up to five eastern North Pacific gray whales.[62] At the 1995 IWC annual meeting, the United States informed the IWC of its intent to submit a proposal on behalf of the Makah.[63] On 22 March 1996, NOAA and the Makah entered into an agreement that committed NOAA, through the United States Commissioner to the IWC, to make a "formal proposal

[54] Ibid. IWC Thirty-Fifth Meeting Report, Note 53 (emphasis added).

[55] Report of the Aboriginal Subsistence Whaling Sub-Committee (hereinafter ASW Report) (15 June 2003), 55 – Rep3.doc. 9 (emphasis added). Available at http://www.iwcoffice.org/2003%20Documents/Reports/55-Rep3(AS).pdf.

[56] 16 U.S.C. §§1531 et seq.

[57] 16 U.S.C. §§1361 et seq.

[58] *Metcalf v. Daley*, (9th Cir. 2000) 214 F.3d 1135, 1138.

[59] 214 F.3d, at 1138. See also 58 Fed. Reg. 3121 (1993).

[60] National Marine Fisheries Service, "Endangered and Threatened Wildlife and Plants: 90-Day Finding for a Petition To List Eastern North Pacific Gray Whales as Threatened or Endangered Under the Endangered Species Act (ESA)" (14 June 2001), 66 Fed. Reg. 32305, 32309.

[61] 66 Fed. Reg. 32310.

[62] *Metcalf v. Daley*, 214 F.3d, at 1138.

[63] Ibid.

to the IWC for a quota of gray whales for subsistence and ceremonial use by the Makah" provided the Makah first prepared an "adequate statement of need."[64] The Agreement also provided that NOAA would cooperate with the Makah in harvest management and, in the event that such a quota was approved by the IWC, that NOAA would revise its regulations to take account of subsistence whaling by the Makah.[65] Because of the precedent that would be set if Makah whaling were approved – authorizing subsistence whaling where there had been a long hiatus in whale hunting by an aboriginal group – and in light of Japan's effort to gain IWC authorization for community-based coastal whaling,[66] the U.S. proposal generated considerable controversy among IWC members. Ultimately, some IWC countries blocked the 1996 U.S. proposal.[67]

In June 1997, two nongovernmental organizations (NGOs), Australians for Animals and BEACH Marine Protection, wrote a letter to NOAA and NMFS alleging that those agencies had violated the National Environmental Policy Act (NEPA)[68] because they had authorized Makah whaling without first conducting an Environmental Assessment (EA) or an Environmental Impact Statement (EIS). In response, a draft EA was issued on 22 August 1997, and a new written agreement between NOAA and the Makah was executed that October.[69] Four days after the parties entered into the new agreement, on 17 October 1997, NOAA/NMFS issued the final EA and made a Finding of No Significant Impact (FONSI).[70] Thus, both the initial and new agreements were executed before the EA was finalized.

Before 1997, the gray whale quota was held only by the Russian Federation on behalf of its aboriginal people. Because its 1996 request had been met with considerable controversy in the IWC, the United States took a different tack in 1997. The United States and the Russian Federation agreed to submit a joint request for a five-year quota of 620 gray whales on behalf of their aboriginal peoples, with the understanding that the average annual harvest of the Chukota people would be 120, whereas the Makah would be limited to an average of four whales per year.[71] Before 1997, only the Russian Federation held a gray whale aboriginal subsistence whaling quota.[72] It is worth noting that 120 eastern North Pacific gray whales represents less than 27 percent of that portion of the stock that the IWC Scientific Committee considers could be hunted sustainably.[73] It represents even a smaller fraction of U.S. estimates.[74] The gray whale agreement was facilitated by a decision by the United States to accommodate Russia's desire to gain an annual ASW quota of bowhead whales for its Chukotka people, a quota that had previously been allocated solely to Alaska natives. Thus, rather than approach the IWC with requests to increase the quotas of bowhead and gray whales to accommodate the needs of the Chukotka people and the Makah Nation – quota increase proposals that

[64] Ibid. at 1139, *quoting* Agreement between Makah and NOAA (22 March 1996).

[65] Ibid.; See also the U.S. Whaling Convention Act, 16 U.S.C. §§916 et seq., enacted to implement the ICRW, and regulations promulgated pursuant thereto, 50 C.F.R. PArt 230.

[66] IWC, Final Press Release (2003). Available at http://www.iwcoffice.org/FinalPressRelease2003.htm.

[67] *Anderson v. Evans*, 371 F.3d, at 484.

[68] 42 U.S.C. §4332.

[69] *Metcalf v. Daley*, 214 F.3d, at 1139.

[70] Ibid. at 1139–1140.

[71] Ibid. at 1140.

[72] National Marine Fisheries Service, "Whaling Provisions: Aboriginal Subsistence Quotas" (6 April 1998), 63 Fed. Reg. 16701, 16703.

[73] ASW Report, note 56, 4; IWC, Report of the Scientific Committee, 56th Annual Meeting (2004), 28. Available at www.iwcoffice.org/_documents/sci_com/SCRepFiles2004/56SCrep.pdf.

[74] 2002 Stock Assessment Report, note 59, at 137–138.

likely would have been very controversial – the United States and Russia effectively traded existing quotas.[75]

Ultimately, at its October 1997 meeting, the IWC approved an ASW quota for gray whales (620 for 2003–2007, with the total not to exceed 140 whales in any given year) and allocated that quota to aboriginal groups "whose traditional subsistence and cultural needs have been recognized."[76] Although IWC members reached broad consensus on the October 1997 ASW quotas, the gray whale quota decision was not without controversy. First, by agreeing to a joint quota, the IWC had effectively short-circuited the role it had envisioned for its ASW Subcommittee in evaluating the merits of proposed aboriginal subsistence whaling quotas. Second, the vague language chosen by the IWC to recognize the quota arguably left two open questions: Which entity or entities had the authority to recognize such needs among aboriginal groups, and which aboriginal groups had been recognized?[77]

With the IWC approval in hand, the Makah Nation approached its first whale hunt in seventy years with a sense of purpose and responsibility. It formed the Makah Whaling Commission, drafted physical and spiritual guidelines, trained prospective crewmembers, and devised a whale hunt management plan. In 1998, NOAA formally authorized the Makah Nation to engage in subsistence whaling.[78] After a seventy-year hiatus, in 1999 the Makah once again went whaling and landed one gray whale.

3.4 The Judicial Proceedings

The coalition opposed to the Makah whale hunt is led by the Sea Shepherd Conservation Society and is comprised of marine conservation organizations, animal welfare organizations, and the whale-watching industry.[79] Approximately 250 animal welfare organizations and 27 conservation organizations have expressed opposition to Makah whaling.[80] However, several notable organizations, including the Sierra Club, Greenpeace, and the World Wildlife Fund (WWF), do not oppose the aboriginal subsistence whaling.[81] Some in the antiwhaling coalition subsequently commenced suit in U.S. courts.

3.4.1 Environmental Impact Analysis and Makah Whaling[82]

In *Metcalf v. Daley*,[83] the Ninth Circuit considered whether NOAA failed to comply with NEPA when it authorized the Makah Tribe to hunt California gray whales. Because the "die had already been cast" by the time the EA was complete – that is, NOAA had already

[75] Gillespie, Note 51, at 88.

[76] ICRW Schedule, Section III, Paragraph 13.b(2), http://www.iwcoffice.org/Schedule.htm#CAPTUREIII.

[77] See Gillespie, Note 51, at 88–89. For a discussion of this issue, see Firestone and Lilley, "An Endangered Species," (2004) 34 *Environmental Law Reporter* (Environmental Law Institute), 10776–10777.

[78] 63 Fed. Reg. 16, 701 (1998).

[79] Alex Dark, *The Makah Whale Hunt* (1999), National Council for Science and the Environment. Available at http://www.cnie.org/NAE/cases/makah/m3.html.

[80] "Ironically, in 1999, protestor boats hit two gray whales and possibly injured them." Miller, Note 7, at 266.

[81] WWF, http://www.panda.org/downloads/species/wwfiwcposition2003final2.pdf; Sierra Club, http://www.sierraclub.org/policy/conservation/marinemammals.asp and http://www.sierraclub.org/marine/mammals/whaling.asp; and Greenpeace, http://whales.greenpeace.org/whaling/subsistence.html.

[82] For a more detailed analysis of the NEPA issue, see Firestone & Lilley, "An Endangered Species."

[83] Note 58.

firmly committed to Makah whaling as witnessed by the 1996 agreement, the court, in a 2–1 decision, held that the government prepared the EA "too late in the decision-making process, i.e., after making an irreversible and irretrievable commitment of resources."[84] In light of the court's decision, NOAA/NMFS abandoned, over the tribe's objection, the 1997 agreement with the Makah and commenced the NEPA process anew.[85] In January 2001, they issued a revised draft EA, which identified a subsistence whale quota of whales and placed limits on the location and time of year of the Makah hunt in an effort to ensure that only migrating whales were targeted.[86] At that time, similar limits on the hunt were contained in the Makah Tribe's Management Plan.[87] The Makah, however, amended the management plan, eliminating geographic limitations on the hunt; the amended plan did, however, contain temporal and geographic limits on the number of "strikes" (but not the number of "takes"[88]) of nonmigrating whales.[89] In July 2001, NOAA and NMFS published the final EA. The final EA was based on the amended management plan and, like the 1997 EA, found no significant environmental impact. On 13 December 2001, NOAA and NMFS established a quota of five landings of gray whales for the years 2001 and 2002.[90]

Once again, antiwhaling advocates challenged the Makah subsistence-whaling quota, contending the government decision violated both NEPA and the MMPA.[91] Turning first to the NEPA issue, an EIS, which requires a more detailed and comprehensive analysis of environmental issues with greater opportunity for public input than an EA, must be prepared whenever a "major Federal action significantly affect[s] the quality of the human environment."[92] The Ninth Circuit, in *Anderson v. Evans*,[93] acknowledged that no one disputed that the Makah hunt would not significantly affect the "overall" California gray whale population. Rather, the dispute was over the localized effect on the whale population in the area where the Makah intended to hunt,[94] with the plaintiffs contending there is a definable "summer resident" group that would be impacted and the government contending otherwise. In the court's view "the answer to this question . . . is sufficiently uncertain and controversial to require the full EIS protocol."[95] By relying on the difference in opinion between government scientists and those employed by the plaintiffs as its basis for "uncertainty," the court, however, appears to have substituted its judgment for that of the NOAA, as the "decision to prepare an EA rather than an EIS is reviewed under the arbitrary and capricious standard."[96] The panel also faulted the EA for failing to properly consider the effect of the decision to permit the Makah to whale on other Native American tribes that may wish to hunt whales as well as its effect on other IWC member countries.[97]

84 214 F.3d, at 1143–1144.

85 *Anderson v. Evans*, 371 F.3d, at 485.

86 Ibid.

87 Ibid.

88 The court appears to be using the term "take" in this context to mean "landed." Both the MMPA, 16 USC 1362(13), and the ESA, 16 USC 1532(19), define "take" considerably broader.

89 *Anderson v. Evans*, 371 F.3d, at 485.

90 66 Fed. Reg. 64,378 (13 December 2001).

91 *Anderson v. Evans*, 371 F.3d, at 486.

92 42 U.S.C. §4332(2)(C).

93 Note 32.

94 *Anderson v. Evans*, 371 F.3d, at 489.

95 Ibid., *489–490.*

96 *Wetlands Action Network v. Army Corps of Engineers* (9th Cir. 2000), 222 F.3d, at 1105, 1116. See also *Anderson*, 371 F.3d at 489 (stating that the court "must defer to the expertise of the agency in evaluating the scientific evidence").

97 Ibid. at 493. See also 40 C.F.R. §1508.27(b)(6) (requiring consideration of the precedential effects of a proposed action).

3.4.2 MMPA, Conservation Necessity, and Abrogation or Modification of Treaty Rights[98]

The more significant issue for indigenous peoples lies in the MMPA issue. The plaintiffs alleged that the MMPA abrogated the Makah's treaty right to hunt whales or, in the alternative, the judicially created "conservation necessity doctrine" otherwise required compliance with the MMPA. The Ninth Circuit Court of Appeals, while finding it unnecessary to reach the question of whether the MMPA abrogated or modified the Makah's whaling rights,[99] held that the conservation necessity doctrine requires the Makah tribe to obtain a permit or waiver under the MMPA.[100] The conservation necessity doctrine originated in the context of *state* regulation (and as we elaborate on later, it is only in that context that the doctrine has a principled basis). States, unlike Congress, do not have the power to modify or abrogate Indian treaty rights. However, in narrowly circumscribed circumstances, states are permitted to regulate the manner in which those rights are exercised "in the interest of conservation."[101] Here, the Ninth Circuit extended the "state-based" conservation necessity doctrine to federal regulation, concluding that applying the MMPA to Makah whaling "effectuate[s] the conservation purpose of the statute" and that its application "goes hand in hand with the principles embedded in the Treaty of Neah Bay itself."[102]

In addition, the court construed the Makah Tribe's reservation of hunting rights "in common with all citizens of the United States," in the Treaty of Neah Bay to support the inference that "the conservation purpose of the MMPA requires it be applied to the Tribe."[103] It noted that, although "the 'fair share' formula might be read to suggest that the Tribe's treaty right gives the Tribe a right to a 'fair share' of whales that are to be taken, . . . [it] does not provide a ready answer in this case, which involves now-protected marine mammals rather than salmon and other fish available, within limits, for fishing."[104] More specifically, the Ninth Circuit concluded that:

> [T]he Makah cannot, consistent with the plain terms of the treaty, hunt whales without regard to processes in place and designed to advance conservation values by preserving marine mammals or . . . whale watching, scientific study, and other non-consumptive uses. . . .
>
> [T]o the extent there is a "fair share" of marine mammal takes by the Tribe, the proper scope of such a share must be considered in light of the MMPA through its permit or waiver process. . . . The procedural safeguards and conservation principles of the MMPA ensure that marine mammals like the gray whale can be sustained as a resource for the benefit of the Tribe and others.[105]

It is true that the MMPA process envisioned by the Ninth Circuit will not necessarily result in a prohibition of future Makah hunts: the process could culminate in a decision permitting a hunt to proceed as contemplated in the EA and Makah Whaling

[98] For a more detailed discussion of conservation necessity and treaty abrogation, see Firestone and Lilley, "An Endangered Species."

[99] *Anderson*, 371 F.3d, at 501.

[100] Ibid. at 501 and Note 26.

[101] *Puyallup Tribe v. Dept. of Game* (Puyallup I) (1968) 391 U.S. 392, 398.

[102] *Anderson*, 371 F.3d, at 497–498, fn. 21 (citations omitted), at 501 and 500.

[103] Ibid; See also *Washington v. Washington State Commercial Passenger Fishing Vessel Association* (1979) 443 U.S., at 684–685.

[104] *Anderson*, 371 F.3d, at 500.

[105] Ibid. at 500–501.

Management Plan or with additional geographic, temporal or other restrictions.[106] Yet, this is not the crux of the matter. Rather, if the MMPA "applies" in a "backhanded way"[107] to the Makah – as a result of the conservation necessity doctrine and/or because it sheds light on the meaning of the phrase "in common with" in the Treaty of Neah Bay – the Ninth Circuit has effectively (while, at the same time, disavowing its intention) concluded that the U.S. Congress modified the Makah's treaty right to hunt whales. Interpreting the MMPA as abrogating or modifying the Makah's right to hunt marine mammals, however, cannot withstand the rigor of the U.S. Supreme Court's *Dion*[108] test. There, the Supreme Court considered whether Congress, in the Bald Eagle Protection Act,[109] modified or abrogated the Yankton Sioux Tribe's treaty right to hunt eagles.[110] Relying on both the plain language of the statute, which provides an exception to its moratorium on taking of eagles, "for the religious purposes of Indian tribes,"[111] and its legislative history, the Court concluded that Congress "considered the special cultural and religious interests of Indians, balanced those needs against the conservation purposes of the statute, and provided a specific, narrow exception that delineated the extent to which Indians would be permitted to hunt the bald and golden eagle."[112] In contrast, there is nothing in the MMPA or its legislative history to suggest that Congress considered the cultural interests of the Makah and other treaty tribes, let alone balanced those interests against the conservation purposes of the MMPA.[113]

Second, even assuming for the sake of argument that the Ninth Circuit did not effectively modify the Makah's treaty right to hunt whales and that such modification is not contrary to congressional intent, the conservation necessity doctrine does not apply under the facts presented here. To begin with, the hunt will not result in the population of the gray whale stock "diminish[ing] below [its] optimum sustainable population."[114] Indeed, as experts in this area note, the eastern North Pacific stock of gray whale is "approaching its carrying capacity."[115] As a result, conservation measures are not "necessary" within the meaning of the doctrine. Moreover, although the "conservation necessity" doctrine represents the Supreme Court's reconciliation of an "Indian tribe's treaty rights to hunt, fish, and gather . . . with a State's sovereignty over the natural

[106] Ibid. at 501 and Note 26.

[107] *Menominee Tribe of Indians v. United States* (1968) 391 U.S. 404, 412. See also Mary Christina Wood, "Fulfilling the Executive's Trust Responsibility Toward the Native Nations on Environmental Issues: A Partial Critique of the Clinton Administration's Promises and Performance" (25)733, *Envtl. L.* (1995), 792–793.

[108] *United States v. Dion* (1986) 476 U.S. 734, 16 ELR 20676. On abrogation and the ESA, see *United States v. Dion*, 752 F.2d 126 (8th Cir. 1985) (en banc) (finding no abrogation), rev'd on other grounds, 476 U.S. 734. On review in *Dion*, the U.S. Supreme Court based its ruling on the Bald Eagle Protection Act and did not reach the ESA issue. 476 U.S., at 745. But see *United States v. Billie*, (S.D. Fla. 1987) 667 F. Supp. 485 (finding abrogation).

[109] 16 U.S.C. §668 et seq.

[110] The Supreme Court considered, but did not resolve, whether the ESA also abrogated the treaty right to hunt. 476 U.S., at 745–746.

[111] 16 U.S.C. §668a.

[112] 476 U.S., at 743–744.

[113] See Marine Mammal Protection Act of 1972, 92 Pub. L. No. 522, §101(b); 86 Stat. 1027, 1031 (21 October 1972), codified at 16 U.S.C. §1371(b) (emphasis added); Pub. L. No. 97–58, §2 (9 October 1981), 95 Stat. 979; H. Rep. No. 228, 97th Cong., 1st Sess., 1981 USCCAN 1458, 1470; 103–238, §14, 108 Stat. 532 (30 April 1994); S. Rep. No. 220, 103rd Cong., 2nd Sess., 1994 USCCAN 518, 535; H.R. Rep. No. 439, 103rd Cong., 2nd Sess., 41 (1994). Also compare the MMPA, 16 U.S.C. §1371(b), with the Magnuson-Stevens Fishing Act, 16 U.S.C. §§1852(a)(1)(F), 1853(a)(2), 1853(a)(1)(B).

[114] 16 U.S.C. §1361(2).

[115] NMFS, "Whaling Provisions: Aboriginal Subsistence Whaling Quotas" (6 April 1998), 63 Fed. Reg. 16704.

resources in the State,"[116] because Congress can modify or abrogate treaty rights legislatively, there is no need to judicially create and accommodate the federal government's interest in the conservation of marine mammals. Indeed, it makes little sense to apply the conservation necessity doctrine to the federal government because that lesser power, if it existed, would be entirely subsumed within a power held solely by Congress – that is, the power to modify or abrogate treaty rights.[117] Finally, the *Anderson* panel's "no-modification" modification works at cross-purposes to the Court's goal of "ensuring legislative accountability for the abrogation [or modification] of treaty rights."[118]

3.4.3 Postscript to Ninth Circuit Decision

On 6 March 2003, NOAA and NMFS notified the public of their intent, subject to a possible rehearing in *Anderson v. Evans, supra*[119] challenging the Makah whaling quota, to prepare an EIS on the Makah annual gray whale subsistence quotas for the years 2003 through 2007.[120] This decision reflected both the Ninth Circuit's original Anderson opinion and the IWC's approval of an aboriginal subsistence quota of 620 gray whales for those years. As of this writing, work on the EIS is ongoing[121] and will consider the Makah Nation's February 15, 2004 request[122] for a limited MMPA waiver.[123]

4 A SUSTAINABLE BIOSPHERE AND SUSTAINABLE INDIGENOUS CULTURES: LESSONS FROM MAKAH WHALING

As we noted at the outset, the Makah whaling controversy raises issues of considerable significance to indigenous peoples and States; it has important implications for the conservation of biodiversity as well. With Makah culture and the legal proceedings providing context, we now attempt to reconcile "seeming" paradoxes behind these issues: (1) the incoherence of whaling to vast segments of the dominant western culture that espouses multiculturalism; (2) the use of nontraditional hunting practices to advance the revival of a traditional cultural practice; (3) the need to engage in aboriginal subsistence whaling in light of several generations of foregoing that practice; and (4) the desire to liberate indigenous peoples, on the one hand, and nature, on the other. Our goal in attempting to reconcile these paradoxes, however, is ultimately broader than any individual paradox. Indeed, we look for messages in these paradoxes to bridge the dominant society-indigenous peoples divide, to forge reconciliation across that divide, and to advance the twin imperatives of a sustainable biosphere and sustainable cultures.

4.1 Reviving an "Incoherent" Cultural Practice

Despite the acceptance of a cultural revival in numerous spheres of Makah life and the current celebration and recognition of multiculturalism more generally, the opponents

[116] *Minnesota v. Mille Lacs Band of Chippewa Indians* (1999) 526 U.S. 172, 204. See also ibid. at 204–205.

[117] *United States v. Eberhardt* (9th Cir. 1986) 789 F.3d, at 1354, 1361.

[118] Ibid.

[119] *Anderson* (9th Cir. 2002) 314 F.3d at 1006.

[120] 68 Fed. Reg. 10703–10704 (6 March 2003).

[121] Makah Whale Hunt NEPA Process, Available at http://www.nwr.noaa.gov/Marine-Mammals/Whales-Dolphins-Porpoise/Gray-Whales/NEPA-Process.cfm.

[122] Overview of Makah Indian Tribe's Waiver Request, Available at http://www.nwr.noaa.gov/Marine-Mammals/Whales-Dolphins-Porpoise/Gray-Whales/upload/waiver-overview.pdf.

[123] 16 U.S.C. §§1371(a)(3) and (5); 371 F.3d, at 501, n. 26.

of Makah whaling have had difficulty accepting the premise that Makah whaling is an "appropriate" twenty-first-century activity. Coming to terms with Makah whaling has been made more difficult for these opponents by the approximate seventy-year lapse between the Makah whale hunts of the 1920s and the culture revival of whaling in the 1990s; for, how can there be a "need" to engage in subsistence whaling, when the Makah have got along just fine for the past several generations without whaling? Irrespective of the merits of the claim that a subsistence need is lacking, a claim that we examine later and find to be wanting, it seems particularly unfair to deny the Makah the right to revive the cultural practice of subsistence whaling when that practice was cut short in large part because "widespread commercial whaling had devastated the population of gray whales almost to extinction."[124]

Moreover, the revival of Makah whaling is consistent with the traditions of the IWC and other efforts at cultural revival by the Makah. For example, the Chukotkas only revived their traditional whale hunting practices in 1994. Before 1994, they relied on whale hunting efforts of the Soviet Union (and Russian Federation) on their behalf to fulfill the IWC quota. Alaska natives revived their practices in the 1970s.[125] Moreover, the IWC accepts the "need" of the aborigines of St. Vincent and The Grenadines despite the fact that their whaling "tradition" only extends back a mere one hundred years[126] and is recognized as meeting cultural rather than nutritional needs.[127] In contrast, reviving a whaling practice of more than one thousand years fits in well with the Makah tribe's successful revival of a number of cultural practices in the aftermath of the significant archaeological find at Ozette. The Ozette excavation led the Makah Nation to create the Makah Cultural and Research Center to manage its cultural resources and to preserve and pass on culture through "research, documentation, exhibition and education."[128] Indeed, over the past twenty years, the Makah have reinstituted numerous "song, dance, and artistic traditions, and operated a program to restore the Makah language to spoken proficiency on the reservation."[129] Since the 1960s, and continually since 1981, long before the gray whale was removed from the ESA, the Makah have provided their children with a whaling curriculum in the schools.[130] As Jennifer Sepez notes, the experience of the Ahoust Band of Nuu-chah-nulth "foreshadows" the Makah experience. The Ahoust temporarily abandoned then resumed whaling in response to species abundance.[131]

Any claim that the Makah effectively slept on their right to whale is neither true to the history of U.S. government policy towards Indians, which has veered back and forth between assimilation and self-determination, nor to the more general notions of cultural revival or renewal. Although American Indian tribal powers have often gone "dormant," and in particular from the 1880s to the 1960s, for the most part, courts have refused to find tribes prejudiced by nonuse.[132] Indian fishing rights of the Makah and other Pacific Northwest tribes provide an apt example. Despite the fact that Indian fishers had harvested less than 10 percent of the twentieth-century salmon catch, that

[124] *Metcalf v. Daley*, 214 F.3d, at 1137.

[125] Miller, Note 7, at 257; IWC, "Forty-Eighth Report of the International Whaling Commission" (1996), 93–94.

[126] http://www.cnie.org/NAE/cases/makah/me.html#18; Alma Soongi Beck, "Comment The Makah's Decision to Resume Whaling," *Environmental L. & LITI* 6.359.397 (1996).

[127] Gillespie, Note 51, at 115 (citations omitted).

[128] Renker, Note 2, at 15.

[129] Ibid. at 14.

[130] Ibid. at 15.

[131] Sepez, Note 4, at 70, citing Philip Drucker, "The Northern and Central Nootkan Tribes." *Bureau Amer. Ethnology Bulletin* (1951), 144.

[132] Wilkinson, Note 26, at 37–38.

Indian fishing had ceased entirely at several traditional fishing locations, and that the State of Washington promoted and regulated commercial and recreational fisheries, which had developed in the interim, the U.S. Supreme Court affirmed a trial court's allocation of approximately 50 percent of the catch to Indians based on their treaty rights.[133] More generally, one would be loath to suggest that long-dormant religious practices of individuals should not be allowed to flourish after a period of oppression and religious intolerance ceases. Likewise, one would not contend that it is somehow improper for African Americans to explore long-dormant African cultural roots and practices. Nor would one claim that languages that have been in hibernation for decades or centuries should not be revitalized simply because they have been in disuse.

James Madison once cautioned that, "[i]f a majority be united by a common interest, the rights of the minority will be insecure."[134] Although majority rule may well be democratic, it is not always equitable. If a minority's interests consistently fall on deaf ears and if the views of a differently opinionated majority always prevail then, as Madison notes, minority rights are "insecure." Whaling is no doubt "culturally incoherent"[135] to many Americans, but should the fact that whales are not thought of as a food source by the majority mean that the minority (for whom whales provide a perfectly legitimate meal as well as a host of other useful products) cannot use them for that purpose either? If society is serious about multiculturalism and the ideals behind that concept, and recognizes the Makah as a distinct and sovereign people, then the members of the Makah Nation have the right to decide for themselves when and under what conditions they exercise their treaty and human rights. We thus see the "essential task" for society as being to "construct a reconciliation" of the expectations of indigenous peoples, which in the United States are embodied in treaties and treaty substitutes, with the expectations of non-Indians, particularly those expectations that are grounded in federal law.[136]

4.2 Traditional Cultural Practices as Opposed to Traditional Methods

The Makah Management Plan sets forth specific guidelines for a hunt, the key points of which are listed here. A whaling team has to include at least one canoe (minimum thirty feet in length) with six paddlers and a harpooner along with at least one chase boat and at least one support boat. Within each chase boat there must be a pilot, a diver, a rifleman, and a harpooner. The diver or an additional crew member must act as a safety officer during the hunt. The rifle must be high-powered (.458 caliber or higher) and after an initial strike on a whale the rifleman is to kill the whale as quickly as possible. The rifleman is not to fire if the safety officer deems it unsafe.[137]

It is clear from these guidelines that there are a number of major differences between a modern-day whale hunt and one that would have been conducted in the past, with the use of a rifle and motorized boats being perhaps the most obvious. For some critics of modern-day Makah whaling, this is a clear statement that adherence to tradition is not important for the Makah and that Makah claims of reviving a traditional cultural

[133] Ibid. at 38–39, 164; *Washington State Commercial Passenger Fishing Vessel Ass'n* (1979), 443 U.S. 658; *United States v. Washington* (W.D. Wash. 1974), 384 F. Supp., at 312, 358, 393.

[134] Lani Guinier, *The Tyranny of the Majority* (Free Press, 1994), 3.

[135] Bradford, "Save the Whales, Save the Makah," 13 St. Thomas L. Rev. 155, 169–170 (2000).

[136] Wilkinson, Note 26, at 23.

[137] Available at http://www.nmfs.noaa.gov/pr/PR2/Conservation_and_Recovery_Program/App%2010.3%20%20MAKAHPLAN.pdf (30 May 2001), 6.

practice are therefore unfounded.[138] Throughout history, the Makah, however, as is the way of many indigenous hunters, frequently made the most of the technology that existed at the time. In the early 1900s, at least one Makah whaler was using a metal head on the end of his traditional harpoon, which was otherwise crafted from yew wood.[139] Likewise, when steam power became more common, Makah whaling canoes would often accept tows from steamers to and from the whaling grounds to save paddling long distances.[140] To assert that the Makah should either whale exactly as they did 150 years ago or not at all demonstrates a lack of understanding of both aboriginal ways and of the connections between culture and development.

The Human Rights Committee (HRC), established by the International Covenant on Civil and Political Rights (IPPRC),[141] has stated that the right to enjoy culture (Article 27 of the IPPRC) need not be confined solely to traditional practices and that modern technology can be used without disrupting cultural continuity. Indeed, the "right to enjoy one's culture cannot be determined *in abstracto* but has to be placed in context."[142] The HRC went on to observe that Article 27's protection extends beyond "*traditional* means of livelihood of national minorities."[143] The HRC thus concluded that, although methods of reindeer herding have been adapted over time and are now practiced with the help of modern technology, one may still invoke Article 27.[144] So it should be for indigenous whaling.[145] In a similar vein, the Australian Law Reform Commission has noted that, "in determining whether [a hunting] activity is "traditional," attention should focus on the purpose of the activity rather than the method."[146]

In addition, it is highly unlikely that a hunt using only traditional methods would be considered humane in today's world. Any criticism of present-day Makah whaling based on this argument therefore defies logic, especially as the IWC and NGOs encourage methods that result in as quick and humane a death as possible.[147] The issue of modern methods in aboriginal whale hunts came before the IWC's Cultural Anthropology Panel in 1979, which, despite some opposition from a number of countries, decided that "the definition of subsistence whaling [did] not prevent the use of modern technology."[148]

Finally, it is worthwhile to return once more to the Treaty of Neah Bay and examine what light it sheds on the usage of modern technology. In *United States v. Washington*, it was noted how, at the time the treaty was constructed, the U.S. government clearly intended the Makah to use any available technology in order to enhance their fishing and whaling.[149] To disallow the Makah the use of modern technology today would

[138] See, for example, Whale and Dolphin Conservation Society, "WDCS Briefing on the Hunt of Gray Whale by the Makah," available at http://www.wdcs.org/dan/news.nsf/webnews/8A415D66D6E27ADA802568FB0063443F; Beach Marine Protection, available at http://www.breach.org/page32.html; West Coast Anti-Whaling Society, http://www.anti-whaling.com/foreward.htm.

[139] Renker, Note 2, at 8.

[140] Ibid.

[141] 999 U.N.T.S. 171 (1966).

[142] *Länsman et al. v. Finland*, Communication No. 511/1992 (1994) U.N. Doc. CCPR/C/52/D/511/1992, ¶ 9.3 (emphasis in original). Available at http://www1.umn.edu/humanrts/undocs/html/vws511.htm.

[143] Ibid. (emphasis in original).

[144] Ibid.

[145] When negotiating with the Makah, the United States promised to provide more modern equipment to assist the Makah in becoming even more effective whalers. *Boldt Decision*, 384 F. Supp. at 363.

[146] Australian Law Reform Commission, "The Recognition of Aboriginal Customary Laws, Report No. 31, Vol. 2" (1986), ¶ 977. Available at http://www.austlii.edu.au/au/other/alrc/publications/reports/31/.

[147] Miller, Note 7, at 264. See also IWC, "Resolution on Whale Killing Issues, Res. 2004–3" (2004). Available at http://www.iwcoffice.org/meetings/resolution2004.htm#3.

[148] Gillespie, Note 51, at 98. See also Note 103.

[149] See also *Boldt decision*, 384 F. Supp, at 363–364.

therefore not only be viewed as being inhumane and patronizing but also would be in direct violation of spirit (if not the text) of the Treaty of Neah Bay.

4.3 Locating Makah Whaling within a Subsistence Context

Makah-whaling opponents point to several 1995 writings[150] in support of their concern over the commercial intentions of the Makah. As noted earlier, this concern is perhaps exacerbated by opponents' view that a true subsistence "need" on behalf of the Makah is lacking. Many of these voices are from principled opponents of whaling who understandably want to ensure an aboriginal hunt is not a mere pretext for commercial exploitation of gray whales and that the Makah hunt does not set a precedent that has implications for whale preservation at the global level.[151] In our view, however, the continued focus on the Makah's commercial intentions, to the extent permitted under the Treaty of Neah Bay, is an unnecessary distraction from the question of the merits of an aboriginal subsistence hunt for local consumption.

It is well documented that, historically, whale products comprised a large part of the Makah diet.[152] It could be argued this historical finding is precisely that – historical – and that it cannot act as a guide to subsistence need in today's world. However, a recent survey and statistical analysis of Makah subsistence practices attests that 99 percent of Makah households participate in subsistence activities.[153] Perhaps more important, among Makah tribal members, annual subsistence consumption of fin fish and shellfish, land and marine mammals, eggs, and birds totals 174 pounds per capita and accounts for between 59 and 71 percent of total meat in the Makah diet.[154] Of the fifty-one animal species consumed, forty-two are marine animals; and marine animals are used by a broader spectrum of Makah households than other animals.[155] Moreover, based on estimates of intended use, the gray whale will once again "take its place among the most important [components of the Makah diet] as delineated by both percent of households using the resource and quantities consumed."[156] Indeed, Renker found that 93.3 percent of those surveyed thought the tribe should continue to hunt whales, with 85.5 and 73.4 percent, respectively, wanting their households to have whale meat and whale oil.[157]

Furthermore, the historical reciprocal networks within the Makah community that allow for the distribution of subsistence goods still exist. With regard to fish, all of the households on the reservation participate in some type of sharing, and there is reason to believe that this will be the case with whale products.[158] More specifically, in a 1988 study, Renker notes how 80.4 percent of the households receive fish that someone else caught;

[150] See Memorandum from Michael Tillman, Deputy Commissioner, Southwest Fisheries Center, NMFS (3 April 1995), available at http://www.safepassing.org/govt/foia1_1.gif; "Notes from the discussion of treaty rights during the April 1995 Pacific Scientific Review Group meeting" and hand-addressed and faxed "To: MFT (Michael F. Tillman) From: RLB (Robert L. Brownell, NMFS Region 4)" (27 April 1995), available at http://www.safepassing.org/govt/foia1_2.gif; "Notes from the discussion of treaty rights during the April 1995 Pacific Scientific Review Group meeting" and hand-addressed and faxed "To: MFT (Michael F. Tillman) From: RLB (Robert L. Brownell, NMFS Region 4)" (27 April 27 1995), available at http://www.safepassing.org/govt/foia1_2.gif.

[151] See Beck, Note 126, at 394–398.

[152] Renker, Note 2, at 10.

[153] Sepez, Note 4, at 81.

[154] Ibid. at 85–86.

[155] Ibid. at 82. Deer and Elk also are important.

[156] Ibid. at 129.

[157] Renker, Note 2, at 11 and 19.

[158] Ibid. at 18.

85.3 percent of households give fish away to other tribal members; and 35.3 percent of households are given money or other goods by a fisherman when there is a good season.[159] Turning to the gray whale, the combined yield of meat and blubber from the whale caught in 1999 was estimated at seven thousand pounds.[160] The village consumed much of this during the course of a large potlatch to celebrate the whale's landing and the remainder was shared among the community. It is estimated that approximately one thousand pounds of meat and thirty-five hundred pounds of blubber where distributed throughout the tribe.[161]

The monetary value of subsistence goods is perhaps put into a clearer context when one considers the economic situation of the Makah. The unemployment rate hovers around 50 percent and almost half of households on the reservation are below the federal poverty level. In fact, the average income for reservation households is $5,000, in contrast to an average of $40,000 in the State of Washington.[162] In addition, 59 percent of Makah housing units are substandard.[163] It is thus clear that subsistence goods are of fundamental economic importance to the Makah.

However, in saying this, the value of a subsistence lifestyle transcends simple monetary gain and there are at least three other ways in which the Makah accrue value from using locally derived food sources. First, there are a number of cultural benefits that are linked to the use of subsistence goods. In Sepez's 1999 study, factors such as strengthening tribal identity, upholding tradition, honoring ancestors, being a good steward of the environment and maintaining a sense of interdependency with nature were all elicited from the interviews with tribal members.[164] Second, there is a social aspect to obtaining subsistence foods. Often families and friends will harvest and consume marine animals (such as gooseneck barnacles and chitons) together and the actual process of collection is as much a part of the social interaction as is the eating.[165] Third, there appear to be certain health consequences for Indians when they move away from a subsistence diet. For example, a high proportion of Makah, who have neither a historic nor a cultural connection to cattle or other dairy animals, have been found to be lactose-intolerant.[166] Comparisons can be drawn between the Makah and other Indian tribes that have experienced diet-related health problems, and there are grounds to suggest that reintroducing whale products, in particular whale oil and the essential fatty acids contained within it, may improve the health of the Makah.[167]

4.4 Makah Liberation and Animal Liberation: Searching for Common Ground

Assuming that we have correctly analyzed the cultural, subsistence, and methodological claims earlier in this chapter, an ethical objection to Makah whaling must still be met, because in killing a whale, harm is done. "The question is not, Can they reason? nor Can they talk? but, Can they suffer?"[168] As a leading deontological animal rights philosopher, Tom Regan, notes, "fundamentally, it is not the number of animals that matters (though the numbers involved compound the wrong). Fundamentally, what matters is that

[159] Ibid.
[160] Sepez, Note 4, at 120.
[161] Ibid.
[162] Ibid. at 18.
[163] Renker, Note 2, at 18 (citations omitted).
[164] Sepez, Note 4, at 130.
[165] Ibid. at 132.
[166] Renker Note 2, at 22.
[167] Ibid. at 22–23.
[168] Jeremy Bentham, *A Introduction to the Principles of Morals and Legislation* (1789) 311.

animals . . . have their life brought to an untimely end."[169] To the extent that whale meat and blubber substitute for other sources of meat (such as subsistence hunted deer or elk or farm-raised pig or cattle) and for seal blubber, however, the taking of whales may decrease the total number of lives involved, and, given their size and the freedom they enjoy while living, may decrease overall suffering as well. Indeed, "[a]part from taking their lives there are also many other things done to [farm] animals in order to bring them cheaply to our dinner table. Castration, the separation of mother and young, the breaking up of herds, branding, transporting, [raising of farm animals in close confinement,] and finally the moments of slaughter – all of these involve suffering and do not take the animals' interests into account."[170]

Again, Tom Regan: "[W]hen we must choose between overriding the rights of the many who are innocent or the rights of the few who are innocent, and when each affected individual will be harmed in a prima facie comparable way, then we ought to override the rights of the few in preference to overriding the rights of the many."[171] If we assume 1:1 substitution – that is, for every pound of whale meat consumed, one pound of another species will not be consumed, then for every whale killed, approximately two cows, two pigs, two lambs, two chickens, two deer, two elk, two grouse, two ducks, and two seals will be saved.[172] Or, looking at it in a slightly different way, in terms of meat, one whale is equivalent to at least seven hundred chickens or one hundred seals or thirty-one bears or twenty-eight deer or fifteen pigs or nine elks or four cows. In terms of blubber, one whale is the equivalent of 180 seals. If all are innocent, we ought to choose to override the rights of the few – that is, the whales.

Some whale advocates may contend that gray whales – so-called charismatic megafauna – are entitled to special treatment or protection by humans because whales[173] are highly intelligent, communal, and communicative creatures and have long gestation periods and low birth rates.[174] Although we appreciate the sincerity of the principled

[169] Tom Regan, *The Case for Animal Rights* (University of California Press, 1985), 336. See also Christopher Stone, *Should Trees Have Standing? Towards Legal Rights for Natural Objects* (Los Altos, CA: William Kaufman, Inc., 1974) (ascribing legal rights to animals); Anthony D'Amato and Sudhir K. Chopra, "Whales: Their Emerging Right to Life" 85(1) *Am. J. Int'l L.* (1991), 21–62, 27 (arguing for an international legal entitlement to inure to whales and be recognized as *opinio juris*). But See Bradford, Note 135, at 212; Jennifer Sepez, "Treaty Rights and the Right to Culture: Native American Subsistence Issues in US Law," 14(2) *Cultural Dynamics* (2002), 143, 154.

[170] Peter Singer, *Practical Ethics* 2nd ed. (Cambridge, UK: Cambridge University Press, 1993), 64. Suffering during the process of dying may work against the Makah to the extent that whales die more slowly or painfully than other sentient animals that the Makah would otherwise consume in the absence of whale meat and blubber. Ibid. at 120. The Makah Management Plan does require the use of methods such as a high-powered rifle after the initial strike in order to minimize suffering. Makah Management Plan, note 137. Yet, the time until death, in the 1999 Makah hunt, was still eight minutes. Environmental Assessment, Note 6, at 50–51. There also may be negative effects of the death of a whale on members of that whale's social group. Singer, *Practical Ethics*, 120.

[171] Ibid. at 305. Regan terms this the "Miniride Principle." This is not to suggest that Regan is pro-whaling. Dale Jamieson and Tom Regan, "Whales are Not Cetacean Resources" in M. W. Fox & L. D. Mickley, eds., *Advances in Animal Welfare Science 1984* (The Hague: Martinus Nijhoff, 1985), 101–111.

[172] Sepez, Note 4, at 120 and Appendix I.B.; Holly Born, "Alternative Meat Marketing, Livestock Technical Note" (May 2000), 6 http://attra.ncat.org/attra-pub/PDF/Altmeat.pdf; Big-game Weights http://www.alaska.com/akcom/trivia/trivcom/bio/story/786154p-860512c.html; and http://www.askthemeatman.com/deer.htm.

[173] See Arne Kalland, "Whale Politics and Green Legitimacy." 9(6) *Anthropology Today* (1993), 3, 4.

[174] See, for example, Howard Scott Schiffman, "The Protection of Whales in International Law: A Perspective for the Next Century." 22(303) *Brooklyn J. Int'l L.* (1996), 320–323.

advocates of this claim who also show reverence and respect for indigenous peoples and culture, we have a number of responses. To begin with, whereas humans "assume a lot of intelligence from whales," a recent study of harbor seals "shows that seals are quite bright little animals too."[175] Moreover, as the Humane Society of the United States (HSUS), one of the plaintiffs in the *Anderson* litigation, and the Seal Conservation Society, respectively, remark, harbor seals are "amazingly graceful"[176] and "gregarious."[177] In addition, although they tend to haul out in small groups, some harbor seal colonies number over one thousand individuals.[178] Finally, seals have low birth rates, giving birth to only one pup per year.[179] In those instances in which similarly sentient and intelligent creatures from two different species (e.g., gray whales and harbor seals) are harmed in a comparable fashion, an argument based on numbers is at its most compelling. Thus, to the extent that the Makah would substitute whale meat and blubber for seal meat and blubber, the contention that whales should not be hunted because they are special falls apart.

Perhaps more damming to whale preservationists' argument, however, is the slippery slope that proponents find themselves on when they engage in comparisons of sentience and intelligence. For example, such an argument could justify differential intraspecies treatment based on mental capacity. Moreover, as Peter Singer, a noted utilitarian ethicist and animal rights advocate, has stated, what is most important is not the relative intelligence[180] or attractiveness of species, but, rather, harping back to Jeremy Bentham, whether and the extent to which an individual within a species is made to suffer.

> The traditional animal welfare organisations concentrate on trying to stop cruelty to animals of those species to which we most easily relate. Dogs, cats and horses are high on their lists, because we keep these animals as pets or companions. Next come those wild animals that we find attractive especially baby seals, with their big brown eyes and soft white coats, the mysterious whales and the playful dolphins. Animal Liberationists are also, of course, opposed to the suffering and killing that is needlessly inflicted on dogs, cats, horses, seals, whales, dolphins and all other animals. They do not, however, think that how appealing an animal is to us has anything to do with the wrongness of making it suffer. Instead they look to the severity of the suffering, and the numbers of animals involved.[181]

Given that cows,[182] pigs, and chickens do not have the same degree of freedom as whales do during their lives, particularly when reared in a factory farm, a desire to minimize suffering during rearing also would support hunting of whales. In light of that

[175] Volker Deecke, quoted in Tom Clarke, "Seals Learn Killers' Clicks" (2002), *Nature*, 14 November 2002 http://www.nature.com/nsu/021111/021111–6.html. See also V. B. Deecke, Slater, P. J. B., & Ford, J. K. B. "Selective habituation shapes acoustic predator recognition in harbour seals." 420 *Nature* (2002), 171–173.

[176] HSUS, Seals, http://www.hsus.org/ace/11735.

[177] Seal Conservation Society, Harbour Seal (*Phoca vitulina*). Available at http://www.pinnipeds.org/species/harbour.htm.

[178] Ibid.

[179] HSUS, Seals, Note 176.

[180] Singer does contend nonetheless that to the extent an animal such as a whale is self-aware and sees itself as "existing over time and thus . . . aspire[s] to a longer life," it would be worse to kill a whale than another animal that lacks that capacity." Singer, Note 170, at 125.

[181] Peter Singer, *The Animal Liberation Movement: Its Philosophy, Its Achievements, And Its Future* (1985). Available at http://www.utilitarian.org/texts/alm.html.

[182] Anderson Plaintiff HSUS had a large picture of a cow on its web homepage, with the motto: "*Promoting* the protection of *all* animals." Available at http://www.hsus.org (emphasis in original).

suffering during rearing, Peter Singer describes the "moral necessity" of avoiding the products of animals that have been reared on factory farms as "the clearest case of all" in which humans ought to look beyond their narrow self-interests.[183] Moreover, because one arranges for the coming into existence of farm animals, it can be argued that one "voluntarily acquire[s] duties to these animals one would not otherwise have."[184]

Although it is true that this argument is premised on a 1:1 substitution, it may be that whaling increases the overall amount of meat in the diet of the Makah. Indeed, from an animal liberationist point of view, the worst outcome would be zero substitution with the result being that one additional creature (the whale itself) is killed for each whale taken.[185] But even at a substitution rate as low as twenty-five percent, the taking of one whale could spare 178 chickens or 25 seals or 8 bears or 7 deer or 2 elk. The point of this argument is not to reach a conclusion – that would take some careful surveying of the Makah – but, rather, to show that when one scratches deeper, the animal welfare argument is not as clear-cut as it is portrayed.

5 CONCLUSION

Although we acknowledge nation-states' recognition in the first half of the twentieth century of indigenous peoples' use and dependence on marine wildlife, we must not forget that instruments such as the ICRW were conceived and crafted by dominant societies and imposed on indigenous peoples based on the values, interests, and norms of those dominant societies. More recently, there has been a growing appreciation that indigenous peoples should be involved in the development and negotiation of international agreements and in the management of their traditionally owned resources. In light of the growing awareness surrounding the role of indigenous people in the international arena, their demands to be viewed as separate autonomous actors are increasingly being heard.[186]

This appreciation can be exemplified by a brief comparison in the construction of international environmental treaties during the twentieth century.[187] The older treaties, for example, the Fur Seals Convention of 1911[188] and – perhaps more relevant here – the ICRW, treated indigenous peoples as being the responsibility of the nation-state in which they were located. Today, they are increasingly seen as being separate entities with their own voice in the decision-making process. This decolonization process, which was stimulated to a large extent by the UN Charter,[189] is reflected in developments at the global level – for example, the Convention on Biological Diversity (CBD), Article 8(j) (access to traditional knowledge and benefit sharing), and the related Ad

[183] Peter Singer, *Animal Liberation*. 2nd ed. (New York: New York Review of Books, 1990), 170.

[184] Regan, Note 169, at 342.

[185] See for example, Sepez, Note 4, at 117–119 (suggesting that demand for seal products outstrips supply).

[186] Benjamin J Richardson, "Indigenous Peoples, International Law and Sustainability." 10(1) *Rev. Eur. Community & Int. Envt'l L.* (2001), 1–12, 3.

[187] See Jeremy Firestone, Jonathan Lilley, and Isabel Torres de Noronha, "Cultural Diversity, Human Rights, and the Emergence of Indigenous Peoples in International and Comparative Environmental Law." 20(2) *Am. U. Int.'l L. Rev.* (2004) 219–292.

[188] Convention between the United States, Great Britain, Russia and Japan for the Preservation and Protection of Fur Seals (7 July 1911) (no longer in force), 37 Stat. 1542. Available at http://fletcher.tufts.edu/multi/sealtreaty.html.

[189] Richardson, Note 186, at 5.

Hoc Working Group, which has been established;[190] the establishment of the Permanent Forum on Indigenous Issues in the UN Economic and Social Council,[191] and the incorporation of indigenous peoples' concerns into decision making of the World Bank,[192] and at the regional level – the Arctic Council,[193] a soft-law agreement among eight "Arctic" States that provides for the inclusion of indigenous representatives as permanent and important participants. The Rio Declaration likewise calls on States to facilitate indigenous peoples' "effective participation" in sustainable development.[194] The Draft Declaration on the Rights of Indigenous Peoples goes further by recognizing that indigenous peoples' participation is at their discretion; that they should choose their own representatives according to their own processes and procedures; and that indigenous peoples' participation is without prejudice to the their right to "maintain and develop their own indigenous decision-making institutions" and "strengthen their distinct political, economic, social and cultural characteristics."[195]

We believe that the Permanent Forum on Indigenous Issues, the changes at the World Bank, the creation of the Arctic Council, and the implementation of the CBD begin to move society in the right direction – towards a recognition of indigenous peoples' self-determination and sovereignty – and provide more principled models of how a pluralistic society and one based on the norm of culture diversity should accommodate indigenous culture, rights, and knowledge. Finally, we believe that the great whales would be better served by those advocates seeking whales' preservation and protection – a broad objective we wholeheartedly endorse – if they focus their energies, talents, and worldwide attention on large anthropogenic threats to whales – that is, climate change, habitat destruction, marine pollution, and fishing by-catch, rather than on preventing the Makah people from exercising their cultural heritage.[196] Indeed, the whaling preservationist camp should see indigenous peoples and indigenous rights under international and national laws (including treaties) as allies in, not impediments to, the quest for a sustainable biosphere.

[190] Repr. 31 I.L.M. (1992) 818, available at http://www.biodiv.org; see also Patricia Birnie & Alan Boyle, *International Law and the Environment* (Oxford University Press, 2002), 568.

[191] Resolution E/RES/2000/22. Available at http://www.un.org/esa/socdev/pfii/mandate.htm.

[192] See, for example, World Bank Operational Policies, Involuntary Resettlement Policy (O.P. 4.12) (Revised April 2004); World Bank Operational Policies, Draft Operational Policy on Indigenous Peoples (OP 4.10), (23 March 2001); World Bank Operational Directives, Indigenous Peoples (OD 4.20) (September 1991); World Bank Operational Policies, Environmental Assessment (O.P. 4.01), (15 January 1999).

[193] Arctic Council http://www.arctic-council.org.

[194] Declaration of the UN Conference on Environment and Development, Rio de Janeiro, 3–14 June 1992, UN Doc. A/CONF.151/5/Rev.1 (1992), Principle 22.

[195] E/CN.4/Sub.2/1994/2/Add.1 at Arts. 4 and 19. See also ibid., Art. 20.

[196] See, for example, Report of the IWC Scientific Committee, IWC/55/Rep1 (2003); William C. G. Burns, "Climate Change and the International Whaling Commission in the 21st Century" in William C. G. Burns & Alexander Gillespie, eds., *The Future of Cetaceans in a Changing World* (Transnational Publishers, 2003), 339–379, 349–350.

PART FIVE

PROCESSES AFFECTING BIODIVERSITY

SECTION A. GLOBAL WARMING

20 Biodiversity and Climate Change Laws: A Failure to Communicate?

David R. Hodas*

1 INTRODUCTION

Climate change driven by global warming is threatening to substantially modify important ecosystems, both marine and terrestrial, because the rate of climate change exceeds rates at which ecosystems and the biodiversity they contain can adapt or migrate. Global warming threatens to destroy great swaths of biodiversity within affected ecosystems. Preservation of biodiversity and avoidance of catastrophic ecosystem collapse depend on global success in reducing emissions of greenhouse gases and stabilizing (or, hopefully, reducing) atmospheric green house gas concentrations. For lawyers, the challenge is how law can be used to achieve this goal.

Two separate sets of laws exist – laws concerning biodiversity and endangered species (e.g., the United Nations Convention on Biological Diversity [CBD], and the U.S. Endangered Species Act [ESA] and comparable laws in other countries) and emerging laws addressing greenhouse gas emissions. Both bodies of law mirror the same analytic questions. That is, to what extent do national and international biodiversity laws consider climate change in their regulatory frameworks? And, to what extent does the emerging climate change legal regime consider biodiversity in its regulatory schemes? Is the extent of incorporation adequate and effective? If not, how could laws be improved to incorporate biodiversity concerns into climate change decisions, and to fold climate change concerns into the operation of biodiversity laws?

This chapter will review the science at the interface of climate change and biodiversity, examine international and national biodiversity legal regimes to see whether they incorporate or could incorporate climate change into biodiversity law and policy, and consider the mirror issue of whether climate change law incorporates biodiversity concerns. The goal of the chapter will be to identify legal opportunities to link biodiversity and climate change in key decision making, and to identify the gaps in the laws that ignore the linkage of these two vital issues.

This analysis is timely, as effects of warming are already being felt by a variety of ecosystems from coral reefs to Arctic sea ice, and, in response, litigation linking biodiversity with climate change has already begun. For instance, the Center for Biological Diversity recently filed a petition with the United States Department of Interior to list the polar bear as a threatened species under the ESA because of the loss of sea ice

* Widener University School of Law Wilmington, Delaware; e-mail: drhodas@widener.edu.

necessary for polar bear survival.[1] According to the group, the Arctic sea ice habitat that polar bears use for feeding, mating, and maternity denning is breaking up earlier each spring and forming later in the autumn, as a result of global warming.[2]

Arguably, listing under the ESA would provide broad protection to polar bears under the ESA §7 mandate that each federal agency action not "jeopardize the continued existence"[3] of endangered or threatened species, or adversely modify their critical habitat. The U.S. Supreme Court has long held that any such action *must* be enjoined.[4] Additionally, polar bear protection could be provided under the §9 prohibition against any "take" of an endangered species.[5] The conceptual issue is to identify those government actions that would violate the no jeopardy requirement by accelerating Arctic sea ice melting as a result of global warming.

Seeking to prevent destruction of critical habitat, the Environmental Law Alliance Worldwide (E-LAW) has petitioned the UNESCO World Heritage Committee to declare three sites to be "In Danger," to take action to protect them, and to "recognize the need to reduce greenhouse gas emissions to protect the World Heritage Sites for future generations."[6] The sites represent a broad range of ecosystems and biodiversity: the Belize

[1] Center for Biological Diversity, "Global Warming to Drive Polar Bears Extinct – Petition Filed to Place Ice Bear on Endangered List," (Online # 359, 25 February 2005), available at http://www.endangeredearth.org/alerts/result.asp?index=1343. ("[T]he Center for Biological Diversity submitted a 154-page scientific petition on 16 February 2005 to place the polar bear on the U.S. endangered species list. Senator Joseph Lieberman, cosponsor of the Climate Stewardship Act, supported the petition: 'The potential listing of the polar bear as an endangered species because of the effects of global warming should set off alarm bells around the world. Global warming is removing the bears' habitat and wreaks havoc in the arctic climates where they live and grow. To spoil the earth for generations to come, and for the creatures that inhabit it, when we knew what we were doing and could have stopped it, would be a moral failing of enormous – and might I add – biblical proportions.' The polar bear is completely dependent on sea ice for hunting, traveling and mating. Its main prey species, the ringed seal, is also associated with the large expanses of sea ice which cover the polar regions for much of the year. Due to global warming, however, the sea ice is melting away.") On 3 February 2006, after being sued by the Center for Biological Diversity for ignoring its petition, the U.S. Fish and Wildlife Service began the formal listing evaluation process by soliciting public comments on the petition. 71 Fed. Reg. 6745 (9 February 2006).

[2] The melting is now so well-recognized that nations surrounding the Arctic are already jockeying for advantageous boundary lines to maximize resource availability, and the "Northwest Passage" sea route may finally be become a reality. Clifford Krauss et al., "As Polar Ice Turns to Water, Dreams of Treasure Abound," *New York Times* (10 October 2005) A1.

[3] 16 U.S.C. §1536(a)(2) ("... Each Federal agency shall ... insure that any action authorized, funded, or carried out by such agency ... is not likely to jeopardize the continued existence of any endangered species or threatened species or result in the destruction or adverse modification of habitat of such species which is determined by ... to be critical ... ")

[4] *TVA v. Hill*, 437 U.S. 153 (1978). In response to this decision, Congress amended the ESA to create the Endangered Species Committee (aka "The God Squad"), which was empowered, after a hearing and in the face of exceptional circumstances, to allow, subject to "reasonable mitigation ... measures ... necessary and appropriate to minimize the adverse effects" on the species, an agency to proceed with projects that would jeopardize the continued existence of a species. 16 U.S.C. §1536(e)–(h). Since 1978, the God Squad has only considered a hand full of petitions, and of those, has legally granted an exception from the jeopardy prohibition only once.

[5] 16 U.S.C. §1538(a). The statute defines "take" to mean "... harass, *harm*, pursue, hunt, shoot, wound, kill, trap, capture, or collect, or attempt to engage in such conduct." 16 U.S.C. §1532(19). Implementing regulations define "harm" to include acts that cause "significant habitat modification or degradation where it actually kills or injures wildlife by significantly impairing essential behavioral patterns, including breeding, feeding or sheltering." *Babbitt v. Sweet Home Chapter of Communities for a Greater Oregon*, 515 U.S. 687 (1995).

[6] "Global Warming Threatens Planet." E-Law Advocate (Autumn 2004), available at http://www.elaw.org/news/advocate/default.asp?issue=2004–4.

Barrier Reef Reserve (coral reefs at risk), the Huascaran National Park (tropical mountain range in Peru), and Sagarmatha National Park (a park in the Himalayas). Among the remedial steps sought in the petition is a reduction in greenhouse gas emissions to protect the sites for future generations.

In Australia, the Wildlife Preservation Society of Queensland (Wildlife Whitsunday) on 22 July 2005 sued the Australian government for refusing to assess in its approval process of a coal mining operation the global warming impacts of burning the forty-eight million tons of coal that the mines are expected to produce; the coal would both be used in Australia and exported. The plaintiff claims that the coal "will largely be burnt in coal-fired power stations producing greenhouse gases contributing to global warming. Global warming is expected to cause severe impacts to the Australian environment, including to the iconic Great Barrier Reef and Wet Tropics Rainforests."[7]

A lawsuit currently in the U.S. courts is seeking the United States Overseas Private Investment Corporation (OPIC) and the Export-Import Bank (Ex-Im Bank) of the United States to include global warming in their environmental impact statement analyses of projects.[8] In the lawsuit, Plaintiffs (Friends of the Earth, Greenpeace, and three U.S. cities) allege that OPIC and the Ex-Im Bank provide financial support to projects that contribute to climate change, but the assistance was approved without including global warming impacts from the projects in their environmental impact statements.

Two NGOs are pursuing a petition before the Inter-American Commission of Human Rights on behalf of the Inuits. The claim asserts that "[I]f global warming continues unchecked it threatens to destroy their culture, render their land uninhabitable, and rob them of their means of subsistence." The petition asks the Commission to recognize the relationship between human rights and the environmental effects of anthropogenic global warming.[9]

In each of these claims, the petitioners are arguing that climate change concerns need to be considered under a variety of existing laws, none of which were designed with climate change in mind. In each instance, the plaintiffs are attempting to use general language addressing endangered species, human rights, general concern for environmental problems, or even seemingly ancient common law concepts to address a new, unique problem – the change of global climate resulting from the historic accumulation of greenhouse gases in the atmosphere. This chapter will argue that existing statutes and laws that deal with biodiversity are not up to the job of slowing climate change to protect the species and ecosystems endangered by global warming. Conversely, climate change law, although motivated in part by biodiversity and ecosystem concerns, does not incorporate biodiversity in shaping adaptation and mitigation regulations.

[7] Press Release, Environmental Defender's Office of North Queensland, Inc. (26 July 2005), available at http://www.climatelaw.org/cases. See also *Australian Conservation Foundation v. Minister for Planning* [2004] VCAT 2029 (29 October 2004) VCAT Reference No. P2257/2004 (holding that a municipality and the government planning board must consider the environmental impacts of greenhouse gas emissions from a brown coal-burning power station before approving a plan to extend the operational life of the station).

[8] *Friends of the Earth v. Watson*, Slip Copy, 2005 WL 2035596, 35 Envtl. L. Rep. 20, 179 (N.D. Cal., 23 August 2005).

[9] Petition to the Inter American Commission on Human Rights Seeking Relief from Violations Resulting from Global Warming Caused by Acts and Omissions of the United States (7 December 2005) Available at http://www.ciel.org/Climate/ICC_Petition_7Dec05.html.

Climate change presents the world's greatest environmental challenge to our market-based legal system. It presents the paradigmatic "tragedy of the commons":[10] each nation keeps the benefits of burning fossil fuels and other means of emitting other greenhouse gases (GHGs) while sharing the adverse effects with the world. Are biodiversity laws up to the challenge of preventing the tragedy by protecting ecosystem biodiversity and preventing species loss from anthropogenic greenhouse gas climate change? This chapter will attempt a preliminary analysis of this problem by considering the international legal regimes and major U.S. laws that can address biodiversity.

2 CLIMATE CHANGE THREATS TO BIODIVERSITY

The precise breadth and depth of potential loss of biodiversity and ecosystem resilience as a result of global warming remains subject to scientific inquiry. But that global warming is adversely affecting biodiversity is now well recognized:

> Human beings are contributing to changing regional temperatures, which in turn are associated with changes in wild species. Therefore human activities are highly likely to be contributing to the changes in regional temperatures, and these human-influenced temperature patterns are significantly associated with discernible changes in plant and animal . . . traits.
>
> . . . All studies taken together demonstrate that recent (at least for the latter few decades on the 20th century) climate changes seen at both the local and nine-grid-box scales, and observed changes in wild species, are highly likely to be forced to a considerable degree by human emissions of GHG & aerosols.[11]

The Convention on Biological Diversity *Ad Hoc Technical Expert Group on Biological Diversity and Climate Change* has summarized these risks as well as evidence of observed changes that verify both the current loss and the imminence of much greater loss of biodiversity.[12] According to the Ad Hoc Technical Expert Group, observed ecosystem modifications associated with global warming include 1) changes in the timing of periodic biological phenomena (e.g., flowering, breeding, migration); 2) changes in species distribution; 3) changes in the form and structure (morphology), behavior, and physiology of many birds, plants, and insects; 4) enlargement of the range, frequency and intensity of pests and diseases, 5) altered patterns of precipitation, floods, droughts, water temperature, stream flows and water quality, which will adversely affect "biodiversity and the goods and services ecosystems provide;" 6) modifications in the length of growing seasons and alteration of species composition in high northern latitude ecosystems; 7) increased mortality of adult penguins; and 8) alterations of weather and temperature sensitive coastal and marine ecosystems such as coral reefs, some fish populations, and Pacific and Arctic marine birds and mammals.[13]

Of course, independent of climate change, biodiversity is already decreasing because of human activity. Ecosystems are already stressed by human population growth, ever

[10] Garrett Hardin, "The Tragedy of the Commons," 162 *Science* (1968), 1243.

[11] Terry Root et al., "Human-Modified Temperatures Induce Species Changes: Joint Attribution." 102 *J. National Academy of Sciences* (2005), *4767.*

[12] Convention on Biological Diversity Ad Hoc Technical Expert Group on Biological Diversity and Climate Change, *Biological Diversity and Climate Change*, UNEP/CBD/SBSTTA/9/INF/12 (30 September 2003). Much of the report is based on work of the Intergovernmental Panel on Climate Change.

[13] Ibid. at 31–32.

more intense land-use patterns and associated ecosystem loss, pollution stresses, and the invasive human spread of exotic species into new ecosystems. Climate change is yet an additional significant pressure on already stressed ecosystems: "while there is little evidence to suggest that climate change will slow species losses, there is evidence that it may increase species losses."[14] For instance, the Technical Expert Group predicts that ecosystem services will be lost as a result of climate change, and with it human welfare will suffer because of ocean warming, sea-level rise, and intense storms that will endanger the very existence of some coastal communities and threaten other coastal communities (those not destroyed) with the loss of the benefits of marine biodiversity, fisheries, and shoreline protection. Wetlands, ranging from reefs, atolls, estuaries, and mangroves to prairies, tropical and boreal forests, and polar and alpine ecosystems, are "natural systems especially vulnerable to climate change because of their limited adaptive capacity, and are likely to undergo significant and irreversible change."[15] The panel also expects presently eroding beaches and barriers to erode further as the climate changes and sea level rises.

From these generalized effects, the Technical Expert Panel then attempted to identify specific adverse impacts that global warming will most likely cause:

> Extinction of wildlife populations may be hastened by increasing temporal variability in precipitation; changes in phenology, such as the date of bud break of plants, hatching, and migration of insects, birds and mammals, have already been observed and are expected to continue; Ecosystems dominated by long-lived species (e.g., long-lived trees) will often be slow to show evidence of change and slow to recover from climate-related stresses. Plant communities are expected to be disrupted. Most soil biota have relatively wide temperature optima, so are unlikely to be adversely affected directly by changes in temperatures, although there is lack of information on the effect of changes in soil moisture. For inland wetlands, changes in rainfall and flooding patterns across large areas of arid land will adversely affect bird species. The lack of thermal refuges and migratory routes in lakes, streams and rivers, may cause contraction of the distributions of many fish species. Species and ecosystems are projected to be impacted by extreme climatic events. The general impact of climate change is that the habitats of many species will move poleward or upward from their current locations. Drought and desertification processes will result in movements of habitats of many species towards areas of higher rainfall from their current locations. The climatic zones suitable for temperate and boreal plant species may be displaced by 200–1,200 km poleward. The species composition of forests is likely to change and new assemblages of species may replace existing forest types. For lakes and streams, the effects of temperature-dependent changes would be least in the tropics, moderate at mid-latitudes, and pronounced in high latitudes. Climate change will have most pronounced effects on wetlands through altering the hydrological regime.[16]

One could drill down still further to evaluate potential biodiversity impacts by regions. For instance, Africa's important biodiversity will be threatened by climate change.[17] Much of Africa is forest (5 million square kilometers), and trees and shrubs (12 million square kilometers). Semiarid and subhumid woodlands and savannahs are

[14] Ibid. at 33–35.

[15] Ibid. at 36–37.

[16] Ibid. at 37–39.

[17] This summary of African biodiversity impacts is taken from David R. Hodas, "Climate Change and Land Use in Africa," in Nathalie J. Chalifour et al., eds., *Land Use for Sustainable Development* (Cambridge University Press, 2007) 45.

at risk from reduced rainfall (increased fires) and more intense land use as a result of population pressure. Global warming will adversely affect ecosystem services, such as water regulation, carbon sequestration, soil fertility, and habitat formation, will be affected. Sub-Saharan Africa contains unique ecosystems whose flora and fauna face risk from climate change. Critical flora biomes include Cape Floral Kingdom, Madagascar, Cameroon, and mountain habitats from Ethiopia to South Africa. Important fauna in danger include savannah and forest species (90 percent of the world's antelope and gazelle species are in Africa) and birds, whose habitat and migratory patterns are in danger from climate change. Biodiversity in Africa is an important source of food, fiber, shelter, fuel, medicine, and income from tourism. Climate change will affect the major mammal migrations in east and southern Africa as well as bird migration. Important, heat-sensitive African habitats, such as the mountain habitat that runs from Ethiopia to South Africa at elevations above two thousand meters and the Cameroon mountain habitats will be impaired as temperature increases. The South African Cape floral kingdom, with seventy-three hundred species, of which about 68 percent only exist there, will be changed by rainfall patterns, warming, and the potential appearance of fires as a result of reduced rain.

3 THE INTERNATIONAL LEGAL RESPONSE TO CLIMATE CHANGE AND BIODIVERSITY LOSS

Although there is a very real link between climate change and biodiversity, and although the major treaties addressing these two topics were concluded and signed at the same place and time, neither treaty refers to the other; nor do they have any conceptual linkage. In 1992, both the Convention on Biological Diversity (CBD)[18] and the United Nations Framework convention on Climate Change (UNFCCC)[19] were concluded and signed at the United Nations Conference on Environment and Development (UNCED) held in Rio de Janeiro. However, the processes that led to their respective results were entirely independent. The CBD began with work at IUCN, and proceeded under the negotiation umbrella of UNEP,[20] whereas the UNFCCC proceeded independently out of work began by the World Meteorological Organization and pushed by the Intergovernmental Panel on Climate Change and others.[21]

In broad strokes, the UNFCCC focuses on reducing the concentration of greenhouse gas emissions in the atmosphere to avoid the dangers associated with rapid global warming. The treaty, without imposing any binding targets and timetables, sought to push developed countries to craft GHG emission reduction plans, assemble emission data and inventories, proceed with essential research, and begin the process of agreeing on what level of anthropogenic greenhouse gas emissions are dangerous, and then establishing specific, binding targets and timetables for reducing GHGs to avoid reaching the dangerous levels. Underpinning the treaty was the concept that market mechanisms should be used to minimize the cost of emission reductions. Because GHG are dispersed

[18] 31 I.L.M. 818 (1992) (signed 5 June 1992; entered into force 29 December 1993).

[19] 31 I.L.M. 849 (1992) (signed 29 May 1992; entered into force 21 March 1994).

[20] Nicholas A. Robinson, "IUCN as Catalyst for a Law of the Biosphere: Acting Globally and Locally." 35 *Envtl. L.* 249 (2005), 273–4.

[21] John Houghton, *Global Warming: The Complete Briefing* 3rd ed., (Cambridge University Press, 2004), 242–246.

throughout the world's atmosphere within weeks of their emission, the location of emissions, emissions reductions, or sequestrations is irrelevant to warming; it is the total atmospheric concentration that is important. Thus, the climate change legal regime envisioned, from the start, the trading of emissions reductions as a central implementation approach. Some pilot concepts were included in the UNFCCC, but full-fledged market mechanisms would be subject to further negotiations. These negotiations, which would flower into protocols to the UNFCCC, would establish emissions targets and timetables, details of trading regimes, and international bodies to oversee the implementation of these commitments. The UNFCCC also recognized the "common but differentiated responsibilities" of all the nations of the world. Initially, only developed nations (including the so-called economies in transition – that is, the countries of the former Soviet Union) would face requirements (the so-called Annex I nations), but ultimately all nations would be required to contribute, to the extent they were able, to the challenge of mitigating climate change. The UNFCCC also included an "additionality" obligation – a commitment of the developed world to provide financial resources over and above (i.e., additional to) existing foreign aid to help developing countries address GHG reduction.

The general procedural terms of the UNFCCC established a Conference of the Parties, which would meet regularly (approximately annually) to negotiate concrete protocols to supplement the more general provisions of the UNFCCC. A Secretariat was also established to support this work. The nations adopting the UNFCCC knew that its commitments would not be sufficient to seriously tackle climate change. At the first meeting of the Conference of the Parties (COP 1 Berlin, March/April 1995), the Parties began ongoing talks to agree on stronger and more detailed commitments for industrialized countries. Two and a half intense years of negotiations later, the Kyoto Protocol was adopted at COP 3 in Kyoto, Japan, on 11 December 1997.[22]

Under the Kyoto Protocol the developed nations agreed to lower their overall emissions to about 5 percent below 1990 levels by the years 2008–2012, with each developed nation agreeing to a specific target, which ranged from an 10 percent increase (Iceland) to a 8 percent reduction from 1990 levels (most of the nations within the European Union).[23] Although originally conceived and advocated by the United States (which was assigned a target of 7 percent reduction), the Kyoto Protocol was rejected by the Bush administration. Nevertheless, with the ratification by the Russian Federation on 18 November 2004, fifty-five nations and Annex I nations accounting for 55 percent of 1990 emissions had ratified the Kyoto Protocol; it thus entered into effect as international law on 16 February 2005.[24]

[22] Available at http://unfccc.int/essential_background/kyoto_protocol/items/2830.php.

[23] Kyoto Protocol, Annex B. The maximum amount of emissions (measured as the equivalent in carbon dioxide) that a Party may emit over the commitment period in order to comply with its emissions target is known as a Party's *assigned amount*. The targets can be grouped as follows: –8 percent EU-15, Bulgaria, Czech Republic, Estonia, Latvia, Liechtenstein, Lithuania, Monaco, Romania, Slovakia, Slovenia, and Switzerland; –7 percent United States; –6 percent Canada, Hungary, Japan, and Poland; –5 percent Croatia; 0 percent New Zealand, Russian Federation, and Ukraine; +1 percent Norway; +8 percent Australia; and +10 percent Iceland.

[24] Available at http://unfccc.int/essential_background/kyoto_protocol/status_of_ratification/items/2613.php.

The Kyoto Protocol elaborates on the general approach of the UNFCCC, in that it concentrates on specific emissions targets (assigned amounts) within a compliance period using market mechanisms. The Protocol establishes three innovative "mechanisms" known as *joint implementation*,[25] the *clean development mechanism*,[26] and *emissions trading*.[27] These are designed to help Annex I Parties cut the cost of meeting their emissions targets by taking advantage of opportunities to reduce emissions, or increase greenhouse gas removals, that cost less in other countries than at home. The approach seeks to rationalize and commodify emissions of the covered GHGs.[28] By assigning each GHG its global warming potential, with CO_2 set as the baseline of 1, the Kyoto Protocol set the stage for trading emission reduction credits across the range of gases. Compliance also may be achieved by removing GHGs from the atmosphere and storing them permanently in sinks.[29] The Kyoto Protocol makes no mention of the CBD or biodiversity. The sole mention of biodiversity in the UNFCCC legal documents is in the Marrakech Accords, which establish the ground rules for the emission trading regimes under Kyoto. Buried deep in the Accords is a brief reference to biodiversity[30] – a requirement that potential afforestation and reforestation projects under the Clean Development Mechanism assess their impacts on biodiversity, among other things.[31]

25 The Secretariat explains that "[u]nder *joint implementation*, an Annex I Party may implement a project that reduces emissions (e.g., an energy efficiency scheme) or increases removals by sinks (e.g., a reforestation project) in the territory of another Annex I Party, and count the resulting *emission reduction units* (ERUs) against its own target. Although the term "joint implementation" does not appear in Article 6 of the Protocol where this mechanism is defined, it is often used as convenient shorthand.

26 Ibid. "Under the *clean development mechanism* (CDM), Annex I Parties may implement projects in non-Annex I Parties that reduce emissions and use the resulting *certified emission reductions* (CERs) to help meet their own targets. The CDM also aims to help non-Annex I Parties achieve sustainable development and contribute to the ultimate objective of the Convention."

27 Ibid. Under *emissions trading*, an Annex I Party may transfer some of the emissions under its assigned amount, known as *assigned amount units* (AAUs), to another Annex I Party that finds it relatively more difficult to meet its emissions target. It also may transfer CERs, ERUs, or RMUs that it has acquired through the CDM, joint implementation or sink activities in the same way. In order to address the concern that some countries could "oversell" and then be unable to meet their own targets, the Protocol rulebook requires Annex I Parties to hold a minimum level of AAUs, CERs, ERUs, or RMUs in a *commitment period reserve* that cannot be traded.

28 Kyoto Protocol, Annex A. The six covered gases are carbon dioxide (CO_2); methane (CH_4); nitrous oxide (N_2O); hydroflourocarbons (HFCs); perfluorocarbons (PFCs); and sulfur hexafluoride (SF_6).

29 The Secretariat explains: "Parties may offset their emissions by increasing the amount of greenhouse gases removed from the atmosphere by so-called carbon "sinks" in the land use, land-use change and forestry (LULUCF) sector. However, only certain activities in this sector are eligible. These are *afforestation*, *reforestation* and *deforestation* (defined as eligible by the Kyoto Protocol) and *forest management*, *cropland management*, *grazing land management* and *revegetation* (added to the list of eligible activities by the Marrakech Accords). Greenhouse gases removed from the atmosphere through eligible sink activities generate credits known as *removal units* (RMUs). Any greenhouse gas *emissions* from eligible activities, in turn, must be offset by greater emission cuts or removals elsewhere."

30 Report of the Conference of the Parties (COP 7), Addendum, Part Two: Action Taken by the Conference of the Parties, Vol. II, U.N. Doc. FCCC/CP/2001/13/Add.2 (21 January 2001) p. 22.

31 Other matters of concern listed before biodiversity are nonpermanence, additionality, leakage, uncertainties, socioeconomic impacts, and environmental impacts (including effects on biodiversity and ecosystems). All but one of the modalities proposed for joint implementation, offsets, and CDM were silent as to biodiversity, David R. Hodas, "Sustainable Development and the Marrakech Accords," in Adrian Bradbrook et al., eds., *The Law of Energy for Sustainable Development* (Cambridge University Press, 2005), 67–73. Only the rules governing afforestation and reforestation projects under the CDM make any mention of biodiversity. The rules contain the procedural requirement that the project proponents prepare an environmental impact assessment of any impacts on biodiversity that project participants or the host nation believe are significant. The project proposal must describe plans to monitor and remedy

The international and legal regime covering biodiversity is governed by two major treaties,[32] the Convention to Regulate International Trade in Endangered Species of Flora and Fauna (CITES)[33] and the CBD. CITES, which has been in effect for more than thirty years, was put into place to control the hunting and poaching to extinction of wild animals and plants. Because much of the exploitation was aimed at obtaining elephant ivory, animal hides, tiger bones, rhinoceros horns, and other animal parts and so on for the economic value these items could attract in the global market, CITES used a trade-based legal regime to eliminate the markets for these animal parts. Under CITES, the party nations agree to a list of species that are endangered, ban all importing and exporting of any specimen of a protected species,[34] and adopt domestic laws to enforce the trade prohibition.

In the United States, implementation is accomplished through the ESA,[35] which bans trade in listed species and parts.[36] The ESA goes beyond the U.S. implementation obligation to ban trade to also ban U.S. government actions that would jeopardize any endangered or threatened species or habitat critical to the survival of those species,[37] and ban conduct that could take or harm those species.[38] Neither CITES nor the ESA make any reference to climate change or its effects on ecosystems or endangered species. This silence is not surprising because at the time the idea that the earth could be warmed by GHGs was only in an embryonic stage.[39]

The CBD takes an altogether different approach to the problem of ecosystems and biodiversity. Instead of banning any particular activity, it seeks to preserve and protect biodiversity by urging more widespread use of environmental impact assessments (EIAs) that incorporate biodiversity impacts into project and program analysis.[40] Other than EIA and information exchange, the only substantive obligation under the CBD is a conditional one: each "Party, as far as possible and appropriate, shall [i]n the case of imminent or grave danger or damage, originating under its jurisdiction or control, to biological diversity within the area under the jurisdiction of other States or in areas beyond the limits of national jurisdiction, notify immediately the potentially affected States of such danger or damage, as well as initiate action to prevent or minimize such danger or damage."[41] This operational focus on using environmental assessment and

any significant impacts that the project participants or the host nation identifies. There is no mention of what happens if the monitoring and/or remedy is inadequate or not carried out. UNFCCC, *Modalities and procedures for afforestation and reforestation activities under the clean development mechanism in the first commitment period of the Kyoto Protocol*, Decision 19/CP.9, Annex, (c) and Appendix B, 3(j)(i) and (l), FCCC/CP/2003/6/Add.2 (30 March 2004), 18, 28.

[32] There are other treaties that address specific species or ecosystems, but CITES and CBD are the two general, overarching conventions. See, for example, International Convention for the Regulation of Whaling, 161U.N.T.S. 72, 10 U.S.T. 952 (1946); Convention on the Conservation of Antarctic Marine Living Resources (1959); Convention on the Conservation of Migratory Species of Wild Animals 19 I.L.M. (1979); Convention on Wetlands of International Importance Especially as to Waterfowl Habitat, 11 I.L.M. 963 (1971); and the Migratory Bird Treaty of 1916 (see *Missouri v. Holland*, 252 U.S. 416 (1920), Oliver Wendell Holmes, Justice: "But for the Treaty and [implementing statute] there soon might be no birds for any power to deal with."). None of these treaties address climate change.

[33] 12 I.L.M. 1085; 993 U.N.T.S. 243 (1973).

[34] CITES Article III.

[35] 16 U.S.C. §§1531(a) and 1537a.

[36] 16 U.S.C. §1538(c) ("It is unlawful for any person . . . to engage in any trade in any specimens contrary to the provision of [CITES], or to possess any specimens traded contrary to the provisions of [CITES] . . . "

[37] 16 U.S.C. §1536.

[38] 16 U.S.C. §1538(a).

[39] See Spencer R. Weart, *The Discovery of Global Warming* (Harvard University Press, 2003).

[40] CBD Articles 7 and 14.

[41] CBD Article 14, paragraph 1(d).

notification of danger from specific actions is supplemented by recognition of the conflict between developing countries and indigenous peoples over ownership and control of traditional knowledge and genetic material as well as vigorous pursuit of this intellectual property by drug companies and other commercial ventures in developed nations.[42] The goal of the CBD was to bring these concerns to the forefront of discussion,[43] with the aim of establishing rules and principles in subsequent protocols and agreements of the Conference of the Parties to the CBD (CBD COP).[44]

The CBD makes no mention of climate change, although some of its provisions contain ideas broad enough that they could be read to support efforts to mitigate or adapt to impacts of climate change.[45] By contrast, the CBD's silence on climate change even though it was drafted simultaneously with the UNFCCC, and both were signed at UNCED in Rio, undercuts any argument that the CBD language was intended to include climate change within the ambit of the treaty. The only direct reference in the CBD to other international law is the requirement that the CBD be implemented "with respect to the marine environment consistently with the rights and obligations of States under the law of the sea."[46]

The lack of direct substantive connection between the CBD and UNFCCC has meant that there has been no legal mandate that each community coordinate its actions with the other.[47] As a result, it is possible that policy adopted in one arena may conflict with or even obstruct policies and goals in the other. For instance, because "invasive alien species can be a very significant ecological problem, . . . it is essential that carbon sequestration measures carried out under the Kyoto Protocol give preference to native species, and that native grasslands and wetlands not be converted to industrial-scale carbon plantations."[48] It is altogether possible to envision carbon dioxide sequestration projects that diminish rather than protect biodiversity. Monoculture afforestation or reforestation projects that maximize rapid sequestration of carbon; increased or excessive use of pesticides, fertilizers, and herbicides; adoption of improper fire management practices, overthinning of forests; and other intensive forestry activities would reduce

[42] CBD Articles 16–19.

[43] "The objectives of [the CBD] . . . are the conservation of biological diversity, the sustainable use of its components and the air and equitable sharing of the benefits arising out of the utilization of genetic resource, including by appropriate access to genetic resources and by appropriate transfer of relevant technology, taking into account all rights over those resources and to technologies, and by appropriate funding." CDB Article 1.

[44] CBD Articles 23–32.

[45] For instance, Article 6 urges Parties to "integrate . . . the conservation and sustainable use of biological diversity into relevant sectoral and cross-sectoral plans, programme and policies." Article 7 requires Parties to identify and monitor "activities which have or are likely to have significant adverse impacts on . . . the sustainable use of biological diversity." Article 8 requires sustainable protection and restoration of ecosystems and adjacent areas, and Parties to "[e]ndeavor to provide the conditions needed for compatibility between present uses and the conservation of biological diversity and the sustainable use of its components." Article 10 calls for including sustainability in decision making and to adopt measures "to avoid or minimize adverse impacts on biological diversity."

[46] CBD Article 22, paragraph 2.

[47] However, at a general level, the CBD does modify the rights and obligations of Parties from preexisting agreements "where the exercise of those rights and obligations would cause a serious damage or threat to biological diversity." CBD Article 22, paragraph 1. However, the UNFCCC was not effective international law when the CBD entered into force on 29 December 1993. The UNFCC did not enter into force until 21 March 1994.

[48] Jeffrey A. McNeeley, "Energy and Biodiversity: Understanding Complex Relationships," in A. J. Bradbrook & R. L. Ottinger, eds., *Energy Law and Sustainable Development* (IUCN, 2003), 31, 41.

species diversity, harm ecosystem vitality, degrade forests, and accelerate biodiversity loss.[49] If projects such as these were approved for tradable carbon reduction credits, they could attract large amounts of capital, resulting in enormous investment in monoculture forests. Conversely, policies adopted under the CBD with respect to ownership of knowledge could, if made without consideration of climate change concerns, increase GHG emissions by promoting land use or other actions that increase use of fossil fuels, the production and release of methane or the release of N_2O. Because neither regime has any mandate to incorporate the goals of the other into its own decisions, long-term commitments could be made that hinder, or even set back, the efforts of the other.

However, there is one idea common to each regime that could enable them to avoid ramming each other like ships in a dense fog – sustainable development. A strong argument can be made that both the UNFCCC and the CBD are treaties that reside under the overarching concept of sustainable development. Language in the UNFCCC explicitly recognizes the treaty as one promoting sustainable development because the climate change challenge involves economics, environment, and human welfare of present and future generations.[50] Additionally, several Article 4 commitments "are directly relevant to the CBD."[51]

The CBD also makes reference to sustainable development as an overarching background theme in its regime, and this makes sense as the CBD is trying to accommodate protection of biodiversity, ecosystems and genetic material with economic interests and with concerns for indigenous peoples – again, a merging of economies, environment, and human equity, the three pillars of sustainable development. The CBD's "objectives . . . are the conservation of biological diversity, the *sustainable* use of its components and the air . . . "[52]

Thus, arguably, decision makers within each regime could, in the name of sustainable development, legitimately include the concerns of the other in their decisions. Although the two treaties could be "mutually reinforcing . . . such mutual reinforcement is not automatic."[53] However, that requires moving beyond the specifics of GHGs or biodiversity to define sustainable development to include those concerns. The principles of sustainable development articulated in the Rio Declaration,[54] Agenda 21,[55] and the Johannesburg Declaration permit this, but do not in their own terms mandate the cross-fertilization, nor do the principles announce how the ideas of global warming and biodiversity should link – or what field takes priority if conflicts emerge.

The best that can be said of the relationship between the CBD and UNFCCC is that there is mild, informal, sporadic evidence of each being aware of the other. In the

[49] Ibid. See also, David R. Hodas, "Sustainable Development and the Marrakech Accords," above note 31.

[50] UNFCCC Article 2 ("The ultimate objective of this Convention and any related instruments that the Conference of the Parties may adopt is to achieve stabilization of greenhouse gas concentrations in the atmosphere at a level that would prevent dangerous anthropogenic interference with the climate system." This level should "be achieved within a time frame to allow ecosystems to adapt naturally to climate change, to ensure that food production is not threatened and to enable economic development to proceed in a sustainable manner."), Article 3, para. 4. ("The Parties have a right to, and should, promote sustainable development."), and Article 4, para. ((d) and (e).

[51] Jeffrey A. McNeeley, Energy and biodiversity, note 48, at 41.

[52] CDB Article 1.

[53] Jeffrey A. McNeeley, Energy and biodiversity, note 48, at 41.

[54] United Nations Conference on Environment and Development, *Rio Declaration on Environment and Development*, 879 U.N. Doc. A/CONF. 151/5/Rev. 1 (1992).

[55] Nicholas A. Robinson, ed., *Agenda 21: Earth's Action Plan* (Oceana Pub., 1993).

climate change analysis world, the IPCC has regularly included impacts of warming on ecosystems and biodiversity in its assessment reports as one of the categories of adverse effects rapid climate change will cause. However, biodiversity is largely missing as an analytic component of policy prescriptions in mitigation and analysis. Moreover, the specific criteria used by the UNFCCC COP to evaluate offset projects for carbon credits under the Kyoto Protocol do not include biodiversity or sustainable development metrics in their rules. Academic literature on the topic of trading is also generally silent on the subject, as is the discussion of market mechanisms.

The CBD does have one project looking at biodiversity and climate change, the Ad Hoc Technical Expert Group on Biodiversity and Climate Change within the CBD's Subsidiary Body on Scientific, Technical and Technological Advice.[56] The Ad Hoc Group actively sought the technical input of the IPCC, which submitted a technical paper and sent a representative to the Ad Hoc Group's meetings. The Ad Hoc Group, on behalf of the CBD, was looking to use this project as a way "to draw to the attention of the Parties to the UNFCCC the need for reducing and mitigating impacts of climate change on coral reefs and forest biological diversity... [a]nd prepare scientific advice for the integration of biodiversity considerations into the implementation of the UNFCCC and its Kyoto Protocol."[57]

4 UNITED STATES DOMESTIC LAW – ENDANGERED SPECIES ACT AND NATIONAL ENVIRONMENTAL POLICY ACT

As a review of two U.S. environmental statutes illustrates, at the level of domestic law, where most law resides, there is little to connect biodiversity and climate change. The Endangered Species Act[58] protects those species the U.S. Department of Interior (DOI) Secretary lists as endangered and threatened, and protects the critical habitat that the Secretary designates as essential for the conservation of those species. The protection is generally provided by two means. First, the statute prohibits the federal government from taking any action that would "jeopardize" any endangered or threatened species or result in the "destruction or adverse modification" of designated critical habitat.[59] Courts *must* enjoin any such actions, irrespective of the sunk financial costs.[60] To implement this provision, the ESA contains a biological assessment process designed to identify federal government action that may jeopardize endangered or threatened species or critical habitat.[61] The first step is for the government agency that is considering undertaking the action (including issuing a permit or license to a private party) to request from the Department of Interior information as to "whether any species which is listed or proposed to be listed may be present in the area of [the] proposed actions." If, "based on the best scientific and commercial data available" the Secretary of DOI or the Secretary of the Department of Commerce[62] determines that a "species may be present," then the government agency wishing to undertake the action, shall conduct a biological

[56] CBD Ad Hoc Technical Expert Group on Biodiversity and Climate Change, *Biological Diversity and Climate Change* (November 2003) UN Doc UNEP/CBD/SBSTTA/9/INF/12.

[57] Ibid. at 11.

[58] 16 U.S.C. §1531 et seq.

[59] 16 U.S.C. §1536.

[60] *Tennessee Valley Authority v. Hill*, 437 U.S. 153 (1978).

[61] 16 U.S.C. §1536(a)–(d). *Roosevelt Campobello Int'l. Park v. U.S.E.P.A.*, 684 F.2d 1041 (1st Cir. 1982).

[62] The Secretary of the Department of Commerce has authority over Cetacea (whales and dolphins), Pinnepedia (seals and sea lions), Marine Fish, Marine Plants, Coral, and Mollusks, and shares authority

assessment for the purpose identifying any endangered species or threatened species which is likely to be affected by [the] action." If a species is likely to be affected, the Department of Interior (or Commerce, as appropriate) must issue a biological opinion that determines, based on the best available scientific and commercial data, whether the action would create a "jeopardy" or "adverse modification" and whether reasonable and prudent alternatives would avoid a violation of the ESA. Although the government agency is not required to undertake the precise alternatives suggested in the biological opinion, it must satisfy the ESA standard that its action not jeopardize the continued existence of an endangered or threatened species or result in destruction or adverse modification of critical habitat.

The ESA also prohibits all persons, private and public, from "taking" an endangered species.[63] Prohibited action under the statute and its implementing regulations includes both direct harm to the species and destruction of habitat necessary for the species continued survival.[64] Both the no jeopardy and no take proscriptions envision restricting action that has a direct, causal effect on the species. So building a dam that will destroy critical habitat for an endangered species of fish is barred, as is hunting an endangered species. However, the Supreme Court requires that the action and effect not be too remote from each other. Rather, there must be an adequately close causal link between the action and the harm, without that proximately causal connection, the statute will not operate to intervene.[65] As a result, the application of the ESA to federal government action that affects GHG emissions because those emissions contribute to global warming is problematic.

Take impacts on the polar bear, for example. First, this is not a situation in which specific, traceable, toxic air emissions are contaminating polar bear habitat. Rather, the historic accumulation of GHG in the atmosphere is slowly warming the planet. This warming is melting Arctic sea ice, the loss of which adversely affects polar bears. The accumulated GHGs were emitted by the entire human population, although to be sure, the United States has been and remains the largest emitter. So, we cannot trace any specific climate problem to any specific action or actions. All emissions are contributing; this is the ultimate case of joint and several liability – we are all liable.[66] Any injunction to require U.S. action to stop or reduce GHG emissions will lessen the rate and amplitude of the warming. In that sense, the action would reduce the risk of jeopardy. Thus, under the ESA no jeopardy and adverse modification prohibitions, it could be argued that any U.S. government action that contributes to global warming must be enjoined unless it represents a reasonable and prudent alternative that reduces the risk of jeopardy or adverse modification of critical habitat.[67]

with the Department of the Interior with regard to sea turtles and anadromous (e.g., salmon) and catrodomous (e.g., eels) species; and the Secretary of the Interior, the remainder.

63 16 U.S.C. §1538.

64 *Babbitt v. Sweet Home Chapter of Communities for a Greater Oregon*, 515 U.S. 687 (1995).

65 Ibid., O'Connor, J., concurring.

66 Even our most extensive laws imposing joint and several liability on a person deemed responsible for releases of hazardous substances do not come close to the scope of this problem. See, for example, Comprehensive Environmental Response, Compensation, and Liability Act (CERCLA) 42 U.S.C. §§9601–9675, which may impose broad joint and several liability on responsible parties, although the nature of the rule is subject to dispute. In the Matter of Bell Petroleum Services, Inc., 3 F.3d 889 (5th Cir. 1993).

67 16 U.S.C. §1536(b)(4)(A)(ii).

Arguably, the National Environmental Policy Act (NEPA) could provide a vehicle to link biodiversity and climate change. It requires agencies that propose actions that could significantly affect the human environment to prepare an environmental impact statement (EIS) as part of the decision making process.[68] However, as presently construed, NEPA is purely procedural, with no substantive bite.[69] Although it requires full consideration of the potential impacts a proposal might have on the environment, and consideration of alternatives (including no action) that might lessen or avoid the environmental impact, NEPA does not require that the agency select the least environmental harmful path. Procedurally, the NEPA process can be combined with the ESA biological assessment process to make information gathering and analysis more cost effective and efficient than if done separately. However, that does not change the purely procedural nature of the statute.

Substantively, NEPA mandates that each EIS include in its analysis of the environmental impact of the proposed action the "relationship between local sort-term uses of man's environment and the maintenance and enhancement of long-term productivity."[70] However, the scope of review of this analysis is limited to a judicial determination of whether the agency considered a reasonable range of alternatives, and whether its actual analysis was arbitrary and capricious.[71] In the biodiversity context, this means that the refusal of an agency to consider conservation biology, habitat fragmentation, or ecosystem approaches to biodiversity impacts of government actions is not agency error.[72] Agency EISs under NEPA generally "(1) focus on species, rather than ecosystems, (2) address the site scale rather than the ecosystem of regional scale; and (3) concentrate on immediate short-term impacts rather than likely future impacts."[73]

Moreover, to challenge an EIS for its failure to consider the global warming effects of the proposal, a citizen must demonstrate that he or she has standing to bring the action. This subject matter jurisdiction hurdle can be difficult,[74] and failure to clear the hurdle is fatal to the case.[75] However, plaintiffs have been able to establish standing in several instances.[76]

Once standing is established, courts may be reluctant to hear the case, opting to avoid the issue by finding global warming to be a political question.[77] If the court does look at the adequacy of the EIS as to global warming, it may not insist on a rigorous

[68] 42 U.S.C. §4321 et seq.

[69] David R. Hodas "NEPA, Ecosystem Management and Environmental Accounting." 14 *Natural Resources & Environment* (2000), 185 (analyzing the U.S. Supreme Court decisions that bleached any substantive power out of NEPA).

[70] 42 U.S.C. § 4332(2)(C)(iv).

[71] *Marsh v. Oregon Natural Resources Council*, 490 U.S. 360 (1989); *Robertson v. Methow Valley Citizens Council*, 490 U.S. 332 (1989).

[72] See *Sierra Club v. Marita*, 46 F.3d 606 (7th Cir. 1995) (court rejected a challenge to the adequacy of an EIS because of the agency's failure to adequately consider ecological principles of biodiversity).

[73] Council on Environmental Quality, *Incorporating Biodiversity Considerations Into Environmental Impact Analysis under the National Environmental Policy Act*, 18 (1993).

[74] *See Massachusetts v. Environmental Protection Agency*, 127 S. Ct. 1438 (2007).

[75] David R. Hodas, "Standing and Climate Change: Can Anyone Complain About the Weather?" 15 *J. of Land Use & Environmental Law* (2000), 451, 454; Bradford C. Mank, "Standing and Global Warming: Is Injury to All Injury to None?" 35 *Envtl. L.* (2005), 1.

[76] See, for example, *Friends of Earth, Inc. v. Watson*, 2005 WL 2035596 (N. D. Cal. 223 August 2005) (Plaintiffs had standing to challenge failure of EX-IM Bank to consider global warming in an environmental impact statement); and *Natural Resources Defense Council v. Mineta*, 2005 WL 1075355 (S.D. N.Y. 3 May 2005).

[77] *Connecticut v. American Elec. Power Co., Inc.*, 406 F. Supp. 2d 265 (S.D.N.Y., 2005).

review of alternatives to reduce GHGs, as the alternatives may too varied, or involve technology forcing, which might be deemed to be outside the range of reasonable scope of alternative analysis.[78] Finally, even if alternatives are reasonably considered, and incorporated into the final proposal, there is no requirement in NEPA that the selected alternative be implemented. Overall, NEPA only has value as a forum for the gathering and review of environmental information, and even at that task it is not robust.

5 PUBLIC NUISANCE

The ancient common law doctrine of public nuisance prohibits unreasonable interference with rights common to the public.[79] Is biodiversity a right common to the public? It should be, according to Prof. Sax[80] and Oliver Wendell Holmes.[81] Under this theory, States, as plaintiffs, can sue actors who are materially harming biodiversity to enjoin the harmful practice. Private suits also may be possible but are subject to the substantial limitations of the "special injury" rule, which permits only those persons uniquely harmed by the conduct to sue.[82] The Public Trust Doctrine also may provide states with some authority to challenge conduct that impairs public trust land and water.[83]

6 THE CAUSATION AND REMEDY PROBLEM

Although many of these statutes and laws establish legal obligations that could be translated at a general level into mandates to avoid conduct that further warms the earth, all face the diffuse causation problem and the problem of what remedy might be imposed. As mentioned earlier, global warming is the product of years of accumulation of GHG in the atmosphere from emissions throughout the world. No single emission can be shown to cause any particular change in climate. Even if warming does affect climate, it may be impossible to separate the effects of warming from natural variability. For example, with more energy in the atmosphere, on average, more storms will be more powerful than in the past.[84] But no one can say how many extra miles per hour of wind in Katrina were due to natural variability and how much as a result of global warming. All that can be said about causation is that the more GHGs an actor emits, the more the earth will warm, and the more climate will change.

Assume that a court were to find that federal funding of a coal-fired power plant would contribute to global warming, which will accelerate melting of Arctic sea ice, thus jeopardizing polar bears. Must the project be enjoined unless the project removes all its GHG emissions from the atmosphere by sequestering carbon in trees or capturing carbon dioxide in the flue gas and pumping it into deep wells? Under *TVA v. Hill*, the

[78] *Vermont Yankee Nuclear Power Corp. v. Natural Resources Defense Council*, 435 U.S. 519 (1978).

[79] David. R. Hodas, "Private Actions for Public Nuisance: Common Law Citizen Suits for Relief from Environmental Harm." 16 *Ecology Law Quarterly* (1989), at 883–888.

[80] See chapter 1 in this volume.

[81] *Missouri v. Holland*, 252 U.S. 416, 435 (1920) (protecting migratory birds is a "national interest of very nearly the first magnitude").

[82] David. R. Hodas, *Private Actions for Public Nuisance*, note 79.

[83] Joseph L. Sax, "The Public Trust Doctrine In Natural Resource Law: Effective Judicial Interpretation." 68 *Michigan L. Rev.* (1970), 471.

[84] P. J. Webster et al., "Changes in Tropical Cyclone Number, Duration, and Intensity in a Warming Environment." 309 *Science* (2005), 1844–1846.

answer would seem to be yes. What about the U.S. Department of Transportation's evaluation of whether to increase fuel efficiency standards on cars or extend them to all vehicles? The failure to do so would contribute to rapid global warming. Must a court order the agency to raise the standards? How much? What about the thousands of other government activities that emit GHGs? Must they all be subject to the ESA and mandatory court injunctions? Courts are simply neither equipped to nor designed to impose GHG policy on government agencies.

The same remedy dilemma exists with respect to the public nuisance and public trust doctrines. Even when harm from air pollution is direct and the polluter is clearly identifiable, courts have been reluctant to use well accepted common law doctrines to create air pollution policy. Instead, common law cases have acted as emergency gap-fillers.[85]

Even when common law doctrine is directly applicable, courts have been hesitant to use their equitable power to engage in crafting environmental regulations. In the leading case of *Boomer v. Atlantic Cement Co.*, landowners sought to enjoin plant operations causing dirt, smoke, and vibrations that damaged their use of their land. Although the plaintiffs made out a sound case that the conduct was a nuisance, the court ordered the company make a one-time payment of permanent damages to the landowners instead of enjoining the injurious activity; an injunction would issue only if the cement company failed to pay the damages.[86] In declining the plaintiffs' invitation to regulate the cement plant activities, the court explained:

> It seems apparent that the amelioration of air pollution will depend on technical research in depth; on a carefully balanced consideration of the economic impact of close regulation; and of the actual effect on public health. It is likely to require massive public expenditure and to demand more than any local community can accomplish and to depend on regional and interstate controls.
>
> A court should not try to do this on its own as a by-product of private litigation and it seems manifest that the judicial establishment is neither equipped in the limited nature of any judgment it can pronounce nor prepared to lay down and implement an effective policy for the elimination of air pollution.

These decisions sent strong messages that unreasonable conduct was occurring, which legislatures must address because the nature and scope of the problem was beyond the capability of courts to address effectively.

7 CONCLUSION

Although all of the various laws reviewed in this chapter fail to link climate change and biodiversity directly, the general theory underlying them could be used for "wake-up" call litigation – suits that would highlight the absence of climate change concerns in our biodiversity laws, and the absence of climate change policy altogether. As was true in

[85] In the United States, federal common law has been used to resolve interstate pollution disputes in the absence of federal legislation addressing the issue, *Georgia v. Tennessee Copper Co.*, 206 U.S. 230, 237 (1907) (interstate air pollution), *Illinois v. Milwaukee*, 406 U.S. 91 (1972) (interstate water pollution). However, once Congress acts, federal common law is thereby preempted. *Milwaukee v. Illinois*, 451 U.S. 304 (1981).

[86] *Boomer v. Atlantic Cement*, 26 N.Y. 2d 219, 257 N.E. 2d 870 (N.Y. 1970).

the 1960s and early 1970s, such litigation could help spur international and domestic legislative responses to the challenge of climate change and biodiversity.

The UNFCCC and CBD protocols could be adopted and ESA and NEPA could be amended to require mitigation or offset of GHG from all new government actions and to require implementation of adaptation measures that could protect biodiversity from adverse global warming effects. However, these legal changes would simply be Band-Aids on a deep wound. Such changes must be part of a larger project to address GHG in national policy and law.

Conversely, in developing climate change law, we must not forget the need to protect and enhance biodiversity. For example, we should discourage carbon sequestration projects that reduce biodiversity and social well-being, such as monoculture afforestation. Instead, we should seek win–win sustainable development solutions that reduce GHGs while protecting and enhancing biodiversity. Some ideas have already been advanced;[87] the next step is to consider concrete policy approaches that could integrate biodiversity and climate change into routine decision making.

[87] Hodas, "Sustainable Development and the Marrakech Accords," note 31.

21 Emissions Trading: A Fantasy for China to Combat Global Warming?

Bo Miao*

1 INTRODUCTION

Since the early 1990s, China has actively been involved in the international effort to address climate change. It has ratified the United Nations Framework Convention on Climate Change (UNFCCC) and the Kyoto Protocol, and focused on how to integrate climate issue with development objectives. Although historically China accounted for only a relatively low percentage (7.3 percent from 1850 to 2000) of globally cumulative greenhouse gas (GHG) emissions, it has increased its share in the last decade to 14.8 percent in 2003. China is, at the beginning of the twenty-first century, the second largest emitter in absolute terms, where GDP and population are decisive determinants.[1]

In sharp contrast with these enormous overall amounts, China's GHG emissions, in per capita terms,[2] depicts a different picture. China only ranks ninety-seventh globally, just slightly higher than the average of developing countries.[3] China could argue that these figures might be deceptive because the cross-country difference in rank may be large but the absolute difference may be rather small, if one compares the U.S. 6.6 tons carbon equivalent per capita to the 1.1 tons of China.[4]

There is also another indicator that China uses to defend itself when asked during international negotiations to take some sort of responsibility to curtail GHG emissions and that is carbon intensity, which is the level of CO_2 emissions per unit of economic

[1] Emissions here include CO_2 from fossil fuels and cement and other five non-CO_2 (CH_4, N_2O, HFC, PFC, and SF_6) gases, but exclude emissions from land-use related emissions, because the latter has a variety of problems, including technical, political, and social obstacles, to be accurately calculated in this stage. However, with the foreseeable development of a reliable accounting approach and close international cooperation, such data will eventually be added to the whole scenario and provide a more comprehensive and solid foundation for researchers to explore further. See Baumert, Pershing, Jonathan, Herzog et al., *Climate Data: Insights and Observations.* Prepared for the Pew Center on Global Climate Change, December, 2004, 13–14.

[2] The indicators of per capita emissions, emissions per unit of Gross Domestic Product (GDP), energy consumption per unit of GDP, or analogous sector-specific indices do differ to some extent. This chapter adopts per capita emissions as the main indicator because it reflects a country's economic activity and evaluates its relative emissions more directly than others. See Baumert et al., note 1, at 16.

[3] Emissions here include CO_2 from fossil fuels and cement and non-CO_2 gases. See Baumert et al., note 1, at 11.

[4] See Baumert et al., note 1, at 9.

* Bo Miao is currently a Ph.D. Candidate in the Center for Environmental Law, Macquarie University, Australia. LLB, The China University of Political Science and Law, LLM, Tsinghua University. The author is especially indebted to Professor Michael Jeffery for his valuable comments.

output. Carbon intensity, a widely agreed variable, not only serves as a strong determinant of a country's overall emissions but also reflects the energy intensity and fuel mix within carbon-related industries.[5] In the past decade, China is the most striking case in this perspective, where carbon intensity fell 47 percent while GDP grew 162 percent from 1990 to 2000.[6] Although there are less optimistic predictions, such as: "It remains to be seen whether these trends are anomalous one-time shifts reflecting particular circumstance ... the opening of China's economy to market forces ... or whether they suggest the potential for a longer-term decoupling of economic and emissions growth,"[7] it would be unreasonable to deny that China indeed has made remarkable progress in improving energy efficiency and thereby brought about some ancillary benefit.

Low per capita emissions, improved carbon intensity, and developing country status, combined together, have in some degree justified China, even as the second-largest emitter in absolute terms, in arguing that it should be under any mandatory obligation to reduce GHG emissions at this time. Furthermore, the issue of equity[8] also serves as a strong shield against any possible attack on China, in that it would not be fair for China to immediately assume any disproportional share because it does not belong to the industrialized group, which historically is the prime cause of global warming. Nor would it be realistic to expect the number two emitter, China, to act first while the greatest emitter, the United States, stands still.

Therefore, why and how to cope with global warming in China has become a critical issue and keeps drawing more and more attention from a wide range of stakeholders, including policy makers. As experience has told us, "States are likely to address climate change only if they believe it is in their interest to do so,"[9] analyzing the following factors may offer some hints with respect to the motivation of China to participate beyond Kyoto.

First, as we still live in a coal-dominant world, China's GHG emissions, even with tremendous uncertainties in national-level projections,[10] are estimated to surpass the United States. China is set to become the world's largest emitter by 2025 as a result of its fast growth rate and population.[11] Although per capita emissions, to some degree,

[5] See Baumert et al., note 1, at 12.

[6] See Baumert et al., note 1, at 8. As a reference, between 1990 and 2000, the GHG "intensity" of the U.S. economy (the ratio of total GHG emissions to economic output) declined by 17.5 percent. See Robert & Kyle, *Designing a Mandatory Greenhouse Gas Reduction Program for the U.S.* Prepared for the Pew Center on Global Climate Change, May, 2003, 4.

[7] See Baumert et al., note 1, at 8.

[8] In this paper, equity, equality, and fairness are treated as interchangeable. Although there are subtle distinctions among these words, they matter little to the points that the author will try to illustrate. See Ashton & Wang, "Equity and Climate: In Principle and Practice," in *Beyond Kyoto: Advancing the International Effort Against Climate Change* (Pew Center on Global Climate Change, Arlington, VA, December 2003).

[9] See Diringer, "Overview: Climate Crossroad," in *Beyond Kyoto: Advancing the International Effort against Climate Change* (Pew Center on Global Climate Change, Arlington, VA, December 2003), 4.

[10] Because of different projecting methods and formula, there are varied projections about China's future emissions, from a 50 percent increase to a 68 percent increase, which also conveys the analysts' confidence in China's economic growth. But all projections unanimously bear out the general trend. See Baumert et al., note 1, at 16.

[11] See Nielsen & McElory, "Introduction and Overiew," in Michael B. McElory, Chris P. Nielsen, & Peter Lydon, *Energizing China: Reconciling Environmental Protection and Economic Growth* (Newton, MA: Desktop Publishing & Design Co., 1998).

will still stand in its favor, China inevitably will face enormous pressure, domestically and internationally, to control GHG emissions.[12]

Second, China is one of the most *vulnerable*[13] countries to climate change, in terms of governance systems, levels of poverty, access to water and sanitation, change in agriculture and fisheries. China is more susceptible to, and possibly not quite capable of coping with, the adverse effects of climate change.[14] Global warming is not a show only taking place in other areas; it is a real threat to China if serious efforts are not made in the foreseeable future. China needs to make genuine environmental progress to grapple with global warming and, hence, inevitably will contribute to some extent in limiting global GHG emissions.

Third, from a historical and equity perspective, industrialized countries have caused the problem of global warming, so they should act first and undertake more responsibility for grappling with this problem. China has always stressed its developing-country status to mitigate against this sort of liability, and so far has been successful. However, some recent trends show that China now seems not to be content with being classified as a developing country in the context of international trade, because that classification means China will not be treated as a market-economy country, putting "made-in-China" at a distinct competitive disadvantage. This has been demonstrated by China's strong position during its recent negotiation of a free trade agreement with Australia.

So what does all of this mean? It could be argued that it reveals China's intent to graduate from the group of developing (or "non-Annex I") countries in an economic sense and join the club of developed ones. This assumption also may be supported by China's subtle unwillingness to stress its *incapacity* of addressing climate problems, but, more often, referring to *equity* as a defence, and thus it would be unfair for it to take on responsibility in the short term.

But there does exist criteria, although not yet officially agreed to in an international sense but detectable in an informal way, for determining the graduation threshold. And it should not require much for China's central government to realize that with the enormous economic benefits the membership could bring, paying the membership fees and pioneering in the global warming campaign would be part of this graduation process.

Fourth, with the Kyoto Protocol's entry into force, China is now actively trying to make effective use of the Clean Development Mechanism (CDM), the flexible mechanism offered by the Protocol to produce mutual economic benefits for both the investing and host countries.[15] It has been reported that several CDM projects are to operate in

[12] China cannot act like the United States in this situation. Just as President Bush declared in this year's G8 summit that the United States will not undertake any mandatory responsibility to reduce GHG that will jeopardize the U.S. economy, it is hard to imagine any Chinese leader explicitly indicating their uncompromising attitude in handling this kind of issue, meaning that China more easily gives in to international pressure concerning economic matters – the latest appreciation of RMB serves as a good example.

[13] The IPCC defines vulnerability as the degree to which a system is susceptible to, or unable to cope with, adverse effects of climate change. See IPCC, 2001. *Climate Change 2001: Impacts, Adaptation and Vulnerability*. Contribution of Working Group II to the Third Assessment Report of the IPCC, J. J. McCarthy, et al., eds., Cambridge University Press.

[14] See Baumert et al., note 1, at 8.

[15] However, some observers do not hold an optimistic attitude toward the future of CDM because verifying the actual effect is very complicated. But the CDM projects seem to have made progress since the

China.[16] Although the long-term effect of these projects remains to be seen, getting deeply involved in international commercial cooperation such as CDM and enjoying the related benefits it brings can help China to contemplate the possibility of further market-oriented participation.[17] After all, in the post-Kyoto stage, less than six years remain for China to resort to the developing country status for support. China inevitably will play a more significant role in the next-stage of bilateral, regional, or multilateral negotiations, whether it chooses to or not.

The question arises: How would China, being in a transitional state, be able to fulfill the obligation to limit or even reduce its GHG emissions? Would the existing environmental institutions be capable of implementing any climate-related scheme? Could it be possible to enable the largest emitter in the electric power sector to control CO_2 emissions in a cost-effective and climate-friendly way?

This chapter will try to explore whether the existing environmental institutions in China would be capable of leading any climate-related program during China's "hybrid" state, and whether the popular and well-documented mechanism, emissions trading, in a political scenario, [18] would be a viable approach under China's specific circumstances. The following sections will examine how the challenge is to be met.

Section 2 discusses the intrinsic value of the often-referred-to shield – *equity* – aiming to provide reasonable support and incentive for China to refute the widespread common unwillingness to share in the responsibility of controlling GHG emissions. Keeping the vulnerable state and graduation threshold in mind, China, domestically or globally, will inevitably enter in stages, first taking on softer, nonbinding obligations, then more demanding commitments. However, as intended effort is ultimately a political quantity, any movement on environmental issues, being inevitably transferred into political issues, depends not only on the amount of political capital China's government is willing to invest on a global stage but also, more essentially, on the domestic infrastructure that already exists, or one that is proposed to be slightly or materially reformed to accommodate such purpose.

Section 3 describes the current domestic GHG emissions, energy consumption profile and its projected trend, policy framework about climate change, and environmental

June 2003 meeting of the CDM Executive Board, six of the first fourteen proposals for baseline and monitoring methodologies were held "sufficiently elaborated" and could be reconsidered expeditiously if the proponents made the required changes. The other eight still require more extensive work and revisions. See Press Release, 10 June 2003 at http://unfccc.int.cdm. Moreover, with the lauch of the EU ETS, the development of CDM has been largely accellerated and it has become an important sources of external credits that could be used to meet the Member States' commitment under the scheme.

[16] See Qiao & Liu. "Opportunity and Challenge for China." Available online at http://www.china5e.com/news/huanbao/200503/200503200069.html.

[17] It has long been a dream for entrepreneurs in China to expect the authority to enact, implement and enforce business-related regulation in a more market-oriented way, and now the new leadership has demonstrated, at least to some degree, the willingness to develop towards a more market-economy way, including the planning political reform which means so much for anyone who intends to run a business in China.

[18] The reason why this paper highlights the political scenario here, rather than not social, cultural or even economic one, is that during the research, it keeps deepening the author's understanding that it is administrative authority, particularly the central government's willingness, and environmental regulator's capability that determine the fate of any nationwide environmental protection program. Though the author does hold hope for China's change towards a more market-oriented economy, the administrative authorities, on which social, cultural, economic-related effects hinge in large measure, does dominates almost every stage of implementing a project, at least it is the case in current state.

institution's performance. Compared with traditional command-and-control (CAC) approaches, emissions trading, the efficiency-driving and market-oriented instruments seem to be an appealing prescription for China to follow. However, it seems unlikely for the current environmental authority to effectively push forward an emissions trading scheme even if it is properly designed. By elaborating on the ongoing economic transformation, structural adaptation, and influential sector-specific interests, a collaborative and centrally powered environmental institution appears to be essential in order to alleviate the ever-existing influence from corporatised state enterprises and other factors characterizing the hybrid political economy. Such fundamental reform therefore may shed light on the implementation of proposed emissions trading programs, of which the essence is to stimulate technology transformation by economic incentive – the only way to dramatically reduce GHG emissions while maintaining economic growth.

Section 4 briefly explores whether the central government would have adequate political will to put emissions trading of GHG into action, and, if so, whether the reformed environmental authority is capable of achieving the desired outcome, which highlights ensuring equity, compliance, and efficiency in the current transitional state. It envisions a multifaceted approach that would seek to justify the claim that the administration's sufficient political will, independent authority, strong enforcement capacity, serious punitive mechanism, and benign relationship with the electric power industry are decisive determinants for any emissions trading scheme to be successful in China.

2 REDEFINING EQUITY[19]

Living in a coal-dominant as well as coal-constrained world, China always faces the dilemma of choosing between economic growth and climate protection. The notion of equity has become the conventional method by which China can satisfy the paramount priority of development and postpone, or even sacrifice, the protection of the environment. However, equity, the most relied-on tool of defence, is now serving somewhat as a two-edged sword for grappling with GHG emissions both in a global sense and a domestic one, and, hence, China must handle it carefully.

Just as improved carbon intensity indicates that China may now be in the preliminary "decoupling" process of economic growth and emissions, the notion of equity starts to fade away when examining China's refusal regarding any mandatory GHG emissions restriction. Equity has been widely and intensely utilized in international negotiations about climate issues over the past two decades. The two major agreements so far achieved – the UNFCCC and Kyoto Protocol – clearly have conveyed the intrinsic value of equity: the solution that people with different interests can all regard as fair, or, at the very least, not demonstrably unfair to one group or another.[20]

China surely is not an exception to that principle, and what hides behind China's abstract "obligations" to climate change explains, more or less, its strong insistence on how to interpret equity. Because we are now in the post-Kyoto stage, is there something

[19] A detailed discussion of dealing with the equity in the realm of climate change has been provided by Aston John & Xueman Wang, "Equity and Climate: In Principle and Practice," in *Beyond Kyoto: Advancing the International Effort against Climate Change* (Pew Center on Global Climate Change, Arlington, VA, December 2003).

[20] See Ashton & Wang (2003, p. 61). One typical example in this regard is the "common but differentiated responsibility" established by the UNFCCC.

different when the perspective of equity is applied in this new context? Is it real that China has less and less room in claiming equity as its defence against any global responsibility? It may help to clarify this doubt if we contemplate equity in the following ways.

In many circumstances, the first response of equity is *responsibility*: it is fair to hold people, individually or as a group, accountable for the damage caused by their behavior, and that is where the accepted "polluter-pays" principle originated. This perspective seems to preclude China from the list of polluting countries bearing historical responsibilities and serves as a powerful tool for China claiming exemptions during the past negotiations.

However, if some other aspects are taken into account, we find the application of the principle of responsibility is not this simple. For example, people may argue that it is unreasonable to hold the polluters responsible if they were not conscious of the damaging effect to climate caused by their behavior or if these effects took place before the international community reached a consensus that human activity affects the climate.[21] Along with the fact that the adverse effect of human-related activities on climate was not widely accepted until recently,[22] there are some obstacles in place that blame industrialized countries for their "deliberately" polluting activity since the Industrial Revolution.[23]

And how should we determine the exact time period of responsibility, as it is hard to find the exact moment showing when this awareness came into polluters' consciousness? Moreover, although it is undeniable that the developed countries did contribute to the majority of cumulative emissions, sharp differences will be found as well if current emissions are compared with historic data.

For example, for the United Kingdom, its historic share is nearly three times its current share. Even for the United States, the emissions drop from 29.8 percent to 20.6 percent,[24] although it is still the largest emitter. Furthermore, if the CO_2 from land-use change is also counted, there appears to be a more pronounced difference in the assessment of contribution – the United States' cumulative emission declines to 15.8 percent.[25] Although China reportedly declines as well, from 14.8 percent to 11.9 percent, the deforestation happening in many rural areas casts a shadow in this optimistic projection.

The chosen time period also influences the calculation of historic contribution and yields very different results. If we compare the emissions from 1850 to 2000 with that of 1990 to 2000, the declining trend in the European Union (EU) and the United States is

[21] See Ashton & Wang (2003, p. 68).

[22] Still now, there are some groups who insist denying the damaging impact of human-related activities on climate, they claim there is not sufficient scientific evidence proving it is not the natural process, but human's behavior that caused global warming. Even among the researchers and environmentalists, there exists some controversy and contentious issues about the effect of global warming, such as, is sea-level-rise accelerating, did scientists forecast a coming Ice Age during the 1970s, are hurricanes more frequent. See, for example, *Dialogue about Climate Tension*. Available online at http://www.pbs.org/newshour/bb/environment/july-dec05/climate_7–5.html. (last visited 4 June 2006). However, after IPCC issued its fourth assessment report and stated that the evidence of human activity on climate is "unequivocal," it can be said that the potential risk of climate change is no long in doubt and the majority of scientists and policymakers have indicated their agreement with the report. See IPCC Fourth Assessment Report (2007), available at http://www.ipcc.ch/SPM040507.pdf. (last visited 2 May 2007).

[23] Estimates of CO_2 emissions from fossil fuels, the principal source of GHG, go back as far as 1850 – the start of industrial revolution. And CO_2 emissions estimates for the period prior to 1850 are available, but for only a few countries. See Baumert et al. (2004, p. 12).

[24] See Baumert et al., note 1, at 12.

[25] See Baumert et al., note 1, at 28.

in sharp contrast with the increasing trend in China.[26] Although per capita emissions still stand in China's favor, it may drop away when China surpasses the United States and becomes the number one emitter in the next few decades. The responsibility we are imposing on others may as well ultimately fall on ourselves.

Should those who decide their own development path and, with it, increase their future emissions most rapidly assume some responsibility for the climate consequences?[27] This time, China cannot escape from the list and may cautiously stay away from claiming the principle of responsibility.

Furthermore, as one of the most vulnerable countries to climate change, China is less prepared to deal with harmful climate-related impacts. Faced with the resulting human consequences, including "dislocation of people from affected areas, intense competition for drinking water or sanitation, disruption of agricultures and fisheries, enhanced threat from agricultural pests and human diseases, and possible conflicts arising from the interplay between these and other stresses,"[28] central government unfortunately lacks adequate financial, human, or political resources, through which it could fulfill its responsibility to its people. It is also extremely difficult to define who should be held accountable for the impact or the exact extent, just as we cannot decide accurately how much China has contributed. This perspective regarding responsibility is no less important here, but it is impractical to apply.

Another issue is the question of distribution. As per capita emissions remain central to any discussion of climate and equity, should we distribute the right to clean air, a given public good, in the form of equal entitlements proportionally among all people, and should their various circumstances be taken into account and become a critical component of equity?

Propositions from the developing world, including China, generally tend to state, sometimes more implicitly, that all humans should enjoy equal entitlement to such public good no matter what situations they are in. Theoretically, it sounds appealingly egalitarian because mankind has experienced how to establish equal entitlements to abstract public goods "*like liberty, security, access to impartial justice, and opportunity to development and benefit from that. . . . If unfortunately not always the case somewhere, everyone at least in theory has an equal right to enjoy them.*"[29]

The case is somewhat different when it comes to more material public goods, such as mineral resources, water, land, and the atmosphere. Questions arise, for example, should the distribution be restricted only to the current generation, or should it include the future generation as well from the viewpoint of intragenerational equity? Is it fair for the already populous countries with the projected fast population growth rate to merely enjoy the potential advantage such proposed distribution would generate? Should not the most populous country, for example, China, assume some responsibility for its own past wrong choice of failing to control its population? This resembles the logic of Western policy makers, who claim unawareness of the adverse effects on climate brought by industrialization as a result of historic limits.

[26] China rose from 7.3 percent to 14.8 percent, while the United States drops from 29.8 to 20.6 and EU 27.2 to 14.0, respectively. See Baumert et al., note 1, at 21–30.

[27] See Ashton & Wang (2003, p. 68).

[28] See Intergovernmental Panel on Climate Change. *The Regional Impacts of Climate Change: An Assessment of Vulnerability.* A Special Report of Working Group II. R. T. Watson, M. C. Zinyoewra, & R. H. Moss, eds., (Cambridge University Press, 1997).

[29] See Ashton, & Wang, note 19, at 73.

With all these caveats in mind, it does not seem to be a wise choice to simply define equal entitlement in absolute terms because we must take into account various circumstances and different aspects. A more acceptable explanation of equal entitlement should not only be based on the absolute amount of people in each state but also, more realistically and specifically, on the level of average energy consumption, or emissions, of the local people that they are used to. And here we should discuss *another dimension* of equity, which has a close relationship with equal entitlement – people's basic needs.

No matter what aspect we adopt in contemplating these dimensions, it is absolutely inhumane to deny the basic needs, which equals surviving necessities, of people striving in some least developed countries. When defining basic needs, we should take into account the widely varied living circumstance of different groups of people.[30] Should the basic needs of those who enjoy a relatively higher standard of living be identified the same way as that of those who are still striving for their survival? Will the former not feel that they are being deprived of some basic needs if their living conditions are lowered substantially, for example, electricity supply for only twelve hours a day (which is pretty common in many places of China)?

Practice tells us that it is unrealistic to allocate equal access to natural resources even when so intended domestically, let alone in a multinational one. China cannot use the idea of meeting all people's basic needs as a defence against any mandatory emissions reductions, because its dramatic growth rate and active application for membership of the developed countries club have collectively demonstrated its strong wish to graduate from the developing group.

The *fourth* perspective of equity is capacity, both in an absolute and a comparative sense. As reflected in the principle of "common but differentiated responsibilities," the efforts that the state should make to combat climate change should correspond to its capability: the capital, human resources, governance system, and available technology. It is widely recognized that the most able should contribute the most, and industrialized countries have better infrastructure and more access to the resources necessary to address the problem.[31] Moreover, the efforts also should be made comparatively, which means that it is fair for the states in similar conditions to assume similar responsibilities.[32]

How China should respond to the capacity issue becomes critical to the policy makers. As mentioned earlier, while still cherishing the developing country status, China is now trying to demonstrate that it should be treated as a market-economy state. Ranking highly in attracting foreign direct investment, China shows its unstoppable developing trend and increasing ability to import climate-related technology, and bring them into the market. It is reported that some projects about renewable energy supported by foreign investment are under operation and accumulating the precious empirical

[30] The proposal of "contraction and convergence" reflects an ideal design that aims to assign every human being an equal entitlement to GHG emissions and all countries should move towards the same per capita emissions. In this way, total global emissions would contract over time and per capita emissions would converge as well. This proposal is appealing to China because it does not require it to reduce its emissions or shift away from the current coal-dominate economy. But, as it easily can be seen, such an idea faces serious obstacles from high emitters because they will suffer a great deal as a result of the related resource transfers, adaptation to new energy, or domestic political pressure derived from such requirements. So experience tells us that any unitary approach will not be feasible. See Ashton & Wang, note 19, at 69. See also the Global Commons Institute. "*Contraction and Convergence" proposal.* Available at http://www.gci.org.uk.

[31] See Ashton & Wang, note 19, at 74.

[32] See Ashton and Wang, note 19, at 75.

lessons for future development in a larger scale.[33] All of these shed some light on the positive attitude about China's capacity to cope with global warming.

However, as we shall see in Section 3, China is currently entrapped in a hybrid (transitional) state and thus is in an awkward position to classify itself. Who should it then compare itself with, if it intends to define its relative capacity to address climate change – developed countries, advanced developing ones, the EU member states in transition, or developing ones? Belonging to any group brings advantages as well as disadvantages. What determines the eventual choice under this circumstance may lie in the ranking of different priorities – which one goes first? Conflicts will arise even among the clearly classified groups. For example, Canada proposed that it receive emissions credits for its exports of clean energy to the United States, its largest trading partner![34]

Furthermore, with the weak environmental institutions, flawed governance system, and limited human resources, China still has a long way to go before it is ready to undertake an appropriate share of the responsibility according to its capacity, whether absolutely or relatively. But this does not constitute any reason for China to shun from making initial steps towards limiting its GHG emissions, because capacity can only be nurtured by endeavoring to develop the required components gradually and persistently. It will not emerge overnight, nor will it fall on China accidentally.

Taking all of these arguments together, something can be drawn from the equity perspective on GHG emissions. The larger the share of cumulative emissions, which varies a lot as a result of different evaluating period, the higher per capita emissions together with per capita GDP are, and the wealthier the state is, the greater should be its responsibility.

With respect to China, while linking climate issues to the international framework of trade and investment and intending to reclassify its international position, it seems not so easy to continue utilizing the issue of equity as a defence against any mandatory international obligations, but, rather, as emissions and income grow, China, ultimately, needs to make related arrangements, take necessary actions to control GHG emissions, and thereby contribute its share – from soft, nonbinding obligations to more demanding commitments along with economic and, more important, political progress.

3 INFRASTRUCTURE REFORM

3.1 Emissions Profile and Trend

It is argued that there are two trends about energy consumption for the foreseeable future: one is that coal will continue to be the primary source of energy; the other is that we are living in a coal-constrained world.[35] In the United States, coal provides 51 percent of all electricity, more than the amount of any other fuel source and fives times more than gas, oil, or hydroelectric power. Australia serves as an extreme case – coal is dominant in the energy mix, providing 85 percent of the nation's electricity.[36]

[33] See, for example, Xin Hua, "China, a Leading Investor in Renewable Energy," May 17, 2006, *China Daily*. Available at http://www.chinadaily.com.cn/china/2006–05/17/content_592759.htm.

[34] See Robert Page, "Kyoto and Emissions Trading: Challenges for the NAFTA family," 28(55) *Canada-United States Law Journal* (2002), 63–64.

[35] Eileen Claussen, *Technology, Public Policy and Coal: Making the Connection.* Speech at Coal 21 Annual Conference. April 5, 2005. Available at http://www.bp.com/centers/energy.

[36] Ibid.

China accounts for 31 percent of the world's coal consumption, whereas domestically, coal represented 74.2 percent in energy manufacturing and 67.1 percent in energy consumption in 2003.[37] Although slightly declining from 1997 to 2000, mostly because of the Asian Financial Crisis, coal resumed its increasing trend immediately from 2001,[38] and at that time the central government claimed that coal still is and will continue to be the dominant energy source in China's economic development.

The Kyoto Protocol, which came into force on 16 February 2005 following ratification by Russia, best demonstrates the idea of multilateral efforts to constrain coal-related emissions. As the bottom line indicates: coal is the most abundant energy source today and it is available at a relatively low cost; "*there is no way that the world can continue to quench its growing thirst for energy without it.*"[39] So how do we reconcile these future scenarios in which the claimed coal constraint seemingly contradicts the long-term reliance on coal use?

The situation is critical for China. Because of the limitation in developing natural gas, oil, hydroelectric, or nuclear power at a faster speed,[40] the economic growth and efforts of enhancing citizens' welfare still rely heavily on coal use in comparison with other countries in the coming future. And CO_2, the main GHG from coal-burning power plants, accounts for the largest share in China's past, current, and projected emissions.[41]

This seems to pose another dilemma for the central government to tackle, in that it cannot afford the costly consequence of sacrificing, or even restricting, coal use as the primary energy, nor is it proper for it sitting there idly and put no constraint on its absolute consumption. The question arises whether China will be capable of limiting coal-related emissions while satisfying the development desire. Practice tells us that the answer hinges, in large measure, on political will, governance systems, environmental institutions, and, essentially, the performance of the environmental authority.

3.2 Relations among Stakeholders

With the structural reform and its consequential achievement of the last decade and a half, it is officially recognized by the central government that China is transforming

[37] Data is available from National Bureau of Statistics of China. Available at http://www.stats.gov.cn.

[38] The coal consumption percent since 1997 dropped from 74.7 percent to 66.1 percent in 2000, but increased again to 67.1 percent in 2003; coal manufacturing rate fluctuated even sharper, from the lowest 66.6 percent in 2000 to as high as 74.2 percent in 2003, but resembles the same trend. Data available online at http://www.stats.gov.cn.

[39] See Claussen (2005).

[40] The financial shortage and conflicting region area-specific interest is delaying some major giant pipeline placing projects for transporting more natural gas from the west to east in China; high oil prices also increases a lot the cost of depending on it as the main energy source; the debate of protecting biodiversity has postponed the construction of several hydroelectric stations, and the expensive installing reinforcing, operating and maintaining expense has prevented China from expanding the number of nuclear power stations. With all these factors, coal, as a relatively cheap energy source, inevitably will continue to play a significant role in China's economic path.

[41] Here this paper only explores the CO_2 from coal-burning power plants, and temporarily excluding that from other sources including vehicles – another major source of CO_2. The reason for this selection is that because the process of infrastructure reform must be a gradual, incremental, not hasty one, it would ruin the whole plan if planners are too ambitious, or greedy to incorporate all-related industries into a multiphase program at the very early stage. Policy makers need to set up the successful example, starting with the group that can relatively easily be targeted, patiently remove doubts of potential participants, and finally step by step, incorporate all interest groups into the grand project. This incremental principle also applies to any emissions trading program to limit CO_2 emissions in China.

from a planned economy, in which State-Owned-Enterprises (SOEs) under the guidance of sector-specific ministries dominated the economic course, to a socialistic market-economy, and has achieved remarkable success. Economic indicators such as dramatic growth rate, incredible GDP, and enhanced living standards all contribute to making this judgment more persuasive. These enormous gains need to be balanced with other aspects if we want to get a fuller picture, because even "*where important political forces are committed to fundamental structural change, this transition is contested and prolonged, and its likely endpoint is difficult to discern.*"[42]

For China, a closer look at what impacts structural reform has had on environmental institutions, particularly, on environmental authority and the regulated party may offer us a different, but clearer, understanding.

As early as the 1990s, the central government established the interministerial National Climate Change Coordinating Committee (later renamed the State Climate Change Coordinating Committee) to lead in addressing climate-related issues in China. However, it will easily mislead the researchers if they take very seriously the several general, abstract, and nonenforceable documents the committee issued as observers need to understand the sharp distinction between words and actions in China.[43] Rather, attention should be paid to analysing whether the regulatory power is exercised independently by the environmental authority, the extent to which other administrative organs affect power plants – the main regulated party – in choosing methods of fulfilling environmental obligations in practice, and whether environmental regulators can provide sufficient incentives and flexibility for the power plants to act efficiently in a climate-friendly way.

Unlike the Environmental Protection Agency (EPA) in the United States, the State Environmental Protection Administration (SEPA) and local Environmental Protection Bureaus (EPBs) do not operate as independent regulatory authorities, but, rather, are heavily constrained by the National Development and Reform Commission (NDRC), which under the Chinese system is in charge of macro-economy issues and coordinates the development plans of major industries, and other sector-specific ministries.

The essence of the interrelationships among all these authorities lies in the way that the State Council identifies them and thereby allocates administrative power. It is not surprising for NDRC to enjoy a superior position to SEPA and to have a more influential impact on the electric power industry because it determines the overall energy policy for China. It is also understandable that the sector-specific ministries, such as the Ministry of Construction, have a more intimate, or benign, relationship with enterprises than SEPA does: the former brings economic benefits whereas the latter always plays the role of troublemaker (although this is not usually the case). And the common case is that SEPA rarely wins over either the debate at the cental level or the dispute of enforcing punitive mechanism on enterprises in practice.

[42] See Heller & Shukla, "Development and Climate: Engaging Developing Countries," in *Beyond Kyoto: Advancing the International Effort against Climate Change* (Pew Center on Global Climate Change, Arlington, VA, 2003), 118.

[43] This can be partly seen from the *national communication* China's government submitted last year at the Tenth Conference of Parties, which, serving as the first official document from the central government, which only offers the climate-related data for 1994. See *The People's Republic of China Initial National Communication on Climate Change: Executive Summary*. 2004. Beijing, October. Available at http://unfccc.int/national_reports/non-annex_i_natcom/items/2979.php.

Such reality is somewhat absurd, and it may occur to observers that their positions seem to be reversed because, as the authority in charge, SEPA is officially entitled with the supervising power and thereby should be more dominant in its relationship with power plants, particularly in the circumstance of China. As a cultural custom and political practice, there has long been a parent–child relationship between the supervising organ and business enterprises in China. Why does the case of SEPA serve as a rare exception?

The answer may be explored from two perspectives.

First, it is the historically weak identification of environmental protection and the relevant authority in charge that puts SEPA in such an awkward position. Despite all the environment-related legislation and associated by-laws issued in the past decades, it has been common practice for the quest of environmental protection to concede to other priorities, whether at a state level or a local one. The difference lies only in the severity of the legislation.

SEPA and local EPBs should work to strengthen enforcement mechanisms, as they were designed to do. They also should develop new approaches to pollution control, and increase public awareness, but the reality depicts quite a different picture.

SEPA used to rank a notch lower than the other sector-specific ministries in the context of hierarchy, and this seemingly slight difference constituted a huge gap politically. If SEPA plans to propose a sector-specific rule dealing with some sort of pollutant, it has to seek the agreement and support from the relevant department in charge and would not achieve anything otherwise. As SEPA ranked lower in the hierarchy, it was always placed at a disadvantage during the collaborating process and thereby faced various unreasonable, sometimes even ridiculous obstacles that can effectively delay, or kill a proposal.

Even after the structural reform, SEPA was nominally elevated to the same position as other sector-specific departments; it still does not have a proportional voice in the State Council.[44] In the case that the relevant departments would not sincerely cooperate with SEPA in implementing a proposed project, SEPA is usually unable to make a loud enough voice to attract the attention or support from the commission in charge, say, NDRC.

An interesting detail in a recent plan about how to regulate CDM projects in China may help us understand more about SEPA's awkward position and such deeply rooted ideas. Among the four members of the committee that is in charge of CDM projects, the name of SEPA, unsurprisingly, appeared last and everyone took it for granted, even the officials within SEPA did not raise a doubt.[45] As the environmental issue was translated into an economic, and finally a political one, SEPA, in this scenario, inevitably was marginalized and had no way to argue for a promotion. SEPA often acts like a shelter when China is attacked for its weak environmental management or inadequate emphasis on climate-related issues, but in reality its awkward position reveals something quite different.

At the local level, conditions are even worse. As the financial and personnel matters are basically in the hand of local governments, the local EPBs, from provincial to city level, are more responsive to local needs and priorities than to SEPA's directives, even though they should actually carry out the enforcement. The polluting enterprises are often allowed to operate because they can ease the unemployment pressure and

[44] The director of SEPA is not a member of the cabinet.

[45] The four members are NDRC, the Ministry of Commerce, the Ministry of Finance and SEPA. See the report at http://www.china5e.com/news/huanbao/200505/200505310021.html.

provide substantial financial income, where the local EPBs are, in most cases, implicitly instructed not to interfere.

Second, the strong lobbying ability of the electric power sector has a tremendous impact on the government's policy choice. It is not unusual for the economic giants to be able to influence policy makers, but the way in which Chinese power plants maneuver, and the degree to which they can achieve their objectives, are typically characterized by the specific circumstance of China.

A dispute about the implementation of Environmental Impact Assessments (EIA) that took place recently in China demonstrates how far the lobbying ability of power plants can go. During this debate, SEPA announced that the construction and operation of more than thirty industrial and power plants, including three started by the China Yangtze Three Gorges Project Corporation, must be temporarily stopped because they did not pass the EIA, which is required by Law on Environmental Assessment (LEAI, promulgated in 2003).[46] Many proenvironmental groups assumed this behavior as a groundbreaking event of arguing for SEPA's independent authority and setting up an unprecedented example.

Unfortunately, the outcome was frustrating. Most of the thirty enterprises did not take this order seriously. Claiming the horrible consequence that stopping operation, even temporarily, would bring, the Three Gorges Project Corporation disregarded the order and even charged SEPA for abusing its supervising power. Later, although it cannot be confirmed whether SEPA was criticized for its abrupt stride by the allies of the electric power industry (relevant administration), or even someone higher (maybe the NDRC), the fact is that it did not take a long time for all these "unlucky thirty" to pass the EIA after paying nominal fines and then resume operating.

The poor authority of SEPA was ruthlessly crushed into the ground. It is not easy to speculate as to the motive that initiated such a radical campaign – it deviated too far from SEPA's persistently conservative style, but the result did indicate the bargaining ability of various stakeholders, and gave insights into how to identify the unique characters of the specific development stage that China is currently in.

3.3 Caught in "Hybrid" State

China is in the midst of a transition from a largely state-centered to a more market-centered system. In reality, "*the process of transition itself has become semi-permanent state that is likely to persist for several decades.*"[47] "*In the hybrid state, political and economic institutes face new incentives and engage in new behavior. The overlapping established and reformed agencies produce contradictory incentives, inducing complex adaptive strategies by private and public actors unsure which system will ultimately take hold.*"[48] Consequently, what deeply affects the relationship among SEPA, sector-specific ministries, and power plants, originates basically from such characters of this transitional state.

As the products of the 1997 structural reform, the corporatized energy-related sectors such as the State Power Corporation[49] (SPC) and the remaining six largest power

[46] See the report at http://smh.com.au/articles/2005/03/25/1111692627792.html.

[47] See Heller & Shukla, note 44, at 118.

[48] See Heller & Shukla, note 44, at 118.

[49] The State Power Corporation was formed in 1997 to take over the business management of China's electric utilities from the former Ministry of Electric Power, as part of China's widespread institutional reforms to separate business management from the administrative and regulatory functions of

group corporations account for more than 80 percent of the national electricity supply,[50] and thus play a key role in improving energy efficiency and limiting CO_2 emissions. In 2004, the SPC was further reorganized into the State Grid Corporation and five regional independent power group corporations following the principle of "separating electricity suppliers and transmitters," but this does not change the basic structure of major electricity suppliers. Without fundamental reform, these business giants, not surprisingly, are mired in bureaucracy and unable to function effectively.

For example, the department responsible for environmental issues in the regional power group corporations, which is originally designed to be responsible for carrying out the power sector's own environmental management systems, prefers to concentrate more on establishing smooth communication channels with regulators or developing newly dependent allies, aiming at easing, or even avoiding their environmental obligations. They are slipping into the "neither state nor private" status that has proven so difficult to subject to the discipline of environmental regulation.

As reflected as the "interest"-oriented, rather than market-oriented companies, these newly established state firms frequently do not accept internally the external faith in competitive markets even as the government announced their conversion, nor do they "*increasingly free of central administration influence, make use of their established political connections to consolidate their inherited national market power, even as they reorganize themselves for international competition.*"[51] They are not administrative agencies but essentially act more like that. And because the environmental regulator only monitors periodically (notification is always given in advance for them to prepare) and relies heavily on the emissions data that the enterprises provide, these electric power giants generally enjoy a friendly relationship with local EPBs, and, in a sense, undertake the major part of the supervising responsibility themselves.

In this hybrid context, if SEPA wants to be capable of enforcing the regulatory power, it must seek to obtain real support from the State Council and shake off its conventional dependent identity.

Just as generic transformation to a market economy has played a more important role than specific energy and environmental policies,[52] the environmental regulator should not restrict itself only within the environmental perspective, but should more actively cast itself into the whole scenario of social transition. The former EIA debate has clearly demonstrated that there are two things SEPA should consider seriously: one is that it should learn how to gain favour from various social classes in enforcing its supervising power or implementing environmental proposals, by which it could gradually draw the leadership's attention and reinforce their willingness to make SEPA an independent body; the other is that it is of equal importance for SEPA to contemplate how to bargain against the public–private coalition of newly autonomous state enterprises and their newly dependent allies in government administrations, how to combat the inclination of sectoral prosperity and expansion, and how to develop a "benign" relationship with the regulatee.

government institutions. See Zu, Li, & Yang, "Overview of Institutional and Market Reforms and Future Prospects in China's Utility Sector," Commissioned by the China Sustainable Energy Program, 21 July 1999.

[50] Available at http://www.stats.gov.cn.

[51] See Heller & Shukla, note 44, at 119.

[52] See Logan Jeffery (2001). "China's air pollution down dramatically, but can it last."

3.4 Proposed Reform

Fighting alone cannot resolve problems immediately, but it can probably ignite wide debate and educate the public. As the electric power industry uses economic growth, public welfare, and social stability as the most effective weapons to fight against emissions constraints, SEPA also should focus on these perspectives in order to stimulate or encourage, rather than force, the power plants to be more efficiency-oriented and climate-friendly.

SEPA must patiently reinforce its independent authority in the transitional state. Traditionally, SEPA lacks horizontal and vertical administrative leverage, faces personnel and budget limitations, and is equipped with vaguely drafted provisions allocating responsibility and liability. Experience also demonstrates that, in the hybrid context, the environmental policy is, in most cases, becoming the instrument to fulfill the ambition of sponsoring coalitions to various resources, monopolized market position, or other means of industrial growth. This principle applies to SEPA and its targeted electric utilities. The question then is, how can the independent status of the regulator be elevated and made relatively robust in handling power plants-related environmental issues?

The revised pollution levy system may offer some hints. By seeking authorization from proposed amendments to the Air Pollution Prevention and Control Law and support from State Council, SEPA successfully increased the pollution levy charge rate and covered all pollutants that exceed the concentration limits, not just the one with the highest concentration, by which the power plants might be effectively targeted in the economic sense. And although it seems impossible to transfer the macrocontrol power from NDRC to SEPA, the latter still can find ways to consolidate and expand its power, thus enabling itself to act more confidently.

Some time ago, SEPA submitted a plan to the State Council, designed to improve its vertical enforcement powers and it received favorable responses.[53] This improvement enabled the local EPBs to be less vulnerable to local government pressure and other priorities at the expense of environmental protection. Furthermore, as revealed by the EIA debate, the positive media and public participation, which is currently a powerful tool used by SEPA, helped to make the environmental regulator well known, favorably labelled, and thus gradually reinforced its authority and became more acceptable to decision makers.

Another challenge for the environmental regulators is how to provide sufficient incentives for the quasi-autonomous state enterprises and other minor facilities to act more like economic actors in dealing with environmental issues. Command-and-control approaches have proved too rigid in stimulating enterprises to install end-of-pipe-cleaning appliances; to invest more on renovating technology; or to change fuels. Alternatively, several Market-Based-Instruments (MBI) serve as appealing alternatives. SEPA, as the supervising agency, needs to adjust the way in which it oversees emitting activity, from stipulating uniform technology standards to providing sufficient flexibility for enterprises to meet their emissions obligation with least abatement cost.

[53] SEPA proposed to strengthen the multilevel EPB network by demoting the lowest level EPBs (county, township, and city) to the level of technical advisors, turning district level EPBs into branch offices, and requiring all local-level EPBs to be appointed by upper-level (provincial and independent municipal) EPBs. The State Council has reportedly approved these changes. See "Reorganization of China's Environmental Institutions." 2(2) *China Environmental Review*, (December 1998–January 1999).

SEPA should be neither friend nor enemy of the electric power industry. It is essential for environmental regulators to be objective. It is not a wise choice for regulators to develop an intimate interrelationship or push itself in the opposite direction. Although gradually reinforcing its authority, SEPA needs to convince the power plants that it is not an intruder, but, rather, a strong supporter offering feasible proposals for them to act in a cost-effective and environmentally friendly way.

For the purpose of entering the program of limiting emissions as an ally and alleviating hostile attitudes from power plants, SEPA needs to redefine its operational style and the consequent conversion to stressing market based incentives. Actually, SEPA has implemented some projects to promote certain kind of MBI (emissions-trading, for example) for more than a decade, during which it provided training for power plant managers to get familiar with MBI, and educated its own staff to broaden their understanding of supervision.[54] Instead of being the mild-tempered or ruthless regulator, SEPA is trying to convert itself into a technical advisor, who also embraces reliable punitive mechanisms, and to nurture a benign relationship with the power plants.

A further problem is that efforts only from the state level will not suffice to put the intended transformation into reality. Local EPBs, in their role as the actual agencies to bear primary enforcement responsibility at various local levels, are confronted with even more difficult obstacles to overcome if they want to exercise power or duty independently.

Some studies by the World Bank reveal that the local EPBs have applied pollution control regulations with a great deal of discretion and flexibility based on local factors, including the sectoral composition of industry, scale of operations, and whether or not a plant is state-owned.[55] It seems that the political capital and mandate of local environmental regulators run thin compared to finance or line ministries and their industrial partners.[56] Recognizing this fact, SEPA has been trying to alleviate the influence from local powers by proposing setting up supervision teams at the national and provincial levels to monitor the performance of lower level EPBs. Unfortunately, the State Council rejected such a proposal mainly because it was predicted to be disruptive; the Council declared that, if any supervision is done, it will be by cross-government teams across a range of functions.[57]

[54] In the early 1990s, SEPA began experimenting with emissions allowance trading through pilot projects in several heavily polluted cities, and these experiments are continuing to be carried out in various degrees. The latest one is in Taiyuan, Shanxi Province, which is designed to target the total SO_2 emissions from local power plants to meet the domestic goal of controlling SO_2 before 2010. However, the actual outcome remains to be seen as the project is just in the baby stage. SEPA also planned to initiate a major emissions trading program to control SO_2 that includes five provinces, two autonomous cities, and Huaneng Power Group in 2003. Nevertheless the program is still in the preparation stage at the moment and it will be too early to comment whether it would make great contribution to the promotion of emissions trading in China.

[55] See Dasgupta, Huq, & Wheeler, "*Bending the Rules: Discretionary Pollution Control in China.*" World Bank Policy Research Department Working Paper, February 1997. See also Dasgupta, Huq, & Wheeler, 1997. "*Surviving Success: Policy reform and the Future of Industrial Pollution in China.*" World Bank, March 1997; and Xiaoying Ma & Leonard Ortolano, *Environmental Regulation in China* (Lanham, MD: Rowman & Littlefield, 2000).

[56] See Finamore, *Taming the Dragon Heads: Controlling Air Emissions From Power Plants In China*, Washington, DC: National Resource Defense Council, June 2000, P20.

[57] See Finamore (2000, p. 21). See also "*Reorganization of China's Environmental Institutions.*" 2(2) *China Environmental Review*, (December 1998–January 1999).

There is a long way to go before the local EPBs become less responsive to other local priorities. However, bearing in mind the converging trend of more internationalized expertise, wider circulation of information, growing concern with the quality of life, and gradual separation of government and enterprises, observers are not deprived of the hope of holding an optimistic attitude towards the future of local environmental regulators. For example, some big cities, such as Beijing, Shanghai, and Shenzhen, have pledged to allocate more resources to environmental agencies, reinforce their enforcing capacity and create an independent stage for them to cope with pollution issues.[58]

Caught in a hybrid status offers specific challenges as well as precious opportunities to environmental authority. Developing a benign relationship with the electric power industry is not a mission impossible, but it does require SEPA and local EPBs to significantly adapt their operational style, cultivate expertise in providing technical advise, enhance familiarity with the implementation of MBI within the agency as well among the public, promote experimental projects to demonstrate attractive MBI models for power plants, and, most important, gradually build independent authority while allying themselves with the power industry to be more acceptable in addressing climate-related issues.

4 EMISSIONS TRADING: A FANTASY?

The main purpose of establishing the independent authority of SEPA to grapple with climate issues is to make the proposed adoption of MBI more effective and practical. SEPA, as the administrative agency in charge, is working to demonstrate the will to push forward emissions-trading, the most popular MBI, to combat air pollution and help participants to comply with their obligations in a cost-effective way. It has been more than ten years since emissions-trading was put in place in China and a recent report informed that a large project of controlling SO_2 from power plants is being implemented among five provinces, two autonomous cities, and Huaneng Power Group.[59] With persistent try-and-test, emissions-trading seems to have become a preferable and right policy choice for China's environmental regulator.

But "*the right policy answers will matter little unless there is sufficient political will to put them into action.*"[60] Will emissions-trading be applied as a desirable approach to cope with GHG emissions by policy makers in China and how to muster the required political will?

It would be unrealistic to take for granted the extension of the government's willingness to apply emissions-trading to the realm of controlling GHG emissions. The reason lies not only in the different nature between GHG and normal air pollutants such as SO_2,[61] but, more often, on the public awareness, media attention, electoral politics,

[58] Only in a deep social reform can the environmental regulators be granted the corresponding power, or obligation. These trends, combined together, indicate some initial step the central and provincial governments adopted to promote environmental protection, though far from enough.

[59] See *Project for Aggregate Amount Control and Emissions Trading for* SO_2. Available online at http://www.zhb.gov.cn/eic/650490891793858560/20030214/1036807.shtml.

[60] See Diringer (2003, p. 3).

[61] Different from conventional air pollutants like SO_2, GHG emissions are evenly dispersed in the global atmosphere, which means a ton of CO_2 emitted in the United Stated has the same effect as a ton of CO_2 emitted in China. That is one of the natural reasons that a single country is unwilling to take action alone because the costly decrease in one region can be easily offset by arbitrary increase in another.

and determination, flexibility, and resourcefulness of governments in fashioning any approach. That is why, "*even though the threat of climate-induced damage is most severe in developing nations, political actors concentrate on immediate issues like local air and water pollution that may help them claim public resources and satisfy popular expectations, rather than on long-term, invisible concerns like climate change.*"[62]

However, observers should not feel discouraged from holding a positive attitude towards the future of emissions trading for CO_2[63] (the GHG at the current stage) in China. The essence of emissions trading is to equip participants with the flexibility to choose the least-abatement-cost approach to meet their obligations,[64] and the goal of implementing such an emissions trading program for China is sustainable growth along a low GHG pathway. Therefore, any proposed emissions trading system will not gain success unless it casts climate action less as a constraint and more as a driver of facilitator of goals such as promoted performance or energy efficiency.

As CO_2 emissions can be dramatically reduced, not at the expense of slowing down economic development, but by transforming the ways we generate and consume energy, technology transformation plays a significant role in achieving such a conversion. Therefore, any proposed emissions-trading program for CO_2 should aim to stimulate power plants to invest more on renovating technology.

No reasonable scenario suggests that the market alone can deliver the needed technology soon enough to stabilize CO_2. The direction and imperative must come from governments.[65] For China, any proposed emissions trading program needs to align emissions control with other paramount priorities, such as improving energy efficiency, adopting renewable energy, or maintaining profitability. Despite the fact that sustainable development and energy conservation have been listed at the top of the agenda by China, adequate technical support or a persuasive demonstrating project pointing out the way for enterprises to achieve the grand goal does not exist. In this case, if a specifically designed emissions-trading program can prove to be salient not only to control CO_2 emissions, but, more impressively, to improve energy efficiency or increase profitability, gaining adequate political will from central government may not seem to be insurmountable.

It is beyond the scope of this chapter to discuss an emissions-trading program that incorporates all GHG emissions or every emitting source. Such an overly ambitious program for current China may gain nothing but ruin the reputation of emissions trading. Targeting CO_2 emissions from the largest emitter, the electric power sector, may serve as the first step towards establishing a multiphased emissions-trading system in China. With this first step, the most important factor necessary for an effective emissions-trading scheme is the capacity of environmental regulators.[66]

[62] See Heller & Shukla (2004, p. 119).

[63] This paper only discuss the possibility of emissions trading on CO_2, but exclude other non-CO_2 GHG, because the CO_2 emitters are relatively concentrated in power plants and other large industrial sources and therefore it is feasible to monitor the emissions and enforce proposed program administratively, but this requirement could not be met by other GHG because their emitting source are generally diverse and incredibly costly to monitor.

[64] The concept of emissions trading was initially demonstrated by Dales (1968), then developed by many scholars, including Montgomery (1972), Tietenberg (1985), and Baumol & Oates (1988).

[65] See Heller & Shukla, (2003, p. 112).

[66] There are many other factors contributing to determining the performance of an emissions trading program, such as available legal system, historical experience or inexperience with market, the level of

It then follows, would SEPA and local EPBs be capable of designing, implementing, and enforcing such a grand emissions trading program even after the preferred structural reform has been made? Could the environmental regulator be qualified to ensure, at least relatively, the required equity, compliance, and efficiency? And how will the hybrid state influence the operation of such a program? Analysis from several aspects may provide for some ideas on these concerns.

Elevating the independent authority of SEPA is essential to ensure that a powerful central environmental regulator is in charge of the whole process of implementing a major program. There are signs indicating that such a promotion may not be a dream.[67] To effectively implement its mandate, although SEPA has to entrust the enforcement rights to local EPBs and rely on them for the inspection work, it is vital for SEPA to maintain a vigorous capacity to supervise the actual effect of local EPBs enforcement, in which case the existing decentralized system should be fundamentally reformed. Hence, the supervising power, in a sense, also has to be centralized mainly because the local EPBs are too weak to fight against local needs in the foreseeable future and the regulated power plants usually rank above the local EPBs. Another reason for arguing that such centralized power probably originates from the worries raised by participants that different levels of enforcement would put the participants with better compliance at a competitive disadvantage.[68] To combat such an unfavorable inclination, a standard supervising team is needed. SEPA needs to set aside financial and human resources specifically for this purpose, and these resources should come mainly from provincial and city EPBs because most participants are at this level.

Although the actual experience as to leading an economy-wide emissions trading program is relatively limited within SEPA, the process of accumulating knowledge may be facilitated by both the empirical learnings from ongoing emissions-trading programs and expertise training offered to environmental officers in various scales. Gaining support from relevant legislation and obtaining authorization from the State Council, SEPA will probably benefit from the structural reform and become the central authority in charge of environmental issues in a real sense.

The concrete operation of an emissions-trading program dominated by SEPA can be analysed from several perspectives to see whether such a proposal would be feasible and attractive to participants. Equity, or fairness to all stakeholders, is surely an essential factor for a successful scheme. In the case of targeting CO_2 from power plants, SEPA

corruption, and public acceptance. These relevant factors are not included in this chapter. However, some researchers hold a pessimistic opinion of China's ability to meet all these requirements and therefore do not support the idea of applying emissions trading to China. See R. G. Bell, *Choosing Environmental Policy Instruments in the Real World.* (OECD, Paris. March 2003).

67 In the emissions-trading program for SO_2, which includes five provinces, two autonomous cities, and one giant electric power corporation, SEPA was appointed as the primary coordinator of implementing this project. This may show the central government's inclination to overcome, or at least alleviate the influence from sector-specific administrations when promoting any program aiming at combating sector-interest. And, in the case of environmental protection, SEPA has the unique advantage of being neutral and thereby more possibly to be given the significant role to play.

68 It is undeniably the fact that due to different level of enforcement, some enterprises suffered from its compliance with the target while some others enjoyed the loose supervision of local governments and thereby become more competitive. This phenomenon conveys unfavorable information that the one who seeks support from some resources other than environmental regulators is probably more successful in the market and establishing a standard supervising team that acts more consistently neutrally will help to reduce this kind of unfairness.

needs to decide, in the first place, the scope of participants and the way to allocate the emissions allowances. As an allowance is actually a de facto currency, it should be no surprise that interest groups affected by the program desired to gain title to as many allowances as possible, and one would certainly expect to see serious rent-seeking with that sort of rent on the table.[69]

As the proportion of each enterprise is generally determined by the data of its historic emissions, output, or input, it could create an incentive for power plants to fake the data in order to gain a larger share. And because SEPA conventionally relies heavily on the data enterprises offer and only monitors emissions occasionally, it will be difficult to ensure the accuracy of historic data and evaluate the allocating criteria. Maybe the experience from the Acid Rain Program of the United States offers a clue, in which the EPA took the average level of emissions of three years from 1985 to 1987 as the baseline for the 1990 allocation.[70] One SO_2 allowance distribution plan proposed by Jiangsu province conveys a similar idea.[71] Although there is no perfect or impartial way to ensure the 100 percent accuracy of historic data in China's situation, it still allows a crude approximation of the emissions baseline by input-based or output-based approaches.

SEPA will then face questions such as, would it be fair to other social groups if the allowance is allocated free to the participants (normally grandfathered as reflected in the Acid Rain Program and European Union Emissions Trading Directive)? In order to address this concern, should the allowance be partly auctioned? Should the program be multiphased so that it can leave some room for later participants, and how? Are funds for technical innovation and education available? Responses from SEPA about these doubts may be positive and full of confidence. Experience claims that grandfathering seems to be the politically feasible way, although an auction may be more economically sound, and an initially modest program is a good start. It also can be assured that flexible mechanisms will be provided for participants in different stages and education for enterprises managers to get familiar with emissions trading is right on the way.

Designing a theoretically proper proposal is no barrier to the environmental regulator. The question is whether SEPA could effectively enforce compliance, and the core issues in the dimension of compliance include accurate monitoring, adequate incentive for participants, and serious punitive mechanisms.

Accurately monitoring the CO_2 emissions from power plants is a vital part of any successful emissions-trading program and has posed a challenge for observers for a long time. In China, it has long been a difficult task for local EPBs to monitor air pollutants such as SO_2. Installing Continuous Emissions Monitors (CEM) surely is the best choice but the costly operation fee makes it least attractive to the power plants. Different from normal air pollutants like SO_2, a practical way to decide the CO_2 emissions may be to calculate the carbon content of the fuel consumed by participants, but this input-based approach may embrace the disadvantage of discouraging power plants from adopting

[69] The fight that took place in the Acid Rain Program has clearly demonstrated the long, hard bargaining process in allocating allowance and how deeply the influences of various stakeholders can affect the outcome of distribution. See Ellerman, Joskow, Schmalensee, Monteto et al. *Markets for Clean Air, The U.S. Acid Rain Program* (New York, NY: Cambridge University Press and Ellerman, 2000), pp. 21–76.

[70] See Ellerman et al. (2000).

[71] See *Plan for Allocating SO_2 among Electric Power Plants in Jiangsu Province.* Available online at http://www.zhb.gov.cn/eic/650490891793858560/20030214/1036808.shtml.

end-of-pipe technology to control the end emissions. Alternatively, an output-based approach may be applied by gauging the carbon content of the final products. It remains to be seen whether a more market-based approach to monitor CO_2 emissions can be found in the coming future. However, experience informs us that it is seldom the technology, but rather the political judgment, that prevents the proposed scheme from being enforced. External factors such as financial, administrative, and criminal penalty mechanisms are also important. Adequate, consistent, and predictable penalties are essential to create the right incentives for compliance. And policy makers in China can benefit a lot from the pioneering U.S. efforts as well as those of the EU regarding the establishment of effective punitive mechanisms.

For efficiency, SEPA is required to be able to provide remedies in case of market failures and combat externalities brought by emissions trading. As the successful Acid Rain Program has proved, arrangement of banking and borrowing allowances are essential to ensure flexibility and efficiency.[72] Compared with monitoring, registering appears to be a minor issue as a result of the development of the Internet and information technology. For example, after establishing the database of allocated SO_2 allowance for Acid Rain Program, EPA only uses two staff to record and track the flow of allowance.[73] Therefore, it would not be unbearably costly even if SEPA wants to create a national database and tracking system for allowances. Another aspect of making the program efficient is to enhance the intellectual base for emissions trading by educating the participants as well as public and gaining media attention.

As characterized by the hybrid state, the major obstacle that SEPA is encountering is the huge pressure from the new quasi-autonomous sectoral coalition. Coming from the former ministry of electric power and the State Power Corporation, the five regional power group corporations are good at utilizing its established political connections to consolidate their inherited regional market power, so do the other electric power giants. As the discussion on the EIA debate has demonstrated, this sectoral coalition has, in some ways, forced the environmental regulator to acede. To combat this, SEPA needs to learn how to align limiting CO_2 emissions with other priorities of enterprises, such as increased capacity and efficiency in energy use that underpins economic growth. Public participation and media power are also the potential allies.

To sum up, the fate of any emissions-trading scheme hinges, in large measure, on the performance of SEPA in China. Although it does not seem to be urgent for China to establish an economy-wide emissions trading program for CO_2 in the near term, it is really urgent to reinforce the independent authority of the environmental regulator and nurture its confidence when grappling with corporatized state enterprises. After all, China will, sooner or later, contribute its share in combatting global warming, and a domestic program therefore is necessary for that purpose. As an intellectually viable approach to cope with this challenge, emissions trading must be adapted to the specific circumstance of China in order not to be a pitiful fantasy, in which the reformed environmental regulator plays the most significant role.

[72] Unfortunately, most of the experimental emissions trading projects in China did not provide participants with the banking or borrowing ability, mainly because of the short-term period of the experiments and worries about participants abusing the flexible mechanism.

[73] A. Denny Ellerman, Paul L. Joskow, & David Harrison. *Emissions Trading in the U.S. Experience, Lessons, and Considerations for Greenhouse Gases.* (May 2003), 17.

5 CONCLUSION

The equity perspective seems unable to serve as the strong shelter for China as it has in the past. With the undeniable trend of ever-increasing GHG emissions accompanying the incredible economic growth, it is just a matter of time until China will assume its appropriate share in the responsibility of limiting, or even curtailing, GHG emissions. The intention of graduating from the group of developing countries also indicates an implicit willingness on the part of the central government to take on soft, nonbinding obligations initially by evaluating the benefits and costs in the context of international trade. Moreover, China's vulnerability to climate change reminds the central government that global warming is not a nightmare only taking place in the Western world, but a real problem that China needs to tackle for its own sake.

Because of the hybrid state in which China is currently entrapped, it seems to be an insurmountable problem for existing SEPA and local EPBs to lead any environmental protection program that deals with a new quasi-autonomous sectoral coalition without revolutionary structural reforms. The current pattern of allocating environmental supervising power among different authorities by the central government, together with the strong established political connection inherited by corporatized state enterprises, has located the environmental regulator in a relatively inferior position. It must be a long and painful path for SEPA to gradually build its independent authority, redefine the relationship with powerful regulated parties, and thereby develop a trustworthy coalition, enhance awareness of and familiarity with, emissions trading within the administration as well as among the public, and enable itself to provide technical advice and stimulate participants to act in a more market-oriented way.

Based on the existing infrastructure and the projected reform, SEPA and local EPBs are able to offer flexible mechanisms necessary for ensuring equity, compliance and efficiency, if they can gain sufficient political will from the central government, and carefully start from a modest step to implement an economy-wide emissions trading program. Hopefully, such political investment is not a dream too far to reach.

SECTION B. LAND MANAGEMENT

22 A Brief Historical Comparison of the Public Land Disposal Policies in Brazil and in the United States

Arlindo Daibert*

1 INTRODUCTION

The theoretical proposition of this work is to examine how the different degrees of environmental degradation, coupled with economic development, present in Brazil and the United States today, basically result from the different strategies adopted by each country regarding the occupation of their territories through the disposal of their public lands. In order to proceed with the comparison, some common ground needs to be established.

One of the first aspects to point out is the similarity in terms of time: before their separate colonization processes began, Brazil and the United States were no more than two vast lands, replete with natural resources. Moreover, although not environmentally friendly according to today's patterns, the practices of the indigenous peoples that originally inhabited the two lands did not exert a significant impact on their ecosystems. In both cases, it was only the arrival of the Europeans that led to significant changes in the environment.

By contrast, it is incontestable that once the first generation of settlers had established themselves in each country, their future independence would be a historical inevitability, as indeed has been the case for every other land subjected to the global colonisation process that started at the end of the fifteenth century.[1] This perspective helps to demonstrate that, at least at one remote point in time, the two countries were perfectly equivalent, that is, to use a modern concept, they were just two developing nations, both in the institutional and in the economic sense.

Another similarity to be noted is that, at the beginning of the colonisation process in each nation, all lands belonged to the British and the Portuguese Crown, respectively, meaning that, until the said lands started to be transferred by the respective governments to private parties, they were deemed by the European courts to be part of the public domain, in spite of any native claims.[2]

Finally, after each country's respective independence, the public domain previously exerted by the British and the Portuguese over the colonial lands was automatically

[1] With the arguable exceptions of those areas colonized by the United States after its independence (Hawaii and the territories taken from Mexico, for instance) and French Guiana.

[2] Warren Dean, with Broadax & Firebrand, *The Destruction of the Brazilian Atlantic Forest* (University of California Press, 1995).

* Arlindo Daibert is with the Attorney-General's office in Rio de Janeiro.

transferred to the new public governmental entities created, the United States and Brazil. Therefore, such lands kept their characteristic of being public property.

In this sense, the similarity of the historical features of Brazil and the United States suggests the beginning of the respective processes of colonization as a fair starting point for a hypothetical "environmental degradation race" involving the two nations. The reference for this "race" shall be how the occupation and the consolidation of each territory took place under the initiative of the public authorities.

The processes shall be examined at two moments: before and after each country's independence, with the former having a tremendous impact on the latter in both cases. The "winner" of the "race," of course, was the United States, as the imaginary "finishing line" here was the declaration of the U.S. Bureau of the Census that the unsettled American west frontier was nonexistent in 1890.

2 HISTORICAL BACKGROUND

Portugal "discovered" Brazil in 1500 and colonised it for three hundred years, beginning a process that left far-reaching consequences that can still be easily observed today.[3] For this reason, in terms of legal institutions, particularly in relation to property, both public and private, it is essential to learn a little about the Portuguese institutions during the colonial period.

In 1375, the Portuguese king Fernando I promulgated an ordinance creating the system of *sesmarias*, regulating the use of land in Portugal. The origins of the word are uncertain. It may be derived from the ancient Portuguese terms *sesma* or *sesmo*, meaning the sixth part of something, or from *caesina*, which in Latin denotes a cut or incision.[4]

The most interesting aspect of this piece of legislation was that it imposed an obligation on the owners of land to make appropriate use of it, which implied a duty to cultivate the area to produce crops in order to help tackle the shortage of food that was affecting the Portuguese at that time. Disobedience of the terms of the law could lead to the seizure of the land without compensation. The land in that case would then be transferred by the crown to a person able to cultivate it in its entirety.[5]

The *sesmarias* were present in the *Afonsinas Ordinances* (1446) and the *Manuelinas Ordinances* (1521), both codifications enacted by Portugal. The model of *sesmarias* would later be adapted by the Portuguese and used by them as a method to foster colonization in Brazil, although not immediately following the "discovery," for it is said that Brazil was "discovered" in 1500 and "forgotten" in 1500.[6] The reason for this was that the Portuguese used to make more money from their trade in the East Indies, tending not to care much about the new lands in Brazil, which were not so lucrative at that time. The first presence of the Portuguese in the Brazilian lands occurred in the form of *feitorias*,[7] a mixture of trading-stations and fortresses, which were established

[3] Caio Prado Jr., *The Colonial Background of Modern Brazil* (University of California Press, 1967).

[4] Ruy Cirne Lima, *Pequena História Territorial do Brasil* (Short Brazilian Territorial History), (Escola de Administração Fazendária, 1988).

[5] Ann Helen Wainer, *Legislacao Ambiental Brasileira – Subsidios para a Historia do Direito Ambiental* (Brazilian Environmental Legislation – Subsidies for the History of the Environmental Law), Editora Forense, 1991.

[6] Caio Prado Jr., note 3.

[7] The *feitorias* had already been used in the Portuguese colonies in Africa for the trade of African slaves, following the same model.

along the coast to be used for coordinating the brazilwood[8] (*pau brasil*) extraction and commerce.

In 1530, the Portuguese took a more active step with the dual purposes of thwarting the French and Spanish efforts to establish a presence on the Brazilian coast, and increasing profits from the new land in addition to those provided by the extraction of *brazilwood*. For that reason, the Portuguese king Dom Joao III ("The Coloniser") divided the colony into thirteen horizontal territories called *capitancies*, as a first strategy, so to speak, to pursue true possession of the new land.

The *capitancies* followed a similar basis to that of the charters used later on by the British Crown to send its first immigrants to America. Basically, a donation charter regulated the duties and rights of the beneficiary before the Crown, setting forth a range of general legal provisions that should be applied within the territory of the *capitancie*.[9] The charter usually granted the beneficiary general powers of administration and law enforcement over all the colonisers with the exception of the members of nobility, who were only subject to the power of the Crown.

The *capitancies* were to be assigned to those willing to undertake the settlement and defense of the territories, assuming full responsibility for the corresponding expenses. In addition, the owner (the *captain*) had the authority to give *sesmarias* – portions of land within the *capitancies* – to those interested in cultivating the soil. The *sesmeiro* (the term for the beneficiary of a *sesmaria*) could be anyone as long as the person was white and Christian.[10]

These *sesmeiros*, in theory, had to fulfill the obligation of yielding a crop from the land within five years; failure to do so would make the beneficiary subject to losing the *sesmaria* rights, as established in the *Afonisnas Ordinances*. However, the main objective of the application of this ancient Portuguese system in Brazil was to encourage the occupation of the new territories rather than to produce food.[11]

The *captain* also had the right to receive 5 percent of the value resulting from the extraction of *brazilwood*, half of the tenth part of the fishing, a tenth of the crown's general income from the area of the *capitancie*, 10 percent of the metals, whether precious or not, and the right of passage in rivers, harbors, and "other waters."[12]

The *capitancies*, therefore, functioned as an emphytheutic[13] contract that ensured the constitution, on the one hand, of a perpetual relationship between the crown and the charter's beneficiary, and, on the other hand, a similar relationship between the latter and those who received the *sesmarias* from him.[14] Private property in Brazil, as noted earlier, was thus totally derived from the Portuguese public domain, which would find

[8] The exploitation of *pau-brasil* (*brazilwood*) began immediately after the "discovery." *Pau-brasil* is called in Tupi native language ibirapitanga, which means "red wood." The tree was crushed to obtain a powder that was used for dyeing fabrics red, a fashionable color at that time, for it was the color of nobility. That is why the wood was called *brasil*, as in Portuguese the word is an adjective that means the quality of something that glows red as an ember. The wood had already been found in Turkey and Egypt, but the Brazilian species was of a much higher quality.

[9] Anne Helen Wainer, note 5.

[10] Paulo de Bessa Antunes, *A Propriedade Rural no Brasil* (The Rural Property in Brazil), Departamento de Publicações da OAB/RJ, 1985.

[11] Anne Helen Wainer, note 5.

[12] Ibid. at 12–13.

[13] "Emphyteusis – A hereditary leasehold; a nonowner's right to use land in perpetuity, subject to forfeiture for nonpayment of a fixed rent or for certain other contingencies." *Black's Law Dictionary*.

[14] Izidoro Martins Jr., as cited by Paulo de Bessa Antunes.

its basis in the international treaties signed with Spain,[15] with no regard whatsoever to the claims of the natives.[16]

The *capitancies* system ultimately did not work, due both to the magnitude of the investments they demanded and to the financial inability of the *capitains* to fulfill their obligations.[17] However, the *sesmarias* did leave profound marks on land ownership in Brazil.

Although modest in the beginning, the size of the *sesmarias* soon reached an average dimension of more than 43 square kilometers. Moreover, after the sugarcane plantations were founded in 1530, as the cultivated land began to become exhausted, the *sesmeiros* would regularly apply for more and more new tracts of land, building up the extension of their already enormous territories instead of recovering any part of what they already owned.

Therefore, the most significant heritage left by the *sesmarias* was a direct consequence of the gigantic size of the tracts of lands that were ordinarily granted to the *sesmeiros*: the *latifundium* (latus = broad + fundus = landed estate). The concentration of great swathes of land in the hands of one owner was destined to be a phenomenon that would continue to affect the Brazilian economy and environment.[18]

A labor force based on white workers was never an alternative for the Brazilian colony,[19] even after the sugarcane cycle commenced (c. 1530). Thus, the decision to opt for the capture and enslavement of the natives was the easiest solution to supply the new enterprise with manpower. This took place despite the fact that the Portuguese had not only already developed a valuable sugarcane technology in the Atlantic islands and in the Mediterranean, but also a whole slave-driven economy in its African colonies, which already supplied the necessary labor force for the former projects. The slavery of Africans only timidly began in Brazil in 1540, although by the end of the century it had exploded in size.

Although the choice to make use of the native slave force was the solution closest to hand, it was not without a cost. Natives refused to work and easily escaped into the forest, which they knew far better than the Portuguese. As a result, by the second half of the sixteenth century, native hunting had intensified tremendously, accompanying the increase in sugarcane activity.[20]

In the pursuit of profit the Portuguese killed natives by means of overwork, "war," starvation, and, finally, for those who happened to survive, by way of transmission of European diseases (smallpox, malaria, measles, respiratory diseases, and even flu). The impact of the Portuguese presence on the native population was so devastating that out of the twelve indigenous villages that surrounded Sao Paulo at the beginning of the sixteenth century, only half remained at the beginning of the seventeenth. Moreover, 95 percent of the Tupi people from Sao Vicente[21] to Cabo Frio[22] had been eliminated. This dramatic decrease in the native population brought about the increasing availability of unoccupied areas ready to be claimed by *squatters*.[23]

[15] Jacob Gorender, as cited by Paulo de Bessa Antunes.
[16] Warren Dean, note 2.
[17] Paulo de Bessa Antunes, note 10.
[18] Paulo de Bessa Antunes, note 10.
[19] Caio Prado Jr., note 3.
[20] Warren Dean, note 2.
[21] A city on the coast of today's State of São Paulo.
[22] A city on the coast of today's State of Rio de Janeiro.
[23] Warren Dean, note 2.

Squatters were free people that occupied any unclaimed land. The practice was illegal, though tolerated as the custom of *posse* (possession). Depending on the way the right of possession had been acquired and exercised, it could possibly lead to the granting of a *sesmaria* to the *squatter*. This often happened because of the practical difficulties in following the legal procedures to obtain a regular *sesmaria*, the granting of which was not based on merit but, instead, on the criterion of having the greatest number of slaves to work for the production of exportable goods. Soon, the ownership of land, as demand increased, became a matter of who had more power and influence. In the end, a *sesmeiro* needed to be not only white and Christian, but, most important, powerful.

In 1548, a new alternative administrative system for the colony was established: the "General Government." One of the first decisions of the General-Governor was the extinction of the *capitancies* rights, although this did not extend to the extinction of the *sesmarias* granted by the captains.[24]

At the same time, the increase in the sugarcane activity entailed deep modifications in the way land was occupied. The industry's two main sources of power were firewood and draft animals, both of which could be supplied locally. Trees were also felled for lumber to be used as building material. Animals were also used as a food source – with beef forming a considerable part of the slaves' diet – as well as for hauling the trees that, given the expansion of the lands cultivated for sugarcane and the consequent devastation of the forests by the slash and burn methods, were only to be found at ever-increasing distances.[25]

Cattle breeding would later on be responsible for the colonization of great parts of the northeast, center-west, and south of Brazil.[26] Nevertheless, the bulk of the colonial occupation still remained mostly concentrated in the coastal zone. However, as Warren Dean noted, "[b]y 1600 the human relationship to the Atlantic Forest was transformed principally because most of its original human inhabitants had disappeared and also because the number of invaders was insufficient to replace them. Along the coast, after a century of constant warfare, enslavement, and epidemics, only seven of the donataries had managed to install any sort of settlement."[27]

This haphazard beginning at least gave the coastal forests a respite. Those locations lacking adequate harbour facilities and that were without *brazilwood* were left in peace,[28] albeit not for long.

In 1603, when Portugal – and hence Brazil – was still under the rule of the Spanish (1580–1640), King Felipe II from Spain enacted *the Filipinas Ordinances*, compiling all the Portuguese rules that had been enacted so far, replacing the *Manuelinas Ordinances*. These ordinances remained applicable in Brazil even after independence and, to a certain extent, even subsequent to the enactment of the Brazilian Civil Code in 1916.[29] The main feature of these ordinances, for the purposes of this work, is that they maintained the validity of the *sesmarias* system and its practice during the whole of the colonial period as the basic means of distribution of public land from the Portuguese crown to private parties.

24 Paulo de Bessa Antunes, note 10.
25 Celso Furtado, *The Economic Growth of Brazil – A Survey from Colonial to Modern Times* (University of California Press, 1965).
26 Ibid.
27 Warren Dean, note 2.
28 Ibid.
29 Anne Helen Wainer, note 5.

On the other side of the hemisphere, it was only at the beginning of the seventeenth century that the British decided to undertake their colonial project in America. When the first British colony (Virginia) was founded 107 years after the Brazilian "discovery," a lot had already happened in the Brazilian environment:

- more than two million *brazilwood* trees had been chopped down, affecting about six thousand square kilometers of Atlantic Forest;[30]
- sugar had been profitably cultivated and commercialised for more than seventy years, opening vast areas of Atlantic Forest through slash-and-burn methods;
- about one hundred thousand people were already living in Brazil, thirty thousand of whom were white.[31]

Another important reference in terms of the difference in the "colonial pace" can be obtained from the Spanish experience in the Americas to that date. At the time of the arrival of the first British pioneers, Spain had already established 160,000 settlers controlling five million natives, two universities (Mexico and Lima, both chartered in 1551), and about two hundred cities and towns in North and South America.

The following 170 years of colonization in British occupied North America would result in thirteen colonies scattered along the Eastern coast of today's United States, squeezed between the Appalachian Mountains and the Atlantic Ocean. Although in the first years of colonization the British had attempted to adopt land disposal practices that resembled the Portuguese *semarias*, that model was soon abandoned. Instead, the use of land for economic purposes and to encourage immigration and agricultural productivity sooner rather than later became the rule.[32]

In the United States, therefore, land was used as an important commodity for development from colonial times. It was sold – although often at cheap prices – to settlers and investors, or exchanged for infrastructure, instead of given away to those who had the right connections with the dominant class, as in Brazil.

Later on, immediately after gaining independence, the new country would undertake the most aggressive, comprehensive and successful process of colonization of new territories, that is, of territories that did not pertain to any of the original thirteen colonies[33] who had participated in the American War of Independence and signed the Articles of the Confederation in 1777.

Indeed, suffice to say that after independence the United States added more than two billion acres to its territory, roughly 92 percent of the country's total area today, not including the Commonwealth of Puerto Rico, the Virgin Islands, and the period when the United States dominated the Philippines. Table 22.1 illustrates the numbers.

[30] Warren Dean, note 2.

[31] Instituto Brasileiro de Geografia e Estatística (Brazilian Institute of Geography and Statistics) – IBGE Web site. Available at http://www.ibge.gov.br.

[32] Historical and geographical data provided about the United States in this work was obtained from Richard N. L. Andrew, *Managing the Environment, Managing Ourselves – A History of the American Environmental Policy* (Yale University Press, 1999), except where otherwise indicated.

[33] Not even the "Indian Country" territories (today, the states of Ohio, Indiana, and part of Michigan) belonged to any of the original states, which only had "claims" on such lands that had been ignored by the British, who before American independence had reserved the areas for its native subjects in a treaty.

Table 22.1. Growth of the United States after independence

Territory description	Size (in acres)	Percentage of America's current territory
America's current territory	2,264 million	100
Original territories of the 13 colonies at the time of independence (1776)	175 million	7.73
Annexation of the Indian Country (1783)	541 million	23.8
Annexation of the area of the central states (French Louisiana purchase – 1803)	523 million	23.1
Annexation of Spanish Florida (1819)	43 million	1.9
Annexation of the "Republic of Texas" (1845)	79 million	3.48
Annexation of the southern part of the Oregon region in the Northwest (1846)	180 million	7.9
Annexation of the Northern Mexican territories (1848)	334 million	14.75
Annexation of other Mexican territories to the Southwestern part (1853)	19 million	0.84
Alaska purchase from Russia (1867)	365 million	16.12
Annexation of the Republic of Hawaii (1898)	6.42 million	0.28
Total of annexed territories	2,089 million	92.27

Conversely, when Brazil declared independence, its boundaries were almost the same as those that are seen on maps today, as the conquest of the bulk[34] of the Brazilian territory had occurred during its colonial period and not afterwards. Indeed, by the end of the seventeenth century, the Portuguese crown was interested in finding new sources of income other than the already diminishing *brazilwood* exploitation and sugarcane production. This led to the financing of colonial enterprises and, in particular, to Portuguese support for the *bandeiras.*

The *bandeiras* were expeditions that penetrated into the interior of Brazil in the search for riches and natives for slavery. To a great extent, these expeditions achieved Portuguese objectives. In addition, although they did not result in the actual occupation of all the territory that was being explored, at least they helped draw the borders of the future country.

In addition, by the middle of the seventeenth century, a clash between the Portuguese and Spanish on one side and the Dutch on the other had resulted in the weakening of the Portuguese position in the East Indies, leading to increased interest in the Brazilian colony. In fact, that situation would make the Portuguese endure a disadvantageous colonial enterprise in Brazilian lands until they succeeded in cultivating spice plants in Brazil, the same plants that had previously led them to the East. For that purpose, in 1677, the Portuguese enacted several regulations encouraging the populating of the

[34] Even considering the territories that Brazil retained after independence as a result of dispute resolution with neighboring countries as annexation, they do not represent more than 10 percent of the total of the Brazilian territory today. They are estimated as amounting to 211 million acres. Source: Brazilian Foreign Affairs Ministry Web site. Available at http://www.mre.gov.br/acs/diplomacia/portg/h_diplom/rv014.htm.

new lands. They also provided for the confiscation of nonproductive properties in the colony in order for them not to cause "damage to the public good."[35]

The northeastern sugar industry experienced a severe decline from the middle seventeenth century, following the expulsion of the Dutch from Brazil and their subsequent partnership with the English in the sugar market of the West Indies, mainly in the Antilles and the southern United States.

Nevertheless, the characteristics of the northeastern sugar and stock breeding industries acquired during the sugar production economy times would remain as a strong influence for the formation of the twentieth-century Brazilian economy.[36] The low maintenance cost of both activities once they were established – cheap or slave workforce, no new technology, and so on – encouraged the producers to continue their activities even when sugar prices plunged. The means of production could not be put to alternative uses. The process continued steadily, with the sugarcane industry losing force while the cattle-breeding sector saw a slight increase for subsistence reasons. "The Northeast was converted from a high productivity economic system into an economy in which the major part of the population produced only what was necessary for its bare existence."[37]

The decay of the sugarcane cycle and the need for a subsistence alternative led to the rise of small low productivity units and, as a result, to the "extinction of the more complex forms of social intercourse, and the substitution of the general law by local custom."[38] Nevertheless, even in their decadence, the sugarcane farms remained as the main – if not the only – source of revenue to the Portuguese and to the colony as a whole, a situation that gave the owners of sugarcane mills more power.

As a result, one other feature of the sugarcane cycle would have a lasting effect on Brazil society: the *senhor de engenho* (lord of the sugarcane mill). He was – and in many parts of Brazil still is – both the law and the final word in the business of those who lived within his *latifúndio*: his wife, children, workers, and whoever else dared to venture onto his land. In reality, the range of his influence usually extended far beyond the borders of his property because the sugarcane *latifúndio* was the only remaining economic reference for the other activities that depended on it for survival. As Brazil remained basically rural until the end of the first half of the twentieth century, other categories of rural lords arose to join the *senhores de engenho* in forming a rural oligarchy that would rule the country from their farms: the *barões do café* (coffee barons), the *caudilhos* (from the south) and cattle ranchers from the *State of Minas Gerais.*

The population in Brazil, nonetheless, grew with the beginning of a new cycle of exploitation, this time of gold. The new economic rush began at the beginning of the eighteenth century in what is today the State of Minas Gerais, leading to a tenfold increase in the number of Portuguese living in Brazil.[39]

As a result of the success of the gold cycle, Brazil was raised to the category of Vice-Kingdom in 1763, when the capital of the colony was moved from the City of Salvador, today the capital of the State of Bahia, to the City of Rio de Janeiro, where the mining business could be better controlled.

[35] Anne Helen Wainer, note 5.
[36] Celso Furtado, note 25.
[37] Ibid.
[38] Ibid.
[39] Celso Furtado, note 25.

This change in political status did not change Brazil, which remained agrarian, undeveloped, and focused on the production of a limited range of goods for exportation. In addition, the country imported everything it needed, not only because of the limitations imposed by the court on attempts to establish any kind of industry, but chiefly for the lack of interest in creating new lines of production, as money could be made in easier ways. The impact of the chase for a fast return, whether from gold or sugarcane, was reflected in the limited amounts of land set aside for the production of food staples, despite the regulatory efforts of the crown to alter that scenario.

From the standpoint of land distribution, the process for granting new properties for mining did not generate conflicts with the *sesmarias*, which had previously been granted, as the development was now being driven toward the unoccupied interior of the territory.

Although important in terms of the consolidation of the territory, the first three hundred years of Brazilian colonization had only borne witness to the Atlantic Forest and parts of the inland (called *sertão* – from desertão, meaning "big desert") giving way to sugarcane plantations, *brazilwood* extraction, cattle breeding, gold mining, and forced labor, of both natives and Africans. There had been no project for planned occupation and development, neither from the court or from the Brazilian inhabitants. It was a model based on the wasteful use of vast tracts of rural property endowed to those that had the right connections, the intensive exploitation of natural resources and merciless slavery. Land, nature, and men were at the service of colonial greed and the sole interest was to make money, without regard to building a new homeland.

Therefore, another important factor that differentiated the two colonial experiences was that settlements were established in British America, whereas there was no effective policy from Portugal or genuine interest from the Portuguese to actually establish themselves in Brazil. This is usually explained by two factors: first, the effortlessness with which profits were extracted from the Brazilian territory, attracting audacious adventurers, rather than settlers to the new lands; and second, the lack of manpower in Portugal, which meant that there was no surplus to send to the colony.

At this point, it is worthwhile noting, by contrast, that the British colonial enterprise in America had only been launched after more than a hundred years of virtual inaction, for, among other causes, including religious disputes, precisely the opposite reason, that is, because of overpopulation.[40]

It is interesting to note when looking at the entire colonial period how advantageous it was for the United States not to have the same "economic appeal" as Brazil. Because of the different degree of importance the two colonies presented to their respective courts, and to the diverse motivation that advanced the interests of the European courts with regard to their respective new lands, the very pace of the colonisation process saved British America from one more century of colonial exploitation and conflict with Britain. In addition, when colonisation really began, the impetus of the British *settlers* toward the new land diverged completely from that of the Portuguese *conquerors*.

Moreover, the political turmoil in England, at the time that colonisation took place, was of great significance, in that it kept the British court reasonably busy with its own internal issues. Meanwhile, the new settlers in the colonies were allowed to carry out their projects in their new homeland in a less turbulent and demanding environment.[41]

[40] Ibid.

[41] Ibid.

Indeed, thanks to such projects, the American colonies were able to achieve a good economic position before gaining independence. This was fundamental to allow the colonies not only to wage the War of Independence against Britain but also to do so at the same time as it developed internal policies that would pave the road to its position of global leadership in the future.

Nevertheless, in one way or another, the fact is that in both Brazil and the United States, at the moment of their independence, the majority of lands were still in public hands. In the case of the new territories annexed by the United States, these also would help build up the amazing stock of public lands. In fact, in the United States, not less than 78 percent of the territory was originally owned by the federal government, and even today roughly a third of the country belongs to this entity.

The historian William Cronon has stated that the:

> U.S. economic wealth came not so much from the application of human labor to the environment [...] but rather from the ease with which limited labor could appropriate the vast abundance of natural value present in the landscape, which had been stored in the public lands by natural processes over millennia before the arrival of Europeans and their export trade economy.[42]

In a slight, although crucial, variation of Cronon's rationale, it could be stated that the difference between Brazil and the United States was not only in terms of the *ease* of the appropriation processes that took place in each country. The distinction also could be seen in to what extent and how quickly public entities made public lands available so that they could be appropriated by private parties. The manner in which those actions were taken amounted to a governmental strategy that completely changed the face of the American land in less than a century, driving human occupation and infrastructure westward, allowing a framework capable of sustaining the appropriation of the natural resources as referred to by Cronon. In other words, the basic dissimilarity resulted from the way public lands were administered and disposed of; or, more accurately, how public land in the one case, Brazil, was handled as a mere privilege of the dominant classes, and, in the other case, the United States, as a valuable commodity in the process to foster territorial occupation and economic growth.

3 LAND AND POLICY

Following independence, both Brazil and the United States kept the juridical systems of the former courts in effect. English *common law* continued to be applied for a long time in the United States, "except those parts which were 'repugnant' to the local constitution or to the rights of the citizens."[43] In Brazil, as observed before, the *Filipinas Ordinances* remained applicable in great part until the first Brazilian Civil Code was enacted in 1916.

In contrast to what happened after independence in Brazil, the United States, immediately after acquiring its sovereignty, initiated a debate about the best policies to adopt regarding public lands. The discussion was epitomised by the controversy between Thomas Jefferson and Alexander Hamilton:

[42] As cited by Richard N. L. Andrews, note 32.

[43] Philip S. Anderson, *Public Trust and Confidence in the Justice System*, in Com*mon Law, Common Values, Common Rights – Essays on Our Common Heritage by Distinguished British and American Authors* (West Group, 2002), 13.

> Jefferson advocated distributing public lands directly to settlers, in small parcels at nominal prices. Hamilton, in contrast, advocated selling public lands, primarily in large blocks, to 'moneyed individuals and companies, who will buy to sell again, and associations of persons, who intend to make settlements themselves.[44]

During U.S. history, those two opposing ideals would alternate positions in driving American land disposal policies, with Jeffersonian opinions eventually prevailing. However, although public land was sometimes disposed of at very low prices, whether to favor a class of large or small property owners, the fact is that in the United States, after independence, land was not given away or disposed of without an economic purpose in mind but, instead, either was sold or offered in exchange for the construction of infrastructure improvements by the private beneficiary.

In the United States, the first use of public land as a commodity had been during the War of Independence, when the colonies distributed about 2.6 million acres of land bounty warrants, "an area somewhat larger than the state of Colorado,"[45] to encourage military enlistment.

Soon after the end of the war, the United States enacted the first legal provisions for land disposal. The Land Ordinance of 1785 and the Land Act of 1796 created a framework for the opening of public land transactions in the country. The laws regulated aspects such as the size of the lands, price, and how the sale should be carried out. The practice adopted was the selling of land blocks in large units ("quarter-townships of 5,120 acres, alternating with 640 acre sections"),[46] by means of auctions, at a minimum price of $5 per acre, with the interested party paying 5 percent in advance and the rest of the price within one year. The limited availability of individual settlers who could afford the terms of the purchase ended up benefiting land companies and investors, as did the fact that no maximum limit of acreage that could be acquired by the interested party had been established.

One of the most important issues, however, was the possibility of allowing the public to choose where these lands would be located, as can be seen in some southern states. The alternative was for the government to organise the process of occupation as the population expanded westward. Free access to land appeared to benefit the use of only the best tracts, favoring speculation. In the end, the system adopted in New England prevailed, with the government establishing:

> clear and systematic boundaries, compact and orderly development patterns, and easy record keeping to prevent claim disputes. Both northern and southern congressmen agreed, therefore, that the 1785 ordinance should incorporate this system.... Its legacy is visible in any aerial of the Midwest: the entire region is laid out in townships six mile square, each divided into thirty-six sections of 640 acres each.... Four of the sections in each township were reserved for government purposes, and one for public schools.[47]

Not even the rush of settlers in the search for new lands that had not yet been designated discouraged the government from its policy, although this policy was one that "followed the settlers rather than leading them."[48]

[44] Richard N. L. Andrews, note 32.
[45] Ibid.
[46] Ibid.
[47] Ibid.
[48] Ibid.

The public land disposal issue in the United States was so intensely debated that before Brazilian independence, the U.S. government had already enacted another three laws regulating the public land disposal system:

- Harrison Frontier Act of 1800, conceding four years' credit for the acquisition of public lands;
- 1804 Law:
  - extending credit to six years;
  - requiring no interest over the balance not yet paid;
  - reducing the minimum size of the land to one-quarter, that is, to 160 acres.
- Land Act of 1820:
  - reducing minimum prices to $1.25 per acre;
  - requiring full cash payment, instead of conceding credit.

Part of the profits made from the sale of public land was used to finance transportation infrastructure to facilitate colonization and the exploitation of the natural resources of the new lands, as well as to carry their production to the East. Five percent of the income generated from land sales went to the state where the land was situated, and 2 percent was invested by the federal government in the construction of roads and further infrastructure developments capable of advancing the policies of land disposal and settlement. The other revenues raised from the sale of public lands helped the nation pay the public debt resulting from the War of Independence, so that in 1806 the U.S. government already had a substantial budget surplus. This led Jefferson to demand the investment of the money in "'roads, rivers, canals, and other objects of public improvement,' rather than reducing taxes."[49]

In 1808, a system of roads and canals formed part of a report prepared for the American Senate, which turned out to be the embryo of a development mechanism financed by the use of public land as a commodity. The U.S. government immediately began to donate rights-of-way to the states for road construction. The American land disposal policy was so aggressive that by 1819 roughly nineteen million acres of public land had been transferred to private initiative.

In Brazil, conversely, independence in 1822 only served to demonstrate that the rural oligarchy had already been, to all intents and purposes, the *de facto* ruling class of the country. Even the urban elite and the bourgeoisie in Brazil were derived from the power of the *latifundiários*. Therefore, it was unsurprising that the fate of the country would continue to be connected to the landowner class, which would bring about all the major political changes for centuries to come.

In terms of land policy, one of the first measures of the new Brazilian Empire was to revoke the system of *sesmarias* in July 1822. The end of the *sesmarias* system, however, did not mean any change in the status quo of those who had already been granted land, nor any harm to the *latifundios*.

The first Brazilian Constitution was promulgated in 1824. It was the emperor's "version," as he had disliked the text first approved by parliament, because, in his opinion, his work was "much more democratic." One of the functions of the constitution was to secure *sesmarias* rights in existence before independence, in Article 179, XXII.

[49] Ibid.

For Brazil, sovereignty did not mean a true opportunity for the country to build its own political identity. Although the Hamilton–Jefferson debate[50] was reproduced in Brazil, to some extent, it took place in a very different political and cultural environment than in the United States. Suffice to say that three hundred years of colonial government, with the distribution of public land based solely on the quality of the beneficiaries' connections with the crown, could not have fostered a propitious environment for a sound land disposal policy. Land distribution had repeatedly worked to favor those who dominated the production of income generating goods. The truth is that there had not been a policy at all but merely a means for the rural oligarchy to evolve.

At that time, Jeffersonian ideas about the need to foster a class of small farmers were to some extent replicated in Brazil by José Bonifácio,[51] although without success, for his opponents were the powerful *latifundiários*, striving to keep their privileges.[52]

In addition, if, on the one hand, the westward expansion of the British American colonies before American independence had been hampered by the crown policy with its neighbors and by geographical limitations, the inward colonisation of Brazil, on the other hand, had been contained by economical stagnation and the *latifúndio* owners.

The discussion concerning a new policy for public lands remained in a stalemate for about thirty years in Brazil. The eventual outcome was the *Lei de Terras e Imigração* (Law of Lands and Immigration), which was not enacted until 1850. During this time, no measures were adopted that gave an economical destination to public land.

Moreover, the climate created by the absence of a land disposal policy and by the lack of the presence of the central authority had facilitated the proliferation of squatters, whose claims and practices would be an additional issue for the new Brazilian government. Bessa Antunes argues that the combination of the rejection of the *sesmarias* method and the fact that no other legal system regulating property was established in Brazil to fill its place were two elements that were seen as legitimising the situation of squatters based on *posse* (possession), that is, *de facto* appropriation of the land.

Meanwhile, in the United States, the policies that used public lands to aid economic growth were reinforced. In addition, the strategy of building river canals to smooth the progress of trade and commerce westward was set in place. This policy was encouraged by means of the enactment of the Rivers and Harbors Act, in 1824, directing funds to the Army Corps of Engineers to work on the project. In that same year, in *Gibbons v. Ogden*, the U.S. Supreme Court confirmed the power of the Union over navigable waters based on the commerce clause in the U.S. Constitution. In 1827, the country disposed of public lands to investors effectively in order to fund canal construction. "The grants [...] donated alternate 640-acre sections on either side within five miles of the route, throughout the length of the canal,"[53] with a guarantee to the investor, after 1838, of another tract, within six to fifteen miles of the canal, for every prior claim in existence on the land granted to him, the so-called lieu lands.

Also in terms of land disposal policy, the United States enacted the Preemption Act in 1830. The law made it possible for settlers to buy lands directly from the government,

[50] In terms of access to land in the United States, which took place just after American independence.
[51] A prominent advocate of the cause of independence.
[52] Paulo de Bessa Antunes, note 10.
[53] Richard N. L. Andrews, note 32.

paying the minimum price required by the government, without participating in auctions. "The effect was to open up virtually the entire public domain to entry and staking claims."[54] The law was ratified by another statute in 1841 and expanded by the 1854 Graduation Act, which "graduated" "the price downward for public lands left unsold (to a dollar per acre after ten years, and as little as twelve and one-half cents per acre after thirty years).

The Californian gold rush and the coincidental annexation of the areas taken from Mexico that later on would become California, Nevada, Arizona, and Utah took place in 1848. At the same time, the demands for the construction of transcontinental railroads increased tremendously, in such a way that:

> between 1862 and 1871 the federal government granted over ninety-four million acres directly to railroad companies. Initial grants typically gave the railroads a right-of-way plus ten alternate sections per mile, plus the right to take timber and stone from the public lands, as well as thirty-year government loans. Later grants gave them sections per mile, and let the railroads select lieu lands virtually anywhere else.
>
> * * *
>
> The railroad thus became the most active and effective promoters of the westward settlement, luring both settlers and investors far beyond the previous areas of settlement and promoting commodity use and tourism as well as further displacement of the indigenous people.
>
> The transportation grants were the most powerful government policy incentives to promote immigration, settlement, and economic exploitation of the continent's assets.[55]

In Brazil, the Brazilian Law of Lands and Immigration was born obsolete. It was not a framework for a policy of land disposal or the utilization of natural resources. Indeed, it emerged as a mere, haphazard attempt to regulate the situations created by the past chaotic system of the *sesmarias* and the consequences it had generated. The law concentrated on the administration of four situations:[56]

a) public lands that had not yet been distributed, called *terras devolutas* (reverted[57] lands);
b) *sesmarias*, in which the definitive ownership had been conferred to the proprietors, according to the Imperial Constitution;
c) *sesmarias* whose claimants (called nonlegitimate *sesmeiros*) had not fulfilled all the legal requirements for the complete acquisition of the property rights over the land;
d) land squatted by persons with no ownership title.

In regard to the legitimate *sesmarias*, the law did not disturb what it considered vested rights. The nonlegitimate *sesmeiros* had their situation validated (Article 2).

Concerning *terras devolutas*, it is relevant to describe the limits of the concept adopted by the law. According to Article 3 of the statute, *terras devolutas* were those that:

[54] Ibid. [55] Ibid.

[56] Otávio Mello Alvarenga, as cited by Paulo de Bessa Antunes.

[57] "[R]reverted, that is, to the crown, which thereby asserted its original ownership," Warren Dean, note 2.

- were not in use for some national, provincial, or municipal public purpose;
- were not subjected to private domain, based on any legitimate title, *sesmarias*, or otherwise;
- were not squatted by parties whose rights of possession were acknowledged by the law.

Article 19 of the statute contained an important innovation about *terras devolutas*: it established that ownership over such public lands could only be acquired by a private party by means of a purchase and no longer bestowed, with the exception of lands situated within sixty square kilometers of the borders of the country with foreign nations, which could still be disposed of gratuitously.

Article 12 of the Law of the Lands established that *terras devolutas* had to be set aside for:

- indigenous colonization [*sic*];
- the foundation of settlements, road construction, and other services, and the establishing of public facilities;
- naval construction.

Article 5 of the statute validated, with conditions that seemed intentionally obscure, the *posses* (possessions, i.e., the rights of the squatters with no title) that had been exerted until that date without any third-party claims. There can be no doubt that this decision played a great part in contributing to the confused ownership system that still plagues Brazil today.

However, the most interesting aspect of the statute was its tentative effort to establish a policy to make access to public lands and the methods of their disposal more democratic. Article 14 provided a set of provisions concerning the standardisation of relatively small size of tracts, procedures for the auction, price, and conditions of payment (full price in cash). Article 16 set obligations on the part of the purchaser for a contribution to the local infrastructure, in terms of road construction, easements and rights-of-way, and access to water. Needless to say, the law, as often still happens in Brazil, "não pegou," that is, did not take hold.

The first delay came in the guise of an expected regulation, necessary for the application of the statute. It took four years for the government to promulgate the regulation which occurred in 1854. The main concern of the regulation, however, was to provide for the creation of a certain:

> General Department of Public Lands, for the measurement of the public lands, revalidation and legitimization of lands and of the procedures aiming at separating public from private property, measurement of lands under private domain based on legitimate title, sale of public lands, reserved lands, reverted lands situated at the borders of the Empire with foreign nations, conservation of reverted lands and other party's lands, record keeping of public lands.[58]

Only twenty-four years after the regulation of the Law of the Lands and Immigration the first reform of the statute was proposed, although the effects on the democratisation of access to public land to a class of small owners remained in the realm of good intentions. The same can be said of the expansion of Brazil to its western frontier, and

[58] Paulo de Bessa Antunes, note 10.

even today there are disagreements involving *sesmarias*, *terras devolutas*, and rights of possession.

During this period, in the United States brought the Homestead Act (1862), which symbolised the final triumph of Jeffersonian ideals. In spite of offering "virtually free public land to actual settlers [. . .] with the right to sell it to someone else so long as the government was paid its due,"[59] the importance of the law for the future of public land in the United States during the twentieth century cannot be underestimated.

In the United States, the ratio of settlements was of seven to ten million acres per year until 1922. In addition, in the nineteenth century, the federal government endowed 148.3 million acres, the equivalent to 6.6 percent of present-day American territory, to the sectors of roads (3.4 million), canals (13.9 million), and railroads (131 million, of which 94 million went directly to private corporations).

In short, the use of public land in the American history "ranked with the tariff as the foremost domestic political issues in the United States, other than slavery,"[60] whereas in Brazil the lack of democratic debate in the past is probably the foremost cause for today's agrarian and urban conflicts. The direct result of the settlement policies and the use of public lands as a valuable commodity in the United States was that "[. . .] by 1890 the superintendent of the census would declare that the unsettled frontier no longer existed."[61]

4 CONCLUSION

As anticipated at the beginning, the United States was the clear "winner" of the "environmental degradation race." Its "prize" could not have been better described than by the words of the author whose work has inspired this chapter:

> In effect, [the U.S. land disposal] policies legalised and promoted all-out commercialization and exploitation of the environment for immediate, private economic gain: what was good for settlers and developers was presumed to be good for the country.
>
> These policies, however, radically transformed the landscape and led to the waste and destruction of its resources. Loggers denuded the Midwestern forests, sometimes for settlement but more often they simply felled the trees and moved on, leaving stumps and often continuing fires behind. Southern farmers exhausted the soil and moved west to new lands rather than put greater expense into fertilization. Hydraulic mining eroded entire hills and mountainsides, washing their soil downstream, Commercial hunting wiped out the passenger pigeon, nearly led to the extinction of the plains bison herds, and destroyed beaver and other species over large areas of their former ranges. The construction of flood control levees 'reclaimed' large areas of riparian lowlands, but in the process exacerbated of catastrophic flooding and silting downstream and encouraged development in low-lying areas at risk of catastrophic future floods. Overall, the United States developed into a prosperous, continental nation, but at a cost of enormous environmental transformation and in some cases permanent destruction.[62]

[59] Richard N. L. Andrews, note 32.
[60] Frank E. Smith, as cited by Richard N. L. Andrews, note 32.
[61] Richard N. L. Andrews, note 32. [62] Ibid.

In Brazil, by contrast, roughly 50 percent of the territory – if not more – lies waiting in pristine condition for whatever destiny has reserved for it. There are still native races inside the Brazilian territory that have never had contact with the white man.

By contrast, Brazil has destroyed 92 percent of the Atlantic Forest ecosystem. From the "discovery" to the 1970s, only 4 percent of Amazonia had been degraded. In the last thirty years, Amazonian degradation is estimated to have increased twofold, as a result, among other reasons, of erroneous measures to encourage the occupation of the rain forest territory, in the pursuit of "economic development."

The worst part is to realise that the process of Brazilian degradation is not so modest, and has been far more inefficient than the American equivalent, as it has not provided advantages in terms of the improvement of living conditions for the Brazilian population.

The land issue in Brazil today is explosive. The Brazilian writer Zuenir Ventura has stated that the distress is so great that the MST, the organization of landless workers, and their equivalents in the urban areas do not advocate an agrarian reform but, rather, a revolution.[63] If from the institutional standpoint the situation is unbearable, for the environmental future of the country's natural resources it signifies disaster. For example, according to the INPE,[64] Brazilian National Institute of Space Research,[65] until 1980 the chief sources of deforestation in Amazonia were agricultural and cattle breeding projects, financed by the federal government, which was interested in settling migrants from the southern states of Brazil. The major cause of the problem today, after the failure of the settlement plans, are agricultural activities carried out on small properties, with a great deal of the responsibility for deforestation being credited to the landless.

The history of misguided policies for public land disposal in Brazil explains many of the causes of agrarian and urban conflicts in Brazil nowadays. It is estimated that 44 percent of rural areas are in hands of only 1 percent of the rural land owners considered as a whole.[66]

The urban disarray is a direct result of a long-lasting exodus from rural areas, resulting from the lack of opportunities in the interior of the country. In 1940, only 31 percent of the Brazilian population lived in cities.[67] Today, 81 percent of the Brazilian population lives in urban areas.[68] Contrary to what some superficial reports have recently suggested, this data does not merely reflect a regular global trend. In contrast to what happens in other countries such as the United States,[69] where the mechanisation of agriculture has eliminated the need for large-scale manpower, in the Brazilian countryside,

[63] Zuenir Ventura, "À beira de um Ataque de Nervos" (At the Edge of a Nervous Breakdown), *O Globo* (Brazilian newspaper) online, 26 July 2003. Available at http://oglobo.globo.com/jornal/colunas/zuenir.asp.

[64] Instituto Nacional de Pesquisas Espaciais.

[65] Thomas Traumann, "Os Novos Vilões" (The New Villains), *Veja* (Brazilian Magazine), 4 February 1998.

[66] See Betto Frei (this gentlemen is known as Frei Betto, which means literally "Friar" Betto), *Terra Encharcada de Sangue* (Land Soaked in Blood), on the MST Web site at http://www.mst.org.br/informativos/mstinforma/mst_informa44.htm.

[67] Source, Instituto Brasileiro de Geografia e Estatística – IBGE. Available at http://www1.ibge.gov.br/home/estatistica/populacao/censohistorico/1940_1996.shtm.

[68] Ibid.

[69] Seventy-nine percent of the American people live in urban centers. Source: U.S. Census. Available at http://www.census.gov/population/censusdata/table-4.pdf and http://factfinder.census.gov/servlet/DTTable?ds_name=D&geo_id=D&mt_name=DEC_ 2000_SF1_U_P002&_lang=en.

regardless of the performance of some agricultural sectors, the bulk of the arable lands are still waiting for the Industrial Revolution. In other words, the Belindia concept is well represented in the agricultural areas. Additionally, the phenomenon of urbanization in Brazil is far more concentrated than it is in the United States, because the number of Brazilian urban centers is much smaller.

None of this means that the American model is to be followed. On the contrary, it once again shows that not everything that is good for the United States may necessarily be good for Brazil.

However, the truth is that both the *favelas* (shantytowns) and the rural conflicts are the reflection of the equivocal land policies so far adopted in Brazil or rather the lack of policies that could responsibly address the land issue in the country.

By contrast, the *favelização* (the growth of shantytowns) in the urban areas and squatting in the rural areas are considered to be the worst environmental villains in terms of devastation of environmentally protected areas.

In addition, a significant proportion of public-owned land contains natural resources and commodities that could be exploited in order to generate jobs and revenue for the country to deal with its social problems.

Does Brazil have the right, as a sovereign nation, to promote the use of its available land and to freely dispose of its natural riches, disregarding the arguments in defense of the environment made by the governments and peoples of other nations, principally developed countries, including the United States? Should the social demands and the land claims of the destitute be granted at the sacrifice of the environment?

Certainly, such questions cannot be answered with a simple "yes" or "no." However, they cannot be addressed without looking back at a history that explains so much of so many present disparities, on which this chapter has attempted to cast some light in order to help discuss common but differentiated responsibilities.

23 Protecting Ecological Functions: Ecological Function Zoning and Conservation Zones in the PRC

Qun Du*

1 BACKGROUND

The major flooding of the Songhua River and Nenjiang River in North-east China in 1998 was the first time that People's Republic of China (PRC) had to face a chaotic disaster that could be attributed solely to poor management of the water, land and forest resources. By 2000 a cycle of frequent and severe dust storms was occurring each spring in Northern China, with more than 20 such episodes in 2002.

These disastrous meteorological phenomena happened in a brief period, and heightened social and political concerns about ecological conservation including natural forest management in northeastern regions. One of the most significant policy responses was that the State Council issued the *National Compendium of the Conservation of Ecological Environment* (NCCEE)[1] in 2000. The NCCEE determined that natural disasters were driven more by human action than by natural forces such as unusual weather. The irrational management and abuse of land, water, and other natural resources were the key human factors to cause adverse environmental effects. The NCCEE proposed a new instrument – ecological function zoning – to address sustainable land use, natural resource utilization, and industrial processing. The objective of ecological function zoning is to provide a scientific baseline to economic growth and safeguard sustainability of the environment.

The authority over ecological function zoning was delegated to two key ministerial-level agencies, the Western Development Leading Group Office (WDLGO) of the State Council and the State Environmental Protection Agency (SEPA). The nationwide demarcation and mapping of ecological function zoning commenced in August 2000. The first phase of ecological function zoning was carried out in the territory of Western Region of PRC by WDLGO, SEPA and all twelve provinces/regions' people's governments that belong to Western Region.[2] The Chinese Academy of Sciences

[1] As the Environmental Protection Law 1989 mostly addressed the regulation of industrial activities in urban or suburban areas, the NCCEE document has been recognized as one of the basic regulatory documents on the conservation of the natural/ecological environment, natural resource use and management, including impacts of agriculture, farming, mining, and so on.

[2] Original eleven provinces (Xinjiang, Gansu, Inner Mongolia, Shaanxi, Ningxia, Qinhai, Tibet, Yunan, Sichuan, Guizhou, and Guangxi) and the Municipality of Chongqing and other supplemented local areas

* Dr. Qun Du is Professor in environmental law and natural resources management, Tongji – UNEP Institute of Environmental Sustainable Development, Tongji University, Peoples' Republic of China. qdu@whu.edu.cn and Cochair of Specialist Group of Sustainable Use of Soil, Commission on Environmental Law, IUCN. This research was one of outcomes of the Research Project of National Science Foundation of PRC (No. 40471056).

(CAS) also participated in the preparatory work of ecozoning in the western region in 2000.

Also in 2002, in the tenth five-year plan for Environmental Protection, WDLGO and SEPA formulated a technical guide for ecological function zoning – the *Interim Rules for Ecological function zoning* (IREFZ) with support from the Centre of Ecological Science of CAS. The IREFZ was issued and took effect on 1 September 2002.[3] By October 2002, provinces or regions in the western region had almost completed the provincial/regional scheme of ecological function zoning. By the middle of 2003, most of provinces/regions in the western region completed their draft work of ecological function zoning. In June 2003, the second phase of national-level ecological function zoning commenced. It focused on ecological function zoning in middle and eastern China. The provinces in the middle and east China[4] conducted provincial/regional investigation of ecological status, and afterward formulated ecological function zoning schemes in late 2003.[5] In June 2004, the second phase of ecological function zoning was completed.

The third phase of ecological function zoning was carried out by SEPA at the national level. In September 2004, the National Technical Expert Group for Ecological Function Zoning (NTEGEFZ) completed the *Draft of National Ecological Function Zoning* by combining the outputs from the first and second phases, and incorporating appropriate data from the draft prepared by each provincial/regional people's government. All feedback and comments on the draft had been collected by experts of the NTEGEFZ of SEPA, and used to modify and improve the *Draft of National Ecological Function Zoning.* In November 2004, NTEGEZ prepared the final version of *National Ecological Function Zoning* for approval by SEPA.

The approved *National Ecological Function Zoning* is a basis for each province/region to revise its draft *Provincial/Regional Ecological Function Zoning.* However, these draft versions will not have official status or be legally binding until the respective provincial/regional people's government has approved it. Some provincial/regional people's governments are more advanced than others.

2 THE PROCESS OF ECOLOGICAL FUNCTION ZONING

2.1 Rationale of Ecological Function Zoning

Ecological functions refer to the service value of natural ecological system that supports human society and economic development; therefore, it is also called "Ecological Service Function" in the Chinese context. The PRC is experiencing an ecological-environmental crisis that impacts on urban and rural areas and threatens economic growth. Manifestations, such as water and soil erosion, land degradation, desertification, elimination of biodiversity, frequent natural disasters, and environmental pollution, are a result of the destruction and deterioration of ecological service functions. The main goal of implementation of ecological protection and construction is to recover and reconstruct the degraded ecological system and their service functions.

constitute the territory of the Western Region. For the provinces/regions of middle and eastern China, see note 4.

[3] *Science Times*, Beijing, 12 September 2002, written by Zhang Qi Yao.

[4] Middle and eastern China includes Beijing, Shanghai, Tianjing, Hebei, Shangxi, liaoning, Jilin, Heilongjiang, Jiangsu, Zhejiang, Anhui, Fujiang, Jiangxi, Shangdong, Henan, Hubeii, Hunan, Guangdong, and Hainan.

[5] SEPA, Document No. [2003] 408, 15 August 2003.

Ecological function zoning depends on differentiating ecological areas according to the environmental elements, environmental sensitivity and mapping the spatial differences according to ecological service functions. The purpose is to provide a scientific basis for: (i) making regional plans of ecological environmental protection and construction; (ii) maintaining regional ecological safety; (iii) guiding the rational use of resources including the overall arrangement of industry and agriculture; and (iv) preserving the regional ecological environment. The purpose of this ecological function zoning is: first, to highlight the importance of service functions of regional ecological systems and ecological environmental sensitivity, and to provide a scientific basis for rational land use (economic and social development plan, ecological environmental protection and construction plan) and ecological environmental decision making; second, to strengthen integration and coordination and reinforce management in accordance with ecological functions and to break the traditional pattern of ecological system management based on exploitable elements (water, forest, etc.); and third, to underpin regulation and planning of industry structure and distribution within the various ecological zones, guide the rational use of natural resources, protect the environment, and recognize and acknowledge the service-providing and supporting function of the regional ecological environment.

In order to achieve these goals, ecological function zoning seeks to clarify the structure, process and characteristics of spatial distribution of ecological systems; shed light on major ecological environmental problems, causes and characteristics of spatial distribution; evaluate ecological service functions of different ecological systems and their effects on regional social and economic development; spell out the distribution characteristics of ecological environmental sensitivity and high sensitivity ecological zones; and clarify ecological environment and social and economic and social functions of each function zone.[6]

2.2 Method of Ecological Function Zoning

The method of ecological function zoning takes the following form:

- assessment of ecological environment status quo,
- assessment of ecological-environmental sensibility,
- assessment of importance of ecological service functions,
- provision of schemes of ecological function zoning, and
- development of a general description of each ecological zone.

The assessment of ecological environment status is the first step of systematic work of ecological function zoning. Status assessment requires analysis of characteristics of the regional ecological environment and the spatial differences so as to define the status and trend of major ecological-environmental problems. The assessment is carried out on the basis of regional ecological environmental survey with the aid of scientific methodologies and technologies, such as remote sensing, and geographical information system (GIS) The areas of assessment include: (i) extent and severity of land degradation

[6] The *Interim Rules for Ecological function zoning* (IREFZ), issued by the Western Development Leading Group Office (WDLGO) of the State Council and the State Environmental Protection Agency (SEPA), September 2002.

(wind-eroded desertification, salinization, water-eroded desertification); (ii) status of water resources and water environment; (iii) status and extent of natural vegetation and forest resources; (iv) biodiversity; (v) status of atmospheric environment including acid rain; (vi) status of sea beach and seashore; and (vii) frequency and severity of natural disasters related to ecological environmental protection (such as landslides, sandstorms, and floods) and other environmental problems (such as soil pollution, estuary pollution, red tides, agricultural nonpoint pollution, and industrial nonpoint source pollution).

The second step of ecological function zoning is the assessment of ecological sensitivity and the importance of ecological functions. The assessment of ecological sensitivity provides fundamental should-be indices for determining the leverage of the conservation of ecological functions in the assessed area. It helps environmental planners and natural resource users to (i) clarify the types of ecological problems in the region, including causal factors; (ii) make comprehensive analysis of sensitivity of particular and multiple ecological problems; and (iii) clarify the distribution characteristics of regional ecological sensitivity. The thematic areas of ecological sensitivity include soil erosion sensitivity, salinization sensitivity, stone desertification sensitivity, and acid rain desertification. The sensitivity assessment is generally classified into five levels, that is, extremely sensitive, very sensitive, medium, slightly sensitive, and not sensitive.

In order to recognize different service functions in the region and their effects and importance on regional sustainable development it is necessary to have a rigorous system of classification and assessment. The types of ecological service function include: (i) biodiversity conservation; (ii) water resources conservation at their source, in catchments and in lakes and rivers; (iii) soil maintenance, including control of desertification; and (iv) seashore protection. The importance of ecological service functions is assigned to one of four levels, that is, extremely important, medium important, important, not important.

Ecological function zone division is the third, and the most important, step of ecological function zoning. It refers to the process of geographical spatial division in accordance with ecological sensitivity, ecological service function importance, and similarities and differences of the characteristics of ecological environment. First, natural ecological zones are divided on a macroscale on the basis of natural climate and geological characteristics; second, subecological zones are divided on the basis of type of ecosystem and its functions; and finally, ecological function zones are formulated on the basis of the importance of ecological service functions, ecological environmental sensitivity, and the magnitude of existing or incipient ecological environmental problems. Boundaries are determined while taking into account natural characteristics such as mountains and rivers, and administrative boundaries. The result of ecological function zoning is shown by maps and charts. Basic maps should include relief maps, climate resources map, plantation maps, soil maps, maps of land use status quo, administrative division maps, and demography maps. Maps of natural division, climate division and agriculture division are also used. New products from the survey work include ecological environment status quo maps, ecological environmental sensitivity distribution maps, ecological service functions importance maps, and ecological function zoning maps.

The general description of ecological division is the summary of ecological function zoning and is the essential reflection of the zoning. It includes description of the following characteristics of each zone:

- natural geological conditions and climate features and typical ecological system types;
- major existing or potential ecological problems;
- driving forces and causes of ecological environmental problems;
- ecological sensitivity of ecological zones and possible major ecological problems;
- ecological function types of ecological zones and their importance; and
- ecological-environmental protection goals of ecological zones and the trend of ecological environment construction and development.

2.3 A Case of Ecological Function Zoning

The earliest case example of ecological function zoning in the PRC is *The Scheme of Ecological Function Zoning in Western China* (*the Scheme*), a concluding document of the ecological function zoning carried out in western China.[7] The scheme initially analyzed the status of the ecological environment in western China. The survey relied on a large existing database as well as new information collected by the teams. It indicated that western China is rich in natural resources and biodiversity, and plays a role in safeguarding the environment of the mainland region of China; however, its ecological functions are fragile and have been severely damaged and are deteriorating. The scheme then made individual analyses of ecological sensitivity and ecological function importance in western China. As for the zoning, the whole territory of western China was divided into 30 ecological zones, 104 subecological zones, and 686 ecological function zones, in which the dominant functional types of ecosystems included water resources conservation, biodiversity protection, water and soil conservation, sandstorm prevention, and ecological resource-supported social and economic development. In the scheme, for each ecological zone, status reports, problem analysis, and proposed protection measures were provided. Finally, the scheme identified twenty-two ecological function conservation zones in four functional types of ecosystems, among which were eight for water resources conservation, seven for biodiversity protection, three for water and soil conservation, and four for sand storm prevention. The scheme further identified existing challenges and potential threats for ecological function conservation zones, and put forward suggested protection measures.

3 THE REGULATORY ROLE OF ECOLOGICAL FUNCTION ZONING

3.1 A New Administrative Instrument

Ecological function zoning is a technical means to catalogue the physical attributes of land, water, and ecological functions. Administrators expect that it can be a new instrument in environmental administration. Mapping data provided by the ecological

[7] *The Scheme of Ecological Function Zoning in Western China*, issued by the Division of Ecosystem and Nature Conservation, SEPA, December 2004, Beijing.

function zoning depicts the status and trend for key natural resources, and physical profiles of ecological functions and mitigating factors. This enables decision makers and resources users to clearly understand the impact on nature of human activities and the interaction between natural change and human behavior. From the administrative point of view, ecological function zoning is a new and effective mechanism to integrate various types of planning on land, water, and other natural resources with social and economic development, and to regulate human behavior according to the types of ecological zones.

The State Council of PRC now requires that ecological function zoning be conducted at two levels – provincial/regional and national. Each level's ecological function zoning should be approved by its respective People's Government and issued to the public. The approved provincial/regional or national ecological function zoning is legally binding and cannot be easily changed. If change to the ecological function zoning is needed, it must go through procedures such as expert appraisal, adjustment of mapping, and governmental approval. (For the process of formulation of ecological function zoning, see Section 2 of this chapter.)

Specific roles of the ecological function zoning in environmental administration are initiated as follows:

1. Identification of national ecological function significance and special conservation zones. Areas with high sensitivity of ecological functions and high significance of ecological service value should be publicized and subjected to special regulative measures to restrict or regulate human activities.
2. Provision of a baseline for natural resource utilization and economic development. In the future, activities of natural resource use and land use should not alter the dominant ecological function of the area to the extent which the landscape could be irrevocably changed. An obligation is that all new constructive projects must be the subject of an ecological function effect-based environmental impact assessment (EIA). If the site of a new project is not in accordance with the approved provincial/regional ecological function zoning, it will not get approved in the course of EIA review. An existing operational project, whose site is not accordance with approved ecological function zoning, will face restrictive orders concerning suspension, disassembly, or relocation and closure in order to comply with ecofunction protection. Its obligation to rehabilitate the destroyed ecofunctions will remain in force.
3. Clarification of objectives of ecosystem protection and management in a given identified area. These objectives would be developed further into targets of ecosystem administration or management for relevant sectors, or be taken into account during routine operation of official ecosystem monitoring, supervision, and examination. More significantly, the ecological function zoning will provide illustrated ecological pictures for the public or administrative supervisors of how to judge or assess environmental accomplishments of head chief administrators within their jurisdiction. The existing situation of environmental management in the PRC is dominated by a top-down approach with a strong emphasis on economic growth. Generally speaking, governors take responsibilities for economic, social, and environmental development; in reality, most governors usually are constrained by quantitative targets for economic growth. The central government has drawn the attention of all

local levels to the fact that governors now need to be aware of environmental health and sustainability and that this will be part of the assessment of performance. The central government also intends to introduce regulations to intensify its ecological conservation mandate. To some extent, ecological function zoning is anticipated as a means to carry out this intent. In the future, governors will be obligated to protect environmental quality in their jurisdiction, with environmental loss and economic gain being two targets to assess their overall accomplishments. To monitor the efficiency of environmental governance, ecological function zoning will be a gauge to judge whether the environmental quality within the jurisdiction has deteriorated or is being conserved at a required standard. Governors who attain a bad record will face punishments, such as demotion or dismissal from their posts. This administrative responsibility could be extended to directors general of state-owned enterprises, the managers of construction projects or other ecoresources users.

4. Creation of a mechanism for various agencies to improve coordination and integrate decision making. Ecological function zoning itself is a mapping-based information system of ecosystem functions and service value that illustrates the bottom line of human interference with nature. Thus, it is a basic requirement that all activities of resources users be consistent with the ecological zoning.
5. Provision of the public with a comprehensive informative tool to participate in ecosystem management. Through this informative tool, the public will be able to understand ecofunction, get involved in the decision-making process and intervene in land-use supervision.

3.2 The Relationship with Existing Zoning and Planning

Zoning already exists and has operated for a long time. The role of ecological function zoning as a new means of environmental management to be introduced into the existing system has been questioned. There already is administrative zoning, geographical zoning, agricultural zoning, and marine function zoning. Administrative and natural zonings are fundamental, respectively, according to social-factored jurisdictional demarcation (e.g., a territory of province, city, and county) and geographical distribution (e.g., a river basin, a mountain). The agricultural and marine function zonings, targeted on industrial production in agriculture and fishery sectors, provide jurisdictional authorities for sectoral resource administration (e.g., the authority of agriculture, or the authority of marine fishery). As to the ecological function zoning, experts state that it is "a special ecological mapping," "a fundamental zoning,"[8] and of a cross-sectoral nature; and therefore, the ecological function zoning should be placed higher than other sectoral zonings in terms of policy function.[9] However, some practitioners in resource management have disagreed with this view.

Planning and zoning have similar connotations in areas of natural resource management. Many types of planning exist under the Chinese environmental and resources legislative frameworks water resource strategic planning, agricultural planning (including animal husbandry and freshwater fishery), land-use comprehensive planning,

[8] *Science Times*, "The Interim Rules for Ecological Function Zoning (IREFZ)" written by Zhang Qi Yao, 12 September 2002, Beijing.

[9] XinhuaNet, 13 September 2002 "Ecological Mapping and Zoning Taking Place in Provinces."

urban development, and construction planning, water and soil conservation planning, desertification control planning, ecological construction planning, and ecological-environmental protection planning, and so on. These types of planning all concern land-use and landscape change by allocation and utilization of natural resources. So what intervention will the ecological function zoning bring into the existing planning system?

Two aspects are likely to provoke conflict. On the one hand, the ideology of ecological function and ecosystem integrated management is understandable to decision makers and practitioners. There is an acceptance of the procedures of ecological function zoning under *the Interim Rules for Ecological Function Zoning* designed by WDLGO and SEPA. It is widely recognized that the system provides a more scientific approach and a rational instrument to conduct tasks of holistic environmental management. On the other hand, challenges to the implementation of ecological function zoning exist. The current management system of natural resources and environmental protection in the PRC is sectoral jurisdiction-based, lacking cross-sectoral cooperation and coordination. Ecological function zoning attempts to provide a framework in which dialogue can take place among resource management authorities when any agency/bureau plans its programs and projects. This should eliminate duplications or fill gaps. However, it is extremely difficult to have every authority committed to this new approach and its new terms of reference.[10]

4 THE CONCEPT OF ECOLOGICAL FUNCTION CONSERVATION ZONES

One objective of ecological function zoning is to provide government and others with fundamental information on ecological significance and environmental sensitivity of a given area and identify "special protected zones for ecological function-significant ecological function conservation zones" (EFCZs). The *National Compendium of Ecological Protection 2000* outlined a series of important areas, for example, origins of rivers and lakes, water sources, wind, and dust shelterbelts, which urgently need protection measures. The *Planning for the Construction of National Ecological Function Conservation Zones*, accomplished by SEPA in late 2004, specified short-term and long-term targets that the State should urgently establish thirty-one national EFCZs and encourage local governments to develop the preliminary administrative and regulatory framework. It will take fifteen to twenty years to establish a series of national EFCZs and develop the administrative, regulatory, and legal framework in this regard. The overall intent of EFCZs is to enhance the ecological functions of national key river basins and watersheds.[11]

4.1 Difference from Existing Nature Reserve Zones

There has been an argument that the EFCZ overlaps the nature reserve zone. However, these two are different in many respects, most importantly in their approaches to management. The former is land open to access; the latter is not. Chinese nature reserve zone systems rely on land closure. According to the *Regulation of Nature Reserve Zones*, except

[10] Discussion from the International Workshop on Integrated Ecosystem Management, held by GEF-PRC OP12, November 2004 Beijing.

[11] *China Environmental Newspaper*, 2 December 2004.

for the perimeter, where some scientific work is permitted, the land under the inner buffer zone and core zone is closed to humans. Hence, most land of nature reserve zones offers just ecological service with very little related social-economic benefit. The reform of nature reserve zone system from complete land closure to restricted land access has been urged. In the EFCZ, protection measures will target protection of dominant ecological functions in the area, and activities that are not linked to dominant ecological functions will be permitted to be conducted in a sustainable manner. The mandatory concept of EFCZs is in accordance with objective-orientated ecosystem management promoted by international practice of GEF and IUCN.

4.2 Links with IUCN Protected Areas System

EFCZs have unique features that also result in differences from the IUCN system of protected area management categories (1994).[12] However, there is some common aspects of the two systems. First, both rely on objectives-approached management, which is essentially neutral about the managing agency or landowner. More particularly, there is no presumption that any conservation area will be owned by the State. Second, conservation measures taken in conservation zones or protected areas are designed based on the degree of environmental modification implied by the human intervention.

However, the specific management objective of EFCZ in the PRC differs from the IUCN-protected areas. IUCN defines a protected area as an area of land/sea especially dedicated to the protection and maintenance of biological diversity as well as of natural and associated cultured resources, managed through legal and other effective means. The categories of IUCN-defined protected areas and PRC's EFCZs are thus different. The IUCN management system of protected areas (1994) (see Annex 1) gives six categories, each highlighting dominant objectives for protection: Category Ia – strict nature reserve/wilderness protection area managed mainly for science or wilderness protection; Category Ib – wilderness area/protected area managed mainly for wilderness protection; Category II – national park, managed mainly for ecosystem protection and recreation; Category III – natural monument, protected area managed mainly for conservation of specific natural features; Category IV – habitat/species management area, protected area managed mainly for conservation through management intervention; Category V – protected landscape/seascape, protected area managed mainly for landscape or seascape conservation or recreation; and Category VI – managed resource protected area, protected area managed mainly for the sustainable use of natural resource. The logical network of categories is shown in Figure 23.1. IUCN urged that land use such as mining and energy exploration should not be permitted in protected areas.[13]

Chinese EFCZ under SEPA's definition is an area dedicated to the protection and maintenance of ecological functions mainly in water catchments enhancement, water-eroded soil control, wind-eroded dust control, wind shelterbelts increase, and flood load of river/lake basins. The mandatory measures for ecological function conservation are aimed at alleviating adverse human interventions (their degree of environmental modification similar to IUCN PAs categories Ia/Ib and II/III) or introducing sound conservation programs, for example, forestation (their degree of environmental modification similar to IUCN PAs categories IV, V, and VI) for the preservation and rehabilitation

[12] See Annex 1 appended at the end of this Chapter. [13] Amman IUCN Congress 2000.

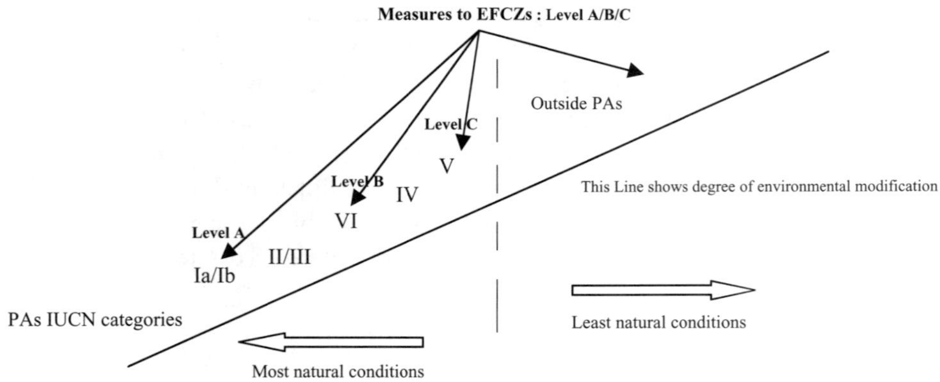

Figure 23.1. The degree of environmental modification implied by the PAs categories and measures for EFCZs.

of conservation zones' functions. According to *the National Compendium for Ecological Protection 2000 and the Guidelines of Formulation of Ecological Function Conservation Plan* (*Interim, 2003*), SEPA divides ecological function zones into six categories according as management objectives: (i) river/lake origin areas; (ii) flood control buffer area of rivers and lakes; (iii) important water catchments areas; (iv) wind shelterbelts and sand fixation areas; (v) water and soil conservation and rehabilitation areas; and (vi) important fishery areas.

Because the system of EFCZ aims at ecofunction conservation and rehabilitation, the judgment (if the area is to be included in EFCZs) is that it should be of significance to ecological function no matter how well the current preservation status of this area is. In other words, even if an area's current status of ecological function is severely deteriorated, if that area is defined as being of ecofunction importance to the region, it still qualifies as an EFCZ; and thus its function has to be rehabilitated by management and conservation projects or measures. This is unlike IUCN management system of protected areas, in which a protected area should be an area whose existing biological diversity and natural and associated cultured resources are in fairly good condition. Therefore, the EFCZs system does not fit well into the IUCN classification system.

Conservation measures in EFCZs are defined at three levels under the Guidelines of Formulation of Ecological Function Conservation Plan (Interim, SEPA, 2003):

Level A – restrictive conservation measures, applied to an area's whose existing ecofunction and associated natural resource and biodiversity are well-preserved; a land closure policy or current nature reserve zone system is recommended to apply;

Level B – regulative conservation measures, to areas where its natural ecosystem has deteriorated; a natural resource or land use ban and management program is imposed;

Level C – constructive conservation measures, to areas whose natural ecosystem and function are severely deteriorated; projects such as water and soil engineering projects and management programs are introduced.

The three levels of measures of EFCZs differ in the degree of human intervention from least to most modified conditions. This implies great conceptual commonality to the IUCN PAs categories, yet as noted earlier, differences remain.

Because the EFCZs is still an ongoing policy initiative in environmental protection in the PRC, little literature on it exists. In the publication of CCICED protected area study, Dr. Kishore Rao, however, commented on the links between EFCZs and PAs, saying that:

> ... from what little is known about the emerging concept of 'ecological function conservation areas', it appears that these seek to put in place conservation oriented land use planning at the broad landscape level or bioregional scale (ecological networks?) and, hence, appear to be more analogous to category V of the IUCN system, but sections could fall under other categories and the larger area could include several other types of protected areas. The maintenance of ecological functions and ecosystems service is considered very important from the Chinese perspective, not just for protecting biodiversity and, hence, the further development and use of the EFCA (EFCZ-author) approach would be extremely relevant.[14]

It needs to be stated that the EFCZs system does not aim at landscape management, although it does start from land-use planning and later impacts the landscape. Another point that also needs to be realized is that although the two systems are concerned with natural conservation, the ultimate intentions are different; the EFCZs system is clearly human needs-oriented and seeks a better flow of goods and services from the nature to human beings, whereas the PAs system is oriented more toward preserving nature.

5 INITIATING A REGULATION FOR ECOLOGICAL FUNCTION ZONING

The general intent underpinning ecological function zoning and EFCZs is to provide a technical tool to determine sustainable natural resources use and ecological conservation conducted in a scientific manner, hence to ensure the protection of ecosystem functions. With the national ecological function zoning and the planning of EFCZs being carried out, the State Council intends to formulate regulations to enhance environmental management by means of ecological function zoning and EFCZs.

Two draft regulations are under consideration. The first is a regulation that would impose ecological function zoning and EFCZs as the main means of environmental management, natural resource exploitation, and land use, and would be applicable to all related construction in the western region development. The proposal, initiated in October 2003 by the Western Region Development Office of State Council and SEPA,[15] was accepted by the legislative office of State Council in 2004, and was brought into the 2004 legislative agenda of State Council. In October 2004, the consultative draft *regulation for the supervision of environmental protection and conservation on the western region development* was completed and handed to State Council. The draft legitimates the system of ecological function zoning, and raises a number of regulatory measures reliant on ecological function zoning as follows:

- a comprehensive decision-making coordinative mechanism, for integrated land and natural resource planning and industrial planning;

[14] Kishore Rao, "Application of IUCN Protected Areas Categories System in the PRC," in Xie Yan, Wang Song, & Peter Schei, *China's Protected Areas* (Beijing, Tsinghua University, October 2004), 108.

[15] A feasibility study on ecological legislation was delegated to Resource College, Beijing Normal University in 2002–2003 by the Western Region Development Office and SEPA. The author was the principal legal expert of the study team.

- procedures of environmental impact assessment needed for planning programs;
- supervision over operations of conservation measures imposed on land-use or natural resource utilization and infrastructure projects;
- accountable environmental governance to prevent environmental harm;
- public surveillance in ecological function conservation;
- senior authority surveillance in ecological function conservation;
- monitoring and an early alarm system for ecological function deterioration; and
- ecological compensation scheme for EFCZs.

It is anticipated that this draft regulation will be approved soon. However, the legislative office of the State Council still questions this regulation. The key disputed points are not on the basic regulatory tool–ecological function zoning, but rather on its application and jurisdiction in the western region. First, the western region is a more of a politically created policy concept than an actual jurisdictional area; second, even if the western region did refer to a certain jurisdictional area, it is unusual for the State Council to create a regulation that applies only to a certain region rather than to the nation as a whole.[16] Optimistically, the State Council will still support this regulation when considering the great ecological significance of the western region and even that of the whole nation.

A draft regulation on EFCZs is also expected to be issued by the State Council. The feasibility study is still ongoing on this draft regulation. The main issue is how to coordinate EFCZs with other types of zones being operated in the PRC, including nature reserve zones, forestry parks, scenic sites, and geological parks. In the tenth five-year legislative plan of the National People's Congress, the nature reserve zone law is expected to be enacted[17]; with drafting beginning in 2006. The first draft was once provided on a mixed technical base of both PRC EFCZs and IUCN PAs systems. It was widely opposed by governmental agencies so that the drafting work has not achieved much progress so far.[18] The debate, which is still ongoing, hinges on the following: should the new law on nature reserve zones be in line with "the unified international language" – the IUCN management and categories system of protected areas? If yes, the IUCN protected areas seem able to embrace all types of zone management; hence, the regulation for EFCZs appears to be a duplication; if not, the necessity for the regulation of EFCZs still remains. It should be remembered that the general intent of IUCN PAs system and PRC EFCZs vary greatly; the former is even narrower than the latter (see earlier). Therefore, the two could not be simply replaced or one cover the other without special interpretations among IUCN PAs system and other types of zone system being operated in the PRC.

No doubt, a special regulation for EFCZs will facilitate environmental protection and management. However, its success will be subject to many conditions. As long

[16] The Interim Regulation for Pollution Control in the Huai River Basin may be the first example of legislation for a given region. However, the Legislative Office of State Council indicated it that should not be regarded as business as normal.

[17] The legislation of the Nature Reserve Zone Law, which was planned in the Legislative Agenda of National People's Congress (2001–2005), commenced in June 2004. Asian Development Bank offers technical assistance in the period of June 2005 to April 2006.

[18] See the first draft of the Nature Reserve Zone Law. It was provided by the Environmental Protection and Resource Conservation Committee of national People's Congress to the International Symposium on Legislation of Nature Reserve Zone Law of PRC in November 2005, Beijing.

as the EFCZs system proves to be a good management model of ecological function conservation, it could still comply with other associated environmental and natural resources laws or regulations, for example, the Environmental Impact Law, the Water and Soil Conservation Law, and so on. Optimistically, there are various ways to introduce the EFCZs to the regulatory and legal framework, for example, the enactment of the Nature Reserve Zone Law, the revision of the Water and Soil Conservation Law, and regulations and provisions for the Environmental Impact Law.

6 CONCLUSION

Ecosystem functions and value have been recognized by the PRC in the case of ecological function conservation. This includes the four-year program of ecological function zoning over all of the PRC, and the program for the establishment of EFCZs. The objective of ecological function zoning and conservation is to identify nationally significant ecological function and to protect the most fragile and sensitive areas for their important ecofunctions.

The programs of ecological function zoning and EFCZs offer technical tools to determine sustainable natural resources use and ecological conservation conducted in a scientific manner, hence ensuring the protection of ecosystem functions. In order to reinforce their roles in environmental protection, initiatives to promote ecological function zoning and EFCZs in legal instruments have been pushed forward since 2003. A regulation as a result of this process is expected to take effect in 2006. Furthermore, there are various other ways to bring the EFCZs to the regulatory and legal framework, for example, the enactment of the Nature Reserve Zone Law, the revision of the Water and Soil Conservation Law, and regulations and provisions for the Environmental Impact Law.

Annex 1. THE IUCN CATEGORIES SYSTEM OF PROTECTED AREAS (1994)

Category Ia: Strict nature reserve/wilderness protection area managed mainly for science or wilderness protection – an area of land and/or sea possessing some outstanding or representative ecosystems, geological or physiological features and/or species, available primarily for scientific research and/or environmental monitoring.

Category Ib: Wilderness area: protected area managed mainly for wilderness protection – large area of unmodified or slightly modified land and/or sea, retaining its natural characteristics and influence, without permanent or significant habitation, which is protected and managed to preserve its natural condition.

Category II: National park: protected area managed mainly for ecosystem protection and recreation – natural area of land and/or sea designated to (a) protect the ecological integrity of one or more ecosystems for present and future generations, (b) exclude exploitation or occupation inimical to the purposes of designation of the area, and (c) provide a foundation for spiritual, scientific, educational, recreational, and visitor opportunities, all of which must be environmentally and culturally compatible.

Category III: Natural monument: protected area managed mainly for conservation of specific natural features – area containing specific natural or natural/cultural features of outstanding or unique value because of their inherent rarity, representativeness, or aesthetic qualities or cultural significance.

Category IV: Habitat/species management area; protected area managed mainly for conservation through management intervention – area of land and/or sea subject to active intervention for management purposes so as to ensure the maintenance of habitats to meet the requirements of specific species.

Category V: Protected landscape/seascape: protected area managed mainly for landscape or seascape conservation or recreation – area of land, with coast or sea as appropriate, where the interaction of people and nature over time has produced an area of distinct character with significant aesthetic, ecological, and or cultural value, and often with high biological diversity. Safeguarding the integrity of this traditional interaction is vital to the protection, maintenance and evolution of such an area.

Category VI: Managed resource protected area: protected area managed mainly for the sustainable use of natural resource – area containing predominantly unmodified natural systems, managed to ensure long-term protection and maintenance of biological diversity, while also providing a sustainable flow of natural products and services to meet community needs.

24 The Successful Ecograss Project and the Policy and Legal Issues Met and Solved

Na Li*, Liu Yanchun**, and Zhang Hui***

1 LOCATION AND NATURAL CONDITIONS OF THE ECOGRASS PROJECT

The Ecograss Project is in the western part of Jilin province, northeast of China. Geographically, Jilin province is divided into three parts: (1) the mountain-forest area in the east, (2) the plain agricultural lands in the middle, and (3) the grass-desert in the west. Because of climate change effects, including the land becoming drier, as well as overuse of the lands by agriculture and raising domestic animals (the number of which is six times normal capacity), approximately 10,000,000 Mu[1] of western lands are in a state of serious degradation, calcification, and desertification, extending eastward at a rate of 1.4 percent per year, threatening the arable lands in the middle and eastern part of the province as well.[2] Under the policy of sustainable development and rehabilitating the vulnerable agricultural land, the provincial government decided in 2000 that 4,200,000 Mu had to be taken out of agricultural and livestock.

2 CAUSES AND IMPACTS OF DESERTIFICATION

Desertification has been an obvious result of climate change in the western part of Jilin. Since the 1930s, rainfall has decreased 0.5 millimeters each year on average,[3] and many rivers, lakes, and wetlands have disappeared, as have the birds. The agricultural and grazing lands have greatly dwindled. Sandstorms from the desert have spread to the entire province, to the north part of China, and even across the border and the ocean to Korea, Japan, and Russia. Thousands upon thousands of people have abandoned their homes because sands covered their housing and lands and led to a shortage of water.

Before the 1930s, the lands in the western part of the province were mainly grasslands for grazing animals. Migrating people from inland China, and large-scale development

[1] Mu is a Chinese measurement of land; 15 Mu is a hectare.
[2] According to the planet distance-sensing data by the Jilin province land-resource bureau; see Dongfang Jian, "Green Goldbach's Conjecture," *Economic Daily Press*, 2005, 5.
[3] This data is issued by the Jilin Meteorology Bureau. See Dongfang Jian, "Green Goldbach's Conjecture," *Economic Daily Press*, 2005, 6.

*Na Li is Professor of Law, Jilin University, PRC, e-mail: nalijd@hotmail.com.
**Liu Yanchun is Head of Jilin Provincial Forest Administrative Bureau, Director of the Ecograss Project.
***Zhang Hui is Lawyer, Legal Advisor to Jilin Forest Bureau Husbandry Administration and on loan to to the forest administration for the Ecograss Project, which plants grass to maintain and restore the ecological system.

since the 1950s have resulted in overpopulation. There are ninety people per square kilometer, exceeding the UN criterion of twenty people per square kilometer for semidry areas. In the late 1950s, there were 644,000 hectares of agricultural land, whereas by the 1990s there were 1,834,000 hectares, almost a threefold increase. Agricultural land expanded at the expense of the grasslands, which has resulted in erosion leading to desertification and abandonment of some land. Overpopulation of animals is another cause of land degradation. In a county, the number of sheep that the grassland can feed is 350,000, but the actual number of sheep has doubled. Seven hundred thousand goats raised in this area in recent years have caused three to five times more damage than sheep. The livestock's trampling of the land, especially in the rain, hardens and compacts the salty land and results in desertification. Underinvestment in the grassland and poor management of projects are also causes of desertification. Collecting medical herbs by digging, grass fuels by combing, and salty soil by broom are common practices in this area that also cause ecological damage.

3 THE INITIATION OF THE PROJECT

In 2000, the provincial forest bureau summed up the causes as to why the desert lands had been unsuccessfully managed and were in such bad condition. Five causes were identified:

1. Prior management overemphasized economic gains from the land.
2. Previous methods of mainly planting trees, but not grass-bush-trees in a combined planting, did not fit the local soil and climate conditions.
3. The administration of such lands were in different departments of government, namely agricultural, livestock-raising-grasslands, and forest agents, separating the unified ecosystem of the lands. The forest bureau was only in charge of trees, and the stock-raising bureau and grasslands stations only in charge of grass. The agricultural department only dealt with crops.
4. There was a reliance on state budgets and management, but no investment or management from enterprises or civil society.
5. Institutional arrangements and mechanisms, such as land ownership, management, operation, and supervision were lacking.

In July 2001, the "changing millions Mu of deserts into green land campaign" was launched. The provincial government decided to give 4,000,000 Mu of the 10,000,000 Mu of damaged lands to the forest bureau administration for the Ecograss Project. In September 2001, the provincial government issued the document to mobilize donations and investment in the project.

The project lands are within three kilometers of the road, which makes them easily accessible. Most have been abandoned by farmers or herdsmen as unproductive. Plant coverage of these lands is 20–60 percent. The project's goal is to increase plant coverage to 85 percent. At this level, after three years grass can be harvested for commercial purposes (stock feeding). The lands in the project are divided into units, each containing a hectare. A 5,000 RMB Yuan[4] donation or investment is required for operating a unit, with

[4] Approximately 477 Euro.

2,500 Yuan for planting, 500 Yuan for fencing the unit and 2,000 Yuan for management and maintenance. The project will last thirty years.

4 CHANGE OF ADMINISTRATION OF THE LANDS

In 2000, the provincial government decided to give the administration of the desert-grassland in the western part to the forest bureau for tree/grass planting. Previously, agricultural land had been governed by the agricultural bureau, and grassland by the livestock-raising bureau's grassland station, with the forest bureau only governing forests. A new policy calls for planting grass and trees on agricultural lands. Therefore relevant government agencies must adjust to this change.

5 REASONS FOR THE ADMINISTRATION CHANGE

In terms of administration, first and economically, the grassland station's work focuses on the utilization of grasslands for raising livestock rather than for maintaining the ecological system, whereas the forest bureau's main task is ecological construction. The state's funds for this purpose are mainly given to the forest bureau. Second, and institutionally, there are a dozen tree farms in every county of the western part of Jilin province. The farms are under the administration of the local forest bureau and can work to plant and maintain grasses.

Third, and in terms of implementation and enforcement, the forest police are powerful and efficient in protecting the Ecograss Project.[5] The grassland station and bureau do not have the same administrative power as the forest police and the police station. When unlawful activities – such as planting crops on grassland and raising livestock on banned areas – cause damage to grassland, the grassland station cannot arrest the wrong-doers. Instead, they can only ask the local police, prosecuting office, or courts to deal with them. It is always the case that the judicial proceedings are so slow that the full course for crops from planting to harvest is completed and the case is still not finished. This makes implementation of the law very weak, and the system is unable to keep the grassland from being sabotaged.

Fourth, and technically, from a scientific point of view, it is almost impossible in the western area of the province to plant trees without first planting grass because of the dry and salty desert and semidesert land. The successful way to vegetate such land is to combine grass, bush, and tree planting. The forest bureau has comparatively rich experience and knowledge of techniques in battling desertification.

6 TECHNOLOGICAL WAYS TO BATTLE AGAINST THE DESERTIFICATION

After many experiments, five technical methods were found to work effectively:

1. Enclose the units of land with fences to forbid livestock entering the area.
2. Choose and plant dry and salt resistant bush and trees to improve the soil conditions for grass growth.

[5] There are forest police, forest courts, and forest prosecuting offices in China. The forest police were set up partly to deal with serious unlawful deforestation and timber traffic, as well as forest fires.

3. On land with 15–30 percent plant coverage, plough to make the hard salty soil loose and then sow grass seeds.
4. On land with less than 15 percent plant coverage, plough and sow grass seeds with machines. Dig wells to irrigate the grass.
5. On land with 80 percent plant coverage (usually after improvement by the project), but with low-quality and quantity grass product, sow and plant better kinds of grass and trees.

7 INVESTMENT AND DONATIONS

In order to attract investment and donations, several policy measures were adopted. Donors' names were engraved on monuments to honor them. Investors' rights of making financial gains, assigning or giving land rights to others as gifts and inheritances are secured. County forest ministries are responsible for administration. Five percent of the land in each unit can be used to build housing for the manager-operator, including fishing ponds and vegetable gardens. The local governments specify lands for biograss production and then give the administration of the lands to the forest bureau. The forest bureau is responsible for attracting donors and investors. There are four kinds of investment:

1. Central and provincial government budget: In the four years since the initiation of the project, 198,000,000 RMB Yuan (USD$ 23,000,000) of such funds have been put in.
2. Raising funds from society: More than thirty-five thousand people have donated 16,000,000 Yuan.
3. Invite private investment:. Dozens of enterprises, especially grass-producing companies, have invested 8,000,000 Yuan more.
4. Local peasant investment: Local peasants are encouraged to engage in the grass-producing businesses; more than thirty peasant households became family businesses with more than 5,000,000 Yuan invested.

8 OWNERSHIP

Prior to the project, the ownership of desert lands was ambiguous and confusing. Some lands were owned by the state and administered by state land resource bureaus such as agricultural, livestock-raising, or forest bureaus; and some lands were owned by collective units of peasants and used by individual peasants. This unclear ownership causes many serious problems. Far example, peasants tend to abuse and overuse the land to get short-term economic gains, but are reluctant to improve the lands because their ownership is uncertain. The project used rights to solve the problem by creating three new types of ownership.

1. Thirty years after the leasehold contract between the owner and manager-operator is formed, the certificate for use of the land is issued. More than 60 percent of the lands have been of this type.
2. Division of interests between the owner and the manager-operator. This is designed to give collective and individual peasant owners some interest in the land. Approximately 35 percent of the lands are of this type.

3. Shift the administration. Local government (usually county government) shifts the administration of the seriously deserted land to the forest bureau. Five percent of lands are in this form.

9 MANAGEMENT

We created three kinds of land management for the Ecograss project:

1. Investor management, in which the investor manages the unit in which he/she invested. The fee for planting and fencing is returned to the investor.
2. Trust management, giving management a qualified grass business company. The company should return to the investor no less than 5 percent of the investment per year after the second year.
3. Forest bureau management. Lands not covered above are directly managed by the local bureau. The bureau employs local peasants to look after the lands, paying them 300 Yuan per month. This is a considerable sum of cash income for a peasant, so they work hard and carefully to keep people and livestock from entering and engaging in damaging activities. The forest bureau gives work harvesting grass seeds to these peasants to increase their income every autumn. Peasants who get the work are very happy and hard-working.

10 ADMINISTRATION TO THE EMERGING PROBLEMS

After years of hard work, some of the desert lands are covered by good grass and look very green. Some peasants graze their livestock on these lands, sometimes on a large scale. Once, twelve thousand livestock were driven onto 10,000 Mu on a rainy day, damaging the grassland forever by trampling, as the salty lands are especially vulnerable during rain. The soil hardens and the grass roots die. The heads of the provincial and county governments as well as the police were called to the site to ease the tense situation. In order to deal with this kind of problem, local peasants were appointed as caretakers of the lands, with one person/family, living in a hut on the lands in charge of (225 Mu) 15 hectares. In addition, sixteen institutes at provincial, city, and county level with seventy-seven personnel have been set up to supervise and patrol the Ecograss lands and to supervise the caretakers' work. However, there have been cases in which livestock-owning peasants have driven their herds onto Ecograss lands and beaten and threatened the caretaking peasants.

11 PROVINCIAL LAW-MAKING FOR THE PROJECT

In September 2004, the Jilin Province Bio-grass Construction Regulations[6] were adopted, officially banning livestock raising, soil and sand digging and collecting, and pollution on project lands. The regulation is to confirm and consolidate the efforts and achievements of the project and put the administration into a legal framework.

[6] This is typical local legislation by the Provincial People's Congress. But, by and large, its adoption must be pushed by local provincial party-government heads, who are pushed in turn by corresponding bureaus, here the head of the provincial forest bureau and its heads do this.

12 BENEFITS THE PROJECT BROUGHT ABOUT TO VILLAGERS

The government requires local peasants to raise livestock in stables feeding the stock with cut grass instead of grazing them on grasslands. These peasants are given priority to cut the grass and to purchase the grass. The local peasants have enjoyed the benefits of Ecograss and they have obtained benefits from the project.

Guo Chunming, a peasant from Taiping village, Daan city, made the following remarks:

> In 1996 a big wind swept the salty sands to be heaped as high as the fencing wall. Pigs climbed onto the roof to eat the maize drying on roof. Since the project, we no longer suffer from the sand storm since the land has been covered by grass. Secondly, we need not go out to cities and towns to be employed.[7]

In 2002, the project used the lands belonging to the village with the interests divided 30–70 percent between the forest bureau and the villagers. It specified that the villagers harvest the grass on their lands to feed their livestock, and the forest bureau employ them to harvest the grass seeds and then purchase the seeds from them. The Guo family made 300 Yuan in one and half days by selling grass seeds.

The head of Longzhao town gave the following data to illustrate the benefits they received from the project Longzhao had 12,000 sheep in 2001, which increased to 40,000 in 2004; the number of geese increased to 145,000. As a result of the project, peasants in the town have increased their income up to 150 Yuan per year on average. The town, which was mainly agricultural, is now tending toward raising livestock as a result of the project.

13 MACROECONOMIC, SOCIAL, BIOLOGICAL, AND CULTURAL BENEFITS BROUGHT ABOUT BY THE PROJECT

After three years' work, biological benefits have improved more than five times. Grasses are ankle high or even much higher in some areas; flora is increased for two hundred pieces per square meter, the grass cover increases 10–15 percent per year. Fresh grass output increased four thousand kilograms per hectare, and dry grass output reached seven hundred kilograms more on the lands that previously had 15–30 percent vegetative coverage. More important, salty lands with less than 5 percent coverage of grass now have 95 percent coverage. The project has completely changed the look of the lands. Biodiversity is remarkably richer; wild animals and birds, such as ducks, cranes, rabbits even foxes, have been seen as well as many kinds of economic flora.

In addition to these biological effects, great economic effects have been achieved. The project can provide employment for one hundred thousand people. Two million ox and cows or twelve million sheep can be raised with the grass produced on the lands. The development of grass products and a processing industry has started. In some of the project's experimental farms, considerable profits have been made from dry grass and grass seeds. It is estimated that investment on 40–60 percent coverage lands can be returned in three to five years, and on less than 20 percent coverage in five to seven years.

[7] See Dongfang Jian, "Green Goldbach's Conjecture," *Economic Daily Press* (2005) 18.

These estimates provide examples for the grassland business and enhance investors' confidence.

14 DISCUSSION

This Ecograss Project is very high profile in China.[8] Antidesertification is a significant issue and a difficult task in China, particularly in recent years when the policy and doctrine of scientific development has been raised by the central authorities.[9] The project contains some policy and legal issues typical for China to deal with this type of environmental problem.

China's policy change from focusing on pursuing economic growth to sustainable development[10] is the general background for the possibility and success of the project. In 1999, the State Council put forward the policy of rehabilitating vulnerable agricultural lands into forests and grasslands, giving grain to the peasants who lose their agricultural lands to conversion as an employment fee, and contracting with them to plant trees and/ grass on the land. In the years following, several official documents by the State Council were issued,[11] there was a policy U-turn,[12] and a campaign was initiated. This is a typical Chinese way to make regulations and to have new policies.

This Ecograss Project was outstanding among many similar projects, most of which were not very well reported in China's mass media. One of the reasons for the project's success was that it had overcome some technical difficulties on a large scale. It showed successful cases in the battles against desertification in semidry and salty land, which are rare nationally or even worldwide. Suitable methods of planting proper grass/trees for various kinds of lands were found. With these methods, we could persuade the relevant leaders and agencies to support this large-scale project.

To launch such a big project in China, the leader's determination, painstaking efforts and personality are important, even key. Without Mr. Liu Yanchun's personal efforts, funds from central and provincial governments, provincial party government's support in many key roles in the project would have been impossible. This is why Mr. Liu was high profile in China's mass media and official assessment. In this sense, the rule of man is prevailing in China rather than the rule of law. Personal capacity and continuing struggles of the responsible officials are very important for a project even if the project is in conformity with policy. Even things such as the provincial lawmaking prohibiting

[8] This project had been reported in several important official newspapers (there is no purely civil, or nonofficial newspapers in China, but the official points of view vary) and some books carrying the stories have been published. Mr. Liu Yanchun, the head of Jilin Provincial Forest Bureau and the director of this project has been selected among the top ten people for the year 2001 in China's reforms.

[9] The policy and doctrine of scientific development was raised in late 2003 in leaders' speeches, including the Party's secretary in chief, Mr. Hu Jintao, and the premier, Wen Jiabao, as well as by several official documents as always in China to launch a campaign or to initiate a major policy. Five harmonizations are key ingredients of this policy. Harmonization between people and nature is one of the five. It emphasizes environmental sound and natural resources saving practice.

[10] China's official term is *doctrine of scientific development*, which is very similar to *sustainable development*. See ibid.

[11] Such documents include *opinions on further the work for experimental sites in rehabilitating lands into forest/grass, 2000; further improving policy measures in rehabilitating lands into forest/grass, 2003*. For the details of these documents, see Gazette of the State Council.

[12] Previously, China's policy had emphasized the planting agricultural crops, as much of wetlands, grasslands, and forests were cultivated for crops.

feeding livestock in the fenced lands must be struggled for by persuading provincial party government heads, instead of lobbying provincial congressmen as in the West.

15 SUMMARY

- It was not difficult to collect and fence the lands for the project at the beginning stage, as much of the land was not productive. When the land was covered with grass after many years' planting, former livestock-raising peasants began to intrude into the fenced grass to feed their livestock. On one rainy day thousands of peasants drove tens of thousands of livestock into the fenced lands causing 10,000 Mu lands to be hardened forever by the livestock's trampling. The provincial government head and hundreds of policemen were called to the site to stop the peasants. Although this was an extreme case, the conflicts between peasants' short-term economic loss and long-term ecological protection of the land for sustainble use remains a problem. There are still complaints and some intrusions into the lands. Tensions between the local grass administration and local peasants still exists. Reducing the number of livestock around the fenced lands and raising livestock in stables with feeding lots will be the solution, but these methods are not yet established in all areas.
- Shifting the administrative power from agricultural and livestock bureaus to the forest bureau is necessary and, to some extent, the guarantee for the success of the project. The shift is considered from administrative capacities, advantages, and conveniences in terms of technology and professional skills, work orientation (agricultural bureau being economically driven, and the forest bureau driven by ecological protection), and enforcing capacity (the forest bureau has its own farm, police, even courts).
- The project was carried out under China's ambiguous property rights legal framework. The local government has powerful control of all the lands – state-owned or collectively owned by the peasants – to actively carry out the projects. The support of local governments (ranging from provincial districts to county governments) is key. Convincing them of the benefits the project will bring to their local people and to the leaders themselves (e.g., political achievements, accounts for career promotion) is our key work. Three kinds of rights on lands were created: land under the forest bureau's direct management, land under leasehold by qualified investors, and land under contract of management with division of any economic gain. So far, the system works well.
- There are still problems to be solved. Only 42 percent of such lands in Jilin province are under the project and 58 percent of them remain laid aside. The project's long-term effects remain to be seen. If the project succeeds in the long run, the remaining 58 percent can be taken into consideration for starting new projects. Funds and investments for the project are still lacking. Conflicts and potential conflicts with some local peasants mainly over potential economic gains and ambiguous property rights, still exist.

PART SIX

BIOSECURITY ISSUES

25 Prevention and Control of Alien Invasive Species – China's Implementation of the CBD

Yuhong Zhao*

1 INTRODUCTION

With the expansion of global trade and international transport and tourism after China's integration into the world economy through the implementation of its open-door policy in the 1980s and the more recent accession to the World Trade Organization (WTO), China's biodiversity is becoming more and more threatened by the potential introduction of nonnative species. According to the very latest statistics from the Ministry of Agriculture, more than four hundred alien species have invaded China, at least twenty in the last ten years.[1] Alien invasive species are found in all of the thirty-four provinces, autonomous regions, and municipalities under direct control of the central government. By May 2002, they had invaded almost all of the fifteen hundred nature reserves nationwide and all types of ecosystems, including forests, farmlands, inland waters, wetlands, grasslands, and urban residential areas.[2] More than half of the world's worst alien invasive species published by the IUCN have invaded China.[3]

The international community has become aware of the serious threat of alien invasive species to the ecosystem, biodiversity, human health, and socioeconomic well-being. Studies have found that the introduction of nonindigenous species is second only to direct habitat destruction in causing loss of biodiversity.[4] In response to the potential irreversible harm created by the invasion of alien species, consensus has been reached under article 8(h) of the *Convention on Biological Diversity* (CBD) that Contracting Parties should, as far as possible and as appropriate, "prevent the introduction of, control or eradicate those alien species which threaten ecosystem, habitats and species."[5] Agenda 21 contains a number of proposals for dealing with the issue of alien invasive species.[6] It

[1] Yao Runfeng, "More than 400 Alien Species Invading China." 22:1 *The Weed Science* (2005), 51.

[2] China Commission on International Cooperation in Environment and Development, *Annual Report of the Biosafety Research Project* (October 2002), available at www.chinabiodiversity.com.

[3] State Environmental Protection Administration (SEPA), *Notice on Strengthening the Prevention and Control of Alien Invasive Species* (2003, no. 6). See also IUCN, *100 of the World's Worst Invasive Alien Species.* The list is available at http://www.issg.org/database/species/search.asp?st=100ss&fr=1&sts=#SpeciesList.

[4] Clare Shine, Nattley Williams, & Lothar Gundling, *A Guide to Designing Legal and Institutional Frameworks on Alien Invasive Species* (Gland, Switzerland, Cambridge, and Bonn: IUCN, 2000), 10 (hereinafter, "*IUCN Guidelines*").

[5] *The Convention on Biological Diversity* was signed at the United Nations Conference on Environment and Development in Rio De Janeiro, 3–14 June 1992 (31 *International Legal Materials* 811).

[6] *Agenda 21* was adopted at the United Nations Conference on Environment and Development (UNCED) held in Rio de Janeiro in 1992.

* Yuhong Zhao is Assistant Professor, School of Law, Chinese University of Hong Kong.

urges States to take action to address the impact of alien species in a wide range of sectors, such as combating deforestation, managing fragile ecosystems, conserving biodiversity, protecting the oceans, seas, and coastal areas, and protecting freshwater resources.

China, as a party to the CBD, is under the international obligation to take proper measures to prevent and control the invasion of alien species. This chapter examines the issue of alien invasive species as a growing threat to biodiversity loss and socioeconomic well-being in China. It reviews and criticizes the current legal and policy responses that address the problem of biological invasion in a piecemeal and fragmented manner. In order to close the gaps and develop more effective mechanisms to prevent and control alien invasive species, the chapter suggests a more integrated approach to law reform and institution building that incorporates fundamental environmental law principles and effective environmental law mechanisms. Section 2 introduces China's experience of the invasion of alien species and the social, economic, health, and ecological impacts caused by the nonindigenous species. Section 3 reviews the current legal frameworks that are being used to respond to the introduction of alien species and the more recent policy development to address the problem of alien invasive species causing biodiversity loss. Section 4 explores how to take a more integrated approach to reform the current fragmented legal framework and to strengthen institutional cooperation to prevent and control alien invasive species in a more effective and efficient manner.

2 ALIEN INVASIVE SPECIES IN CHINA AND THEIR IMPACTS

The CBD uses the term "alien species" without defining it.[7] A possible definition is found in the *Guiding Principles for the Prevention, Introduction and Mitigation of Impacts of Alien Species that Threaten Ecosystems, Habitats or Species*[8] (hereinafter as the Guiding Principles), which is "a species, subspecies or lower taxon, introduced outside its natural past or present distribution; includes any part, gametes, seeds, eggs, or propagules of such species that might survive and subsequently reproduce." A species is considered to be native in its past or present natural range (the habitats and ecosystems where it lives or lived) and within its natural dispersal potential (the area it can reach using its own legs, wings, or wind/waterborne dispersal systems). The term "invasive" is often related to the concept of "adverse impact" in the form of damage inflicted on the receiving species, habitats, or ecosystem. The CBD defines "alien invasive species" as alien species that threaten ecosystems, habitats, or other species.[9] Many introduced alien species may not become invasive, although there is always uncertainty and much debate about the point at which an alien species may be defined as "invasive."

Introduced alien species that spread beyond human control may die out after a certain period of time or remain in the areas without disrupting local biota or ecosystem. Invasion occurs when an alien species not only persists but also proliferates and becomes a threat to another native species, the local habitat, or the ecosystem. It is extremely difficult to predict accurately which introduced alien species will have benign effects

[7] *Convention on Biological Diversity*, Article 8(h).

[8] It was developed under the framework of the CBD Subsidiary Body on Scientific, Technical and Technological Advice, and submitted for consideration to the fifth meeting of the Conference of Parties in Nairobi in May 2000 as "Interim Guiding Principles." It was adopted at the sixth meeting of the Conference of Parties in The Hague in April 2002 as the *Guiding Principles for the Prevention, Introduction and Mitigation of Impacts of Alien Species that Threaten Ecosystems, Habitats or Species* (UNEP/CBD/COP/6/20).

[9] *Convention on Biological Diversity*, Article 2.

and which may become invasive in a new habitat. To make things more complicated, invasiveness may be triggered by diverse events such as habitat alteration or the arrival of another alien species and interactions with it.

2.1 Invasion of Alien Species into China

Invasion of alien species occurs as a result of three categories of activities with legitimate economic or other objectives: first, intentional introduction for use in biological production systems of agriculture, forestry, and fishery, and in landscaping for recreational and ornamental purposes; second, intentional introduction for use in containment or captivity such as zoos, aquaria, and the pet trade, from which there is known risk of escape or release to the wild; and, third, unintentional introduction of species, organisms or pathogens through pathways involving trade, transport, travel, and tourism.

After carrying out a nationwide investigation from 2001 to 2003, China's State Environmental Protection Administration (SEPA) compiled detailed data on the origins, pathways, and ecological and economic impacts of 283 alien invasive species.[10] These species have caused significant harm to China's ecosystem, biodiversity, and socioeconomic well-being. According to inconclusive statistics, the annual economic loss caused by alien invasive species has amounted to RMB119.88 billion *yuan*.[11]

According to SEPA's preliminary investigation, China has 107 species of alien invasive weeds, 58 percent of which were introduced intentionally for the purposes of pasture, foodstuff, vegetables, ornamental plants, medicinal herbs, and so on. Others were introduced unintentionally, entering China with imported goods, passenger luggage, and other means of transportation. There are thirty-two species of alien invasive pests and twenty-three alien pathogens. These are mostly the result of unintentional introduction, having been transported with imported plants and other goods.[12] Even some of China's nature reserves and well-known scenic sites have become threatened to various degrees by alien invasive species.

Crofton weed originates in America. It spread into Yunnan Province in the 1940s and now grows commonly in the southwestern region including in Yunnan, Guizhou, Tibet, Guangxi, and Sichuan provinces. The plant is aggressive and powerful and grows very quickly.[13] It has occupied large areas of farmlands, orchards, forests, grasslands, and lands along roads. Ragweed (bitterweed) originates in North America and was transmitted into China in the 1930s. It expanded into Shanghai and many big cities in Liaoning, Heilongjiang, Jilin, Shandong, Hunan, Zhejiang, Anhui, and Jiangxi provinces. With

[10] "China Has Established Detailed Information on Alien Species," *China Environment News* (24 May 2004). According to the report, such alien invasive species include 19 micro-organisms, 18 aquatic plant species, 170 terrestrial plant species, 25 aquatic invertebrate species, 33 terrestrial invertebrate species, 3 amphibian species, 10 fish species, and 5 mammal species.

[11] That is approximately $USD15 billion. Biodiversity Clearing-House Mechanism of China, "Alien Invasive Species," available at: http://www.biodiv.org.cn, an official Web site managed by the Bureau of Nature and Ecological Protection of the State Environmental Protection Administration. Also see "China Has Established Detailed Information on Alien Species," *China Environment News* (24 May 2004).

[12] The State Environmental Protection Administration, *China's Second National Report on the Implementation of the Convention on Biological Diversity*, at 37–38 (submitted to the CBD Secretariat in 2001). See also Cai Lei et al., "Control Alien Invasive Species to Conserve Biodiversity," 8 *Environmental Protection* (2003), 27–34, at 27.

[13] Crofton weed covered 110,000 square kilometers in 1985 and expanded to 247,000 square kilometers in 1995. It is now expanding into Eastern and Northern parts of China at a rate of sixty kilometers per year. *SEPA Submission of Case Studies on Alien Species to the CBD Secretariat* (8 October 1999).

strong reproduction and competition capacity, it excludes other plants and grasses, causing significant economic and aesthetic damage.[14]

2.2 Economic Impacts of Alien Invasive Species

Introduced species often bring economic and sociocultural benefits at least to certain groups of stakeholders. Even when alien species have known invasive characteristics, some interest groups may strongly support their continuous introduction and use. The perceived "benefits" are visible, whereas the negative impacts may take a long time to emerge and the environmental costs are always difficult to quantify and sometimes not fully understood by the policy makers.

The outbreak of alien invasive species has caused heavy economic losses to China. The invasion of pests, such as lobdelly pine mealybug, American white moth, and giant African snails, and weeds, such as crofton weed, mile-a-minute weed, alligator weed, ragweed, smooth cord-grass, siam weed, and water hyacinth, are causing economic losses to agriculture and forestry in the amount of RMB57.4 billion *yuan* each year on average, according to conservative estimates.[15] Another study has put the figure of total annual loss caused by alien invasive species to be RMB119.88 billion *yuan*, which includes both direct annual economic loss of RMB19.86 billion *yuan* and indirect annual economic loss resulting from the harm done to ecosystems, species, and genetic resources in the amount of RMB100.02 billion *yuan*.[16] According to preliminary investigation, invasive pests cause RMB7 to 8 billion *yuan* of economic loss and alien weeds cause as high as RMB900 million *yuan* of loss to China's agriculture.[17]

Despite the great efforts to quantify the economic loss caused by the invasion of alien species, these figures can by no means be viewed as exhaustive given the difficulty of valueing components of native biodiversity or the benefits freely provided by ecosystem services in the form of clean and abundant water, clean air, sediment control, and so on that may be degraded through invasions.[18]

2.3 Ecological Impacts of Alien Invasive Species

Species existing outside their historic area of distribution are no longer subject to the natural checks limiting their population growth. Alien invasive species are found in all taxonomic groups, from viruses and fungi to plants and mammals. A high number

[14] *SEPA Submission of Case Studies on Alien Species to the CBD Secretariat* (8 October 1999).

[15] China Commission on International Cooperation in Environment and Development, *Annual Report of the Biosafety Research Project* (October 2002). Available at: http://www.chinabiodiversity.com.

[16] Biodiversity Clearing-House Mechanism of China, "Alien Invasive Species," available at http://www.biodiv.org.cn, an official Web site managed by the Bureau of Nature and Ecological Protection of the State Environmental Protection Administration.

[17] The State Environmental Protection Administration, *China's Second National Report on the Implementation of the Convention on Biological Diversity*, at 38 (submitted to the CBD Secretariat in 2001).

[18] According to the *IUCN Guidelines*, elements for assessment need to include items such as: reduction in the value of agricultural land; increased operating costs and loss of income; collapse of buildings and power failures; inefficient irrigation and lowered water tables; seed contamination, spread of disease, and incremental pest control costs; loss of sport, game, endangered species, and biodiversity; ecosystem disturbance and protection, monitoring, and recovery costs; loss of scientific value; loss of opportunity, and ecosystem services for future generations; and loss of equitable access to resources. Clare Shine et al., note 4, at 9.

of documented extinctions have been caused by alien species, with the irretrievable loss of native species and ecosystems.[19] Crofton weed, originating from Latin America (especially Mexico and Costa Rica) is now widely found in southwest China, causing the fall and disappearance of indigenous plants.

When alien invasive species have successfully invaded the new habitat and the growth is out of control, they can cause irreversible damage and serious "biological pollution." Water hyacinth originates from South America. It has now spread all over China and invaded the inland waters (rivers, lakes, and ponds) of most provinces and cities in north, east, central, and south China. It has become the worst weed in many aquatic habitats, leading to the loss of both plant and animal species. The seriously affected one-thousand-hectare Dianchi Lake in Yunnan Province has water hyacinth covering its surface, critically destroying the structure and function of the water ecosystem and reducing indigenous plants and animals from over two hundred species to a mere twenty or so. The excessive growth of the water hyacinth has forced the suspension of a famous tourist cruise line as the navigation was literally blocked by the plants.[20]

Alligator weed originates in South America and entered Shanghai and the eastern part of China in the 1930s. It has been used as foodstuff to feed pigs in many areas in southern China since the 1950s and has been grown widely. Nowadays, it occupies extensive areas in Hebei, Shaanxi, Henan, Anhui, Jiangsu, Zhejiang, Jiangxi, Hubei, Hunan, Taiwan, Sichuan, Guizhou, and Yunnan provinces. The weed can reproduce easily, grows rapidly, and is hard to eradicate. It can grow in both aquatic and terrestrial environments. In China, it is mainly found on the land, invading orchards and farmlands, affecting the growth of indigenous fruits, rice, beans, corns, and cotton. With a density as high as three hundred pieces per square meter, it creates great damage to fruit trees and agricultural farms, causing a direct economic loss of around RMB600 million *yuan* per year.[21]

The invasion of smooth cord-grass into the shallow coastal marine and estuarine environment has severely affected the water quality and induced "red tide," causing the disappearance of large areas of mangroves.[22] The outburst of the red turpentine beetle, which entered China from the United States with the import of timber products, killed one-third of the pine trees in Shanxi province within months in 1999.[23]

In the ecosystems in which human destruction of habitats is strictly controlled and prohibited, alien invasive species have become the primary cause of ecological degradation and loss of biodiversity. The invasion of alien species is already the top threat for inland waters and tropical and subtropical ecosystems in China. Alien fish species have been the primary cause of the extinction of native fish species in Yunnan Province.[24]

[19] Ibid., at 10.

[20] Li Mingyang & Xu Haigen, "Economic Assessment of the Impact of Invasive Species on Wetland Ecosystem," *Journal of Central South Forestry University* (2004), 24(5) 53–56.

[21] SEPA Submission of Case Studies on Alien Species to the CBD Secretariat (8 October 1999).

[22] Cai Lei et al., "Control Alien Invasive Species to Conserve Biodiversity." 8 *Environmental Protection* (2003), 27–34, at 27. For more, see Li Mingyang & Xu Haigen, note 20.

[23] Chen Sai, "Invasion of Alien Species and Principles for Environmental Legal Control." 24/4 *Xinjiang Environmental Protection* (2002), 31–33.

[24] China Commission on International Cooperation in Environment and Development, *Annual Report of the Biosafety Research Project* (October 2002). Available at http://www.chinabiodiversity.com.

2.4 Health Impacts of Alien Invasive Species

The introduction of alien species presents opportunities for the transmission of certain strands of micro-organisms that affect the health of humans and animals. Transmission occurs through vectors such as mosquitoes, domestic animals and ballast water. Alien invasive species may serve as hosts of diseases that affect human and animal health. The West Nile virus carried by mosquitoes affecting New York City is an example.[25] Alien invasive species are seriously affecting human health at a cost of RMB2.9 billion *yuan* per year in China.[26] Ragweed (also known as bitterweed), which has now invaded fifteen provinces and cities in northeast, north, east, and central China, is found to be the main cause of pollen allergy, causing "dry weed fever" syndrome. According to preliminary statistics, about 1 percent of the target population is affected to various degrees by the pollen, and each year at least one million people are hospitalized seeking treatment for such syndrome.[27]

3 CURRENT LEGAL REGIME AND ITS LIMITATIONS

China's current legal regime dealing with alien invasive species can be described as piecemeal and fragmented, and there exists a huge gap between China's efforts and the expectations of international instruments. The regime has mainly focused on the control of unintentional introduction of harmful pests, weeds, and diseases.[28] Generally speaking, relevant provisions are distributed across quarantine legislation and wildlife protection laws.

3.1 Quarantine Legislation

China relies heavily on quarantine measures to control the unintentional introduction of alien species and diseases. The targets of quarantine control are those products found to be particularly dangerous and harmful to agriculture, forestry, husbandry, and fishery sectors.

The *Frontier Health and Quarantine Law*[29] was enacted to institutionalize quarantine inspection for the purpose of preventing the spreading of infectious diseases into or out of China in order to protect human health.[30] Although the act was not intended to prevent or control the introduction of alien species, some provisions could be relied on to prevent the entry of certain species that carry diseases or that are harmful to

[25] Clare Shine et al., *IUCN Guidelines*, note 4, at 10.

[26] Biodiversity Clearing-House Mechanism of China, "Alien Invasive Species," available at http://www.biodiv.org.cn, an official Web site managed by the Bureau of Nature and Ecological Protection of the State Environmental Protection Administration.

[27] SEPA Submission of Case Studies on Alien Species to the CBD Secretariat (8 October 1999).

[28] "Hitchhiker" organisms are inadvertently transmitted through diverse pathways of trade, travel, and transport. The risk of traded commodities being contaminated with alien animals, plants, or microorganisms is real for large trading nations such as China. Livestock can bring in seeds in their gut, timber can bring in pests, soil on roots can harbor diseases for native plants, and seed consignments may be contaminated with weeds. Contamination problems can be detected and managed by strict border and quarantine controls, combined with improved cleaning, packaging, and transport methods and techniques, and more and more stringent international sanitary and phytosanitary measures.

[29] *The Frontier Health and Quarantine Law of the People's Republic of China* was adopted at the 18th Meeting of the Standing Committee of the Sixth National People's Congress, promulgated by Order No. 46 of the People's Republic of China on 2 December 1986. The Law became effective on 1 May 1987.

[30] *Frontier Health and Quarantine Law of the People's Republic of China*, Article 1.

human health. For example, transportation vehicles subject to border entry quarantine inspections are required to be disinfected or treated with other sanitation measures, if rodents or pests, which are carriers of disease, are found.[31] Similar measures are carried out on luggage, goods and postal parcels subject to quarantine inspection.[32] The *Law on Animal Epidemic Prevention*[33] was enacted to prevent, control, and eliminate animal epidemics in order to protect human health.[34] The main targets of control are infectious animal diseases and parasitic animal diseases.[35]

The *Law on Entry and Exit Quarantine of Animals and Plants*[36] is more relevant to the control of alien species as it goes beyond the mere control of infectious or parasitic diseases. It also aims to prevent the entry of pests and weeds dangerous to plants, and other harmful organisms into China. The goal remains the protection of agriculture, forestry, animal husbandry, and fishery production together with human health.[37] Five years after the adoption of this law, the State Council promulgated the *Implementing Regulation*, providing more detailed and concrete provisions.[38] Under the National Administration of Quarantine for Animals and Plants, more than two hundred port quarantine departments have been established, formulating a relatively comprehensive network of supervision and monitoring for pests and weeds harmful and dangerous to the agriculture, forestry, and fisheries.[39]

Under the *Law on Entry and Exit Quarantine of Animals and Plants*, China prohibits the entry of pathogenic micro-organisms of animals and plants (including seed cultures of bacteria and viruses), pests, and other harmful organisms.[40] It also prohibits the entry of animals and plants as well as their products that originate in countries or regions with prevalent epidemic animal or plant diseases.[41] The law has established strict entry quarantine mechanisms that could contribute to a certain degree of control over the introduction of alien species, although the primary purpose remains the control of diseases. Prior approval is required for the import of all animals, animal products, plant seeds, seedlings, or other propagating materials. Relevant parties must submit an application in advance and go through the formalities of examination and approval of quarantine inspection.[42] Imported animals, plants, and their products are subject to quarantine inspection at the port of entry. When necessary, the imported animals and plants and their products may be quarantined in isolation as required by the port animal and plant quarantine office.[43] If they pass the quarantine inspection, they are allowed to enter China.[44]

[31] Ibid., Article 13.

[32] Ibid., Article 14.

[33] The *Law of the People's Republic of China on Animal Epidemic Prevention* was adopted at the 26th Meeting of the Standing Committee of the Eighth National People's Congress and promulgated by Order No. 87 of the President of the People's Republic of China. It enters into force on 1 January 1998.

[34] Ibid., Article 1.

[35] Ibid., Article 3.

[36] *The Law of the People's Republic of China on the Entry and Exit Quarantine of Animals and Plants* was adopted at the 22nd Meeting of the Standing Committee of the Seventh National People's Congress and promulgated by Order No. 53 of the President of the People's Republic of China. The Law enters into force on 1 April 1992.

[37] Ibid., Article 1.

[38] The Implementing Regulations of the Law on Entry and Exit Quarantine of Animals and Plants was promulgated by the State Council on 2 December 1996 and became effective on 1 January 1997.

[39] The State Environmental Protection Administration, *China's Second National Report on the Implementation of the Convention on Biological Diversity*, at 38 (submitted to the CBD Secretariat in 2001).

[40] *The Law on Entry and Exit Quarantine of Animals and Plants*, Article 5(1).

[41] Ibid., Article 5(2).

[42] Ibid., Article 10.

[43] Ibid., Article 14.

[44] Ibid., Article 15.

For the imported animals that fail quarantine inspection, the port animal and plant quarantine office issues a quarantine treatment notice to the owner or its agent, asking it to return or slaughter all the animals if Class A infectious or parasitic diseases are found, or asking it to return or slaughter animals affected by Class B infectious or parasitic diseases and to keep the in-contact animals at a designated place of isolation for observation.[45] The Class A and Class B infectious or parasitic diseases are designated by the Ministry of Agriculture.[46]

For imported plants and plant products found to be contaminated with "diseases, pests or weeds dangerous to plants" after quarantine inspection, the plant quarantine office issues a quarantine treatment notice to the owner or its agent, asking it to conduct such treatment as disinfections and pest control, or to return the item to its place of origin or even on-site destruction. Those that pass the quarantine inspection after treatment are allowed to enter China.[47] The "diseases, pests and weeds dangerous to plants" are designated by the Ministry of Agriculture.[48]

If the quarantine inspection discovers that imported animals and plants and their products are contaminated with diseases, pests, or harmful organisms not covered by the catalogues promulgated by the Ministry of Agriculture according to Article 18, but are nevertheless extremely harmful to agriculture, forestry, animal husbandry, and fishery, the port animal and plant quarantine office shall notify the owner or its agent to conduct such treatment as disinfection and pest control, or to return the item to its place of origin or even on-site destruction. Those that pass the quarantine inspection after the treatment are allowed to enter China.[49]

3.2 Wildlife Protection Law

The *Wild Animal Protection Law*[50] was passed to protect and rescue precious and endangered wild animals, to preserve, develop, and rationally utilize wild animal resources and to maintain ecological balance.[51] According to the *Wild Animal Protection Law*, the State Forestry Administration and the Fishery Administrative Authority are responsible for the management of terrestrial and aquatic animals respectively.[52] As a result, the State Forestry Administration promulgated the *Regulation for Protection of Terrestrial Wild Animals* with the approval of the State Council on 1 March 1992, and the Ministry of Agriculture promulgated the *Regulation for the Protection of Aquatic Wild Animals* with the approval of the State Council on 5 October 1993.

For the introduction of terrestrial wild animals from foreign countries or from other provinces, autonomous regions or municipalities under direct control of the Central Government for reproduction and cultivation, the relevant parties must take proper measures to prevent accidental escape of the animals into the wild. When it is necessary to release the animals into the wild habitat, the responsible parties must file

45 Ibid., Article 16.
46 Ibid., Article 18.
47 Ibid., Article 17.
48 Ibid., Article 18.
49 Ibid., Article 19.
50 The *Wild Animal Protection Law* was first adopted at the fourth meeting of the Standing Committee of the Seventh National People's Congress and promulgated by Order No. 9 of the President of the People's Republic of China on 8 November 1988. The Law went into force on 1 March 1989. It was substantially amended in 2004.
51 The *Wild Animal Protection Law*, Article 1.
52 Ibid., Article 7.

an application with the forestry administration authority at the provincial level, which will designate a science research institute to carry out scientific assessment. The case will then be submitted to the State Forestry Administration or its authorized body for approval. The release of introduced wild animals into the wild or the escape by the animals resulting from improper management will render the parties responsible to take remedial measures including being ordered to capture the released or escaped wild animals within a specified period of time.[53] Similar control can be found against the introduction of water-based wild animals. Anyone introducing aquatic wild animals from foreign countries should submit an application to the provincial level fishery administration authority, which will designate a science research institute to carry out scientific assessment. The case will then be submitted to the Fishery Administration of the Ministry of Agriculture for approval.[54]

The *Wild Plant Protection Regulation*[55] was passed to protect, develop, and rationally utilize wild plant resources, conserve biodiversity, and maintain ecological balance.[56] The Ministry of Agriculture promulgated the *Provisions on the Protection of Agricultural Wild Plants*[57] in accordance with the *Wild Plant Protection Regulation* to provide more concrete rules and measures to protect and rationally utilize rare and endangered wild plant resources and conserve biodiversity. The Regulation and the Provisions have focused on the protection of the habitats and prohibition of illegal harvesting, sale, and export of the relevant plants.

3.3 Limitations

The legal and institutional frameworks in China treat alien invasive species in a fragmented manner. There is a widespread lack of clear principles, procedures, and criteria for analyzing risk and dealing with eradication and control across all taxonomic groups. First, there is an absence of strategic approach to the problem of alien invasive species. The issue of biological invasion generally has been ignored or has very low visibility in the national environmental and biodiversity planning process. Second, there are low levels of coordination among agencies responsible for phyto-sanitary matters, trade, natural resources, and biodiversity conservation and other sectors, with regard both to international standard setting and to legislative development and implementation. Third, the dispersed character of existing provisions and inconsistent legislative treatment seriously affect the effective implementation of prevention and control mechanisms. Fourth, the objectives have been defined too narrowly, only prohibiting introduction of pests and weeds that are harmful to agro-forestry or fisheries interests. That is, there is no protection of all components of biodiversity against invasive processes, as mandated in the CBD. Finally, there is a total lack of postentry or postrelease control and management of alien invasive species, including an absence of a mandatory monitoring requirement and crisis response mechanisms.

[53] *Regulation for the Protection of Terrestrial Wild Animals*, Article 23.
[54] *Regulation for the Protection of Aquatic Wild Animals*, Article 22.
[55] *The Wild Plant Protection Regulation* was promulgated by the State Council on 30 September 1996. It went into force on 1 January 1997.
[56] The *Wild Plant Protection Regulation*, Article 1.
[57] The Ministry of Agriculture first promulgated the *Provisions on the Protection of Agriculture Wild Plants* on 6 September 2002. The Provisions went into force on 1 October 2002. It was amended on 1 July 2004.

In addition to the low visibility of the issue of alien species at the policy-making level, public awareness of the issue has remained minimal. Units and individuals engaging in the introduction of alien species have little knowledge of the potential ecological impact of such introduction, and there is no scientific risk assessment being carried out. Furthermore, the lack of proper management and control of introduced species has led to their escape and release from designated plantations or farms to the natural environment, subsequently becoming invasive species.

4 LAW REFORM FOR BETTER IMPLEMENTATION OF CBD

Under CBD, member states should design laws that make use of incentives as well as employ conventional regulatory approaches.[58] The CBD Secretariat has suggested a three-stage hierarchical approach to control alien species. First of all, priority should be given to prevent entry of potential invasive alien species, both between and within States. Second, if entry has already taken place, actions should be undertaken to prevent the establishment and spread of alien species: the preferred response would be eradication at the earliest possible stage. Third, if eradication is not feasible or cost-effective, containment, and long-term control measures should be considered.[59] A well-designed legal framework is essential to prevent and minimize the risk of unwanted introductions and to provide a basis for effective eradication and control measures. This framework not only prohibits or restricts certain acts but also promotes desired goals through provision of economic and other incentives. Furthermore, it strengthens institutional mechanisms to implement the laws and regulations and ensure compliance.

The Chinese government has demonstrated its commitment to fulfill its obligation under Article 8(h) of the CBD. In 2000, the concept of biosafety for the first time attracted the attention of policy makers and the issue was addressed in *the Compendium of National Ecological Conservation*.[60] Article 14 provides that "all the alien species have to go through a risk assessment process. The import quarantine work has to be strengthened to prevent any harmful alien species from entering into China." More recent efforts made by SEPA are found in two important documents issued in 2003. One is "Notice on Strengthening the Prevention and Control of Alien Invasive Species,"[61] and the other is "Notice on Issuing the First Catalogue of Alien Invasive Species in China," jointly promulgated with the Chinese Academy of Science.[62]

Despite the efforts made by policy makers to better manage alien invasive species, there is still urgent need for China to improve its current legal regime in order to

[58] *Convention on Biological Diversity*, Article 11. [59] CBD Guiding Principles, note 8.

[60] *The Compendium of National Ecological Conservation* was promulgated by the State Council on 26 November 2000. It is a most important policy statement by the central government on its commitment to combat ecological degradation and to conserve natural resources.

[61] SEPA, *Notice on Strengthening the Prevention and Control of Alien Invasive Species* (2003, no. 6), note 4.

[62] SEPA Document, 2003, no. 11. The Catalogue lists the sixteen most harmful alien invasive species found in China and provides their characteristics, places of origin, distribution in China, pathways, impacts, and methods of control. The sixteen species are crofton weed, mile-a-minute weed, alligator weed, ragweed (bitterweed), darnel rye-grass (poison darnel), smooth cord-grass, bitter bush (siam weed), water hyacinth, Johnson grass, banana moth, lobdelly pine mealybug, red turpentine beetle, American white moth, giant African snail, Amazonian snail (apple snail), and American bull frog.

effectively control and mitigate the adverse impact of alien invasive species. A comprehensive legal framework on the management and control of alien species should incorporate fundamental environmental law principles and the environmental mechanisms that have been tested and proved to be effective.

4.1 Defining Legislative Objectives

The establishment of a comprehensive legal framework starts with a clear definition of its objectives. Explicit objectives are necessary to provide a conceptual basis to develop the legislation itself, guide implementation, set priorities, and build awareness. According to the IUCN Guidelines, specific objectives for alien species legislation should include: protection of animals, plants, plant products, and human health against alien pests, including pathogens; protection of species, subspecies, and races against contamination, hybridization, and extinction or extirpation; protection of native biodiversity, biological resources, and ecological processes against adverse impacts generated by alien invasive species; protection against biosecurity threats, defined as matters or activities that, individually or collectively, may constitute a biological risk to the ecological welfare or to the well-being of humans, animals, or plants of a country.[63]

4.2 Incorporating Fundamental Environmental Law Principles

4.2.1 The Preventive Principle

The preventive principle seeks to minimize environmental damage by requiring action to be taken at an early stage and, if possible, before harm is done. Under the preventive principle, a state may be under an obligation to prevent damage to the environment by means of appropriate regulatory, administrative and other measures.[64] Although taking a preventive approach does not impose an absolute duty on States to prevent all harm, it does require them to exercise due diligence and act reasonably and in good faith in prohibiting and regulating activities that could have such results. They also should put measures in place to prevent or minimize damaging consequences of activities that are permitted. Once an introduced species becomes invasive, it will be both difficult and expensive to eradicate. If much time has elapsed, eradication becomes impossible, and the damage irreversible. Prevention is more cost-effective and environmentally desirable than remedial measures taken after the introduction or establishment of an alien invasive species. For these reasons, prevention of unwanted introductions should be the priority of any legal regime to control and manage alien invasive species.

Although there are no settled criteria for the minimum damage, spread, or size of population needed for a species to be considered invasive, past experience shows that a very small number of individuals, representing a small fraction of the species' genetic variation in its native range, can be enough to generate massive environmental

[63] Clare Shine et al., *IUCN Guidelines*, note 4, at 43.

[64] Philippe Sands, *Principles of International Environmental Law*, 2nd ed. (Cambridge University Press, 2003), 246–249.

damage.[65] Therefore, every alien species needs to be treated for management purposes as potentially invasive, unless and until there is reasonable evidence to indicate otherwise.

Preventive actions will be different for intentional and unintentional introductions. For intentional introductions, prevention may take the form of total prohibition or partial prohibition, usually under a permit to which conditions may be attached. For unintentional introductions, the likelihood of unwanted introductions should be minimized by identifying and controlling common pathways through appropriate controls, such as quarantine systems.

4.2.2 The Precautionary Principle

Precaution relates to decision making in situations of scientific uncertainty. One formulation of the precautionary principle holds that the lack of full scientific certainty shall not be used as a reason for postponing cost effective measures to prevent environmental degradation.[66] The principle was reiterated in the CBD Preamble, in slightly modified form, in which it states that "lack of full scientific certainty should not be used as a reason for postponing measures to avoid or minimize" a "threat of significant reduction or loss of biological diversity."[67]

Precaution is particularly relevant to alien invasive species issues because of the inherent scientific uncertainty and limitations on predictive capacity.[68] The precautionary principle provides a legal basis for using risk analysis tools to inform decision makers of proposed introductions, activities and control strategies. It requires decision makers to take into account scientific uncertainty and to judge the level of acceptable uncertainty in a given context based on the scientific evidence that is available.

4.2.3 The Polluter Pays Principle

The polluter pays principle requires that the costs of pollution should be borne by the person responsible for causing the pollution. It first appeared as a guiding principle endorsed by the OECD Council to allocate costs of pollution prevention and control measures to encourage rational use of environmental resources and avoid distortions in international trade and investment.[69]

The polluter pays principle can work in the context of alien invasive species to internalize the "external" cost of environmental damage. A party who imports an alien invasive species could be viewed as a polluter and liable under the polluter pays principle. This holds the polluter who creates an environmental harm liable to pay the costs of preventing and remedying that harm. The natural or legal person responsible – who

[65] Scientists have found that factors affecting the establishment and proliferation of alien species include demographics, environment, natural catastrophes, and genetics. M. L. Shaffer, "Minimum Population Sizes for Species Conservation." 31 *Bioscience* (1981), 131–134. It is possible that invasion is independent from population size if density-independent factors – such as weather, habitat conditions and the size of the habitat patch – are the main determinants of persistence or if the population's numerical increase allows initially small populations to escape rapidly the risk of extinction. National Research Council, *Predicting Invasions of Nonindigenous Plants and Plant Pests* (National Academy Press, 2002).

[66] *Rio Declaration*, Principle 15.

[67] *Convention on Biological Diversity*, Preamble.

[68] For the difficulties and uncertainties involved in the prediction of the invasion of alien species, see National Research Council, supra note 65.

[69] OECD Council Recommendation C(72)128 (1972), 14 *International Legal Materials* (1975), 236.

often stands to benefit commercially from the activity or process that generates the pollution – therefore should bear the cost of pollution prevention and control measures.

Adoption of the polluter pays principle can improve the existing liability scheme practiced in China, which can be characterized as administrative in nature. In its Notice to Provincial Level Environmental Protection Bureaus (EPBs), SEPA mandates that any units or individuals engaged in the work of introducing and applying alien species should take preventative measures such as setting up insulation or buffer zones, and should carry out environmental monitoring and establish the relevant monitoring files and records.[70] Although no clear legal liabilities are attached to the relevant parties, SEPA has directed the local EPBs to implement a reward and disciplinary system. Those who have achieved significant progress in preventing and controlling alien invasive species will be rewarded. Those who have not carried out effective supervision and management will be criticized and ordered to take proper measures within a limited period of time. When heavy loss is caused by a failure to implement the prevention, control, and eradication plan, relevant leaders will be considered responsible. When significant loss is caused to the ecosystem and the economy as a result of illegal introduction of alien species, the relevant parties shall be held criminally liable.[71]

4.3 Adopting Essential Mechanisms

4.3.1 Risk Analysis

The State Council has declared its policy statement on alien species in the *Compendium of National Ecological Conservation*, which provides that risk assessment must be carried out on introduced alien species and that import sanitary measures must be strengthened in order to prevent the entry of harmful alien species into China.[72]

The risk analysis process seeks to identify the relevant risks associated with a proposed introduction and to assess each of those risks by three steps: risk assessment, risk management, and risk communication.[73] "Assessing risk means looking at the size and nature of the potential adverse effects of a proposed introduction as well as the likelihood of them happening. It should identify effective means to reduce the risks and examine alternatives to the proposed introduction."[74]

To promote transparency and accountability, each stage of the risk analysis procedure should be documented and become publicly available. In the context of intentional introduction of alien species, the analysis should identify the likely ecological, social and economic consequences of introduction; identify, and compare alternative measures, including likely ecological, social, and economic implications, and their feasibility; review the choice of management strategies; evaluate the likelihood of introduction, spread, or establishment of alien species under the proposed control or management measures; and determine how the proposed measures can be effectively implemented, including evaluation, monitoring, and adjustment in light of new information.[75]

70 SEPA, note 3.

71 Ibid.

72 *Compendium of National Ecological Conservation (2000)*, Article 14.

73 Clare Shine et al., *IUCN Guidelines*, note 4, at 35.

74 IUCN – The World Conservation Union, *Guidelines for the Prevention of Biodiversity Loss Due to Biological Invasion* (2000).

75 Clare Shine et al., *IUCN Guidelines*, note 4, at 36.

Risk management frameworks for unintentional introductions have to focus on a particular pathway or process rather than on a specific alien species or group of species. Sectoral activities that are often pathways for introduction include fisheries, agriculture, forestry, horticulture, shipping, ground and air transportation, construction projects, landscaping, ornamental aquaculture, tourism, and game-farming. "Risk assessments are most reliable when the identity and biological characteristics of a pest likely to be associated with a commodity are well documented and when the availability and vulnerability of potentially affected plants and their communities are known."[76] Although some pathways are known to present high risks of unintentional introductions, such as ballast water discharges, regulatory controls should not be limited to already identified pathways. Consistent with the precautionary principle, the legal framework needs to be sufficiently flexible to respond to new and emerging pathways that were previously considered as low risk.

4.3.2 Environmental Impact Assessment

The CBD suggests carrying out environmental impact assessments (EIAs) for projects, programs, and policies likely to have a significant adverse impact on biodiversity and notifying, exchanging information, and consulting with neighboring countries that may be affected by damaging processes and activities.[77] The EIA as mandated under the CBD is not only for specific projects but also for programs and policies that are likely to have significant adverse effects on biodiversity. Parties to the CBD are urged to integrate EIA into work programs on alien species.[78] The Guiding Principles recommends the use of EIA before making a decision on whether or not to authorize a proposed introduction of an alien species.[79]

SEPA has emphasized the precautionary principle in preventing alien invasive species. In order to strengthen the supervision and control of the introduction of alien species, SEPA proposed the establishment of an environmental impact assessment regime whereby not only the economic values will be considered but also the potential impacts on biodiversity and ecosystem will be assessed. Only those species that have proved to be biologically safe through scientific risk assessment and relevant tests can be introduced, applied, and commercialized.[80]

The EIA seeks to ensure that adequate and early information is available on the likely environmental consequences of a project, on the possible alternatives, and on the measures to mitigate harm.[81] As a general prerequisite for undertaking decisions or for approving designated processes or activities, EIA serves to inform decision makers

[76] National Research Council, note 65, at 16.

[77] *Convention on Biological Diversity*, Article 14.

[78] CBD Decision V/18.

[79] CBD Secretariat, *Guiding Principles for the Prevention, Introduction and Mitigation of Impacts of Alien Species That Threaten Ecosystems, Habitats or Species* (UNEP/CBD/COP/6/20), Principles 10 and 11. Adopted at the sixth meeting of the Conference of Parties in The Hague in April 2002.

[80] SEPA, note 3.

[81] In applying this tool to alien species, Shine et. al., provides a nonexhaustive list of factors that should be considered: (1) the cumulative, long-term, long-distance, direct, and transboundary effects of alien species introductions; (2) alternative actions, including prohibiting the proposed introduction; (3) measures to avert or minimize the potential impact of the proposed introduction; and (4) a periodic review and monitoring to determine whether the introduction is in compliance with the conditions set out in the approval, and to evaluate the effectiveness of mitigation measures. Clare Shine et al., *IUCN Guidelines*, note 4, at 36.

of the environmental consequences of their decisions, and to integrate environment matters into the broader social and economic policy-making process.

4.3.3 Permit Control Mechanism

For intentional introduction of alien species, an effective and flexible control mechanism can be established in the form of a permit/license system, or equivalent authorization procedures.[82]

Obviously, the approach most consistent with the precautionary principle is to control all categories of alien species proposed for introduction or release, whatever their origins or the purpose of their introduction. That is, no intentional introduction should take place without proper authorization in the form of a permit or license. When it is impossible to apply the permit system to all alien species legally or administratively, listing techniques may be adopted for the operation of the permit system. The lists can be compiled with reference to established databases and in close collaboration with competent authorities in neighboring countries or key trading partners and be regularly updated. Blacklists are used to identify alien species that are deemed to be high risk.[83] Their intentional introduction, even into situations of containment, should be prohibited, as should their possession, sale, and transport, because they may be inadvertantly introduced. Blacklists make an important contribution to border control and monitoring, but are not successful management tools by themselves. They are reactive: species are listed after they have been proved to be invasive, often based on a crisis management approach. These lists can never be fully accurate or exhaustive or up-to-date.[84]

The permit control mechanism allows for a case-by-case, tailor-made regulatory control mechanism to be implemented with relative flexibility. When an introduction permit is granted, legislation should provide a basis for attaching conditions, consistent with the precautionary principle, to minimize the risk of alien species escaping from human control and becoming invasive.[85] Noncompliance with permit conditions should result in revocation of permits in addition to other sanctions.

4.3.4 Special Protection Zones

In line with the precautionary principle, introduction of alien species to protected areas and vulnerable ecosystems should be prohibited or subject to extremely strict regulation.

[82] Basic components for a workable permit system should include: a clear statement of which species are subject to the permit requirement; a clear statement of information to be supplied by the applicant; public access to information on applications, criteria, hearings, and decisions; risk analysis and environmental impact assessment based on scientific principles and evidence; provision of objective and technically sound information to guide decision makers in determining permit applications; the possibility of permit conditions (monitoring, emergency plans, containment procedures); the possibility of allocating the cost of permit procedures to the applicant; sanctions for breach and noncompliance with the permit. Clare Shine et al., *IUCN Guidelines*, note 4, at 52.

[83] They may be known as pests elsewhere in the region or be considered to be capable of reproducing in the wild in the country concerned. Species on such lists pose a serious threat to ecosystems, habitats, and species. Clare Shine et al., *IUCN Guidelines*, note 4, at 53.

[84] Clare Shine et al., *IUCN Guidelines*, note 4, at 54.

[85] Appropriate conditions may include preparation of a mitigation plan, monitoring procedures, containment requirements, and emergency plans. Permit conditions make it possible for those responsible for introductions to be bound by enforceable rules, which can be flexibly designed to individual circumstances and to ensure a flow of information to the competent authorities. Financial charges (fees, levies, and deposit bonds) may be attached to permits. See Clare Shine et al., *IUCN Guidelines*, note 4, at 59.

It is important to implement complementary measures around protected areas to avoid creating refuges of native biodiversity in close proximity to degraded areas vulnerable to invasion.

Certain ecosystems can be particularly vulnerable to alien invasive species and the risk of subjecting them to potentially irreversible damage caused by alien invasive species are too high to take. SEPA has made it clear that it is strictly prohibited to introduce or apply alien species in the country's nature reserves, well-known scenic sites, protected ecological function zones, and other special and vulnerable ecosystems.[86] In addition, SEPA directs local EPBs to work with relevant local government departments to identify key alien invasive species and establish key protection zones. Such key protection zones include nature reserves, protected ecological function zones, well-known scenic sites, special and vulnerable ecosystems, and inland waters.[87]

4.3.5 Special Conditions for Containment Facilities

Many intentional introductions involve the import of alien species for contained use or situations of captivity.[88] A major control mechanism is to restrict the location of such containment facilities. They should not be set up in the vicinity of protected areas, areas of high biodiversity or on small islands. When a complete ban is not possible, such establishments should be subject to even stricter security conditions than elsewhere. Aquaculture and mariculture facilities are associated with particularly high risks of escape and invasions. Such facilities should be prohibited where there is communication with open water and should be located outside the one-hundred-year or even five-hundred-year flood zone.[89]

4.3.6 Monitoring and Database Building

The CBD mandates identification and monitoring processes and categories of activities that may have significant adverse impacts on conservation and sustainable use of biodiversity,[90] and, when a significant adverse effect on biological diversity has been determined, a regulation or management of the relevant processes and categories of activities.[91]

An accurate scientific and technical knowledge base is essential for any effective legal regime on invasive species. Where statistics are incomplete, impacts of invasions tend to be underestimated, which makes it hard to build political will for new or improved legislation. Timely information is needed to make responsible decisions on proposed introductions, allocation of scarce resources and implementation of effective control options. Lack of information makes it hard to promote consistent and coordinated decision making by administrators holding different positions at different times and in different geographical areas.[92]

An effective monitoring mechanism is essential in any effort to prevent, control, or eradicate alien invasive species. SEPA, with a widespread monitoring network all over

[86] SEPA, note 4.

[87] Ibid.

[88] Relevant facilities include zoos, aquaculture and mariculture installations, research institutions, captive-breeding facilities, horticultural establishments where artificial propagation is carried out, pet shops, and even traveling circuses. See Clare Shine et al., *IUCN Guidelines*, note 4, at 59.

[89] Ibid at 60.

[90] *Convention on Biological Diversity*, Article 7(c).

[91] Ibid., Article 8(l).

[92] Clare Shine et al., *IUCN Guidelines*, note 4, at 39.

China at the local level of EPBs, can play a supervisory and coordinating role in that regard. The maintenance of a nationwide catalogue of alien invasive species would provide valuable assistance to regulators, parties involved in introduction and application of alien species and the general public, in terms of prevention, control, monitoring, and awareness-raising. The IUCN publication of the one hundred World's Worst Invasive Alien Species[93] provides valuable guidance to the international community in developing national legal and institutional frameworks against alien invasive species. China has taken the first step by publishing a catalogue of the sixteen most harmful alien invasive species.[94]

Legal frameworks should provide a formal basis for monitoring and surveillance of both terrestrial and aquatic environments. Detection and early warning systems are essential preconditions for rapid responses against new invasions. The results of research and monitoring should then be fed back into the relevant knowledge base. China has not yet established systematic legal procedures to detect alien species invasions through monitoring, which is one reason why responses to invasions are often piecemeal, delayed, and ineffective. Legal frameworks should not only support identification and monitoring of alien species, but also provide the backing for the establishment of a knowledge base.[95]

The legal requirements of monitoring may vary depending on the nature of the introduction. Where an introduction or release is intentional, there is a known responsible party and the relevant permit may be subject to monitoring and reporting conditions. Where an introduction is unintentional or unlawful, detection has to rely on general and targeted surveys. Resource constraints may further limit the scope of the surveys in accordance with the predicted levels of risk.[96] Coordination and compilation of information on alien invasive species is particularly important where legal frameworks are fragmented. The IUCN suggests the use of a focal point or lead agency to record, collate, and maintain all such data.[97]

4.4 Control of Alien Invasive Species: Eradication and Containment

SEPA has directed local EPBs to come up with prevention and eradication plans based on the investigation of alien invasive species for their jurisdictions. They should carry out regular inspection of alien species and if the species are found to be invasive, the local EPBs must order the relevant parties to immediately stop introduction and take

[93] IUCN, *100 of the World's Worst Invasive Alien Species*. The list is available at http://www.issg.org/database/species/search.asp?st=100ss&fr=1&sts=#SpeciesList.

[94] SEPA, supra note 62.

[95] Such a knowledge base should include the following as suggested by the IUCN: information on the status, distribution, and characteristics of alien species known to exist in each country and, where applicable, its subnational units; case histories on past invasions, including information on time lag, which can obscure human perception of the invasion process; information on ecological and economic impacts associated with different alien invasive species to improve prevention and prioritise mitigation strategies; records of commercial practices leading to invasions and other pathways to provide a basis for developing new regulations; technical advice and support to border control and quarantine officers for use in applying regulations and developing contingency plans and rapid response tools. This may include generating advance lists of likely pests so that they can be identified and appropriate responses developed before they arrive and inventorying areas that are pest-free or of importance for biodiversity or other reasons so that particularly stringent contingency plans and required resources or technical personnel can be put in place. Clare Shine et al., *IUCN Guidelines*, note 4, at 40.

[96] Ibid at 67.

[97] Ibid.

measures to control and eradicate the relevant species. The local EPBs shall report such cases to both the local people's governments and the environmental authority at a higher level. For those established as alien invasive species, local EPBs shall develop practical plans and take mechanical, chemical, physical, and biological measures to eradicate the species. For those that cannot be eradicated immediately, measures shall be taken to contain and control further spread.[98] Mechanical control involves removing the species by hand or with appropriate machines such as harvesting vehicles (in the case of water hyacinth), or firearms or traps. Chemical control involves the use of herbicides and insecticides, ensuring that only the target species are extirpated and avoiding the potential problem of resistance that develops over time. Biological control involves the intentional use of populations of natural enemies of the target alien invasive species or other methods. It may provide long-term suppression of an alien invasive species without recurrent costs.

Where financial resources are limited, priority is given to areas needing special protection such as nature reserves, well-known scenic sites, ecologically special and vulnerable areas, and inland waters.

The Ministry of Agriculture ran pilot schemes known as "One Province and Five Counties" in 2003 to eradicate pests and weeds. The scheme was extended to "Ten Provinces and One Hundred Counties" in 2004 with more targets for eradication including crofton weeds, ragweeds (bitterweeds), and alligator weeds.[99]

4.5 Institutional Coordination

The CBD suggests integration of biodiversity-related considerations into sectoral and cross-sectoral plans, programs, and policies.[100] The prevention and control of alien invasive species involves many different sectors including environmental protection, agriculture, forestry, customs, quality inspection, science and technology, foreign affairs, international trade, and so on. The IUCN suggests that States should consider the establishment of a scientific authority for alien species control. The authority would provide scientific input to planning and decision-making procedures, including EIA and risk analysis, and advise on the design and amendment of regulatory measures and criteria. Legislation should specify the respective functions of the regulatory and scientific authorities and provide for necessary cooperation mechanisms between the two bodies.[101] In China, the role of this scientific authority is played by the Chinese Academy of Science. Responsibility for alien invasive species control is shared between the relevant sectoral institutions and agencies. Coordination is essential to ensure consistent practice. Mechanisms enacted for this purpose may take the form of cross-sectoral commissions or committees involving the representatives of all governmental institutions involved. In 2003, the Ministry of Agriculture took the lead in establishing the Alien Species Management Office, which coordinates the nationwide alien species prevention taskforce including SEPA, the State Quality Inspection Administration, the State Forestry Administration, the Ministry of Science and Technology, the Customs Administration, and the State Ocean Administration.[102]

[98] SEPA, note 3.
[99] Yao Runfeng, "More than 400 Alien Species Invading China." *The Weed Science* (2005), 22(1) 51.
[100] *Convention on Biological Diversity*, Article 6(b).
[101] Clare Shine et al., IUCN Guidelines, note 4, at 42.
[102] Yao Runfeng, see note 98.

4.6 Public Education and Public Participation

Promotion of public education and awareness is an important and integral part of any effective efforts to prevent and control alien invasive species.[103] Regulatory frameworks alone cannot solve all the problems presented by alien invasive species. They need to be complemented by nonregulatory efforts, particularly information, education and awareness-raising campaigns. A well-educated public is a prerequisite for the successful implementation of a well-designed legal system. Effective enforcement of any legal regime to a large extent depends on the participation and cooperation of parties involved. Members of the public can play a vital role in monitoring the implementation and enforcement of the law.

Up to now, there has been a daunting lack of knowledge, awareness, and commitment with regard to the issues of alien invasive species in China. Educating the public about the potential danger, risk, and harm of alien invasive species by all possible means including newspaper, websites, TV programs, and radio broadcasting can keep the public informed and get them involved in the efforts to prevent and control alien invasive species.

Furthermore, because the planning and decision-making processes on alien species issues are complex, they may require the involvement of governmental and non-governmental stakeholders in different sectors and at all levels. Open and transparent procedures involve creating opportunities for the participation of affected and interested parties, communities, and even the general public, in planning, permit-issuance, and the development of mitigation and management strategies. Such participation will have educational effects and raise public awareness without which no regulatory system can be effective. Participatory approaches need to be complemented by judicial review procedures to guarantee individual rights. Affected parties should be given the right to appeal permits denials, whereas interested individuals/groups should have the judicial remedies to challenge administrative decisions that they believe to be unlawful or inconsistent.

5 CONCLUSION

Although it might be complex, it is desirable for China to enact core legislation for the control and management of alien invasive species. It will help harmonize the legislative goals, control criteria and management procedures that currently exist in a piecemeal and fragmented manner in various laws, regulations, rules, and policy statements. Such a core enactment could implement and enforce international standards in quarantine measures and transport controls. It should incorporate the preventive principle, the precautionary principle and polluter pays principle, using a variety of regulatory tools including risk analysis, environmental impact assessment, and permit control to prevent and manage alien invasive species. In addition, the enactment should prohibit or strictly regulate the introduction or release of alien species into or near vulnerable ecosystems and protected areas. Furthermore, the law should provide for monitoring, early warning, and emergency response systems to support crisis management, when biological invasions are detected. It should mandate timely measures foreradication and control of species that are already invasive or likely to become invasive in the future.

[103] *Convention on Biological Diversity*, Article 13.

The law also should strengthen compliance by public, commercial, and private actors and support research, training, education, and public awareness.

By improving government capacity to prevent unwanted introductions, through better knowledge, improved laws, and greater management capacity, backed by quarantine and customs systems that are capable of detecting and intercepting alien invasive species, China will be able to implement fully its obligations under article 8(h) of the CBD and better conserve biodiversity and ensure biosafety for both China and the world.

SECTION B. GENETICALLY MODIFIED ORGANISMS

26 Who Is to Blame? Liability and Redress Related to GMOs

Loretta Feris*

1 INTRODUCTION

Although scientists and farmers have for centuries engaged in plant manipulation and cross-breeding, it was not until the discovery of the DNA molecule in 1953 that a new mode of genetic manipulation was made possible.[1] Agricultural biotechnology now utilizes recombinant DNA techniques to transfer genes between species and from one cell to another.[2] As such, the resultant genetically modified organisms (GMOs) can draw from a more diverse gene pool and offer valuable phenotypes not available through conventional breeding.[3] The so-called first generation GM crops, that is, those modified for resistance to insect pests, herbicides, and viruses, have mostly benefited producers of GMOs,[4] whereas second-generation crops are in the process of development and they are more likely to benefit consumers.[5]

The development of genetically modified foods has mushroomed since 1953. It is now estimated that the United States has 72 percent, Argentina 17 percent, and Canada 10 percent of its agricultural land planted with genetically modified crops.[6] The technology of genetically modified organisms is still relatively new, however, and, as with any new technology, it carries some level of risk. Harm can occur in a number of circumstances from the cradle to the grave route of biotechnology and some risks such as safety and health hazards are as yet undetermined. Other risks have been clearly established. For example, approximately nine class action suits have been brought in the United States against the biotech company Aventis over the contamination of corn.[7] This includes an action by government on the basis that the company did not adequately educate farmers on separating animal feed from human food. It also includes a lawsuit by restaurants and food companies relating to the damage they suffered as a result of

[1] Edith Weiss, & John Jackson, eds., *Reconciling Environment and Trade* (Ardsley, New York: Transnational Publishers, 2001), 571.

[2] Ellen Messer, "Food Systems and Dietary Perspective: Are Genetically Modified Organisms the Best Way to Ensure Nutritionally Adequate Food?" 7 *Indiana Journal of Global Legal Studies* (2001), 65, 72.

[3] Ibid. at 66.

[4] Jennifer Thompson, *Genes for Africa: Genetically Modified Crops in the Developing World* (University of Cape Town Press, 2002), 28.

[5] Ibid. at 50.

[6] Available at http://www.developmentgateway.org (last visited 12 December 2003).

[7] *LA Times* 9 June 2001. Available at http://www.latimes.com/news/front/20010609/ (last visited 12 December 2003).

* Loretta Feris is Associate Professor of Law, Faculty of Law, University of Pretoria.

being linked to the use of Aventis' Starlink corn. These lawsuits are indicative of the quagmire of legal issues that can arise from the potential detrimental impacts of GMOs.

They also illustrate the need to regulate legal responsibility for GMO-related harm. Legal liability regimes satisfy this function and create observance of environmental principles such as precaution, prevention, duty of care and the polluter pays. First, the existence of a liability regime may lead to a cautious approach in the import, export, production, handling, moving, use, and so on of GMOs. In this respect, it serves the purpose of prevention and urges an actor *ex ante facto* to avert the imposition of liability.[8] Second, a liability regime promotes compliance with environmental regulatory measures and as such serves to enforce environmental laws. It provides the injured party with an instrument to secure his or her legally protected interests and covers the punitive function of liability. As such a liability regime plays a corrective function.[9] Third, a liability regime ensures that redress is provided for in those instances where unlawful actions cause injury to the environment or to third parties. A liability regime thus serves a reparative function, which shifts the detrimental costs of harmful conduct in whole or in part from the victim to the author of the conduct.[10]

The concept of liability is not uncommon in environmental law and forms part of both domestic and international law. In international law, liability regimes have been created in various areas of the law such as nuclear regulation, oil pollution, marine pollution, hazardous waste, and so on. In fact, the duty on States to prevent environmental harm dates as far back as 1941. In the Trial Smelter Arbitration,[11] the panel found that, although a company operating in the United States, adhered to U.S. laws, it had a duty to prevent environmental harm from occurring outside of its jurisdiction. Thus, a state may manage its environment within its jurisdiction, but it cannot allow the environmental effects and damages to spread outside of the country's jurisdiction. This duty against transboundary harm does not only prohibit a State from doing harm that reaches the jurisdiction of another State but also to refrain from doing harm beyond the limits of national jurisdiction.[12] Principle 2 of the Rio Declaration states: "States have ... the sovereign right to exploit their own resources pursuant to their own environmental and development policies, and the responsibility to ensure that activities within their jurisdiction or control do not cause damage to the environment of other States or of areas beyond the limits of national jurisdiction."[13]

The law has not, however, kept pace with the rapid advances in biotechnology. Many countries do not provide for biosafety regulations, whereas others are underregulated.[14] It is key, therefore, that environmental liability for GMO-related harm be addressed globally and in a uniform way.

[8] René Lefeber, *Transboundary Environmental Interference and the Origin of State Liability* (Brill Academic, 1996), 1.

[9] Ibid.

[10] Ibid.

[11] United Nations, Trail Smelter, *Reports of International Arbitral Awards*, Vol. III, 1965–1966.

[12] Birnie and Boyle argue that "international law does not allow states to conduct or permit activities within their territories, or *in common spaces* [emphasis added], without regard of other states or for the protection of the environment." See Patricia Birnie & Alan Boyle, *International Law and the Environment* (Oxford University Press, 2002), 104.

[13] United Nations Conference on the Environment and Development (UNCED) held in Rio de Janeiro, Brazil, June 1992.

[14] Karen Graziano, "Biosafety Protocol: Recommendations to Ensure the Safety of the Environment." 7 *Colorado Journal of International Environmental Law and Policy* (1996), 179.

This chapter examines liability and redress schemes in the context of international law. It identifies the various types of risks associated with GMOs and the potential legal claims that may result from GMO-related damage, followed by a consideration of different aspects of a liability regime for harm associated with GMOs. It then assesses the current state of play on an international level and highlights some of the legal challenges in creating a uniform liability scheme for GMO associated harm to the environment.

2 IDENTIFYING THE RISKS ASSOCIATED WITH GMOs

Biotechnology carries both benefits and risks. Genetic engineering has the potential to help increase production and productivity in agriculture, forestry, and fisheries.[15] It also can be utilized to increase the nutritional value of foods. For instance, crops can be genetically engineered to increase vitamin contents as in the case of so-called golden rice, in which the rice has been genetically transformed to incorporate pro-vitamin A (beta-carotene) and iron.[16] Through genetic modification, livestock and poultry can become disease-resistant and can have breed improvement.[17] Genetic engineering also can help to reduce the transmission of human and animal diseases through new vaccines.[18] It can, furthermore, spur the development of pharmaceutical products through genetically engineered micro-organisms[19] and have various other environmental benefits, including remediation of oil spills and pollution control through the use of GMOs.[20]

Scientists, academics, and nongovernmental organizations, however, also have called attention to the risks of biotechnology to both human and animal health and safety and to the environment overall. GMOs are able to "interact with other forms of life, reproduce, transfer their characteristics and mutate in response to environmental influences." Once GMOs have been released they cannot be recalled and risks can occur to biodiversity through contamination and cross-pollination and the transfer of undesirable genetic traits to other species.[21] Opponents to GMOs also argue that through these kinds of gene transfers genetic modification will produce pests and weeds immune to pesticides and herbicides.[22] GM species may thus become pests that "displace existing plants and animals, disrupt the functioning of ecosystems, reduce biological diversity, alter the composition of species, and even threaten the extinction of various species and change climate patterns."[23]

[15] Howard Davies, "The Role of Science and the Scientist in the GMO Debate; Identification of Risks, Uncertainties and Benefits." Conference presentation available at http://wwwexternal.scri.sari.ac.uk/SCRI/nmsruntime/saveasdialog.asp?lID=902&sID=1422 (last visited 12 December 2003).

[16] Ibid.

[17] John Elkington, "Double Dividends? US Biotechnology and Third World Development." *World Resources Institute Paper No. 2.* WRI, Washington, DC, 13. On file with the author.

[18] FAO Special Programme for Food Security. Available at http://www.fao.org/spfs/ (last visited 15 December 2003).

[19] Dan Burk, "Introduction: A Biotechnology Primer." *University of Pittsburgh Law Review* 55(3) (1994), 611, 625.

[20] Howard, note 15.

[21] Lonie Boens, "Glyphosate-Resistant Soybeans: An Introduction." 6 *Great Plains Natural Resources* (2001) *Journal* 36, 44.

[22] Rahul Dhanda, *Guiding, Icarus: Merging Bioethics with Corporate Interests* (New York: John Wiley & Sons, 2002), 37.

[23] Richard Repp, "Biotech Pollution: Assessing Liability for Genetically Modified Crop Production and Genetic Drift." 36 *Idaho Law Review* (2000) 585, 591 (quoting M. Melton, *Biotechnology and the Environment: A Primer on the Environmental Implications of Genetic Engineering* 8 [1988]). A few years

Health and safety risks include the likelihood of allergens and other side effects harmful to human health.[24] Concerns associated with human health pertain mostly to food safety and the uncertainties with regard to unknown health risks and potential allergic reactions.[25] Given the techniques of genetic modification, which requires the insertion of genes from one species into the genetic code of another, someone allergic to the donor species could suffer an allergic reaction by consuming the host species.[26] It is also argued that GMOs could have adverse effects on people with "specific dietary requirements [due to their] ethical, religious, or cultural beliefs."[27]

In addition to the environmental and health risks, it has been argued that GMOs may have a negative effect on poor farmers and especially farmers in the developing world.[28] It poses a risk to traditional farming systems as the technology has been developed in a way that seeds cannot be reused, a practice used by farmers around the world. In addition, crops are engineered to resist pesticides and herbicides and promote reliance on specific chemicals. Farmers are thus forced to buy a particular type of pesticide or herbicide.[29] This could in effect lead to the creation of "monopolies" in the biochemical industry.

Farmers also may run some financial risks as a result of cross-pollination. As mentioned earlier, cross-pollination can lead to crop contamination, which is particularly harmful to organic farmers. A study conducted in the United Kingdom identified pollen from genetically modified crops that bees carried 4.5 kilometers away from the test site.[30] The researchers also found airborne genetically modified pollen up to 475 meters away from the test crops.[31] The economic injuries sustained in such cases can be extensive, especially considering the costs involved when an organic farmer has lost the organic status of his crop.[32]

ago, for example, a Cornell University study found that pollen from corn genetically modified to produce the toxin Bacillus thuringiensis (Bt) could be fatal to monarch butterflies. Scientists engineered these corn plants to produce this Bt toxin in order to kill European corn borers that feed on corn plants and did not necessarily foresee the demise of the Monarch Butterfly as the outcome of this experiment. *San Francisco Chronicle*, 20 May 1999.

[24] Anne Marie Solberg, "Genetically Engineered Produce Travels North America under NAFTA: An Issue Ripe for Consideration." *Hamline Law Review* 18(3) (1995), 551, 556.

[25] Tanya Vollendorf, "Genetically Modified Organisms: Someone Is in the Kitchen with DNA: Who Is Responsible When Someone Gets Burned?' 21 *Mississippi College Law Review* (2001), 43, 44. See also Julie Nordlee et al., "Identification of a Brazil-Nut Allergen in Transgenic Soybeans." 334 *New England Journal of Medicine* (1996), 688. The report talks about Pioneer Hi-Bred's efforts to increase amino acid levels in soybeans through genetic modification. The modification transferred to the soybean the same genetic material that occurs naturally in Brazil nuts and causes allergic reactions in some people.

[26] Ibid. at 45.

[27] Ibid.

[28] Ibid. at 37.

[29] Ibid. at 45.

[30] Ibid.

[31] Ibid. In the United States, the so-called StarLink case is probably the biggest case around contamination and may lead to the some of the largest litigation in the area of GM technology. The case arises out of the fact that GM StarLink and "buffer corn" became co-mingled with large quantities of other corn in the harvesting, transportation, storage, and marketing processes. StarLink was approved for human consumption, but in September 2000, traces of cry9C DNA, contained in StarLink, were discovered in taco shells, other corn food products, and corn export shipments. As a result, various food products containing StarLink were recalled. Numerous lawsuits have since been filed against the company Aventis, alleging StarLink-related damages to corn producers and consumers. Uchtman, D., "StarLinkTm – a Case Study of Agricultural Biotechnology." 7 *Drake Journal of Agricultural Law* (2001), 195, 162.

[32] An organic tortilla chip processor, for instance, was forced to recall and destroy eighty-seven thousand units of certified organic tortilla chips from Europe after tests revealed the presence of genetically modified corn. The company traced the corn used to make the recalled chips back to the specific organic farmer

Although the risks to human health, to the environment, and to property have not in all cases been clearly established, the potential GMO-related risks do, however, raise a number of legal issues. In particular, when the risk result in actual damage, those responsible for such damage can be held legally liable. In this respect, it would be of value to consider the scope of a regime that would regulate liability and redress for GMO related damage in a comprehensive manner.

3 DESIGNING AN EFFECTIVE LIABILITY REGIME

Environmental regulation is first and foremost aimed at protecting the environment. Principles such as "the polluter pays" have, therefore, been developed and adopted at both and international and domestic level. Integral to this principle is the notion that violators of environmental law rules and regulations who, in the process of such violation cause injury to the environment, should be punished. This usually happens by way of administrative or even criminal sanctions. A further step requires such polluter to remedy the damage caused. A liability regime plays an important role in realizing the objective of holding a polluter responsible for existing damage, future damage, and for subsequent remediation of the environment.

In drafting a liability regime, a number of legal issues need to be considered. These include the scope and content of concepts such as damage and the range of claims that can be brought, the standing to bring such claims, the identification of actors covered by such a regime, that is, the channeling of liability, the standard for liability, the scope of redress, and the provision for financial security. In international law, additional questions relates to whether an international instrument should provide for state liability or civil liability. Questions also arise as to the form of such a regime. Possible approaches to a state liability regime range from guidelines or framework documents to the creation of a legally binding instrument.

3.1 The Scope of Damage under a Liability Regime

Delineating the scope of damage involves a range of questions such as the nature of the damage, that is, direct versus indirect damage, reversible versus irreversible damage, continuous or contained damage, and whether the damage will result in public claims or private claims or both. Should these claims be restricted to economic loss or should it be wider and include the cost of response measures, including the cost of restoration? Should it maybe also cover some novel areas such as claims for cultural loss, for example, loss of plants or animals of cultural value? Should damage be circumscribed and, for example, only cover severe, major, or considerable damage? Should there be a threshold for damage and should such a threshold be a qualitative or a quantitative threshold?

The 1997 Protocol to Amend the Vienna Convention on Civil Liability for Nuclear Damage defines damage to include: (i) economic loss arising from loss or damage to person or property; (ii) the costs of measures of reinstatement of impaired environment; (iii) loss of income deriving from an economic interest in any use or enjoyment of the

who grew the corn, and it was found that the most likely cause of the presence of genetically modified corn was pollen from genetically modified corn in nearby fields cross-pollinating with the farmer's organically grown corn. Cheryl Hogue, "Organic Farmers, Greenpeace, Others Ask Court to Pull Bt Crop Registrations." 22 *International Environmental Report* (1999), 195, 196 (BNA).

environment, incurred as a result of a significant impairment of the environment; and (iv) the costs of preventive measures. Article 2(7) of the Lugano Convention on Civil Liability for Damage Resulting from Activities Dangerous for the Environment (Lugano Convention) has an equally wide definition of damage, which includes: (a) loss of life or personal injury; (b) loss of or damage to property other than to the installation itself or property held under the control of the operator, at the site of the dangerous activity; (c) loss or damage by impairment of the environment in so far as this is not considered to be damage within the meaning of subparagraphs a or b provided that compensation for impairment of the environment, other than for loss of profit from such impairment, shall be limited to the costs of measures of reinstatement[33] actually undertaken or to be undertaken; and (d) the costs of preventive measures[34] and any loss or damage caused by preventive measures.

From this definition, one can assert three general types of damage that potentially could be included in a liability regime: damage to the environment, damage to property and damage to humans, and, more specifically, damage to human health or life.

Although one needs to acknowledge that not every biosafety related impact on the environment would necessarily equate to or result in damage, claims for those impacts that do result in harm can be wide-ranging. Ideally, a liability regime should therefore cover harm to animal and plant life or health, which should include natural habitats. For example, the recently adopted EC Directive on Environmental Liability with Regard to the Prevention and Remedying of Environmental Damage[35] (EC Directive) specifically delineate "environmental damage" in such a way to include "damage to protected species and natural habitats," "water damage," and "land damage."[36]

Given the threat of cross-pollination to biodiversity, damage also should include loss of biodiversity. It should be recognised, however, that the current definition of biodiversity (as defined by the Convention on Biodiversity), that is, "the variability among living organisms from all sources including, inter alia, terrestrial, marine and other aquatic ecosystems and the ecological complexes of which they are part" does not make it easy to extend the scope of a liability regime to biodiversity. For instance, measuring "variability among living organisms" may prove to be rather tricky. Equally complex would be establishing a threshold for such damage.[37] This would depend largely on the extent to which countries have already acquired baseline data regarding their existing biodiversity. Another murky issue is at what point does changes to flora and fauna actually constitutes "damage"? If one accepts that it is a customary trait for plants to cross-pollinate, how does one establish the damage and how is remediation achieved, given that it may not be possible to restore biodiversity?[38]

[33] In terms of Article 8, "measures of reinstatement" means any reasonable measures aiming to reinstate or restore damaged or destroyed components of the environment, or to introduce, when reasonable, the equivalent of these components into the environment. Domestic law may indicate who will be entitled to take such measures.

[34] In terms of Article 2(9), "preventive measures" refers to measures taken after an incident has occurred to prevent or minimise loss or damage.

[35] Directive 2004/35/CE of the European Parliament and Counsel.

[36] Article 2(1)(b). Land damage is, however, limited in that it relates only to "land contamination that creates a significant risk of human health being adversely affected . . . "

[37] This has been the argument of the European Commission in excluding biodiversity from the definition of environmental damage. See Explanatory Memorandum COM 2002 17 Final 17.

[38] Ulla Oehler, *Environmental Liability and GMOs in the EU and Germany*. LLM Dissertation, Exeter, 2004. On file with the author, at 25.

The extent of damage to the environment will depend largely on the definition of environment itself. An expansive definition may include cultural practices and provide the scope for claims related to such practices. For example, traditional knowledge pertaining to the medicinal, cosmetic, and other value of specific fauna and flora may disappear if the species it relies on become extinct.

Damage to property may equally lead to a wide range of claims. One of the most contentious issues in this regard relates to genetic drift in agriculture. The phrase "genetic drift" is used to describe the problem of inadvertent spreading of GMOs from a farm choosing to use that technology to a neighboring farm that has chosen not to include GMOs as part of its crop.[39] Genetic drift could potentially lead to two types of claims: first, an intellectual property claim, in which a person knowingly uses a plant containing the patented gene without having paid for the seed or having signed the requisite technology use agreements.[40] In other words, it could result in a claim for the "theft" of genetic technology resulting from cross-pollination. Second, it also could include a claim by the property owner for the "contamination" of his property. These claims may include loss of income when his crops are rejected as a result of the contamination and future income (for instance, when an organic farmer looses his or her organic license or certification[41]). Farmers also may have to deal with increased production and equipment costs, restoration costs, and depressed market prices.

Not all impacts on the environment will affect human health, yet the potential for GMOs to do so has been established. As indicated earlier, injury may result if someone allergic to a donor species suffers an allergic reaction if consuming food that contains such donor species. Damage to human health and, in some severe instances, human life, is, therefore, possible and ideally should be covered under a liability regime. These types of claims may include costs associated with health screenings, vaccinations, treatment, and so on.[42] A regime also should take into account fact that damage may only become

[39] Hilary Preston, "Drift of Patented Genetically Engineered Crops: Rethinking Liability Theories." 81 *Texas Law Review* (2003), 1153, 1154.

[40] See, for instance, *Monsanto Canada Inc. v. Schmeiser* [2001] F.C.T.D. 256 (Sask.), aff'd, [2002] F.C.A. 309 (Fed. Ct. App. Canada), which dealt with question of whether genetic drift can lead to patent infringement. The defendant farmed with conventional canola while his neighbours used Monsanto's Roundup Ready canola, a genetically modified canola engineered to be resistant to glyphosate, an herbicide present in Roundup. Monsanto's patent for the gene inserted to make Roundup Ready seeds mandates that every purchaser of the seed sign a Grower's Agreement and a Technology Use Agreement that prescribe the conditions under which a farmer may use the patented seeds. The farmer can use the seed for one-time planting and may only sell it to a commercial purchaser authorized by Monsanto for consumption. The farmer may not sell or give the seed to anyone else, and he is prohibited from saving the seed for replanting the following year. Roundup Ready canola was detected on Schmeiser's property by Monsanto. Schmeiser argued that the GM canola arrived either by wind drift of seeds from neighbouring farms or passing trucks or by cross-pollination from those farms. Monsanto maintained, however, that Schmeiser intentionally planted the Roundup Ready canola. The court held that Schmeiser violated Monsanto's patent and awarded damages to Monsanto.

[41] Roger McEowan, "Legal Issues Related to the Use and Ownership of Genetically Modified Organisms." 43 *Washburn Law Journal* (2004), 611, 625. It also could include damages related to the inability to meet contract obligations or obtain higher premiums, and costs relating to violation of identity-preserved crop contracts.

[42] It has been stated that food allergies affect approximately two and one-half to five million people in the United States and that adverse symptoms range from mild discomfort to a severe and even fatal reaction known as anaphylactic shock. Endres, Brian, "'GMO': Genetically Modified Organism or Gigantic Monetary Obligation? The Liability Schemes for GMO Damage in the United States and the European Union." 22 *Loyola of Los Angeles International and Comparative Law Review* (2000), 453, 457.

clear over time and may not be initially apparent. Although injury to human health is incorporated in some international agreements, most domestic law regimes already provide for personal injury claims by way of legislation or the common law.

3.2 Standing to Bring a Claim

Standing represents a crucial element of a liability regime as it determines who has access to justice. Under international law, a multilateral regime on liability limits standing to State actors. This is in line with the principle that international law is a body of rules and principles that binds States in their relations with one another.[43]

The EC Directive also has limited standing to State authorities.[44] Natural or legal persons only have the ability to request the designated authority to act.[45] This limits access to justice. Standing provisions should be wide enough to provide private citizens the power to act in the interest of the environment. Thus, in designing an effective liability regime standing should preferably be expanded and not be restricted.

It has been argued here that a liability regime should broadly cover damage to the environment, damage to property, and damage to human health. With respect to the latter two aspects, litigants will have to indicate a personal interest. However, widened standing provisions are required to allow for claims on behalf of the environment. In this respect, an effective liability regime should create the opportunity for private actors to seek redress for environmental wrongs and bring a claim on behalf of the environment.

3.3 Channeling of Liability

An important aspect of any liability regime is, of course, the question "who should we blame"? Channeling of liability may depend on the type of damage, extent of risk, and who has operational control. International law (and to some extent domestic law) often channels liability towards the "operator" or "actor" of an activity.[46] In this regard, international agreements utilize a civil liability regime where private parties (the operator) predominantly control the activities at issue.[47] Depending on the definition of "operator" liability may fall only to the producer or developer of GMOs or also may include the end-users of GMOs.

Some agreements also may place liability on the State in instances in which it may act as an operator[48] or in which it may have failed to satisfy its obligations under the

[43] John Dugard, *International Law, A South African Perspective* (Cape Town: Juta, 2000), 1.

[44] Article 11 states that a "competent authority" shall be designated by Member States to fulfill the duties under the Directive. Thus, the State through its designated authority has standing to ensure that environmental damage is prevented and remedied.

[45] Article 12(1).

[46] The Basel Protocol on Liability and Compensation (Basel Protocol), for example, places liability on the notifier, disposer, exporter, importer, or reimporter of hazardous wastes. Article 2(6) of the EU Directive on Environmental Liability also uses "operator," which is defined as any natural, or legal, private or public person who operates or control the occupational activity, or who holds economical power over the technical functioning of the activity, or the holder of a permit or authorization of the activity, or the person registering or notifying the activity.

[47] See, for example, Vienna Convention on Civil Liability for Nuclear Damage and the International Convention on Civil Liability for Oil Pollution Damage.

[48] See, for example, Annex on Liability to the Environmental Protocol of the Antarctic Treaty.

agreement.[49] There also may be a number of different actors in which case the notion of joint liability will come into play.

3.4 Standard of Liability

Strict liability is the preferred standard for environmental offences. For strict liability, the commission of an act is sufficient to establish the offence, thus making it easier to establish liability. Strict liability is normally utilized in those circumstances in which abnormally dangerous activities are carried out.[50] The determination of whether an activity is abnormally dangerous involves an inquiry into the following factors: (a) existence of a high degree of risk of some harm to the person, land, or chattels of others; (b) likelihood that the harm that results from it will be great; (c) inability to eliminate the risk by the exercise of reasonable care; (d) extent to which the activity is not a matter of common usage; (e) inappropriateness of the activity to the place where it is carried on; and (f) extent to which its value to the community is outweighed by its dangerous attributes.[51]

Arguably, some biosafety-related activities may come within the scope of this description[52] and some form of strict liability should be included in a biosafety regime. Most international liability regimes, however, do provide for exceptions to strict liability. Exceptions would typically exclude harm as a result of armed conflict or civil war, natural disasters, compliance with a compulsory measure, or third-party action.[53]

Other possible liability standards may include fault-based liability, which would require intent or some form of negligence or absolute liability in which no defenses are permitted. A liability regime may even provide for a combination of liability standards

[49] See, for example, International Convention on the Establishment of an International Fund for Compensation of Oil Pollution Damage, International Convention on Liability and Compensation for Damage in Connection with the Carriage of Hazardous and Noxious Substances at Sea.

[50] See, for example, the Basel Protocol. Strict liability applies when both importing and exporting countries are parties and when trading with a nonparty for damages caused while the waste is in possession of the country that is a party.

[51] The Restatement (Second) of Torts.

[52] See Vollendorf, note 25, at 8, who argues: In terms of the first element the risk of harm from cross-pollination has been identified and documented. The concerns over the effects of GMOs on biodiversity and the potential unknown risks of harm meet the second requirement. This third element requires an examination of the situation to determine if the exercise of reasonable care would eliminate any potential risks. Once GMOs are released into the environment, no amount of due care can prevent all forms of cross-pollination. Such a risk cannot be eliminated. With the fourth element, common usage is evaluated. Currently, it may be difficult to make a determination as to whether the use of GMOs is common usage, but the use of GMOs has increased dramatically over the past few years and the industry is still evolving through experimentation. The fifth element involves the inappropriateness of the location of the activity. As the acceptance of GMOs continues to grow, "a plaintiff may establish that the use of GMOs is inappropriate or uncommon in a particular location," rather than being generally inappropriate. If the plaintiff can establish that the location is inappropriate, then the fifth element is met. Finally, the sixth element involves the value of the activity to the community in relation to the dangerous attributes of the activity. This entails a balancing test. Public policy concerns are heavily considered and viewed favorably. Such public policy concerns include increased crop yield for growing populations, socially desirable industrial activities, and overall economic benefits. In this situation, courts could utilize strict liability to balance the risks involved. By planting GM crops near traditional or organic crops, the defendant has created an imbalance of risks by subjecting neighbors to potential harm to which the defendant is not subjected – the defendant's crop will not be harmed by cross-pollination.

[53] See, for example, Article 4 of the Basel Protocol and Article 8 of the Lugano Convention.

such as the Basel Protocol that provides for a combination of strict and fault-based liability.[54]

3.5 Redress and Financial Provisions

A central aim of a liability regime is the nature of redress, once liability is established. In cases of environmental damage, response action that would prevent, contain, or limit the damage plays an important role as an initial step. A liability regime should, therefore, place a positive duty on operators to take preventive measures to avoid environmental damage, which has not yet occurred, but continues to present an imminent threat.

When damage has already occurred, operators should be liable for cleaning up and should be obliged to take steps to control, contain, remove, or otherwise manage the damage so as to limit or to prevent further environmental damage and further adverse effects on human health.[55] In addition, when the damage has occurred, a notification requirement can be imposed and the operator can be obliged to inform the competent authority of all relevant aspects of the situation without delay. This would provide authorities with the choice to either issue instructions in respect of the immediate steps to be taken, or take the necessary remedial measures themselves.[56] Such a notification requirement is especially important in those situations in which the operator fails to comply with a directive to take action from the appropriate authorities or in which the operator cannot be identified or is not liable under domestic law.

Once environmental damage has occurred, however, the remediation or restoration of the environment, preferably to its original state – in other words, *restitutio in integrum* – is a fundamental requirement. Given the permanency that GMO-related damage may pose to the environment and to biodiversity in particular, restoration or reinstatement may not be possible. In such a scenario, monetary compensation must be considered and, in this regard, the compensation must be based on the costs of alternative solutions, aiming at the establishment of natural resources equivalent to the destroyed natural resources.[57]

Redress measures such as preventive measures, response actions, and remedial actions may become a costly affair. Operators would thus benefit from taking out insurance that would cover such liability. From the perspective of governments, requiring such insurance or financial security would guarantee that redress would take place. A number of international regimes thus require mechanisms for financial security that will ensure recourse for redress.[58] Several options exist that includes instruments such as compulsory insurance, the provision of bonds, and the establishment of a fund for cleanup costs.

[54] The EC Directive similarly provides for a combination of strict liability on the operators of certain regulated activities listed in Annex III and fault-based liability on operators of other, nonregulated activities but only in respect of damage to habitats and species. Owen McIntyre, "The New European Community Directive on Environmental Liability: Substantive Content and Practical Implications." (2004), 5. On file with the author.

[55] See, for example, Article 6(1)(a) of the EC Directive.

[56] See, for example, Article 6(2) of the EC Directive.

[57] Elizabeth Dual, "A Liability and Redress Regime for Genetically Modified Organisms under the Cartagena Protocol." For example, 36 *George Washington International Law Review* (2004), 173, 193.

[58] See, for example, the Lugano Convention, the Vienna Convention on Civil Liability for Nuclear Damage and Protocol to Amend the Vienna Convention on Civil Liability for Nuclear Damage, and the OECD Paris Convention on Third Part Liability in the Field of Nuclear Energy.

4 INTERNATIONAL DEVELOPMENTS IN ESTABLISHING A LIABILITY REGIME FOR GMO-RELATED DAMAGE

4.1 The Cartagena Protocol on Biosafety

GMOs are frequently developed in one country and exported for use to another country. As a result, disputes related to GMOs may be transboundary in nature. Problems related to transboundary environmental disputes are numerous and include questions around a forum with universal jurisdiction, access to national procedures and remedies, uncertainties around state responsibility for environmental damage, the absence of clarity concerning the remedies available to states and their scope, and private international law problems such as jurisdiction and choice of law.[59] It has been argued that public international law can play a role in alleviating these complexities by providing an international regime that would harmonize national laws dealing with environmental damage and thus ensuring that adequate national remedies are available to plaintiffs in transboundary cases.[60]

The Convention on Biological Diversity established that the Parties consider the need for and modalities of a protocol setting out appropriate procedures in the field of the safe transfer, handling, and use of GMOs, the Conference of the Parties (COP) adopted the Cartagena Protocol on Biosafety on 29 January 2000, entered into force on 11 September 2003.[61] The Protocol regulates the "transboundary movement, transit, handling and use of living modified organisms (LMOs)[62] that may have adverse effects on the conservation and sustainable use of biological diversity, taking also into account risks to human health."[63] Article 27 of the Cartagena Protocol requires that the Parties to the Protocol "at its first meeting, adopt a process with respect to the appropriate elaboration of international rules and procedures in the field of liability and redress for damage resulting from transboundary movements of living modified organisms, analysing and taking due account of the ongoing processes in international law on these matters, and shall endeavour to complete this process within four years."

Thus, an "Open-Ended Ad Hoc Working Group of legal and technical experts on liability and redress in the context of the Protocol" was established in terms of Decision BS-1/8. The terms of reference of this working group include *inter alia* a mandate to analyse legal issues "relevant to liability and redress with a view to building understanding and consensus on the nature and contents of international rules and procedures referred to in Article 27 of the Protocol." In doing so, it must:[64]

(a) Analyse general issues relating to:
   (i) The potential and/or actual damage scenarios of concern that may be covered under the Protocol in order to identify the situations for which international rules and procedures referred to in Article 27 of the Protocol may be needed;

[59] Birnie & Boyle, note 12, at 267.
[60] Ibid., 269.
[61] Available at http://www.biodiv.org/biosafety/background.asp (last visited 15 December 2003).
[62] The term "living modified organism" is defined as any living organism with a novel combination of genetic material obtained through biotechnology. Article 3(g) Cartagena Protocol on Biosafety to the Convention on Biological Diversity, available at www.biodiv.org/biosafety (last visited 15 December 2003).
[63] Article 4. Except those used as human pharmaceuticals and addressed by other relevant international agreements, those in transit, and those destined for contained use.
[64] Available at http://www.biodiv.org/biosafety/issues/liability2.aspx (last visited 14 June 2005).

(ii) The application of international rules and procedures on liability and redress to the damage scenarios of concern that may be covered under Article 27 of the Protocol;

(b) Elaborate options for elements of rules and procedures referred to in Article 27 of the Protocol, which may include, *inter alia*:

(ii) Definition and nature of damage, including scope of damage resulting from transboundary movement of living modified organisms;
(iii) Valuation of damage to biodiversity and to human health;
(iv) Threshold of damage;
(v) Causation;
(vi) Channelling of liability;
(vii) Roles of Parties of import and export;
(viii) Standard of liability;
(ix) Mechanisms of financial security;
(x) Standing/right to bring claims.

The first meeting of the Ad Hoc Group on Liability and Redress took place in Montreal, Canada, 25–27 May 2005. As expected, there were disagreements among member states over the details of the proposed liability regime. Although many developing countries are pushing for a strong liability regime, the European Union (EU) has indicated that it is now no longer in favor of an "international legally-binding instrument."[65]

The obligations contained in the Cartagena Protocol may give rise to a number of difficulties in negotiating the scope and content of a liability regime for GMOs and Parties may face some severe challenges in finalizing such a regime. The first hurdle may lie in deciding what form the liability regime will take and whether to negotiate a legally binding agreement or nonbinding guidelines. Although a comprehensive legal agreement ensures legal certainty and provides scope for actual corrective action, history shows that States are less likely to sign an international agreement that creates binding obligations on liability for environmental harm.[66] A nonbinding instrument may thus allow for broader participation given its inherent flexibility. It also would provide the scope for creating more ambitious goals, but it will not secure compliance with the aim of a liability regime, and the broader goals of prevention, correction, and reparation may be defeated.

A tricky issue will also be the question of non-Parties, as Article 24 mandates Parties to encourage non-Parties to adhere to the Protocol. Major exporters of GMOs such as the United States and Australia are not members to the Protocol, whereas countries such as Argentina and Canada have signed, but not ratified, the agreement. The efficacy of a liability regime will be hampered significantly if the major trading countries fall outside of the reach of a prospective international agreement on liability.

[65] "EU dashes hopes of global liability regime on GMOs." Available at http://www.genet-info.org/ (last accessed 14 June 2005).

[66] International agreements on environmental liability that has not entered into force as a result of insufficient signatories include the Council of Europe Lugano Convention on Civil Liability for Damage resulting from Activities Dangerous to the Environment, the IMO International Convention on Liability and Compensation in Connection with Carriage of Hazardous and Noxious Substances by Sea, Basel Protocol on Liability and Compensation for Damage Resulting from Transboundary Movement of Hazardous Wastes and their Disposal, IMO International Convention on Civil Liability for Bunker Oil Pollution Damage and the UNECE Protocol on Civil Liability and Compensation for Damage Caused by the Transboundary Effects of Industrial Accidents on Transboundary Waters.

Other areas of concern include the scope of activities and damage covered by the Protocol. The Protocol itself is narrow in scope and does not cover pharmaceuticals,[67] or derivatives of GMOs. Liability will thus potentially only attach to GMOs intended for release into the environment and GMOs destined for food or feed, or for processing. This leaves out a range of GMOs (such as vaccines, biowarfare agents, bioremediation products, bioreactors for antibodies, and industrial chemicals) that may potentially impact adversely on the environment.

Furthermore, the Protocol adopts two separate procedures to ensure adequate protection in transboundary movements of LMOs. The first is the so-called Advanced Informed Agreement (AIA). The AIA only applies to the "first intentional transboundary movement of LMOs for the intentional introduction into the environment of the Part of import"[68] and provides for advanced notification of the introduction of LMOs into a country of import. This would apply to the environmental release of plants and seeds, for example. Any plants or animal product destined for food, animal feed, or processing are explicitly excluded.[69] The second less stringent procedure applies to a Party's final decision regarding domestic use, including placing on the market of LMOs that may be subject to transboundary movement for direct use as food or feed, or for processing. When a Party makes a final decision regarding the domestic use of such an LMO, it has the obligation to inform the other parties of that decision within fifteen days through the Biosafety Clearing-House of the Protocol. The philosophy behind the two procedures seemed to be linked to the notion that GMOs destined for food or feed, or for processing, are less likely to cause environmental harm, which begs the question whether separate liability standards would be an appropriate approach.

Parties also may have to consider Article 26, which provides for the consideration of socioeconomic concerns arising from the impact of GMOs on the conservation and sustainable use of biodiversity, especially with regard to the value it holds for indigenous and local communities. It has already been noted that when considering the scope of damage in a liability regime consideration should be given to issues such as traditional knowledge that is based on bioresources and that possible related claims may flow from any harm to biodiversity. The term "sustainable use of biological diversity" in Article 26 as well as in Article 4, which defines the scope of the Protocol, may affect the extent of the damage concept in a liability regime.

In dealing with the channeling of liability, an important consideration is whether to provide for state liability, civil liability or a combination or variation on both. A number of liability regimes provides for civil liability, for example the Council of Europe Lugano Convention on Civil Liability for Damage resulting from Activities Dangerous to the Environment, IMO International Convention on Civil Liability for Bunker Oil Pollution Damage, and the UNECE Protocol on Civil Liability and Compensation for Damage Caused by the Transboundary Effects of Industrial Accidents on Transboundary Waters. A civil liability regime recognises the fact that private actors are primarily responsible for operating within the environment and claims for damage should thus be brought against them directly. By contrast, it is argued that "a regime that does not attribute private conduct to the State would significantly reduce the effectiveness of a liability regime and ignores the existence of obligations on States to regulate and control the conduct of

[67] Article 5.

[68] Ibid., Article 7.1.

[69] Ibid., Article 7.2.

private persons within its jurisdiction or control."[70] I do not agree. Regardless of State liability, States have a primary responsibility to regulate and control the conduct of private persons within its jurisdiction or control. In those scenarios in which States act as operators, however, it is important to provide for State liability, whether it is primary State liability or shared civil liability. Thus, channeling of liability in the Cartagena Protocol should depend on the extent to which States act as private operators in the transboundary movement of GMOs.

With regard to the standard of liability, international instruments may employ strict liability, fault-based liability, or a combination thereof. Fault may be difficult to prove when it comes to GMO-related harm. The harm often occurs as a result of unintentional contamination or cross-pollination and despite any reasonable measures taken to avoid such harm. Some measure of protection against absolute liability may be build into the liability regime by providing for defenses. Typical defenses include *force majeur*, acts of war or civil unrest, intervention by a third party, and compliance with compulsory measures. The current draft of the Protocol's liability regime also include as a possible defense "the state-of-art in relation to the activities that were not considered harmful according to the science and technical knowledge at the time they were carried out". This would mean that the "operator" would not be held liable in those instances in which the activity in question was not considered likely to cause damage to the environment at the time that the activity took place. Given the lack of clarity on the long-term impacts of GMOs, this defense may serve to exclude liability in many instances and it has been argued that it challenges the "strictness" of strict liability.[71] By contrast, it should be taken into account that the development of and trade in GMOs may be stifled or even completely halted if operators bear the burden of liability despite unforeseen risks.

Finally, with regard to redress, the challenge lies in providing for a system of redress where the damage to the environment may be irreversible. As noted earlier, one option would be to provide for monetary compensation that would be utilized in replacing lost fauna and flora. The greatest value of a liability regime under the Protocol may, however, not lie in its reparative or corrective function, but in its preventive function as the mere existence of such a regime may encourage operators to avert the imposition of liability.

5 CONCLUSION

Technological advancement can undoubtedly benefit society as a whole, but inevitably it also can produce harmful results. The law plays an important role in ensuring that risks are managed and mitigated and, where harm occurs, remedied. The law should thus balance this responsibility with the potential benefits that can be derived from technology and specifically biotechnology.

Internationally, the Cartagena Protocol addresses this balancing requirement by obliging member states to institute national biosafety laws. The Protocol's liability regime would place similar requirements concerning liability and redress. Such a regime would fill an important legal vacuum in this arena, as the ultimate goal of an international agreement is the adoption of a harmonized system on national levels. Legal harmonization can contribute greatly to resolving transboundary conflicts, particularly

[70] Dual, note 59, at 198.

[71] Oehler, note 38, at 26.

in terms of clarifying the responsibilities of transboundary defendants, limiting conflict of laws predicaments, and balancing the interests of plaintiffs.

Creating a comprehensive uniform liability regime may, however, pose a challenge. History has shown that States are not willing to adopt liability agreements that provide for a wide scope of possible claims. The test will thus be to achieve consensus around the scope of a liability regime that will reflect the different interest of member States, while still meeting the mandate of Article 27 of the Cartagena Protocol.

27 The Reality and Effect of "Advance Informed Agreement" under the Cartegena Protocol

Rosemary Lyster*

There is considerable controversy about whether, and to what extent, genetically modified organisms (GMOs)[1] pose a threat to the biodiversity of the earth.[2] It is important, for the purposes of this chapter, to note that GMOs are organisms, plants, or animals that are *not* derived from traditional breeding techniques. They are produced using biotechnological methods known as recombinant DNA, which is the latest evolution of genetic engineering. It involves the transfer of an alien gene into the genetic code of an organism such that the organism bears certain "desired" new characteristics. The potential risks presented by GM crops for biodiversity include: the impact on nontarget organisms such as insects, birds, and micro/fauna and flora; gene transfer from the GM crop into related species; persistence or invasiveness of GM crops; the potential adverse effects of altered farm management practices, required by GM crops, on biodiversity; and the potential adverse impact on the centre of the origin of species.[3] Yet, there are many who extol the environmental benefits of GM crops that require fewer fertilisers, herbicides, and pesticides. Others point to the fact that there will be nine billion people by 2050 concentrated in developing countries. Their food security is tenuous given the shrinkage of available farmland and decreasing productivity caused by housing, infrastructure, and climate change.

However, given the potential threats posed by GMOs, it seems axiomatic that their release into the environment must be regulated in accordance with the principles of ecologically sustainable development. This requires adherence to the conservation of biological diversity,[4] the principles of intergenerational equity,[5] the precautionary

[1] This term is preferred by the author but may be used interchangeably with the term "living modified organisms," as adopted in the *Cartagena Protocol.*

[2] See, for example, S. Kolehmainen, "Precaution before Profits: An Overview of Issues in Genetically Engineered Food and Crops." 20 *Vancouver Environmental Law Journal* (2001), 267.

[3] See T. Simpson, "Environmental Risk Assessment of GMOs under Directive 2001/18: An Effective Safety-Net or a 'Collective Illusion.'" 25(2) *European Intellectual Property Review* (2003), 79, 81.

[4] *Convention on Biological Diversity*, available at http://www.biodiv.org/doc/legal/cbd-en.pdf (last visited 1 October 2005).

[5] *Rio Declaration* Principle 3. Intergenerational equity requires current rates of development to equitably meet the development and environmental needs of present and future generations.

* Rosemary Lyster is Associate Professor in the Faculty of Law at Sydney University and Director of the Australian Centre for Environmental Law.

principle,[6] and the polluter pays principle.[7] Public participation is an essential element of sustainable development. These principles are enunciated in the *Rio Declaration*,[8] *Agenda 21*,[9] and the *Convention on Biological Diversity*,[10] which are the international environmental instruments establishing the foundations of sustainable development.

In this chapter, the author questions the reality and effect of the "advance informed agreement" procedure that exists under the *Cartagena Protocol*[11] to the *Convention on Biological Diversity*. The *Protocol* requires that such agreement must be given before a Party can export a genetically modified organism to another country. However, the *reality* of informed consent given by most proposed importing developing countries must surely be questioned when one ascertains the capacity of the "competent national authority" (CNA) to fulfill its *Protocol* responsibility to decide whether or not to allow the importation of the GMO. Ideally, agreement to the importation should be based on a thorough assessment of the risks of the GMO to the biodiversity of the importing country. The preferable approach would be for the proposed importing country to have in place a comprehensive regulatory framework for risk assessment, supported by rigorous scientific studies, scientific peer review, and public participation processes. Yet, a lack of capacity on the part of governments in developing countries to achieve the multitudinous environmental objectives required of them by international environmental law is so well known that capacity building has become a cornerstone of all of the instruments supporting sustainable development.[12] In the likely absence, in developing countries, of such a framework, the CNA might be heavily influenced by the fact that the GMO has been "approved" in its country of origin.

To emphasise the difficulty of deciding whether or not to allow the importation of an "approved" GMO, this chapter elucidates the widely differing regulatory regimes that govern the release of GMOs into the environment in three jurisdictions – the United States, the European Union, and Australia. The label "approved for release into the environment in the United States/EU/Australia" will mean nothing unless the CNA satisfies itself that the approval processes, adopted by those jurisdictions, meet the standards for the sustainable regulation of GMOs.

The *effect* of the "advance informed agreement" is also questioned here since the *EU–US Biotech* dispute,[13] discussed extensively here, has foreshadowed that even where a developing country dares to say "no" to the importation of GMOs, trade agreements

[6] Ibid., Principle 15, which states that where there are threats of serious or irretrievable damage, lack of full scientific certainty shall not be used as a reason for postponing cost-effective measures to prevent environmental degradation.

[7] Ibid., Principle 16, which envisages the internalisation of environmental costs and the use of economic instruments, taking into account the approach that the polluter should, in principle, bear the cost of pollution.

[8] Available at http://www.unep.org/Documents.Multilingual/Default.asp?ArticleID=1163&DocumentID=78&l=en (last visited 1 October 2005).

[9] Available at http://www.un.org/esa/sustdev/documents/agenda21/English/agenda21toc.htm (last visited 3 October 2005).

[10] 31 ILM 818 (1992).

[11] Available at http://www.biodiv.org/doc/legal/cartagena-protocol-en.pdf (last visited 1 October 2005).

[12] See, for example, Principle 9 of the *Rio Declaration*, Principle 37 of *Agenda 21*, Article 4(5) of the *United Nations Framework Convention on Climate Change*, and Articles 12, 16, and 18 of the *Convention on Biological Diversity*.

[13] European Communities – Measures Affecting the Approval and Marketing of Biotech Products, Request for Consultations by the US, WT/DS291/1; see also Request for Consultations by Canada, WT/DS292/1, and Request for Consultations by Argentina, WT/DS293/1.

may require a WTO panel to declare the refusal unlawful in accordance with WTO law. This would be despite all the objections made by the country, and more particularly by the community in the country, to which the GMO is intended to be exported.

The fact that communities are able to express strong views on GMOs, which may ultimately be trumped by trade agreements, is amply demonstrated by one of the most extensive public debates on GMOs to be held in recent times – the United Kingdom's 2004 "GM Debate?" The debate emanated from the recommendation the Agriculture and Environment Biotechnology Commission (AEBC) made in its 2001 report *Crops on Trial.*[14] The Commission stressed the importance of encouraging a broader national debate stating that:

> It will be crucial for the public to be involved in the important decisions which need to be taken. We have to find a way to foster informed public discussion of the development and application of new technologies.[15]

The debate was extensive, involving 675 local meetings, 3.9 million hits on the "GM Nation?" Web site, and twelve hundred letters and e-mails. The findings of the public debate were that: there is a general unease about GMOs; the more people engage with GMOs the harder their attitudes become; there is little support for early commercialisation; there is a desire for more information and further research; and there is a deep mistrust of government and multi-national companies.[16]

With respect to the sense of unease among those people who took an active part in the debate about GM crops, their attitudes of caution, doubt, suspicion, scepticism, hostility, or rejection far outweighed any degree of support or enthusiasm for GMOs. The majority rejected any suggested benefits from GMOs. Just over half of the active participants never want GM crops to be grown in the United Kingdom under any circumstances. The remainder seeks varying periods of delay so that new research can identify, eliminate, or reduce, to an acceptable level, any risks to the environment or human health.

The mistrust of government was caused by the suspicion that government has already taken a decision to promote GMOs while using the debate to camouflage its decision. This seemed to link in with a general mistrust of modern governments, which are perceived to pursue secret agendas and ignore the public's views. There is also a lack of trust in the government's ability or will to defend the public interest, especially as they may be too closely aligned with the interests of multinational corporations. The public was suspicious of information about GMOs disseminated by multinational corporations that are regarded as pursuing profit rather than meeting society's needs. Overwhelmingly, people wanted to be provided with information that was independent and that they could trust. Essentially, they were looking for an agreed set of "facts" acceptable to all interested and affected stakeholders.

Of course, a similar debate held in another country may produce very different outcomes. Nevertheless, one could justifiably regard the United Kingdom's GM Debate as an excellent example of public participation, supporting the public's democratic right to express its views on a very controversial issue. The outcomes of the debate should certainly be taken into account, and given serious consideration, by the U.K.

[14] For an explanation, see http://www.gmnation.org.uk/ut_09/ut_9_1.htm (last visited 18 November 2004).

[15] AEBC Crops on Trial available at http://www.aebc.gov.uk/aebc/pdf/crops.pdf at para 68.

[16] GM Nation? Findings available at http://www.gmnation.org.uk/ut_09/ut_9_6.htm. See also M. Grekos "GM Public Debate – Findings Published" *Journal of Planning & Environment Law* (2003), 1530.

government in deciding how to proceed with the regulation of GMOs. Yet, a country that refuses to allow the importation of GMOs may be forced by a WTO Panel to either accept the importation of GMOs or pay substantial penalties to uphold the ban. This is fundamentally undermining of the notions of democracy. It is the author's view that adverse WTO rulings are a very real danger facing the CNA of a country that decides not to allow the importation of a GMO.

Before expanding on these issues, it is necessary to discover the provisions of the international environmental law instruments that cover the field under discussion.

1 THE CONVENTION ON BIOLOGICAL DIVERSITY AND THE CARTAGENA PROTOCOL

The objectives of the *Convention on Biological Diversity* are the conservation of biological diversity, the sustainable use of its components, and the fair and equitable sharing of the benefits arising out of the utilization of genetic resources, including by appropriate access to genetic resources and by appropriate transfer of relevant technologies, taking into account all rights over those resources and to technologies, and by appropriate funding.[17] The handling of biotechnology and the distribution of its benefits is provided for by requiring the parties to consider the need for a "protocol setting out appropriate procedures, including, in particular, advance informed agreement, in the field of the safe transfer, handling and use of any living modified organism resulting from biotechnology that may have an adverse effect on the conservation and sustainable use of biological diversity."[18]

This Article in the Convention gave rise to the negotiation of the Cartagena Protocol, which acknowledges the growing pubic concern over the rapid expansion of modern biotechnology and its potential to impact adversely on biological diversity and human health.[19] It also recognises, however, that if modern biotechnology is used with adequate safety measures for the environment and human health, it has great potential for human well-being. The *Protocol* specifically acknowledges that many countries, particularly developing countries, have little capacity to cope with the potential risks associated with living modified organisms.

Consequently, the objective of the *Protocol* is to ensure an adequate level of protection for the safe transfer, handling and use of living modified organisms (hereafter "organisms") derived from modern biotechnology. Relying on the precautionary principle, the level of protection should take into account risks to biological diversity, human health, and should focus on transboundary movements.[20] The *Protocol* does not apply to the transboundary movement of organisms which are pharmaceuticals for humans as these are regulated under other relevant international agreements or organisations.[21]

The centerpiece of the *Protocol* is the "advance informed agreement procedure," which requires the exporting Party to notify the CNA[22] of the importing Party about its first intentional transboundary movement of an organism.[23] The importing Party

[17] Note 4, Article 1.
[18] Note 4, Article 19.
[19] H. Baumuller, "The Cargegena Prrotocol on Biosafety-Environmental Perspectives." 18 (1). *Environmental and Planning Law Journal* (2001), 46 and B. Eggers & R. Mackenzie "The Cartagena Protocol on Biosafety" *Journal of International Economic Law* (2000), 525.
[20] Note 11, Article 1.
[21] Note 11, Article 5.
[22] Note 11, Article 19.
[23] Note 11, Articles 8–10 and 12. Annex I of the *Protocol* sets out the information that must be included in such notification.

must acknowledge receipt of the notification[24] and then decide, within ninety days of notification, whether the importation can proceed with or without the written consent of the importing party.[25] The importing Party is required to carry out an assessment of the risk posed to biodiversity and human health by the organisms, taking into account recognised risk assessment techniques and the precautionary principle.[26] The exporting Party can be required by the importing Party to undertake a risk assessment and bear the cost.[27] If importation is only allowed on written consent, the importing Party must notify the notifier and the Biosafety Clearing-House[28] of its decision to: approve the import, with or without conditions, including how the decision will apply to subsequent imports of the same organism; prohibit the import; or request additional relevant information.[29] The advance informed agreement procedure does not apply to organisms in transit or destined for contained use in the importing country.[30] Different provisions apply to organisms intended for direct use as food or feed, or for processing.[31]

Parties also should develop risk management strategies to deal with the risks associated with the transboundary movement of organisms.[32] They must also notify potentially affected States and the Biosafety Clearing-House[33] if an unintentional transboundary movement occurs.[34] Parties also must ensure that organisms that are subject to intentional transboundary movement are handled, packaged, and transported under conditions of safety, taking into consideration relevant international rules and standards.[35]

Appropriate domestic measures aimed at preventing and penalising illegal transboundary movements of organisms should be adopted by parties. The affected Party also may request the Party of origin to dispose of the organisms by repatriation or destruction at its own expense. The Biosafety Clearing-House must be informed of all cases of illegal transboundary movements.[36]

2 THE REALITY OF ADVANCE INFORMED CONSENT: CHALLENGES FACING COMPETENT NATIONAL AUTHORITIES IN DEVELOPING COUNTRIES

International environmental conventions place a considerable raft of responsibilities on developing countries. On the domestic front, environmental agencies in developing countries are expected to regulate pollution, environmental planning and assessment, and natural resource management. Yet these agencies are typically fragmented, under-resourced, and often relegated to a junior status in government. In addition to domestic regulation, government agencies must work towards achieving the multifarious obligations imposed by international environmental laws, in accordance with the principle of common but differentiated responsibility.

[24] Note 11, Article 9.

[25] Note 11, Article 10(2).

[26] Note 11, Articles 10(1), 10(6), 12.

[27] Note 11, Articles 15, 16.

[28] Note 11, Article 20. The Biosafety Clearing-House provides a mechanism to facilitate the exchange of scientific, technical, environmental, and legal information on, and experience with, living modified organisms; and assists Parties to implement the Protocol, taking into account the special needs of developing countries and small island States.

[29] Note 11, Article 10(3). This notification must take place within 270 days of notification by the exporting Party.

[30] Note 11, Article 6.

[31] Note 11, Article 11.

[32] Note 11, Article 16

[33] Note 11, Article 20.

[34] Note 11, Article 17.

[35] Note 11, Article 18.

[36] Note 11, Article 25.

The current difficulties experienced by developing countries in fulfilling their obligations under the *United Nations Framework Convention on Climate Change* (UNFCCC) may shed some light on the likely capacity of CNAs in developing countries to decide whether or not to grant "advance informed agreement." This comparison is instructive because the *UNFCCC* is a fairly recent international environmental law convention, and the difficulties faced by developing countries to comply with the convention are well documented. It is also relevant given the important impacts on biodiversity from global climate change, and the duty on all signatories of the *UNFCCC* to identify adaptation and mitigation strategies to minimise damage to biodiversity. The crucial point to be made here is to acknowledge that developing country obligations under the *UNFCCC*, or the *Cartagena Protocol* for that matter, represent only one aspect of the enormous burden placed on regulatory agencies. Whether they can adequately protect their own interests in the GMO context, is a moot point.

Under the *UNFCCC*, developing country obligations are primarily the following: to develop, update, publish, and make available national inventories of anthropogenic emissions and removal of sinks;[37] to enact effective legislation to achieve the objectives of the *UNFCCC*; to formulate, implement, publish, and update national and regional programs to mitigate climate change;[38] to sustainably manage sinks and reservoirs of greenhouse gases;[39] and to take climate change into account when undertaking environmental impact assessment.[40] As is well known, developing countries did not commit themselves to any binding targets under the *Kyoto Protocol*; however, those that ratified the *UNFCCC* remain obliged to comply with their commitments.

The *Protocol* also provides that developed countries should provide new financial resources to assist developing countries to meet their commitments.[41] The provision of funding[42] in itself imposes burdens on developing country governments which must comply with funding criteria before receiving it. As well, if a developing country wishes to participate in clean development mechanisms (CDM) projects[43] under the *Kyoto Protocol* it must establish a "designated national authority" (DNA).[44] The DNA must issue written approval of the project stating that participation is voluntary and that the CDM project contributes to sustainable development in the host country.[45]

[37] *United Nations Framework Convention on Climate Change* Article 4.1(a).

[38] Ibid., Article 4.1(b).

[39] Ibid., Article 4.1(d).

[40] Ibid., Article 4.1(f).

[41] The *Kyoto Protocol*, Article 11.

[42] Three different funds assist developing countries to meet their commitments. Under the UNFCCC, the Special Climate Change Fund finances projects relating to adaptation; technology transfer and capacity building; energy, transport, industry, agriculture, forestry and waste management; and economic diversification. The Least Developed Country Fund, also under the UNFCCC, assist LDCs to carry out, inter alia, the preparation and implementation of national adaptation programmes of action. The Adaptation Fund, established under the *Kyoto Protocol* to support the implementation of concrete adaptation projects and programs; see http://unfccc.int/cooperation_and_support/funding/items/2807.php (last visited 28 September 2005).

[43] Note 37, Article 12. The Clean Development Mechanism (CDM) allows developed countries to invest in emission reducing projects in developing countries, and to obtain certified emission reductions toward meeting assigned amounts. This allows developed countries not only to meet their emission reduction targets outside of their own jurisdictions but also to find a ready export market for their sustainable energy technologies.

[44] Just to add to the mix of responsibilities, see also the responsibilities of designated national authorities under the *Rotterdam Convention*, available at http://www.fao.org/documents/show_cdr.asp?url_file=/docrep/007/y5423e/y5423e07.htm (last visited on 29 September 2005).

[45] In accordance with cl. 29 of the Modalities and Procedures for a CDM (Annex decision 17/CP.7 para. 40), available at http://cdm.unfccc.int/DNA (last visited 29 September 2005).

The Subsidiary Body for Implementation of the UNFCCC noted in October 2004,[46] that a lack of capacity, financial resources, and good quality data were frequently reported in the national communications of developing countries. With respect to preparing national greenhouse gas inventories, developing countries expressed the need for improvements to the scope and quality of national activity data, relevant emission and conversion factors, continuous collection, archiving, and management including the establishment of databases, and modeling to assess greenhouse gas emissions in the agriculture sector especially those emanating from rice fields and savannah burning. In the context of preparing national communications, developing countries expressed the need for the building and upgrading of research capacity, data collection, and analysis in order to be able to undertake vulnerability assessment and adaptation options. In addition, a lack of financial resources, human capacity, and technical support has restricted the capacity of institutions and agencies in developing countries responsible for collecting, collating, managing, and using meteorological and hydrological data.

This report by the Subsidiary Implementation Body highlights poignantly the very real difficulties facing regulatory agencies in developing countries when they attempt to comply with their international obligations. It throws into sharp relief the difficulties that developing countries may face with respect to the functions of the CNAs under the *Cartagena Protocol.*

3 CHINA'S EXPERIENCE WITH BIOSAFETY REGULATION

The lengths to which developing countries should go in assessing whether or not to allow the importation of a GMO is well illustrated by Wang Xi et al.[47] when they describe the assessment process adopted in the People's Republic of China with respect to biosafety. In the first place, they note that China only ratified the *Cartagena Protocol* on 8 June 2005, and that it came into force only on 6 September 2005. One of the reasons for the delay was the difficulty of deciding which of many ministries should be appointed as the CNA. The State Environment Protection Agency has had carriage of protecting China's biodiversity since the start of negotiations on the *Convention on Biological Diversity.* The Ministry of Agriculture is responsible for managing biosafety issues relating to agricultural GMOs, whereas the Minister of Health monitors GM foods. Finally, the Quality Supervision Administration is the authority for regulating the importation of GMOs.[48] The Ministry for Agriculture has now been appointed the CNA. The principal piece of legislation regulating biosafety issues in China is the Regulation on Biosafety Management of Agricultural GMOs,[49] which must be read together with Provisions on Labelling of GMOs, Provisions on Safety Management of the Importation of GMOs, and Provisions on Safety Assessment of Agricultural GMOs.[50] Essentially, these laws require that a Party wishing to import a GMO into China must obtain a biosafety certificate from the Ministry of Agriculture and the GMO must be appropriately labeled.

[46] See Subsidiary Body for Implementation, "Report on the assessment of funding necessary to assist developing countries to fulfill their obligations under the UNFCCC." Fccc/SBI/2004/18, 21 October 2004, available at http://unfccc.int/resource/docs/2004/sbi/18.pdf (last visited 29 September 2005).

[47] Wang Xi, Qin Tianbao, & Fu Lu, "Cartagena Protocol on Biosafety and China's Practice." 3–4 *Asia Pacific Journal of Environmental Law* (2004), 67.

[48] Ibid. at 81.

[49] Decree No. 304 of State Council of the People's Republic of China.

[50] For a full discussion of these, see Wang Xi et al., note 34, at 84–90.

Before granting the certificate, the Minister must have complied with the extensive risk assessment processes set out in the legislation.

One might conclude, based on the analysis provided by Wang Xi et al., that proposed importations of GMOs into China would probably undergo a thorough risk assessment. What is clear is that in order to establish its extensive regulatory framework and to identify the appropriate ministry to act as CNA, the Chinese government has committed considerable resources to the issue of biosafety. It is fair to ask whether developing countries that lack China's considerable financial resources would be able to invest in the type of regulatory framework that is clearly needed to protect biodiversity from the possible threats posed by GMOs.

Given the onerous requirements of the "informed advance agreement" procedure, how much easier would it be for a CNA in a developing country to simply approve the importation of a GMO because it is "approved" elsewhere in the world? But this raises the next obvious question, which is, what does that "approval" amount to at the end of the day? The wide diversity of regulatory approaches to assessing the risks of GMOs to biodiversity, and human health, becomes apparent when one analyses the regulatory regimes in three contexts: the United States, the European Union, and Australia. This indicates that without undertaking its own risk assessment procedures, a CNA might be misguided by assuming that all "approvals" granted under any of these three regimes entail the same standards of risk assessment.

4 REGULATING GMOs IN THE UNITED STATES

The uptake of, and public acceptance of, GMOs in the United States is notable. GMOs are now grown on over one hundred million hectares of farmland. This is up from six million hectares in 1996. Interestingly, 81 percent of soybeans, 40 percent of corn, 73 percent of cotton grown, and over 50 percent of canola and papaya are derived from GMO seeds. Grocery Manufacturers of America estimates that 70 percent of food on grocery shelves is GM food. This includes cereals, crackers, juice, soda, salad dressing, and sauces. These statistics show an enormous tolerance, and acceptance, on the part of the U.S. public for GM crops. This sense of security is not in direct relation to the regulatory scheme governing the release of GMOs into the environment and the commercialization of GM food.

GMOs are regulated in the United States under three principal pieces of legislation and by three administrative agencies. Releases into the environment are governed by the *Plant Protection Act.*[51] The relevant agency is the Department of Agriculture's Animal and Plant Health Inspection Service (APHIS), which exercises its powers under *Regulation 7 CFR 340.* APHIS states that it has overseen the "safe" release of ten thousand GMOs, and the deregulation for purposes of commercialisation of sixty genetically engineered (GE) products.[52] The safety of commercial food is regulated by the Food and Drug Administration (FDA) under the *Public Health Act,*[53] whereas the U.S. EPA has authority under the *Federal Insecticide, Fungicide, and Rodenticide Act.*[54]

[51] 7 U.S.C. 7701.

[52] See APHIS New Release No. 0033.04, available at http://www.usda.gov/Newsroom/0033.04.htm (last visited 17 August 2004).

[53] 21 U.S.C. 342(a)(1) s. 402(a)(1).

[54] 7 U.S.C. 136.

5 RELEASES INTO THE ENVIRONMENT IN THE UNITED STATES

In order to release a GMO into the environment, the developer of the organisms must apply for a field test permit. If the plant falls under APHIS's "eligibility criteria," a streamlined permitting method known as the Notification Process is used. This means that the developer does a risk assessment of the possible impacts on the environment and human health and notifies APHIS that there is no risk associated with the GMO. The release into the environment is then authorised. The only public participation provisions are where APHIS releases lists of notifications to "interested parties" *on request.* If the plants are not "eligible," APHIS prepares an Environmental Assessment and issues a permit subject to detailed conditions. Penalties exist for noncompliance with these conditions. According to APHIS, 99 percent of all field tests, importations, and interstate movements of GMO plants take place under this notification system. When the developer has sufficient field test data, it may apply to APHIS for deregulation of the tested organism so that it can be commercialised. APHIS then issues a notice in the *Federal Register* that it has undertaken an Environmental Assessment and copies must be *ordered* by members of the public for the purpose of making submissions. There is no postderegulation monitoring by APHIS for unexpected impacts. APHIS does not subject data supplied by the developer of the GMO to external scientific review. The only role that the U.S. EPA plays in the scheme is under the *Federal Insecticide, Fungicide, and Rodenticide Act* (FIFRA),[55] which gives the agency the power to regulate GM pest-protected plants as "pesticides," and pesticide residues in food. It does not have regulatory authority to ensure that releases of GMOs into the environment do not impact on biological diversity.

On 29 June 2004, the U.S. National Academy of Sciences warned APHIS that its regulation of transgenic plants (to produce pesticides) was "superficial," as most are approved using the Notification Process. The Academy noted that APHIS was relying too heavily on scientific literature rather than requiring the developer to develop experimental data.[56]

Because of increasing public concern about GMOs, in 2003/2004 APHIS announced its intention to enhance its risk assessment procedures for field testing GMOs.[57] APHIS intends to introduce specific risk-based categories for different types of engineered plants to replace the notification system. It will revise the regulation regarding the release of plants engineered to produce pharmaceutical or industrial compounds, noxious weeds risks, and biological control agents. New biological and safety information will be required of the developer as part of the application process, as well as information on confinement conditions, including greater opportunities for public participation. The date for making submissions on these proposals has closed very recently. Also in 2003 a new compliance and enforcement unit was established under APHIS Biotechnology Regulatory Service.

[55] Ibid.

[56] See http://www4.nationalacademies.org/news.nsf/isbn/0309092094?OpenDocument (last visited 18 April 2005).

[57] *Federal Register,* Vol. 69, No. 15/ January 23, 2004/ Notices 3271–3272, see also http://www.aphis.usda.gov/lpa/issues/biotechcomp/biotechcomp.html (last visited 26 August 2004).

6 CONCLUSIONS ABOUT THE SUSTAINABILITY OF U.S. REGULATIONS GOVERNING THE RELEASE OF GMOs INTO THE ENVIRONMENT

If we analyse the GMO regulatory framework in the United States, we may well have some concerns about whether it satisfies international norms of sustainability.[58] As can be seen, the philosophy of regulators, until 2003/2004, has been that there is no difference between GMOs and other types of plant breeding regulation, and consequently risk assessment of releases into the environment, has been minimal.

As a result of this, there may well be risks for present and future generations. In the entire regulatory framework, there is not one mention of the precautionary principle, and risk assessments submitted to, or undertaken by, APHIS are not subjected to external scientific review. Given this, and the minimal role played by the U.S. EPA in the scheme, can we be satisfied that potential risks to biodiversity are adequately assessed? The legislation provides for penalties for failure to observe permit conditions, but no direct liability for compensation is imposed on developers for the detrimental effects of their products. Also, there is minimal public participation in the decision-making processes of agencies. Generally this occurs only where interested and affected stakeholders request further information, order copies of environmental impact assessment statements, or make FOI applications.

It may be concluded that the GMO regulatory scheme in the United States does not seem to satisfy the criteria for sustainable regulation.

7 REGULATING THE RELEASE OF GMOs INTO THE ENVIRONMENT: THE EU

The release of GMOs into the environment is governed by *Directive 2001/18/EC on the Deliberate Release of GMOs, the Placing of GM Products on the Market and Labelling.*[59] In accordance with the precautionary principle, the objective of the Directive is to provide a common regulatory framework in the Member States (MSs) to protect human health and the environment when deliberately releasing GMOs into the environment, and when placing on the market GMOs as, or in, products within the Community.[60] MSs must ensure that all appropriate measures are taken to avoid adverse effects on human health and the environment that might arise from these activities.[61] Before releasing a GMO into the environment a person must carry out an environmental risk assessment (ERA). When carrying out an ERA, particular consideration must be given by MSs to GMOs containing genes expressing resistance to antibiotics for medical or veterinary use. By 31 December 2008, MSs should identify and phase out antibiotic resistance markers in GMOs which may have adverse effects on human health and the environment.[62] MSs also must ensure that any adverse effects that may occur through gene transfer from

[58] See R. Bratspies, "The Illusion of Care: Regulation, Uncertainty, and Genetically ModifiedFood Crops." 10 *New York University Environmental Law Journal* (2002), 297; G. N. Mandel, "Gaps, Inexperience, Inconsistencies, and Overlaps: Crisis in the Regulation of Genetically Modified Plants and Animals." 45 *William and Mary Law Review* (2004), 2167.

[59] CONSLEG: 2001L0018 – 07/11/2003.

[60] Ibid., Article 1.

[61] Ibid., Article 4(1).

[62] Ibid., Article 4(2).

GMOs to other organisms are accurately assessed on a case-by-case basis.[63] A competent authority must be designated by MSs to take responsibility for obligations imposed by the Directive,[64] and such authority must organise inspections and measures to ensure compliance with the Directive.[65]

The ERA process is spelt out in Annex II of the Directive.[66] It comprises the following steps:

Step 1: Identify characteristics that may cause adverse effects.
Step 2: Evaluate potential consequences of effects.
Step 3: Evaluate likelihood of occurrence of potential adverse effect.
Step 4: Estimate risk posed by each identified characteristic of GMO.
Step 5: Apply management strategy for risks arising from deliberate release of GMO.
Step 6: Determine overall risk of GMO.

The ERA should be carried out in a scientifically sound and transparent manner based on available scientific and technical data. An analysis of "cumulative long-term effects"[67] also must be carried out. If new information on the effects of GMOs becomes available, the ERA may need to be readdressed.[68]

After conducting an ERA, conclusions must be drawn about the potential environmental impacts or the placing on the market of GMOs, with reference to the following: the likelihood of GMOs becoming persistent or invasive in natural habitats; any selective advantage or disadvantage conferred to the GMO becoming realised under conditions of release; the potential for gene transfer to other species; the potential immediate or delayed environmental impact of the direct and indirect interactions between the GMO with target, nontarget organisms;[69] human and animal health;[70] and biogeochemical processes.

Having undertaken an ERA, and drawn the necessary conclusions, the person wanting to release the GMO into the environment must notify the competent authority. The person must provide the competent authority with a technical dossier containing information about the GMO as well as the ERA and conclusions drawn. Bibliographic references and indications of methods used also may be supplied.[71] Having acknowledged receipt of the notification, the authority must advise the notifier within ninety days either that the release may proceed in conformity with any conditions, or that the notification does not fulfill the requirements of the Directive and is rejected.[72] If

[63] Ibid., Article 4(3).

[64] Ibid., Article 4(4).

[65] Ibid., Article 4(5)

[66] See also *Commission Decision of 24 July 2002* [OJ L 200/22, 24.7.2002] establishing guidance notes supplementing Annex II to *Directive 2001/18/EC of the European Parliament and of the Council*, note 60, on the deliberate release into the environment of genetically modified organisms, repealing Council Directive 90/220/EEC [OJ L 117/15 8. 5. 1990].

[67] These are spelt out under the Principles for the ERA in Annex II as effects on human health and the environment including flora and fauna, soil fertility, soil degradation of organic material, the feed/food chain, biological diversity, animal health, and resistance problems in relation to antibiotics; note 60, at 28.

[68] Note 59, Annex II, B. General Principles.

[69] Here the impacts on population levels of competitors, prey, hosts, symbionts, predators, parasites, and pathogens must be considered; ibid., Annex II, D. Conclusions on the Environmental Impact from the Release or the Placing on the Market of GMOs.

[70] Here consequences for the feed/food chain resulting from consumption of the GMO also must be considered; ibid.

[71] Note 59, Article 6(1)–(3).

[72] Note 59, Article 6(5)–(8).

there are any modifications or unintended changes to the release of the GMOs, which could have impact on human health or the environment, the competent authority must be informed and measures must be taken by the notifier to protect human health and the environment.[73]

MSs must ensure that the public is consulted on proposed deliberate releases and that all information on such releases within their territory is made publicly available.[74] The information required in such notifications is set out in Annex III of the Directive and includes information relating to: the GMO; the conditions of release and the receiving environment; the interactions between the GMO and the environment; and information on monitoring, control, waste treatment, and emergency response plans.

After release, and at any intervals laid down in the consent, the notifier must send the competent authority the result of the release in respect to any risk to human health or the environment.[75] The Directive also contains provisions for consultation with the relevant Scientific Committee and the European Group on Ethics in Science and New Technologies.[76]

In addition to this sophisticated body of rules for releasing GMOs into the environment, the EU has placed specific liability for environmental damage on those who release the GMOs.

8 PLACING LIABILITY ON DEVELOPERS OF GMOs TO PREVENT AND REMEDY ENVIRONMENTAL DAMAGE

Liability for the prevention and remedy of environmental damage is placed on those who release GMOs into the environment, and is imposed under *Directive 2004/35/CE Placing Liability on Developers of GMOs to Prevent and Remedy Environmental Damage.*[77] The objective of this Directive is to establish a common framework for the prevention and remedying of environment damage[78] at a reasonable cost to society. Of particular concern are the significant health risks posed by the many contaminated sites in the Community, and also the dramatic acceleration in the loss of biodiversity[79] over recent decades. GMOs are brought within the ambit of the Directive as a result of their specific mention in Annex III.[80]

The Directive refers specifically to the principle of sustainable development and the polluter pays principle. The Directive does not apply to cases of personal injury, to damage to private property, or to any economic loss, and does not affect any right regarding these types of damages.[81] The liability mechanism will only be effective where there is an identifiable polluter, the damage is concrete and quantifiable, and a causal link

[73] Note 59, Article 8.

[74] Note 59, Artcle 9.

[75] Note 59, Article 10; note also *Commission Decision of 29 September 2003* [OJL 254/21, 8.10.2003] establishing pursuant to *Directive 2001/18/EC of the European Parliament and of the Council*, note 60, a format for presenting the results of the deliberate release into the environment of genetically modified higher plants for purposes other than placing on the market.

[76] Note 59, Articles 28, 29.

[77] OJL 143/56, 30.4.2004.

[78] This includes damage done by airborne elements so far as they cause damage to water, land or protected species or natural habitats.

[79] The Directive refers to other Council Directives on the conservation of wild birds [OJL 103, 25.4.1979], the conservation of natural habitats and of wild fauna and flora [OJL 206, 22.7. 1992] and in the field of water policy [OJL 327, 22.12. 2000].

[80] Note 77, Annex III s. 11.

[81] Note 77, Preamble section (14).

between the damage and the polluter can be drawn. So the mechanism is not particularly well-suited to diffuse and widespread environmental effects that cannot be traced back to individual actors.[82] Operators also should be encouraged to lodge appropriate forms of financial security to provide effective cover in the event that they are held liable under the Directive.[83] Operators are required to take remedial[84] or preventive action[85] where environmental damage has, or has not yet occurred, and to bear the costs of such action.[86] Persons affected by environmental damage, with a sufficient interest relating to the damage, or alleging the impairment of a right, can request a competent authority to take action under the Directive.[87]

9 TRACING AND LABELING GMOs

The traceablity and labeling provisions are found in *Regulation (EC) 1830/2003 Concerning the Traceability and Labelling of Genetically Modified Organisms and the Traceability of Food and Feed Products Produced from Genetically Modified Organisms.*[88] The Regulation provides a harmonised Community framework for the traceability and labeling of GM foods to allow the internal market to function effectively. According to the Regulation, traceability of GMOs facilitates the withdrawal of products if unforeseen adverse impacts on the environment or animal and human health are detected. It also facilitates the implementation of risk-management measures in accordance with the precautionary principle.[89] Accurate labeling of GM foods is also enhanced.

The person who places the GM product on the market is required to give the receiver of the product (both parties being known as "operators") both the information that the product contains or consists of GMOs and the unique identifier assigned to the GMOs.[90] This information must be continually transmitted in writing throughout the supply chain. Operators who place GM products on the market and who receive them must have in place systems and standardised procedures for holding the necessary information about the product for a period of five years after each transaction.[91] An operator placing GM food and feed on the market must give the receiver of the product the following: an indication of each of the food ingredients which is produced from GMOs; an indication of each of the feed materials or additives that is produced from GMOs; and in the case of products for which no list of ingredients exists, an indication that the product is produced from GMOs.[92]

Operators are also required to label pre-packaged products consisting of or containing GMOs with the words "This product contains genetically modified organisms"

[82] Note 77, s. 13.

[83] Note 77, s. 27.

[84] Note 77, Article 6.

[85] Note 77, Article 5.

[86] Note 77, Article 8. Note that where the competent authority has taken preventive or remedial action, the costs of the action can be recovered from the operator. Exceptions apply where the damage was caused by a third party, or the operator was ordered to comply with a compulsory administrative order, or the operator demonstrates that it was not at fault; see ibid., Article 8(3) (4).

[87] Note 77, Article 12. Note that it is for the MSs to determine what constitutes a "sufficient interest" and an "impairment of a right."

[88] OJL 268/24, 18.10.2003. See, A. MacGregor & E. Brown, "EU: GMO Regulation – Progress." 9(2) *International Trade Law & Regulation* (2003), N17.

[89] Ibid., Preamble (3), (4).

[90] The Commission must establish a system for the development and assignment of unique identifiers to GMOs; ibid., Article 8.

[91] Note 88, Article 4 A. Traceability.

[92] Note 88, Article 5.

or "This product contains genetically modified [name of organism(s)]". For non–prepackaged products offered to the final consumer, the same words must appear on, or in connection, with the display of the product.[93] Consistent with *Directive 2001/18/EC*,[94] exemptions apply to the traceability and labeling of products that contain traces of GMOs below thresholds established under the Directive.[95] MSs have the obligation of ensuring that inspection and monitoring systems are put in place to ensure compliance with the Regulation in accordance with a technical guidance developed by the Commission. MSs also must lay down rules on penalties for infringements of the Regulation.[96] Also, the Commission must ensure that a central register is available at the Community level containing all available sequencing information and references for GMOs that are authorised. Information also should be included about GMOs that are not authorised.[97]

10 RECORDING INFORMATION ABOUT GMOs ON PUBLIC REGISTERS

In addition to the requirements for making information publicly available under *Directive 2001/18/EC*, detailed arrangements are in place for the operation of GMO registers. This is done under the *Commission Decision 2004/204/EC Providing for Public Registers to Record Information on GMOs*.[98] The following information must be included in the registers: details of the notifier and persons responsible for placing GM products on the market (where they are different from the notifier); general information concerning the GMO; information on the nucleotide sequence of the insert; information concerning detection and identification methods; and information on the lodging, storage, and supply of samples.[99] Registers must be publicly available, although confidential data on the registers will only be accessible to the MSs, the Commission, and EFSA.[100] Competent national authorities are responsible for extracting all of the information they receive in notifications and submitting this to the Commission either at the time of submitting the assessment report, or within two weeks thereafter. Links to other registers and databases such as the opinion of the EFSA, the assessment report of the competent authority, and the Biosafety Clearing-House, also may be provided.[101] The registers must be updated.[102]

11 REGULATING THE TRANSBOUNDARY MOVEMENT OF GMOs

Clearly, European states have an interest in being informed about the transboundary movement of GMOs. This is provided for under *Regulation (EC) 1946/2003 on Transboundary Movement of GMOs between European States*.[103] This Regulation is expressly intended to adopt the *Cartagena Protocol* into EU law.[104] Hence, the advance informed agreement procedure contained in the *Protocol* is replicated in the Regulation. The definition of "transboundary movement" excludes the intentional movement of GMOs between Parties within the Community. The Regulation deals with GMOs intended for

[93] Note 88, Article 4 B. Labelling.
[94] Note 60, Article 21.
[95] Note 88, Article 4 C. Exemptions.
[96] Note 88, Article 11.
[97] Note 88, Article 9.
[98] OJL 65/20, 3.3.2004.
[99] Ibid., Article 3.
[100] Ibid., Article 4.
[101] Ibid., Article 5.
[102] Ibid., Article 6.
[103] OJL 287/3, 5, 5.11.2003.
[104] Ibid., Article 1.

deliberate release into the environment,[105] GMOs intended for direct use as food or feed, or for processing,[106] and GMOs intended for contained use.[107] The Regulation does not cover GMOs intended for deliberate release if the Conference of the Parties to the *Convention on Biological Diversity* has already decided that the GMO is not likely to have adverse effects on the conservation and sustainable use of biological diversity, taking into account risks to human health.[108] MSs are required to take appropriate measures to prevent unintentional transboundary movements of GMOs.[109] MSs are also required to inform the Biosafety Clearing-House and the Commission of all national legislation and guidelines that implement the *Protocol*.[110]

12 THE CENTRALITY OF THE PRECAUTIONARY PRINCIPLE IN THE EU CONTEXT

As already mentioned, the precautionary principle is a fundamental principle of sustainable development. Analysis of EU regulation governing GMOs indicates that the EU recognises that the precautionary principle has a crucial role to play in assessing the risks relating to GMOs, and in the making of decisions based on that assessment.[111] Reference to the precautionary principle in all the EU law mentioned above should be read together with the *Communication from the Commission on the Precautionary Principle*[112] in order to understand how the precautionary principle will be applied in the context of GMO decision making. What is most notable is that the EU believes that an assessment of the risks associated with GMOs should be made not only in accordance with the precautionary principle, but that the assessment should be politically determined.

It is not surprising that the EU has taken this stance given that the precautionary principle is specifically mentioned in the *Treaty Establishing the European Community*,[113] in which it is stated that:

> Community policy on the environment shall aim at a high level of protection taking into account the diversity of situations in the various regions of the Community. It shall be based on the precautionary principle and on the principles that preventive action should be taken, that environmental damage should as a priority be rectified at source and that the polluter should pay. Environmental protection requirements must be integrated into the definition and implementation of other Community policies.[114]

Nowhere in the *Treaty*, nor the documents mentioned earlier, is the precautionary principle specifically defined. However, reference may be made to a well-known definition of the precautionary principle. It is that:

[105] Ibid., Ch. II, s. 1.
[106] Ibid., s. 2.
[107] Ibid., s. 3.
[108] Ibid., Article 8(1).
[109] Ibid., Ch. III, Article 14.
[110] Ibid., Ch. IV, Article 15.
[111] See N. Salmon, "A European Perspective on the Precautionary Principle, Food Safety and the Free Trade Imperative of the WTO." 27:2 *European Law Review* (2002), 138. See also A. Nucara, "Precautionary Principle and GMOs: Protection or Protectionism." 9(2) *International Trade Law & Regulation* (2003), 47.
[112] Brussels, 02.02.2000, COM(2000) 1.
[113] OJ C 325/33, 24.12.2002.
[114] Ibid., Article 130r.

> Where there are threats of serious or irretrievable damage, lack of full scientific certainty shall not be used as a reason for postponing cost-effective measures to prevent environmental degradation.[115]

The Court of Justice of the European Community and the Court of First Instance have had occasion recently to develop case law relevant to the precautionary principle and GMOs. In *Monsanto Italia SpA and Others v. Presidenza del Consiglio dei Ministri*,[116] the Court stated that;

> the precautionary principle allows protective measures to be taken without having to wait until the reality and seriousness of risks become fully apparent, even if a full risk assessment proves impossible because of the inadequate nature of the scientific data available.[117]

In this case, Monsanto notified the Commission of its intention to place cornflour derived from genetically modified maize grain (Bt-11 and MON 810) on the market. It relied on an assessment of substantial equivalence by the competent authority in the United Kingdom. The Commission subsequently notified the Member States. In 2000, the presence of residues of transgenic protein (expressed by the inserted gene) in the corn flour were noted by an Italian scientific institute. However, opinion as to whether or not they posed any risk to human health was divided. Italy subsequently adopted a decree on 4 August 2000 providing for the precautionary suspension of the trade in and use of products derived from those maize lines. Monsanto and others subsequently challenged the Italian decree, which they considered to be in breach of Community law. The Court found that where use of the "simplified procedure" is not warranted, a Member State can, as a preventive measure, temporarily restrict or suspend the marketing of those foods in its territory without first being required to challenge the lawfulness of the procedure.

Despite the lack of definition of the precautionary principle, the *Communication* states that applying the precautionary principle is a key tenet of its policy that it has the right to establish a level of environmental, human, animal and plant health that it deems appropriate.[118] Furthermore, that the principle should be considered within a structured approach to the analysis of risk which comprises risk assessment, risk management and risk communication, with the principle having particular relevance to risk management. However, the *Communication* goes on to say that "judging what is an 'acceptable' level of risk for society, is an eminently *political* [*sic*] responsibility." It also emphasises that the precautionary principle is not concerned simply with short- or medium-term risks but with long-term risks and the well-being of future generations.[119] As a result, the decision-making procedure should be transparent and involve all interested parties as early as possible, and to the extent reasonably possible.[120] As well,

[115] UNEP, note 7, Principle 15.

[116] *Monsanto Italia SpA and Others v. Presidenza del Consiglio dei Ministri* (C-236/01) [2003] ECR I-8105.

[117] *Regulation (EC) No. 258/1997 Concerning Novel Foods and Novel Food Ingredients* [OJ L 253 of 16.09.1997] provided that foods that are produced from genetically modified organisms *but no longer contain them* may be placed on the market within the Community under a "simplified procedure." This procedure requires the person to notify the Commission that it intends to place a product on the market. A competent national authority must have already concluded that the GMOs are *substantially equivalent* to comparable traditional foods.

[118] Note 113, at 3.

[119] Ibid. at 8.

[120] Ibid. at 4.

"all interested parties should be involved to the fullest extent possible in the study of various risk management options that may be envisaged once the results of the scientific evaluation and/or risk assessment are available and the procedure be as transparent as possible."[121]

It is clear that the EU believes that the assessment of risk relating to the release of GMOs must be done in accordance with the precautionary principle and that its application, in practice, must be politically determined.

13 CONCLUSIONS ABOUT THE SUSTAINABILITY OF GMO REGULATIONS IN THE EU

It is clear from the preceding discussion of EU law governing the deliberate release of GMOs into the environment and the placing of GM food and feed on the market, that the precautionary principle is a central tenet of the regulatory scheme. This is in direct contrast with the U.S. regulatory scheme where the principle is not mentioned, even once, in all the legal and policy documents regulating GMOs. Purely from this perspective, one could affirm that the EU scheme is more closely aligned with the principles of sustainable development enunciated earlier. Of course, this is true for a number of other reasons, not least of which is the detailed body of law that attempts to cover all the elements of a sustainable regulatory framework for GMOs – rigorous risk-assessment procedures, reference to expert panels, opportunities for public submissions, access to information, provisions that attribute liability to those who cause harm, and proper labeling requirements. As a result of all of these provisions, we might conclude that the EU framework is likely to present fewer risks for present and future generations and to biodiversity than the U.S. scheme.

14 REGULATING THE RELEASE OF GMOs INTO THE ENVIRONMENT IN AUSTRALIA

In Australia, GMOs are regulated under a number of different Acts including the *Gene Technology Act 2000 (Cth)*, the *Food Acts*[122] in the States that in the case of GM foods must be labeled consistently with *Standard A18*,[123] the *Quarantine Act 1908 (Cth)* and the *Imported Food Control Act 1992 (Cth)* in respect of which the Australian Quarantine and Inspection Service is the relevant agency and the *Customs Act 1901* vesting various powers in the Australian Customs Service.

For the purposes of releasing GMOs into the environment, the most relevant legislation is the *Gene Technology Act*. This Act regulates "dealings"[124] with GMOs (defined as live, viable organisms that have been modified by techniques of gene technology) and dealings with GM products not currently regulated by existing regulators. A "dealing" includes conducting experiments with making, developing, producing, manufacturing,

[121] Ibid. at 17.

[122] See *Food Act 2003 (NSW), Food Act 2001 (ACT), Food Act 2006 (Qld), Food Act 2001 (SA), Food Act 2003 (Tas), Food Act 1984 (Vic)*.

[123] On 28 July 2000, ANZFSC agreed on a genetically modified food labelling regime and Standard A18 now requires the labelling of food and food ingredients: where novel DNA and/or protein is present in the final food or where the food has altered characteristics. However, the Standard allows an ingredient to contain up to 1 percent unintended presence of genetically modified product.

[124] See the *Gene Technology Act 2000 (Cth)* Part 4 of the Act.

breeding, propagating, using in the course of manufacture of a thing, growing, raising, culturing, or importing. The Act prohibits any "dealing with" GMOs unless the dealing is exempt, a notifiable low risk dealing,[125] is licensed, or is on the Register of GMOs. The Act is administered by the Gene Technology Regulator (GTR) who reports directly to Parliament and is the final decision maker on applications relating to "dealings." These include GM agricultural crops, GM animals or fish, GM micro-organisms designed for bioremediation, and GM viruses and vaccines. The Act also requires the establishment of a publicly available database of all approvals of GMOs and GM products in Australia.[126]

Three advisory committees[127] are established under the Act: the Gene Technology Technical Advisory Committee to advise exclusively on licence applications; the Gene Technology Ethics Committee and the Gene Technology Community Consultative Group. The Consultative Group comprises twelve members appointed by the Minister who have skills and experience in environmental issues, consumer issues, the impact of gene technology on the community, issues relevant to the biotechnology industry, issues relevant to gene technology research, and public health issues.

If the GTR is satisfied that a "dealing" involving the intentional release of a GMO into the environment may pose significant risks to the health and safety of people, before approving the "dealing," the GTRs must prepare a Risk Assessment and Risk Management Plan. Public participation is only called for if the GTR believes that the "dealing" will pose a significant risk to health and safety of people and environment. The Regulator also must seek advice on the risk assessment and the risk management plan from: the States; the Gene Technology Technical Advisory Committee; each Commonwealth authority or agency prescribed by the regulations for the purposes of this paragraph; the Environment Minister; and any local council that the Regulator considers appropriate.[128]

There are no third party appeals or statutory standing for judicial review.[129] Also the GTR is not specifically required to take the precautionary principle into account in making a decision whether or not to licence a "dealing," but the principle is included in the Act as a means of achieving the object of the Act.[130] The object is "to protect the health and safety of people, and to protect the environment, by identifying risks posed by or as a result of gene technology, and by managing those risks through regulating certain dealings with GMOs."[131]

15 STATE MORATORIUM ON PLANTING OF GM TRIAL CROPS

Given Australia's federal system of government, even if an intentional release of a GMO crop into the environment is authorised by the GTR, there is no guarantee that it can be released into the environment. This is because a number of state governments in Australia have placed moratoria on the planting of GM crops in their jurisdictions. The New South Wales government, for example, enacted the *Gene Technology (GM Crop*

[125] Before the Governor General declares that a "dealing" is a notifiable low risk dealing, the Regulator must be satisfied that the "dealing" would not involve the intentional release of a GMO into the environment; ibid., s. 74(2).

[126] Ibid., Part 9, Division 6.

[127] Ibid., Part 8.

[128] Ibid., Part 5, Division 4.

[129] Ibid., Part 12, Division 2.

[130] Ibid., s. 4.

[131] Ibid., s. 3.

Moratorium) Act 2003 (NSW), which designates NSW as an area in which certain GM plants may not be cultivated for marketing purposes. The moratorium was initially intended to expire on 3 March 2006 but has been extended to 2008. The moratorium operates to the extent that the Minister can prohibit the cultivation in NSW of a specified GM food plant or class of GM food plants. A breach of the Act is an offence attracting a fine of $125,000 for a corporation, or $50,000 or imprisonment for two years, or both, for a person who cultivates the GM food plant, either intentionally or negligently. A person can be ordered to destroy a plant or the Minister can seize and dispose of an offending plant. Inspectorial powers are conferred on persons appointed by the Director-General. Exemption from the operation of the moratorium order may be conferred.

To indicate the effect of the NSW moratorium, in July 2003, the Federal Gene Technology Regulator made a decision, under the *Gene Technology Act*, to issue a licence in respect of application DIR 021/2002 from Bayer CropScience Pty Ltd. This was the first step in the phased commercial release of InVigor® canola in Australia. However, the NSW government released Moratorium Order Number 1 prohibiting cultivation of InVigor canola in New South Wales.[132] In May 2004, the NSW Minister for Agriculture then granted an exemption from the moratorium with respect to three sites in NSW. The exemption was for GM canola to be planted as part of research trial by Bayer CropScience Pty Ltd (Bayer).[133]

The Minister attached the following extensive conditions of consent: Bayer must notify the Director General in writing of the date of the planting, and forecasted date of flowering and harvesting of the canola and must notify neighbours of the date of planting and the location of the site, Bayer also must provide evidence to the Director General that planting equipment has been cleaned after the planting; a buffer zone of at least fifty meters must extend in all direction from the edge of the site, which must be inspected at least once every thirty-five days commencing fourteen days before the forecasted flowering of the GM canola at the site and concluding when flowering of the GM canola ceases. If plants in the buffer zone are detected, then the GM canola at the site must be destroyed; Bayer also must give the Director General evidence of the measures taken to clean equipment after the harvesting of the GM canola.

After harvesting, the canola seeds must be stored in a locked, sealed container and marked "GM canola seed," or rendered unviable by autoclaving or burning, or transported in an unbreakable and sealed container to a location outside NSW; Bayer must provide evidence to the Director General of measures taken to clean equipment used to transport the GM canola from the site; Bayer must, within three months of the harvest, or after rain, lightly till the site when germination of any canola seed is likely. Grazing is prohibited unless the tillage has taken place, and deep cultivation (i.e., to a depth of more than fifty millimeters) is prohibited in the twelve months following the harvest. After the harvest, GM must not be planted at the site before 3 March 2006 unless authorised by the Director General. The site must be inspected for volunteer plants until 3 March 2006 and records of the inspection must be kept; Bayer must make available to the Director General any data relating to the trials conducted at the site, including but not limited to the trial design, results of experiments, and any other results required by the Director General within seven days of written request; Bayer must hold and maintain, and must ensure that all subcontractors are beneficiaries under, a public

[132] *NSW Government Gazette*, Special Supplement No. 119, 25 July 2003.

[133] *NSW Government Gazette* Special Supplement, Exemption Orders Number's 4, 5, 6, No. 89, 25 May 2004.

liability insurance policy that provides coverage to the equivalent of ten million Euros for any losses that it may incur in connection with the cultivation of GM canola in research trials conducted in accordance with the exemption.

Ultimately, Bayer decided not to proceed with the trial sites citing unfavourable agricultural conditions in NSW.

16 CONCLUSIONS ABOUT THE REGULATION OF GMOs IN AUSTRALIA

Compared with the United States, Australia has a fairly strict regime for licensing "dealings" with GMOs and it would seem to present fewer risks for present and future generations. However, in spite of this, the *Gene Technology Act* does have a number of weaknesses. These include a concern that the precautionary principle is not applied to all decision making; and that the risk assessment and risk management process is not sufficiently rigorous and should be subjected to external peer review so as to avoid any risks to biodiversity. The participatory procedures are also weak and it would be preferable for the Act to allow for participation at every level of decision making, and the merits appeals and judicial review proceedings to be liberated. Nevertheless, the Act does contain quite significant penalties for GMO "polluters." It is not altogether certain that the Act satisfies the requirements for a sustainable regulatory framework.

17 THE EFFECT OF REFUSING TO GRANT ADVANCE INFORMED CONSENT

This discussion shows that it is not really adequate for CNAs to assume that because GMOs have been "approved" in a particular jurisdiction, that their safety has been adequately assessed. The other pressing concern, however, is that trade agreements may radically undermine the attempts of nation-states to regulate GMOs in accordance with their democratic mandates, and in accordance with the principles of ecologically sustainable development. This concern is well articulated in the academic literature.[134]

It is the author's view that international environmental agreements, generally, are far too glib in assuming that conflicts between trade agreements and environmental agreements can be easily resolved. For example, the Preamble of the *Protocol* states that trade and environment agreements should be framed in a way that is supportive of sustainable development.[135] Principle 12 of the *Rio Declaration* states that:

> States should cooperate to promote a supportive and open international economic system that would lead to economic growth and sustainable development in all countries, to better address the problems of environmental degradation. Trade policy

[134] See D. Morgan, "International Trade Rules and their Implications for Biotechnology Regulation." 3–4 *Asia Pacific Journal of Environmental Law* (2004), 177; C. Hutchinson, "International with International Trade Law: A Compatibility Analysis of the Cartagena Protocol to the Convention on Biological Diversity with the Environmental Law Attempts to be 'Mutually Supportive' World Trade Organisation Agreement on Sanitary and PhytoSanitary Measures." 4 *Journal of International Wildlife Law and Policy* (2001), 1; S. Lively, "The ABCs and NTBs of GMOs: The Great EU–US Trade Debate – Do European Restrictions on the Trade of GMOs Violate International Trade Law?" 23 *Northwestern Journal of International Law & Business* (2002), 239; P. Phillips & W. Kerr, "Alternative Paradigms: The WTO versus the Biosafety Protocol for Trade in Genetically Modified Organisms." 34(4) *Journal of World Trade* (2000), 63; O. Rivera-Torres, "The Biosafety Protocol and the WTO." 26 *Boston College International and Comparative Law Review* (2003), 253; and H. Krenzler & A. MacGregor, "GM Food: The Next Major Transatlantic Water?" *European Foreign Affairs Review* (2000), 287.

[135] Note 11, Preamble.

> measures for environmental purposes should not constitute a means of arbitrary or unjustifiable discrimination or a disguised restriction on international trade. Unilateral actions to deal with environmental challenges outside the jurisdiction of the importing country should be avoided. Environmental measures addressing transboundary or global environmental problems should, as far as possible, be based on an international consensus.

Meanwhile, the *Plan of Implementation*[136] negotiated at the World Summit on Sustainable Development states that the Parties must "[p]romote mutual supportiveness between the multilateral trading system and the multilateral environmental agreements, consistent with sustainable development goals, in support of the work programme agreed through WTO, while recognizing the importance of maintaining the integrity of both sets of instruments."[137]

18 THE EU–U.S. BIOTECH DISPUTE: A CASE STUDY ON THE SANITARY AND PHYTOSANITARY AGREEMENT

The *EU–U.S. Biotech* dispute illustrates that the reconciliation between environmental and trade objectives is far more complicated than the multilateral agreements on the environment suggest. It points to the next aspect of this chapter which is – what is the ultimate effect of a CNA saying "no" to the importation of GMOs? The types of arguments that could be raised by the intending importer of GMOs into a developing country are illustrated in the EU–U.S. dispute. Although the issues raised and the decision will be discussed shortly, it is instructive to note that the WTO Panel itself encountered significant difficulties in attempting to reach a decision. The difficulties are exemplified by the fact that the Panel postponed the making of its decision initially from September 2004 to March 2005. Then, on 13 June 2005, the Chair of the WTO Panel announced that as a result of the complex scientific reports presented to the Panel, and its limited resources, the decision would only be released in October 2005. Ultimately, the interim report was released by the Panel on the 8 February 2006, whereas the final report was released on 19 May 2006. This suggests that the CNAs in developing countries face a considerable challenge in assessing the scientific data relating to the GMOs, which are the subject of the proposed importation.

18.1 Issues Raised in the Dispute

As Morgan explains,[138] the history to the dispute is that in 1997 individual EU MSs of the EU imposed national bans on GM corn and canola that had already been approved for import into and/or cultivation in EU, and even though EU Scientific Committees found the MSs reasons not to be justified. Then in 1998 a number of MSs indicated they would block further approvals for GMOs used as food or feed under *Directive 90/220/EEC*, thereby placing a "de facto moratorium" on the planting or use of any new GMOs in the EU.

[136] Available at http://www.johannesburgsummit.org/html/documents/summit_docs/2309_planfinal.htm (last visited 3 October 2005).

[137] Ibid., Cl. 92.

[138] Morgan, note 135, at 193–194.

The essence of the complaints made by the United States[139] was that the EU moratorium on biotech approvals, the EU's failure to approve a number of specific biotech products (referred to as "product-specific measures"), and national-level bans in several EU member states on the marketing and import of specific biotech products, after the products had been approved at the EU level, constituted breaches by the EU of its obligations under the Sanitary and Phytosanitary Agreement (SPS).

The SPS does recognise the right of Members to impose measures: to protect human, animal (including wild fauna), or plant (including forest or wild flora) life or health;[140] to determine the level of risk they judge acceptable and to adopt their own measures if international standards do not meet this level of protection.[141] However, measures (including all relevant laws, decrees, regulations, requirements, and procedures) must apply to: risks arising from the entry, establishment, or spread of pests (including weeds), diseases, disease-carrying organisms or disease-causing organisms; risks arising from additives, contaminants, toxins, or disease-causing organisms in foods, beverages, or feedstuffs; and risks arising from diseases carried by animals, plants, or products thereof, or from the entry, establishment, or spread of pests, or to prevent or limit damage within the territory of the Member from the entry, establishment, or spread of pests.[142]

18.2 What Did the WTO Panel Decide?

On 7 February 2006, the Panel made a preliminary finding[143] that the EU had in fact applied a general "de facto" moratorium on approvals of biotech products between June 1999 and August 2003. The panel noted that the moratorium had resulted in a failure to complete individual procedures without undue delay, and so had violated Article 8 and Annex C of the SPS Agreement. These provisions relate to Control, Inspection, and Approval processes. The panel did not agree with the complainants that the moratorium was not based on a risk assessment (Article 5 of the SPS) or on scientific principles (Article 2 of the SPS). As it turned out, it was not necessary for the Panel to make recommendations about the moratorium since it found that the moratorium had already ended with the approval of "a relevant biotech product" in 2004.

With regard to the product-specific measures, the Panel argued that the completion of the approval process had been unduly delayed for the vast majority of the biotech products, and required the EU to complete the approval process for the outstanding applications without delay.

With regard to the national bans, the EU had argued that they were taken as precautionary measures under Article 5.7 of the SPS Agreement, which allows WTO Members to provisionally adopt SPS measures where there is insufficient scientific evidence in respect of a matter. However, the Panel concluded that a risk assessment could have been conducted because the EU's Scientific Committee had already assessed the risks of the biotech products and judged them to be safe. Therefore, there was sufficient

[139] As mentioned earlier, joined by Canada, Argentina, Australia, Brazil, Chile, Colombia, India, Mexico, New Zealand, and Peru.

[140] Ibid., Article 2.

[141] Ibid., Article 3.3.

[142] Annex A, paragraph 1 as cited by Morgan, note 135, at 88.

[143] Note that the preliminary and final rulings by the Panel have not been released to the public. However, the author has had access to a number of reputable websites which have released information regarding the outcome of the dispute to the public.

scientific evidence. For this reason, the Panel concluded that the EU member states had not undertaken risk assessments in line with the requirements of the SPS Agreement that would "reasonably support the prohibition." Consequently, the Panel ruled that the national-level bans must be brought into conformity with WTO law, which implies revoking them or providing an SPS Agreement-compliant risk assessment to justify the measures.

The interim findings of the Panel were confirmed in its final decision delivered on 10 May 2006.

19 THE GATT AND THE TBT: A CASE STUDY

In addition to arguments that may be made regarding whether or not bans on the importation of GMOs are noncompliant with SPS provisions, such bans, sought to be imposed by the CNAs of developing countries, also might fall foul of the Agreement on Technical Barriers to Trade (TBT) and the General Agreement on Tariffs and Trade (GATT). With respect to both the *GATT* and the *TBT*, the essential question is whether or not a ban on GMO products amounts to discrimination against a "like product."[144] So, for example, are GM corn and canola-derived products "like" their conventional counterparts'? There is no simple answer to this question, as the differences in approach to this question between the U.S. and EU regulatory philosophy to GMOs indicates.

The regulatory approach in the United States to the placing of GM food on the market is that the United States regards it as food that is no different from food derived using more conventional methods of plant breeding. GM food is regulated in the United States under the *Federal Food Drug and Cosmetic Act.*[145] The relevant administrative agency is the Food and Drug Administration (FDA), which is given broad authority to initiate legal action against a food that is adulterated or misbranded within the meaning of the Act. Producers of new foods have an obligation to ensure that the foods they offer consumers are safe and in compliance with applicable legal requirements.[146] According to the FDA, the Act is used most frequently to regulate the presence of contaminants such as lead, mercury, dioxin, and aflatoxin in foods.[147] The FDA first disclosed its regulatory approach to regulating GM Foods in its *1992 Statement of Policy: Foods Derived from New Plant Varieties.*[148] Here, the FDA stated that:

> In most cases, the substances expected to become components of food as a result of genetic modification of a plant will be the same as or substantially similar to substances commonly found in food, such as proteins, fats and oils and carbohydrates.[149]

[144] See *GATT* Article 1 (General Most Favoured Nation Treatment) and *TPP* Article 2.1 (Non-Discriminatory Treatment of Like Products) both extensively discussed by Morgan note 135, at 186–188 and again at 197–200.

[145] 21 U.S.C. 343–1.

[146] Under s. 402(a)(1) of the Act, food is deemed to be adulterated and unlawful if it bears or contains an added poisonous or deleterious substance that may render the food injurious to health or a naturally occurring substance that is ordinarily injurious. Foods that are adulterated are subject to a range of enforcement measures including seizure, injunction, and criminal prosecution.

[147] *Federal Register*, Vol. 57, No. 104/ May 29, 1992/ Notices 22985, at 22989.

[148] Ibid.

[149] Ibid. at 22985.

The FDA also states that it is the responsibility of the producer of a new food to evaluate the safety of its products, relying on the guidance in the *Statement of Policy*. Where producers are not certain of the safety of their foods they are *encouraged* (not required) to consult with the FDA. However, it seems likely that whether or not producers are likely to consult with the FDA depends on the agency's policies regarding certain types of foods. This statement regarding the FDA's view on GM modification of a plant does not suggest that consultation is needed.

The FDA also has authority to regulate "food additives"[150] and where a GMO has in fact altered the composition of a plant such that it is not "generally recognised as safe" (GRAS) it will be regarded as a "food additive." However, the *Statement of Policy* expressly states that:

> With respect to transferred genetic material (nucleic acids), generally, FDA does not anticipate that transferred genetic material would itself be subject to food additive regulation. . . . Likewise, minor variation in molecular structure would not require regulation as an additive . . . it is possible, however, that the intended expression product in a food could be a protein, carbohydrate, fat or oil that differs significantly in structure, function or composition from substances found currently in food . . . and may require regulation.[151]

With respect to labeling, the *Statement of Policy* states that "the agency does not believe that the method of development of a new plant variety[152] is material information and would not usually be required to be disclosed in labeling."[153]

The *Statement of Policy* includes an extensive Guidance for Industry for foods derived from new plant varieties to assess the safety of their foods.[154]

More recently, in 2001, the FDA issued a proposed rule requiring *Pre-Market Notice Concerning Bioengineered Foods*[155] giving the FDA authority to declare that the safety of GM food had not been proved prior to release onto the market. In this *Notice*, the FDA recognised that because the consultation process is voluntary, domestic and overseas food producers could choose not to notify the FDA about the placement of GM food on the market. The FDA also acknowledged for the first time that, because a wider range of sources for genetic engineering of plants has become available to bioengineers, GM food might be significantly different from substances historically consumed in food. Consequently, the proposed rule would require a notifier to submit a premarket biotechnology notice (PBN) to the FDA 120 days before the food is marketed. The PBN contains seven parts and is very detailed.[156] Under the proposed rule, the notifier will be encouraged to consult with the FDA regarding the safety of the food. Information about the consultation will become public under the Freedom of Information Act[157] unless it could be shown to be confidential. The PBN will then be sent to the Center for

[150] 21 U.S.C. 348 s. 409.

[151] Note 154, at 22990.

[152] Including hybridisation, chemical or radiation-induced mutagenesis, protoplast fusion, embryo rescue, somacional variation, or any other method; ibid. at 22991.

[153] Ibid.

[154] *Federal Register*, note 41, see s. VII.

[155] *Federal Register*, Vol. 66, No. 12/January 18, 2001/4706.

[156] See ibid., s. 192.25. Information needed includes a letter, a synopsis, an administrative statement about the status of review of the food by other federal agencies or by foreign government; data or information about the method of development; a discussion of any newly inserted genes that encode resistance to an antiobiotic; data or information about substances introduced into or modified in the food; and data or information about the food.

[157] 5 U.S.C. 552.

Food Safety and Applied Nutrition and the Center for Veterinary Medicine. The FDA will evaluate the PBN and inform the notifier either that the food is, or is not, safe or that the FDA needs more time to evaluate it. The FDA's evaluation of the food will be placed on the Internet or in a newspaper for public review. The tone of the proposed rule is that the FDA is not expecting to find that GM foods are significantly different from those developed using traditional plant breeding methods.

Also in 2001, the FDA released a Guidance for Industry entitled *Voluntary Labelling Indicating Whether Foods Have or Have Not Been Developed Using Bioengineering.* The Guidance is voluntary because the FDA reiterates its view that bioengineered food does not require special labeling, as bioengineering is not a "material fact." Nevertheless, consumers may be interested in having the information, hence the Guidance.[158] There have been no updates on this Guidance by the FDA.

When the the U.S. regulatory approach to GM food is compared with the EU's regulatory framework governing the commercialisation of GM crops, the placing of GM foods on the market, and the labeling of GM foods, the dispute between the EU and the U.S. and to whether GM products are "like" products is exemplified. The placement of GM food on the market in the EU is governed *by Regulation (EC) No 1829/2003 on Genetically Modified Food and Feed.*[159] The Regulation applies to GMOs for food use, food containing or consisting of GMOs, and food produced from or containing ingredients produced from GMOs.[160] It also applies to GMOs for feed use, feed containing or consisting of GMOs, and feed produced from GMOs.[161] Food must not have adverse effects on human health, animal health or the environment; mislead the consumer; or differ from the food that it is replacing such that its consumption would be nutritionally disadvantageous to the consumer. No person can place on the market, use, or process such food without an authorisation granted under the Regulation.[162]

The following information must accompany the application for authorisation: where applicable, information complying with the *Cartagena Protocol*; a detailed description of the method of production and manufacturing; a copy of studies, including independent peer-reviewed studies, which demonstrate that the food does not have adverse effects on human health, animal health, or the environment; an analysis that the food is not different from its conventional counterpart; a reasoned statement that the food does not give rise to ethical or religious concerns; the conditions for placing the food on the market, including specific conditions for use and handling; a proposal for postmarket monitoring; and others.

In addition, the complete technical dossier regarding information about a GMO required under Annexes III and IV of *Directive 2001/18/EC* must be included. Information and conclusions about the ERA carried out under the *Directive* as well as any authorisation under Part C of the Directive must be provided to the competent authority. The monitoring plan for environmental effects prepared under the Directive also must be produced.[163]

[158] U.S. Food and Drug Administration, Center for Food Safety and Applied Nutrition, January 2001.

[159] OJL 268/5, 18.10.2003. This Regulation should be read together with *Regulation* (*EC*) No. 178/2002 [OJL 31/1, 1.2.2002] laying down the general principles and requirements of food law, establishing the European Food Safety Authority and laying down procedures in matters of food safety.

[160] Ibid., Ch. II.

[161] Ibid., Ch. III. Note that although it is clear the feed given to animals may harm human health, these provisions are not discussed in any detail in this article, which focuses on GMO food.

[162] Ibid., Article 16.

[163] Ibid., Article 5.

On receiving an application, the competent authority must notify the European Food Safety Authority (EFSA) and supply it with all the relevant information to enable the Authority to formulate an opinion on the safety of the food. EFSA must forward its opinion, within six months, to the Commission, the MSs and the applicant, with a report describing its assessment of the food and stating the reasons for its opinion and the information on which its opinion is based, including the results of any consultation with competent authorities.[164] Within three months of receiving this opinion, the Commission shall inform the Standing Committee on the Food Chain on Animal Health[165] of its draft decision. Once a final decision is made, the applicant is notified and the authorisation lasts for ten years, and may be renewed.[166]

The difference in regulatory philosophies between the EU and United States regarding whether or not GM products are "like products" serves to shine a light on yet another controversial aspect of the dispute between the two countries.

20 CONCLUSIONS ABOUT THE EFFECT OF REFUSING TO GRANT CONSENT TO THE IMPORTATION OF GMOs

Given the extensive coverage of the implications of trade agreements for biotechnology regulation in the academic literature, there is no need for an exhaustive restatement of the issues here. However, what this chapter has attempted to show, using a number of case studies, is that even when a CNA has the capacity to actually assess the risks posed by GMOs and to refuse consent to their importation, this refusal may be totally ineffectual given the overriding considerations contained in WTO agreements such as the SPS, the GATT, and the TBT.

21 IS THERE ANY EVIDENCE THAT TRADE AGREEMENTS MAY BE DETRIMENTAL TO THE ENVIRONMENT?

Lest it be thought that the concern about the impact of trade agreements on the environment is idle and speculative, it is instructive to note that on 20 September 2005, the United National Environment Program (UNEP) warned of the serious environmental consequences of trade liberalization for developing, when effective environmental policies are not properly linked at the outset with trade agreements.[167] UNEP points to six case studies undertaken on the effect of trade agreements concerning the rice sector in China, Colombia, Indonesia, Nigeria, Senegal, and Vietnam. The reports point to soil degradation caused by increased pesticide use, water pollution, loss of biodiversity, and the destruction of forests and wetlands as the consequences of environmentally insensitive trade agreements. As well, although trade agreements are supposed to lift people in developing countries out of poverty, in these countries there were serious impacts on the earning of local producers, especially small-scale farmers and also consumers because cartels often do not pass on the price reductions. The "winners" from trade liberalization were identified as importers, middlemen, large-scale producers of rice, and the government. Conclusions drawn from the rice sector studies were that:

[164] Ibid., Article 6; see this Article generally for details relating to the formulation by the Authority of its opinion.
[165] Established under Article 58 of *Regulation (EC) No. 178/2002.*
[166] Note 165, Article 7.
[167] See http://www.unep.ch/etb/index.php (last visited 2 October 2005).

the minimization of environmental damage should be addressed at the moment that trade policies are designed; high economic costs can result from the environmental damage caused by liberalization; decision makers should be made aware of these consequences and encouraged to adopt strengthened environmental policies; policy response packages should reflect local conditions, needs, and priorities; there should be interministerial coordination in the policy-making process; and this process should involve the participation of multistakeholders.

22 CONCLUSION

This chapter has sought to analyse the *reality* and *effect* of the "advance informed agreement" procedure contained in the *Cartagena Protocol*, which is supposed to protect developing countries from the possible biosafety threats posed by GMOs. The author does not at any stage seek to declare that there are any threats to biodiversity associated with the importation of GMOs for release into the environment. The scientific uncertainty regarding this issue is notorious, and makes a precautionary approach to the importation and release of GMOs all the more crucial. Rather, the author has shown that, although the *Protocol* provides formal protections to developing countries, these may prove far more difficult, substantively, to achieve. The reality of the "agreement" is undermined by a lack of capacity in developing countries to fulfill many of the obligations required of them by international environmental agreements. This chapter also shows that if a CNA agrees to the importation of a GMO simply because it has been "approved" elsewhere, biosafety is not assured given the varying regulatory approaches to assessing the risks associated with releasing GMOs into the environment. Furthermore, a refusal to allow the importation of a GMO, based on issues of biosafety, may have no *effect* at all. This is because of the inevitable conflict between the biosafety concerns expressed in the *Protocol* and the trade-related imperatives contained in the *SPS*, the *GATT*, and *TBT* and other trade agreements.

Ultimately, if it is eventually proven scientifically that the release of GMOs into the environment has no identifiable impacts on biodiversity, then the concerns raised in this chapter have no resonance. But, if the scientific evidence points to material biosafety risks, then the project to expose the weaknesses inherent in the *Protocol* will have been worthwhile. Unfortunately, by then it may be too late to guard against the risks. Leaving aside questions of whether or not it can ever be achieved, it lies in the realms of imagination to consider who, globally, will pay the costs of remedying the damage.

PART SEVEN

ACCESS AND BENEFIT-SHARING

28 Access, Obligations, and Benefits: Regulating Bioprospecting in the Antarctic

Alan D. Hemmings* and Michelle Rogan-Finnemore**

The term "bioprospecting" is a relatively new one, and as yet there is no consensus on its precise legal meaning. But what it appears to cover are the range of activities associated with searching for, discovering, and researching unique biodiversity for potential commercial applications. The Antarctic region, which we will take to be the entire area south of the Antarctic Convergence, is a region containing such uniqueness. Bioprospecting has already been underway in the Antarctic for some years.

Bioprospecting in the Antarctic presents the familiar generic challenges associated with the activity anywhere. It also, however, carries with it additional and particular challenges because of the region's contested and unresolved territorial sovereignty situation, which is managed through a delicate (and itself periodically contested) form of international governance through the Antarctic Treaty System.

The principle achievements of the Antarctic Treaty System include: practical demilitarisation of the region, ensuring freedom of scientific investigation (including free availability of scientific observations and results) and the establishment of science as the currency of national presence, containing the territorial sovereignty problems, safeguarding the environment, and establishing activity-specific responses to issues (sealing, marine harvesting, minerals activities, and [currently] tourism) as they arise.

Thus, bioprospecting arises in Antarctica in a context of a novel entrenched role for science, in a community that involves both developed and developing states of significantly differing technical and economic capacity, within a regime that itself crosses terrestrial and marine environments, and against a background of other non-Antarctic Treaty System legal regimes such as the UN Convention of the Law of the Sea and the Convention on Biological Diversity, with which jurisdictional boundaries are unclear.

Some quite profound questions therefore arise: whether management of Antarctic bioprospecting can be done through the Antarctic Treaty System at all; if it can, the consequences for existing norms of Antarctic activity – logistic cooperation, openness, free availability of information, avoidance of sovereignty issues, environmental protection; and how to address issues of equity – both across the present diverse state membership of the system, and between the Antarctic Treaty System as a whole and the wider international community. Recalling the annual "Question of Antarctica" at

* Alan D. Hemmings is Senior Fellow at Gateway Antarctica Centre for Antarctic Studies and Research, University of Canterbury, Christchurch, New Zealand; E-mail: alan.d.hemmings@bigpond.com

** Michelle Rogan-Finnemore is Centre Manager, Gateway Antarctica Centre for Antarctic Studies and Research, University of Canterbury, Christchurch, New Zealand; E-mail: michelle.finnemore@canterbury.ac.nz

the General Assembly in the 1980s and 1990s suggests a new resource issue may again attract wider international interest than the present forty-eight Parties[1] to the several Antarctic instruments.

1 THE BASIS FOR INTEREST IN BIOPROSPECTING IN THE ANTARCTIC

Globally, commercialisation of products or processes sourced from natural biochemical or other materials increasingly underpins major and lucrative industries. Pharmaceutical products developed from globally sourced natural products for the cancer market alone were worth US$16 billion in 1998.[2] In 2005, it is estimated that this market will be worth US$24 billion.[3] "Bioprospecting" is the term applied to the process (or parts thereof) whereby such natural sources are discovered and exploited.

Bioprospectors are interested in the region's biodiversity, examining its plants, animals and micro-organisms, across a range of Antarctic environments. The likelihood of isolating a novel or useful biochemical compound ordinarily increases with biodiversity; the greater the biodiversity, the greater the likelihood of a "hit."[4] Therefore, bioprospecting efforts are often linked with efforts to scope the biodiversity of an area.[5] Indeed, differentiating the point where "science" becomes "bioprospecting" may sometimes be problematic. Of particular importance to bioprospectors are those organisms found in extreme environments, defined as those where physical (e.g., temperature, radiation, pressure) and chemical (e.g., salinity, acidity) conditions approach or exceed the usual tolerances for life.[6] Some organisms – for which the term "extremophiles" has been coined – thrive under such conditions and do not survive outside them.

Although Antarctica's terrestrial biodiversity is, overall, low, the marine environment of the Southern Ocean supports significantly greater biodiversity, including a diverse range of micro-organisms. The Antarctic ice sheet, and lakes and other limnological features in the McMurdo Dry Valleys are known to contain micro-organisms; and hot spots around volcanic areas such as Mount Erebus are extremely biodiverse zones.

Underpinning Antarctic bioprospecting is the massive scientific enterprise grounded in the 1957 International Geophysical Year and the consequential establishment of science as the currency of national engagement on and around the continent following the adoption of the Antarctic Treaty and its subsequent expansion into the Antarctic Treaty System.[7]

Although bioprospecting has been underway in the Antarctic for a number of years,[8] there is no mention of "bioprospecting" *per se* in any of the Antarctic Treaty System legal

[1] See "Parties to the Antarctic Treaty System's Component Instruments," in Alan D. Hemmings & Michelle Rogan-Finnemore, eds., *Antarctic Bioprospecting* (2005) Appendix D, 295–297.

[2] Murray Munro, "Biodiversity and Bioprospecting in Antarctica" (Presentation delivered at the Graduate Certificate in Antarctic Studies Programme, Christchurch, 9 December 2003, copy on file with authors.)

[3] Ibid.

[4] Ibid.

[5] Roberta L. Farrell & Shona M. Duncan, "Uniqueness of Antarctica and Potential for Commercial Success," in Alan D. Hemmings & Michelle Rogan-Finnemore, eds., *Antarctic Bioprospecting* (2005), 10–40; See also, Munro, note 4.

[6] Peter Doran, "Antarctica as an extreme environment and extraterrestrial analogue" (Presentation at the University of Canterbury Science Prestige Lecture, Christchurch, 8 June 2005, copy on file with authors).

[7] See, for example, Richard Herr & Robert Hall, "Science as Currency and the Currency of Science," in John Handmer, ed., *Antarctica: Policies and Policy Development* (1989), 13–24.

[8] The situation in relation to the high seas appears analogous – see David K. Leary, "Bioprospecting and the Genetic Resources of Hydrothermal Vents on the High Seas: What Is the Existing Legal Position, Where

instruments.[9] Even the Protocol, adopted as recently as 1991 and covering all human activities subject to the Antarctic Treaty, does not specifically mention bioprospecting.

Despite the fact that the legal machinery of the Antarctic Treaty System appeared to ignore the activity, groups of Antarctic scientists recognised very early on the potential benefits from bioprospecting-related research and have been engaged, to one extent or another, in the activity ever since. To date, no one has been able to ascertain the precise nature and full extent of current Antarctic bioprospecting activities.[10]

However, there have been groups from a number of Antarctic Treaty Consultative states actively involved in Antarctic bioprospecting on the continent and in the marine environment since at least 1995. This work has been carried out by a range of universities, research institutes, and companies, which tend to act within consortia groups which are a mixture of public and private bodies.[11] The funding for such research also usually represents a mixture of public and private sources.

2 ANTARCTIC GOVERNANCE

2.1 Geopolitical Context

The Antarctic, which we take to comprise the continent, surrounding islands, ice shelves, and marine area south of the Antarctic Convergence/Polar Front, has an essentially unique juridical status and a resulting novel form of international governance. Seven states[12] claim Antarctic sectors, three of these substantially overlap[13] and are mutually contested. One claim[14] has undefined southern or northern boundaries, and one sector[15] is claimed by nobody (Figure 28.1). Two further states[16] reject all seven claims, while maintaining that they themselves have a basis to claim should they choose to do so. For the rest of the 191[17] state members of the United Nations, no claims or bases for claims are recognised and Antarctica is seen instead as a global commons or common heritage area, or subject to some sort of *de facto* condominium managed by the Antarctic Treaty System.

2.2 The Antarctic Treaty System

The Antarctic Treaty System is an international governance arrangement grounded in the 1959 Antarctic Treaty[18] and three subsequent treaties in force: 1972 Convention for

Are We Heading and What Are Our Options?" 1 *Macquarie Journal of International and Comparative Environmental Law*, (2004), 137–178.

9 Alan D. Hemmings, "A Question of Politics: Bioprospecting and the Antarctic Treaty System," in Alan D. Hemmings & Michelle Rogan-Finnemore, eds., *Antarctic Bioprospecting* (2005), 107.

10 United Nations University/Institute of Advanced Studies (UNU/IAS), *The International Regime for Bioprospecting: Existing Policies and Emerging Issues for Antarctica* (2003), 6.

11 Ibid.

12 Argentina, Australia, Chile, France, New Zealand, Norway, United Kingdom.

13 The claims by Argentina, Chile, and the United Kingdom.

14 Norway.

15 The sector between 150° W and 90° W, between the claims of New Zealand and Chile.

16 Russia and the United States.

17 List of Member States, UN Web site, 1 June 2005. http://www.un.org/Overview/unmember.html.

18 *The Antarctic Treaty*, opened for signature 1 December 1959, 402 UNTS 71 (entered into force 23 June 1961) (hereafter *Antarctic Treaty*).

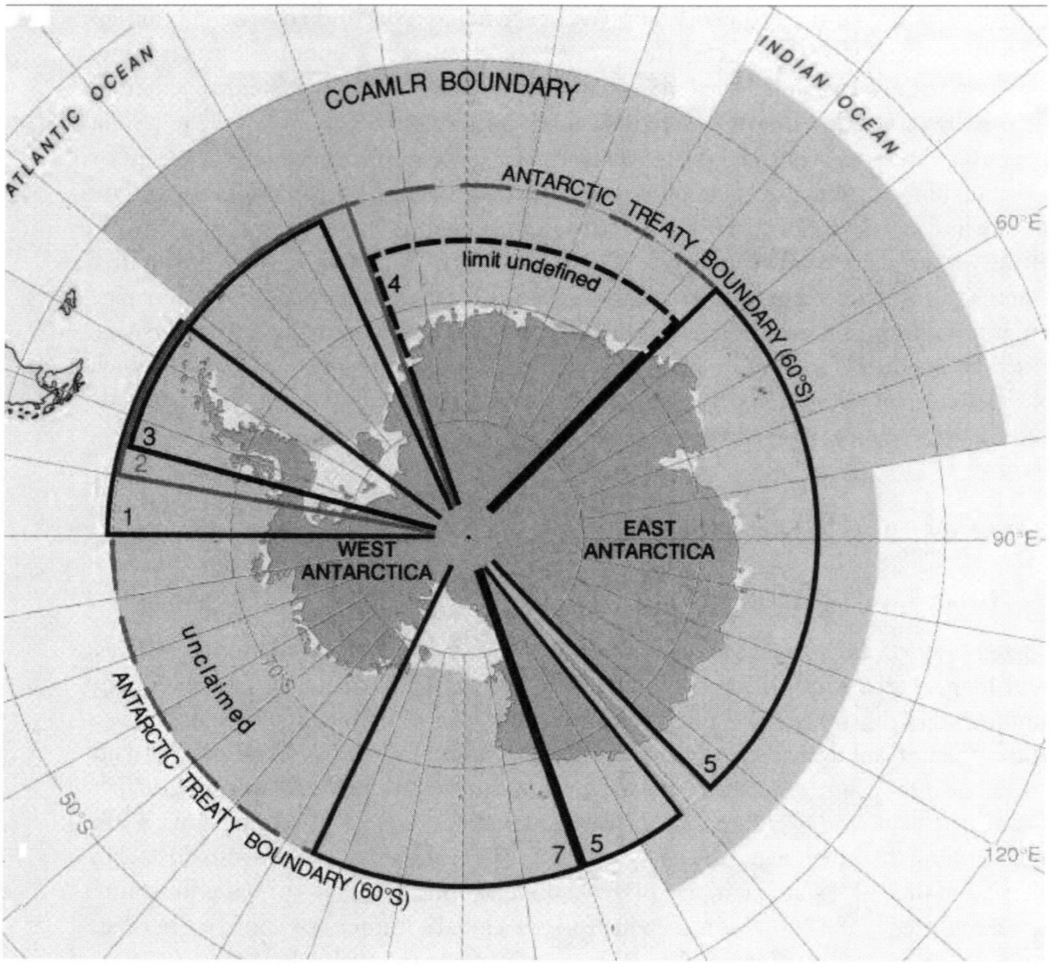

Figure 28.1. Map showing the Antarctic territorial claims, the boundaries of the Antarctic Treaty area and Convention for the Conservation of Antarctic Marine Living Resources area. (Note: All of the territorial claims, except Norway's, converge at the south geographic pole.)

The seven sections refer to the following territorial claims:

1 Chile
2 United Kingdom
3 Argentina
4 Norway (undefined northern and southern limits)
5 Australia (in two parts, separated by the French claim)
6 France
7 New Zealand

the Conservation of Antarctic Seals[19] (CCAS), 1980 Convention on the Conservation of Antarctic Marine Living Resources[20] (CCAMLR), and the 1991 Protocol on Environmental Protection to the Antarctic Treaty[21] (Protocol). The 1988 Convention on the

[19] *Convention for the Conservation of Antarctic Seals*, opened for signature 1 June 1972, 11 ILM 251 (1972) (entered into force 11 March 1978) (hereafter *CCAS*).

[20] *Convention on the Conservation of Antarctic Marine Living Resources*, opened for signature 20 May 1980, 19 ILM (1980) (entered into force 7 April 1982) (hereafter *CCAMLR*).

[21] *Protocol on Environmental Protection to the Antarctic Treaty*, opened for signature 4 October 1991, 30 ILM (1991) (entered into force 14 January 1998) (hereafter *Protocol*).

Regulation of Antarctic Mineral Resource Activities[22] (CRAMRA) has not entered into force, nor is it likely to, having been adopted but then essentially abandoned in favour of the Protocol, which includes a specific prohibition on mineral resource activities.

Although the Antarctic Treaty, CCAS, and Protocol have effect over an area with a common northern boundary (coincident with most claims) at 60° South, CCAMLR's boundary approximates the Antarctic Convergence and is variably set at 45°–60° South.

Membership of all or parts of the Antarctic Treaty System now involves forty-five states, including the most powerful states in both the developed and less-developed world. This community has cooperated to preserve what it sees as its particular rights and obligations for the region against inroads by the wider international community and historically has viewed the Antarctic Treaty System, rather than the United Nations, as the appropriate institution through which states should engage on Antarctic issues, and one consistent with the reference to "Regional Arrangements" in the Charter of the United Nations.

This international system has sought to balance the positions of both claimant and nonclaimant states. It extends across a whole continent, numerous surrounding islands, and the entire Southern Ocean – some 10 percent of the surface of the planet.

2.3 Antarctic Treaty

The Antarctic Treaty established science and scientific cooperation[23] as the bedrock of national activity in Antarctica, limited its use to peaceful purposes and prohibited military activities (but not the use of military equipment or personnel),[24] nuclear testing (and dumping without international agreement),[25] ensured freedom of access to all parts of the area,[26] and "froze" positions on sovereignty.[27] Although it did not address what would now be termed resource or environmental issues, through its establishment of a consultative process among the parties it provided the mechanism whereby these matters might subsequently be addressed.[28] A permanent Antarctic Treaty Secretariat, servicing both Antarctic Treaty and Protocol issues, was only agreed in 2001[29] and became functional on 1 September 2004.

2.4 Convention for the Conservation of Antarctic Seals

The Convention for the Conservation of Antarctic Seals was driven by the belief in the late 1960s that a resumption of commercial sealing in Antarctica was possible, and that there was a jurisdictional gap in relation to seals in the marine area, including on pack ice. The 1964 Agreed Measures for the Conservation of Antarctic Fauna and Flora,[30] which established, *inter alia*, the obligation to avoid harmful interference, the category of "Specially Protected Species," and "Specially Protected Areas," were seen as

[22] *Convention on the Regulation of Antarctic Mineral Resource Activities*, opened for signature 25 November 1988, 27 ILM (1988) (not in force) (hereafter *CRAMRA*).

[23] *Antarctic Treaty*, Articles II, III.

[24] *Antarctic Treaty*, Article I.

[25] *Antarctic Treaty*, Article V.

[26] *Antarctic Treaty*, Article VII.

[27] *Antarctic Treaty*, Article IV.

[28] *Antarctic Treaty*, Article IX (1)(f) refers to "preservation and conservation of living resources in Antarctica."

[29] Decision 1 (2001) of XXIV ATCM, St. Petersburg, 2001.

[30] Recommendation III VIII ATCM, Brussels, 1964.

insufficient to secure potential target seal species in the marine environment[31] should the industry recommence. CCAS establishes a mechanism for regulating commercial sealing should it recommence[32] and an obligation for permits for other uses of any of the six seal taxa found in the Antarctic Treaty area. To date, commercial sealing has not eventuated, and thus the core provisions of the convention have not been used. CCAS has no obvious likely role in relation to bioprospecting.

2.5 Convention on the Conservation of Antarctic Marine Living Resources

The Convention on the Conservation of Antarctic Marine Living Resources (CCAMLR) applies to the marine area south of the Antarctic Convergence. Its objective is "the conservation of Antarctic marine living resources," although "conservation" is taken to include "rational use."[33] Marine living resources are defined as "the populations of fin fish, molluscs, crustaceans and all other species of living organisms, including birds, found south of the Antarctic Convergence."[34] Marine harvesting is set in a context of maintaining the marine ecosystem.[35]

Final management responsibility is assigned to a CCAMLR Commission comprising state parties,[36] and it gives effect to these obligations through, *inter alia*, Conservation Measures.[37] Underpinning the Commission's actions is an advisory Scientific Committee[38] and a permanent Secretariat.[39]

2.6 Protocol on Environmental Protection to the Antarctic Treaty

The Protocol establishes generically applicable obligations across the range of all human activities, governmental and nongovernmental, regulated by the Antarctic Treaty (but *not* the activities regulated by CCAS, CCAMLR, or the 1946 International Convention for the Regulation of Whaling[40] through its International Whaling Commission [IWC]). It is a framework convention comprising a main body of twenty-seven articles, a schedule on arbitration, and technical annexes (which legally form an integral part of it). The Protocol designates Antarctica "a natural reserve, devoted to peace and science",[41] establishes "environmental principles",[42] and an advisory Committee for Environmental Protection (CEP)[43] to facilitate protection of the Antarctic environment and "dependent and associated ecosystems." There are currently five annexes in force addressing: I Environmental Impact Assessment; II Conservation of Antarctic Fauna and Flora; III Waste Disposal and Waste Management; IV Prevention of Marine Pollution; and V Area Protection and Management.

Annexes can be individually amended, to keep pace with technical developments, best-practice, and changing circumstances, without the necessity to revisit the core agreements of the main text. Additional annexes also can be added. A sixth annex

[31] Although two taxa – Fur seals (*Arctocephalus* spp.) and Ross Seal (*Ommatophoca rossii*) – formed the Specially Protected Species listed in its Annex A.

[32] *CCAS*, Article 3, Annex.

[33] *CCAMLR*, Article 2.

[34] *CCAMLR*, Article 1, paragraph 2.

[35] *CCAMLR*, Article 2.

[36] *CCAMLR*, Article 7.

[37] *CCAMLR*, Article 9.

[38] *CCAMLR*, Articles 14, 15.

[39] *CCAMLR*, Article 17.

[40] *International Convention for the Regulation of Whaling*, opened for signature 2 December 1946 161 UNTS 72 (entered into force 10 November 1948) (hereafter *ICRW*).

[41] *Protocol*, Article 2.

[42] *Protocol*, Article 3.

[43] *Protocol*, Articles 11, 12.

(Liability Arising from Environmental Emergencies) was adopted in June 2005 and has not yet entered into force.[44]

2.7 System Functioning in Practice

The Antarctic Treaty System conducts its substantive business through two annual two-week meetings of states parties: the Antarctic Treaty Consultative Meeting (ATCM) addressing Antarctic Treaty and Protocol business (and allowing reporting in relation to CCAS) and the CCAMLR Meeting. Both meetings assign agenda items to standing working groups that report back to plenary sessions. Positions agreed by consensus are codified in various mechanisms, including Decisions, Resolutions, and Measures at the ATCM and Conservation Measures at the CCAMLR Meeting. The Reports of ATCMs and CCAMLR Meetings reproduce these and include language summarising the discussions on the various agenda items.

Additional substantive technical (scientific, legal, operational) work is conducted through intersessional meetings and electronic exchange. Aside from conventional diplomatic communications, there also may be some limited real-time capacity (or potential) for management and reaction outside the annual meetings through the CCAMLR and Antarctic Treaty secretariats.

3 BIOPROSPECTING

3.1 No Agreed Definition

There is no universally agreed definition of "bioprospecting," and no international legal agreements that specifically define the term.[45] Even the Convention on Biological Diversity 1992[46] (CBD) and The Bonn Guidelines on Access to Genetic Resources and Benefit-Sharing[47] (Bonn Guidelines), recently created legal instruments whose objectives involve the sustainable use and protection of biological diversity and regulation of access to and benefits derived from living resources, do not use the term.

3.2 Some Approaches to a Definition

There have, however, been recent attempts by various authors to compose a legal definition of the term. For example, Jones defines bioprospecting as:

> the search for and sourcing of organisms from the natural environment with the purpose of extracting of compounds for further investigation of their potential development in therapeutic or industrial applications.[48]

[44] Measure 1 XXVIII ATCM (2005) Annex VI to the Protocol on Environmental Protection to the Antarctic Treaty – Liability Arising from Environmental Emergencies.

[45] See Donald R. Rothwell, "Southern Ocean Bioprospecting and International Law," in Alan D. Hemmings & Michelle Rogan-Finnemore eds., *Antarctic Bioprospecting* (2005), 211.

[46] *Convention on Biological Diversity*, opened for signature on 5 June 1992, 31 ILM (1992) (entered into force 29 December 1993) (hereafter *CBD*).

[47] *Bonn Guidelines on Access to Genetic Resources and Fair and Equitable Sharing of the Benefits Arising out of their Utilization*, COP VI Decision VI/24 (hereafter *Bonn Guidelines*).

[48] Judith Jones, "Regulating Access to Biological and Genetic Resources in Australia: A Case Study of bioprospecting in Queensland." 5 *The Australasian Journal of Natural Resources Law and Policy* (1998), 1, 89.

It can be seen from this definition that the activity seems to consist of a number of stages. This is also reflected in the *Bioprospecting in the High Seas* conference report where it is noted that bioprospecting is being viewed as "a broad concept embracing a number of phases to investigate a region's biodiversity and to collect samples of biological organisms."[49] Accordingly, the suggestion has been made that the activity be characterised by two distinct terms: "bioprospecting," used in its narrowest sense, and "biodiscovery."[50]

Bioprospecting would encompass phase one, the initial phase of scientific research into a region's biodiversity including sample collection, where generally the initial size of any collected sample is small and the environmental impact is minimal. In some cases, this phase may utilise *ex-situ* samples that were collected from a region for another purpose and are no longer needed for that purpose, or have been described and archived.

Biodiscovery would cover the second and subsequent phases, including the recollection, if required, of the biological organism for the purpose of further investigation. Jabour-Green and Nicol[51] describe the subsequent phases as:

- Isolation, Characterisation, and Culture;
- Screening for . . . Activity; and
- Development of Product, Patenting, Trials, Sales, and Marketing.

Phase one of the activity is simply the start of any process that may produce a commercial outcome.[52] The process requires in many cases a long lead-in time before any commercialisation might be realised. In the Antarctic context, phase one is the only stage of the activity that is undertaken in the Antarctic region itself, unless recollection of the material is required. Any subsequent phases of the activity are usually carried out in the home country of the investigator.

Beyond these individual definitions, states have begun to develop their own bioprospecting policies and definitions. The Australian Government, for example, has recently finalised documentation[53] specifically dealing with bioprospecting on Australian territory. It is noted in the report that there is no standard definition and "there are different views on how far bioprospecting extends down the commercialisation path."[54] Their policy document defines *bioprospecting* in its broader sense to reflect what it called common usage as:

> The search for valuable chemical compounds and genetic materials from plants, animals and micro-organisms. The term is sometimes used more narrowly to refer only to the initial collection of biological material for subsequent use for biodiscovery.[55]

Biodiscovery is then defined in the Australian document as: "The extraction and testing of molecules for biological activity, identification of compounds with promise for further development, and research on the molecular basis for the biological activity."[56]

[49] Julia Jabour-Green, *Bioprospecting in the High Seas* (Report from the Bioprospecting in the High Seas Conference, Dunedin) 28–29 November 2003.

[50] See, for example, Standing Committee on Primary Industries and Regional Services, House of Representatives Parliament of Australia, *Bioprospecting: Discoveries Changing the Future* (2001), para. 1.8.

[51] Julia Jabour-Green and Dianne Nicol, "Bioprospecting in Areas outside of National Jurisdiction: Antarctica and the Southern Ocean." 4 *Melbourne Journal of International Law,* (2003), 76, 85–87; Jabour-Green and Nicol define four phases in the whole process: 1) Sample Collection; 2) Isolation, Characterisation and Culture; 3) Screening for Pharmaceutical Activity; and 4) Development of Product, Patenting, Trials, Sales and Marketing.

[52] Farrell and Duncan, note 5, at 33.

[53] Note 50.

[54] Ibid., paragraph 1.7.

[55] Ibid., paragraph 1.8.

[56] Ibid., glossary.

The Australian document, in its discussion regarding ownership of biological materials, points out that ownership of biological resources is unclear and particularly challenging in both the marine and Antarctic environments.[57] There are also, of course, complicated issues in Australia and other states involving compensation for traditional knowledge, benefit-sharing with indigenous people, and ownership or stewardship of native flora and fauna.

3.3 A Working Definition

For the purposes of this chapter, bioprospecting will be defined in its broadest sense, inclusive of all phases of the process from search and discovery through to any commercial development. Specifically, bioprospecting is here taken to be:

> The search for valuable chemical compounds and genetic materials from plants, animals and micro-organisms; the extraction and testing of those compounds and materials for biological activity; and the research and commercial development of those that show activity.[58]

4 REAWAKENING CHALLENGE TO THE ANTARCTIC TREATY SYSTEM?

Interest in bioprospecting in the Antarctic poses challenges similar to those presented by earlier resource exploitation interests such as whaling, sealing, fishing, and mining, and potentially, too, the current interest in tourism.

4.1 Territorial Sovereignty Issues

The recurrent legal challenge that these have presented to the system, and that now faces us with bioprospecting, stem first from the tension between the asserted territorial sovereignty of a few states and the nonrecognition of these assertions by just about every other state; and, second, from the tension between the regional quasi-condominium of the Antarctic Treaty System as a whole, and the wider international community in relation to rights, benefits, and obligations there. The second tension is ironic, of course, arising as it does, in part, from the attempt to address the first.

The crux of the Antarctic problem is that, in a world still largely organised around the system of state sovereignty and clear territorial jurisdiction, we lack a generally recognised sovereign in the Antarctic. So how, in such a place, are we to manage bioprospecting?

4.2 Competing Values

The issue is further complicated because of the various (and frequently conflicting) values and uses already argued for the Antarctic (both within the Antarctic Treaty System and outside it). These include the value of the region for scientific research; the increasing value of the region in economic terms; and the environmental value

[57] Ibid., paragraph 3.32.

[58] This encompasses the definition of both biodiscovery and bioprospecting as presented in the Australian document; see also Michelle Rogan-Finnemore, *The Legal Implications of Bioprospecting in the Antarctic* (LLM, University of Canterbury, 2005) 59.

of Antarctica, including intrinsic and wilderness values, recognised in the Protocol. Assorted pressures on, or threats to, these values are argued.

4.3 Regulating Bioprospecting

Antarctic sovereignty is a subject well covered in the literature and accordingly the focus here is on factors that appear most apposite to the bioprospecting question.

For a state asserting a claim to Antarctic territory, several consequences may follow. The claimant believes it has particular prerogatives in relation to the assignment of access and use rights within its claim. Notwithstanding Article IV of the Antarctic Treaty, it is likely to wish it might "license" bioprospectors in "its" territory, in some way. Abstaining from asserting its claimant interests is hard when potential benefits are at stake. This potentially threatens the *modus vivendi* in relation to sovereignty under the Antarctic Treaty. It clearly puts the claimant at odds with those states (both within and without the Antarctic Treaty System) that see the Antarctic as common heritage or global commons.

For states outside the Antarctic Treaty System, this conflict presumably kicks in even if bioprospecting is managed by the Antarctic Treaty System as a whole – this is, after all, the basis for the "Question of Antarctica" in the General Assembly through the 1980s and 1990s during the discussion within the Antarctic Treaty System of a minerals regime. Here is fertile new ground for conflict between north and south about access to global benefits. After a decade on the shelf, Antarctica may be about to be dusted off and be placed back in the front line of international contention.

There are likely to be practical dilemmas at the operational level, too. As a product of the historic commitments to science, and scientific and logistics cooperation in Antarctica, sharing of facilities and transportation is common. Scientific openness – and the free availability of results and data – is the norm. But is such a norm sustainable when the activity is potentially commercial? Will cooperation persist when the activity involves a potential commercial (and national?) competitor? Will legislators remain happy for their taxpayers to subsidise (say) transportation for a direct rival to one of their own national entities? Will full and frank disclosure of scientific data persist if such data has a clear (or even merely potential) pecuniary value?[59]

By virtue of its territorial assertion, an Antarctic claimant state is likely to see itself as a coastal state *sensu* UN Convention on the Law of the Sea[60] (UNCLOS) – with consequential standing in relation to territorial seas, exclusive economic zones (EEZs) and the possibility of further rights over the continental shelf beyond two hundred nautical miles. This, too, threatens the *modus vivendi* in relation to sovereignty under the Antarctic Treaty. To the extent that CCAMLR may have standing in relation to management of some bioprospecting activities, it also threatens the *modus vivendi* in relation to sovereignty under that instrument. But perhaps even more significant is the fact that we now enter an area seen (by most states) as high seas and thus properly subject to UNCLOS and the Deep Seabed Authority.

[59] See the discussion of these themes in Alan D. Hemmings & Michelle Rogan-Finnemore, "The Issues Posed by Bioprospecting in Antarctica," in Alan D. Hemmings & Michelle Rogan-Finnemore, eds., *Antarctic Bioprospecting* (2005), 234–244.

[60] *UN Convention on the Law of the Sea*, 21 ILM (1982), 1261 (entered into force 16 November 1994) (hereafter *UNCLOS*).

Although the lead players might well be different in relation to bioprospecting from those states which challenged Antarctic Treaty System hegemony in relation to the minerals issue in the 1980s and early 1990s,[61] that period of "external" challenge to the Antarctic Treaty System should perhaps be taken as a warning to the system about the need to consider the wider international community in relation to Antarctic resource access. Having spent a decade taking the sting out of the annual "Question of Antarctica" in the General Assembly, Antarctic Treaty Consultative Parties will hardly wish to see it reinvigorated via bioprospecting.

5 EXISTING OBLIGATIONS

5.1 Antarctic Treaty

When one begins to consider what the regulation of Antarctic bioprospecting might entail, one immediately must consider the obligations that state parties have already agreed to within the Antarctic Treaty System, as these would continue to exist in addition to any specific bioprospecting regulation.

The Antarctic Treaty lays down at least two fundamental legal obligations, which are:

1. Peaceful use of the Antarctic Treaty region; *and*
2. Freedom of scientific investigation and cooperation toward that end, in the Antarctic Treaty region.

The question that might be asked is, what is the extent of the Treaty obligations of peaceful purposes and freedom of scientific investigations in regards to Antarctic bioprospecting? Answering this question requires consideration of Articles I, II, and III of the Antarctic Treaty.

From the start of the negotiation of the Antarctic Treaty, the "peaceful use" of Antarctica "constituted the fundamental objective."[62] What peaceful use or peaceful purposes specifically means, and, more important, what it practically does, is not defined within the Antarctic Treaty System. In a strict sense, a "peaceful purpose" carries with it a negative connotation of not doing anything with a military purpose in the region, but even here things are far from clear.[63] This interpretation made sense in 1959 when the Antarctic Treaty was negotiated and signed, as the United States in particular did not wish to see the Cold War spread into the Antarctic region. Although the objective of maintaining a nonmilitarised zone in the region was of critical importance in the

[61] Malaysia, the lead state outside the Antarctic Treaty System challenging it in relation to the minerals question mounted a sustained critique. See, for example, UNGA 1984 document A/39/583 (Part II). Question of Antarctica; Study requested under General Assembly Resolution 38/77. Report of the Secretary-General. Part Two: Views of States, Vol. II (Malaysia, pp. 107–111) and UNGA 1999 document 54/99/32 (1C-3) Statement by Ambassador Hasmy Agam, Permanent Representative of Malaysia to the United Nations on Agenda item 66: Question on Antarctica at the First Committee of the 54th Session of the United Nations General Assembly New York, Thursday 11 November 1999. Subsequently, Malaysia has been courted as a possible Party to the Antarctic Treaty and is now involved in Antarctic institutions: See "Malaysia Antarctic Research Program," nonpaper presented by Malaysian invited representative to XXVIII ATCM, Stockholm, June 2005.

[62] Peter J. Beck, *The International Politics of Antarctica* (1986), 70.

[63] See Alan D. Hemmings, "Is Antarctica Demilitarised?" in Richard Herr, Rob Hall & Marcus Haward, eds., *Antarctica's Future: Continuity or Change?* (1990).

late 1950s when the Treaty was negotiated and signed, the science of the International Geophysical Year (IGY 1957–1958) became the primary means of implementing the peaceful purposes objective. So the obligation has come to be interpreted to mean that scientific investigation and associated activities represent examples of peaceful purpose.

Bioprospecting appears, *prima facie*, to be an activity with a peaceful purpose, which not only has high scientific value-adding to our understanding of the biodiversity of the region but also potentially generates other benefits that could be applied for the good of all mankind (and be of commercial value). One potential problem with bioprospecting in Antarctica then is that any commercial activity related to resource extraction, especially in an area where sovereignty is undetermined, while initially carried out for a peaceful purpose and otherwise legitimate has the ***potential*** to create internal and external conflict in the region.[64] This conflict opens up the possibility that the Antarctic region could become the scene of international discord, and that would be contrary to the peaceful purposes objective laid down in the Antarctic Treaty.

Generally, there appears to be at least the perception with respect to any commercial activity in the Antarctic that, if the stakes get too high, the activity could generate expectations and pressures leading to actions that threaten the peaceful purposes objective of the Antarctic Treaty. When mining was perceived to have this capacity to disrupt, the solution was the same that applied to the strictly military and nuclear activities in the region, that is, these activities are prohibited.

The few discussions to date surrounding the legal obligations of bioprospecting in the Antarctic have focused on Article II and III of the Antarctic Treaty. Exactly what the extent of these represent for Antarctic Treaty state parties and, whether bioprospecting is an activity that can legally be carried out in the Antarctic, while allowing state parties to continue to meet these obligations, is problematic.

Freedom of scientific investigation is first mentioned in the preamble of the Treaty and is stated in a general way in its Article II, saying that "Freedom of scientific investigation in Antarctica and co-operation toward that end, as applied in the International Geophysical Year, shall continue . . . " Article III then goes on to give specific indications of what was foreseen by the Treaty parties in Article II. Article III states:

1. In order to promote international cooperation in scientific investigation in Antarctica, as provided for in Article II of the present Treaty, the Contracting Parties agree that, to the greatest extent feasible and practicable:
   a. information regarding plans for scientific programs in Antarctica shall be exchanged to permit maximum economy of and efficiency of operations;
   b. scientific personnel shall be exchanged in Antarctica between expeditions and stations;
   c. scientific observations and results from Antarctica shall be exchanged and made freely available.

Whatever the current extent of the obligation, it appears that the "freedom of scientific investigation" obligation has historically been met by all Antarctic Treaty State parties. Through the cooperative arrangement of the Antarctic Treaty Consultative Meeting system and related organisations such as the Council of Managers of National

[64] See, for example, a discussion of this in the context of minerals and CRAMRA in Rudiger Wolfrum, *The Convention on the Regulation of Antarctic Mineral Resource Activities* (1991), 11–15.

Antarctic Programmes (COMNAP), National Antarctic Science Program information is prepared and presented to all Treaty parties at the annual meetings.

Many of the programs operate cooperative arrangements when providing air, marine, and surface support, so that generally there is no restriction on freedom of scientific investigation in a practical sense. It is the more specific obligation laid down in Article III(1)(c) that may prove to be the most difficult to interpret and apply in the context of bioprospecting activities in the Antarctic. The precise nature of the disclosure and exchange requirements imposed by this section is uncertain.[65] There has been particular concern that protection of intellectual property rights associated with Antarctic biodiversity may be in breach of the obligation for the free availability of scientific information and results from Antarctica. Nevertheless, patents in relation to organisms sourced from Antarctica and the Southern Ocean do exist.

Interestingly, the first explicit response to bioprospecting to come out of the Antarctic Treaty System is a Resolution[66] (an hortatory document) adopted at XXVII ATCM in Stockholm in June 2005, which:

> reaffirm[s] the importance of Article III(1) of the Antarctic Treaty with regard to scientific activities relating to biological prospecting in that . . .

It then goes on to reproduce, verbatim, the three sections (a, b, and c) found in Article III(1). The Resolution then recommends that:

1. Their governments draw to the attention of their national Antarctic programmes and other research institutes engaged in Antarctic biological prospecting the provisions of Article III(1) of the Antarctic Treaty;
2. Their governments continue to keep under review the question of biological prospecting in the Antarctic Treaty Area, and exchange on an annual basis information and views relating to that question as appropriate.

A critical success of the Antarctic Treaty was the transparency which it introduced to the operations and plans of states operating in Antarctica, and several articles in the Treaty relate to this point. The Article III exchanges of personnel, and observations and results were important. So, too, was the commitment to advance notification of:

> all expeditions to and within Antarctica, on the part of its ships or nationals, and all expeditions to Antarctica organized in or proceeding from its territory.[67]

A practice of revealing some internal categories of activity has arisen in relation to the annual exchange of information documents resulting from this obligation. Potentially, this is a mechanism whereby bioprospecting activities and intentions might be flagged by Consultative Parties. But a difficulty is already evident. Another practice – not inherent in the Article VII obligation – has arisen whereby vessels engaged in fishing activities (and those engaged in activities regulated by the IWC) are not ordinarily deemed to constitute "expeditions" in the sense of the article. Presumably, this practice reflects a particular and narrow reading of the Treaty's reach given the reservation of high seas freedoms in Article VI. The question this seems to pose, in relation to bioprospecting, is whether an expedition directed to this activity also would be ignored in the exchange of

[65] Jabour-Green and Nicol, note 151, at 104.
[66] Resolution 7 XXVIII ATCM (2005) Biological Prospecting in Antarctica.
[67] *Antarctic Treaty*, Article VII 5(a).

information, whether or not the activity was subject to CCAMLR. It may be premature to go much further on this point, other than to suggest that maintaining transparency across all activities in the area seems desirable.

5.2 Convention on the Conservation of Antarctic Marine Living Resources (CCAMLR)

Although it has not itself addressed bioprospecting, and merely kept a watching brief in the discussions of the issue at the ATCM in recent years,[68] to the extent that Antarctic marine living resources are the target of bioprospecting interest, CCAMLR obligations apply. A significant issue is whether marine microbial taxa fall under CCAMLR. Some further comments in relation to CCAMLR are offered below in relation to the use of existing legal tools.

5.3 The Protocol

In addition to the obligations established by the Antarctic Treaty, the more recently enacted Protocol lays down further fundamental obligations to protect the Antarctic environment and its dependent and associated ecosystems.

The Protocol designates Antarctica as a "natural reserve, devoted to peace and science,"[69] a position that seems at best neutral in relation to the (subsequently emerging) question of bioprospecting. To the extent that the argument that bioprospecting is merely an extension of science, conceivably it bolsters its status. A set of "Environmental Principles"[70] is at the heart of the Protocol. Activities in the area are to be planned and conducted to avoid significant risk to established (and identified) values and uses, and signs of the precautionary principle can be detected. Cooperation is emphasised.[71]

A three-level system of prior environmental impact assessment (EIA) is established for all activities covered by the Protocol.[72] Many states assume an obligation to address the full range of obligations in the main text of the Protocol and all five technical annexes currently in force in the course of meeting the EIA obligations. Reporting is required for some levels of EIA. Various review and oversight capabilities are provided – through the advisory CEP,[73] on-site inspection provisions,[74] and mechanisms for dispute settlement are provided.[75]

For the sorts of activities anticipated by the Protocol, and across activities over which it has standing, the Protocol offers a reasonable basis for managing any environmental issues posed by bioprospecting. The difficulty is that this presently appears to be the only facet of bioprospecting for which an existing Antarctic Treaty System instrument provides any specific guidance.

Organisms of interest to bioprospectors exist across a range of environments, both terrestrial and marine. These environments extend across the boundaries of the Antarctic legal instruments – that is, some parts of a single activity may fall under the Antarctic Treaty and the Protocol and some other parts under CCAMLR (Figure 28.2). Some

[68] See Alan D. Hemmings, "A Question of Politics: Bioprospecting and the Antarctic Treaty System," in Alan D. Hemmings & Michelle Rogan-Finnemore, eds., *Antarctic Bioprospecting* (2005), 122.

[69] *Protocol*, Article 2.

[70] *Protocol*, Article 3.

[71] *Protocol*, Article 6.

[72] *Protocol*, Article 8 and Annex I.

[73] See *Protocol*, Article 12 for its functions.

[74] *Protocol*, Article 14.

[75] *Protocol*, Articles 18–20.

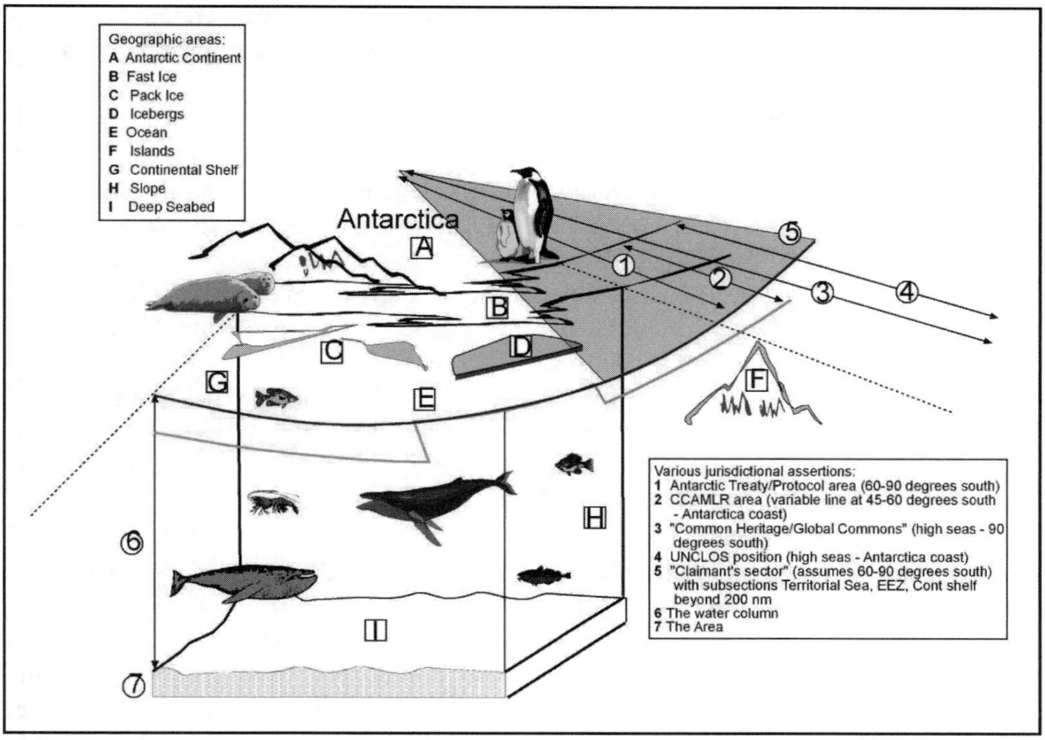

Figure 28.2. Diagram showing the various geographies (letters) present in the Antarctic region with corresponding and often overlapping legal jurisdictions (numbers).

uncertainty may therefore arise as to where responsibility resides, and how to thread an activity through multiple instruments.

6 BENEFIT-SHARING

With any utilization of resources, benefit-sharing is an area that requires consideration; there are differing interests of stakeholders and broad implications in the word "benefit-sharing." In the global context, there has been considerable discussion, and subsequent law and policy development, as regards benefits and benefit-sharing from the use of biodiversity/biogenetic resources and from the use of knowledge, including traditional knowledge, relating to these resources. In the past thirty years, at least three important international agreements have resulted from these discussions, including the Convention on Biological Diversity[76] (CBD).

6.1 Convention on Biological Diversity

The CBD is "a framework agreement that outlines goals and policies for the conservation of biological diversity... but which leaves states to operationalize the principles"[77] to reach those goals and implement policy. The CBD commits parties to take steps to

[76] *Convention on Biological Diversity*, opened for signature on 5 June 1992, 31 ILM (1992) (entered into force 29 December 1993) (here in after *CBD*).

[77] Karin Timmermans, "Intellectual Property Rights and Traditional Medicine: Policy Dilemmas at the Interface." 57 *Social Science and Medicine* (2003), 745, 747.

achieve three objectives: conserving biological diversity, using natural resources sustainably and fairly, and equitably sharing benefits derived from the use of genetic resources.[78] This section focuses on the final objective.

The CBD reaffirmed[79] in Article 3 that states have a sovereign right to exploit their own resources pursuant to their own environmental and developmental policies. Article 15 provides that the authority to determine access to genetic resources rests with national governments and is subject to national legislation and where access is granted it should be on "mutually agreed terms." Contracting parties are also required to adopt measures that aim to achieve the fair and equitable sharing of benefits arising from the commercial (and other) utilisation of genetic resources, and the results of research and development, with the state that provided the resource.[80]

The CBD's Conferences of the Parties (COPs) discuss intellectual property rights (IPRs) frequently in the context of benefit sharing. The 6th COP included the development of the Bonn Guidelines on Access to Genetic Resources and Fair and Equitable Sharing of the Benefits Arising Out of their Utilisation[81] (Bonn Guidelines). They are nonbinding but provide guidance on matters such as the negotiation, monitoring and evaluation, implementation and enforcement of access and benefit-sharing agreements, procedures for obtaining prior informed consent and mechanisms for benefit-sharing.[82]

Ownership of relevant IPRs is listed as only one of a number of possible benefits in Appendix II of the Bonn Guidelines. Other, nonmonetary, benefits include: sharing of research and development results; collaboration, cooperation and contribution in scientific research and development programs, particularly biotechnological research activities, where possible in the provider country; participation in product development; collaboration, cooperation, and contribution in education and training; and admittance to *ex situ* facilities of genetic resources and to databases.

All of the original twelve signatory states to the Antarctic Treaty have signed the CBD. All seven of the territorial claimant states have ratified the CBD; however, although the United States has signed, it has not ratified the Convention. Although the Antarctic Treaty System on the whole cannot be a party to the CBD, a SCAR Working Paper (subsequently withdrawn[83]) in 2002 recognised the value that the CBD provided. The withdrawn Working Paper stated that:

> it would now appear that the Antarctic is now the only part of the world, excluding the High Seas, to which the Convention (on Biological Diversity) does not apply. Yet it might reasonably be expected that . . . such a globally accepted progressive approach . . . would be entirely appropriate.[84]

It remains to be seen how appropriate the CBD and Bonn Guidelines will be in the context of the Antarctic Treaty System and the Antarctic region, especially given that the

[78] Kevin Grey, "Accomplishments and New Directions?" 52.1 *International and Comparative Law Quarterly* (2003), 256, 261–263.

[79] *CBD*, Article 3 is identical to *Stockholm Declaration* (1972), Principle 21, which was the first international agreement to formally state this principle; see also UNGA Resolution 1803 (1962).

[80] *CBD*, Article 15(7); See also *CBD* Articles 16 and 19 regarding access to and transfer of technology and handling of biotechnology and distribution of its benefits.

[81] *Bonn Guidelines, CBD* COP Decision VI/24.

[82] See Kim Connelly-Stone, "Patents, Property Rights and Benefit-Sharing," in Alan D. Hemmings & Michelle Rogan-Finnemore, eds., *Antarctic Bioprospecting* (2005), 69–97.

[83] See Alan D. Hemmings, "A Question of Politics: Bioprospecting and the Antarctic Treaty System," in Alan D. Hemmings & Michelle Rogan-Finnemore eds., *Antarctic Bioprospecting* (2005), 108–110.

[84] Ibid.

United States has not ratified the CBD and the significant, although nonclaimant, role that the United States plays in the Antarctic region. The CBD, based as it is on sovereign ownership, does however mention in its Article 5 that:

> Each Contracting Party shall . . . cooperate with other Contracting Parties . . . through competent international organizations, in respect of areas beyond national jurisdiction and on other matters of mutual interest, for the conservation and sustainable use of biological diversity.[85]

This article could be relied upon by the contracting state parties to work together within the Antarctic Treaty System to regulate any utilization of Antarctic biodiversity.

6.2 Who Are the Stakeholders?

Within a sovereign state generally, benefits from bioprospecting within its territory accrue to that state primarily for the benefit of its people. Benefits should (in some manner) be equitably shared between the parties involved in the bioprospecting. In states where there is an indigenous population and where a discovery is based on traditional knowledge of the resource, the parties involved include the indigenous people of the region. As Antarctica has no indigenous population, no question surrounding traditional knowledge and indigenous culture, and intellectual property arise and the list of stakeholders cannot include an "Antarctic citizen." The list of stakeholders clearly includes the seven territorial claimant states, the other Consultative State parties and, arguably, the Nonconsultative State parties to the Antarctic Treaty. There are also arguments that support enlarging the list of stakeholders to include the remaining UN member states, which are currently outside of the Antarctic Treaty System as the system proposes to be "in the interest of all mankind." Any arrangement for benefit-sharing that falls short of maximum inclusion is likely to be seen by the wider international community as self-serving and evidence that the Antarctic arrangements continue to be a "rich man's club."

7 A WAY FORWARD?

How might Antarctic bioprospecting actually be managed? At this point, there appear to be a number of options theoretically available. One would have to say that on the basis of the limited discussions in the Antarctic Treaty System, and in other places, so far it is hard to discern particular preferences, beyond perhaps an inclination to stall in the hope that things become clearer.

7.1 Utilizing Existing Legal Tools

Within the context of the Antarctic Treaty System, it is arguable that there are already adequate tools to regulate the envisioned, or potential, environmental impacts from bioprospecting in the Antarctic. At least, this can be argued for the area subject to the Protocol where a variety of environmental management obligations and tools (including prior EIA) are in place. The picture across parts of the marine environment may, however, be more complex – with intra-Antarctic Treaty System jurisdiction issues to

[85] *CBD*, Article 5.

resolve and (in the case of CCAMLR) a less developed environmental regime (e.g., no EIA, although capacity to apply some environmental management through Conservation Measures) and a particular focus on facilitating resource access and use.

What currently does not exist within the system as a whole is a mechanism for regulating extraction of resources. Of course, CCAMLR is largely directed to doing precisely this, but its direct experience is with different taxa to many of those most likely to attract near-term bioprospecting interest. CCAMLR is also focussed on harvesting, and although some bioprospecting may merge into this sort of activity, much will not. These considerations pose the question whether, in the event that marine bioprospecting is seen as legally falling within CCAMLR's purview, it has the competence (at least in the short term) to actually regulate the activity. There is nothing to stop it developing such competence of course.

No part of the Antarctic Treaty System appears to offer any existing mechanism to address benefit-sharing, and although the issue has not formally been discussed in any Antarctic fora, members of the system may exhibit similar polarisation on benefit-sharing in the Antarctic to that seen elsewhere.

Because the issues surrounding Antarctic bioprospecting are not simply those issues falling within the environmental category, there is an implication that if bioprospecting continues in the Antarctic, new regulations specific to the activity will need to be developed and adopted.

Although there are some lessons to be learned from both the development of CCAMLR and the development (and subsequent abandonment) of CRAMRA, there are other legal instruments outside the Antarctic Treaty System that are clearly relevant to the issues posed by bioprospecting in the Antarctic. These other instruments include the CBD and Bonn Guidelines noted above. In the context of intellectual property rights generally, and patents in relation to Antarctic products or processes specifically, the Agreement on Trade-Related Aspects of Intellectual Property Rights (TRIPS)[86] is clearly a significant instrument. Also of profound significance for bioprospecting in the marine environment is UNCLOS. Both are considered briefly here.

7.2 UNCLOS

The legal regime for the Southern Ocean is complex. Within the Antarctic Treaty System itself, many of the major legal instruments including CCAS, CCAMLR, and the Protocol regulate, to one extent or another, activity in the Southern Ocean. Outside of the Antarctic area, away from the few and small sub-Antarctic islands subject to national jurisdiction, the Southern Ocean is solely subject to the 1982 UN Convention on the Law of the Sea (UNCLOS).

Under UNCLOS, coastal states enjoy certain rights over a range of maritime zones. Beyond these zones are high seas areas, that is, those areas beyond national jurisdiction. As there is no recognised coastal state, or states, for Antarctica, there are, therefore, no marine zones, so that the marine area of the Southern Ocean is generally considered high seas. Rothwell notes, "Whilst in the overwhelming majority of cases around the world bioprospecting will be regulated within coastal State maritime zones, there are

[86] *Agreement on Trade-Related Aspects of Intellectual Property Rights*, opened for signature 15 April 1994, 1869 UNTS 229 (entered into force 1 January 1995) (hereafter *TRIPS Agreement*).

significant challenges in doing so in the Southern Ocean."[87] This is a result of the unresolved nature of Antarctic sovereignty.

7.3 TRIPS Agreement

The TRIPS Agreement is now the key international agreement promoting standardization of national Intellectual Property Right regimes.[88] It states in Article 27 (1) that "patents shall be made available for any inventions ... provided they are new, involve and inventive step and are capable of industrial application ... without discrimination as to the place of invention, the field of technology and whether products are imported or locally produced." Although TRIPS has been regarded as highly beneficial by some, it has also been criticised[89] by others, especially with regard to the needs of developing nations.

How TRIPS may impact Antarctic bioprospecting remains unclear. It does appear, however, that because every Antarctic Treaty Consultative Party is a signatory to the TRIPS Agreement, to deny a patent application simply because of the Antarctic-origin of the materials involved in the application, would be a breach of the TRIPS agreement. However, further consideration of this issue may be required.

7.4 New Legal Mechanisms

Although some have argued the sufficiency of existing legal mechanisms within the Antarctic Treaty System for bioprospecting management, it is here argued that none of the existing instruments, as they currently stand, could effectively deal with issues associated with living resource use – outside of conventional marine harvesting. Existing approaches such as the adoption of a Measure, or a bioprospecting-specific Annex to the Protocol could well be taken. In practice (even in combination) they seem to offer little hope of a comprehensive and internally coherent approach to bioprospecting in the Antarctic. They may be particularly problematical when it comes to any provision for benefit-sharing with the wider international community, and may even be inadequate in relation to benefit-sharing *within* the Antarctic Treaty System.

Existing mechanisms represent the conceptual middle of a putative bioprospecting management spectrum. If one considers what might be termed the extremities of the spectrum, two obvious theoretical options present themselves – some sort of moratorium on bioprospecting, and the elaboration of a new Antarctic bioprospecting-specific instrument.

7.5 A Moratorium

As with early Antarctic minerals discussions, there has been little discussion in principle on whether bioprospecting activities *should* be allowed in the Antarctic region. Aside what this may say about the depth of consideration of important matters relating to

[87] Donald R. Rothwell, "Southern Ocean Bioprospecting and International Law," in Alan D. Hemmings & Michelle Rogan-Finnemore, eds., *Antarctic Bioprospecting* (2005), 226.

[88] Graham Dutfield, *Intellectual Property, Biogenetic Resources* (2004), 25.

[89] See, for example, Commission on Intellectual Property Rights, *Integrating Intellectual Property Rights and Development Policy* (2002).

some 10 percent of the planet, an obvious difference from the minerals issue is that bioprospecting in the Antarctic is already occurring. Any proposal for – and any agreement to impose – a moratorium would mean halting an activity already underway. This is a very different situation to that in the 1980s and early 1990s in relation to minerals resource activities. These activities had not commenced, and difficult as it clearly was to get international agreement, this required the foregoing of presently unrealised rights and benefits, not the cessation of activities already underway. Furthermore, minerals activities or "mining" were conceptually distinct activities, defined and understood in other contexts.

Bioprospecting, still without agreed definition and merging from science at one end to harvesting at the other with much in the middle that is entirely novel, is not such a simple target. Also, the likely adverse effects of bioprospecting are not seen as of the same magnitude as those generally associated with mining. It also should be recalled that the minerals moratorium was initially at least not an end in itself, but a holding-action while a minerals convention was negotiated. Only later did the interim measure of a moratorium itself become the basis of a new dispensation, when CRAMRA was abandoned in favour of the Protocol with its explicit prohibition on mineral resource activities.[90]

For bioprospecting, it is therefore unlikely, given that it is already occurring in Antarctica and the Southern Ocean, and given its connections to other scientific research in National Antarctic Programs, that any moratorium could now be agreed. There would undoubtedly be subsequent problems associated with adequate policing and enforcement of such a ban. Any samples that have already been legally extracted could still be used for commercial development without breaching a moratorium on extraction from Antarctica, as the samples are already part of national and private collections scattered throughout the world. But a moratorium might, for the time being, make it easier to move territorial sovereignty issues to the back burner.

Although a moratorium may not be feasible at this time, a prohibition on the patenting of any product or process derived from the Antarctic might stop derivation of any economic benefit from bioprospecting. This would limit, at least for the time being, any upstream product development and any need to source Antarctic materials. It would, however, be difficult, or even impossible, to enforce as it would require reliance on national patenting offices to stop any Antarctic-related application. It also may conflict with state's obligations under the TRIPS agreement, which all Antarctic Treaty Consultative Parties have ratified.

Thus, moratoria appear unlikely to win support. That may be seen as unnecessary, at this stage, given the present low level of activity in the Antarctic and the general feeling that currently the activity is causing little environmental impact. And one would face the reasonable question of "What losses [commercial, medical, industrial or otherwise] would we incur if we did not conduct bioprospecting in the Antarctic?"[91]

Currently, all bioprospecting in the Antarctic is carried out within, and therefore presumably with the approval of, national Antarctic research programs. Consultative Parties may decide that as long as the activity poses little to no environmental problems

[90] *Protocol*, Article 7.

[91] See Alan D. Hemmings & Michelle Rogan-Finnemore, "Science and Commercial Issues," in Alan D. Hemmings & Michelle Rogan-Finnemore, eds., *Antarctic Bioprospecting* (2005), 246–253.

then the activity may proceed as is, that is, within the context of their research programs and without formal, specific, regulation, although hopefully subject to EIA. The nexus, however, between scientific research within national Antarctic research programs and the potential for the research to lead to a commercial benefit for the state (or states) involved, may prove to be a conflict of interest that prevents Antarctic Treaty Consultative Parties from acting truly in good faith in their discussions of Antarctic bioprospecting. The likelihood of now enacting or enforcing a moratorium appears very low because of this close connection.

7.6 Antarctic Bioprospecting Convention

A reasonable rationale exists for elaborating a specific Antarctic bioprospecting regime. This, after all, is the model established by previous Antarctic Treaty System practice in relation to sealing, fishing, and mining (and whaling was already subject to a separate arrangement before the negotiation of the Antarctic Treaty). As each specific Antarctic resource issue has arisen, Antarctic practice has been to elaborate a particular new instrument to address it. These successive resource-specific instruments have been the building blocks whereby we arrived at the Antarctic Treaty System. For convenience, the bioprospecting analogue is here referred to as the "Antarctic Bioprospecting Convention."

Exactly what form such an Antarctic Bioprospecting Convention could or should take is a matter of debate. Our working assumption is that it would be another stand-alone convention forming part of the Antarctic Treaty System. Its membership would likely include most present parties to the other instruments. On the assumption that the past is some guide to the future, one would expect the negotiation of a new Antarctic instrument to attract additional states (who may then in turn either voluntarily accede to some or all of the earlier instruments, or be required as a condition of participation to do so by existing members).

Plainly, the details of a convention that has not even been formally mooted are uncertain. In the event that such a convention was, in principle, agreeable to the present Antarctic states, it would be likely to cross the terrestrial and marine boundaries of the Antarctic environment, as there seems little sense in continuing a terrestrial/marine divide. If that is the case, then the Antarctic Bioprospecting Convention will inevitably differ in a strategic sense from earlier conventions; it will not be able to claim to be entirely without prejudice to rights and obligations under preexisting instruments. If bioprospecting is to be managed here, it cannot also be managed under the Antarctic Treaty/Protocol and CCAMLR (bioprospecting activities might of course still have specific obligations in relation to these other conventions – for example, advance notice and exposure to inspection under the Antarctic Treaty; EIA and other technical standards under the Protocol; consideration of effects on marine ecosystems under CCAMLR). Otherwise, all one has achieved is greater complexity and uncertainty about where responsibilities reside.

Any stand-alone legal instrument would also require Antarctic Treaty System states to consider overlapping international conventions and regimes beyond the Antarctic regime, such as UNCLOS, the CBD, and TRIPS, discussed earlier. Relationships with these instruments may be difficult (even impossible) to resolve through a regionally focussed instrument of the sort canvassed here – and if that is so, it may say something significant about the medium-term prospects for continued management of Antarctica by any regional mechanism. But possibly the difficulties are less when one is initiating a new instrument (open to participation by any state) than when one is asserting a right to manage an activity under existing, regional instruments with an existing (and small) membership.

At the next level down, one can pose some suggestions about likely areas of attention. These might include: a precautionary approach to living resource use; establishment of robust access and benefit-sharing provisions; administrative provisions for database creation, development, and management. It might be expected (by analogy with CCAMLR's Scientific Committee and the CEP advising the ATCM in relation to Protocol issues) that a scientific committee would be established to advise on sustainable management of any use of Antarctic biogenetic resources.

There is a continuing and quite fundamental importance to maintaining the Antarctic Treaty's Article III obligation for free availability of scientific information and results, and the Article IV formulation in relation to positions on territorial sovereignty. In the case of bioprospecting, any restatement of Article III of the Antarctic Treaty should be accompanied by a clear explanation of the extent of that obligation, especially in the context of patenting and other intellectual property rights.

Both Articles III and IV would likely be reiterated in an Antarctic Bioprospecting Convention (as in each of the existing Antarctic Treaty System instruments). Whether, and if so how, the new convention would consider the emerging view of the wider international community in relation to common heritage arguments and the regulation of the Antarctic region, or at least the biota of that region, as part of the global commons, is unclear. These would be likely issues to arise – and may be the sorts of concerns that some existing Antarctic states may have about considering a new resource convention. Failure to adequately address these could reignite debate about United Nations involvement in the Antarctic or could see other nonstate actors, such as commercial companies, with a greater role.

The key provision of any convention must be the objective of the convention – and herein may be the basis for the most fundamental debate. It seems clear that defining key terms, including probably parts of the activity-sequence referred to as bioprospecting, will be critical. It will also be important to include definitions of other key terms, such as, *inter alia*, "biota," "living resources," and "biodiversity." For these terms, the Antarctic Treaty System could rely on exiting international legal instruments, such as the CBD, which contain relevant and useful definitions that have already been agreed to by a majority of states also involved in the Antarctic Treaty System.

Although only the initial phases of bioprospecting may be carried out in the Antarctic region, in order to address fundamental issues such as benefit-sharing, the convention would surely have to address in some way the subsequent phases, even when carried out elsewhere. Convention states would, therefore, through this instrument, have some interest in all phases of the process, from search and discovery, through to commercialisation of a product or process.

Some clear provisions on access to and benefit from Antarctic bioprospecting would be required. CRAMRA relied on sponsoring-state provisions for access to Antarctic mineral resources. Whether this sort of tight relationship between states and their corporations remains politically acceptable almost twenty years on from CRAMRA is an interesting question. Although it may be that this type of provision and sponsorship might look useful in relation to some facets of bioprospecting, the fact that the activity relies on the harvesting of relatively small amounts of biodiversity may mean that the "search" and "discovery" phase could be implemented simply through access to an Antarctic biodiversity database. That is, access may be provided by way of the database, not by providing access for every bioprospector to the Antarctic region itself. Populating the database with biodiversity would be the responsibility of National Antarctic programmes, but the database would be the combination of efforts by the National Antarctic programmes as a whole. That is, the database would contain biodiversity data and information from all Parties conducting biodiversity research in the Antarctic region.

Establishing a database seems to offer a number of benefits. It provides a mechanism to protect the Antarctic environment; creates a resource (the database) available for use by states that may not have independent capacity to carry out research activity in Antarctica; and allows for control over Antarctic biodiversity *per se*. Such control would itself aid in creating the wider awareness necessary to ensure that benefit-sharing was taken seriously.

The establishment of such a database provides an opportunity for the Antarctic Treaty System, to demonstrate that it is indeed acting in the benefit of all mankind, which is a claim implicitly made in the Preamble to the Antarctic Treaty.

8 CONCLUDING REMARKS

Although bioprospecting has now been underway in Antarctica (and using material already collected in Antarctica back home) for some years, as a subject for management and international regulation these are early days.

Antarctic Treaty states encounter bioprospecting in this region in a context of unresolved territorial sovereignty and jurisdiction amongst themselves, a wider international community that may not concede unlimited special rights to them, overlapping jurisdiction across a raft of international instruments, and in the face of uncertainty about individual national policy toward bioprospecting in general.

Their likely preferred "solution" – business as usual with whatever minimal regulation (and regulatory development) secured through the Antarctic Treaty System – is itself not without complication, given the central role these states have given to science in the system and the seamless transition from conventional Antarctic science to the industrial, commercial, resource activity that bioprospecting may become. The consequences of such a transition, not only for the conduct of science and scientific cooperation in Antarctica, but for a whole range of norms in the Antarctic Treaty System are presently unclear. But it does seem evident that whereas the Antarctic Treaty System has been slow to commence serious political and legal consideration of what may be required by way of response on its part, in other communities and other international fora there is substantial interest.

Whatever the difficulties, if the Antarctic Treaty System does not engage with bioprospecting, we may be seeing the first Antarctic resource issue since the inception of the Antarctic Treaty System where that system is not the key determinant of the way in which it is resolved. Could the Antarctic regime survive such a discovery?

ACKNOWLEDGMENTS

We extend our appreciation to participants in the *Bioprospecting in Antarctica* Workshop, Gateway Antarctica, University of Canterbury, Christchurch, 7–8 April 2003, and participants in the *Bioprospecting in the High Seas* Workshop (associated with *Deep Sea 2003*), Dunedin, 28–29 November 2003, and its convenor Julia Jabour-Green. ADH extends appreciation to delegates involved in considering bioprospecting at the *XXVIII Antarctic Treaty Consultative Meeting*, Stockholm, 6–17 June 2005. Although we have benefited from discussions at, and ideas emanating from, these fora, and acknowledge that here, the participants are not implicated in our interpretations.

We are grateful to Marney Brosnan and Paul Bealing, Geography Department, University of Canterbury, for assistance in realising Figure 28.2.

SECTION B. INDIGENOUS INTELLECTUAL AND CULTURAL PROPERTY RIGHTS

29 Biotechnological Innovations, Genetic Resources, and Traditional Knowledge: Current Developments at the World Intellectual Property Organization

Burton Ong*

1 INTRODUCTION

At its General Assembly in 2000, the World Intellectual Property Organization (WIPO) proposed the constitution of a special taskforce to look into intellectual property issues arising from the exploitation of genetic resources, traditional knowledge, and expressions of folklore at the request of its Member States.[1] This resulted in the establishment of the Intergovernmental Committee on Intellectual Property and Genetic Resources, Traditional Knowledge and Folklore (IGC), which has spearheaded WIPO's exploratory efforts in shaping an international response to the misappropriation of these resources to develop products over which intellectual property rights are secured. Five years later, thousands of pages of text have been produced in a plethora of discussion materials, consultation papers, technical reports, survey result compilations, and numerous document drafts by the IGC and the WIPO Member States, which have responded to its calls for participation in the international process. Having held eight official sessions[2] to analyse and discuss the intellectual property issues that have arisen in the context of these topical controversies, what progress has the IGC achieved in reaching a global consensus on the Intellectual Property community's response to these issues?

This chapter seeks to distil the output generated by the IGC and to evaluate the draft recommendations it has put forward in its recent sessions, identifying the key developments that have occurred at this forum and the directions in which they appear to be heading. The focus of this chapter will be on the IGC's work on intellectual property–related issues connected to genetic resources and traditional knowledge (which is distinguishable from issues relating to folklore and other traditional cultural expressions), with emphasis placed on the impact of these proposals on the development of biotechnological innovations by users of genetic resources and traditional knowledge.

[1] The Twenty-Sixth (12th Extraordinary) Session was held in Geneva, from 25 September to 3 October 2000. See WO/GA/26/6. All publications issued by WIPO are available from its Web site at http://www.wipo.org.

[2] The most recent meeting of the IGC, at the time of writing, was held between 6 June and 10 June 2005. The documents produced for consideration at these meetings are available online at the following Web address: http://www.wipo.int/meetings/en/topic.jsp?group_id=110.

* Burton Ong is Associate Professor, Faculty of Law, National University of Singapore.

Three areas of the IGC's work deserve special attention:

(1) the development of "Guide Contractual Practices" with intellectual property aspects as part of a wider policy framework regulating access to genetic resources and the equitable sharing of benefits obtained from the used accessed resources;
(2) the draft provisions on the protection of traditional knowledge using existing and *sui generis* legal frameworks (positive protection); and
(3) the development of strategies to strengthen the recognition of genetic resources and traditional knowledge within the existing patent system (defensive protection).

Before discussing the current state of the IGC's progress on these matters, it might be useful to summarise the international legal and political backdrop against which these developments have taken place. In the next section of this chapter, a brief overview of the nature of the problem that WIPO was asked to respond to will be provided along with an account of its origins in the provisions of the Convention on Biological Diversity (CBD). This will be followed by an analysis of the WIPO Committee's contributions to current developments in the three areas identified earlier.

2 GENETIC RESOURCES, TRADITIONAL KNOWLEDGE, AND THE CBD

The basic problem that WIPO has sought to address, through the efforts of the IGC, relates to misconduct by users of genetic resources and associated traditional knowledge which amounts to what is commonly referred to as "biopiracy."[3] A classic scenario would involve the use of genetic resources from a biologically diverse country, possibly in conjunction with the traditional knowledge associated with such resources, to develop biotechnological innovations over which intellectual property rights may be acquired. The resources may be accessed in circumstances that do not fully reflect the prior informed consent of the relevant stakeholders, and the benefits obtained from the development of these innovations and the commercial exploitation of products that embody them are not shared equitably with the resource providers and traditional knowledge holders. The reprehensible character of such an act of misappropriation is further magnified where the patent system is used to secure a legal monopoly over an innovation which it should not be entitled to lay claim to – where the claimed invention is based on a traditional practice or some other aspect of a community's cultural heritage,[4] for example. The commodification of a local or indigenous community's

[3] There is no agreed definition of this term, which was coined by a nongovernmental organization formerly known as RAFI (the Rural Advancement Foundation International) but now known as the ETC group (Action group for Erosion, Technology and Concentration) to refer to "the appropriation of the knowledge and genetic resources of farming and indigenous communities by individuals or institutions who seek exclusive monopoly control (patents or intellectual property) over these resources and knowledge." Available at http://www.etcgroup.org/key_defs.asp.

[4] The most noteworthy examples of allegations of biopiracy involve the patenting of traditional plant-based technologies that have been practiced for centuries by members of indigenous and local communities based in biodiversity-rich developing countries. For a survey of the rise and fall of the Neem patents, arguably the most well-known case in which patents were revoked after strenuous lobbying from NGOs based in India, see Shubha Ghosh, "Globalization, Patents and Traditional Knowledge" 17 *Colum. J. Asian L.* (2003), 73 Other examples include a patent for the use of Turmeric to heal wounds and a patent for Basmati rice, both of which are food crops that were well-established members of India's agricultural and botanical heritage. For a detailed examination of these and other famous biopiracy cases, see Philip Schuler, "Biopiracy and Commercialization of Ethnobotanical Knowledge," in J. Michael Finger & Philip

Box 29.1

Article 8(j) (In situ conservation) requires Contracting Parties to:

"Subject to its national legislation, respect, preserve and maintain **knowledge, innovations and practices of indigenous and local communities** embodying traditional lifestyles relevant for the conservation and sustainable use of biological diversity and promote their wider application with the approval and involvement of the holders of such knowledge, innovations and practices and **encourage the equitable sharing of the benefits** arising from the utilization of such knowledge, innovations and practices"

Article 15(7) (Access to Genetic Resources)

"Each Contracting Party shall take legislative, administrative or policy measures, as appropriate . . . with the aim of **sharing in a fair and equitable way** the results of research and development and the benefits arising from the commercial and other utilization of genetic resources with the Contracting Party providing such resources. Such sharing shall be upon mutually agreed terms."

Article 16(5) (Access to and Transfer of Technology)

"The Contracting Parties, recognizing that patents and other **intellectual property rights** may have an influence on the implementation of this Convention, shall cooperate in this regard subject to national legislation and international law in order to ensure that such rights are supportive of and do not run counter to its objectives."

Article 18(4) (Technical and Scientific Cooperation)

"The Contracting Parties shall, in accordance with national legislation and policies, encourage and develop methods of cooperation for the development and use of technologies, including **indigenous and traditional technologies**, in pursuance of the objectives of this Convention. For this purpose, the Contracting Parties shall also promote cooperation in the training of personnel and exchange of experts."

customs and traditions, which may be closely tied to its cultural identity or have a spiritual significance, raises urgent ethical and legal objections that the IGC and many other international bodies have sought to address.

These concerns were reflected in the CBD, signed at the Rio Earth Summit in 1992, which currently has an impressive list of 188 countries that are parties to it. Apart from promoting the conservation of biological diversity and the sustainable use of biological resources, the CBD also seeks to encourage the fair and equitable sharing of benefits obtained from the utilisation of genetic resources[5] and any associated traditional

Schuler, *Poor People's Knowledge: Promoting Intellectual Property in Developing Countries* (World Bank, 2004).

[5] "Genetic resources" are defined in Article 2 of the CBD as "genetic material of actual or potential value," whereas "genetic material" means "any material of plant, animal, microbial or other origin containing functional units of heredity." It has been pointed out by the Food and Agriculture Organization (FAO) that this definition may be too restrictive because it does not cover genetic resources holistically. By restricting its scope to biological material containing genetic material, the definition would not include other organic substances derived from biological sources (such as resins and ligneous products) that do not contain genetic material. The definition would also not cover artificially synthesized chemically inert products derived from genetic resources after the active ingredient has been identified.

knowledge.[6] The provisions from the CBD, indicated in Box 29.1, reflect these aspirations quite clearly.

In 2000, the CBD Conference of Parties set up an Ad Hoc Working Group on Access to Genetic Resources and Benefit Sharing (ABS)[7] to develop guidelines for parties to implement national legislation that gives effect to these objectives of the Convention. At its first meeting in Bonn, the Working Group developed a set of draft guidelines on access to genetic resources and the fair and equitable sharing of the benefits arising from their utilisation. The *Bonn Guidelines* lay a broad framework for Member States to implement the various elements of an access and benefit-sharing regime in their national laws: principles of prior informed consent, mutually agreed terms, mechanisms for benefit-sharing, and so forth. A number of suggestions are made in the *Guidelines*, as to the possible role of intellectual property rights in contractual arrangements for access to genetic resources and benefit-sharing. Apart from royalty payments and licensing fees that may be agreed on by the relevant parties, benefit-sharing arrangements that involve joint ownership of intellectual property rights are identified in the *Guidelines* as both monetary and nonmonetary benefits that Member States may wish to include on a menu of choices from which the relevant stakeholders can choose.[8] These *Guidelines* were subsequently adopted by the CBD COP in 2001,[9] when the parties to the Convention also extended an invitation to WIPO for its assistance on matters related to intellectual property (see Box 29.2).

In 2004, the Working Group on ABS was mandated by the CBD COP "to elaborate and negotiate an international regime on access to genetic resources and benefit-sharing with the aim of adopting an instrument to effectively implement the provisions of Article 15 and Article 8(j) of the Convention and the three objectives of the Convention."[10] The development of this international regime to regulate access to genetic resources is currently ongoing within the consultative processes of the CBD and runs parallel to the efforts put in by the WIPO Committee to develop international legal norms relating to the use of intellectual property institutions in the development of biotechnological innovations from genetic resources and traditional knowledge. At the same session of the CBD COP, a more detailed request for assistance was also put forward to WIPO in Decision VII/19 (see Box 29.3).

Cooperation between the CBD Working Group on ABS and WIPO is currently ongoing against this backdrop of international legal processes. A consultation process

[6] There is no internationally agreed definition for "traditional knowledge," but it is generally regarded as knowledge that is generated, preserved, and transmitted in a traditional context. This body of knowledge is distinctively associated with the traditional or indigenous culture of a community that is passed down from generation to generation. Traditional knowledge systems may encompass a wide range of social, cultural, environmental and technological contexts which relate to the use of indigenous biological resources. See WIPO/GRTKF/IC/5/8 at paragraph 69 and WIPO/GRTKF/IC/5/12, at paragraph 45.

[7] Decision V/26, paragraph 11, CBD COP 5 (Nairobi, Kenya. 15–26 May 2000).

[8] See Appendix II of the *Bonn Guidelines, Monetary and Non-Monetary Benefits.*

[9] Decision VI/24, Annex, *Bonn Guidelines on Access to Genetic Resources and Fair and Equitable Sharing of the Benefits Arising out of their Utilization*, CBD COP 6 (The Hague, The Netherlands, 7–19 April 2002).

[10] Decision VII/19, Access and benefit-sharing as related to genetic resources (Article 15), Part D: International Regime on access to genetic resources and benefit-sharing, CBD COP 7 (Kuala Lumpur, Malaysia, 9–20 February 2004). The idea for an International Regime on Access and Benefit-sharing was put forward earlier at the World Summit on Sustainable Development (Johannesburg, September 2002) where a Plan of Implementation was adopted, including (at para. 44(o) of the WSSD Plan of Implementation) a call for action to "negotiate within the framework of the Convention on Biological Diversity, bearing in mind the Bonn Guidelines, an international regime to promote and safeguard the fair and equitable sharing of benefits arising out of the utilization of genetic resources."

Box 29.2

"C. Role of intellectual property rights in the implementation of access and benefit-sharing arrangements

The Conference of Parties:

* * * *

4. Invite the **World Intellectual Property Organization** to prepare a technical study, and to report its findings to the Conference of the Parties at its seventh meeting, on methods consistent with obligations in treaties administered by the World Intellectual Property Organization for **requiring the disclosure within patent applications** of, *inter alia*:

(a) Genetic resources utilized in the development of the claimed inventions
(b) The country of origin of genetic resources utilized in the claimed inventions;
(c) Associated traditional knowledge, innovations and practices utilized in the development of the claimed inventions;
(d) The source of associated traditional knowledge, innovations and practices; and
(e) Evidence of prior informed consent."

* * * *

9. Encourage the World Intellectual Property Organization to make rapid progress in the **development of model intellectual property clauses** which may be considered for inclusion in **contractual agreements** when mutually agreed terms are under negotiation;

10. Recognize the importance of the work being undertaken by the World Intellectual Property Organization on international models and encourage the World Intellectual Property Organization to also consider **means by which Parties could collaborate to protect traditional knowledge** for further consideration by the Conference of the Parties;

11. Urge the World Intellectual Property Organization to provide to the Conference of the Parties with the results of its deliberations of relevance to access to genetic resources and benefit-sharing related to traditional knowledge.

has been initiated by WIPO, with an extremely comprehensive first draft response[11] issued to the Working Group in early 2005 for its consideration.[12] This fairly recent formal collaboration between WIPO and the CBD Working Group adds an extra facet to the increasingly crowded international playing field in which various intergovernmental processes are being simultaneously developed in relation to genetic resources and associated traditional knowledge. Apart from WIPO's own efforts to develop an international policy framework relating to the IP-related aspects of genetic resource and traditional knowledge use, as well as the CBD Working Group's development of an international access and benefit-sharing regime, other international organisations engaged in parallel work on the same, or closely related, issues include the Food and Agriculture Organization of the United Nations (FAO) and the Consultative Group of International

[11] WIPO/IP/GR/05/01, Examination of Issues Relating to the Interrelation of Access to Genetic Resources and Disclosure Requirements of Intellectual Property Rights Applications (Prepared by the WIPO Secretariat).

[12] The third meeting of the CBD Working Group was held in Bangkok, Thailand, from 14 to 18 February 2005, at which WIPO's report was considered and recommendations for further action were made for its fourth meeting in Spain (to be held in March 2006).

Box 29.3

E. Measures, including consideration of their feasibility, practicality and costs, to support compliance with prior informed consent of the Contracting Party providing genetic resources and mutually agreed terms on which access was granted in Contracting Parties with users of such resources under their jurisdiction

The Conference of Parties:

* * * *

8. Invites the **World Intellectual Property Organization** to examine, and where appropriate address, taking into account the need to ensure that this work is supportive of, and does not run counter to, the objectives of the Convention on Biological Diversity, issues regarding the **interrelation of access to genetic resources and disclosure requirements in intellectual property rights applications**, including, *inter alia*:

(a) Options for model provisions on proposed **disclosure requirements**;
(b) Practical options for intellectual property rights application procedures with regard to the triggers of disclosure requirements;
(c) Options for incentive measures for applicants;
(d) Identification of the implications for the functioning of disclosure requirements in various World Intellectual Property Organization-administered treaties;

Intellectual property-related issues raised by proposed international certificate of origin/source/legal provenance; and **regularly provide reports** to the Convention on Biological Diversity on its work, in particular on actions or steps proposed to address the above issues, in order for the Convention on Biological Diversity to provide additional information to the World Intellectual Property Organization for its consideration in the spirit of mutual supportiveness.

Agricultural Research (CGIAR).The FAO has, for example, a specialised international regime for plant genetic resources for food and agriculture, which takes into account concerns about global food security, the diffused origins of agricultural food crops that make it difficult to identify their specific countries of origin, and the international interdependence of countries in relation to food crops. Access to these plant genetic resources is regulated by the International Treaty on Plant Genetic Resources for Food and Agriculture (ITPGR) by way of a Multilateral System of Access and Benefit-Sharing, as well as an International Code of Conduct for Plant Germplasm Collecting and Transfer.[13] The CGIAR participates in these access and benefit-sharing regimes through the International Agricultural Research Centres (IARCs), which house *ex situ* collections of plant genetic resources for food and agriculture.

3 WIPO AS AN INTERNATIONAL LEGAL NORM-SETTING FORUM

The invitations made by the CBD COP to WIPO to work on developing legal norms for the intellectual property-related aspects of an international policy framework, which regulates access to genetic resources and protects traditional knowledge, reflect the

[13] The text of these international legal instruments administered by the FAO are available online at http://www.fao.org.

highly specialised nature of the work involved. Reforming the Patent System to reflect the imperatives of the CBD, or accommodating new forms of positive or defensive protection for traditional knowledge (either as a species of quasi-intellectual property of otherwise), requires substantial expertise in the field of Intellectual Property and an intimate familiarity with the various international legal instruments (many of which were developed, and are administered, by WIPO) that shape national intellectual property laws.

WIPO is ideally positioned as an intergovernmental organisation to lead the global community in addressing these issues. First, the nature of the problem – the misappropriation of genetic resources and traditional knowledge – is primarily transnational in character. Biopiracy, which takes place within the country of origin of the genetic resources or traditional knowledge, where the end product developed from access to the resource or knowledge is only exploited domestically, is not a real problem as sanctions can be easily meted out against the unscrupulous user within the domestic legal framework. The real problem arises when the user of the genetic resources or traditional knowledge is based in a foreign country, and where intellectual property rights are secured in foreign jurisdictions with larger markets for the end product that the user has developed. In such circumstances, legal redress in the foreign jurisdiction is only available to the providers of the genetic resources or traditional knowledge (the State from which the resources were harvested or the communities from which the knowledge was obtained), if the foreign State recognises that their rights have been violated under that State's national laws, and if appropriate national legal mechanisms are in place to ensure that there are incentives for users to conduct their affairs in a manner consistent with the values articulated by the CBD. The need for international harmonisation in this area of the Law is particularly pronounced when intellectual property rights are concerned – given the territorial nature of these rights and that national intellectual property frameworks have to be relied on to challenge the validity of any application for, or grant of, intellectual property rights over biotechnological innovations developed from genetic resources or traditional knowledge.

Second, achieving an international consensus on how international intellectual property standards should be tinkered with, requires the political competence of an organisation such as WIPO, which has been instrumental in shaping a wide gamut of international agreements (both binding and nonbinding) concerning the recognition and protection of a very wide variety of subject matters. More significantly, WIPO's membership includes the United States of America, which, unlike most other countries around the world, has not become a party to the CBD. Given that the United States is viewed as a primary market for those developing products or services based on genetic resources and traditional knowledge, and that its patent system is typically the first stop for users seeking to acquire intellectual property protection for their biotechnological innovations, any attempts to introduce new legal norms would have to involve the participation of the United States in order for these standards to make a practical impact on its domestic legal framework.

WIPO's work on the intellectual property aspects of access to, and the protection of, genetic resources and traditional knowledge has been fairly holistic, although this has come at the price of a diffused focus on the wide spectrum of related issues. The multipronged approach it has taken is best illustrated diagrammatically with reference to a timeline over which a biotechnological innovation is developed from the use of genetic resources and traditional knowledge as raw materials (see Figure 29.1).

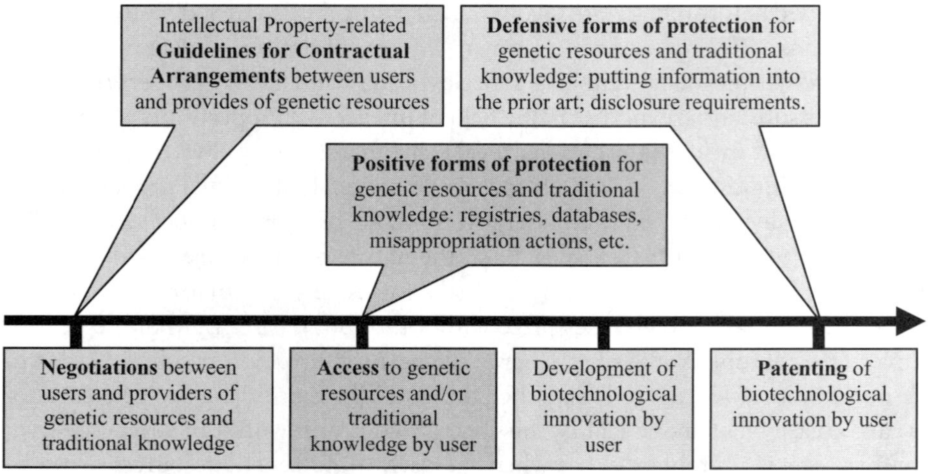

Figure 29.1. WHO's multipronged approach.

As can be seen in Box 29.4, the legal and policy frameworks that are being developed by WIPO to address the intellectual-property related issues arising from the exploitation of genetic resources and traditional knowledge fall within three broad categories, each corresponding to a different stage of a biotechnological innovation's development. The first two categories involve "front-end" legal controls that seek to ensure that the CBD principles of prior informed consent and equitable benefit-sharing are built into the contractual relationship between the user and provider of genetic resources and traditional knowledge, and that the rights (proprietary or otherwise) of the provider over the subject matter utilised are formally recognised by the legal system. The third category of legal mechanisms is a "back-end" measure, which takes effect only at the stage when the user seeks to acquire or enforce a patent over the biotechnological innovation that has emerged from his utilisation of the genetic resources or traditional

Box 29.4

Principle 1: The IP-related rights and obligations set out in [the Guide Contractual Practices] should recognize, **promote and protect all forms of formal and informal human creativity and innovation**, based on, or related to, the transferred genetic resources.

Principle 2: The IP-related rights and obligations set out in [the Guide Contractual Practices] should take into account **sectorial characteristics of genetic resources** and genetic resource policy objectives and frameworks.

Principle 3: The IP-related rights and obligations set out in [the Guide Contractual Practices] should ensure the **full and effective participation of all relevant stakeholders** and address process issues related to contract negotiation and the development of IP clauses for access and benefit-sharing agreements, including in particular **traditional knowledge holders** where traditional knowledge is covered by the agreement.

Principle 4: The IP-related rights and obligations set out in [the Guide Contractual Practices] should distinguish between different kinds of use of genetic resources, including commercial, non-commercial, and customary uses.

knowledge. This may require, for example, direct legal reform of the Patent System to incorporate the values of the CBD by way of additional disclosure requirements by the patent applicant. These measures are not mutually exclusive but are being developed by WIPO as complementary tools that comprise a comprehensive package of legal strategies that may be implemented by its Member States.

4 REGULATING ACCESS TO GENETIC RESOURCES AND TRADITIONAL KNOWLEDGE: CONTRACTS WITH INTELLECTUAL PROPERTY–RELATED ASPECTS

One of the more well-developed areas of its work in which the WIPO Committee has made significant progress is the formulation of its "Draft Guide on Intellectual Property Aspects of Agreements on Access and Equitable Benefit Sharing Relating to Genetic Resources"[14] (the draft Guide Contractual Practices). Although the final version of the Guide has not been released yet, the current draft version reflects a principled, articulate, and holistic body of guidelines that have been designed to facilitate the creation of mutually acceptable access and benefit-sharing contractual arrangements between users and providers of genetic resources and traditional knowledge. These guidelines were formulated as a result of an international survey of the empirical experiences of Member States with these sorts of agreements, all of which has been assembled in a useful database for reference and information-sharing purposes.[15]

The draft Guide Contractual Practices offer parties with little expertise in intellectual property–related transactions a useful checklist of issues to consider when negotiating agreements (including letters of intent, permits, IP licences, material transfer and confidentiality agreements, and so forth) with those who seek to access to genetic resources or traditional knowledge. Although these guidelines are entirely voluntary and do not create any binding legal obligations, they serve a valuable role in capacity building and have an important normative aspect to them. By articulating the wide menu of options available to providers of genetic resources and traditional knowledge holders, the Guide facilitates capacity building by information dissemination such that these parties are in a better position to make fully informed choices on the contents of their agreements. The normative aspect of these guidelines lie in the "advice" that it offers the parties on how to approach these negotiations, bearing in mind the different sociocultural perspectives of each party toward the genetic resources to which access is sought.

At the core of the draft Guide lie four basic principles that have received "broad support" from the WIPO Committee (see Box 29.4).[16]

These principles reflect a number of important characteristics of the draft Guide. First, it only seeks to offer suggestions on the IP-related aspects of the agreements entered into between users and providers of genetic resources. The first principle also emphasises that the subject matter of these agreements should encompass genetic resources as well as any traditional knowledge associated with these resources. Second, these guidelines are intended to be consistent with, and complementary to, the legal and policy frameworks

[14] See the Annex to WIPO/GRTKF/IC/7/9.

[15] The Contracts Database is available at http://www.wipo.int/tk/en/databases/contracts/index.html. The survey and online database was the first stage of the development of the Guide Contractual Practices which was put on agenda of the WIPO Committee's first meeting. See Task A.1, WIPO/GRTKF/1/3.

[16] See WIPO/GRTKF/IC/2/3.

developed at other international fora, including the CBD and FAO, which articulate their own principles, guidelines, or concepts related to particular kinds of genetic resources. Third, these guidelines envisage the full participation of all the relevant stakeholders – including indigenous peoples and local communities and other traditional knowledge holders when there is associated traditional knowledge that is intrinsically linked to the genetic resources that are sought – in the negotiation process from which access and benefit-sharing agreements are created. The guidelines are therefore drafted with these frequently marginalised parties in mind, such that its contents offer detailed commentary that is clearly and practically drafted. Fourth, the guidelines are drafted in a way that is conscious of the need to distinguish between the various categories of uses (commercial and noncommercial, for example) to which genetic resources and associated traditional knowledge may be put. These distinctions are important to the types of intellectual property provisions that need to be incorporated, if at all, into the agreements entered into between the parties.[17]

Bearing in mind that, ultimately, the validity and enforceability of any access and benefit-sharing contract depends on its compliance with the proper law chosen by the parties (presumably the law of the country of origin of the genetic resources or traditional knowledge), and the actual provisions of each contract will vary significantly according to the specific transaction in question, the draft Guide Contractual Practices can only articulate the broad structural and strategic considerations that parties ought to take into account when shaping the intellectual property–related aspects of their contracts.[18] These include guidelines on general intellectual property issues that require a bird's-eye view of the transaction and the relationship of the parties involved (which parties assume which obligations, which party owns the IP rights that may be secured, and so forth), as well as more specific guidelines relating to individual categories of intellectual property (patents, copyright, and trademarks) and the unique considerations arising from each of them. The guidelines offer a step-by-step approach[19] to analyse the intellectual property-related consequences that parties might encounter down the road after access to the genetic resource or associated traditional knowledge has been granted. Parties are asked to address, for example, the following framework of short-term and long-term intellectual property-related issues when drafting their access agreements:

- What IP could result from the access to the genetic resources?
- What conditions or restrictions should apply to the acquisition of IP rights?
- How should those IP rights be owned, maintained, and licensed?
- What approach in obtaining, holding, and exercising those rights best promotes a mutually beneficial outcome, and the equitable sharing of benefits from the permitted access?

[17] For a more detailed treatment of these four basic principles, see WIPO/GRTKF/IC/7/9 at paragraphs 13 to 21.

[18] This is recognised explicitly in the draft Guide, at paragraph 7 (see note 14), which states that the guidelines "are intended to provide practical information and support for those who choose to negotiate terms of access to genetic resources. However, they are limited to IP aspects only, and they are an adjunct and an aid, to be used as a resource, rather than a stand-alone guide to negotiating and concluding contracts and agreements on access and benefit-sharing."

[19] A section of the draft Guide Contractual Practices is dedicated to the intricacies of intellectual property licensing, offering a long checklist of issues that include the definition of the subject matter under licence, the modes of control and ownership, the scope of the licence, the exclusivity of the licence, cross-licensing issues, and ancillary licensee obligations. See paragraph 61 of the draft Guide, referred to in note 14.

Box 29.5

"22. One key to an equitable and enduring partnership, and appropriate provisions concerning IP, is a **shared understanding of the value of the contributions that are made by each party** – on the one hand, the value of genetic resources and associated TK that are being provided, and on the other hand, the value of research, development, risk management and investment that is involved in the use of the resource. Each party may need to understand the **limitations of their contributions to the potential arrangement as well as the valuable attributes of their contributions**. It will be helpful, for instance, for both parties to recognise the **different expectations and perceptions** of value that each brings to the discussions.

23. A recipient of genetic resources and associated TK may need to understand that the value of a genetic resource or insight into the workings of biological material (including traditional knowledge) may **not be limited to monetary value in the eyes of the provider of that resource or insight**. What is viewed by the recipient in simple terms as a raw input for research may be seen by the custodian and provider as a vital part of their heritage, cultural identity and spirituality. The resource and TK, for instance, may be associated with spiritual or cultural values of the provider that can not easily be defined in economic terms or within a brief time frame. Genetic resources may be the result of many generations of conservation, selection and development by indigenous and local communities. If the resource provider is a government body, a public agency or a community, broader public interests – e.g. sustainable resource management, environmental protection, social equity, appropriate grass roots development and technology transfer – are likely to be valued more highly than more immediate technological or commercial goals. Non-monetary and longer-term benefits may be preferred over short-term or monetary benefits.

24. Understanding of the value and use of genetic resources, and associated TK, from the perspective of the public and community interests of the provider, may be the key to reaching an equitable agreement on IP. Indigenous communities and scientists working in academic institutions alike may have committed years, decades or a lifetime of work to arrive at the genetic resource or insight into a particular biological component. Both the resource and the knowledge of its present utility may have developed over generations."[20]

- What applicable laws, apart from the Law of Intellectual Property, should be taken into consideration when analysing these questions? Are there any applicable international, regional, or national laws or regulations, including *sui generis* legislation protecting traditional knowledge or customary laws?

In addition to raising questions for users and providers of genetic resources to consider when formulating their access and benefit-sharing agreements, the Guide Contractual Practices also shed light on the different worldviews that these parties might have and how this may affect their respective interests at the negotiating table. Box 29.5 is an example of how the guidelines attempt to contextualise the negotiation process for which parties have to prepare themselves.

The degree of cultural sensitivity demonstrated in the guidelines reproduced here is not commonly observed in the other intellectual property–related materials produced by

[20] See note 14, paragraphs 22 to 24.

WIPO. They reflect the great deal of care that has been taken by the IGC to incorporate the sociological and ethical dimensions to such agreements, as well as the need to consider all the diverse perspectives of the multiple stakeholders which are typically involved. With its thorough coverage of the intellectual property-related issues and its insightful presentation of the nonlegal facets of access and benefit-sharing arrangements, the draft Guide Contractual Practices make valuable contribution[21] to WIPO's efforts to respond to the international community's implementation of the principles espoused by the CBD.

The IGC's work in this area is not complete and it will involve further refinements of the draft Guide Contractual Practices, the development of operational principles for implementing these guidelines on the ground, and the development of model intellectual property–related contractual provisions as requested by the CBD COP.

It has been pointed out that using access and benefit-sharing agreements to protect the interests of providers of genetic resources and associated traditional knowledge holders is essentially a "privatist" approach to giving effect to the objectives of the CBD.[22] Such a "decentralised" strategy fails to give adequate recognition to the multinational character of the biopiracy problem, which requires an international legal regime with mandatory provisions with which all parties have to comply. As contracts are voluntarily arranged and optional legal instruments, they are unlikely to be effective tools to combat biopiracy because of the vastly unequal bargaining positions of the parties involved, particularly when indigenous or local communities from developing countries are involved. Although these criticisms are valid, it should always be borne in mind that the draft Guide Contractual Practices is just one piece in a larger puzzle of concerted legal mechanisms being developed, by WIPO and other international agencies, to tackle the international problem of biopiracy. It is therefore necessary to consider the progress that WIPO has made in developing other legal mechanisms that may be used to protect the rights of those who provide access to genetic resources and any associated traditional knowledge.

[21] These guidelines are not without their critics, who question whether WIPO should expend so much effort on matters that relate to national contract law rather than issues related more directly to intellectual property systems. The delegation from India, for example, urged the IGC to concentrate its efforts on reforming the international standards set for intellectual property regimes, particularly in the law of patents, and to leave the contract-related matters for consideration within the CBD process. The Indian delegation has argued that the outcome of any privately negotiated arrangement between users and providers of genetic resources will always be to the prejudice of the latter because of their unequal bargaining power: "However carefully any model contract is drafted, however ardently such contracts try to correct the huge imbalance between the provider and the user, such an approach simply cannot lead to anything remotely resembling a fair and equitable regime." See WIPO/GRTK/IC/7/15 Prov. 2 at paragraph 175.

[22] The delegation from Peru, for example, has argued that the realization of the CBD's objectives of fair and equitable benefit-sharing cannot be approached purely as a matter for private regulation. In response to the draft Guide Contractual Practices, the following observation was made: "The ideas underpinning the proposals contained in WIPO/GRTKF/IC/7/9 approach this issue as though it were confined to the realm of private interests. Such an approach to access to GR seems to run counter to the international dimension recognized as the necessary path towards a system aimed at curbing biopiracy. In other words instead of devising a system in which the States maintain the regulatory powers concerning this particular subject, the only means by which an international framework is possible, the rationale underlying these contractual guidelines would seem to lead in the opposite direction; that is to say, to a fragmented kaleidoscope of contractual provisions that provide no real response to biopiracy." See WIPO/GRTK/IC/7/15 Prov. 2 at paragraph 183.

5 POSITIVE PROTECTION FOR TRADITIONAL KNOWLEDGE: DRAFT RECOMMENDATIONS

Designing a legal framework to help prevent the unfair exploitation of traditional knowledge is more challenging than the protection of tangible genetic resources. When the subject matter of legal protection has a physical form – biological organisms, their component parts or substances derived from them, for example – the creation of property-related rights over them is fairly straightforward. By contrast, the conceptual, practical, and political issues encountered when trying to protect the "knowledge" associated with the use of those genetic resources poses a formidable challenge, even for a body such as WIPO, which has had a lot of experience dealing with the legal protection of intangible intellectual products.

For starters, no clear consensus has been reached on how the subject matter of protection should be defined. Unlike cultural expressions of folklore, which requires the intellectual product to be embodied in a form that is perceptible (a drawing, a dance, or a song, for example), traditional knowledge relating to the use of genetic resources may exist in an unrecorded form and transmitted across generations through a form of customary oral traditions. Different communities may have different conceptions of what they consider to constitute the body of "traditional knowledge" over which they should have rights. The IGC takes the view that these definitional difficulties should not operate as a barrier to the formulation of an international legal framework for protecting traditional knowledge. Drawing from WIPO's experience with other international intellectual property treaties and conventions, the definition of the protected subject matter need only be expressed in general terms at the international level,[23] with any additional eligibility criteria separately specified in the substantive provisions, leaving it to national laws that implement these legal standards to decide how it should be defined.[24]

Definitional difficulties aside, it is clear to the IGC that international legal standards are necessary to establish positive modes of protection for traditional knowledge at the ground level. What is unclear is whether proprietary modes of protection should be employed and the form in which the international legal framework should take. Even though WIPO's expertise lies in the area of intellectual property law, it also recognises the difficulty in reaching a consensus on whether traditional knowledge should be protected within existing intellectual property systems, through modified or adapted intellectual property systems, or by designing stand-alone *sui generis* quasi-intellectual

[23] For example, the Paris Convention for the Protection of Industrial Property does not define the terms "patents" and "trademarks," whereas the Berne Convention defines the subject matter of copyright protection ("literary and artistic works") in very broad terms ("include every production in the literary, scientific and artistic domain . . . ").

[24] See WIPO/GRTKF/IC/7/6, at paragraph 40: "A relatively general approach to definition may be called for in relation to traditional knowledge as the subject matter of protection, in contrast to the areas of intellectual property already surveyed here. TK subject matter is particularly dynamic and variable, and more likely to be shaped by local, cultural factors than other forms of IP. Moreover, there have been calls in the work of the Committee for there to be some recognition of customary law as an element in the definition and protection of TK. If there is to be reflection of customary law in the characterization of traditional knowledge, this would necessarily involve a more general form of definition at the international level, given the diverse and distinct quality of customary laws; equally, if weight is to be given to local cultural factors, this could also entail a general umbrella definition at an international level."

property rights. As the IGC has noted, many of WIPO's members have voiced strong objections to the creation and assertion of property rights of any kind over traditional knowledge because of its association with notions of individual-centred ownership, exclusive rights, and commodification.[25] Nonproprietary legal options for protecting traditional knowledge include the use of information registries (including inventories and databases), unfair competition laws, cultural heritage laws, customary laws, and laws regulating access to genetic resources and benefit-sharing.

It should be noted that there are severe limitations to the protection of traditional knowledge by way of conventional intellectual property systems. Technical knowledge relating to genetic resources, for example, may not meet the stringent qualifying standards required for patentability or protection as confidential information. Trying to identify the "owner" of the intellectual property right, a very fundamental concept in conventional intellectual property regimes, may be difficult where the traditional knowledge is more properly associated with a dynamic community rather than individuals. The limited duration of protection available to the various species of intellectual property may not be sufficient to meet the objectives of protecting traditional knowledge, whereas the incentive-based justifications that underpin many intellectual property regimes are irrelevant to the growth of traditional knowledge systems. In addition, conventional intellectual property systems are designed for standardised categories of protected subject matter and may not be flexible enough to accommodate the diversity in the characteristics and cultural content demonstrated by different traditional knowledge systems.

WIPO's work in developing an international legal framework for traditional knowledge protection has proceeded on the basis that the final decision as to whether property-based legal mechanisms are employed lies with each member state. The focus of the IGC's current output is to articulate broad legal norms that set out the types of conduct involving the misuse of traditional knowledge that should be prohibited when national laws are implemented. Having surveyed numerous existing national laws that provide intellectual property or *sui generis* protection for traditional knowledge,[26] the IGC has drafted a preliminary document that sets out broad substantive standards, "which may provide the content of international standards for the protection of collectively held TK against misappropriation, without requiring the assertion of new exclusive property rights over TK (but leaving open this option for when TK holders themselves elect

[25] Dialogues held as a part of WIPO's background consultations with traditional knowledge holders revealed that some stakeholders "believe that the [IP] system is unsuitable as a modality to protect TK because of what they regard as the system's private property, exclusive rights and individual author/inventor-centric nature. One of the bases expressed for this criticism was that TK and the kind of innovation and creativity that the IP system was established to protect are too different. Certain of these persons are critical of the IP system *per se*, while others expressed opposition merely to its deployment in the TK arena. The latter stressed the holistic and communally-shared nature of TK, which, they said, should not become the subject of private IPRs in the hands of outside parties." See *Needs and Expectations of TK Holders*, WIPO, 2201, at 90.

[26] Summaries of some of these national laws are available at WIPO/GRTKF/IC/5/INF/2 and WIPO/GRTKF/IC/5/INF/4. These include the African Model Law 2000 (Model Legislation for the Protection of the Rights of Local Communities, Farmers and Breeders, and for the Regulation of Access to Biological Resources), Brazil's Provisional Measure No. 2186–16 of 2001 (Regulating Access to the Genetic Heritage, Protection of and Access to Associated Traditional Knowledge), India's Biodiversity Act of 2002, Peru's Law No, 27,811 of 2002 (Introducing a Protection Regime for the Collective Knowledge of Indigenous Peoples Derived from Biological Resources), and Portugal's Decree Law No. 118 of 2002 (Establishing a Legal Regime of Registration, Conservation, Legal Custody and Transfer of Plant Endogenous Material).

Box 29.6. Article 1. Protection against Misappropriation

1. Traditional knowledge shall be protected against misappropriation.

2. Any acquisition, appropriation or utilization of traditional knowledge **by unfair or illicit means constitutes an act of misappropriation.** Misappropriation may also include deriving commercial benefit from the acquisition, appropriation or utilization of traditional knowledge when the person using that knowledge knows, or is negligent in failing to know, that it was acquired or appropriated by unfair means; and other commercial activities **contrary to honest practices that gain inequitable benefit** from traditional knowledge.

to take it up)".[27] The "Draft Provisions for the Protection of Traditional Knowledge: Policy Objectives and Core Principles"[28] (the Draft Provisions) attempts to identify and consolidate the legal norms shared by the various Member States from their individual experiences with the protection of traditional knowledge under their national laws. Accompanying the Draft Provisions are ancillary reports that document the existing measures that various Member States have taken to protect traditional knowledge, offering a "menu of options to assist policymakers and communities in making practical choices about protection."[29]

The Draft Provisions have a three-part structure that is based on a widely supported framework document submitted by the African Group:[30] the first part ("Policy Objectives") sets out the common general directions for protection and provide a consistent policy framework, the second part ("General Guiding Principles") articulates general principles that are meant to ensure consistency, balance and effectiveness of the substantive provisions, and the third part ("Substantive Principles") defines the basic characteristics of the legal protection envisaged, with a focus on the suppression of acts of misappropriation of traditional knowledge rather than the creation of new private rights over traditional knowledge. The focus on the broad substantive principle of "misappropriation of traditional knowledge" at this stage reflects a conscious decision to accommodate the concerns of Member States who are against the creation of *sui generis* quasi-intellectual property rights at this stage. A conscious decision was also taken by the IGC to "leave flexibility for national authorities to give effect to the principles in a manner compatible with their own legal systems and to hold national policy consultations with TK holders."[31]

The centrepiece of the substantive principles which underlie the Draft Provisions can be found in Article 1 of Part III (see Box 29.6).

[27] See WIPO/GRTKF/IC/8/5, at paragraph 3.

[28] At the time of writing, the most current version of this draft is available in the Annex of WIPO/GRTKF/IC/8/5 (prepared on 8 April 2005).

[29] See WIPO/GRTKF/IC/7/6, at paragraph 9. The international aspects of traditional knowledge protection are addressed in WIPO/GRTKF/IC/8/6.

[30] See WIPO/GRTKF/IC/6/12 (Submission by the African Group: Objectives, Principles and Elements of an International Instrument, or Instruments, on Intellectual Property in Relation to Genetic Resources and on the Protection of Traditional Knowledge and Folklore).

[31] See WIPO/GRTKF/IC/8/5, at paragraph 11.

Box 29.7

i. acquisition of traditional knowledge by **theft, bribery, coercion, fraud, trespass,** breach or inducement of **breach of contract**, breach or inducement of **breach of confidence** or confidentiality, breach of fiduciary obligations or other relations of trust, **deception, misrepresentation**, the provision of misleading information when obtaining prior informed consent for access to traditional knowledge, or other **unfair or dishonest means**;

ii. acquisition of traditional knowledge or exercising control over it in violation of legal measures that require prior informed consent as a condition of access to the knowledge, and use of traditional knowledge that violates terms that were mutually agreed as a condition of prior informed consent concerning access to that knowledge;

iii. false claims or assertions of ownership or control over traditional knowledge, including **acquiring, claiming or asserting intellectual property rights over traditional knowledge-related subject matter** when those intellectual property rights are not validly held in the light of that traditional knowledge and any conditions relating to its access;

iv. if traditional knowledge has been accessed, commercial or industrial use of traditional knowledge **without just and appropriate compensation** to the recognized holders of the knowledge, when such use has gainful intent and confers a technological or commercial advantage on its user, and when compensation would be consistent with fairness and equity in relation to the holders of the knowledge in view of the circumstances in which the user acquired the knowledge; and

v. wilful offensive use of traditional knowledge of particular moral or spiritual value to its holders by third parties outside the customary context, when such use clearly constitutes a **mutilation, distortion or derogatory modification** of that knowledge and is contrary to *ordre public* or morality.

Article 1(3) goes further to explain that legal means should be provided by Member States to prevent the following acts of misappropriation (see Box 29.7).

In essence, the Draft Provisions identify the traditional knowledge-related problems that Member States need to respond to in their national laws without prescribing the actual manner in which this should be achieved. In its commentary on the General Guiding Principles that comprise Part II of the Draft Provisions, the IGC indicates its preference for a further elaboration and discussion of the guiding principles that the substantive provisions seek to give legal expression to.[32]

At this stage, it appears that the IGC is unwilling or unable to commit itself to either the specific mode of protection which should be offered to traditional knowledge (whether through quasi-intellectual property means or otherwise), or the legal status of the Draft Provisions down the road. The reasons for not advocating a specific mode of protection rest largely on the diverse nature of traditional knowledge systems and out of respect for the freedom of traditional knowledge holders to decide what is most

[32] These guiding principles are viewed as "a key step in establishing a firm foundation for development of consensus on the more detailed aspects of protection" and that "broad agreement on core principles could put international cooperation on a clearer, more solid footing" and "could build common ground, and promote consistency and harmony between national laws, without imposing a single, detailed legislative template." See WIPO/GRTKF/IC/8/5 at Annex, 9.

appropriate for them in accordance with their individual needs and customs.[33] The reasons for remaining neutral on the legal nature of the end product that emerges from the Draft Provisions can probably be explained as the result of a political compromise between Member States that are presently unable to arrive at a consensus as to whether they should be held to a legally binding international agreement for the protection of traditional knowledge.

The experience of existing traditional knowledge protection regimes that WIPO has studied offer these legal doctrines as possible options that Member States might adopt as a basis for implementing the Draft Provisions:[34]

- The grant of **exclusive property** rights for traditional knowledge, either through the use of existing IP rights, modified or extended versions of conventional IP rights, or *sui generis* measures for newly defined exclusive rights;
- A legal requirement that the traditional knowledge is acquired in accordance with principle of **prior informed consent**, as part of national laws that regulate access to genetic resources and benefit-sharing, where the consent of the traditional knowledge holder or an appropriate proxy has to be obtained;
- A **compensatory legal regime** that requires those who make use of traditional knowledge to make some form of equitable compensation or remuneration available to the traditional knowledge holder, either directly or through a state-administered fund for the benefit of those communities recognised as traditional knowledge holders, without creating private property rights over specific parts of the traditional knowledge system;
- An approach based on the **law of unfair competition**, which does not grant exclusive rights over any intangible property but confers on the traditional knowledge holder the right to suppress deceptive trade practices, unjust enrichment, passing off and the taking of an unfair commercial advantage; or
- The use of **customary law** mechanisms and protocols to govern whether the elements from a traditional knowledge system may be accessed by third parties, if at all, and how it may be used thereafter.

As for the legal status of the Draft Provisions, which the IGC has carefully explained "to be neutral with regard to, and entirely without prejudice to, the legal nature of the

[33] See WIPO/GRTKF/IC/8/6, at paragraph 14, in which it is observed that "it may be considered an inappropriate intrusion for the Committee to endeavour to delimit or stipulate what laws and practices should apply within the traditional context, in particular within the original community. To the contrary, the draft provisions, in capturing the main points of the Committee's deliberations, have not sought to intrude in the traditional domain but rather to articulate how norms and practices established under local, customary law may be supplemented and buttressed by international safeguards against the misappropriation and misuse of TK.... Equally, the provisions do not propound the creation of distinct and discrete property rights as such, given the broader range of legal mechanisms that the Committee has explored, and the preference expressed by some to avoid such mechanisms. The draft provisions do, naturally, respond to the choice for specific rights that a number of national and regional *sui generis* laws create, and intangible property rights are one mechanism among several for addressing misappropriation and misuse.... Yet in distilling a possible common international outcome that allows sufficient space for diversity while promoting convergence around shared norms, the provisions may need to look beyond specific legal mechanisms such as property rights, and instead concentrate on clarifying the acts of third parties that are considered illegitimate."

[34] For a detailed exposition on the various potential implementation options which member states have at their disposal, see WIPO/GRTKF/IC/7/6, Annex I, at paragraphs 13–25.

instrument in which or through which they might be contained or expressed,"[35] it is possible that this may evolve into one of the following:[36]

- A **binding legal instrument** that prescribes standards for states to implement in their respective national laws, or a protocol to an existing international agreement;
- A nonbinding statement or **recommendations** for Member States to consider reforming their domestic laws to give effect to prescribed standards;
- **Guidelines** or **Model Provisions** that provide a basis for cooperation between Member States, the convergence of their national laws, and the mutual compatibility of their legislative initiatives;
- An authoritative or persuasive **interpretation** of existing legal instruments that encourage Member States to interpret their existing international obligations in a particular way which enhances the protection of traditional knowledge; or
- An international **political declaration** espousing core principles and establishing the needs and expectations of traditional knowledge holders as a political priority, providing a political basis for further work aimed at more precise legal outcomes.

The IGC, however, based on its past experience with other intellectual property–related conventions is, quite optimistic that these current uncertainties will eventually resolve themselves. These conventions have used very broad language to establish general principles that signatories have to implement in their national laws, thereby giving some scope for wide variations between the laws of the signatories. For example, the Washington Treaty on Intellectual Property in Respect of Integrated Circuits provides that "each Contracting Party shall be free to implement its obligations ... through a special law ... or its law on copyright, patents, utility models, industrial designs, unfair competition or any other law or combination of laws."[37] Therefore, leaving it up to individual Member States to decide if they wish to introduce proprietary rights in respect of traditional knowledge, or if some other legal mechanism would be more suitable to prevent its misuse or misappropriation, is quite consistent with the approaches taken in the development of other international intellectual property–related agreements. As for the undisclosed direction in which its work on the Draft Provisions is heading, the IGC has maintained that its options remain open because of the contents have been deliberately expressed in a neutral form, thereby making it possible for a "phased approach" in which initially nonbinding instruments evolve into international conventions.[38] Drawing again from past experience with intellectual property-related conventions, such as how the FAO's International Treaty on Plant Genetic Resources for Food and Agriculture was developed from earlier nonbinding International Undertaking, the IGC's

[35] See WIPO/GRTKF/IC/8/5, at paragraph 13.

[36] See WIPO/GRTKF/IC/8/6, at paragraph 29 and WIPO/GRTKF/IC/6/6, at paragraph 34.

[37] See Article 4 of the Washington Treaty. Other examples of such permissive and flexible provisions in international intellectual property conventions can be found in Article 7 of the Rome Convention for the Protection of Performers, Producers of Phonograms and Broadcasting Organisations 1961, Article 3 of the Geneva Convention for the Protection of Producers of Phonograms against Unauthorised Duplication of their Phonograms 1971, and Article 2 of the Satellites Convention.

[38] See WIPO/GRTKF/IC/8/5 at paragraph 13 and WIPO/GRTKF/IC/8/6 at paragraph 30: "As noted, past WIPO recommendations have been employed in drafting national laws, have been weighed by judicial authorities, and have given rise to proposed binding treaty language ... experience in other domains suggests the possibility of a phased approach, in which one mechanism for framing international standards and for promoting the desired approach to protection in national standards leads in turn to further elaborated or revised mechanisms, with increasing expectation of compliance and increasing legal effect."

current approach appears to suggest that it expects its work on the positive protection of traditional knowledge to progress by way of incremental crystallisation rather than the attainment of an immediate global consensus. If a multilateral agreement cannot be reached through WIPO's political processes, then it may be left up to individual Member States to lead the way forward by entering into bilateral[39] or regional agreements as a means of imposing obligations on Member States to implement national laws that protect traditional knowledge holders.

At this stage, the contents of the Draft Provisions have been significantly influenced by the positions taken under existing national laws as they have been reported to WIPO, on its request for Member States to share their experiences with the legal protection of traditional knowledge. One important lacuna in the national laws surveyed is the status of foreign traditional knowledge holders and the availability of legal protection to these parties – whether these foreign parties have the necessary legal standing to gain access to the county's legal system and whether they are subject to the same legal criteria that is applied to domestic traditional knowledge holders. In addition, the legal basis on which foreign right holders receive protection under national laws has not been resolved as far as traditional knowledge protection is concerned.

Are foreign traditional knowledge holders eligible for protection:

(1) on the same nondiscriminatory basis as domestic traditional knowledge holders (National Treatment),
(2) with the same legal privileges as those enjoyed by traditional knowledge holders from other countries (Most-Favoured Nation),
(3) if they satisfy some basic criterion such as a relationship with a country that is party to a certain legal treaty (Universality), or
(4) if they are based in a jurisdiction that offers similar protection to traditional knowledge holders who are nationals of the state (Reciprocity)?

These are critical issues that the Draft Provisions have not properly addressed[40] and should be high on the IGC's list of priorities because of transnational character of many examples of traditional knowledge misappropriation – the users of the traditional knowledge who stand to enjoy commercial benefits from its exploitation are likely to be based in jurisdictions that are different from that in which the providers of that traditional knowledge are located.

The practical experience of the various countries surveyed by the IGC has shown that any *sui generis* legal framework for the protection of traditional knowledge is never implemented in isolation.[41] Corresponding changes to existing national intellectual

[39] For example, compliance with WIPO's Joint Recommendation Concerning Provisions on the Protection of Well-Known Trade Marks (a nonbinding statement of enhanced legal standards that encourages member countries to implement in their national laws) has been a popular inclusion in many free-trade agreements that include IP-related chapters.

[40] This was an issue raised at the IGC's Eighth Session in June 2005 and will probably be on its radar screens for some time in the future. See WIPO/GRTKF/IC/8/6, at paragraphs 32–51.

[41] See WIPO/GRTKF/IC/7/6, at paragraph 6: "... the documented practical experience of many Member States reflects that existing IP rights and *sui generis* measures are not mutually exclusive but are complementary options. A comprehensive approach is likely to consider each of these options, and apply them judiciously to achieve the objectives of protection, accepting the practical reality that the boundaries between these options are not rigid. Effective protection may therefore be found in a combined and comprehensive approach, with a menu of differentiated and multiple levels and forms of protection."

property laws are made to complement their efforts to address the problem of biopiracy holistically, putting legal mechanisms in place at both the "front end"and the "back end" of the process through which biotechnological innovations are developed from genetic resources and traditional knowledge. Legal mechanisms for the positive protection of traditional knowledge and genetic resources are enhanced when they work in tandem with defensive modes of protection that prevent the acquisition of patent rights[42] over biotechnological innovations that have been developed in circumstances that are prejudicial to the rights of genetic resource providers and traditional knowledge holders. This brings us to the third major area of the IGC's work – which WIPO is quite clearly the most competent authority among the global community of international organisations – the development of defensive mechanisms within and around the patent system to ensure compliance with the legal norms echoed in the Draft Guide Contractual Practices and the Draft Provisions discussed earlier.

6 DEFENSIVE PROTECTION FOR GENETIC RESOURCES AND TRADITIONAL KNOWLEDGE

The notion of "defensive protection," when applied in the context of the IGC's work, refers to a broad range measures that can be taken to prevent the acquisition of intellectual property rights over traditional knowledge or genetic resources by parties other than their customary custodians. WIPO has placed particular emphasis on devising defensive strategies centred on the patent system in a number of areas.[43] These strategies fall within three general categories. The first category focuses on disclosures by genetic resource providers and traditional knowledge holders and how, through their conduct, they may defeat patent applications by third parties by placing appropriate information about their resources or knowledge into the prior art. The second category focuses on enhancing the procedural aspects of patent system, with particular attention paid to the role of patent authorities and administrators in making accurate evaluations of the patentability of biotechnological innovations developed from genetic resources and traditional knowledge. The third category focuses on reforming the substantive provisions of the Patent System by requiring the patent applicant to make additional disclosures that would help in the detection of acts of misappropriation and enable the patent system to respond accordingly.

Considerable progress has been made in the first two categories of defensive protection, whereas the third category is very much still a work in progress because of fundamental disagreements over the types of additional disclosures that patent applicants should be required to make and the consequences of noncompliance. In the first category, a number of strategies have been formulated and implemented to place information relating to genetic resources and traditional knowledge into publicly accessible

[42] For example, the Andean Community Decisions 391 (Common Regime on Access to Genetic Resources 1996) and 486 (Common Regime on Industrial Property 2001) allow Member States of the Andean Community of Nations to amend their patent laws such that patent applicants are required to disclose the origins of any genetic resources or traditional knowledge that form part of the invention. Decision 486 also requires patent applicants to provide evidence of prior informed consent and equitable benefit-sharing when they incorporate traditional knowledge into a claimed invention.

[43] For a detailed overview of the various forms of defensive protection discussed by the IGC, see WIPO/GRTKF/IC/5/6.

sources, which make them part of the prior art that is taken into account when assessing the novelty or nonobviousness of a claimed invention. To this end, the following deliverables have already been achieved:

- The compilation of **inventories**[44] of existing traditional knowledge-related periodicals that document and disclose traditional knowledge for use by patent search authorities when examining patent applications;
- The establishment of **online databases**[45] to facilitate the electronic exchange of public domain data regarding genetic resources and traditional knowledge, with the application of WIPO's existing IP documentation standards to this subject matter;
- The adoption of a draft **Toolkit**[46] for IP Management when documenting traditional knowledge and genetic resources to assist stakeholders in the documentation process and its IP-related implications, should they wish to put information into the public domain as part of a defensive protection strategy.

These measures do have their limitations, particularly when the resource providers or knowledge holders do not have the technical or financial means to engage in the documentation process, or when it may not be in their interests to do so as public disclosure may facilitate the undesirable uses by third parties.[47] The "tension between the objective of disclosure for defensive purposes, and protecting TK against unauthorised use and misappropriation by third parties" highlights the need for complementary forms of positive protection for genetic resources and traditional knowledge – the other components of the IGC's work discussed earlier – which empower stakeholders with the ability to actively prevent acts of misappropriation.[48]

The second category of defensive strategies is closely linked to the first, in which procedural reforms are made to the international patent system to facilitate a more rigorous patent search and examination process for biotechnological innovations involving the use of genetic resources and traditional knowledge. First, changes have been made to the International Patent Classification (IPC)[49] system to take better account of genetic resources and traditional knowledge-related innovations, particularly in relation to medicinal products based on plant extracts. The primary function of the IPC is to assist patent examiners by classifying patent documents and patent-related literature into industry categories, which are useful when prior art searches are carried out in

[44] The IGC has put together two such nonexhaustive inventories: the "Inventory of Traditional Knowledge-related Periodicals" and the "Inventory of Traditional Knowledge-related Databases." See WIPO/GRTKF/IC/3/5 and WIPO/GRTKF/IC/3/6, as well as WIPO/GRTKF/IC/5/6, at paragraphs 36–43.

[45] The IGC has set up the WIPO Portal of Online Databases of Disclosed TK and Genetic Resources, with links to the CGIAR's electronic System-wide Information Network on Genetic Resources (SINGER), to facilitate international patent searches and examinations. The WIPO Industrial Property Documentation Standard ST.9 is applied to these databases and registries. See WIPO/GRTKF/IC/5/6, at paragraphs 60–78.

[46] See WIPO/GRTKF/IC/4/5 and WIPO/GRTKF/IC/5/6, at paragraphs 55–59.

[47] The IGC has clearly recognised, for example, that "documentation of oral TK, including for the sake of patent procedures, can accelerate or facilitate its misappropriation, including its commercial use by third parties without the prior informed consent of the holders of TK." See WIPO/GRTKF/IC/6/8, at paragraph 17.

[48] WIPO/GRTKF/IC/7/8, at paragraph 10 and at paragraph 6 of the Annexed Questionnaire directed at national patent authorities.

[49] This was developed from the WIPO-administered Strasbourg Agreement Concerning the International Patent Classification of 1971, which entered into force in 1975.

assessing the novelty or patentability of a claimed invention. A WIPO-led Task Force has developed a new subject group for the IPC (designated A61K 36/00), with approximately two hundred subgroups, in the field of medicinal preparations containing plants. This would enable documents or literature that is related that fall into these categories to be properly classified and easily located by patent examiners who make use of the IPC.[50]

In addition, efforts to revise the minimum documentation requirements of the WIPO-administered Patent Cooperation Treaty (PCT) have been initiated to enhance the visibility of literature in the field of genetic resources and traditional knowledge. The PCT is a legal mechanism that enables a single international application filed by a patent applicant to have the legal effect of multiple simulaneously filed applications in a large number of countries around the world that are members of the PCT. Utilising the PCT requires the applicant to submit a prescribed list of documents to the International Searching Authority for onward transmission to national patent authorities. This list of prescribed documents, commonly referred to as the PCT minimum documentation, is found in the PCT Regulations and includes certain national patent documents, published applications, inventors' certificated and "such other published items of non-patent literature as the International Searching Authorities shall agree upon and which shall be published in a list by the International Bureau when agreed upon for the first time and whenever changed."[51] To improve the availability of traditional knowledge-related information to the International Search Authorities, the IGC has recommended adding periodicals, gazettes, and other nonpatent literature that document traditional knowledge onto the minimum documentation list. This will increase the likelihood that additional traditional knowledge-related information will be given greater recognition during the international search and examination process and cited against the patent application, even before the international applications enter the national phase within individual jurisdictions. This also will help ensure that the relevant traditional knowledge will be given full consideration as part of the prior art when the application reaches the national level.[52]

To complement these amendments to the procedural framework for international patent applications, the IGC is also preparing guidelines for national patent offices regarding the search and examination process for intentions, linked to traditional knowledge or genetic resources. The goal is to assist patent authorities with little background in traditional knowledge systems in their review of the prior art, by giving them a better understanding of the subject matter, thereby putting into practical effect the developments that have taken place in relation to the IPC and PCT. A questionnaire[53] was sent out to all WIPO Member States and other relevant stakeholders to survey current national practices in the recognition of traditional knowledge and genetic resources as part of the relevant prior art, especially in evaluating the novelty and nonobviousness of claimed inventions. The results obtained from this exercise are being incorporated

[50] See WIPO/GRTKF/IC/5/6, at paragraphs 44–53, and WIPO/GRTKF/IC/6/8, at paragraphs 5–9.

[51] Rule 34.1(b)(iii) of the PCT Regulations, read together with Article 15(4) of the PCT.

[52] See WIPO/GRTKF/IC/5/6, at paragraphs 31–35, and WIPO/GRTKF/IC/6/8, at paragraphs 10–15. The amendments to the PCT regime are carried out by the Meeting of International Authorities on the PCT (See PCT/MIA/9/4).

[53] See WIPO/GRTKF/IC/Q.5 (Questionnaire on Recognition of Traditional Knowledge and Genetic Resources in the Patent System, July 2004), annexed to WIPO/GRTKF/IC/7/8.

into the guidelines that the IGC is currently preparing – "Draft Recommendations on the Recognition of Traditional Knowledge in the Patent System."[54] WIPO hopes that these recommendations will be useful to the national patent authorities of Member States in developing patent procedures that ensure that relevant traditional knowledge is properly taken into account when patent applications are examined, as well provide background guidance for policy makers involved in reviewing and developing national or regional patent systems.

The third category of defensive strategies relates to the process of reforming the Patent System by imposing additional disclosure requirements on patent applicants in situations in which the claimed invention is linked to traditional knowledge or genetic resources. This is perhaps the least developed area of WIPO's work and probably the most contentious.[55] Currently, patent applications already have to make a number of disclosures about the identity of the inventor and provide sufficient information to explain how the claimed invention works to the hypothetical skilled person. The imposition of additional mandatory disclosure requirements[56] is contemplated as a means of encouraging patent applicants to ensure that they have conducted themselves in a manner consistent with the legal norms articulated by the CBD, and to enable patent authorities to flag potential cases of misappropriative conduct before the patent is actually issued. As mentioned earlier, the express invitation for WIPO to consider how enhanced disclosure requirements might facilitate the defensive protection of genetic resources and traditional knowledge from acts of biopiracy, by preventing the acquisition of patent rights over the claimed invention, was extended by the CBD COP to the WIPO General Assembly in 2004.[57] Work is currently in progress within WIPO[58] to examine the various options for enhancing disclosure requirements for claimed inventions developed in connection with traditional knowledge or genetic resources, with the participation of the IGC and the Standing Committee on the Law of Patents

[54] The interim draft, issued on 5 June 2005, can be found at WIPO/GRTKF/IC/8/8. In the draft recommendations, the various issues raised in the ongoing international debate about the relationship between patents and genetic resources and traditional knowledge are concisely explained, with a clear exposition on the use of defensive protection as a means of promoting the interests of traditional knowledge holders. The draft recommendations also highlight the legal issues arising from the prior art status of traditional knowledge (when examining a patent application for novelty or nonobviousness) and the practical issues encountered in searching for traditional knowledge in the prior article.

[55] Members of the IGC were unable to reach a consensus among themselves as to how they should proceed in response to the CBD's invitation to work on the issue of disclosure mechanisms as a defensive protection measure; they had to refer the invitation to the WIPO General Assembly for its consideration. See WIPO/GRTKF/IC/6/14, at paragraphs 142–188.

[56] The possibility of contractually created disclosure requirements, imposed by providers of genetic resources or traditional knowledge on users in the terms of the access and benefit-sharing agreements between these parties, has already been considered elsewhere by WIPO. See WIPO/GRTKF/IC/7/9, at paragraph 28.

[57] See text above accompanying notes 10–12.

[58] Consideration of the CBD COP's specific request appears to have been taken outside of the IGC forum, although the IGC has considered disclosure issues in its previous sessions. See WIPO/GRTKF/IC/6/9, at paragraph 9, and WIPO/GRTKF/IC/6/14, at paragraph 172. A distinct process within WIPO (an Ad hoc Intergovermental Meeting) has emerged to consider the broader conceptual linkages between access and benefit-sharing frameworks and specific existing IP agreements, as well as questions arising from their compatibility with, and integration into, each other. It is thus unclear how the IGC will proceed on these patent disclosure issues in its work on developing defensive protection strategies. See WIPO/GRTKF/IC/8/9, at paragraphs 44–45, and 50.

(SCP, which is responsible for the Substantive Patent Law Treaty) and the Working Group on PCT Reform. The following options are being considered as potentially new disclosure requirements which patent applicants should have to include in their patent applications:[59]

- The acknowledgement of coinventorship by a traditional knowledge holder, where appropriate, if the traditional knowledge holder has contributed to the claimed inventive concept;
- A declaration that traditional knowledge comprises part of the relevant prior art; or
- Specific disclosures relating to:
  - The **origin** of the genetic resources or traditional knowledge utilised;
  - The **legal circumstances** in which genetic resources or traditional knowledge were accessed;
  - Proof of **prior informed consent** from providers of genetic resources and traditional knowledge holders;
  - Proof of **access and benefit-sharing agreements** entered into with providers of genetic resources and traditional knowledge holders in accordance with national laws of the country of origin.

Additions to the patent disclosure requirements of the existing international patent agreements are likely to take some time to materialise, if at all, given the sharp differences in the positions taken by Member States[60] and the strong lobby against the imposition of additional burdens on users of the patent system.[61] In addition to the difficulties in reaching an agreement on which disclosures a patent applicant should make, there are also a wide range of options from which to choose the consequences of noncompliance with these additional disclosure requirements.[62] Nevertheless, this is probably the most current frontier of WIPO's work in the relation to genetic resources and traditional knowledge and could have a profound impact on how the patent system responds to the need for defensive mechanisms against biopiracy.[63]

[59] See WIPO/IP/GR/05/01, at pages 39–41. A number of proposals were also canvassed for when these disclosure requirements should be "triggered" – see paragraph 114 – including circumstances in which 1) access to the genetic resources or traditional knowledge is necessary to carry out or replicate the claimed invention or to implement the preferred embodiment of the invention described in the patent; 2) the applicant knows that the traditional knowledge forms part of the prior art and is relevant to the assessment of novelty or prior art; 3) the genetic resources or traditional knowledge were "directly used in developing the invention"; 4) where "the invention made immediate use of the genetic resource" (because it depends on the specific properties of the resource); or 5) where the genetic resources or traditional knowledge "were used in the course of research that led to the invention and were essential to deriving the invention."

[60] Contrast the positions taken by European Community and Peru in their recent submissions to the IGC on the approach which should be taken toward the role of the patent system and disclosures of origin of genetic resources and associated traditional knowledge. See WIPO/GRTKF/IC/8/11 and WIPO/GRTKF/IC/8/12.

[61] See the vigorous objections made by the representative from the Biotechnology Industry Organisation (BIO) toward proposals for additional patent disclosure requirements: WIPO/GRTKF/IC/7/15, at paragraph 198.

[62] These consequences could range from a suspension in the patent application process, to the total invalidation of the patent claims, to a transfer of ownership of the patent. See note 58.

[63] Details of the outcomes reached at the WIPO Ad hoc meeting, which was scheduled for 3 June 2005, to respond to the CBD COP's invitation have not been released at the time of writing.

7 CONCLUSION

WIPO and its constituent subgroups, particularly the IGC, have undertaken a very wide scope of work on the intellectual property–related issues connected to genetic resources and traditional knowledge over the last five years. These include the development of positive and defensive modes of protection, both from a "front end" and from a "back end" perspective. The output it has generated has been staggering though a lot of its proposals and recommendations for legal instruments remain as drafts at the present stage. The progress made by the IGC in the various areas of its work has varied according to the degree of political polarisation demonstrated by Member States on the issues at stake. It appears as if the more direct an impact a proposal for legal reform will have on the Patent System, the more it is likely to encounter fierce dissension from those Member States concerned about the burdens that will be imposed on their biotechnology industries. This is unsurprising given WIPO's traditional role as an advocate for the interests of intellectual property holders, including patentees, and the ways in which the position of these proprietors have been strengthened progressively with each successive international legal instrument which has emerged from the organisation's auspices. However, if genetic resource providers and traditional knowledge holders are accorded the same degree of respect as authors, inventors, and other IP creators, such that the value of their contributions to the conservation and sustainable use of biological diversity is appropriately recognised in the eyes of the Law of Intellectual Property, then perhaps an ethically satisfying resolution may ensue.

POSTSCRIPT:

In the two years or so since this chapter was written, there has been limited substantive progress by WIPO in the three broad areas of its work discussed above – (a)) the draft Guide Contractual Practices (dealing with IP-related contractual provisions relevant to access and equitable benefit sharing), (b) the Draft Provisions concerning the protection of Traditional Knowledge (recommendations concerned with positive modes of protection), and (c) the various defensive strategies for preventing the improper acquisition of patent rights over innovations based on traditional knowledge or genetic resources. The IGC has spent the last two years in a period of consolidation, with most of its recent efforts directed towards getting feedback from its members on its various drafts and refining its discussion papers while waiting for a clearer mandate from the WIPO General Assembly as to how it should proceed with its various proposals, guidelines and recommendations. At the IGC's most recent meeting (its Eleventh Session, which was held from July 3 to July 12 of 2007), many of the materials prepared by the Secretariat sought to "provide a distillation of past more voluminous documentation in a more readily accessible form."[64]

Where(a) is concerned, the IGC is considering disseminating its latest draft on guide practices more widely by making more accessible to the relevant stakeholders, while exploring the possibility of developing licensing practices "in the field of genetic resources which extends

[64] See WIPO/GRTKF/IC/11/8(a), at paragraph 15. A concise summary of the IGC's work thus far was produced by the IGC Secretariat – see WIPO/GRTKF/IC/11/9 "Overview of Activities and Outcomes of the Intergovernmental Committee" – in support of its recommendations to the next WIPO General Assembly, which will be held in 2008, that its current mandate be renewed as set out in WO/GA/30/8. See WIPO/GRTKF/IC/11 at paragraph 8 ("Decision on Item 10: Future Work").

the concepts of distributive innovation or open source from the copyright field, drawing on experiences such as the Global Public License and other similar experiences in the copyright field."[65]

Where (bi) is concerned, the IGC has re-issued a draft set of "Revised Objectives and Principles for the Protection of Traditional Knowledge"[66] *after an extensive survey of the various policy options and legal mechanisms which national and legal systems around the world have employed to implement these objectives and principles.*[67] *The IGC has declared that the text of this document was "prepared without prejudging their status or legal implications" and is intended only to "present in coherent and focused form the kind of specific questions that may need to be weighed by policymakers at national, regional and international level(s), when considering the appropriate form and means of protection . . . of TK."*[68]

Where ci) is concerned, the IGC appears prepared to publish a full set of draft recommendations on how traditional knowledge can be recognised within the patent system, drawing upon its survey of the experiences which national patent authorities have had with traditional knowledge issues in their respective search and examination processes.[69] *It has also been suggested that the "activities successfully completed for TK be translated, applied and executed in relation to disclosed genetic resources," such that the technical measures and strategies that have been developed to strengthen the patent search and examination process in the context of traditional knowledge-based inventions are extended to patent applications involving genetic resources.*[70] *No consensus appears to have been reached by the IGC on the issue of whether, and in what form, a specific disclosure requirement (for information relating to genetic resources or traditional knowledge which have been utilised in a claimed invention) should be introduced into the patent system as a defensive measure to reduce the likelihood of improperly granted patents. As a result, no model provisions for national or regional patent laws, guidelines or recommendations have been issued by the IGC on the disclosure requirement. Instead, the IGC's attention appears to have been diverted towards considerations of how legal reforms of the patent system can be carried out so as to optimise linkages and synergies with non-patent legal mechanisms that effectuate access and benefit-sharing regimes.*[71]

After eleven meetings spanning the last seven years, the IGC has expended a phenomenal amount of effort and resources in identifying, exploring and analysing the multifaceted issues that have emerged from the commercial exploitation of genetic resources and traditional knowledge. With the likely renewal of the IGC's mandate by the WIPO General Assembly in 2008, the next phase of the IGC's work on these issues will, hopefully, move towards concrete reforms of specific WIPO-administered treaties, such as the Patent Cooperation Treaty and the draft Substantive Patent Law Treaty, so as to implement the various draft proposals, guidelines and recommendations that it has so painstakingly put together.

[65] See WIPO/GRTKF/IC/11/8(a), at paragraph 20(C).

[66] See WIPO/GRTKF/IC/11/5(c), which is identical to the text circulated at the 8th, 9th, and 10th sessions of the IGC's meetings.

[67] See WIPO/GRTKF/IC/9/INF/5, WIPO/GRTKF/IC/11/5(a) and WIPO/GRTKF/IC/11/5(b).

[68] See WIPO/GRTKF/IC/11/9, at paragraph 83.

[69] See the Annex to WIPO/GRTKF/IC/11/7 ("Recommendations on the Recognition of Traditional Knowledge in the Patent System: Consultation Paper").

[70] See WIPO/GRTKF/IC/11/8(a), at paragraphs 6 and 16.

[71] See WIPO/GRTKF/IC/11/8(a), at paragraphs 7, 8, 17, and 20(B).

30 Sharing All the Benefits: The Challenge of Legal Recognition of Indigenous Intellectual and Cultural Property Rights in the Fiji Islands

Pio E. Manoa* and Isoa Korovulavula**

1 INTRODUCTION

There is currently no legal recognition of indigenous intellectual and cultural property rights in the laws of Fiji. Although the Constitution of the Republic of Fiji[1] obligates parliament to make provision for the application of customary laws and for dispute resolution in accordance with traditional Fijian processes, it does not provide for the protection of indigenous intellectual and property rights at the national level. The provision is passive and urges the need for serious attention.

Indigenous cultural rights and intellectual property rights are complementary, fused, and cannot be separated. The very essence of indigenous rights flow from the existence, practice, and innovations of a culture, and such rights are inalienable and indefeasible. They are inherent and owned by the members of an indigenous unit, although, in specific cases, such rights can be owned by an individual member. Protection is vital to the culture and for the economic survival and development of indigenous peoples.[2]

This chapter begins with a discussion of the administration of indigenous property rights in Fiji and the recognition of communal rights by the courts. It then assesses the types of intellectual property recognised and limitations of laws relating to biodiversity and access and benefit-sharing. Pertinent economic issues identified support the establishment of a register at the provincial level and comprehensive supporting provisions in national law that, among other things, provide the nature, extent, and duration of the property right.

2 ADMINISTRATION OF INDIGENOUS PROPERTY RIGHTS

Fiji was ceded to Britain on 10 October 1874 and was a dependency for ninety-six years. Fiji's legal system was thus influenced greatly by the British Crown, her representatives, and her subjects. The Deed of Cession signed in 1874 is regarded as the "fundamental charter of the Fijian people's rights and liberties under the British Crown, in particular

[1] *Constitution Amendment Act 1997*, Act No. 13 of 1997 as amended by Act No. 5 of 1998.

[2] UN Sub-Commission of the Prevention of Discrimination and Protection of Minorities, resolution 1992/35.

* Pio E. Manoa is with the School of Marine Studies, University of the South Pacific, Suva, Fiji Islands. Tel.: +679–323 2942; fax: +679–3231526. E-mail: manoa_p@usp.ac.fj.

** Isoa Korovulavula is with the Institute of Applied Science, University of the South Pacific, Suva, Fiji Islands.

as confirming them in ownership of their lands."[3] A few days before the signing of the Deed, eminent Chiefs met Sir Hercules Robinson, representative of Queen Victoria, and stated that they would "trust to the Queen's justice and generosity as their Sovereign and Highest Chief to return to them all or whatever part of their gift she may think right," and "to govern them righteously and in accordance with native usages and customs."[4] Protection of indigenous customs and interests is recognised in the Deed. This influenced the creation of a separate legal system for natives in addition to that provided for Europeans and other foreigners.

A central element of the native legal system was the use of customary law by the judiciary. Fiji's first substantial Governor Sir Authur Gordon (later Lord Stanmore), while speaking on the revocation of a 1905 law allowing for the alienation of native land in the House of Lords on 16 July 1907, said that at Cession "we told them that their customs and laws, so far as they were not absolutely objectionable and immoral, should be maintained."[5] Even after leaving Fiji, Gordon espoused the view that native customs and laws not "objectionable and immoral" were valid and binding on natives. Native regulations were developed in conformity with customary laws and practices. So native magistrates and European magistrates in provincial courts were required to be familiar with customary law and language.[6]

A year after assuming office, Gordon enacted the *Native Affairs Ordinance*, which enabled the creation of the Native Regulation Board (NRB) with powers to make regulations with regard to marriage and divorce of natives, succession to property, powers of native courts and magistrates in civil and criminal proceedings, and other matters for the good government and welfare of Fijians.[7] Later the NRB was replaced by the Fijian Affairs Board. Although regulations of the NRB required approval of the Legislative Council, this was generally given without question.[8] The NRB was able to provide for a fine of up to £50 or a term of imprisonment not exceeding a year, or both. The first regulation made by the NRB permitted the appointment of native officials with administrative responsibilities in various provinces.[9] The administration was supervised by the Secretary for Native Affairs, with the assistance of provincial chiefs (*roko*) and district officials (*buli*) across twelve provinces and eighty-two districts.

The first native lands ordinance enacted in 1880 established the Native Lands Commission (NLC), which was responsible for the survey of land boundaries of different native-owning units, settling boundary disputes, and keeping records of surviving members of landowning units in a list called "Na i Vola ni Kawa."[10] Native land ownership was recorded in the register of native lands and surveyed boundaries on NLC sheets. These records are vital to the administration of native land in Fiji because they provide information on ownership and boundaries of native land and when consent needs to be sought.

[3] H. Luke, *Islands of the South Pacific.* (London: George G. Harrap, 1962), 97.

[4] G. K. Roth, *Native Administration in Fiji during the Past 75 Years: A Successful Experiment in Indirect Rule.* London, Royal Anthropological Institute, Occasional Paper No. 10, 1951, 1.

[5] A. Burns, *Fiji.* (London, Her Majesty's Stationary Office, 1963), 105.

[6] Roth, note 4, at 3.

[7] A. A. Wright, ed., *The Colony of* Fiji, 3rd ed. (Suva: Government Printer, 1931), 18.

[8] J. W. Coulter, *The Drama of Fiji: A Contemporary History.* (Melbourne: Paul Flesch & Company, 1967), 127.

[9] Roth, note 4, at 2.

[10] J. N. Kamikamica, "Fiji: Making Native Land Productive," in R. Crocombe, ed., *Land Tenure in the Pacific*, 3rd ed. (Suva: University of the South Pacific, 1987), 226–239, 226–227.

The "Na i Vola ni Kawa," now commonly referred to as the "Vola ni Kawa Bula" or register of the living, is relied on to determine ownership of native land and fishing grounds, and whether one is Fijian.[11] Eligibility for registration is governed by custom, tradition, and practice. A person whose father or any of whose male progenitors in the male line is or was the child of parents both of whom are or were indigenous inhabitants of Fiji is eligible to be registered. Across Fiji, custom differs in rules on the choice of whether a person be registered as a part of the mother or father's unit. Generally, an illegitimate child can be registered if the mother is registered and the mother's unit approves of the registration, but customs, traditions, and practices prevailing in the area concerned must be adhered to.[12]

The rights of a child in the mother's unit vary across Fiji. Children are referred to as *vasu* by the mother's unit. Depending on the prevailing custom, tradition, and practice, *vasu* can enjoy the same if not more rights than other members of the unit, especially if their mother is of chiefly status. Hence, for the purposes of legal interests in indigenous and cultural intellectual property, *vasu* rights need to be accommodated in accordance with prevailing custom and practice. For instance, the indigenous and cultural intellectual property rights of the traditional firewalkers from the island of Beqa are likely to be shared between the practicing *mataqalis* and their *vasu*.

In 1940, an eminent Fijian chief and scholar Ratu Sir Lala Sukuna proposed a law for the creation of the Native Land Trust Board (NLTB) to control and administer native land on behalf of indigenous owners. The resulting ordinance complemented the work of Sir Authur Gordon by precluding the sale of native land; native land cannot be used without the consent of the NLTB and could only be appropriated by the Crown for a public purpose.

The Native Fisheries Commission, formed in 1958, is responsible for determining customary fishing rights ownership and the delineation of boundaries of the respective owners. According to section 14 of the *Fisheries Act* Cap. 158, the Commission is obligated to determine customary fishing rights in each province of Fiji that are "the rightful and hereditary property of native owners." Although Native Land Commissioner David Wilkinson carried out some work on customary fisheries boundaries and ownership in the 1890s, most of the investigations and enquiries were undertaken between 1958 and 1967.[13]

Legal ownership of native land is vested in the NLTB, whereas indigenous owners have beneficial ownership. For native land reserved for the maintenance of the landowning unit, members of the unit had more freedom to use the property compared to unreserved land. Unreserved land could be leased by the NLTB to a member of the unit or another person. It is important to note that control and access to reserved native land lies with the owning unit, whereas, for unreserved land, initial control rests with NLTB. However, on granting of a lease or licence, the lessee or licensee holds power to control access.

[11] See, for instance, *Ah Koy v. Registration Officer for Suva City Fijian Urban Constituency* [1993] 39 FLR 191.

[12] Section 21 *Native Lands Act* and sworn affidavit of Ilaitia Kurukace Caginavanua of 6 April 1992 in *Ah Koy v. Registration Officer.*

[13] S. Waqairatu, "The Delimitation of Traditional Fishing Grounds – The Fiji Experience," in G. R., South, D. Goulet, S. Tuqiri, & M. Church, eds., *Traditional Marine Tenure and Sustainable Management of Marine Resources in Asia and the Pacific.* (Suva: IOI-South Pacific, 1994), 79–84, 81.

A major weakness of the administration of native land is that the system has yet to provide for the protection of indigenous cultural and intellectual property rights. For activities such as bioprospecting on native land, standard lease or licence provisions do not provide conditions that need to be satisfied by the bioprospector before, during, and after accessing and collecting biological or other material from the land. This loophole has been exploited by many. Informal approval given by landowning units gives rise to further exploitation and use of information and material without any benefit to the owning unit.

The protection of indigenous cultural and intellectual property rights in the marine environment is of concern. Given the demarcation of 410 traditional fishing grounds under customary ownership, one would think that indigenous rights within these areas are clear. However, as on land, there is no clear provision relating to the protection of indigenous cultural and intellectual property rights. Since Cession, the State owns all intertidal land, seabed, subsoil, and reefs, in addition to controlling use and access to traditional fishing grounds. Indigenous owners are only given preferential usage rights, but this, too, is ambiguous. Section 13 of the *Fisheries Act* Cap. 158 states that:

> ...it shall be an offence for any person to take fish on any reef or any kai (cockle) or other shellfish in any area in respect of which the rights of any mataqali or other division or subdivision of the Fijian people have been registered by the Native Fisheries Commission in the Register of Native Customary Fishing Rights, unless he shall be a member of such mataqali, division or subdivision of the Fijian people who does not require a licence...

The draft Customary Fisheries Bill 2005 would return legal ownership of land within traditional fishing areas to the NLTB and, subject to a few exceptions, would give customary owners exclusive possession of their traditional fishing areas. Although this is a positive step towards providing indigenous peoples with ownership and control or their traditional fishing areas, commercial or research activity within traditional fishing areas still requires the approval of a statutory authority. Furthermore, there is no enabling provision in the Bill or the *Fisheries Act* that provides for the protection of indigenous intellectual and cultural property rights.

Nevertheless, on the basis of the tasks carried out by the Native Land Commission and Native Fisheries Commission, it is possible to investigate and to collect existing cultural and intellectual property rights of each indigenous owning unit for the development of a database or register.

3 COMMUNAL RIGHTS

Although the most common communal owning unit, the *mataqali*, is not a recognised legal entity, current practice has seen the establishment of trusts or companies that own units to function as the *mataquli*'s legal face. Posey and Dutfield[14] identify two bases for vesting in communities custodial rights of an innovation; the first is a constructive trust and the second is a "higher trust." With the first, community leaders are appointed as trustees acting for the benefit of the whole community. Constructive trusts are already in operation in the many indigenous communities in Fiji that have established trusts

[14] D. A. Posey & G. Dutfield, *Beyond Intellectual Property: Toward Traditional Resource Rights for Indigenous Peoples and Local Communities.* (Ottawa: International Development Research Centre, 1996), 98.

for specific projects or endeavors. The role and powers of trustees are laid out in the deed of trust and regulated by the *Trustee Act* Cap. 65. Despite the absence of a *mataqali* trust that holds legal ownership of cultural or intellectual property rights on behalf of the *mataqali*, a constructive trust is possible. The second basis, the "higher" trust, is less attractive because of conflict between indigenous desires and political priorities and the composition of the wider community. Ideally, a State works at all times for and on behalf of its nationals, yet in a situation in which there are indigenous communities and other ethnic groups within the country, a State cannot devote all of its attention to or exercise sovereign rights for the ultimate benefit of the indigenous alone. If anything, the Fijian experience shows clear conflicts of interest in the role of State with respect to the administration of natural resources and the interests of the indigenous, which are subordinate to international obligations and national priorities.

The courts play an important role in defining the legal position of the *mataqali*. It is now clearly established that where land is owned by a *mataqali*, an individual member cannot sue and recover damages personally where damage has been suffered by the *mataqali*.[15] However, if an individual's personal rights as an owner have been directly infringed, s/he can bring an action for a remedy resulting from such infringement.[16]

Although not a legal entity, the *mataqali* is recognised as an unincorporated association and is not alien to the Fiji common law.[17] Cullinan J., in *Waisake Ratu No 2 v. Native Land Development Corporation & anor* (1987) Civil Action No. 580 of 1984, said at page 52 of his judgment:

> I do not consider that a mataqali or a tokatoka is an institution which is alien to the applied law of Fiji. I cannot see why the courts, without any ingenuity on their part, could not equate either of those bodies to an unincorporated association. The original coming together to form the group was no doubt the action of the present members' ancestors. Nonetheless they remain in free, communal association, the members thereof sharing a communal proprietary interest: while landholding may be individual in places, they are none the less communal proprietary rights, such as those over the veikau or forest. Such groups are of common agnatic descent, the individual membership and leadership and the physical location and proprietary rights of which are by statute recorded in the Register of Native Lands, preserved by the Registrar of Titles. Not only has the mataqali been recognized as a central proprietary unit by the statute law of Fiji for over a hundred years now (to the extent indeed that the law provides for the devolution of the lands of an extinct mataqali), so also have all the individual divisions of the Fijian people by the act of statutory registration. How then can any of those groups be regarded as alien to such statute law?

The approach adopted by Cullinan J. is supported by a formidable body of authority in the common-law world.[18] Recently, the Fiji Court of Appeal in *Narawa v. NLTB*[19] supported the approach and added that a *mataqali* can, by representative action or by

[15] *Meli Kaliavu & ors v. Native Land Trust Board* (1956) 5 FLR 17 per Hammet J. Adopted, for example, in *Naimisio Dikau No 1 & ors v. Native Land Board & anor* CA No 801/1984.

[16] *Serupepeli Dakai No 1 & ors v. Native Land Development Corporation & ors* Civ. App. No. 30/1982 FCA: CA. 543/1979; *Waisake Ratu No 2 v. Native Land Development Corporation & anor* (1987) Civil Action No. 580 of 1984.

[17] In contrast see Rooney J. in *Naimisio Dikau No 1*, note 15, at 6.

[18] See, for instance, *In re Southern Rhodesia* [1919] AC 211, per Lord Sumner; *Amodu Tijani v. The Secretary of Southern Nigeria* [1921] 2 AC 399, per Viscount Haldane, at 403.

[19] Civil Appeal No. ABU0012 of 1999S per Sheppard JA, Tompkins JA, & Smellie JA.

action brought by all those belonging to the *mataqali* as an unincorporated association, institute proceedings in the court seeking common-law or equitable remedies for any breach of rights it is able to establish.

Although this neatly provides the foundation on which a *mataqali* may institute legal proceedings for a breach of rights, there can be no action when there is no recognised right. The Fiji Constitution, in its passive provisions only, provides a framework that parliament must make provision for the application of customary laws and for dispute resolution in accordance with traditional processes and with regard to customs, traditions, usages, values, and aspirations.[20] Protection of cultural and indigenous intellectual property rights falls beyond the ambit of the Constitution because customary laws apply only to the indigenous and can only be enforced at the village, district, or provincial levels. As with many indigenous cultures in the Pacific, Fijians have an oral culture through which knowledge, folklore, and secrets are transmitted from one generation to another. Within this traditional system, there are mechanisms to avoid disclosure to others, such as the transmission of traditional healing knowledge only within a particular family. Customary law by its very nature does not provide for specific contemporary mechanisms relating to access, prior informed consent, and benefit-sharing, although this is woven, in general and crude forms, into intra- and inter-community relationships and the fabric of society.

4 INTELLECTUAL PROPERTY RECOGNISED

There are two types of intellectual property expressly recognised in Fiji law: patents and copyright. Both have severe limitations with relation to the protection of indigenous cultural and intellectual property rights. Since 1879, "any manner of new manufacture and every new process of manufacture and every new method of application of known processes and improvements in any known process" could be patented.[21] Since 1967, an inventor has been able to gain sole exclusive rights to and in her/his invention for a period of fourteen years from the date that a patent is issued, and could sell, use, make, or authorise others to do the same. However, among other things, an invention has to be novel and has to be of use. Given that indigenous cultural and intellectual property rights have developed over many generations and are used primarily within the community, the requirements of novelty and utility have little application.

Patents aside, copyright law in Fiji is governed by the *Copyright Act* 1999. According to section 5 of the Act, items that may receive copyright protection are literary, dramatic, musical or artistic work, sound recording, audiovisual work, or a broadcast or cable program. The author or creator of the work can be a natural person or a body corporate or a combination of both in cases in which there is joint authorship. Authorship does not necessarily equate to ownership of the copyright.[22] Duration of copyright in literary, dramatic, musical, or artistic works is fifty years after the end of the calendar year in which the author dies. Works of unknown authorship also attract copyright protection for fifty years after the year of authorised publication of the work. Copyright in audiovisual works and sound recordings expires after fifty years from the later of the year the work is made or is first made available to the public or is published. Over many decades, the collection of video footage and sound recordings of traditional oratory, rituals, dances,

[20] Sections 186(1) and (2).

[21] Ordinance No. 3, 1879.

[22] See Copyright Act 1999, section 8.

or ceremonies have exploited the indigenous community who have not been recognised as authors, individually or collectively. The *Copyright Act* merely consolidates fragments of copyright law previously in force and continues to disadvantage the indigenous community in Fiji.

Moreover, patents and copyrights protect the rights of the inventor and promote individualism. With respect to traditional knowledge (TK) and folklore, for instance, a community as a whole should be able to claim exclusive rights to legal protection of TK and folklore. Ownership rights of such a community cannot be alienated regardless of the mode of performance or publication. As well, recognition will need to be given to those who, with special talents and interests, tell legends and stories, or to a composer who creates a dance. Although communal rights need to attract *sui generis* international legal protection, rights of raconteurs and individual composers or creators also deserve recognition.[23]

5 BIOLOGICAL DIVERSITY

As a party to the 1992 Convention on Biological Diversity[24] and in accordance with Article 8(j), Fiji is obliged to encourage the sharing of benefits arising from the use of knowledge, innovations, and practices of indigenous communities for the conservation and sustainable use of biological diversity. Indeed, an objective of the Convention is "fair and equitable sharing" of benefits arising from the use of genetic resources. Much depends on national activities to document and protect indigenous cultural and intellectual property rights relating to biodiversity, yet even more depends on recognition and clarity at the international level.

The work of the CBD Conference of the Parties (COP) and particularly the Ad Hoc Open-Ended Working Group on Access and Benefit-Sharing is important.[25] In 2002, the Bonn Guidelines on access to genetic resources and the fair and equitable sharing of benefits was adopted by the COP, and measures on its implementation have been identified by the Working Group. At its February 2005 meeting, the Working Group, among other things, proposed options towards the development of an international regime on access and benefit sharing in accordance with the CBD.[26] Although the main components of the regime – namely, access to genetic resources, fair and equitable sharing of benefits, and the protection of traditional knowledge, innovations, and practice associated with genetic resources – do not change, the options include the development of legally binding or nonbinding instruments. In the short term, the use of soft law options cannot compel a State party to act, but in the long term such nonbinding instruments may contribute to the corpus of customary international law. Legally binding instruments are preferred and can act to provide protection of indigenous intellectual property rights inherent in traditional knowledge, ensure compliance with

[23] W. Weeraworawit, "International Legal Protection for Genetic Resources, Traditional Knowledge and Folklore: Challenges for the Intellectual Property System," in C. Bellmann, G. Dutfield, & R. Melendez-Ortiz, eds., *Trading in Knowledge: Development Perspectives on TRIPS, Trade and Sustainability.* (London, Earthscan Publications, 2003), 157–165, 159.

[24] 31 *ILM* (1992). Fiji signed CBD on 9 October 1992 and ratified on 25 February 1993.

[25] For example, see Santiago Carrizosa, Stephen B. Brush, Brian D. Wright, & Patrick E. McGuire, eds., *Accessing Biodiversity and Sharing the Benefits: Lessons from Implementation of the Convention on Biological Diversity.* (Gland, Switzerland, and Cambridge, UK: IUCN, 2004), xiv, 316.

[26] Report of the Ad Hoc Open-Ended Working Group on Access and Benefit Sharing on the Work of its Third Meeting, Bangkok, 14–18 February 2005, UNEP/CBD/WG-ABS/3/7, 24.

prior informed consent of indigenous owners, and promote fair and equitable sharing of benefits. However, the regime has to be consistent with international human rights laws and norms and national laws have to accommodate indigenous cultural and intellectual property rights at the outset.

Biodiversity laws in Fiji are in their infancy. The *Endangered and Protected Species Act* 2002 and its 2003 regulations and the *Environment Management Act* 2005 constitute the key laws relating to biological diversity. The former works to regulate and control the international trade, domestic trade and possession, and transportation of species protected under the Convention on International Trade in Endangered Species of Wild Fauna and Flora (CITES),[27] whereas the latter serves to protect natural resources, control and manage development, control pollution, and establish a national environment council. Both laws therefore are not equipped for the protection of traditional knowledge, innovations, and practices associated with genetic resources.

Be that as it may, there are efforts to collect information relating to traditional knowledge and culture and the work of the Institute of Fijian Language and Culture is an example. Established under the auspices of the Ministry of Fijian Affairs, the Institute is the lead government agency responsible for the collection of information on Fijian language and culture. Information is collected and kept by the Institute. Legal ownership of the information or traditional knowledge does not rest with the informants.

Legislation in Costa Rica, Brazil, and Peru offer a model framework for the recognition and protection of indigenous cultural and intellectual property rights. Although these laws provide that the State will exercise total and exclusive sovereignty over components of biodiversity, Costa Rica's Biodiversity Law of 1998 expressly recognises *sui generis* community intellectual rights including knowledge, practices, and innovations of indigenous peoples and local communities related to the use of components of biodiversity. Community intellectual rights exist and are legally recognised by the mere existence of the cultural practice or knowledge related to biodiversity and do not require prior declaration or official registration.[28] An inventory of such rights is maintained and uses and the sharing of benefits is enabled.

Brazil's Indigenous Societies Act (Bill 2057/1991) recognises that intellectual property rights of indigenous communities are perpetual and offers broader protection to indigenous communities including customs, languages, beliefs, and traditions. The Act provides for the right to maintain secrecy of traditional knowledge; the right to refuse access to traditional knowledge; the right to apply for protection of intellectual property granted in the name of the community or the society; the right of prior informed consent in writing for access to, use, and application of traditional knowledge; the right to co-ownership of research data, patents, and products derived from research; and the right of communities to nullify patents derived from their knowledge.[29] Brazil Provisional Measure No. 2.052 of 21 December 2000 gives local communities the right to benefit from their knowledge and be compensated for its economic use, but it has been acknowledged that recent access and benefit-sharing laws need further improvement.[30]

[27] 993 UNTS 243; 12 *ILM* 1085 (1973) (1 July 1975).

[28] Article 82.

[29] Posey & Dutfield, note 14, at 152.

[30] C. M. do Amaral Azevedo, "Regulation to Access to Genetic Resources and Associated Traditional Knowledge in Brazil" 5(1) *Biota Neotropica* (2005). Available at http://www.biotaneotropica.org.br/v5n1/pt/abstract?point-of-view+BN00105012005.

Peru's 2002 Law No. 27811 establishes a special protection regime for the collective knowledge of indigenous peoples that is connected with biological resources. The law establishes three registers for the registration of collective knowledge – the public national register, the confidential national register, and the local community register, as well as a fund for the development of indigenous communities. Under Article 42, indigenous peoples are protected against the disclosure and acquisition or use of their collective knowledge without their consent or in an improper manner, provided that the collective knowledge is not in the public domain.

Recognition of indigenous community ownership of intellectual property rights in Fiji can follow the enactment of a law that recognises and protects such rights. Such a law will be consistent with Article 186(1) and (2) of the Constitution. These provisions mandate parliament to make provision for the application of customary laws and for dispute resolution in accordance with traditional Fijian processes and to have regard to "customs, traditions, usages, values and aspirations." Inherent in customary law is its protection and transfer within the community, so making provision for the "application" of such laws by default also mandates protection for its existence, use, and application within the indigenous community. The limitation, however, is in its protection and transfer to external users.

6 PROBLEMS WITH ACCESS AND BENEFIT-SHARING

In Fiji, there is a need to develop a legal basis on which access and benefit-sharing can be regulated. The same need as well as the absence of any kind of market oversight or regulation has been identified at the international level.[31] The most common mechanism for benefit-sharing available today is in relation to the leasing or licensing of native land. The NLTB currently takes 15 percent from any dealings for the administration and maintenance of native land; the remaining 85 percent is distributed half-yearly in accordance with the *Native Land Trust Act.* Under the Act, the heads of the landowning unit, tribe, and the district receive 15, 10, and 5 percent, respectively, of the financial benefits, whereas members of the landowning unit collectively receive 70 percent. This formula has been criticized by members of landowning unit, who generally are of the view that there is no reason to compensate those that do not dwell in the village, including heads of districts. Furthermore, although sought in practice by the NLTB, the Act does not expressly require the consent of landowners for the leasing of unreserved native land. Noninclusion of the requirement of consent by landowners can result in dealings that impinge on the rights of landowners.

In the case of an indigenous cultural and intellectual property system for Fiji, prior informed consent of indigenous owners must be an essential requirement. Thus, consent will need to be sought and obtained at two levels – from the owning unit and, later, from the State. Without the approval of indigenous owners, the State should not have the authority to grant access to or approve of the use of indigenous cultural and intellectual property. The rationale lies in the potential for conflicts of interest; the State cannot act as a trustee for indigenous communities while promoting its own interests. Consent

[31] T. R. Young, "Legal Issues Regarding the International Regime: Objectives, Options and Outlook," in C. Santiago, S. B. Brush, B. D. Wright, & P. E. McGuire, eds., *Accessing Biodiversity and Sharing the Benefits: Lessons from Implementation of the Convention on Biological Diversity.* (Gland, Switzerland, and Cambridge, UK: IUCN, 2004), 271–294, 284.

of indigenous owners is therefore of paramount importance and will need express recognition in legislation and policy.

The involvement of indigenous communities in benefit-sharing arrangements is another prerequisite recognised in Article 8(j) of the CBD. Ten Kate and Laird[32] submit that constraints in the policy environment and in the benefits available to communities from bioprospecting results are two major barriers inhibiting the value of such agreements to local communities. Access and benefit-sharing at the local level in Fiji can be addressed in two ways. The first involves the creation of a register at the provincial level that documents indigenous and cultural intellectual property; the second promotes the creation of trusts within the owning community.

7 ECONOMIC ISSUES

There are a number of key questions that ought to be addressed as the basis of understanding the economics of the establishment of an intellectual and cultural property rights administration and management system at the provincial and national levels in Fiji.

- What is the characteristic of the indigenous and cultural knowledge property right?
- What is the appropriate mechanism to ensure that benefits and costs are adequately captured in an economic analysis?

7.1 What Are the Characteristics of the Indigenous and Cultural Intellectual Property Rights?

The primary reason for analysing the characteristics of indigenous and cultural knowledge property rights is to identify key features that create incentives for their sustainable (or unsustainable) and efficient (or inefficient) use. These features are comprised of five major characteristics that can be used to explain why (i) markets fail to appear, and (ii) unsustainable and inefficient resource use occurs. The five characteristics are:

- exclusivity (appropriability);
- enforceability;
- duration;
- divisibility; and
- transferability.

Exclusivity (or "appropriability") describes the extent to which all the benefits and costs from using the resource accrues to the individual holder of the rights. Similarly, exclusivity encompasses the extent to which non–rights holders are excluded from acquiring any benefit from the use of the resource.[33] This is closely tied in with the physical attributes of goods, which allow physical exclusion of people from a resource.

[32] K. ten Kate & S. A. Laird, "Bioprospecting Agreements and Benefit Sharing with Local Communities," in J. M. Finger, & P. Schuler, eds., *Poor People's Knowledge: Promoting Intellectual Property in Developing Countries.* (Washington, DC: World Bank/Oxford University Press, 2004), 133–158, 155–156.

[33] P. Lal, P. Holland, J. Veitayaki, & I. Korovulavula, *Economics for Community-Based Project Management in the Pacific.* Apia, International Waters Programme/SPREP, 2004.

In this instance, intellectual and cultural knowledge are "goods." If the users of goods and services "appropriate" all costs and benefits, they will choose to use resources in the way that creates the most benefit to them. This is because they will experience all of those benefits personally. By comparison, if some of the benefits or costs of using the good or service accrue to someone else, these will not be accounted for by the person in deciding whether to proceed with using the good or service in that way.

Enforceability describes the extent to which people are able to enforce their rights over a good or service.[34] For instance, imagine that *mataqali* A in a particular village has a unique traditional healing practice of curing fever. Because of this unique traditional knowledge of healing, *mataqali* A has the right to exclude other clans in the village from possessing this knowledge. However, if somehow this traditional healing knowledge is made known to other *mataqalis*, this traditional healing knowledge will no longer be unique; it will be public knowledge and liable to be "exploited," possibly for large-scale pharmaceutical commercialisation. Thus, lack of enforceability will lead to the loss of the benefit to *mataqali* A in the commercialization of their traditional healing knowledge.

Duration refers to the length of time that a right to use a good or service lasts. People have a greater incentive to protect the quality of an environmental good or service – or to ensure that it is not excessively extracted – if they have continued access to it in the future. Continued access means that people will be able to reap the future rewards of any conservation measures they make now. By contrast, short-term access to resources creates incentives for unsustainable resource use. This is because there are no incentives to invest in resources if the benefits cannot be reaped.

Divisibility refers to the ability of people to divide up a good or service into smaller parts. This is a function of the physical nature of the resource. Usually, rival goods are divisible, whereas nonrival services are not.[35] Divisibility creates incentives for sustainable resource use when it enables more uses of a good or service to occur, thereby satisfying more demands. For example, a type of sponge found on a coral reef may be valuable to a bioprospector for pharmaceutical purposes and a dive company that wants to tour the reef. It might appear that these two uses of the reef are not compatible; however, it might be possible to zone certain parts of the reef as "take" areas and others as "no-take" areas in order to meet both needs.

Transferability refers to the extent to which ownership or use of the resource is transferable. Transferability creates incentives for efficient resource use when it enables competing users of a good or service to negotiate for access to it and to reach settlement. In other words, transferability provides a key feature of markets. For intellectual and cultural property rights, transferability may be possible if there is an established system to ensure that the rightful owners of the intellectual and cultural property right are fairly compensated.

Seen from the perspective of *vasu*, transferability within an owning unit gives rise to many complexities. If a *mataqali* recognises that its *vasu* also have legal rights, will the *vasu* be accorded similar rights or lesser benefits? Also, the national system needs to accommodate the extent of recognition of the children of *vasu* and when rights and benefits no longer accrue.

[34] Ibid.

[35] Ibid.

7.2 What Mechanism Could Ensure that Benefits and Costs Are Adequately Captured in an Economic Analysis?

The following are key questions in the establishment of an appropriate mechanism to capture net economic benefits as well as oversee and monitor the legal recognition of indigenous intellectual and cultural property rights.

- Who will finance such a system?
- Will there be any net financial benefits envisaged in developing such a system?
- How can any net financial benefits be shared fairly to all affected parties, particularly the original owners of the intellectual and cultural knowledge?
- How can a cost recovery system or structure be developed in order to sustain administrative and operational functions of such system?

8 FRAMEWORK FOR A NATIONAL SYSTEM

Taking economic questions into account, a preliminary assessment supports a national system resting with the Fijian administration at the provincial level. Provincial offices exist and are more accessible to indigenous communities and appreciate customs, traditions, and practices of a particular province compared to administrators at the national level. The documentation of indigenous and cultural intellectual property in each province will need to be led by provincial administrators who, in most cases, are from the same province. Entries in the register at the provincial level will need to identify the potential for overlapping rights between *mataqali* or other units providing the same knowledge and information. The register will need to have public and private components, to allow for public access and the protection of secret knowledge and information, respectively.

To complement provincial registers, legal recognition and protection at the national level is essential. Constitutional provisions may be broadened in scope to recognise indigenous and cultural intellectual property rights in addition to facilitating the making of laws based on customary practices. National law should elaborate on legal rights and privileges of the rights holders and provide the framework for access and benefit-sharing. Full and active participation of the owning unit at all stages should be promoted. It follows that for international dealings, consent of the owning unit(s) is necessary before the State grants its consent. Representatives of owning units need to participate in any agreement relating to their rights and be satisfied with financial and other benefits accruing. The legal rights and interests of *vasu* will need to be accommodated in accordance with custom and practice of the owning unit. Thus, the enabling provisions in national law must allow for some flexibility to recognise *vasu* if that is in accordance with the wishes of the owning unit.

9 CONCLUSION

Legal recognition of indigenous intellectual and cultural property rights is important for the enhancement and protection of indigenous culture in Fiji. Although the courts have provided that the most common owning unit, the *mataqali*, has *locus standi* to institute legal action for a breach of its rights, recognition of the indigenous and cultural intellectual property rights and concomitant privileges and benefits do not exist. Constitutional provisions need to be broadened in scope to allow for such rights and national laws enacted vesting ownership. An international *sui generis* regime is best composed of binding legal instruments able to compel user and provider States to adhere to fairer and equitable benefit-sharing. Without a legal mechanism at the national level and an international binding framework, illegal, unreported, and unregulated use of indigenous intellectual and cultural property rights will continue.

The establishment of a national system responsible for the identification, recording, and registration of such rights will be centered at the provincial level and will be legally enabled and recognised at the national level. More work needs to be undertaken on the nature and characterization of rights, the extent and duration of protection, and other pertinent issues such as the rights of *vasu.* Active participation of owning units in providing prior informed consent and in negotiations relating to access and benefit-sharing should be included without question. However, the major obstacle in current practice relates to legal ownership in land and fisheries resources currently vested with a statutory authority and the State, respectively. Market system can operate efficiently only if the property rights are well defined. In areas in which the intellectual and cultural property rights are vague or nonexistent, appropriate institutional systems should be established to ensure efficiency and fair distribution of benefits. Ultimately, fair and equitable sharing of the financial benefit can occur only if ownership and intellectual and cultural property rights of the indigenous are recognised and promoted at all levels. Thus, identification of appropriate economic mechanisms to capture and effectively manage all the financial benefits is undoubtedly the key to sustaining the intellectual and cultural-knowledge property rights administrative and legislative system.

Index